W9-ARS-966

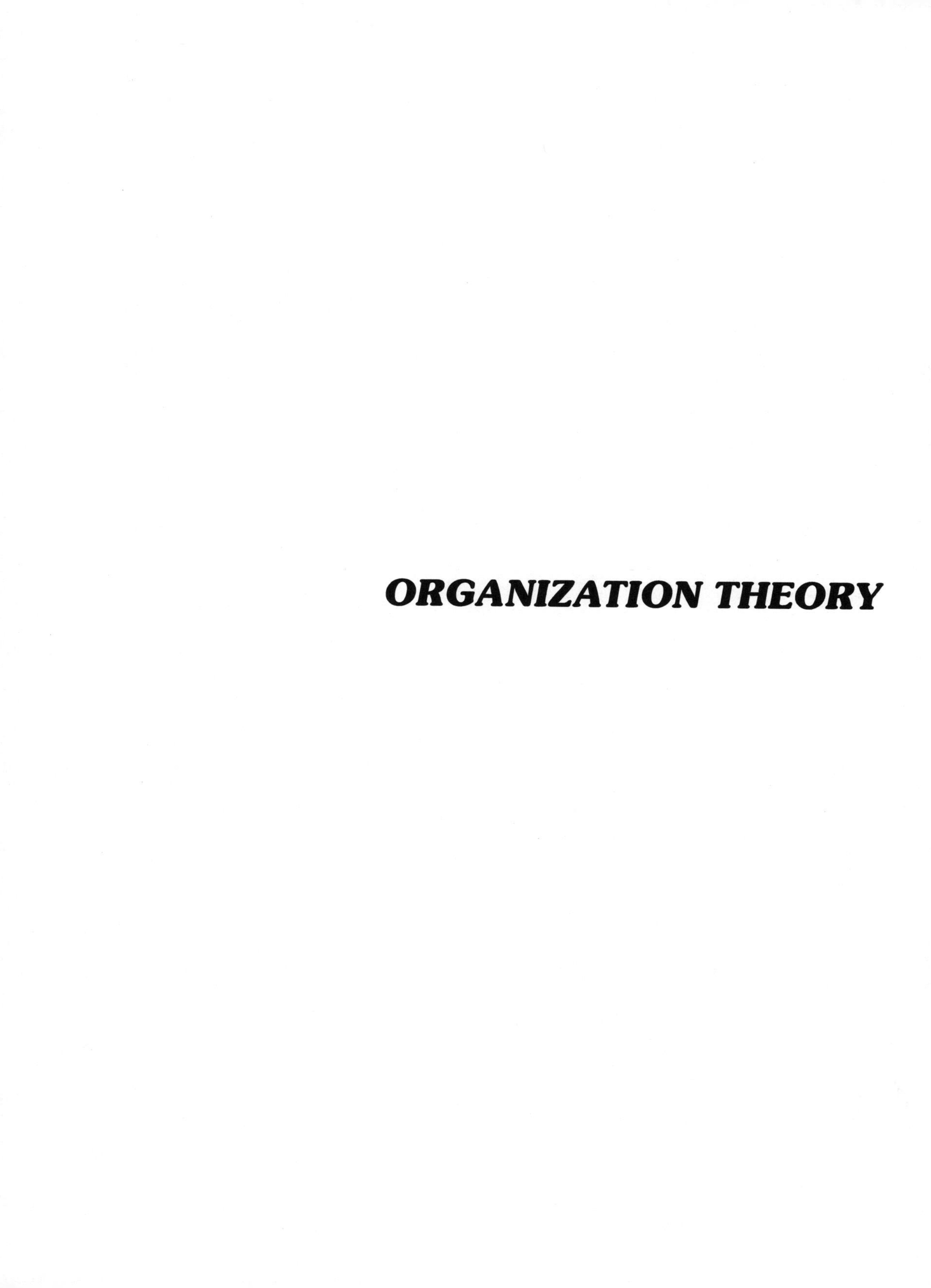

ORGANIZATION THEORY

Gary Dessler
Florida International University

ORGANIZATION THEORY
Integrating Structure and Behavior
Second Edition

Prentice-Hall, Inc., Englewood Cliffs, New Jersey 07632

Library of Congress Cataloging-in-Publication Data

DESSLER, GARY
Organization theory.

Includes index.
1. Organization. 2. Management. I. Title.
HD31.D4875 1986 658.4 85-12117
ISBN 0-13-641903-8

Editorial/production supervision and
interior design: Pamela Wilder
Cover design: Ben Santora
Manufacturing buyer: Ed O'Dougherty

Printed in the United States of America

10 9 8 7 6 5 4 3 2 1

ISBN 0-13-641903-8 01

Prentice-Hall International (UK) Limited, *London*
Prentice-Hall of Australia Pty. Limited, *Sydney*
Prentice-Hall Canada Inc., *Toronto*
Prentice-Hall Hispanoamericana, S.A., *Mexico*
Prentice-Hall of India Private Limited, *New Delhi*
Prentice-Hall of Japan, Inc., *Tokyo*
Prentice-Hall of Southeast Asia Pte. Ltd., *Singapore*
Editora Prentice-Hall do Brasil, Ltda., *Rio de Janeiro*
Whitehall Books Limited, *Wellington, New Zealand*

For my Family

Contents

Preface

The subject of organization theory is concerned primarily with the question of how to understand, explain, and predict how to best structure an organization to fulfill its goals, and is a very exciting subject. Few of the decisions managers make are more crucial than how they organize their firms, and in studying organization theory, students have a chance to learn a theory or set of principles that will aid them in more effectively designing their own departments and enterprises.

Many changes have taken place in the field of organization theory since the first edition of this book was published, many of which have been incorporated in this book. These include Peters and Waterman's study *In Pursuit of Excellence*, Mintzberg's new approach to organizing, and works by various authors that underscore the need to take the company's "culture" into account before reorganizing.

Which brings us to the unique aspects of *Organization Theory: Integrating Structure and Behavior*. First, Peters and Waterman point out in their study that "there is no such thing as a good structural answer apart from people considerations, and vice versa," a conclusion with which I heartily agree. Readers of *Organization Theory* will therefore find a heavy emphasis on purely macro, structural matters, combined with an adequate treatment in the body of the text of the sorts of behavioral issues (like culture, conflict, and power) without which one can't reorganize a firm. More behavioral issues, such as motivation and leadership theories, have been placed in chapter appendixes, for instructors or students who want to cover or review this purely behavioral material in more depth.

Several major changes have been made in this second edition. First, this new edition places a much greater emphasis on macro issues than did the first, with four more chapters now devoted to organization structure and design, and two fewer chapters devoted to organization behavior. The behavioral material itself has been revised to make it more relevant to the macro issues stressed in the text. Traditional organization-behavior topics like motivation and leadership theory are confined to appendixes, as noted above. All the chapters have, of course, been updated, and several new chapters have been added, including Chapter 9, "Organization Design," devoted primarily to an explanation of Mintzberg's design approach; 8, on formalization; 4, on strategy, structure, and effectiveness; 10, on job redesign; and 13 on "Leadership, Values, and Culture."

I want to thank several people for their assistance on this book. Reviewers, including Martin Marsh at Humboldt State University, Michael Moore at Michigan State University, and Pamela Specht at the University of Nebraska at Omaha, made extremely useful comments on the book, for which I am sincerely grateful. At Prentice-Hall, Alison Reeves, editor of Business Management and Industrial Relations, was a source of encouragement and assistance and greatly facilitated the process of revision. Last but not least, I want to thank my family for letting me borrow the time from them to complete this book.

Introduction to Organization Theory

THE NATURE OF ORGANIZATION THEORY

By 1980 it had become apparent to General Motors' top managers that the organization structure that had served them so well for decades had to be changed.[1] In a series of events that were prompted in part by the fuel crunch, increased foreign competition, and recession, the auto giant found itself repeatedly embarrassed by problems with its J-cars, and with locking X-car brakes, faulty diesel engines, malfunctioning V-8-6-4 engines, and delays in introducing front-wheel-drive replacements for its biggest cars. And in what was perhaps the biggest problem of all, GM's five car divisions—each of which for years had produced its own unique line of cars—were saddled with look-alike models that confused consumers and contributed to a drop in GM's market share.

The problems can be traced back to the 1960s. For years, the decentralized, divisionalized organization of GM had been used by experts as a textbook example of how to manage a large company with autonomous product divisions. In fact, though, the divisions had already become much less autonomous by the 1960s, when GM—in an effort to reduce duplication and thus cut costs—began to require more interdependencies among the five formerly independent car divisions: Chevrolet, Pontiac, Buick, Oldsmobile, and Cadillac. Previously, the five car divisions had each carried out most of the design, engineering, manufacturing, and sales work associated with their own cars. This worked well enough while GM had only five car lines, each with one basic model. However problems began to crop up in the 1960s as the company began adding more and more models. Since it would have been too expensive to have duplicate engineering, design, and manufacturing operations for all these new models within each of the five car divisions, GM decided to spread the tasks across divisions. Thus, whereas each division had formerly carried out most of its own engineering, the engineering effort was reorganized and distributed across divisions, with, for example, Pontiac engineering the rear suspensions and Buick the brakes. Similarly, assembly operations were taken away from the divisions and grouped under a new GM assembly division.

So by the 1970s, the idea promulgated by Alfred P. Sloan, longtime GM president, of having five independent, self-contained divisions, each with its own general manager to oversee all the car-producing functions—so brilliant in its simplicity—had already become muddled. Increasingly, it became apparent that no one person was responsible for all the steps in designing, engineering, producing, and selling a car or car line, as had previously been the case; instead, for example, the general manager of the Chevrolet division had to depend on engineering staffs in the other divisions to get changes made that he felt were vital to his own car line. The organization chart, which had formerly been unambiguous, became confused. The chart became even more complicated after the 1972 oil embargo, when GM began downsizing all its cars. To manage this enormous task, centralized project centers were established with a mandate to coordinate all product development. Although these centers accomplished their tasks, the costs of producing GM cars began to drift out of control, partly because no single group had power over all aspects of product development and sales, and partly because during these years, GM's middle management had tripled in size.[2]

As a result of problems like these, GM is now embarked on the most extensive organizational restructuring ever. Under the plan, GM will continue to market autos through the same five car divisions—Chevrolet, Pontiac, Oldsmobile, Buick, and Cadillac—but these divisions will be consolidated within two new divisions. Small cars will be engineered and built by the Chevrolet–Pontiac–GM Canada group, and intermediates and large cars will be developed by the Buick–Cadillac–Oldsmobile group. Each of these two groups will have its own group executive, who will report to the newly created position of Executive Vice-President for North American Passenger-Car Operations. Under the plan, GM's engineering will now be consolidated rather than spread throughout the corporation's various divisions, insofar as each of the two car groups will now have its own engineering group, created by consolidating engineering staff from the existing car divisions. The five car divisions themselves will continue to exist, but primarily as marketing arms of the two car groups. An entirely new and independent car company has also been set up to design and produce the firm's new Saturn car.

GM's top management believes that the massive reorganization will boost the company's organizational effectiveness. It will do this by, for instance, helping the company launch its new models on schedule, boosting quality control, providing more cost control, and allowing the divisions to build more distinctive models instead of the current look-alikes.

ORGANIZATION THEORY DEFINED

When managers sit down to reorganize an enterprise, they ideally need a theory that would let them understand, explain, and predict the implications of making various structural changes. In the case of General Motors, for instance, what would be the merits of simply going back to the organization structure it had used for 50 years, giving each division's general manager almost total control over all aspects of designing, engineering, producing, and selling that division's own cars? What are going to be the drawbacks of organizing into two giant divisions and relegating the five former car divisions to basically marketing roles? Will the benefits derived from centralizing the engineering functions in just the two main car units outweigh the duplication costs of doing so (since there may now be, say, two engineering teams working on developing better brakes at the same time)?

The subject of *organization theory* is aimed at answering questions like these. It is concerned mostly with the question of organization structure—in other words, with how to design an organization structure that ensures the firm's effectiveness. *Organization theory* itself can be defined as the subject concerned with *understanding, explaining, and predicting how to best structure an organization to fulfill its goals*. In physics, there is a theory that explains how contained gases react under pressure; in biology, a theory explains how man evolved from lower animals; and in psychiatry, Freud proposed a theory that helps an analyst explain a patient's behavior and predict which type of treatment to use. *Organization theory* serves about the same purpose in management: By consolidating what we have learned from observing organizations, organizational experts have developed a set of rules (or a *theory*) that can help managers reorganize their companies effectively.

Yet organization theory can't just focus on organization charts and on the narrowest questions of organization structure (such as "span of control"), since in practice you can't design a structure without considering employee behavior. For example, before deciding on the best span of control (the number of subordinates reporting to a manager), you'd have to take into account behavioral issues like, What is the optimal group size for encouraging all group members to actively participate in decision making? Similarly, you will find that some committed people do well even with no apparent chain of command, whereas some highly structured firms fail for lack of motivated employees. There is, in other words, *no such thing as a good structural answer apart from people considerations, and vice versa.*[3] Our study of organization theory will thus also take us into the realm of behavior, since in practice, structural realignments can't be made as if behavioral factors like "power" and "groups" don't exist.

THE PLAN OF THIS BOOK

This book is aimed at explaining the theory and practice involved in structuring an organization; thus it necessarily focuses on structural issues like departmentation and coordination and those behavioral factors (like leadership and company culture) that affect how an enterprise is structured. In outline form, the chapters in this book will cover the following topics:

Chapter 2: "Classical Organization Theories." The main purpose of this chapter is to discuss the milestones in the evolution of management and organization theory from preindustrial times to just after the First World War. A recurring theme here is that the organizations prescribed by these early classical theorists were generally very centralized and bureaucratic, a fact that probably reflected the relatively simple and unchanging environment in which these early organizations competed.

Chapter 3: "Contemporary Organization Theories." In this chapter we continue our discussion of the evolution of organization theory with a treatment of the period from roughly 1930 to the present. This period, as we will see, was marked by an increase in the rate of change facing organizations; there was a consequent change in direction for organization theory, which thereafter focused more on structuring the enterprise for creativity and innovation.

Chapter 4: "Strategy, Structure, and Organizational Effectiveness." This chapter defines more clearly what is meant by organizational effectiveness and explains how the organization's strategy—its plan for matching the company's resources and skills and the environmental opportunities and risks that it faces—determines the environment in which the organization will have to compete as well as the structure it will need to be effective.

Chapter 5: "Environment, Technology, and Organization." The purpose of this chapter is to explain how an organization's *context*—its environment, technology, and size—affect how it is structured. Here we follow up on the previous three chapters, in which the stage was set for explaining the effect an organization's context has on its structure and management.

Chapter 6: "Departmentation and Coordination." This chapter explains how to organize the departments in an organization and how to achieve coordination among them.

Chapter 7: "Organizational Hierarchy and Delegation." In this chapter, we discuss the process of decentralization, including the factors that drive an enterprise to decentralize and the various ways in which decentralization can take place. Note that whereas Chapter 6 focused on the horizontal aspects of structuring an enterprise, Chapter 7 turns to an explanation of the vertical aspect of organizing and to the concepts of delegation, decentralization, and organizational hierarchy.

Chapter 8: "Formalization and Communication." This chapter explains the nature, determinants, and effects of organizational *formalization*—the extent to which procedures, instructions, and communications are written. Here we will see that formalization complements the horizontal and vertical aspects of organization structure, insofar as it further elaborates what each jobholder is expected to do, and how he or she is expected to do it.

Chapter 9: "Organization Design." In this chapter, we describe how to design an organization structure by focusing on five ideal or "pure" structural configurations: simple structure, machine bureaucracy, professional bureaucracy, divisionalized form, and adhocracy. We will actually get into the details of how to structure an enterprise by fitting the appropriate configuration to the nature of the enterprise's task.

Chapter 10: "Job Redesign and Enrichment." The main theme of this chapter is how to design the specific jobs that occupy the organization structure and, in particular, the degree to which each job should be specialized and routine or enriched and multifaceted. Your decisions here, as we will see, have a marked effect on the emergent morale and motivation in your enterprise.

Chapter 11: "Power and Control in Organizations." This chapter explains the techniques that managers use to impose control on employees and, in particular, the concepts of power, authority, and organizational control. All three of these concepts are used by managers to help ensure the dependable behavior of employees within the confines of the organization structure that the managers design.

Chapter 12: "Motivation and Innovation." The subject of this chapter is how to elicit intrinsic motivation—motivation that comes from within the person and is derived from his or her ability to satisfy higher-order needs for competence, self-determination, and self-actualization. Whereas formalization, close supervision, or imposed controls can be used to ensure compliance in bureaucratic organizations, self-control of the sort explained in Chapter 12 is essential in the more free-wheeling "adhocracies;" where the looseness of the formal structure tends to demand a tight system of values and self-controls to keep employees in line.

Chapter 13: "Leadership, Values, and Culture." In this chapter, we discuss the determinants of organizational culture—in particular, leadership and how the leader's actions mold the organizational culture. Culture, as we'll see in this chapter, plays a crucial role in maintaining compliance in the relatively free-flowing "organic" structure, since it is in part through company culture that management ensures that all employees' values are consistent with those of the company at large.

Chapter 14: "Group Processes and Organization Theory." Groups play a critical role in organization theory for two reasons, and the main purpose of this chapter is to explain the reasons. First, groups affect how their members define their self-interest and therefore affect their motivation. Second, groups influence (and are influenced by) the organization structure itself—for instance, by filling the gaps in an inadequate structure.

Chapter 15: "Intergroup Relations and Conflict." This chapter deals with the origins and management of intergroup conflict—conflict, for instance, between line and staff units, or between production and sales departments. We'll see that the effectiveness of a structure depends on the departments' working together effectively, and intergroup conflict can undermine the structure's effectiveness by reducing interdepartmental communication and collaboration.

Chapter 16: "Managing Change." Here we explain how to manage organizational change. Organizational change and development is important to a study of organization theory because it involves the modification of structure, tasks, technology, and/or people in the organization for the purpose of increasing the organization's effectiveness.

• *An Overview*

We assume in this book that organizations are systems—that they are purposeful social units and consist of people who carry out differentiated tasks which are coordinated to contribute to the organization's goals. This definition has several implications, including the fact that we need to view the topics in this book (division of work, leadership, groups, and so on) not as separate entities but in terms of their relation to each other, to the organization, and to the organization's effectiveness.

Context First, in this book we asume that the organization's "context"—its environment, technology, and size—influences how it is organized and managed. In Chapter 4, we explain how an organization's strategy—its basic long-term plan—answers the question, "What business are we in?" and thereby determines the environment in which the organization must compete, as well as its technology and size. In turn (as we'll see in Chapter 4) the organization's context has a major influence on how the organization is structured and managed. For example, we'll see that in firms where efficiency is emphasized, effective organizations tend to be "mechanistic." They stress adherence to rules and to the chain of command, and they have a specialized division of work and directive leadership. At the other extreme, organizations like research labs may have unpredictable, nonroutine tasks. Here, creativity and entrepreneurial activities are emphasized, and to encourage such activities, these organizations tend to be "organic." They don't urge employees to "play it by the rules" or to abide closely by the chain of command. Similarly, jobs here tend to be less specialized, and leadership tends to be more "participative." The processes of decision making, communications, and information processing (discussed in Chapter 5) help explain the link between the organization and its context.

Structure and Compliance Next we assume that there are two basic aspects of organizations (their *structure*, and how *compliance* is ensured) that organization theorists have focused on and that we should therefore stress in this book. First, in Chapters 6 through 10, we address the question of *organization structure and design*—the question, in other words, of how to distribute specific tasks and responsibilities among the members of the organization. Here we discuss structural dimensions like departmentation, span of control, and coordination, and how context affects each dimension.

But from the point of view of an organization theorist (or manager), it is not enough to simply assign tasks to individuals; in addition, *you have to ensure that those tasks are in fact carried out*—that *compliance* takes place. For an organization to be able to function with any degree of effectiveness, each person must be able to assume that the people he or she directs will comply with orders and carry out their tasks. The president who directs the vice-president to increase efficiency, the shipping manager who directs the truckers to make certain deliveries, and the production foreman who directs an employee to tighten a bolt all issue orders on the assumption that those orders will be carried out. To the extent that orders are carried out, tasks can be accomplished in such a way that they contribute in an integrated manner to the organization's goals. To the extent that orders are not obeyed, there is no way to ensure that the logic of the organization's structure will function effectively. Therefore, we discuss motivation and compliance in Chapters 11, 12, and 13. We thus assume that *compliance* and *structure* are two major theoretical issues to be dealt with, and that both are influenced by the context of the organization.

Social Influences However, although having an effective structure and ensuring compliance are important determinants of organization effectiveness, other factors also influence effectiveness (often through their effects on structure and compliance). In Chapters 14 through 16, we discuss four such influential factors—leadership, work groups, intergroup conflict, and organization change and development—with a particular focus on the question, "How does this particular factor influence organization structure and compliance?"

APPENDIX TO CHAPTER 1
Designing Research Studies

THE SCIENTIFIC METHOD[4]

In the most general sense, a science is a body of knowledge that is systematically acquired and arranged. Physics, biology, and chemistry are thus sciences, as are psychology and other behavioral sciences.

Stripped to its essentials, the scientific method involves a cycle of observation, generalization, and experimentation; a phenomenon is observed, a general hypothesis is developed to explain this phenomenon, and an experiment is carried out to test the hypothesis. In practice, this cycle is never-ending, and the frontier of the science is pushed ever forward as scientists, through observation, generalization, and experimentation, collect new bits of information that are woven into the tapestry of their evolving theories. An important point is that when scientists make an observation that does not agree with their hypothesis, they may conclude that either the hypothesis or the observation is wrong. If, after redesigning the experiment, the researchers determine that the observation is valid, they then discard the hypothesis or adjust it to account for the new observation. Hypotheses are therefore constantly refined and elaborated through a constant cycle of observation, generalization, and experimentation.

A hypothesis is a "tentative theory," a theory to be tested but that has not yet received enough empirical support to gain the position of a full-fledged theory. Hypotheses are tested through the scientific method, which has several distinguishing characteristics. Its procedures are public, and the scientific report contains a complete description of what was done so that other researchers can follow each step of the study. Definitions are precise, so that it is clear to those reading the report how each term was defined. Data collecting is objective; in fact, objectivity is a key feature of the scientific approach. The findings must be replicable; other researchers attempting to test the results of the study should be able to reproduce them. Finally, the scientific approach is systematic and cumulative, and its ultimate purposes are to explain and predict phenomena.

The scientist works through experimentation, and his or her reliance on experiments suggests a final characteristic of the scientific approach. Experiments are always carried out to test clearly formulated hypotheses under *controlled conditions;* ideally, therefore, the scientific method is a carefully controlled approach, one in which all the conditions are known and under the control of the experimenter. In this way, a cause-and-effect relationship can be established: For example, the researcher can be reasonably sure that employee performance improved as a result of a new training program rather than as a result of "uncontrolled" changes (like an increase in pay) that took place between the training program and the time when performance was measured.

The basic objective of any experiment is thus always *to eliminate alternative explanations for the researcher's findings.* In the case of the training program, for example, a researcher would want to design an experiment in such a way that another scientist could not come back and challenge his or her conclusion that it was the training program that improved performance. The simplest way to design such an experiment is to randomly assign subjects to an "experimental" and a "control" group, observe the performance of each group at a particular time, expose the subjects in the experimental group to the training program, and then subsequently measure the performance of *both* groups again. If the performance of the subjects in the experimental group has improved but that of the subjects in the control group has not, the researcher can be reasonably sure that the training program has been effective, since in virtually all other respects, the two groups were treated in the same way.

Once a hypothesis has been supported by a large body of different types of observations and experiments, it becomes a theory, or general principle. A good theory grows and relates additional facts as they become known. However, there are strikingly few unassailable theories even in the physical sciences, a fact that many behavioral scientists often seem to overlook. Even in the physical sciences, where experimental conditions are relatively controllable, it is rare that scientists can be more than "reasonably sure" that X is the cause of Y. In applying the scientific method to *managerial* decisions, the problem is even more acute, because in most cases, it is difficult (and often impossible) to carry out a controlled experiment.

• *Experimental Validity*

In order for any experiment to be meaningful, it should meet two basic criteria: First, you should be able to confidently attribute the effect you obtained to the independent variable that was manipulated. This is called *internal validity*. It is the *sine qua non* for enabling you to meaningfully interpret the results of an experiment. (Thus, if productivity went up after the training program, you should be able to say confidently that it was the training program and not some other factor, like extra pressure from the supervisor, that resulted in higher productivity.) The second criterion asks the question of generalizability: To what populations and settings can your findings be generalized? This is called *external validity,* and although it is not an essential characteristic of an experiment, it is an important one. In the following sections, we discuss several methods that can help reduce the dangers to internal validity. Dangers to external validity are traditionally reduced by using unobtrusive measures (so that subjects don't know they are being studied) and/or by choosing subjects and an experimental situation that is the same as or close to those to which you want to generalize your findings.

• Random Assignment of Subjects

Random assignment refers to any procedure in which subjects are assigned to groups in such a way that every subject has an equal chance of being assigned to any of the experimental groups. This reduces the chance that observed differences among the groups after treatment will be due to initial differences in the samples rather than to the effects of your treatment. Random assignment is aimed at eliminating what is known as the *selection* danger to internal validity. A selection problem may occur when the subjects in one or more of the experimental groups are dissimilar from those in the other groups (for example, when most of the subjects in your treatment group are female and most of those in your control group are male). Random assignment of subjects is used to assign participants to your groups in such a way that all groups can be deemed equivalent, at least as far their constituencies are concerned.

EXPERIMENTAL DESIGNS

An experiment is a study carried out under controlled conditions. In an experiment, you establish a situation that will enable you to discover the effects of some change that you have introduced. The aim is to try to specify a cause-and-effect relationship as precisely as possible under a known set of conditions. Ideally, all the conditions should be known and under your control.

• Poor Experimental Designs

The three experimental designs we discuss here are actually not experimental designs at all. They are presented as examples of designs to be avoided.

In discussing these and the other designs in this section, we will use the following shorthand notation:

- *R* indicates *random assignment* of subjects to groups.
- *O* refers to the *observation* or measurement.
- *X* refers to the experimental *treatment,* such as a training program.

The left-to-right dimension indicates the temporal order, and Xs and Os presented vertically refer to simultaneous activities:

O X O

O O

This means that for the first group, there is a "before" observation, then a treatment (such as a training program), and then an "after" training observation to see if there has been any observable change. In the second group, an observation is made each time an observation is made in the first group. Thus, the only difference in those two groups should be the training the first group received.

The "One-Shot Case Study" Much of the research in management today conforms to the following design:

X O

In this design, a single group is studied only once, subsequent to some treatment that is presumed to cause some change. For example, a group of employees is trained and then their performance is tested. Such a design is completely lacking in control. There is no pretest, so you have no way of testing the effects of the treatment (the training program), nor can you assess the effects of other changes (such as a companywide raise) that may have accompanied the training program. There is no experimental control group that can be used as a standard of comparison.

The One-Group Pretest–Posttest Design This involves a "pre- and post-" comparison of a single group that underwent some treatment, and can be diagrammed as follows:

O X O

In this design, one group of subjects is tested on some factor (such as morale). They receive a treatment (such as a training program), and their morale after the training is then tested. This "design" is widely used. For example, assume that a consultant administers a morale survey to employees in a company and finds that morale is low. He suggests a training program for employees, and the employees are trained. After the training program, the consultant again administers his morale questionnaire and finds that morale has increased.

Why has morale increased? Using this non-design, it is impossible to tell. The experiment is internally invalid, since there are many rival hypotheses that could explain the consultant's findings. A companywide pay raise and the hiring of a new, more considerate boss are among the sources of invalidity that are not controlled, because there is no "control," no comparative group that would have been exposed to the companywide pay raise or new boss but not to the experimental treatment.

The Static-Group Comparison This is a design in which a group that has experienced a treatment is compared with one that has not, for the purpose of determining the effect of the treatment. It may be diagrammed as follows:

X	O
	O

In this experiment, a group that has not experienced the treatment is found for comparison with one that has. For example, suppose a researcher wants to assess the effect of required overtime on employee morale. He chooses two companies, one in which overtime is required and one in which it is not. He uses a questionnaire to assess the level of morale in both companies and finds that morale is higher in the company without the required overtime.

Why is morale higher in the "no-required-overtime" company? Again, there are so many rival hypotheses that our researcher can draw no conclusion. The study suffers first from the "selection" danger to internal validity. Specifically, if the observations (the level of morale) for the two groups differ, this difference could well be a result of the differential recruitment of persons making up the groups. In other words, the groups might have differed anyway, without the occurrence of the treatment. "Mortality" is a second problem. Thus, the two groups might have originally been identical, but the group exposed to the treatment experienced a relatively high dropout rate.

• *Some Important True Experimental Designs*

A "true" experimental design has three basic characteristics: Subjects are randomly assigned to groups, there is a control group, and an independent variable is manipulated. The three true experimental designs we discuss next meet these conditions. They are the currently recommended designs in the methodological literature and should result in internally valid experiments.

The Pretest/Posttest Control-Group Design This is perhaps the simplest true experimental design and may be diagrammed as follows:

R	O	X	O
R	O		O

This design contains both a control group and random assignment of subjects. The experimental subjects are randomly assigned to the two groups to be compared. And it is randomly determined which group will serve as the control group and which will serve as the experimental group. Because of these procedures, it can be assumed that the two groups are equivalent at the time of the initial observations. The existence of the control group means that the effect of companywide changes—a pay raise or appointment of a new boss, for instance—can be assessed, since, it is assumed, the companywide change would have affected both "control" and "experimental" group subjects. But only those in the experimental group were exposed to the experimental treatment.

The Posttest-Only Control-Group Design The posttest-only control-group design can be diagrammed as follows:

R	X	O
R		O

Because there is no pretest here, others cannot argue that the researcher gets the results he does only when he first "pretests" subjects (thus letting them know they are part of a study—the so-called "Hawthorne effect"). And, like the preceding design, this posttest-only control-group design adequately controls for many of the sources of internal invalidity. This design also requires about half the effort of the other design, since there is no pretest. Furthermore, many research problems occur for which pretests are unavailable, inconvenient, or likely to be reactive in that they "cue" subjects to the nature of the study; for this reason, too, the posttest-only design is recommended.

The Solomon Four Group Design The Solomon four group design can be diagrammed as follows:

R	O	X	O
R	O		O
R		X	O
R			O

Although it is more cumbersome than the last two designs, the Solomon four group design is an extremely effective one that not only eliminates sources of internal invalidity but deals with several of the dangers to external validity as well. In this design, two groups are exposed to the pretest and two are not. Thus, the researcher can compare the final results for the pretested and nonpretested groups that underwent treatment and can therefore determine whether or not the results can be generalized only to situations in which pretests are given. Thus, with this design, the effects of the pretest and treatment can be assessed separately.

Footnotes

[1]See "Can GM Solve Its Identity Crises?" *Business Week,* Jan. 23, 1984, pp. 32–33.

[2]"Can GM Solve Its Identity Crises?" pp. 32–33.

[3]Thomas Peters and Robert Waterman, Jr., *In Search of Excellence* (New York: Harper & Row, 1982), p. 9.

[4]Donald T. Campbell and Julian C. Stanley *Experimental and Quasi-Experimental Designs for Research* (Chicago: Rand McNally & Co., 1963); John M. Neale and Robert M. Liebert *Science and Behavior: An Introduction to Methods of Research* (Englewood Cliffs, N. J.: Prentice-Hall, Inc., 1973); Richard Bagozzi and Lynn Phillips, "Representing and Testing Organizational Theories: A Holistic Construal," *Administrative Science Quarterly,* Vol. 27, No. 3 (September 1982), 459–89.

2

Classical Organization Theories

OVERVIEW

The purpose of this chapter is to discuss the milestones in the evolution of management and organization theory from preindustrial times to just after the First World War. A recurring theme here is that the organizations prescribed by these early classical theorists were generally highly centralized and bureaucratic. These theorists advocated close adherence to the chain of command and the use of discipline, rules, and close supervision for ensuring compliance—all recommendations that were generally in keeping with the environment and tasks that these early theorists focused on. As we'll see, the pace of life was comparatively slow, organizations were seldom called upon to make high-speed decisions, and work tasks called for routine effort, not creativity. In this environment and with these kinds of tasks, the rigid mechanistic prescriptions of the classical theorists and their predecessors worked quite well.

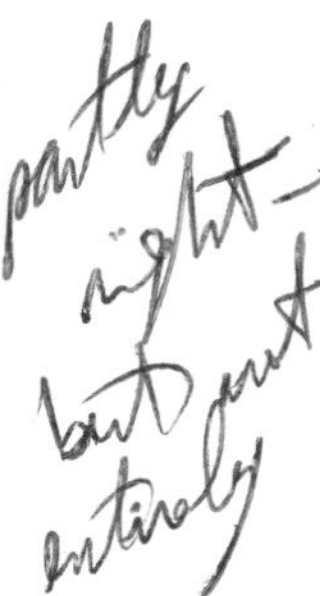

The outline of this chapter is as follows:

- **A** Background: The preindustrial period
  - **1** Egypt, Greece, and Rome
  - **2** The medieval period
  - **3** The capitalistic ethic and economic individualism
  - **4** The legacy
  - **5** The industrial revolution
- **B** Scientific management
  - **1** Frederick Winslow Taylor

C The administrative theorists
  1 Henri Fayol
  2 Urwick and Gulick; Mooney and Reilly
  3 Max Weber and bureaucratic organization theory
  4 Criticism of administrative and bureaucratic organization theories

BACKGROUND: THE PREINDUSTRIAL PERIOD

Many of the structures and assumptions of classical theory had their genesis in this early, preindustrial period, so an understanding of this background is important for putting the classical theories in perspective.

• *Egypt, Greece, and Rome*

The first large-scale organizations were Egyptian state monopolies, used for carrying out such projects as irrigation, canal building, and the construction of pyramids. At the top of the organization was the pharaoh, who based his authority on divine right and delegated certain authority to his vizier. The vizier acted as prime minister, chief justice, and treasurer, and was directly responsible for an elaborate bureaucracy at the base of which were tens of thousands of slaves. The Egyptian economy was an almost totally agrarian one, and a major function of the bureaucracy was to forecast and utilize the rise and fall of the Nile River.

Although the Old Testament and Babylonian documents indicate that commerce existed during this period, it was not until the rise of ancient Greece that trade began to flourish. But ironically, as Tilgher points out, the aristocratic or philosophical Greek found that "any activity which brings the spirit into close contact with the material world . . . [was] a painful and humiliating necessity . . . truth alone being the only true concern."[1] Business in general, and money-lending in particular, were therefore carried out by slaves and less-than-respectable citizens; manual workers and merchants, in fact, were not permitted citizenship in the Greek democracy. To the high-placed Greek, commerce was necessary but distasteful.

The Romans inherited this disdain for business and left these activities in the hands of Greek and Oriental freemen. Although the aristocracy entered into agreements with business in return for the provision of money for its wars, there was a persistent distrust of the merchant. Yet trade flourished, and the Roman state became increasingly involved in all aspects of economic life, largely because of the requirements for commercial standardization and a state-guaranteed system of weights, measures, and coins. In addition, the state levied tariffs and fines and regulated the guilds. Superimposed over these various state functions was the military autocracy, which, through the dual concepts of discipline and functionalism, ran the empire with an iron hand. Functionalism vested itself in a highly specialized division of work among the various military and governmental agencies, while discipline ensured the compliance that enabled a rigid, hierarchical, centralized structure to be utilized in carrying out the various functions.

As the autocratic Roman military organization reached its apex, the popularity of the Catholic Church began to spread. Church leaders found this popularity to be a two-edged sword, however, and in the second century A.D., they began to recognize that the growth of new sects was threatening the foundations of the Church. This concern manifested itself in a number of activities aimed at defining more rigorously the objectives, doctrine, and conditions for membership within the organization. The result was the development and establishment of scriptural canons, doctrine, and a centralized source of authority, all of which were aimed at ensuring the compliance of Church members and officers.

The Medieval Period

The period between the fall of Rome and the Renaissance was characterized by stagnation and a lack of economic and social development. The feudal system dominated the economic life of Europe, and the serf, who was legally free but almost entirely dependent on the manor lord, replaced the slave at the base of the economic social order. The Church was the dominant institution and prevailed over virtually all areas of human activity, both secular and spiritual. Salvation was stressed, and European man was taught to lead a subsistent, monastic life in return for an eternity in heaven.

With the Church as superstate, the warnings against lending for interest or desiring anything in this life perpetuated the idea of business as a necessary evil. But the Church, which Harbison describes as a paradox—"a divine church, with human worldly organization"[2]—became the largest landholder in Europe and employed thousands of serfs. There was a noticeable shift in Church views of business activities during the latter part of the medieval period, consistent with the growing commercialism. Even with these relaxations, however, the dominant view was that trade and commerce were to be tolerated as necessary evils. For example, Tawney describes the medieval period and its views of commerce as follows:

> At every turn, therefore, there are limits, restrictions, warnings against allowing economic interests to interfere with serious affairs. It is right for man to seek such wealth as is necessary for a livelihood in his station. To seek more is not enterprise, but avarice, and avarice is a deadly sin. Trade is legitimate; the different resources of different countries show that it was intended by Providence. But it is a dangerous business. A man must be sure that he carries it on for the public benefit, and the profits which he takes are no more than the wages of his labor. Private property is a necessary institution, at least in a fallen world; men work more and dispute less when goods are private than when they are common. But it is to be tolerated as a concession to frailty, not applauded as desirable in itself.[3]

This negative view had its origin in ancient Greece and still persists among certain groups and cultures. Before industrialization could take place, it had to be counterbalanced with a new view, that of the capitalistic ethic.

• *The Capitalistic Ethic and Economic Individualism*

This new ethic had religious, political, and economic roots and had its origin in the Crusades, which were themselves a result of feudalism. The Crusades stimulated commerce by establishing new trade routes and exposing the parochial civilization of Europe to the wealth of the Orient. The first cracks began to appear in the Church's facade as the Crusaders, who had embarked on their journeys with unshakable religious conviction, were struck by the realization that the Middle Eastern culture was in many ways superior to theirs—particularly in trade and industry. In brief, the Crusades stimulated commerce by opening new trade routes, contributing to the rise of towns and a new middle class, and weakening the dominance of Christian belief.

Gradually, the spread of prosperity, the loosening of religious bonds by the Crusades, and the excesses of the Church resulted in the undermining of the Church's various secular duties. Slowly, throughout Europe, its three key powers of appointment, taxation, and jurisdiction were circumscribed by monarchs. In Germany, which had the weakest of national governments, Martin Luther proclaimed his 95 Theses and opened the first hole in the religious dike holding back individualism.

Economic individualism, which Harbison has described as "more a coincidence of the reformation than an effect of it,"[4] would have its foundations in Luther's ideas of *a calling.* This idea discarded Catholic notions of subsistence living by urging the individual to fulfill the obligation imposed upon him in this world—that is, his calling. In addition, Luther's emphasis on the Bible (not the Church) as authority and on the whole community of Christ as the Church attracted wide acceptance. His ideas were espoused by workers, who felt they would be free of *both* Church and secular bonds; by the middle class, who saw in them the first visions of a religious rationale for trade and business; and by the governing class, who looked enviously at Church lands.

Whereas Luther's eyes were on the past, Calvin's were on the present, and he accepted the advanced commerce of his day. He developed the concept of the *elect,* who were those predestined to be saved. Each man must consider himself one of the elect; if he did not, his lack of self-confidence would be interpreted as a lack of faith. To attain this self-confidence, each man must engage intensely in work, for this activity could dispel religious doubts and give certainty of grace.

Although Protestantism did not condone the pursuit of wealth, it did encourage intense activity as the goal of the good life. Similarly, the wasting of time and unwillingness to work were the deadliest of sins, and the division and specialization of work was the result of a divine will, if it led to an increase in the quality and quantity of production. Furthermore, this division of work placed each man in his calling and required him to do his best; those workers who were nonspecialized demonstrated a lack of grace and therefore of predestination.

Religion, which once had a moderating effect on industry, now gradually took on a facilitative accelerative function. Unlike the Catholic of the Middle Ages, who was taught to strive for a subsistent, monastic existence while hoping for salvation, a Puritan was taught to believe that hard work reflected the fact that he was predestined. In particular:

> If an individual's destiny hangs on a private transaction between himself and his maker, what room is left for human intervention . . . the Puritan flings himself into practical activities with the daemonic energy of one who, all doubts allayed, is conscious that he is a sealed and chosen vessel.[5]

These were powerful ideas, and, as Tawney notes:

> Like traits of individual character which are suppressed until the approach of maturity releases them, the tendencies in Puritanism, which were to make it later a potent ally of the movement against the control of economic relations in the name either of social morality or of the public interest, did not reveal themselves till political and economic changes had prepared a congenial environment for their growth.[6]

Economically, the Middle Ages had been a sterile period, since the relatively simple, localized economies required no sophisticated theories of resource allocation. Toward the end of the Middle Ages, increased trade resulted in the growth of the domestic or "putting-out" system of production. Under this system, a merchant would act as a middleman in both procuring raw materials and selling the completed product. Upon obtaining the materials, he would allocate them to individual workers or families, who would use their own equipment in manufacturing the finished product for a wage. This system was well suited to the period: Trade was still in its infancy, a high-volume demand for goods had not yet been developed, and the nature of the domestic system itself militated against a standardization of either raw materials or the finished product. As the volume of trade grew, however, this system proved increasingly inefficient, and civilization moved inexorably toward the Industrial Revolution.

By the 16th century, international trade and the rise of centralized governments had resulted in the economic philosophy of mercantilism, which gave the government a strong central role in the financing and regulating of trade. In the 18th century, the Physiocratic School of economic thought, under François Quesnay, advocated laissez-faire capitalism, a philosophy that in turn influenced Adam Smith. In his *Wealth of Nations,* Smith called for the separation of government and economy, and described how the "invisible hand" of the market would ensure that resources flowed to the best consumption and their most efficient reward. The economic rationality and self-interest of each person and nation, acting in a fully competitive market, would bring about the greatest prosperity for all. For Smith, the division and specialization of work was a pillar of the free, competitive market mechanism and would lead to enormous increases in productivity and output. John Locke's essay, "Concerning Civil Government," was also published in this period; in it he attacked the divine right of kings and stated the principles of the English Bloodless Revolution of 1688. Justice, equality, and the rights of man became the prime movers of political action.

By about 1750, the ideological and cultural stage was set for the advent of the Industrial Revolution. Economic theory emphasized the utilitarian rationality and self-interest of man; *every man supposedly weighed the economic alternatives open to him and consistently chose the one that resulted in his highest net gain. For the worker, this was the highest possible wage.* Furthermore, the benefits of division of work were claimed as the economic rationale for the factory system. In conjunction with these two concepts, Protestantism—and particularly the later Puritanism—provided a religious rationale for hard work, specialization, and competition.

Ironically, though, the ideas of economic rationality, self-interest, and predestination acted in some respects as counteracting forces to the new ideas of political liberty. A legal–rational authority based on private property and technical competence was simply substituted for the traditional social-class authority founded on the divine right of kings. Leaders and entrepreneurs, who had previously based their autocratic treatment of workers on the concept of divine right and on philosophies like those of Machiavelli and Hobbes, now had the Protestant Ethic to guide them. The result was that many management writers in future years would continue to view the worker, as March and Simon put it, as an "inert instrument performing the task assigned him . . . as a given, rather than as a variable in the system."[7]

• *The Legacy*

The major organizational legacy of this later preindustrial period reflected the traditional, social-class concept of authority, the Greek view of work, and the command philosophy of leadership reflected in the works of Machiavelli and Hobbes. Historically, structures were highly centralized, the work tasks were specialized into functional units, and discipline, dogma, and fear were used to ensure the compliance of workers. A rigid, hierarchical chain of command was the norm, and authority and communications emanated from the top. In turn, these inflexible organizations largely reflected a stable, relatively unchanging environment. As Toffler has noted:

> Each age produces a form of organization appropriate to its own tempo. During the long epoch of agricultural civilization, societies were marked by low transience. Delays in communication and transportation slowed the rate at which information moved. The pace of individual life was comparatively slow. And organizations were seldom called upon to make what we would regard as high-speed decisions.[8]

• *The Industrial Revolution*

The new economic, religious, and political ideas emerging at the time combined to produce a catalytic climate in which the scientific and technological discoveries of Galileo, Gilbert, Harvey, Watt, and others could contribute to industrialization. The Industrial Revolution, recognized as having centered in England around the 1780s, was characterized by a monumental event: the substitution of machine power for manpower. England during this period had a stable, constitutional government, a sensitivity to laissez-faire economics, and a strong spirit of self-reliance. It was therefore a logical epicenter for the industrial changes taking place.

Organizationally, industrialization resulted in an almost total emphasis on the strategy of resource accumulation and company growth. This was necessitated by the availability of capital and the widely recognized and accepted productivity advantages of division of work. Division of work and specialization require volume and stability, and growth therefore resulted in increasing returns; as sales, volume, and stability increased, unit costs decreased. In an age without mass communication or transportation, efficiency experts, research and development, or government interference, this strategy of resource accumulation was an effective one that helped protect the production facility from the vagaries of the marketplace.

Enlarged operations, however, created many problems for the entrepreneur. First, he found (as did managers before him) that he alone could not direct and control all the activities of his organization; whereas the Church could resort to dogma and the military to discipline, managers in the new factory system found themselves unable to properly monitor the work of submanagers and workers. In addition, there was a severe shortage of both managers and skilled labor, and the skilled labor that was available frequently resisted the standardization of parts, methods, and tools required by the interchangeable-parts method of production.

Management These early entrepreneurs—faced with the dilemma of rigorous competition on the one hand, and an uncertain labor force on the other—quickly adopted the structures and principles of older organizations. Such ideas as centralization, clear hierarchy, specialized division of work, and autocratic leadership were implemented as competitive pressures for size demanded increasingly predictable results from a frequently unwilling labor force. But it is important to remember that this emphasis on structure and imposed compliance also reflected the prevailing economic, religious, and political philosophies. Specifically—and this is important—these philosophies (particularly those of predestination, the religious benefits of division of work, and economic self-interest and rationality) combined to permit the entrepreneur to view his "human inputs" as little more than another tool, a view that would last through the first two decades of the present century. In addition, the competitive environment was one over which the entrepreneur had little control, except what he could exert through increased size. Therefore, the organizations of the period did not have to be structured for adapting to a rapidly changing and complex environment; instead, the entrepreneur had to exert all his energies and abilities toward the accumulation of more resources for the purpose of increasing the size and productivity of his manufacturing facility.

SCIENTIFIC MANAGEMENT

This race to accumulate resources and increase factory size was particularly pronounced in America. The War of 1812 had severed America economically from England and spurred the growth of manufacturing operations. Technological advances included the steamboat, the cotton gin, the iron plow, the telegraph, the electric motor, and the expansion of a railroad and canal network that opened new markets for producers. In turn, these new markets provided the volume that was a fundamental requirement for the division of work.

Chandler has pointed out that during the late 1800s, many new industries were completing the resource-accumulation stage of their existence and beginning to move into a "rationalization" stage.[9] The rationalization of the newly accumulated resources was necessary not only because of industry's pressing need for efficiency but also because of the crude forms of planning, organizing, controlling, and administering then in existence. Given the nature of the environment and of mass-production techniques, this rationalization was more crucial in the production shop than elsewhere in the organization. Production—and in particular, mass production—demanded, in addition to high volume, stability in raw materials, labor, and production techniques for its very existence. In total, therefore, the stage was set for the American economy to move into its rationalization phase.

• *Frederick Winslow Taylor*

Frederick Winslow Taylor was a mechanical engineer whose ideas were strongly influenced by a paper delivered in 1886 by Henry Towne to the American Society of Mechanical Engineers. The paper, entitled, "The Engineer as Economist," asked engineers to build a management literature of "Science and Practice." Taylor had always shown an affinity for scientific investigation, research, and experimentation, and for improving things from a basis of fact; Towne's speech provided a direction for his energies.

The major theme of scientific management was that work, and especially blue-collar work, could be studied scientifically. Taylor believed that the objective analysis of data collected in the workplace could provide the basis for determining the "one best way" to organize work, and with his Quaker–Puritan background, he pursued this goal relentlessly.

In his two major works, *Shop Management* and *The Principles of Scientific Management,* Taylor proposed the framework for his new science of work. He suggested a system that can be summarized as consisting of four principles:

1 *Finding the "one best way."* First, management—through observation and "the deliberate gathering in . . . of all the great mass of traditional knowledge, which in the past has been in the heads of the workmen . . ."—finds the "one best way" for performing each job.

2 *Scientific selection of personnel.* This next principle requires "the scientific selection and then the progressive development of the workmen." This involves finding each worker's limitations and "possibilities for development" and giving him the required training.

3 *Financial incentives.* Taylor knew that putting the right worker on the right job would not by itself ensure high productivity, and that some plan for motivating workers to do their best and to comply with their supervisor's instructions was necessary. He saw, in other words, that organization structure and division of work was only half the problem faced by an organization theorist: the other half involved finding some way to ensure that each worker performed his or her task effectively. Taylor, always the Puritan, proposed that a system of financial incentives be used, in which each worker was paid in direct proportion to how much he produced rather than simply according to a basic hourly wage. An incentive plan thus served much the same purpose in Taylor's organization theory as did the discipline, dogma, and threats of earlier military, religious, and feudal managers.

4 *Functional foremanship.* Finally, Taylor called for a division of work between manager and worker such that managers did all planning, preparing, and inspecting while the workers did the actual work. Taylor proposed using specialized experts ("functional foremen"), each of whom was to be responsible for some specific aspect of the worker's task, such as finding the best machine speed, deciding on job priorities, or inspecting the work. The worker was to take orders from each of these foremen, depending upon whether the matter concerned planning, machine speed, or inspecting, for example.[10]

Taylor as an Organization Theorist As a theorist, Taylor dealt explicitly with both the structure and compliance questions of organization theory. With respect to structure, he focused not on questions of overall organization but rather on the best way for dividing the work at the workplace itself. Here, he prescribed functional foremanship and, more important, the scientific observation and analysis of each separate job in order to find the "one best way" for performing it.

The question of compliance—of how to get each worker to do his or her best—was probably Taylor's overriding concern, and it was one that manifested itself in both his incentive plan and his equating scientific management with a "mental revolution." Although Taylor was often criticized as the man who proposed a degrading, demoralizing, machinelike existence for the worker, his objectives were probably just the opposite. He said that scientific management was "not just an efficiency device, or a new scheme of paying men, or a bonus system," but instead:

> . . . involves a complete mental revolution on the part of the working man engaged in any particular establishment or industry—a complete mental revolution on the part of these men as to their duties toward their work, toward their fellow men, and toward their employees. And it involves the equally complete mental revolution on the part of those on the management side—the foreman, the superintendent, [etc.]. . . .
>
> The great revolution that takes place in the mental attitude of the two parties under scientific management is that both sides take their eyes off the division of the surplus as the all-important matter, and together turn their attention toward increasing the size of the surplus until the surplus becomes so large that it is unnecessary to quarrel over how it shall be divided. They come to see that when they stop pulling against one another and instead both turn and push shoulder to shoulder in the same direction, the size of the surplus created by their joint effort is truly astonishing.[11]

Taylor's ideas were firmly founded upon a desire for worker–management harmony and increased worker benefits. The problem lay not in Taylor's motives but in his assumptions, which were the prevailing utilitarian–rational assumptions of the day. The concepts of man as a rational being, and division of work as a manifestation of religious grace, allowed Taylor and his disciples to largely disregard the variables of human behavior in organizations. Furthermore, his idea of an increased surplus referred only to dollars, and he overestimated the extent to which wages were the sole concern of workers.

Scientific management was therefore a product of its times. Born and nurtured in an era of laissez-faire economics, the Protestant Ethic, and national optimism and dedication to efficiency, it was a reasonable and probably necessary method for rationalizing the recently accumulated resources of industry. Furthermore, the fact that the environment was still relatively stable, combined with Taylor's inherent production orientation, allowed him to largely disregard the environment as a vital force to which organizations must adapt.

As Thompson points out:

> Scientific management, focusing primarily on manufacturing or similar production activities, clearly employs economic efficiency as its ultimate criterion . . . and achieves conceptual closure of the organization by assuming that goals are known, tasks are repetitive, output of the production process somehow disappears, and resources in uniform qualities are available.[12]

THE ADMINISTRATIVE THEORISTS

The concepts and methods of scientific management were not generally applicable to the broader questions of organizational design. In fact, with the exception of planning and supervising, managerial functions like organizing, controlling, and staffing were not analyzed. These functions and questions were analyzed by subsequent theorists, to whom we now turn.

• *Henry Fayol*

Background Henry Fayol was born and educated in France, and his working life (although spent entirely with the Commentry-Fourchambault Mining Company) fell into four periods.[13] From 1860 to 1872, he was a subordinate, working mainly on technical problems of mining engineering, such as the fire hazards of coal mining. From 1872 to 1888, he was the director of a group of mining pits, and his mind turned to the geographical problems of the area. From 1888 to 1918, he held the top position of managing director of the entire company, and he proved to be a remarkably effective chief executive. (When he was appointed in 1888, the company was on the verge of bankruptcy, and many of its divisions were showing heavy losses. Almost from the day he took charge, losses decreased, and by the time he retired at the age of 77, the firm's financial and managerial situation was unassailable.) Toward the end of this period, his work *General and Industrial Management* was first published in French. From 1918 until his death in 1925, he devoted himself to popularizing his theory of administration, which (unlike Taylor's production-shop orientation) viewed management from the general perspective of a chief executive. *General and Industrial Management* was first translated into English in 1929 but was apparently not published in the United States until the 1940s.

Fayol's Definition of Management Fayol said that all industrial activities could be divided into one of six groups:

1 Technical activities (production, manufacturing, adaptation)
2 Commercial activities (buying, selling, exchange)
3 Financial activities (search for an optimum use of capital)
4 Security activities (protection of property and person)
5 Accounting activities (stock taking, balance sheets, costs, statistics)
6 Managerial activities (planning, organization, command, coordination, control)

Fayol felt that although management was only one of the six groups of activities necessary in companies, it was perhaps the most important one, and it was the only one he focused on in his writings. He also thought there was an absence of management teaching in schools and that this was due to the fact that there was "no generally accepted theory of management emanating from general discussion." He set out to present such a theory, based upon two concepts: principles of management, and elements of management.

Fayol's Principles of Management Fayol prescribed fourteen principles of management, each of which, he emphasized, was "flexible and capable of adaptation to every need; it is a matter of knowing how to make use of them, which is a difficult art requiring intelligence, experience, decision and proportion." (Although he stressed that the principles should be applied flexibly, he also referred to them as "acknowledged truths regarded as proven on which to rely.")[14] He said these fourteen were the principles he most often used as a manager, but that many other principles could also be identified.

His fourteen principles (along with some of his comments on them) were as follows:

1 *Division of work.* The worker, always on the same part, and the manager, concerned always with the same matters, acquired ability, sureness, and accuracy, which increased their output.
2 *Authority and responsibility.* Authority is the right to give orders and the power to exact obedience. Distinction must be made between a manager's official authority, deriving from office, and personal authority, compounded of intelligence, experience, moral worth, and ability to lead.
3 *Discipline.* The best means of establishing and maintaining [discipline] are: good superiors at all levels; agreements as clear and fair as possible; sanctions [penalties] judiciously applied.
4 *Unity of command.* For any action whatsoever, an employee should receive orders from one superior only. . . .
5 *Unity of direction.* There should be one head and one plan for a group of activities serving the same objective.
6 *Subordination of individual interests to general interests.* This principle means that in a business, the interests of one employee or group of employees should not prevail over those of the concern. . . . Means of effecting it are: firmness and good example on the part of superiors; agreements as far as is possible; constant supervision.
7 *Remuneration of personnel.* Remuneration should be fair and as far as possible afford satisfaction to both personnel and firm.
8 *Centralization.* The question of centralization or decentralization is a simple question of proportion; it is a matter of finding the optimum degree for the particular concern. What appropriate share of initiative may be left to intermediaries depends on the personal character of the manager, on his moral worth, on the reliability of his subordinates, and also on the condition of the business. The degree of centralization must vary according to different cases.
9 *Scalar chain.* The scalar chain is the chain of superiors ranging from the ultimate authority to the lowest ranks. . . . It is an error to depart needlessly from

the line of authority, but it is an even greater one to keep to it when detriment to the business ensues.

10 *Order.* For social order to prevail in a concern, there must be an appointed place for every employee and every employee must be in his appointed place.
11 *Equity.* For the personnel to be encouraged to carry out its duties with all the devotion and loyalty of which it is capable, it must be treated with kindliness, and equity results from the combination of kindness and justice. Equity excludes neither forcefulness nor sternness. . . .
12 *Stability of tenure of personnel.* Time is required for an employee to get used to new work and succeed in doing it well, always assuming that he possesses the requisite abilities. If, when he has gotten used to it, or before then, he is removed, he will not have had time to render worthwhile service.
13 *Initiative.* Thinking out a plan and ensuring its success is one of the keenest satisfactions for an intelligent man to experience. . . . This power of thinking out and executing is what is called initiative. . . . It . . . represents a great source of strength for business.
14 *Esprit de corps.* "Union is strength." Harmony, union among the personnel of a concern, is a great strength in that concern. Effort, then, should be made to establish it.

The Elements of Management Fayol turned next to a discussion of his "elements" of management—planning, organizing, commanding, coordinating, and controlling—and for each he presented some prescriptions; for example:

1 *Planning.* The general features of a good plan of action include . . . unity, continuity, flexibility, precision.
2 *Organizing.* The general form of an organization depends almost solely on the number of its employees. . . . The personnel of enterprises of all kinds is constituted in similar fashion to that of industrial concerns, so much so that all organizations at the same stage of expansion are alike. This likeness is explained by the fact of there being identity of functions in business of the same type.
3 *Command.* The organization, having been formed, must be set going, and this is the mission of command. . . . While it is taken for granted that every manager has authority to exact obedience, a business would be ill-served where obedience is obtained only by fear of oppression. . . . Some leaders get obedience, energy, zeal, and even loyalty without apparent effort; others never succeed at it . . . but managers should also conduct periodic audits of the organization, bring together their chief assistants by means of conferences, not become engrossed in detail, and aim at making unity, energy, initiative, and loyalty prevail among the personnel. They can do this by allowing them the maximum share in activity consistent with their position and capability even at the cost of some mistakes, whose magnitude, however, may be circumscribed by means of watchful attention.[15]
4 *Coordination.* In a well-coordinated enterprise, each department works in har-

mony with the rest; and in each department, divisions and subdivisions are precisely informed as to the share they must take in the communal task. There is a weekly conference of department heads which has for its aim to inform management about the running of the concern. . . . If such meetings are impractical, the gap must be filled as far as possible by the use of liaison officers at meetings.

5 *Control.* In an undertaking, control consists in verifying whether everything occurs in conformity with the plan adopted, the instructions issued, and the principles established. It has for its object to point out weaknesses and errors in order to rectify them and prevent recurrences. It operates on everything—things, people, actions. . . .

Fayol as an Organization Theorist As a theorist, Fayol dealt primarily with the question of organization structure, but his prescriptions touched on employee compliance as well. With respect to structure, he leaned toward recommending a more centralized, functionally specialized organization structure in which everyone and everything had a precisely defined place. (His narrative, however, contains frequent reference to his experience in his mining and steel firm, and you should keep in mind that to this day, most firms of this type will still reflect this "mechanistic" structure.) He concluded erroneously that all organizations at the same stage of development should have the same functional division of work and structure, and that the number of employees was the main determinant of the "general form of organization."

When he did address the problem of compliance, he usually prescribed the use of "sanctions" (penalties), "constant supervision," and a subordination of individual interests to those of the firm. About the only explicit statement he makes in regard to using something other than sanctions or close supervision in motivating workers is his mention of managers' "setting a good example" and also letting subordinates make more decisions in order to tap their initiative.

• *Urwick and Gulick; Mooney and Reilly*

During the 1920s and 1930s, a number of other theorists—primarily those engaged in management or consulting practices—set forth their views, following the concepts laid down by Fayol. Two of these, Luther Gulick and Lyndall Urwick, utilized their broad managerial experience in elaborating on Fayol's principles, and in 1937 they coedited *Papers on the Science of Administration.*[16] Their book included papers by Fayol, by Gulick (who was then a professor at Columbia University), by Urwick (then a management consultant), and by James D. Mooney (then a vice-president at General Motors Corporation).[17]

Gulick, Urwick, and Organization Theory In their *Papers,* Gulick and Urwick popularized principles governing *division of work, coordination, creating depart-*

ments built around "purposes, process, persons, and place," and *the use of "staff."*[18] Their work emphasized questions of organization structure. For example, they explain the pros and cons of different ways of dividing and coordinating the work of the organization, how to make use of line and staff personnel, the best span of control, and the advantages of specialization. But while stressing structure, they at least make reference to the need for encouraging motivation and compliance; Gulick says, for example:

> Any large and complicated enterprise would be incapable of effective operation if reliance for coordination were placed in organization alone. Organization is necessary; in a large enterprise it is essential, but it does not take the place of a dominant central idea as the foundation of action and self-coordination in the daily operation of all the parts of the enterprise. Accordingly, the most difficult task of the chief executive is not command, it is leadership; that is, the development of the desire and will to work together for a purpose in the minds of those who are associated in any activity. Human beings are compounded of cogitation and emotion and do not function well when treated as though they were merely cogs in motion. Their capacity for great and productive labor, creative cooperative work, and loyal self-sacrifice knows no limits provided the whole man, body, mind, and spirit, is thrown into the program.[19]

Yet, having mentioned the idea that "the development of the desire" is important, they provide almost no guidelines for implementation. They simply suggest that "personnel administration"—selecting qualified employees—is important, that professionalism among workers should be encouraged, and that "dominant ideals" in which all organizational members can believe are crucial:

> Men of intelligence and goodwill will find little difficulty in working together for a given purpose even without an organization. They do not need to be held in line or driven to do a specific task in a specific way at a specific time. They carry on because of their inner compulsion, and may in the end accomplish a far better result for that very reason.[20]

Their statements (particularly the last one) stand as a brilliant insight into the compliance problem of organization theory; yet their papers were devoted almost entirely to questions of organization structure.

Mooney and Reilly's Principles of Organization In 1931, James Mooney and Allen Reilly published their book, *Onward Industry,* which had a major influence on management practice in America.[21] In it, they stressed three principles of organization that they had found displayed in governmental, religious, military, and business organizations. In their words:

1 *The coordinative principle.* Organization begins when people, even if they be only two or more, combine their efforts for a given purpose. A simple illustra-

tion is two people combining their strength to lift and move a weighty object. The efforts of these two lifters must be coordinated. If first one lifted and then the other, there would be no unity of action, and hence no true organization of effort. . . . Coordination expresses the principles of organization "in toto." . . .

2 *The scalar process.* It is essential to the very idea and concept of organization that there must be a process, formal in character, through which the supreme coordinating authority operates throughout the whole structure of the organized body. . . . The scalar process is the same form in organization which is sometimes called hierarchical. . . . It means the graduation of duties, not according to differentiated functions, for this involves another and different principle of organization, but simply according to degrees of authority and corresponding responsibility.

3 *The functional effect.* By the term functionalism, we mean the differentiation or distinction between kinds of duties.

Mooney, Reilly, and Organization Theory Like Gulick and Urwick, Mooney and Reilly emphasized organization structure. Mooney states, for example:

> But what, in industrial organization, are the conditions necessary to the highest efficiency of considered effort? If we addressed this question to a score of representative executives, we would of course get many valuable and inspirational answers. But I wonder how many of these answers would give the structural principles of organization the importance that I believe they deserve?[22]

Yet they too at least recognize the importance of the human element. Mooney states, for example:

> In this outline of the structural principles of organization I have done no more than expose the scaffolding, the framework out of which it is made. In stressing the importance of the framework, I hope no one will think I am overlooking the major importance of the human factor. Humanly speaking, the strength of any organization is simply the aggregate strength of the individuals who compose it.[23]

However, this "aggregate strength" is best tapped by designing an efficient organization structure:

> We cannot forget, however, that the strength of the individual, whatever that strength may be, can only attain the highest measure of effectiveness through soundly adjusted relationships, and it is here that we see the fundamental importance of the structural principles. If we truly coordinate the jobs as such, we shall find that the more efficient and harmonious coordination of the people on the jobs is immensely facilitated.[24]

Max Weber and Bureaucratic Organization Theory

Background Max Weber was a contemporary of both Taylor and Fayol, and his work, first published in Germany in 1921, bears remarkable similarity to that of Fayol, Urwick, and Gulick. However, it was not translated and published in America until 1947 and was apparently unknown to theorists of the 1930s.

Unlike most of these writers, Weber did not write from the vantage point of a manager, but from that of an intellectual. He had been born in 1864 to a well-to-do, cultured family and attended Heidelberg University, where he studied law, history, economics, and philosophy under a succession of eminent scholars. He served a year in the German army, and then resumed his university studies in Berlin and Goettingen; then, after practicing law, he accepted a chair as professor at Heidelberg.

Bureaucracy Writing during the 1920s, Weber saw the growth of the large-scale organization and correctly predicted that this growth required a more formalized set of procedures for administrators. Today, he said,

> . . . it is primarily the capitalistic market economy which demands that the official business of the administration be discharged precisely, unambiguously, continuously, and with as much speed as possible.[25]

In line with this, Weber adopted the idea of an ideal or "pure form" of organization, which he called *bureaucracy*. This term, as developed by Weber and his followers, was not used in the now popularized sense of red tape and inefficiency. The bureaucratic model possesses certain structural characteristics that are found in every complex organization, and the model refers to these characteristics of organizational design. For Weber, bureaucracy was the most efficient form of organization, and could most effectively be used with the complex organizations that arose out of the needs of modern society. Weber described bureaucracy as having:

1. A well-defined hierarchy of authority
2. A clear division of work
3. A system of rules covering the rights and duties of position incumbents
4. A system of procedures for dealing with the work situation
5. Impersonality of interpersonal relationships
6. Selection for employment and promotion based on technical competence[26]

Such an organization was technically superior to any other form of organization:

> The fully developed bureaucratic mechanism compares with other organizations exactly as does the machine with the non-mechanical modes of production . . . precision, speed, unambiguity, continuity, discretion, unity, . . . these are raised to the optimum point in a strictly bureaucratic administration.[27]

Weber felt that these attributes were necessary because of the "extraordinary increase in the speed by which public announcements, as well as economic and political facts, are transmitted." He saw that the tempo of administrative action was increasing and concluded that "the optimum of such reaction time is normally obtained only by a strictly bureaucratic organization."[28]

One of the ironies in the development of organization theory is that bureaucracy, which has come to mean a ponderous and unadaptive organization, was originally advocated as the best form for dealing with a changing environment. And yet, in the context of its time, the idea made a good deal of sense. The codified rules, predictable relationships, and clear job descriptions permitted these organizations to make faster decisions than before.

One of the work problems that the bureaucratic model was developed to deal with was what Bennis has described as:

> . . . the personal subjugation, nepotism, cruelty, emotional vicissitudes and subjective judgments which passed for managerial practices in the early days of the Industrial Revolution. . . .[29]

Bureaucracy, Weber points out,

> . . . is like a modern judge who is a vending machine into which the pleadings are inserted together with the fee and which then disgorges the judgment together with reasons mechanically derived from a code.[30]

Similarly, the individual bureaucrats or officeholders in this ideal organization are described as virtually mechanical objects:

> The individual bureaucrat cannot squirm out of the apparatus in which he is harnessed . . . in a great majority of cases, he is only a single cog in an ever moving mechanism which prescribes to him an essentially fixed route of march. . . .[31]

Although the image of a mechanical organization, manned by automatons, has cast bureaucracy in an unfavorable light, remember that Weber's ideal model was usually very successful in dealing with the contemporary environment. As Bennis points out, there was a good reason for this:

> It was an ideal weapon to harness and routinize the human mechanical energy which fueled the Industrial Revolution. It can also function in a highly competitive, fairly undifferentiated and stable environment. The pyramid structure of bureaucracy where power was concentrated at the top—perhaps by one person or a group that had the knowledge and resources to control the entire enterprise—seemed perfect to "run a railroad." And undoubtedly for the routine tasks like building railroads, bureaucracy was and is an eminently suitable social arrangement.[32]

Weber and Organization Theory Weber's bureaucratic theory was primarily a theory of organization structure. In it, Weber tried to show how an ideal organization (one with clearly defined jobs, a stable hierarchy of authority, a system of written documents and procedures, and so on) was superior to less rationally conceived organizations.

Weber actually has very little to say about motivation or compliance in his essay, "Bureaucracy," but his thinking in this regard is made clear in another essay, "The Meaning of Discipline."[33] Discipline, Weber says,

> . . . is nothing but the consistently rationalized, methodically trained and exact execution of the received order, in which all personal criticism is unconditionally suspended and the actor is unswervingly and exclusively set for carrying out the command. . . .

From this essay, it is clear that Weber believed discipline to be a necessary prerequisite to bureaucracy, which he called discipline's "most rational offspring."[34] And discipline, he felt, grew out of workers' economic motives. On the one hand, he recognized that leaders sometimes use "emotional means of all sorts," such as inspiration and reference to a common cause, to evoke discipline. Yet, he says, even in war, *economic rationality* ensures the discipline of soldiers: "In the past the fully disciplined army has necessarily been a professional army, and therefore the basic problem has always been how to provide for the sustenance of the warriors." Similarly, he applies this thinking to industrial organizations:

> No special proof is necessary to show that military discipline is the ideal model for the modern capitalist factory. . . . Organizational discipline in the factory is founded upon a completely rational basis. With the help of appropriate methods of measurement, the optimum profitability of the individual worker is calculated like that of any material means of production. On the basis of this calculation, the American system of "scientific management"[35] enjoys the greatest triumphs in the rational conditioning and training of work performances. The final consequences are drawn from the mechanization and discipline of the plant, and the psycho-physical apparatus of man is completely adjusted to the demands of the outer world, the tools, the machines—in short, to individual "function." . . .[36]

• *Criticism of Administrative and Bureaucratic Organization Theories*

Criticisms of these two theories, most of which also apply to scientific management, concern characteristics that fall into one of four categories:

1. Conflicting principles and lack of empirical validity
2. Inadequate assumptions about workers
3. Inadequate assumptions about the organization's tasks
4. Unanticipated consequences

Conflicting Principles and Lack of Empirical Validity Prof. Herbert Simon has argued that the principles these theories embody are nothing more than proverbs that have neither empirical validation nor universal application. Simon points out, for example:

> It is a fatal defect of the current principles of administration that, like proverbs, they occur in pairs. For almost every principle one can find an equally plausible and acceptable contradictory principle. Although the two principles of the pair will lead to exactly opposite organizational recommendations, there is nothing in the theory to indicate which is the proper one to apply.[37]

Inadequate Assumptions about Workers Second, some say these theories tend to view workers as little more than machines. March and Simon say that they tend to view the employee as "an inert instrument performing the tasks assigned to him." These machine theories, they say, "have largely ignored factors associated with individual behavior and particularly its motivational basis."[38] Massie complains that these theories assume that people do not like to work, always act rationally, and require detailed guidance and clear job limits in order to perform adequately.[39] Another writer notes that "these are the implicit assumptions about man on which classical organizational theory seems to be based: He is lazy, short-sighted, selfish, liable to make mistakes, has poor judgment, and may even be a little dishonest."[40]

Although some of these allegations may be exaggerated, it does seem apparent that by assuming that man is primarily a rational, money-oriented decision maker, the "machine theorists" were able to relegate workers to a dependent, passive role in organizations. In other words, while clearly recognizing the importance of what Fayol called "keen" performance and "enthusiasm" on the part of the workers, these theorists *erroneously assumed that financial incentives combined with an efficient organization structure would result in optimal performance.* It is therefore not stretching the point too far to say that, despite their occasional disclaimers, these theorists tended to view organizations as something akin to machines—machines that could be laid out in blueprints (organization charts), designed to provide the most efficient service, and oiled periodically (with financial incentives) to keep all the human "parts" operating as they were designed to.

Inadequate Assumptions about the Organization's Tasks Third, as Thompson has pointed out, these organizational theories invariably assume that goals are known, tasks are repetitive, production output somehow disappears from the factory, and the organization is a closed system and impervious to all but major changes in environment.[41] Similarly, others note that Taylor was most concerned with the kinds of tasks performed on the production floor or in clerical departments, and that these tasks are largely repetitive.[42] As a result, the tasks these theories (especially scientific management) were concerned with can usually be explained in terms of overt behavior like tightening a bolt or turning a screw, and the applicability of classical prescriptions to more creative tasks must be suspect.

Unanticipated Consequences Finally, the classical theorists generally prescribed imposed controls (like rules and close supervision) for ensuring employee compliance, and one criticism of such controls is that they result in unanticipated consequences. Robert Merton, for example, says that in these theories, the techniques used to secure reliability include standard operating procedures and constant supervision. Consequences, he says, include a reduction in the amount of personalized relationships in the organization, and an internalization of the rules of the organization by participants whereby the rules, which are meant to be means to an end, become ends in themselves.[43]

Alvin Gouldner made a study of this phenomenon. He found that in practice, work rules provide cues for employees beyond those intended by the manager who developed the rules. Rules, for example, make it clear to employees what *un*acceptable behavior is, and the rules therefore become the minimum standards that employees know they can "get by" with.[44] (For example, the manager who tells his employees they can take only one hour for lunch may find that they rarely take more, but also never less.) The problem with this, of course, is that

> . . . for effective organizational functioning, many members must be willing on occasion to do *more* than their job prescriptions specify. If members of the system were to follow the precise letter of job descriptions and organizational protocol, things would soon grind to a halt. Many acts of spontaneous cooperation and many anticipations of organizational objectives are required to make the system viable. . . .[45]

Yet such unanticipated consequences need not—in fact do not—always occur. Where jobs are in fact routine, where unexpected occurrences and atypical cases do not exist, and where creativity and initiative are not required of employees, unanticipated consequences would not be a serious problem. Such a description may fit the organizations that theorists like Fayol and Mooney were most familiar with, and to that extent, their prescriptions make a great deal of sense. However, we now recognize that even though people may be "rational," the "benefits" they try to maximize include things other than money, and so using rules, close supervision, and financial incentives to maintain compliance is bound to be inadequate.

More important, in the late 1920s organizations were moving into a new era, one in which the tempo of competition and change and the demand for organizational responsiveness increased. At the same time, as we will see in the next chapter, the tasks workers were called upon to do increasingly required a problem-solving ability and creativity not foreseen by early classical theorists. Man's values changed, the tempo of technological change increased, and the world moved toward what William Scott has called the period of collision.

SUMMARY

What can we conclude from this discussion of classical organization theories? Perhaps the best way to frame an answer to this is in terms of these four questions:

What prescriptions did each theorist have for how to best structure organizations? The highly centralized and mechanistic structures of classical theory had their genesis in the state monopolies of Egypt and the military empire of Rome. Faced with the need for structures through which to manage their new organizations, Industrial Revolution-era managers quickly adopted the structures and principles of the older, preindustrial organizations, and centralization, clear hierarchy of command, and specialized division of work soon became the norm. By and large, the classical theorists themselves—Taylor, Fayol, Urwick and Gulick, Mooney and Reilly, and Weber—generally focused on the question of organization structure, and their prescriptions tended to reflect the mechanistic structural prescriptions (for centralization, specialization of work, and so on) of preindustrial writers. This was due partly to the fairly routine tasks facing the classicists' organizations, and partly to the fact that Protestantism and the concept of economic individualism that prevailed in the early 1900s put great stress on the religious and economic advantages of highly specialized work.

What prescriptions did each theorist have for how to best ensure compliance—to ensure, in other words, that each worker carries out the task to which he or she is assigned? Preindustrial managers emphasized discipline, dogma, and fear in obtaining compliance, techniques that were probably effective where workers were slaves, serfs, or soldiers. But with the advent of the Industrial Revolution, scores of new workers had to be hired and controlled, and new techniques had to be developed to ensure employee compliance. Here, early managers and the later classical theorists found a rallying point in the economic individualism of Protestantism. Protestantism did not condone the pursuit of wealth but did encourage intense activity as the goal of the good life, and such activity was generally measured in economic terms. As a result, classical theorists were able to substitute a network of financial incentives for the discipline and fear of earlier managers. Classical organization theory is thus replete with reference to the need for financial incentives and for close supervision for ensuring employee compliance.

What was it about the workers' tasks *each theorist focused on that influenced the prescriptions for how to structure organizations and obtain compliance?* During this period, the tasks facing workers were relatively routine and repetitive: Efficiency, rather than creativity or adaptability, was the rule. Jobs like these could be objectively measured and closely supervised, and so close supervision and financial incentives were useful techniques for ensuring compliance. Similarly, there was little or no need for workers to make problem-solving-type, creative decisions, and so most decisions could be made centrally and then enforced through the chain of command.

What was it about the environment *of the organizations each theorist focused on that influenced the prescriptions for how to structure organizations and gain compliance?* The answer to this was perhaps best summarized by Toffler, who said:

> Each age produces a form of organization appropriate to its own tempo. During the long epoch of agricultural civilization, societies were marked by low transience. Delays in communication and transportation slowed the rate at which information moved. The pace of individual life was comparatively slow. And organizations were seldom called upon to make what we would regard as high-speed decisions.

During this period, in other words, organizational environments (including competitors, customers, sources of labor, and so forth) were relatively simple and unchanging. Particularly during the early 1900s, most managers found a strong demand for their products and could focus attention on efficiency rather than on developing new products or adapting to a competitor's new product. And in this relatively undifferentiated and stable environment, an emphasis on efficiency (and therefore, centralized decision making, highly specialized jobs, financial incentives, and close supervision) made a good deal of sense. The most effective organizations, in fact, were those that could focus on efficiency and thus minimize their costs and selling prices.

Organizational environments and tasks thus emerge as important determinants of how an organization is structured and managed. How will the prescriptions of organization theorists change when the prevailing organizations must cope with complex, changing environments and creative, entrepreneurial tasks? This is a topic we turn to in the next chapter.

DISCUSSION QUESTIONS

1 Describe how developments during the preindustrial period contributed to later organization theory.
2 How did Protestantism influence classical organization theory?
3 Compare and contrast the organization theories of Taylor, Fayol, and Weber.
4 Discuss the criticisms of administrative and bureaucratic organizational theories. To what extent do you think these criticisms are valid?
5 What are the implicit assumptions of the classical organization theories?
6 "Organization theory and values tend to reflect the prevailing environment in which they develop." Discuss whether you agree or disagree with this statement. Include specific references to the various theories we discussed in this chapter.

FOOTNOTES

[1]Adriano Tilgher, *Work,* trans. Dorothy C. Fisher (New York: Harcourt, Brace, 1930), pp. 5–6, quoted in Richard Eells and Clarence Walton, *Conceptual Foundations of Business* (Homewood, Ill.: Richard D. Irwin, 1961), p. 21. For an excellent discussion of the evolution of management thought, see

Daniel Wren, *The Evolution of Management Thought* (New York: Ronald Press, 1972). See also F. Kast and J. Rosenzweig, *Organization and Management* (New York: McGraw-Hill, 1974), 25–73.

[2]E.H. Harbison, *The Age of Reformation* (Ithaca, N.Y.: Cornell University Press, 1955).

[3]R.H. Tawney, *Religion and the Rise of Capitalism* (New York: New American Library, 1954), p. 35.

[4]Harbison, *The Age of Reformation.*

[5]Tawney, *Religion and the Rise of Capitalism,* p. 191.

[6]*Ibid.,* pp. 188–89.

[7]James G. March and Herbert A. Simon, *Organizations* (New York: John Wiley, 1958), p. 29.

[8]Alvin Toffler, *Future Shock* (New York: Bantam Books, 1971), p. 143.

[9]Alfred Chandler, *Strategy and Structure* (Cambridge, Mass.: M.I.T. Press, 1932).

[10]D.S. Pugh, *Organization Theory* (Baltimore: Penguin, 1971), pp. 126–27.

[11]Frederick W. Taylor, "What Is Scientific Management?" reprinted in Michael Matteson and John Ivancevich, *Management Classics* (Santa Monica: Goodyear, 1977), pp. 5–8.

[12]James D. Thompson, *Organizations in Action* (New York: McGraw-Hill, 1967), p. 5.

[13]Much of the information on Fayol was derived from Henri Fayol, *General and Industrial Management,* trans. Constance Storrs (London: Sir Isaac Pitman, 1949).

[14]*Ibid.,* p. 42.

[15]*Ibid.,* pp. 102–3.

[16]Luther Gulick and Lyndall Urwick, eds., *Papers on the Science of Administration* (Clifton, N.J.: A.M. Kelley, 1972).

[17]Also papers by, among others, Elton Mayo, Mary Parker Follett, and V.A. Graicunas.

[18]Gulick and Urwick, *Papers,* p. 3.

[19]*Ibid.,* p. 37.

[20]*Ibid.,* p. 38.

[21]James Mooney and Allen Reilly, *Onward Industry* (New York: Harper & Row, 1931).

[22]*Ibid.,* p. 92.

[23]*Ibid.,* p. 96.

[24]*Ibid.,* p. 96.

[25]Max Weber, "Bureaucracy," in *Essays in Sociology,* trans. and ed. H.H. Gerth and C. Wright Mills, copyright 1946 by Oxford University Press; reprinted in Joseph A. Litterer, *Organizations: Structure and Behavior* (New York: John Wiley, 1969), p. 34.

[26]Based on Richard D. Hall, "Intraorganizational Structure Variation: Application of the Bureaucratic Model," *Administrative Science Quarterly,* Vol. 7, No. 3 (December 1962), 295–308.

[27]Weber, "Bureaucracy."

[28]*Ibid.*

[29]Warren G. Bennis, "Organizational Development and the Fate of Bureaucracy," address to the Division of Industrial and Business Psychology, American Psychological Association, September 5, 1964. Reprinted in L.L. Cummings and W.E. Scott, Jr., *Organizational Behavior and Human Performance* (Homewood, Ill.: Richard D. Irwin and Dorsey, 1969), p. 436.

[30]R. Bendix. *Max Weber: An Intellectual Portrait* (New York: Doubleday, 1960), p. 421. Indeed, Weiss has recently taken the position that Weber was primarily concerned not with organizational efficiency or effectiveness but with dominance in organizations, and how to best reduce its adverse effects. See Richard Weiss, "Weber on Bureaucracy: Management Consultant or Political Theorist?" *The Academy of Management Review,* Vol. 8, No. 3 (April 1983), 242–47.

[31]Weber, "Bureaucracy," p. 37.

[32]Bennis, "Organizational Development," p. 443.

[33]In Weber, *Essays in Sociology,* pp. 253–64.

[34]*Ibid.,* p. 254.

[35]Weber had spent some time traveling in the United States.

[36]Weber, "The Meaning of Discipline," p. 261.

[37]Herbert A. Simon, *Administrative Behavior* (New York: Free Press, 1976), p. 20.

[38]March and Simon, *Organizations,* p. 29.

[39]J.L. Massie, "Management Theory," in *Handbook of Organizations,* ed. J.G. March (New York: Rand McNally, 1965).

[40]Mason Haire, "The Concept of Power and the Concept of Man," in *Social Science Approaches to Business Behavior,* ed. George B. Strother (Homewood, Ill.: Dorsey, 1962), p. 176.

[41]Thompson, *Organizations in Action,* p. 35.

[42]March and Simon, *Organizations,* p. 14.

[43]Robert Merton, *Social Theory and Social Structure,* rev. ed. (New York: Free Press, 1957).

[44]Alvin Gouldner, *Patterns of Industrial Bureaucracy* (New York: Free Press, 1954).

[45]Daniel Katz and Robert Kahn, *The Social Psychology of Organizations* (New York: John Wiley, 1966).

3

Contemporary Organization Theories

OVERVIEW

In this chapter we continue our discussion of the evolution of organization theory with a treatment of the period from roughly 1930 to the present. This period was marked by an increase in the rate of change facing organizations and with the emergence of work tasks that called for more creativity and problem solving on the part of employees. We will see that these new environments and tasks influenced the prescriptions of contemporary organization theorists. This new environment—characterized by increased diversity and change—combined with the advent of human-relations management to create a new direction for organization theory.

The outline of this chapter is as follows:

3 Tavistock studies
4 Homans
5 Likert
6 McGregor
7 Argyris
8 Katz and Kahn

D The quantitative school
1 Management science/operations research
2 Arguments against the use of management science

E Toward a situational theory

HUMAN-RELATIONS MANAGEMENT: THE PERIOD OF COLLISION

• *The Changing Environment*

As early as 1900, events were occurring that, culminating in the late 1930s, would drastically alter man's view of himself, his organizations, and his environment. William Scott has proposed that the individualistic optimism of the 19th century slowly gave way to an era of conflict, which he called the Period of Collision.[1] The collision effect results from "environmental conditions which draw people into inescapable proximity and dependency on one another."[2] The factors leading to the dependency and proximity may be categorized as technology and population dynamics.

The technological factors were primarily products of the rapid industrialization of the period. Mechanization was rapidly replacing manpower, and standardization, division of work, and specialization were widely emphasized on both the production and organizational levels. In turn, such a division of work results in interdependency and a need for tight coordination. Furthermore, the nature of mass production and specialization necessitates a large number of functions, thus adding to worker proximity. The industrial factors were in turn compounded by the improving communications and transportation of the period. In addition to making the country "smaller," these factors contributed to expanded markets and therefore to increased industrialization. Dependency and proximity were also aggravated by the population trends of the early 1900s: The population in America doubled between 1890 and 1930, and the proportion of city dwellers rose from 20 percent in 1860 to over 50 percent by 1920.

These factors might not have added up to a "collision effect" had they not occurred simultaneously with the closing of the American frontier. The frontier, Scott says, had acted as a safety valve and contributed to a spirit of optimism and growth during the 19th century; with its closing, the proximity and dependency caused by technology and population growth resulted in conflict and collision:

> If left unharnessed, the collision effect would breed brutal competition, then conflict, to end in the degeneration of society.[3]

However, this did not occur, because the collision effect coincided with a change in societal values, characterized by a deemphasis on the individualistic ethic and a corresponding emphasis on a social ethic. This change manifested itself in a number of ways. Government became increasingly involved in economic matters, and a variety of suits based on the Sherman Act were initiated by President Theodore Roosevelt and his successors. The Progressives' movement became popular and with it their objectives of enfranchising women, electing senators by popular direct vote, establishing a minimum wage, and encouraging trade unions. The literature of the period became increasingly antiindividualistic and, as Allen has pointed out, "there was a continuing disposition among Americans, young and old, to look with a cynical eye upon the old Horatio Alger formula for success."[4] The factories poured forth products in abundance, and the fetish for efficiency was replaced by an emphasis on consumption. People craved security, and the need to belong became prevalent in American industrial life.

• *Hawthorne*

In 1927, a series of studies was begun at the Chicago Hawthorne plant of the Western Electric Company that would eventually add an entirely new perspective to the analysis of organizations and management. We analyze these studies in detail in Chapter 14, but because of their importance to the present topic, we discuss them briefly at this point.

The original Hawthorne studies were based on a number of traditional scientific-management assumptions. In particular, the initial study was formulated to determine the relation of the level of illumination in the workplace to the efficiency of workers; but to the surprise of the researchers, their findings showed no consistent relation between these two factors. In fact, when the experiment was reversed and the illumination reduced, output actually continued to increase. These findings led to additional studies aimed at explaining the mysterious discrepancy between traditional assumptions about worker behavior and their actual behavior.

The Hawthorne results suggested that variables other than physical working conditions might be affecting worker behavior and output. Initially, this possibility was studied by examining the relationships between output and working conditions like length of the working day and rest periods. The researchers continued to find that regardless of how the physical conditions varied, production continued to increase. They finally hypothesized that the increases in output were not the result of physical job conditions but rather of the changed social situations of the workers—in particular, changes in their motivation, group norms, satisfaction, and patterns of supervision.[5] For the first time, the notion that workers' behavior depended on something more than just financial incentives and physical work conditions became popular.

• *The End of an Era*

The Hawthorne experiments were ended in 1933 as the country fell deeper into the Great Depression. Between 1929 and 1933, the unemployment rate rose from 3.2 percent to 30 percent. Businesses were failing, unemployment was widespread, incomes were dropping, and national morale was low. The period of optimism and prosperity was gone; the old guideposts of individualism and self-help had failed, and the notion of the self-made man as a guarantee of economic order was rejected. Increasingly, the social ethic of the times played down achievement by individuals and emphasized the importance of the group and of getting along with others.

Changes were also occurring in economic theory. For years, people had been taught to believe that saving money was a virtue, and that the "invisible hand" of the market would ensure that each person, working in his own self-interest, would unknowingly contribute to and ensure society's maximum welfare. British economist John Maynard Keynes attacked these assumptions, and showed in convincing terms that saving could actually diminish a nation's productive strength, and that government spending should be used—in fact *had* to be used—to breathe life back into the faltering economy.[6] His work provided a theoretical foundation for the new social ethic and cast doubts on the classical assumption of rationality as well.

As a result of the new social ethic, the depression, and the Hawthorne studies, a new set of assumptions about work and workers had to be formulated. Whereas leaders from the dawn of civilization to the classical organization theorists had viewed the worker as an inert tool, they would henceforth have to view him as a significant variable in the system. Organization theories would have to allow for interaction between the formal system and its human components. Furthermore, as we shall see, the environment in which organizations were operating was becoming increasingly complex, and this would result in a new emphasis on organizational adaptability and the fuller utilization of employee problem-solving potential. New techniques for eliciting creativity had to be developed.

BRIDGING THE ERAS: FOLLETT, BARNARD, AND SIMON

The work of the writers described in this section does not fit neatly into any one school of organization theory. Although Follett wrote during the scientific-management era, her work pointed the way to human relations in management. Similarly, Barnard and Simon are often considered members of a "decision-theory" school, but their contributions actually spanned a number of schools and contributed to the development of an integrated theory of organizations.

• *Mary Parker Follett*

Mary Parker Follett was trained in philosophy and political science and became interested in social psychology early in her career. She was an admirer of a philosophy in which the freedom of the individual was subordinated to that of the group. For Follett, democracy did not mean individualism, but rather the development of a social consciousness. The true democracy was to build from small neighborhood groups to community groups, and so on. She consistently stressed the need for "integration," which involved finding a solution that satisfied both sides without having one side dominate the other.

Integration as a principle, however, could not be implemented until a new concept of authority and power was developed. She sought to develop such a concept by advocating power *with* rather than power *over,* and by abolishing many aspects of the roles of boss and subordinate. "One person," she concluded, "should not give orders to another person, but both should agree to take their orders from the situation."[7]

• *Chester Barnard*

Writing several years later, Chester Barnard used his experience as an executive to develop an important new organization theory. He was the president of New Jersey Bell Telephone Company and, at various times, president of the United Service Organization (the USO of World War II), president of the Rockefeller Foundation, and chairman of the National Science Foundation. His book, *The Functions of the Executive,* "is a direct outcome of Barnard's failure to find an adequate explanation of his own executive experience in classic organization or economic theory."[8]

Barnard's contributions lie in three areas: First, his was the first organization theory to attempt to explain the importance and variabililty of individual behavior at work. Second, he developed a classic explanation of compliance, an explanation that emphasized the importance of both financial and nonfinancial incentives. Third, he presented a new theory of organization structure, one that focused on the organization as a communication system. We will discuss each of these three contributions.

The Importance of Individual Behavior Classical organization theorists tended to focus on questions of organization structure. They largely neglected the question of compliance by assuming that workers were economically rational and would perform in direct relation to their financial incentives. People, in other words, were viewed as "givens" in the system, like the mechanical devices of an engineer.

Barnard was the first major theorist (after the Hawthorne studies) to emphasize the importance and variability of the individual in the work setting. He said, for example, that "an essential element of organizations is the willingness of persons to contribute their individual efforts to the cooperative system." And he added that "the individual is always the basic strategic factor in organization. Regardless of his history or his obligations, he must be induced to cooperate, or there can be no cooperation." Such remarks may seem obvious today, but when they were written in the mid-1930s, they represented a clear and important break with the classical theories.

Barnard's Theory of Compliance Besides emphasizing the importance of individual behavior, Barnard developed a theory of motivation and compliance in organizations. It consisted of four basic elements:

1 *The willingness to cooperate is a basic requirement of organization.* First, Barnard states that compliance—the willingness of individuals to cooperate—is a basic element of organization.[9]
2 *In complying, the individual must "surrender" his personal preferences.* According to Barnard, an order has "authority"—it will be carried out—when it is such that the person getting the order is willing to surrender his own preferences and carry it out. Willingness, says Barnard, means "the surrender of control of personal conduct, the depersonalization of personal action."[10]
3 *The order must fall within the person's "zone of indifference."* Why should a person be willing to carry out his superior's orders? Because there exists, says Barnard, a "zone of indifference" in each individual in which orders are acceptable *without conscious questioning of their authority.*[11]
4 *The inducements and contributions determine how wide the zone of indifference is.* But why should a person be willing to unquestioningly suspend his own judgment? Incentives, says Barnard, provide the answer. He says that the willingness to cooperate is the expression of the net satisfactions or dissatisfactions experienced or anticipated by each person and that each, in effect, asks himself, "Is it to my advantage to carry out this order?"[12] Since orders must be "accepted" to be carried out, it behooves organizations to see to it that the advantages (of suspending judgment and carrying out the order) outweigh the disadvantages; for this, inducements (or incentives) must be used. Barnard, in a clear break with the classicists, states that material incentives by themselves are not enough: "The unaided power of material incentives, when the minimum necessities are satisfied, in my opinion is exceedingly limited as to most men. . . ."[13] Instead, several other classes of incentives, including "the opportunities for distinction, prestige, personal power . . ." are also necessary. The extent to which the advantages outweigh the disadvantages (or the inducements outweigh the contributions) then determines the width of the zone of indifference: It will be "wider or narrower depending on the degree to which the inducement exceeds the burdens and sacrifices. . . ."[14] Finally, if an organization cannot provide adequate incentives, then coercion is sometimes used.

Barnard's Theory of Organization Structure Barnard also made contributions to the theory of organization structure. He stressed that the organization was a structure of decision makers and emphasized the importance of communications in organizations. He stressed the role of the informal organization and explained how it aids communication and cohesiveness. He was also probably the first to take a "systems" view of organizations, including in the latter investors, suppliers, and others whose actions contribute to the firm.

• *Herbert Simon*

Barnard's view of the organization as a network of decision makers in which inducements play a major role was refined and developed by Herbert Simon.[15] Whereas Barnard wrote from the vantage point of an executive, Simon was a scholar who had a mastery of organization theory, economics, natural science, and political science.

Simon's Theory of Compliance Like Barnard, Simon viewed developing and maintaining compliance as a major problem facing managers, and he said:

> Decisions reached in the higher ranks of the organization hierarchy will have no effect upon the activities of operative employees unless they are communicated downward. Consideration of the process requires an examination of the ways in which the behavior of the operative employee can be influenced. These influences fall roughly into two categories: (1) *establishing in the operative employee himself* attitudes, habits, and a state of mind which lead him to reach that decision which is advantageous to the organization, and (2) *imposing on the operative employee* decisions reached elsewhere in the organization. The first type of influence operates by inculcating in the employee organizational loyalties and a concern with efficiency, and more generally by training him. The second type of influence depends primarily upon authority and upon advisory and informational services. It is not insisted that these categories are either exhaustive or mutually exclusive. . . .[16]

Thus, according to Simon, there are various types of influence an organization can use to ensure employee compliance, and to a large extent, these types are interchangeable. First, you can *impose authority* on an employee.[17] Here, a subordinate is said to accept authority whenever he permits his behavior to be guided by the decision of his superior, but "if you attempt to carry authority beyond a certain point (the "zone of acceptance," which is equivalent to Barnard's zone of indifference), disobedience will follow."

What then determines the "width" of the person's zone of acceptance? Primarily, according to Simon, the nature and magnitude of the incentives the organization offers. These incentives include salary, status and prestige, opportunities for promotion, and other material and nonmaterial rewards.[18]

However, inducements are not the only methods of ensuring acceptance of authority. There are also sanctions (like the possibility of losing one's job) and the "social sanctions" that come from accepting the job in the first place. Specifically, joining the organization and accepting a "subordinate" role automatically "establishes an area of acceptance in behavior within which the subordinate is willing to accept the decisions made for him by his superior."[19]

But, according to Simon, there is an alternative to *imposed* authority. The organization can also establish in the employee *self-control*—the "attitudes, habits, and a state of mind which lead him to reach that decision which is advantageous to the organization."[20] Simon cites three factors contributing to the development of such self-control. One is *organizational loyalty* or identification. Here, the person identifies with the organization, and its goals become his own. The second is inculcation in employees of *the criterion of efficiency*. Here, the employee is motivated "to take the shortest path, the cheapest means, toward the attainment of the desired goals."[21] *Training* is a third method for developing self-control: It "prepares the organization member to reach satisfactory decisions himself, without the need for the constant exercise of authority or advice."[22]

Thus, according to Simon, managers can ensure that employees carry out their tasks in one of two ways: They can *impose* control (through the use of authority), or they can develop *self-control* (through training, the criterion of efficiency, and organizational identification or loyalty). And, in comparing these two, Simon notes:

> Administrators have increasingly recognized in recent years [the early 1940s] that authority, unless buttressed by other forms of influence, is relatively impotent to control decision in any but a negative way. The elements entering into all but the most routine decisions are so numerous and so complex that it is impossible to control positively more than a few. Unless the subordinate is himself able to supply most of the premises of decision, and to synthesize them adequately, the task of supervision becomes hopelessly burdensome.[23]

Written when it was, this was a perceptive and useful insight. It helped to explain, for example, how the classical theories—dependent as they were on the exercise of authority, and on imposed control—had been so useful. As long as tasks were simple, repetitive, and routine, no complex decision making was necessary. And where the rules always apply—where they cover every contingency, and the employee is never called upon to do more than what the rules tell him to—few controls beyond rules and close supervision are required.

However, and this is very important, few jobs can be laid out in advance with such perfect detail. Especially in the changing environment after World War II, employees have had to innovate—to do more than what is called for in the rules—to carry out their tasks satisfactorily. At the extreme, the job may depend so much on the employees' creativity and problem solving that relying on imposed authority for ensuring performance is virtually impossible. Here, other modes of influence (like

Simon's "organizational identification") that encourage self-control are necessary; and "the broader the sphere of discretion left to the subordinate, the more important become those types of influence which do not depend upon the exercise of formal authority."[24]

Simon's Theory of Organization Structure Simon also contributed to our understanding of organization structure by elaborating on Barnard's idea of an organization as a network of decision makers. For example, Simon and his associates classified decision making as routine versus creative, and then drew conclusions about what types of structures were best for facilitating each type of decision making. He was also one of the first to explain clearly why decentralized decision making is often preferable:

> It has been assumed that given ample time, the superior could make more accurate decisions than the subordinate and that centralization is therefore preferred. This will be true, however, only if the information upon which the decision is to be based is equally accessible to both. When decisions must be made against a deadline, or when the organization is characterized by geographical dispersion, this may be far from the case.[25]

• *Summary*

The work of Follett, Barnard, and Simon, emerging as it did at about the time of the Hawthorne studies, resulted in a significant change in direction for organization theory. Up to this time, theorists were preoccupied with organization structure and with designing jobs as efficiently as possible. Employees were viewed as "givens," as little more than mechanical parts that could be expected to perform as ordered as long as financial incentives were adequate. There is little in the classicists' writing to indicate that they viewed man as worthless or lazy, and yet the ends were the same: By assuming that man was motivated by money alone, they were able to discount the variability in human behavior and instead devote their full energies to efficient organization design.

The work of the theorists we discussed in this section changed the course of organization theory. Most significantly, they introduced the idea that orders need not always be accepted, and that such acceptance was actually a function of a variety of material and nonmaterial inducements. Their work, in other words, turned the attention of theorists to the second major question of organization theory: the question of compliance—of how to ensure that employees carry out their assigned tasks. And whereas prior researchers had focused on organization structure and disregarded the question of compliance, later theorists would do the opposite: They focused almost entirely on questions of motivation, control, and compliance, often relegating questions of structure to a position of secondary importance.

THE BEHAVIORAL-SYSTEMS SCHOOL

• The Environment: Increased Diversity and Change

Chandler has suggested that after accumulating and rationalizing resources, managers traditionally move into a third stage, in which organizations attempt to utilize these resources by developing new products and new markets. Movement into this third stage was hampered by the Depression; but as Chandler points out, the presence of excess production capacity during the Depression did stimulate research and development activities, which led to product diversification.[26] Furthermore, although World War II required industrial conversion to military production, the technological and managerial advancements of the war years resulted in a postwar reconversion that finally shifted most of American industry into Chandler's stage 3.

This period was characterized by product diversification and by increasingly differentiated, complex, and rapidly changing environments. Even before World War II, many companies had embarked upon extensive research and development activities, with the objective of developing new products and thereby better utilizing their resources. In fact, some companies, such as du Pont and General Electric, had already begun strategies of diversification, although these strategies generally did not become widespread until after the war. At General Electric and Westinghouse, research and development activities resulted in the manufacture of plastics and alloys, as well as a variety of other products based upon the science of electronics. And the automobile companies had already begun to produce airplane engines, electrical equipment, and household appliances before the war years. After the war, companies in the rubber industry—such as United States Rubber and B.F. Goodrich, which had concentrated on tire manufacturing—entered into systematic research and development and began to market latex, plastics, flooring, and so forth. Similarly, postwar gasoline companies began to diversify by developing a wide range of petrochemicals. Steel and aluminum companies also undertook strategies of diversification by developing more complete and wide-ranging product lines. Somewhat later, the large food-processing and -marketing organizations began to develop a wide variety of breakfast cereals, prepared foods, and other end products.[27]

These environmental changes were important for the development of organization theory for several reasons. First, as we will see, the increased rate of change and novelty meant that managers and management theorists could no longer view organizations as closed systems that were isolated from their environments.[28] Second, there was a corresponding shift in emphasis toward making organizations more adaptable, as evidenced by a trend toward decentralization.[29] Decentralization, however, required a new organizational philosophy. In particular, by placing a new emphasis upon the decision making and problem solving of people at all levels of the organization, it accentuated a number of the trends of this period. Managers increasingly found it necessary to elicit the self-control of their employees; and words such as *democratic* and *participative leadership* began to appear frequently in the management literature.

The first theorists who tried to deal with this new milieu may be called "behavioral-systems writers," since they focused on organization *behavior* and on the organization as a *system*. The classicists had designed the organization for efficiency and assumed that compliance would follow automatically through the use of financial incentives. The behavioral systems writers had the opposite point of view. Employees, they emphasized, are human beings who are motivated by a vast array of wants and needs. The main focus of organization theory should be on the question of motivation and compliance, and they therefore focused on developing theories and prescriptions for motivating employees. The classicists said, "Build the organization structure, and employees will comply." The theorists we discuss in this section said, "Focus on motivating employees, and structure your organization to increase motivation and morale."

• *Kurt Lewin*

Most behavioral-systems writers are primarily social psychologists, who look upon Kurt Lewin as the founder of their school. Lewin's major contributions were in the area of group dynamics; in this context, he developed the idea of Field Theory, which holds that group behavior is an intricate set of interactions and forces that affect both group structure and individual behavior.[30]

Lewin's work, carried out in the late 1930s, was motivated by his desire to link human behavior and the environment. He developed a model describing the relationship between an individual and his environment:

$$B = f(P,E)$$

Lewin's model proposes that a worker's behavior in a factory (B) is a function of or is influenced significantly by the personality or personal characteristics of the worker (P) as well as the factory's environment or climate (E).

Although this model seems simple enough today, it is important to remember the conceptual jump it represented in the 1930s. What Lewin emphasized was that a person's behavior is not just some function of economic rewards. Instead, it is a complex product of the person's personality and the environment in which he works. Lewin's theory helped to emphasize that employee behavior was a *variable*, not a *given* in the organization.

Lewin's stress upon the relationship between the individual, group, organization, and environment was pursued by a number of researchers. At Yale, for example, a researcher studied the New England Telephone Company to determine how the company and the union were bound together in an integrated social system. His studies provided a new perspective that was a building block for later work carried out at the Tavistock Institute for Social Research in England.

• *Tavistock Studies*

Researchers at the Tavistock Institute focused on the relationship between the technical and the social systems in organizations. In one study at the Glacier Metal Company, for example, researchers found that a technological change had drastically altered the organization's social system.[31] In another Tavistock study, Trist and his associates made an analysis of the British coal industry.[32] A new "long-wall" technology had been implemented that required the breakup of small, cohesive work groups and the substitution of specialized larger groups working in shifts. The logical efficiency of the long-wall method had resulted in severe emotional disturbances, low productivity, and an increasing sense of anomie. The conclusion in both cases was that the imperatives of efficiency had so disrupted the social organization that the hoped-for advantages of the new method never materialized.

• *Homans*

Writing at about the same time, George Homans tried to conceptualize how an organization's social and technical systems are related. As seen in Figure 3-1, he divided the social system of a group into an internal and external system. The external system contained certain *required* actions, interactions, and sentiments, whereas the internal system was characterized by a number of *emergent* actions, interactions, and sentiments. Homans stressed that all the various elements in his model interacted with each other and that they all needed to be considered in the design of the organization.

• *Likert*

The work of Rensis Likert is another example of the trends in organization theory during this period. Likert's thesis is that effective organizations differ markedly from ineffective ones in a number of ways. The effective organization encourages its supervisors to "focus their primary attention on endeavoring to build effective work groups with high performance goals." This can be contrasted with the less-effective organization, which usually follows the prescriptions of classical organization theory. These less-effective, "job-centered" organizations:

1 Break the total operation into simple component parts or tasks
2 Develop the best way to carry out each of the component parts
3 Hire people with appropriate aptitudes and skills to perform each of these tasks
4 Train these people to do their respective tasks in the specified best way

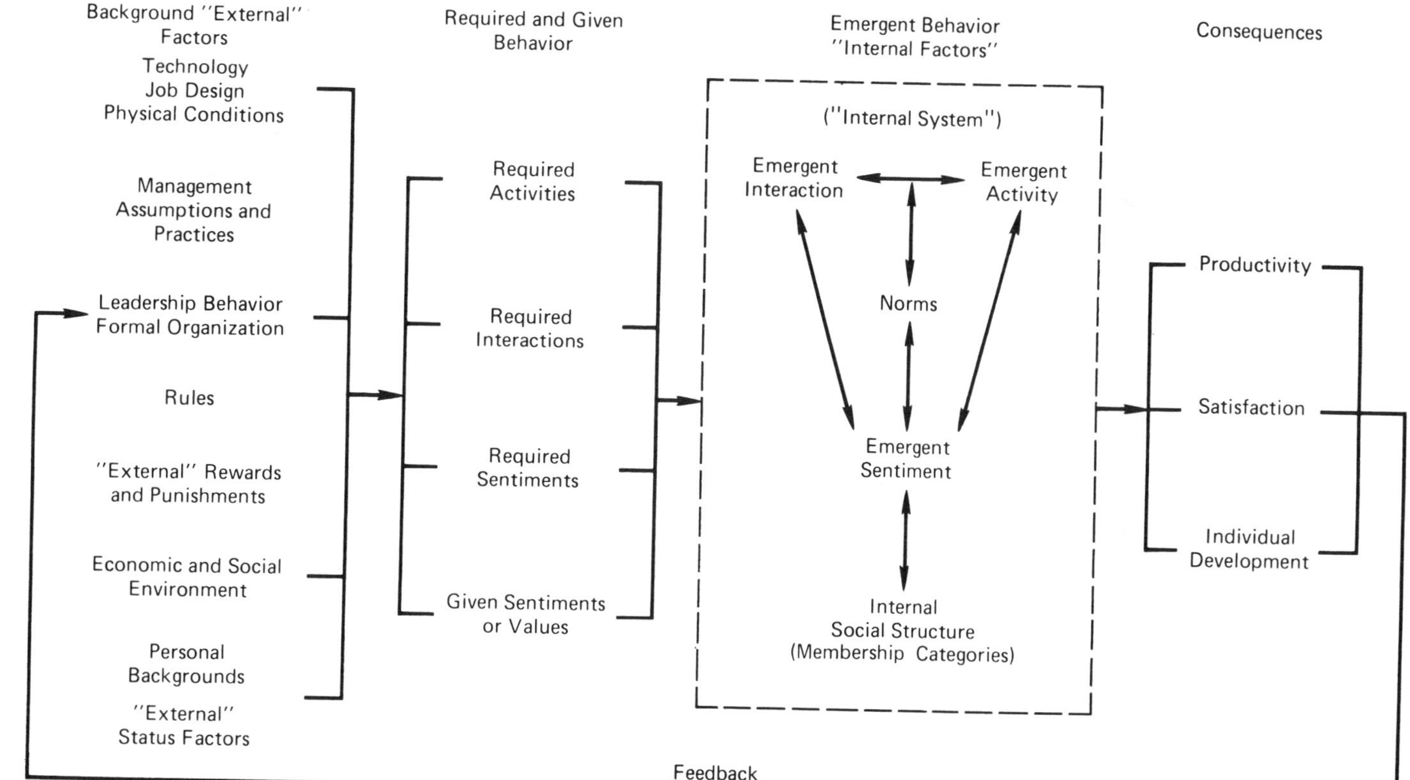

FIGURE 3-1 How Work-Group Behavior Is Related to "External" Factors such as Technology and Environment. *Source:* Arthur N. Turner, "A Conceptual Scheme for Describing Work Group Behavior," in Paul R. Lawrence and John A. Seller, *Organizational Behavior and Administration,* rev. ed. (Homewood, Ill.: Richard D. Irwin and Dorsey, 1965), p. 158.

5 Provide supervision to see that they perform their designated tasks, using the specified procedure and at an acceptable rate as determined by such procedures as timing the job
6 Use incentives, where feasible, in the form of individual or group wage rates[33]

For Likert, structure was only a means to an end, that end being the improved motivation and morale of employees. He says, for example:

> The leadership and other processes of the organization must be such as to ensure a maximum probability that in all interactions and all relationships with the organization each member will, in the light of his background, values, and expectations, view the experience as supportive and one which builds and maintains his sense of personal worth and importance.[34]

In addition, he asserts that management will fully utilize its human resources only when each person in an organization is a member of one or more effectively functioning work groups that have a high degree of group loyalty.[35] And the most effective leaders in such groups are perceived as supportive, friendly, and helpful by their subordinates.

Notice the change that has taken place in organization theory between the classicists and Likert. Whereas the former stressed organization structure and assumed employee compliance, Likert stresses the importance of motivating employees and building a structure to serve that purpose. The classicists stressed efficiency, centralization, and narrow spans of control. Likert, seeking a structure to boost motivation, prescribes a flexible structure in which subordinates make important decisions and in which supervision is supportive and friendly. Thus, compared with that of the classicists, Likert's approach formed a totally new theory, a theory in which questions of human motivation, self-control, and compliance were paramount.

• *McGregor*

Working independently, Douglas McGregor arrived at conclusions concerning the interaction between the individual and the organization that were strikingly similar to those of Likert. According to McGregor, the traditional organization, with its highly specialized jobs, centralized decision making, and top-down communications, was not simply a product of economic necessity but rather a reflection of certain basic assumptions about human nature.[36] These assumptions, which McGregor somewhat arbitrarily classified as "Theory X," held that most people dislike work and responsibility and prefer to be directed; that people are motivated not by the desire to do a good job, but simply by financial incentives; and that therefore, most people must be closely supervised, controlled, and coerced into achieving organizational objectives.

McGregor questioned the truth of this view and, in doing so, naturally questioned whether such management practices as centralization and specialized division of work are appropriate for the sorts of tasks faced by many organizations today. He felt that management needed new organizations and practices, and that these in turn had to be based on a revised view of the nature of man. What emerged was an alternate set of assumptions, which McGregor called "Theory Y." Unlike the Theory X assumptions, these held that people could enjoy work and that, if the conditions were favorable, they would exercise substantial self-control over their performance. Implicit in these Theory Y assumptions is the belief that people are motivated by the desire to do a good job and by the opportunity to affiliate with their peers, rather than simply by financial rewards.

Based upon these Theory Y assumptions, McGregor proposed a new approach to organization structure and compliance, one aimed at encouraging self-control.[37]

For the purpose of developing such self-control, McGregor suggested several new techniques, some of which involved restructuring organizations. He said *decentralization* and *delegation* should be the norm in order to free people from the "too close control of conventional organization." *Job enlargement* (in which the variety of tasks an employee performs is increased) should be encouraged so that workers' jobs are made more challenging and interesting. *Participative management* (which he said would give employees "some voice in decisions that affect them") would similarly enhance self-control. Finally, he proposed using *management by objectives;* here, subordinates set goals jointly with their superiors and then are measured on the accomplishment of these goals, thus avoiding the need for day-to-day close supervision.

• *Argyris*

Chris Argyris has reached similar conclusions, but he approaches the problem from a different perspective.[38] According to Argyris, the traditional highly structured organization inhibits people from maturing to the point where they can utilize their full potential. He says:

> The classical design for a formal organization has some very serious flaws. The nature of these flaws is apparent when we set side by side two pictures: first, a view of how human beings need to behave in our society in order to be healthy, productive, growing individuals; and second, how a formal organization (a factory, business, or hospital) requires them to behave. Comparing these pictures, we see that the organization's requirements, as presented by "classical" descriptions, are sharply opposed to the individual's needs.[39]

Healthy people go through a maturation process, says Argyris, one that involves seven changes in the personality of the individual. Specifically, as the person approaches adulthood, he moves to a state of increased activity, independence, and stronger interests. Furthermore, he becomes capable of behaving in a greater variety of ways and tends to have a much longer time perspective. Finally, he matures from the subordinate position of a child to one of an equal or superordinate position as an adult and, in addition, develops an increased awareness and control over himself. Argyris contends that in many instances, the formal structure, control, and other practices of the classical organizations inhibit these normal maturation changes by encouraging employees to be dependent, passive, and subordinate.

The most insidious aspect of classical organization theory, according to Argyris, is that the organization it prescribes is "rational"—"that is, it has been 'designed' and its parts are purposefully related within this design."[40] People, says Argyris, are forced to "stick to the rules," and the efficiency advantages of specialization force workers to perform increasingly specialized, routine, unchallenging jobs.

The total effect of applying these classical principles, Argyris says, is that employees work in an environment where they have little or no self-control and are encouraged to be dependent and passive. Thus, in the long run, the classicists' "efficient" organization is not really so efficient, since workers whose maturation is hampered become frustrated, apathetic, and less efficient. The classical assumptions, he implies, are not only incorrect but are actually unhealthy and harmful to employees. The solution is to decrease the dependency, subordination, and submissiveness of employees by developing (among other things) enlarged jobs and participative leaders. For Argyris (as for McGregor), organization structure is not something to be designed for efficiency without regard to employee behavior. Instead, structure is a vehicle for increasing the motivation and self-control of employees.

• *Katz and Kahn*

The Organization as an Open System Katz and Kahn are social psychologists who worked closely with Rensis Likert at the University of Michigan, and their backgrounds in social psychology help explain their unique approach to organization theory.[41] They believe that classical organization theories emphasized organization structure while overlooking the organization's people, whereas more recent behavioral approaches often focused on people while overlooking the organization structure existing around those people.[42] They sought therefore to more fully merge the "macro" subject of organization structure with the "micro" subject of individual behavior and to show the relations between the two.

Katz and Kahn's Theory of Motivation/Compliance Katz and Kahn say that because organizations are responsive, open systems, managers are constantly faced with the problem of somehow ensuring that the tasks they delegate are in fact carried out. The classicists' answer to this problem was to install a network of incentives, rules, and close supervision—to *impose* compliance. Yet such imposed or "legal" compliance has its shortcomings. For one thing, they say, "creativity is difficult to legislate,'' and so some jobs don't lend themselves to this type of compliance. Of even greater importance is the fact that:

> For effective organizational functioning many members must be willing, on occasion, to do more than their job description specifies. If members of the system were to follow their precise letter of job descriptions and organizational protocol, things would soon grind to a halt.[43]

The solution, say Katz and Kahn, is that managers can't just rely on *imposed compliance* like rules or close supervision; instead, three other "patterns of compliance" should also be used.

One involves the use of *rewards* for inducing the required behavior. Here, rewards are linked to desired behaviors, and the employee's actions thus supposedly become instrumental to his obtaining specific desired rewards. A second involves *job identification*. Here the job is challenging and the employee thus has opportunities for self-expression and achievement. He or she receives satisfaction from the job and so is motivated to perform it.[44]

Finally, at the opposite end of a continuum from *imposed* compliance is compliance based on the employee's *internalization* of the organization's goals. Here, employees adopt the organization's goals as their own, and they comply because by doing so, they are also contributing to their own goals.

Katz and Kahn's Theory of Organization Structure Katz and Kahn also dealt with the question of structure. Here they stressed that organizations were open systems that had to continually respond and adapt to their environments. And they elaborated on this idea by distinguishing among five types of formal organizational subsystems: production, maintenance, boundary, adaptive, and managerial. Members of the *production* subsystem are concerned with task accomplishment and may include employees in the production and distribution departments. The *maintenance* subsystem aims at maintaining stability and predictability in the organization. (Here, selection procedures are developed for screening employees, and raw materials are screened by quality control, for example.)

There are also *boundary* systems for procurement and disposal. These directly support the production system but, unlike the production system, necessarily carry on transactions with the environment. (Marketing and advertising influence the buying public, for example.)

Adaptive systems deal with the problems of planning. For example, there may be a long-range-planning committee, or a research and development group, to fill this role.

Finally, there is the *managerial* system, which "cuts across all of the operating structures of production, maintenance, environmental support, and adaptation." This subsystem coordinates the other subsystems, resolves conflicts between organizational levels, and coordinates external requirements with organizational resources.[45]

THE QUANTITATIVE SCHOOL

• *Management Science/Operations Research*

After World War II, a trend developed toward applying quantitative techniques to the solution of a wide range of managerial problems. This movement is usually referred to as *operations research* or *management science* and has been described as "the application of scientific methods, techniques, and tools to problems involving the operations of systems so as to provide those in control of a system with optimum solutions to the problems."[46]

Management science has three distinguishing characteristics. First, management scientists generally deal with problems that are well defined and that have clear and *undisputable standards of effectiveness.* They want to know, for instance, that "inventory costs have been too high and should be reduced by 20 percent," or, "How many items should be produced at each of our five plants so as to minimize transportation costs to the following customers? . . ." Second, management scientists generally deal with problems that have *well-defined alternative courses of action.* Thus, there might be four alternative plants from which to ship products, or various levels of product A and product B that can be produced in order to maximize sales revenue. Finally, management scientists must *develop a theory* or model concerning how the relevant factors are related. Like any scientists, management scientists must thus be able to carry out experiments (by manipulating the various factors in the model) and be able to understand the problem and relationships clearly enough so that the relationships can be formulated in a model. For example, the management scientist might develop an inventory model that takes into consideration such diverse variables as projected sales, storage costs, and cost of raw materials. This model could then permit the manager to calculate optimal ordering quantities, even though such basic variables as projected sales change over time.

The idea of applying scientific methodology and quantitative analysis to large-scale problems is not new; primitive mathematical models were used by economists in the 1700s.[47] But the first use of organized operations research occurred during the Battle of Britain in 1941. Teams of British scientists were asked by the British military to analyze and solve a variety of diverse problems, including the optimal use of radar and the setting of antisubmarine depth charges. The multidisciplinary team of scientists, by applying the scientific method and quantitative analysis, so increased military effectiveness that other teams were quickly organized. After the war, it seemed logical to extend this approach to the solution of industrial problems, and operations-research groups began springing up around the industrialized world.

Historian Daniel Wren points out that operations research/management science has "direct lineal routes in scientific management."[48] Like Taylor and his disciples, today's management scientists try to find optimal solutions to management problems. And just as Taylor and his people tried to scientifically find the "one best way" for doing the job, management scientists seek to apply the scientific method to finding the best solution to industrial problems. The difference in the two approaches is (1) that modern-day management scientists have at their disposal much more sophisticated mathematical tools and computers, and (2) that their goal is not to try to find a *science of management* (as did Taylor) as much as to use *science in management.*

• Arguments Against the Use of Management Science

The first industrial applications of management science took place in the relatively well controlled environment of the production shop, and here the results these people achieved was fairly good. But as they tried to apply their techniques to broader organizational problems, their mathematical models became complex, since they now had to include unpredictable factors like competitors' reactions. Particularly with respect to using management science for making major organizationwide or "strategic" decisions, management science has thus been attacked on several grounds.

A study by Mintzberg is typical of the sort of attacks made here. Mintzberg argues that the process of making strategic decisions relies heavily on intuition, creativity, and judgment, all human activities that are not very amenable to modeling and computerization. In one study, he found that in only 18 out of 83 cases did managers mention using explicit analyses in arriving at a strategic decision. Sometimes the choice was arrived at after considerable bargaining among managers, but more often, judgment was used to arrive at the decision. "Typically, the choices and all kinds of data associated with them were pumped into the mind of a manager, and somehow a choice later came out. How was never explained." As a result, says Mintzberg, management science (with its emphasis on a systematic, quantitative approach to decision analysis) may be exactly *the opposite* of the sort of approach needed to make major strategic decisions.[49] Instead, a more intuitive approach may be best.

Argyris makes a similar point. He says that any scientist collects data, makes observations, and manipulates a model to support or to refute some predetermined hypothesis or theory. He says that although this hypothesis-testing approach is effective when the situation to be analyzed is clear and controllable, it becomes increasingly less effective when, as in the social sciences, the situations are so complex that virtually any researcher can mislead himself into finding just the data he needs to prove his pet theory.[50] Argyris claims that the problem here is that organizational managers cannot be entirely objective when comparing alternative courses of action and that, basically, they tend to approach the alternatives with a closed mind. For example, if a product manager was responsible for deciding to sell product X, he might react to dwindling sales of the product *not* by dropping the product entirely (which would question his previous decision) but instead by assuming that working harder to advertise and sell the product would eliminate the problem. Argyris contends that the reason such mistakes occur is that *everyone is guided by unstated, implicit theories that govern what data they seek and how they interpret them,* just as the product manager was governed by the implicit, unstated theory that the product should continue to be sold. These unstated theories, says Argyris, govern the data that managers collect as well as how they interpret those data. One effect is that the results of a mathematical model can be changed dramatically by a manager who chooses the data to fit the conclusion he or she wants to achieve. As two writers put it:

> Given the wealth of data that abounds in virtually all large-scale organizations, a committed proponent of a particular point of view can almost always find and therefore muster significant empirical support for his policy by consciously and unconsciously selecting the evidence most favorable to his case. The moral seems to be that management science can be a strong work horse but only if both its strengths and drawbacks are kept in mind.[51]

TOWARD A SITUATIONAL THEORY

The 20th century has been a period of diversity and change. Examples abound of swift changes and improvements in communication techniques, transportation, energy generation and consumption, economic growth, and knowledge accumulation.

Organizationally, this rapid change has manifested itself in more diverse, interwoven markets, the use of advanced technologies, the widespread use of specialists, and larger, more complex organizational structures, among other phenomena. In turn, these have resulted in an increasing concern for development of a general organization theory that managers could use in dealing with the greater number of variables they must now take into account in their decision making.

This need for a general theory and a number of interrelated events beginning late in the 1950s combined to create a significant milestone in the evolution of organization theory. First, two reports—one commissioned by the Ford Foundation, one by the Carnegie Corporation—produced sharp indictments of the state of business education in the United States. They reported that business schools were adhering to worn-out precepts and were emphasizing "vocationalism." The reports stressed that problem solving, organization theory, management principles, and human relations should be integrated into business-school curricula. A second event was the publication in 1961 of a paper entitled, "The Management Theory Jungle," by Harold Koontz. In it, Koontz said that the variety of management schools, terminology, and assumptions had resulted in confusion and "jungle warfare" among the various groups.[52] The direct result of this article was a symposium in California, attended by a group of eminent scholars and practitioners with diverse research and analytical approaches to management. These incidents encouraged a renewed interest in principles, giving rise to questions about the universality of the classical principles and the tackling of other pressing problems—all in the search for a unified organization theory.

Finally, along with these developments, a number of organizational-research studies were being carried out in England and America. Their combined effect was to underscore the need for a "situational" view of organization theory—one in which the appropriateness of the organization and management system was contingent upon the rate of change in organizational environment and technology. In one such study, Burns and Stalker carried out an analysis of a number of industrial firms in England and concluded that whether a "mechanistic" or an "organic" management system was appropriate depended upon the nature of the organization's environment. They wrote:

> We have endeavored to stress the appropriateness of each system to its own specific set of conditions. Equally, we desire to avoid the suggestion that either system is superior under all circumstances to the other. In particular, nothing in our experience justifies the assumption that the mechanistic systems should be superseded by organic in conditions of stability. The beginning of administrative wisdom is the awareness that there is no one optimum type of management system.[53]

Also in England, Joan Woodward and a group of researchers from the Tavistock Institute analyzed the relationship between the organization and the technology of a group of firms in the South Essex area. The organic, flexible system described by Burns and Stalker appeared to be more appropriate in firms with either small-batch or continuous-process production systems, whereas the mechanistic, classical system was appropriate where mass-production technology was utilized.[54]

These findings and others like them have culminated in what can be called a situational approach to organization theory. As Lawrence and Lorsch, two of the original investigators in this area, put it:

> During the past few years there has been evident a new trend in the study of organizational phenomena. Underlying this new approach is the idea that the internal functioning of organizations must be consistent with the demands of the organization's task, technology, or external environment, and the need of its members if the organization is to be effective. Rather than searching for the panacea of the one best way to organize under all conditions, investigators have more and more tended to examine the functioning of organizations in relation to the needs of their particular members and the external pressures facing them. Basically, this approach seems to be leading to the development of a "contingency" theory of organization with the appropriate internal states and processes of the organization contingent upon external requirements and member needs.[55]

The implications of this new "situational" theory of organizations will be pursued in the following chapters.

SUMMARY

The period from roughly 1925 to the present saw a drastic change in organization theory. To fully appreciate these changes, we can answer the questions posed in the last chapter and compare our answers with those that were presented on pages 35–36.

What prescriptions did each theorist have for how organizations should be structured? The behavioral-systems writers prescribed a radically different form of organization from that of classical theorists. The structure of the classicists was a "mechanistic" one in which decision making was centralized, there was close adherence to the chain of command, employees were told to "stick to the rules," jobs were highly specialized, and employees were rarely asked to participate in decision making. In contrast, writers like Likert, Argyris, and McGregor were more concerned with the mental health and motivation of employees, and they saw organization structure as a means toward improving that health and motivation. They therefore prescribed structures in which decision making was pushed to the lowest level possible, jobs were varied and unspecialized, and managers were not preoccupied with adherence to the chain of command or enforcing rules; the organization, in other words, was more "organic." The efficiency-oriented, machine-like structure of the classicists was thus replaced by the adaptive, relatively open structure of the behavioralists.

What prescriptions did each theorist have for how to best ensure compliance—that employees carry out their assigned tasks? It was on the question of compliance that the writers we discussed in this chapter differed most markedly from the classicists. The latter emphasized the use of rules, close supervision, and financial incentives for ensuring that workers accomplished their tasks. The writers discussed in this chapter, on the other hand, emphasized gaining the self-control of employees, rather than imposing controls on them. Barnard, for example, said that the power of material incentives, when the minimum necessities are satisfied, "is exceedingly limited as to most men," and he prescribed nonmaterial inducements like prestige for ensuring compliance. Simon made a similar distinction and said that through training, organizational loyalty, and instilling the "criterion of efficiency," managers can elicit self-control. Behavioral-systems writers like Likert, McGregor, and Argyris built upon these ideas and prescribed specific techniques, like management by objectives, participative leadership, job enlargement, and delegation, for building self-control.

What was it about the workers' tasks these theorists focused on that influenced their prescriptions for how to structure organizations and obtain compliance? Tasks studied by the classical theorists tended to be routine, repetitive, and easily measured. Taylor, for example, focused almost entirely on jobs in the production shop, where jobs tended to be routine and mechanical. By the mid-1900s, however, employees' tasks were no longer uniformly routine. Several things, including product research and development and the growth and size of organizations, resulted in more jobs of a problem-solving, creative nature; in many industries, the emphasis on efficiency thus gave way to an emphasis on adaptability and creativity.

What was it about the environment of the organizations each theorist focused on that influenced his or her prescriptions for how to structure and obtain compliance? The environment faced by classicists was relatively simple and unchanging, and prevailing values emphasized economic individualism and hard work. But by the 1930s, various factors had combined to drastically alter the environment faced by organization theorists. The depression forced many to question the underlying values of economic individualism and resulted in a partial replacement of the work ethic with a social ethic. More important, perhaps, World War II had stimulated research and development activities, and by the end of the war, many firms had embarked on strategies of diversification. Gradually, the environments of organizations became increasingly complex as firms found themselves more and more dependent upon the actions of previously unrelated firms. Change and novelty became the rule, and managers soon found themselves flooded with information—on new products, competitors, new technologies, and so forth—from their environments.

To understand an organization theory, one must understand the milieu in which it evolved; this seems especially true when viewed in the light of our discussions from this and the preceding chapter. Scientific management, bureaucracy, and administrative theory are all appropriate responses to the problems classicists faced—problems centering on efficiency, on environments that were relatively unchanging, on tasks that were simple, and on organizations of limited size. In such situations, it would seem, prescribing centralized decision making, specialized jobs, rules, incentives, and close supervision made sense.

The writers we discussed in this chapter, on the other hand, faced very different situations. New-product development, technological advances, increased competition, diversity, and increased organization size required that companys change their strategys from *efficiency* to *diversification and adaptability*. Environments were no longer simple and unchanging and, related to this fact, an increasing number of work tasks required initiative, creativity, and problem solving. The new organization theories we discussed in this chapter were aimed at dealing with these new conditions. In the next chapter, we pursue this line of thought and turn our attention to a more detailed analysis of the relationships between environment, task, and organization.

Discussion Questions

1 What are some of the trends that have been leading to increasing complexity in the environments of organizations? What effect do you think this complexity is having on organization theory and values?

2 How would you account for the emergence of a contingency or situational approach to organizations and management?

3 What are the implicit assumptions of the behavioral-systems writers' organization theory? How do these compare with the assumptions of the classical organization theorists?
4 What role did financial incentive play in Barnard's theory of compliance? How did it relate to his "zone of indifference"?
5 What specific techniques did McGregor prescribe for developing self-control? Why didn't the classical organizational theorists prescribe such techniques?

FOOTNOTES

[1]William Scott, *Organization Theory* (Homewood, Ill.: Irwin, 1967). For an excellent discussion of the evolution of management thought, see Daniel Wren, *The Evolution of Management Thought* (New York: Ronald Press, 1972).

[2]Scott, *Organization Theory,* p. 48.

[3]*Ibid.,* p. 52.

[4]Frederick Lewis Allen, *The Big Change* (New York: Harper & Row, 1952), p. 132.

[5]F.J. Roethlisberger and William J. Dickson, *Management and the Worker* (New York: John Wiley, 1964).

[6]John Maynard Keynes, *The General Theory of Employment, Interest and Money* (New York: Harcourt, Brace, 1964).

[7]Mary Parker Follett, *Creative Experience* (London: Longmans, Green, 1924), p. 59.

[8]Chester Barnard, *The Functions of the Executive* (Cambridge: Harvard University Press, 1968).

[9]*Ibid.,* p. 83.

[10]*Ibid.,* p. 84.

[11]*Ibid.,* p. 167.

[12]*Ibid.,* p. 85.

[13]*Ibid.,* p. 143.

[14]*Ibid.,* p. 169.

[15]Herbert A. Simon, *Administrative Behavior* (New York: Free Press, 1976).

[16]*Ibid.,* p. 11.

[17]*Ibid.,* p. 226.

[18]*Ibid.,* pp. 116–17.

[19]*Ibid.,* p. 133.

[20]*Ibid.,* p. 11.

[21]*Ibid.,* p. 14.

[22]*Ibid.,* p. 15.

[23]*Ibid.,* p. 227.

[24]*Ibid.,* p. 225.

[25]*Ibid.,* p. 238.

[26]Alfred Chandler, *Strategy and Structure* (Cambridge, Mass.: M.I.T. Press, 1932), pp. 19–51.

[27]See also F.E. Emery and E.C. Trist, "The Causal Texture of Organizational Environments," *Human Relations,* Vol. 18 (August 1963), 20–26.

[28]Warren G. Bennis, "Organizational Development and the Fate of Bureaucracy," address to the Division of Industrial and Business Psychology, American Psychological Association, September 5, 1964. Reprinted in L.L. Cummings and W.E. Scott, Jr., *Organizational Behavior and Human Performance* (Homewood, Ill.: Richard D. Irwin and Dorsey, 1969), p. 436.

[29]Alvin Toffler, *Future Shock* (New York: Bantam Books, 1971), pp. 124–51.

[30]Kurt Lewin, *Field Theory and Social Science* (New York: Harper & Row, 1951), p. 241.

[31]W.B.D. Brown and E. Jaques, *The Glacier Project Papers* (London: Heineman, 1965).

[32]E. Trist and K. Bamforth, "Some Social and Psychological Consequences of the Long Wall Method of Coal-Getting," *Human Relations,* Vol. 4, No. 1 (1951).

[33]Rensis Likert, *New Patterns of Management* (New York: McGraw-Hill, 1961), p. 6.

[34]*Ibid.,* p. 103.

[35]*Ibid.,* p. 104.

[36]Douglas McGregor, *The Human Side of Enterprise* (New York: McGraw-Hill, 1960). See also Byron G. Firman, "An Investigation of the Relationships among Supervisory Attitudes, Behaviors, and Outputs: An Examination of McGregor's Theory Y," *Personnel Psychology,* Vol. 26 (Spring 1973), 95–105.

[37]Douglas McGregor, "The Human Side of Enterprise," in Edward Deci, B. von Haller Gilmer, and Harry Karn, *Readings in Industrial and Organizational Psychology* (New York: McGraw-Hill, 1972), p. 123.

[38]Chris Argyris, *Integrating the Individual and the Organization* (New York: John Wiley, 1964).

[39]Chris Argyris, "Being Human and Being Organized," *Transaction,* Vol. I (1964), 3–6. Reprinted in Deci et al., *Readings,* pp. 68–73.

[40]*Ibid.,* p. 69.

[41]Daniel Katz and Robert Kahn, *The Social Psychology of Organization* (New York: John Wiley, 1966).

[42]*Ibid.,* p. 336.

[43]*Ibid.,* p. 340.

[44]*Ibid.,* p. 345.

[45]*Ibid.,* p. 94.

[46]C. West Churchman, Russel Ackoff, and E. Leonard Arnoff, *Introduction to Operations Research* (New York: John Wiley, 1957), p. 18.

[47]Harvey Wagner, *Principles of Operations Research, with Applications to Management Decisions* (Englewood Cliffs, N.J.: Prentice-Hall, 1969), pp. 3–31.

[48]Daniel Wren, *The Evolution of Management Thought* (New York: John Wiley, 1979), p. 512.

[49]Henry Mintzberg, "Planning on the Left Side and Managing on the Right Side," *Harvard Business Review,* July–August 1976, pp. 49–58.

[50]Chris Argyris, "Double-Look Learning in Organizations," *Harvard Business Review,* Vol. 15 (September–October 1977), 115–25.

[51]Ian Mitroff and James Emshoff, "On Strategic Assumption Making: A Dialectical Approach to Policy and Planning," *Academy of Management Review,* Vol. 4, 2–3.

[52]Not everyone agreed with this conclusion. Simon, for example, stated that there was no confusion and that he was "exhilarated by the progress we have made." See Harold Koontz, ed., *Toward a Unified Theory of Management* (New York: McGraw-Hill, 1964), p. 79.

[53]Tom Burns and G.M. Stalker, *The Management of Innovation* (London: Tavistock, 1961), p. 125.

[54]Joan Woodward, *Industrial Organization: Theory and Practice* (London: Oxford University Press, 1965), pp. 64–65.

[55]Jay W. Lorsch and Paul R. Lawrence, eds., *Studies in Organization Design* (Homewood, Ill.: Richard D. Irwin and Dorsey, 1970), p. 1.

Strategy, Structure, and Organizational Effectiveness

OVERVIEW

In the preceding two chapters, we introduced the idea that to be effective, the organization's structure and management system had to be appropriate for or "fit" its environment and task. The purpose of the present chapter is to define more clearly what is meant by *organizational effectiveness,* and to explain how the organization's strategy—its plan for matching the company's resources and skills with the environmental opportunities and risks that it faces—determines the environment in which the organization will have to compete as well as the structure it will need to be effective.

The outline of this chapter is as follows:

A What is organizational effectiveness?
- **1** Introduction
- **2** Single-criterion measures of effectiveness
- **3** Multiple-criteria measures of effectiveness
- **4** Comparison of multiple-criteria models

B Strategic Planning
- **1** The nature of strategic planning
- **2** Developing a strategic plan
- **3** Four characteristic strategies
- **4** Strategy and structure
- **5** Beyond strategy and structure
- **6** Managing the environment

WHAT IS ORGANIZATIONAL EFFECTIVENESS?

• Introduction

The fact that some organizations are more effective than others is a basic assumption of economic and organization theory and, indeed, is implicit throughout this book. Whenever we organize an enterprise, we do so on the assumption that one design will prove more effective than another; in other words, that the organization will be more effective if designed in a certain way.

But what is organizational effectiveness? Is an organization that maximizes profits by keeping its costs to a minimum the most effective? Or does *organizational effectiveness* also imply that other criteria, like the organization's ability to adapt and survive, are important as well?

• Single-Criterion Measures of Effectiveness

Profit Maximization Early models of organizational effectiveness generally focused on a single criterion of organizational success. The most popular of these was (and probably still is) *profit maximization.*

The idea that firms seek to "maximize profits" and that effectiveness should primarily reflect profits is a fundamental assumption accepted by most economists. Technically, they assume that the object of the firm is to obtain as large a difference as possible between total revenue and total costs, provided that the difference is greater than or equal to zero.[1]

Yet even though profit maximization is the most familiar criterion of organizational effectiveness, no one has yet shown that firms do in fact act as if they seek to maximize profits at the exclusion of other, equally important goals, and, in fact, economists themselves disagree as to the supreme position of profit maximization. William Baumol, for example, suggests that firms seek to maximize not their profits but their *sales revenue,* on the assumption that the managers who run our large organizations (as opposed to the stockholder-owners) want their firms as large as possible.[2] And many economists point out that "profit maximization" is as much a convenient device as an unassailable assumption. Stigler, for example, says:

> The extent to which the entrepreneurial behavior can be explained by efforts to maximize profits is a celebrated debating ground for economists. We shall nevertheless use this assumption without extensive defense, and on two grounds. First, and most important, it yields a vast number of testable conclusions, and by and large these conclusions agree with observation. Second, no other well-defined goals have yet been developed and given empirical support.[3]

Similarly, Ferguson notes:

> Without doubt, not all producers try to maximize profits at all times. Entrepreneurs may indeed be seekers after multiple goals. Nonetheless, a business cannot long re-

> main viable unless profits are earned; and it is a very unusual businessman who treats profits in a cavalier fashion. . . . Whether profit maximization is a reasonable assumption is a question long debated in economics. Several important criticisms have been brought to bear; however, these criticisms do not overcome the supremely important fact that the assumption of profit maximization is the only one providing a general theory of firms, markets, and resource allocation that is successful in both explaining and predicting business behavior.[4]

Satisficing Organization theorists have proposed various alternatives for evaluating the effectiveness of organizations, but perhaps the most complete and enduring argument against profit maximization has been proposed by Herbert Simon. According to Simon, managers (and firms) do not maximize but instead "satisfice." That is, "we must expect the firm's goals to be not maximizing profits but attaining a certain level or rate of profit, holding a certain share of the market or a certain level of sales."[5] Firms do not seek to maximize profits, in other words, but instead set a minimum level of acceptable profits and, once this is met, do not aggressively seek to exceed this level.

One example that may support this position was a phenomenon that occured just after World War II. At one point, the price of new cars was actually lower than that of used cars, and the explanation for this, say proponents of "satisficing," is that car manufacturers set a target level of acceptable profits and did not seek to exceed this level. Contemporary examples include the recent attempts by large oil firms to depress reported profits, and by auto insurers in Florida to reduce their "excessive" profits by returning huge sums to their customers. Of course, these examples may simply reflect, say, attempts by the firms to develop better "public relations," rather than satisficing behavior.

Other Single-Criterion Measures Many other single-criterion measures have been proposed. For example, in one recent review, John Campbell identified 19 different variables that have been used to reflect organizational effectiveness. The most widely used were:

- *Overall performance,* as measured by employee or supervisory rating
- *Productivity,* as measured typically with actual output data
- *Employee satisfaction,* as measured by self-report questionnaires
- *Profit, or rate of return,* based on accounting data
- *Withdrawal,* based on historical turnover and absenteeism data[6]

In summary, many "single-criterion" measures of effectiveness have been proposed and used. However, none have proved to be entirely satisfactory as the sole or universal measure.

• Multiple-Criteria Measures of Effectiveness

Even though single-criterion measures of organizational effectiveness are still widely used, most of the modern effectiveness models measure effectiveness as a function of *several* criteria, such as productivity, flexibility, and stability.

The idea that managers do in fact pursue multiple goals simultaneously has received some support in research studies. In one study, George England surveyed organizational goals as expressed by American managers. He found that managers rated a variety of goals, including "organizational efficiency," "high productivity," "profit maximization," and "organizational growth," as both highly important and significant for corporate success. And in a literature review, Richard Steers surveyed multiple-criteria models and found that each model defined effectiveness in terms of *several* interdependent factors (like productivity and flexibility). However, there was very little consistency among models.[7]

We will briefly discuss four illustrative examples of multiple-criteria effectiveness models—models that try to define and measure organizational effectiveness in terms of several criteria simultaneously—in this section.

The Yuchtman-Seashore Model Yuchtman and Seashore reject the idea that managers seek to attain any single goal. Instead, they see the organization as an open system and view effectiveness in terms of how successful the organization is at acquiring "scarce and valued resources." As a result, they define organizational effectiveness largely in terms of "bargaining position," and:

> The concept of "bargaining position" implies the exclusion of any specific goal (or function) as the ultimate criterion of organizational effectiveness. Instead it points to the more general capability of the organization as a resource-getting system.[8]

According to these writers, a firm's bargaining position is itself determined by several factors, including how efficiently it uses it resources. This conception of organizational effectiveness thus focuses not on the specific goal toward which the organization is striving, but rather on the organization's behavior, "conceived as a continuous and never-ending process of exchange and competition over scarce and valued resources."[9] To these writers, *the successful acquisition of scarce and valued resources* and the *control of its environment* are thus the two major criteria of organizational effectiveness.

The Bass Model Psychologist Bernard Bass says that traditional effectiveness indexes like productivity or profits are not sufficiently broad for evaluating the success of an organization.[10] Instead, an organization's effectiveness should also reflect "the worth of the organization to its individual members and the worth of both individual members and the organization to society." Specifically, an organization should be evaluated in terms of:

1 The degree to which it is productive, profitable, self-maintaining, and so forth
2 The degree to which it is of value to its members
3 The degree to which it and its members are of value to society

Bass believes that these have become recognized criteria of organizational effectiveness, as substantiated by several facts. For example, he notes that federal and state worker-safety and antitrust laws assume that an organization's worth to the individual and to society are both important effectiveness criteria. And even though Bass's work on effectiveness was begun over 25 years ago, his criteria make even more sense today. For example, a multitude of new laws have been enacted establishing the "social responsibility" of business, with the goal of ensuring the worth of the organization to society. Other laws, like the Occupational Safety and Health Act and the Civil Rights Act, are aimed at ensuring the worth of the organization to its individual members. Similarly, interest is increasing among organization theorists and managers in the concept of "quality of work life." Prof. J. Lloyd Suttle defines this as "the degree to which members of a work organization are able to satisfy important personal needs through their experiences in the organization," and many today are coming to view this as an important criterion of organizational effectiveness."[11]

Currently, therefore, there is obviously more interest—even more than when Bass proposed his three criteria in the early 1950s—in measuring an organization's effectiveness not just in terms of productivity, but in terms of the organization's worth to its individual members and to society as a whole.

The Bennis Model Warren Bennis says the basic flaw in present effectiveness criteria is their inattention to the problem of adapting to change.[12] In his view, "the main challenge confronting today's organization, whether it is a hospital or a business enterprise, is that of responding to changing conditions and adapting to external stress," and measures of organizational effectiveness must therefore include criteria like adaptability and problem-solving ability. He bases his argument on the findings of writers like Emery and Trist, who, as we saw in Chapter 3, found that the environments in which organizations are operating are becoming increasingly uncertain and turbulent.

Bennis feels that the "methodological rules" and problem-solving techniques an organization uses are the critical determinants of its effectiveness. According to him, these rules and procedures closely resemble the rules of inquiry that are an implicit part of scientific investigation, and therefore:

> . . . the rules and norms of science may provide a valuable, possibly necessary model for organizational behavior.[13]

Organizations must exhibit two basic aspects of the scientific approach, says Bennis, if they are to exist in a changing environment. First, there must be an emphasis on scientific methodology, and in particular on the spirit of inquiry and desire for experimentation that characterize the scientific approach. In other words, organizations (and their managers) must be willing to approach problems openly and develop solutions with tentativeness and caution, and having done this, they must be willing to expose their tentative conclusions to empirical testing. It is this constant interplay of hypothesis *development* and *testing,* says Bennis, that is the essence of the scientific approach and a major factor in the effectiveness of organizations.

Second, for this spirit of scientific inquiry to flourish, there must be a certain "democracy" in the organization, one that "accents freedom of opinion and dissent, and respect for the individual."[14] Bennis argues, therefore, that the way organizations can come to grips with their problems and survive and prosper in an uncertain environment is by establishing social conditions in which the scientific attitude flourishes. To Bennis, such social conditions would be built on "Theory Y"–type assumptions and would reflect the organizational trust, supportiveness, and democracy found in organizational models like Likert's System IV.

In summary, Bennis's argument is that the most crucial problem facing organizations is to survive and adapt in a changing environment, and that for them to do so, an open, scientific spirit of inquiry must prevail in the organization. Thus, adaptability, an ability to clearly identify the organizational identity, and the capability for "reality testing"—for correctly identifying problems and their solutions—are the major criteria of organizational effectiveness, in Bennis's opinion.

The Peters and Waterman Model Peters and Waterman, in their search for excellence among American companies, take a pragmatic approach to assessing effectiveness, one that combines the issues of profitability, growth, and innovation.[15] Their criteria include "hard" measures of effectiveness, including compound asset growth, the ratio of market value to book value, and average return on capital. In addition, "as a last screen, we applied a measure of innovativeness per se. We asked selected industry experts (e.g., businessmen from within the industry) to rate the company's 20-year record of innovation, defined as a continuous flow of industry bellwether products and services and general rapidness of response to changing markets or other external dynamics."[16] So to Peters and Waterman, effectiveness must be measured in terms of profitability, growth, adaptability, and innovation.

• Comparison of Multiple-Criteria Models

What conclusions can be drawn from a comparison of multiple-criteria models of organizational effectiveness? There are two points of view. Steers believes that the evidence suggests a "lack of consensus as to what constitutes a useful and valid set of effectiveness measures."[17]

Table 4-1 shows the frequency of occurrence of effectiveness criteria mentioned in 17 models of organizational effectiveness. As you can see, adaptability–flexibility was mentioned most often, followed by productivity and satisfaction. However, only adaptability–flexibility was mentioned in more than half the models. From this, Steers concludes:

> . . . the effectiveness construct is so complex as to defy attempts at model development. Perhaps more flexible, comprehensive models are required.[18]

On the other hand, some writers take a more positive approach to the question of organizational effectiveness. For example, Jeffrey Pfeffer and Gerald Salancik say that the effective organization is *the one that satisfies the demands of those in its environment from whom it requires support for its continued existence,*[19] a conclusion similar to that reached by Yuchtman and Seashore, with their bargaining approach to effectiveness. Pfeffer and Salancik point out that organizations are faced with frequently competing demands from a variety of interest groups, and that their effectiveness—their ability to create acceptable outcomes and actions—can be measured only in terms of the interest group being considered. For example, *stockholders* of a company may consider effectiveness in terms of profits, or rate of growth. To *employees,* decent wages and quality of work life might be crucial. To the *community* surrounding the firm, the firm's support of community projects, such as Little League baseball teams, might be paramount. In summary, these writers propose a

TABLE 4-1 Frequency of Occurrence of Evaluation Criteria in 17 Models of Organizational Effectiveness

Evaluation Criteria	*No. of Times Mentioned (N = 17)*
Adaptability–flexibility	10
Productivity	6
Satisfaction	5
Profitability	3
Resource acquisition	3
Absence of strain	2
Control over environment	2
Development	2
Efficiency	2
Employee retention	2
Growth	2
Integration	2
Open communications	2
Survival	2
All other criteria	1

Source: Richard Steers, "Problems in Measurement of Organizational Effectiveness," *Administrative Science Quarterly,* Vol. 20, No. 4 (December 1975), 549.

multifaceted concept of effectiveness and hold that managers seek to satisfy several aims (and interest groups) simultaneously.

There is some support for the notion that effectiveness is multifaceted and can be described only with respect to particular interest groups. England found that managers do in fact pursue a variety of goals, and these seem to be aimed at different interest groups. The results of another study (see Table 4-2) point up one of the dilemmas managers face if this multifaceted view of effectiveness is correct. The data from this study suggest that satisfying one group (owner, community, government) implies very little about satisfying any other groups, and that the groups' interests may occasionally conflict. For example, there was some indication that satisfying the owners' goals was occasionally incompatible with satisfying those of the government.

In summary, we can conclude that the firm's ability to survive and effectively "bargain" with and adapt to crucial interest groups and create acceptable outcomes and actions is perhaps the ultimate criterion of organizational effectiveness; this is a basic point made by Yuchtman and Seashore, and by Pfeffer and Salancik. And in this regard, Bennis's prescriptions for organizational democracy and a spirit of scientific inquiry provide one approach for achieving this ultimate objective; the recent trend toward organizing companies as "adhocracies" reflects, as we will see, the need for such an approach.

TABLE 4–2 Intercorrelations of Satisfactions of Seven Parties-at-Interest

	Satisfaction of					
	Community	*Government*	*Customer*	*Supplier*	*Creditor*	*Employee*
Owner satisfaction	.23*	−.12	.37*	.14	.00	.25*
Community satisfaction		.16	.04	.16	.14	.22*
Government satisfaction			−.09	.11	.20*	−.07
Customer satisfaction				.17	.23*	.23*
Supplier satisfaction					.08	.17
Creditor satisfaction						.08

*Significant relationships.

Source: Reprinted from Hall Pickle and Frank Friedlander, "Seven Societal Criteria of Organizational Success," *Personnel Psychology*, Vol. 20 (1967), Table 1, p. 171.

STRATEGIC PLANNING

• *The Nature of Strategic Planning*

Given the supreme importance of adapting to shifting environmental demands, it should come as no surprise that one of top management's crucial tasks involves matching organizational competencies with the opportunities and risks created by environmental change. *An organization's strategy is the match between the organization's resources and skills and the environmental opportunities and risks it faces.*[20] It reflects, in other words, the *course of action* through which the organization plans to adapt to the threats and opportunities in its environment and thereby maintain its effectiveness.

An organization's strategy provides the overall direction for the enterprise. It clarifies the domain of the organization by specifying what business it is in and the courses of action it will pursue, such as, "Expand sales in Europe," and, "Diversify by adding two new product lines." It answers the questions, Who are our customers? What product or services will we sell? Where will we sell our product or services? and Why are we unique as compared with the competition? Ideally, a strategy should identify three things:

1 The firm's domain in terms of the product or services it will render, and to whom. The domain answers the question, "What business are we in?"
2 The basic strategic moves the firm plans to make—for instance, in terms of diversifying, or expanding overseas.
3 The basic goals the firm hopes to achieve—for instance, in terms of market share or profits.[21]

Thus the strategy summarizes, in broad terms, how the organization's top management wants to have the organization compete in, adapt to, and interact with its environment. This environment consists of competitors, suppliers, customers, stockholders, governments, and employees. Notice that the strategy does not provide a detailed step-by-step plan showing how the firm is to achieve its goals, since this is the purpose of short-term planning. Instead, the strategy identifies the firm's broad direction and the basic strategic moves (like "diversify," or "cut costs") it must perform to move there. As an example, in the 1920s, President Alfred P. Sloan of General Motors stated the following cost-reduction strategy for that company:

> Management should now direct its energies toward increasing earning power through increased effectiveness and reduced expense . . . efforts that have been so lavishly expended on expansion and development should now be directed at economy in operation. . . . This policy is valid if our cars are at least equal to the best of our competitors in a grade, so that it is not necessary to lead in design.[22]

Another well-phrased strategy, this for a women's apparel firm, is as follows:

> Our strategy is to increase market penetration by 30 percent by increasing our market share in the low-priced segment of the women's apparel business, with a limited line of fashion items that can be sold on the basis of style and low prices to national retail chains catering to budget-conscious women. During this period, no diversification efforts will be undertaken and all available internal funds will be allocated to debt retirement, increased marketing efforts, and improved production methods in

that order of priority—so that we emerge as a uniquely cost-effective women's apparel manufacturer.[23]

• Developing a Strategic Plan

Developing a strategic plan involves the following steps:

Step 1 Determine the current domain of the enterprise in terms of how it defines its current "business."[24] First, management answers the question, Who are we now? by determining the firm's domain—the business or businesses it is in at present—in terms of four things: product scope, integration, geographic coverage, and differential advantage.

- *Product scope* is the range of products or services the organization provides. In the auto industry, for instance, some companies specialize in producing a single, specialized car (like the Ferrari); others (like General Motors) market several lines of cars, as well as trucks and products like refrigerators and washing machines.
- Management's policy regarding *integration* is another element that helps define "what business we are in." Most apparel manufacturers, for instance, simply purchase textiles, produce their garments, and then sell them to wholesalers or retailers. Yet some firms, like Genesco, have chosen to vertically integrate—to manufacture garments and also sell them through company-owned retail stores.
- Management policy regarding *geographic coverage* also helps to define the organization's business. The *New York Times,* for instance, competes mostly in one section of the country. On the other hand, *The Wall Street Journal* has pursued a policy of increasing its geographic coverage to the point that it is now sold throughout the United States.
- The organization's *differential advantage* is anoher important aspect of its current domain. The differential advantage is the special competitive strength the organization stresses. During its early years, for instance, the Ford Motor Company relied on its competitive edge—its emphasis on specialization efficiency—to maintain a low-priced car for the mass market.

Step 2 Make a strategic forecast. That is, management tries to identify the environmental opportunities and threats it faces. Specific questions here include:

- What are the *political, social, and economic trends* we have to consider? For example, is there new legislation on the horizon that might affect our organization in the way that antipollution and gas-conservation laws affected the auto industry? What social trends do we have to consider? What is the implication of the fact, for instance, that the average age of the U.S. population is increasing?

- What are the trends in the *markets* for our product and services? Is the market demand growing, diminishing, or remaining about the same? Are there any untapped special segments or niches in the market that we could capitalize on?
- What *product and/or technological changes* do we anticipate will affect our organization? For example, are there new products on the horizon that could make ours outmoded, the way that hand-held calculators did slide rules?
- Who are the *competitors*? How do we compare, and who will our competitors be? Are we wearing blinders in regard to identifying our competitors? In 1965, for instance, few watch manufacturers would have believed that Texas Instruments, the calculator manufacturer, would be one of their main competitors within ten years.

Step 3 Determine current strengths and weaknesses. Here, management analyzes the organization's operational, financial, and managerial strengths. Operationally, for instance, ask, Do we have any special competitive edge, the way Ferrari has in building high-quality, sophisticated sports cars? Financially, do we have the resources to compete effectively in our industry today, or in the industry we are considering in the future? Managerially, do we have the managerial talents to carry out the organizational changes we want to make, or should we develop new managers first?

Step 4 Develop alternatives: Test for consistency; make a choice. This step is to develop alternatives and to analyze each in the light of the organization's strengths and weaknesses and the opportunities and threats it faces. (Sometimes, the best "strategic move" is to just continue with the status quo. Often, though, the best strategic move involves changing the firm's product line, integration, geographic coverage, or differential advantage. Thus, McDonald's might decide to branch out geographically by opening restaurants in Europe, or to integrate vertically by buying a cattle farm, or to diversify its product line by also offering salads.) Here, the manager endeavors to compare what the company is able to do with respect to its strengths and weaknesses, and what is possible in the light of its forecasted opportunities and constraints. For example:

> The success of Dr. Pepper in the soft-drink industry illustrates the coupling of realistic knowledge of corporate strengths with sound industry analysis to yield a superior strategy. Coca-Cola and PepsiCola dominate Dr. Pepper's industry, where many small producers compete for a piece of the action. Dr. Pepper chose a strategy of avoiding the largest-selling drink segment (colas), maintaining a narrow flavor line, forgoing the development of an (expensive) captive bottler network, and marketing heavily. The company positioned itself so as to be least vulnerable to its competitive forces while it exploited its small size.[25]

Step 5 Set specific objectives. Once the strategy has been identified, it is quantified in terms of goals, such as, "Obtain a 20 percent share of the soft-drink market within five years," and, "Double advertising expenditures each year for the next three years." Then, with these specific goals as targets, short-term plans can be developed that specify how the goals will be attained, and what each department must do to contribute to their attainment.

• *Four Characteristic Strategies*

Although a multitude of strategies are possible, Miles and Snow have found that there seem to be four characteristic classes of strategies and strategy makers.[26] *Defenders* pursue strategies of specialization; their main aim seems to be to become the best at producing and marketing one specialized product or service. Top managers in this type of organization are highly expert in their organization's limited area of operation and do not search outside their traditional domains for new opportunities. These organizations therefore seldom need to make major adjustments in their production methods or organization structures. Instead, they focus almost exclusively on improving the efficiency of their existing operations.

Prospectors are continually searching for new market opportunities and experimenting with new products and services. For the top management of an organization like this, product and market innovation is more important than efficiency. For instead, instead of focusing exclusively on specialized metal cans, as does the Crown Cork & Seal Company, the canning firm that is a prospector might be continually seeking out new footholds in related markets, like packaging quick-frozen foods.

Analyzers try to combine the efficiency advantage of defenders with the innovation and new-product-development advantages of prospectors. Analyzers are therefore more cautious than prospectors and are unwilling to let introducing new products completely overshadow their desire for maintaining stable and efficient operations for their traditional products or services. Some college textbook publishers are analyzers, for instance. A main concern in this highly competitive industry is to produce good books as inexpensively as possible. To facilitate this, centralized departments are created that handle the editing, manufacturing, and sale of all books. And, since there is usually a sufficiently high volume of books to keep everyone in the department busy, there is little downtime between projects; these departments tend to be relatively efficient and to process a high number of books per employee. But these publishers also want to make sure that they do not miss out on adapting to new, innovative markets. As a result, they have established research and development divisions that are involved in marketing new and innovative learning devices, such as video cassettes at the college level.

Reactors are organizations that always seem to be followers, or that are inclined to pursue "status quo" strategies. Here, top managers frequently perceive changes occurring in their environment (such as the introduction of digital watches).

But, like the top managers at some traditional firms, they are unwilling or unable to respond effectively. They therefore continue to do business as usual even as the market for their goods is going through profound changes.

• *Strategy and Structure*

The Chandler Study Historian Alfred Chandler studied the relations between a firm's strategy, its environment, and its structure, and he concluded that "structure follows strategy." Specifically, his findings suggest that a strategy of diversification typically leads to the need for a firm to decentralize. Chandler investigated this thesis by analyzing the administrative histories of about 100 of America's largest industrial enterprises. Information was obtained from such sources as annual reports, articles, and government publications, as well as selected interviews with senior executives.

He found that a changing economic environment in America led companies to develop new strategies, which in turn necessitated new organizational structures:

> The prospect of a new market or the threatened loss of a current one stimulated [the strategies of] geographical expansion, vertical integration, and product diversification. Moreover, once a firm had accumulated large resources, the need to keep its men, money, and materials steadily employed provided a constant stimulus to look for new markets by moving into new areas, by taking on new functions, or by developing new product lines.[27]

Eventually, the linking together of these three basic strategies resulted in the need for the decentralized, divisionalized structure:

> Expansion of volume, . . . [g]rowth through geographical disperson, . . . [and finally] the developing of new lines of products . . . brought about the formation of the multi-divisional structure. . . . [28]

Among the industries that widely accepted the new, decentralized structure with its autonomous product divisions were the electrical and electronics, power-machinery (including automobiles), and chemical industries; all but two of the 20 leading companies in these industries were managed in 1960 through a multidivisional administrative structure.[29]

What is it about these three industries that made them choose this form of organization? Chandler found that companies in these three industries all placed an emphasis upon research and development and on a strategy of expansion through diversification. The two giants of the electronics industry, Westinghouse and General Electric, had specialized before World War II in producing and marketing equipment for providing electric power and light. The majority of these products went directly to other industrial firms, the one exception being the marketing of light bulbs directly to mass consumers. This latter market, however, was highly differentiated from the companies' industrial markets. Furthermore, the complexities of designing and producing electrical and electronic components created an atmosphere in which research and development activities thrived.

The ensuing rapid rate of new-product development and further differentiation of markets rendered ineffective the centralized organizational structure in these two firms. As a Westinghouse executive pointed out:

> All of the activities of the company were divided into production, engineering, and sales, each of which was the responsibility of a vice-president. The domain of each vice-president covered the whole diversified and far-flung operations of the corporation. Such an organization of the corporation's management lacks responsiveness. There was too much delay in the recognition of problems and in the solution of problems after they were recognized.[30]

In other words, because these firms' products were so diverse, and because new products were introduced so often, an organization in which the same production department, sales department, and so on served all products became unresponsive. As a result, these firms decentralized by setting up self-contained product divisions. At Westinghouse, merchandise divisions were established for various electric appliances. These allowed division executives to make most of the sales, engineering, and manufacturing decisions for products in their divisions. Similarly, General Electric established a decentralized organization with vice-presidents for such divisional groups as consumer products, aerospace, and construction materials.

On the other hand, Chandler found that the trend in other industries, such as steel, was toward increased centralization of operations. The differences between the steel and electrical industries are informative. Whereas the demands facing the latter could be described as diverse, differentiated, and rapidly changing, the demands of the steel industry could best be described as routine, undifferentiated, and stable. These differences reflect similar differences in the strategic issues facing the two industries. For example, research, development, and engineering seem consistently paramount in the electrical industry. However, the strategic issue facing steel firms has historically been production efficiency. In turn, this emphasis was closely associated with a need for a high-volume output and predictable demand.

This stress on production and the closely associated need for maintaining stable and predictable markets led to centralized organizations in the steel industry. For example, the organizational structure of the United States Steel Company evolved from a relatively decentralized one in the early 1900s to a centralized one today. In fact, by 1950, two-thirds of the corporation's steelmaking activities were consolidated into "central" operations:

> [A] single set of executive vice-presidents became to a large extent responsible for the administration of their different functions in every part of the corporation. The executive vice-president in charge of production had under him vice-presidents for coal, steel, and fabricating.[31]

Thus, structure followed strategy. A strategy aimed at increasing volume and production efficiency led to an environment that was relatively stable and undifferentiated. A strategy of diversification led to an environment in which technology, markets, and sources of supply were rapidly changing; and in such a situation, the defects of the centralized organization structure became apparent. Organizational adaptation and effectiveness were impaired, and firms faced with such environments found it necessary to take on the new decentralized form.

Similar findings have been obtained in a developing country. Researchers collected data from 30 manufacturing firms in India, a variety of industries that included chemicals, pharmaceuticals, cosmetics, machine tools, and soft drinks.[32] The researchers used "degree of market competition" (degree of price competition, number of alternatives available to the consumer, and so on) as their measure of environmental predictability. They found that the results of their study "provide further evidence in support of a contingency theory of organizations." They could not conclude that dynamic, competitive market conditions necessitated decentralization whereas stable conditions necessitated centralization. However, they did find that the decentralized structure was "more important" for a firm's effectiveness when the environment was dynamic than when it was stable.

• *Beyond Strategy and Structure*

The structure-follows-strategy thesis has been questioned on several grounds. First, some argue that *strategy often follows structure,* or that at least the relation is reciprocal: A company organized for, say, innovation may be driven to develop more new and varied products, whereas one organized for efficiency may seek ways to maintain the status quo, so that their strategies each reflect, to some degree, the way they are organized and managed.

Others contend that the structure–strategy fit *may not matter at all,* at least if the firm is not operating under competitive conditions. Thus, "if a firm has power over its environment so that it can control prices because of monopoly position, tariffs, or close ties to government, it can maintain effective economic performance even if there is a mismatch between strategy and structure."[33]

One recent study concludes that even though organizational structure and strategy may be related, they are so mostly because of organizational size. As a company ages, these writers say, it tends to diversify, a strategy that results in a growth in organizational size. In turn, this increased size demands changes in the organization's structure.[34]

Yet another point of view is expressed by Peters and Waterman, who contend that the structure-follows-strategy thesis is simply incomplete, insofar as "there is no such thing as a good structural answer apart from people considerations, and vice versa."[35] They conclude that "any intelligent approach to organizing "has to treat as interdependent at least seven variables: structure, strategy, people, management style, systems and procedures, guiding concepts and shared values, and the present or hoped-for corporate strengths or skills." True organizational effectiveness, they say, comes not from just a match between strategy and structure, but from a match between these two and factors like shared values among employees, and the right people as well.

• *Managing the Environment*

Pfeffer and Salancik take a different approach to the structure–strategy issue and contend that to survive and prosper, the organization can react to environmental demands defensively, offensively, or both. Defensively, it can engage in organizational change and development activities—for instance, by defensively changing its structure or shared values in such a way that the organization "fits"—becomes more appropriate for—dealing with its environmental demands. This more defensive, reactive posture is generally the one we'll stress in the following chapters.

But organizations can also react offensively. And explaining specific ways the organization can act offensively to reduce its dependence on "outside factors" by modifying its environment is one of Pfeffer and Salancik's key themes. They say an organization can manage environmental demands by *avoiding influence, altering dependencies, negotiating with the environment,* or *legislatively creating a new environment.*[36]

First, it can *avoid* or manage the conditions of external control without actually changing those conditions. One way to do this is by playing off the demands of one group against those of another. Thus, an organization faced with an affirmative-action suit might seek to avoid government influence by putting the blame for its hiring practices on the union. Another technique for avoiding influence is to control communications and information so that groups like unions, government agencies, and stockholders have insufficient information on which to hold the organization accountable.

A more potent way to manage environmental demands involves reducing or *altering the organization's interdependencies.* And, according to these writers, "the most effective strategies for dealing with dependence which arises from reliance on a single product or market are those which alter the purpose or structure of the organization so that it no longer requires only a limited range of inputs or serves only a few markets." For example, the organization can diversify, perhaps by adding new products, moving into new geographic locations, or offering products in a wider range of prices: By increasing the number and variety of its customers, the firm becomes less dependent on any one of those customers. Mergers are a second technique for reducing a firm's dependence on outside elements. Thus, by following a strategy of vertical integration, a car manufacturer might merge with or purchase a steel firm in order to reduce the uncertainties surrounding its steel acquisition. Growth is another technique for reducing dependence, since an increase in size should make the firm more powerful and therefore less dependent on outside elements.

Organizations need not totally absorb crucial outside groups in order to gain some control over them. An alternative is for the firm to *renegotiate its environment*—for example, by setting up trade associations, cartels, trade agreements, coordinating councils, and joint ventures. All these are negotiated agreements through which interdependent firms can coordinate their efforts and thereby reduce conflict and uncertainty.

Finally, organizations can legislatively alter or *create environments*. For example, auto-industry lobbyists try to reduce pollution standards, and apparel manufacturers try to have quotas put on imported clothing.

In summary, Pfeffer and Salancik say that organizational effectiveness is multifaceted, and that since each outside group evaluates the organization by its own criteria, effectiveness is always relative: An organization might be simultaneously effective in the opinion of stockholders and very ineffective from the point of view of community groups or government agencies. Yet the organization cannot depend on just a single group for its support, since, in addition to stockholders, it needs the support of its suppliers, retail outlets, clients, and so forth. The effective firm is thus the firm that can survive and prosper in the face of the competing demands from all influential groups, and the firm that can reduce its dependence on outsiders increases its chances for survival. Four techniques for reducing the uncertainty, interdependence, and conflict in environments are *avoiding* the influence, *altering* the dependencies, *negotiating* with the environment, and legislatively *creating* a new environment.

As an alternative, of course, the firm can also deal with its dependencies through a process of organizational change and development. Structurally, for example, it can establish self-contained, differentiated departments, each of which "co-opts" an environmental segment and pays close and continuous attention to it. It is this more "defensive" approach to survival and effectiveness that we stress in this book.

SUMMARY

In this chapter we focused on *organizational effectiveness,* which we defined as the firm's ability to survive and effectively bargain with and adapt to crucial interest groups and to create acceptable outcomes and actions. Specific measures of effectiveness that we discussed included single-criterion measures like profit maximization; multiple-criteria measures like profitability, growth, and innovation; and Pfeffer and Salancik's concept that the effective organization is the one that satisfies the demands of those in its environment from whom it requires support for its continued existence.

Given the importance of adapting to shifting environmental demands, it should come as no surprise that one of top management's main tasks involves strategic planning, matching organizational competencies with the opportunities and risks created by environmental change. An organization's strategy (as explained in this chapter) is the match between an organization's resources and skills and the environmental opportunities and risks it faces. It reflects, in other words, how the organization plans to adapt to the threats and opportunities in its environment and thereby maintain its effectiveness. The strategy identifies, among other things, the market niche in which the enterprise will compete, as well as its product scope, geographic coverage, and differential advantage. It thus helps to determine the firm's effectivness.

But strategy may also affect a firm's effectiveness indirectly, through its effects on structure. Historian Alfred Chandler was the first to popularize the idea that the organization's structure depends partly on its strategy. He found that effective companies that had pursued strategies of diversification had almost invariably organized around self-contained divisions, apparently as a result of a need to reduce the diversity and quantity of information with which the chief executive had to cope. In the next chapter, we turn our attention to a more detailed analysis of the relation between the organization's context—its environment, technology, and size—and its organization structure.

Discussion Questions

1 How would you define "organizational effectiveness"?
2 Explain Pfeffer and Salancik's concept of organizational effectiveness.
3 Explain the relationship between strategy and structure.
4 Define what is meant by "environment."
5 Explain how to develop a strategic plan.

Footnotes

[1]Richard Bilas, *Micro Economic Theory* (New York: McGraw-Hill, 1967), pp. 150–51.

[2]Richard Lipsey and Peter Steiner, *Economics* (New York: Harper & Row, 1969), p. 369.

[3]George Stigler, *The Theory of Price* (New York: Macmillan, 1966), p. 177.

[4]C.E. Ferguson, *Micro Economic Theory* (New York: McGraw-Hill, 1966), p. 191.

[5]Herbert Simon, *Administrative Behavior* (New York: Free Press, 1957).

[6]John P. Campbell, "Research into the Nature of Organizational Effectiveness: An Endangered Species?" working paper, University of Minnesota, 1973, quoted in Steers, "Problems in the Measurement of Organizational Effectiveness."

[7]G.W. England, "Organizational Goals and Expectant Behavior of American Managers," *Academy of Management Journal*, Vol. 10 (1967); Richard Steers, "Problems in Measurement of Organizational Effectiveness," *Administrative Science Quarterly*, Vol. 20, (December 1975).

[8]Ephraim Yuchtman and Stanley Seashore, "A System Resource Approach to Organizational Effectiveness," *Administrative Science Quarterly*, Vol. 32 (December 1967), 377–95.

[9]*Ibid.*

[10]Bernard Bass, "Ultimate Criteria of Organizational Worth," *Personnel Psychology*, Vol. 5 (1952), 157–73.

[11]See, for example, J. Richard Hackman and J. Lloyd Suttle, *Improving Life at Work* (Santa Monica, Calif.: Goodyear, 1977).

[12]Warren Bennis, "Towards a 'Truly' Scientific Management: The Concept of Organizational Health," in W. Bennis, *Changing Organizations* (New York: McGraw-Hill, 1966). Jaisingh Ghorpade, *Assessment of Organizational Effectiveness* (Pacific Palisades, Calif.: Goodyear, 1971), pp. 116–43.

[13]*Ibid.,* p. 128.

[14]*Ibid.,* p. 129.

[15]Thomas Peters and Robert Waterman, Jr., *In Search of Excellence* (New York: Harper & Row, 1982), p. 23.

[16]*Ibid.*

[17]See Steers, "Problems in the Measurement of Organizational Effectiveness," pp. 547–51.

[18]*Ibid.,* p. 549.

[19]Jeffrey Pfeffer and Gerald Salancik, *The External Control of Organizations* (New York: Harper & Row, 1978).

[20]Charles Hofer and Dan Schendel, *Strategy Formulation: Analytical Concepts* (St. Paul: West, 1978), p. 11.

[21]Based on William Newman and John Logan, *Strategy, Policy and Central Management* (Cincinnati: South-Western, 1981).

[22]Quoted in William R. Hall, "Survival Strategies in a Hostile Environment," *Harvard Business Review,* Vol. 58, No. 5 (September–October 1980), 79.

[23]Adapted from Arthur Thompson, Jr., and A.J. Strickland III, *Strategy Formulation and Implementation* (Dallas: BPI, 1980), p. 66.

[24]See Hugo Uyterhoven, Robert Ackerman, and John Rosenblum, *Strategy and Organization* (Homewood, Ill.: Irwin, 1977), pp. 7–17.

[25]Michael Porter, "How Competitive Forces Shape Strategy," *Harvard Business Review* (March–April 1979), p. 143. See also Donald Hambrick and Steven Schecter, "Turnaround Strategies for Mature Industrial-Product Business Units," *Academy of Management Journal,* Vol. 26, No. 2 (June 1983), 231–48; and Anil Gupta and V. Govindarajan, "Business Unit Strategy, Managerial Characteristics, and Business Unit Effectiveness at Strategy Implementation," *Academy of Management Journal,* Vol. 27, No. 1 (March 1984), 25–41.

[26]R.E. Miles and C.C. Snow, *Organizational Strategy, Structure and Process* (New York: McGraw-Hill, 1978). Hambrick, in a study of the Miles and Snow theory, concluded that "in every type of environment examined, defenders outperformed prospectors in terms of current profitability and cash flow" and that "the costs and risks of product innovation appeared significant." On the other hand, prospectors outperformed the defenders in terms of market-share gains, but only in "innovative" industries where they were rewarded for their adaptive stance. In summary, says Hambrick, his study supports the idea that choice of strategy should be a function of the requirements of the environment and the type of performance being sought at the time. Donald Hambrick, "Some Tests of the Effectiveness and Functional Attributes of Miles and Snow's Strategic Types," *Academy of Management Journal,* Vol. 26, No. 1 (March 1983), 5–26.

[27]Alfred Chandler, Jr., *Strategy and Structure* (Cambridge, Mass.: M.I.T. Press, 1962), p. 15.

[28]*Ibid.,* p. 14. Franko obtained similar findings in a study of 127 European companies. He found that approximately one-half had changed to the divisionalized structure. However, the changes seemed more in response to "specific changes in the competitive environment . . . than as a result of changes in product diversification strategies." Lawrence G. Franko, "The Move toward a Multivisional Structure in European Organizations," *Administrative Science Quarterly,* December 1974, pp. 493–505. See also Robert J. Pavan, "Diversification and the Division Structure in Italy," paper presented at the 34th annual meeting, Academy of Management, Seattle, Washington, August 18–21, 1974.

[29]Chandler, *Strategy and Structure,* p. 362.

[30]*Ibid.,* p. 366.

[31]*Ibid.,* p. 335.

[32]Anant R. Negandhi and Bernard Reimann, "A Contingency Theory of Organization in the Context of a Developing Country," *Academy of Management Journal,* Vol. 15, No. 2 (June 1972), 137–46. For an application of this concept to multinational companies, see William Egelhoff, "Strategy and Structure in Multinational Corporations: An Information Processing Approach," *Administrative Science Quarterly,* Vol. 27, No. 3 (September 1982), 435–58.

[33]Jay Galbraith and Daniel Nathanson, *Strategy Implementation: The Role of Structure and Process* (St. Paul: West, 1978) p. 139.

[34]Peter Grinyer and Masooud Yasai-Ardekani, "Strategy, Structure, Size and Bureaucracy," *Academy of Management Journal,* Vol. 24, No. 3 (September 1981), 471–86.

[35]Peters and Waterman, *In Search of Excellence,* p. 9.

[36]Pfeffer and Salancik, *The External Control of Organizations,* p. 257.

CASE FOR CHAPTER 4
THE DIFFICULT TASK OF CHANGING CORPORATE CULTURE: THE CASE OF CORNING GLASS*

Ann Hughey

Corning Glass Works' management-training program, so the joke on Wall Street goes, consists of three weeks of polo, three weeks of squash, and three weeks of platform tennis.

Corning clearly has a reputation for a laid-back management style—a reputation that observers inside and outside the company say is deserved. They blame the company's 41 percent drop in net income since 1979 partly on management's unwillingness to make difficult, but necessary, decisions on cost cutting, acquisitions, and divestitures.

Last week, however, Corning decided to try to change course. Amory Houghton, Jr., Corning chairman and chief executive for almost two decades, stepped down at age 56 and was replaced by his 47-year-old brother, James R. Houghton. The new boss, who had been vice chairman, has a reputation for toughness and is the chief architect of strategy, including management reorganization and extensive write-offs, that Corning hopes will revive its sagging fortunes.

"I'm viewed around here as a little bit of a hard ass," says the new chairman, who confesses to having just reread Machiavelli's *The Prince.* "I have a reputation for asking hard questions and sometimes not being very nice in meetings. I guess I don't put up with too much explanation for lots of problems."

*Reprinted by permission of *The Wall Street Journal.* Ann Hughey is a staff reporter for *The Wall Street Journal.*

• *Changing a Culture*

Still, most people believe he won't have it easy. It is hard to change a corporate culture, and the one at Corning has been around a long time.

Moreover, that culture of paternalism and an easygoing, risk-averse style has been provided by the Houghton family, which started Corning 130 years ago here in upstate New York. Houghtons traditionally provide the chief executive, and the family still controls 30 percent of the shares.

The younger Mr. Houghton is called "Jamie" by everyone, just as his brother is universally called "Amo": The company prides itself on the personal touch. Jamie joined Corning in 1962 after a traditional Houghton education: St. Paul's prep school in Concord, New Hampshire; Harvard College; and Harvard Business School.

But Corning's problems extend beyond its perhaps too-soft management style at the top. The company also has been slow to react to new opportunities and slow to shelve declining business.

• *Some Steps Taken*

Television bulbs, for instance, once produced most of Corning's profits, but that's been a declining business for several years. Yet the company has been slow to cut back on it. Corning's laboratory glassware products have been steadily replaced on the market by more sophisticated, high-technology medical devices that Corning only recently invested in.

Amory Houghton, Jr., did take some steps. In March 1982 he cut the pay of 7,500 salaried employees by 5 percent to avoid layoffs. But it wasn't enough; about 20 percent of Corning's domestic hourly employees have been laid off, while salaried employment is down 8 percent from last year. Earnings fell 28 percent last year to $74.5 million, or $3.52 a share, from 1981.

Last January, Corning announced a major retrenchment, beginning with the closing of a television-bulb plant. The company's moves resulted in a $46 million net write-down against 1982 earnings.

The January plan had been devised by James Houghton, who revealed more changes last week, the day he took over as chairman and chief executive.

• *Avoiding the "Baron System"*

He divided the company into three groups: electronics and communications, consumer and industry, and health and sciences. Previously, the company had one president. Now the head of each Corning group has the title of president, and each reports to the chairman.

Mr. Houghton named the three presidents to the six-member management committee that will help make major operating decisions. Amory Houghton, Jr., had an advisory committee, but it had only one member with direct line responsibility.

The new chairman says he wants a tighter, faster-reacting committee. He put the three operating presidents on the committee, he says, to create peer pressure and to force them to think in terms of the whole company. He says he wants to avoid "the baron system," where line managers worry only about their own turf.

It's also clearer now which divisions will grow and which will retrench.

The bulk of Corning's traditional businesses, such as television tubes and Corelle dishes, have been combined into the consumer and industry group. That's where Mr. Houghton plans to cut because, he says, "there are some questionable businesses where we have very high market share, a lot of competition, and margins are eroding a bit."

Corning also has been pulling out of the light bulb business, which it developed in the 1880s at the request of Thomas Edison, as well as its European laboratory glassware business. Corning won't say what is next, but an analyst speculates that the axe will hit some consumer glassware lines, refractory bricks used to line furnaces, and some foreign operations.

Corporate resources will be concentrated in biotechnology and fiber optics, the tiny glass strands that are expected to replace traditional wiring in communications systems. Mr. Houghton describes fiber optics as "the envy of the corporation because regardless of what it wants, we just keep pouring more money and people into it." Corning holds fiber-optic patents and, in addition to producing fiber-optic materials, has issued licenses and formed joint ventures to take advantage of its technology.

• *Research Priorities*

Biotechnology is part of the health and sciences group that Corning has built through recent acquisitions and joint ventures. Last week, Corning said that a joint venture with Genentech, Inc., has signed a big Danish firm, Chr. Hansen's Laboratorium A/S to market rennin, an enzyme used to make cheese and a product of biotechnology.

Corning also reordered priorities for its approximately $90 million research budget. Mr. Houghton says that 80 percent of research money will remain in glass and ceramics. "We're number one in the world in glass and ceramics, and if we ever lose that, we're stupid," he says. But he adds: "Before, there was a little empire up there [at Corning research], and they'd work on what they wanted to work on." Now, he says, the operating units will decide what the research division will work on, with research costs charged to the individual units.

The idea, he says, "is to be able to move faster. We used to be in a position where we could be pretty sleepy. We would come up with a development and nurse it along and take our time, and whenever we got ready, the marketplace would accept it. That's gone.''

Despite all these moves, Mr. Houghton realizes that his goal of ''a respectable level of profitability'' won't be easy to attain. And it might be even harder to maintain.

''I think there are a lot of people in the company who think we're restructuring now, and once that's done . . . it's back like the 1940s and 1950s,'' Mr. Houghton says. He says people think that ''every business can grow because the economy's growing. That just isn't going to be the case.''

QUESTIONS

1 How has James Houghton changed Corning's strategy? What structural changes has this strategic change required?

2 What exactly has Mr. Houghton done to ensure that Corning ''is to be able to move faster'' in the future?

Environment, Technology, and Organization

OVERVIEW

In the previous chapter we introduced the idea that the firm's environment (for instance, in terms of diversity and change) seems to affect its structure. The purpose of this chapter is to expand on this idea and to explain how an organization's *context*—its environment, technology, and size—affects how the organization is structured. The studies by Burns and Stalker and by Lawrence and Lorsch show how different types of environments affect the organization and how it is managed. The Woodward and New Jersey studies show that technology—the means an organization employs to produce its goods or services—also affects the organization and its management.

The outline of this chapter is as follows:

- **A** Studies in environment and organization
  - **1** Introduction
  - **2** The Burns and Stalker studies: organization and environment
  - **3** The Lawrence and Lorsch studies: differentiation and integration
  - **4** The Emery and Trist studies
- **B** Technology and organization
  - **1** The Woodward studies
  - **2** The Aston studies
  - **3** The New Jersey studies
  - **4** Toward a broader view of technology

- C Organization size and structure
  - 1 Positive findings
  - 2 Negative findings
  - 3 Research problems
  - 4 Discussion
- D Uncertainty, complexity, and organization
  - 1 Uncertainty: a central element
- E Appendix: Human information processing and decision making

STUDIES IN ENVIRONMENT AND ORGANIZATION

• Introduction

Any organization—whether General Motors, City Hospital, or the United Way—operates within an environment, and it stands to reason that its environment will help determine how it behaves. The environment—including (as explained in Chapter 4) political, economic, and social trends, market trends, competitive trends, and product/technological trends—forces varying degrees of complexity and change on the enterprise, and so it is the enterprise that can adapt and innovate that will best survive. This point is illustrated by the three studies described in this section.

• The Burns and Stalker Studies: Organization and Environment

Burns and Stalker studied some 20 industrial firms in the United Kingdom in order to "describe and explain what happens when new and unfamiliar tasks are put upon industrial concerns organized for relatively stable conditions." They believed that when an organization's environment—its competitors, customers, and suppliers, for instance—start changing rapidly, "a fundamentally different kind of management system becomes appropriate from that which applies to a relatively stable commercial and technical environment."[1] Companies they studied included a rayon manufacturer, a large engineering firm, and a number of electronics firms. We can illustrate their findings by distinguishing among three types of environments: the stable environment, the changing environment, and the innovative environment.

Organizing in a Stable Environment A stable environment can be characterized as follows:

1. Demand for the organization's product or service is stable and predictable.
2. There is an unchanging, stable set of competitors.

3. Technological innovation and new-product development are evolutionary rather than revolutionary, in that required product changes can be predicted well in advance and the required modifications made at a leisurely pace.
4. Government policies regarding regulation of the industry and taxation are stable and change little over time.

As an example, the watch industry until 1970 (when digital watches were introduced) had a stable environment. Demand for jeweled-lever-movement watches was stable, there was a stable set of competitors in the industry, technological innovation and new-product development were at most evolutionary, and government policies regarding taxation and regulation of the industry were consistent over time.

The rayon mill Burns and Stalker studied operated in a stable environment. In order to be successful in this highly competitive industry, the parent firm had to keep costs to a minimum and be as efficient as possible. Therefore, its very existence depended on keeping unexpected occurrences to a minimum and the level of sales orders high and stable, so that (from the point of view of the mill itself) the environment seemed stable.

The researchers found that the organization structure that had evolved in this mill seemed to reflect this stable, unchanging environment and emphasis on efficiency. The organization was a "pyramid of knowledge," in that top management made most decisions and communicated these downward via the chain of command. Decision making in the plant was highly centralized, and it was run on the basis of an elaborate network of policies, procedures, rules, and tight production controls. Job descriptions were carefully defined, and everyone from the top of the organization to the bottom had a very specialized job to do. Coordination was achieved via the chain of command.

Organizing in a Changing Environment A changing environment is characterized as follows:

1. Demand for the organization's product or service fluctuates but can still be predicted with some accuracy several years in advance.
2. Competitors enter and leave the industry, but although these changes can affect the firm's demand, the effects are usually not drastic.
3. Technological innovation and new-product development proceeds in an orderly, sequential fashion, with the required changes well understood a year or more in advance.
4. Government policies regarding regulation and taxation are changing, but these changes can generally be predicted well in advance and planned for.

The U.S. auto industry is characteristic of one that now competes in a changing environment. Demand fluctuates with the economy, but the basic demand for cars can be predicted well in advance, although this market may be changing as competition from foreign car makers increases and as commuters turn to more fuel-efficient transportation like buses. In order for a firm to maintain market demand in the face of increased fuel costs and new government antipollution requirements, technical innovations, such as electronic fuel injection, will continue to demand more development efforts than were necessary in the auto industry ten or 20 years ago. Similarly, government policies regarding fuel efficiency, safety, and pollution are becoming more stringent, although the fact that the laws are "phased in" over several years gives the industry time to plan all required changes.

Burns and Stalker found that a small electrical engineering firm that produced electrical devices was competing in such a changing environment. Design and production of these devices "was on fairly standard lines," but "every contract required some special units, and there was a constant flow of design improvements."[2]

As a result, this firm could not afford to focus entirely on efficiency (as could the rayon mill), but instead had to organize in a way that allowed it to remain responsive to its customers. Here, Burns and Stalker found that there was a deliberate avoidance of clearly defined jobs and lines of authority. Tasks were less rigidly defined even at the lower levels, and employees tended to regard their work as a contribution to the overall task of the firm. Communications, aided by committee meetings, tended to flow easily outside the formal chain of command.

Organizing in an Innovative Environment An innovative environment is characterized by the following:

1 Demand for the organization's product or service can change dramatically, sometimes overnight, as competitors introduce radically improved products.[3]
2 Sudden, unexpected changes occur in the nature of the organization's competitors.[4]
3 There is an extremely rapid rate of technological innovation and new-product development. Organizations in innovative environments usually rely heavily on research and development for their survival.
4 Government policies regarding regulation and taxation are evolving quickly, trying to keep pace with the stream of new, more technologically advanced products being introduced by firms.

Innovative environments are typified by the "third-wave" industries that Toffler says will dominate the industrialized world for the foreseeable future. These include electronics and computers (including fiber optics, computers, digital watches, and the like), the space industry (satellites, space platforms, and so on), the deep-sea industry (for new sources of food and minerals, for instance), and the gene industry (for high-yielding crops, "oil-eating" bacteria, and so forth).

For example, innovation is epitomized by the changes taking place in the microchip industry. A microprocessor is similar to a tiny "computer"—one that, when suitably instructed, can perform certain basic arithmetical operations on data presented to it. The first microprocessor was commercially developed in 1971.[5] Today, chips are used in many applications, including electronic fuel injection in cars, General Motors' Cruise Control, and video games. And as the market for these chips has exploded, their capabilities have increased as well. Today, even industry giants like Texas Instruments have found it difficult to keep up with the technological innovations in this area.[6]

Burns and Stalker found that several of the electronics firms they studied were in fact competing in this sort of innovative environment. Therefore, these firms' existence depended on their ability to continuously introduce new and innovative electronic components. They also had to be always on the alert for innovations by their competitors, so flexibility and creativity (rather than efficiency) were paramount for these companies.[7]

In these firms, the researchers found a "deliberate attempt to avoid specifying individual tasks."[8] Each worker's job, in other words, might change daily, as employees rushed to respond to the "problem of the day."[9] Most important, all employees here recognized the need for sharing common beliefs and goals, and these common goals (such as, "Let's make sure we produce only first-rate products.") ensured that all could work together with little or no guidance. In turn, this pervasive self-control helped the firm adapt quickly and "unbureaucratically" to its rapidly changing environment. The head of one firm, in fact,

> . . . attacked the idea of the organization chart as inapplicable in his concern and as a dangerous method of thinking about the working of industrial management. The first requirement of management, according to him, was that it should make the fullest use of the capacities of its members; any individual's job should be as little defined as possible, so that it will shape itself to his special abilities and initiative.[10]

Mechanistic and Organic Organizations Their findings led Burns and Stalker to distinguish between two different types of organizations, which they called *mechanistic* and *organic*. The rayon mill was typical of mechanistic, classical-type organizations; the electronics firms were typical of organic, behavioral-type ones. Mechanistic organizations, they contend, are characterized by:

- Close adherence to the chain of command
- A functional division of work, through which the problems and tasks facing the concern as a whole are broken down
- The highly specialized nature of each task
- The use of the formal hierarchy for coordination
- Detailed job descriptions that provide a precise definition of rights, obligations, and technical methods for performing each job
- A tendency for interaction between employees to be vertical; i.e., "between superior and subordinate"
- A tendency for operations and working behavior to be governed by the instructions and decisions issued by superiors

Organic organizations, according to Burns and Stalker, are characterized by:

- Little preoccupation with adhering to the chain of command
- A more "realistic," divisional-type division of work
- "The shedding of responsibility as a limited field of rights, obligations, and methods" (employees do not respond to requests by saying, "That's not my job," for instance)
- Jobs that are not clearly defined in advance, but are instead continually adjusted and redefined as the situation demands
- More of a network or matrix structure of communication
- Lateral rather than vertical communication and an emphasis on consultation rather than command; communication here generally consists of information and advice rather than instructions and decisions
- A pervasive commitment to the organization's tasks that motivates employees to maintain self-control (as opposed to having performance controlled solely through a system of rewards and penalties, as is often the case in mechanistic organizations)[11]

The Lawrence and Lorsch Studies: Differentiation and Integration

The Lawrence and Lorsch studies (first mentioned in Chapter 3) are important because they show that in large, multidepartment organizations, each department must often contend with its own environment and thus have its own unique structure. In a company like Texas Instruments, for example, we might expect the marketing, research, and new-product-development departments to face innovative environments, while the firm makes every effort to ensure that manufacturing faces a stable environment. Consequently, we might expect the manufacturing department to be organized mechanistically and the other departments organically.

The Study The basic question Lawrence and Lorsch sought to answer was, What kind of organization does it take to deal with various economic and market conditions?[12] Their research was carried out in two steps. In the first, six firms in the plastics industry were analyzed. This analysis provided a qualitative understanding of the relationship between environment and organizational structure. Second, a highly effective organization and a less effective one in each of the plastics, food, and container industries were studied and compared. These three industries were chosen because they seemed to display important differences in environmental uncertainty and diversity. For example, the industries examined had a "different rate of technological change in both products and processes."[13]

Lawrence and Lorsch were concerned with two interrelated issues. First, in line with the Burns and Stalker findings, they wanted to analyze the relationship between the uncertainty of an organization's environment and its internal structure. Specifically, Lawrence and Lorsch drew a distinction between three main subsystems of an organization—marketing, economic—technical, and scientific—and hypothesized that the structure of each subsystem or "department" would vary with how predictable its own environment was. Their hypothesis was that "the greater the degree of certainty of the relevant subenvironment, the more formalized the structure of the subsystem."[14]

Information concerning the stability and predictability of the environments of each department was collected in interviews with the top executives in each firm. To Lawrence and Lorsch, "environmental uncertainty" reflected things like "the rate of change in environmental conditions" (such as how often new products are introduced); and "time span—how long it took to get feedback" (for example, on the success of a new product after it is introduced).[15]

Findings As Table 5-1 shows, Lawrence and Lorsch found that subsystems within each organization tended to "develop a degree of formalized structure related to the certainty of their relevant environment."[16] For example, production, with a more certain subenvironment, tended to have the highest structure in all but one organization, and fundamental-research subsystems tended to have the least structure. Sales subsystems with moderately certain tasks tended to be more structured than research subsystems, but usually less structured than production.

The second, related question focused on what they called "differentiation and integration." They felt that differences in the subenvironments might result in corresponding differences in the structures and orientations of each of the three subsystems and that therefore the organization would be "differentiated." This differentiation, in turn, necessitates "integration," or the "process of achieving unity of effort among the various subsystems in the accomplishment of the organization's task."[17] They found that the more differentiated the departments were, the more elaborate were the methods used to achieve "integration" (coordination).

TABLE 5-1 Lawrence and Lorsch Subsystem-Structure Scores Ranked from Low to High

Subsystem	*Firm I*	*Firm II*	*Firm III*	*Firm IV*	*Firm V*	*Firm VI*
Fundamental research	1	1.5	1	1	1.5	1
Applied research	2.5	1.5	2	2	1.5	2
Sales	2.5	3	3	4	3	3.5
Production	4	4	4	3	4	3.5

Numbers are rank orders: 1 = low structure, 4 = high structure. Fundamental-research units usually had the most uncertain environments, production units the most predictable.

Summary The studies by Lawrence and Lorsch (as well as those by Burns and Stalker) help illustrate how environments and organization are related. Organizations in stable, unchanging environments tend to develop structures that are mechanistic and formal. Those that must deal with more uncertain, innovative environments develop more organic, adaptive structures. Since different departments within organizations usually have their own "subenvironments" to contend with, organizations are differentiated, with each department having its own degree of structure. In turn, this "differentiation" between departments in each firm contributes to the need for different types of "integration" or coordination techniques. In their study they found that in successful organizations in the container industry (where all departments faced stable environments and were therefore mechanistically structured), the chain of command was usually sufficient for achieving coordination. In the plastics industry, on the other hand (where departments faced different environments in terms of stability, and each department had its own unique structure), coordination was more difficult to achieve, and special "integrators" had to be appointed.[18]

• *The Emery and Trist Studies*

Organizational environments are becoming more complex, diverse, and unpredictable. A major contribution of the Emery and Trist case studies is that they help illustrate how environments evolve from simplicity and stability to complexity and change.

Emery and Trist distinguish among four "ideal types" of environments, each of which differs in the complexity, "relevant uncertainty," relatedness, and overall "causal texture" with which constituent organizations must cope.[19] These may be summarized as follows:

- *Type 1, placid, randomized.* This type of environment is the simplest and corresponds to the economist's classical market. The organization, unable to predict what its environment will do, can operate independently of it. Therefore, "the best tactic . . . can be learned only by trial and error."
- *Type 2, placid, clustered.* Here, it is possible to make probability estimates of the relation between causes and effects of events, although the environment is still not changing rapidly. Unlike the case with the first type, "survival becomes critically linked with what an organization knows of its environment." To gather and adapt to environmental information, the organization must now construct a master plan and see to it that resources are appropriately allocated.
- *Type 3, disturbed, reactive.* The significant difference between this and the preceding type is the existence of a number of similar organizations, a fact that becomes the dominant characteristic of this environment. In addition to considering its counterparts, which it meets at random, the organization must now consider that what it knows can also be known by the others. "This type is comparable to the economist's oligopolistic market." Here, strategies must be

worked out that take into consideration not only the reaction of the market and the long-run goals of the organization, but also the probable reactions of competitors. Therefore, the relatively simple cause–effect relations of the type 2 environment give way in type 3 to a more complex, uncertain situation in which reactions of competitors must be considered. The organization must decide not only where it is going but how to get there "while insuring that others . . . do not." Adapting to the reactions of others requires greater flexibility, however; and "the flexibility required encourages a certain decentralization and also puts a premium on quality and speed of decision. . . ."

- *Type 4, turbulent field.* In this type of environment, dynamic processes "arise from the field itself" and not merely from the interactions of components. "The turbulence results from the complexity and multiple character of the causal interconnections." This is the most complex, rapidly changing environment and arises as a result of three interrelated trends. First, in order to adapt to the demands of the type 3 environment, organizations grow and become linked until they begin to alter the nature of their environment. Second, there is "a deepening interdependence between the economic and the other facets of the society." Finally, and perhaps most important, "the increasing reliance on research and development . . . leads to a situation in which a change gradient is continuously present in the environmental field."

Emery and Trist present a case history that, along with others not described in their paper, led them to develop their ideas about types of environments. The case history involved a British food-canning company that decided to install highly automated machinery, only to find the markets for its goods rapidly changed. The changes were wrought by a number of seemingly unrelated factors in the firm's environment, such as the emergence of the quick-freezing process, a decrease in the price of tin for cans, and an increase in competition. Thus, the "causal texture" of the environment had changed, resulting in new complexities and uncertainties for the firm.

TECHNOLOGY AND ORGANIZATION

• The Woodward Studies

Introduction Woodward's contribution lies in her discovery that a firm's production technology (the processes it uses to produce its products or services) also affects how the firm should be organized. Woodward's research team began its studies in 1953 in an attempt to survey the organizational practices of local firms and to develop research hypotheses.[20] The researchers chose the area of south Essex, England, which surrounded their college, and studied virtually all the firms in that area that employed at least 100 people, thereby securing a sample of 100 firms in widely diverse lines of business.[21]

For each of these firms, the team collected data on the following aspects of the organization and its management through interviews, observation, and analysis of company records:

1 History, background, and objectives
2 Description of the manufacturing processes and methods and of the organization structure
3 Forms and procedures through which the firm was organized and operated
4 Facts and figures that could be used to assess the firm's commercial success

Finally, the team evaluated each firm, determining whether it was organic or mechanistic, in line with the Burns and Stalker findings.[22]

Initial Findings The research team used this information to identify interorganizational differences in structure and management practices. At the outset, some obvious differences in organization structure were identified. For example, the number of managerial levels varied from two to twelve, and the spans of control of the chief executives from two to eighteen. Furthermore, the ratio of production workers to staff personnel varied from less than one to one to more than ten to one.

These differences stimulated the research team to seek the causes, but a review of their data led to some surprising findings. First, they found that the differences did not relate to the size of a firm or to its general industrial category. On the average, for example, large companies were no more mechanistic than small ones. Furthermore, the 20 firms assessed "above average" in success had little in common (in terms of organization structure), nor did the 20 firms assessed as "below average."[23]

Therefore, the classical "principles of organization" that were often stressed appeared to be unrelated to success for the companies the Woodward team had studied. Over half the successful firms, in fact, tended to operate under the relatively free-wheeling organic system of management rather than the classical, mechanistic type of structure.

Relating Technology to Organization The researchers then turned to the problem of explaining these findings. The final unused data consisted of information relating to technology—"the methods and processes of manufacture."[24] As Table 5-2 shows, the researchers hit upon the idea of classifying the firms into three main groups, according to technology:

1 Unit and small-batch production, such as custom-built cars
2 Large-batch and mass production, such as mass-produced cars
3 Long-run process production of the same product, such as chemicals

66 **TABLE 5-2** Woodward's Technology Classifications

		Number of Firms			*Number of Firms*
67 68					
69	(I) Unit and Small-Batch (Job-Order) Production	5	I	Production of Units to Customer's Requirements	17
		10	II	Production of Protypes	
		2	III	Fabrication of Large Equipment in Stages	
		7	IV	Production of Small Batches to Customer's Orders	
70 71	(II) Large-Batch and Mass Production	14	V	Production of Large Batches	32
		11	VI	Production of Large Batches on Assembly Lines	
		6	VII	Mass Production	6
72 73	(III) Process Production	13	VIII	Intermittent Production of Chemicals in Multipurpose Plant	13
74		12	IX	Continuous-Flow Production of Liquids, Gases, and Crystalline Substances	12

75

76 *Source:* Joan Woodward, *Industrial Organization: Theory and Practice* (London: Oxford University Press, 1965), p. 39.

Once the firms were classified by technology, it became apparent that different organization structures seemed to be appropriate for different technologies. For example, as summarized Table 5-3, there was a clear line–staff distinction in mass-production firms, but no distinction in unit or process firms. The chief executives' span of control also varied with technology, with managers in process-manufacturing facilities having the widest spans. Departmentalization was functional in mass-production firms, but divisional in unit and process firms. Furthermore,

> There was a tendency for organic management systems to predominate in the production categories at the extremes of the technical scale (unit and process), while mechanistic systems dominated the middle ranges. Clear-cut definition of duties and responsibilities was a characteristic of firms in the middle ranges, while flexible organization with a high degree of delegation both of authority and of the responsibility for decision making, and with permissive and participating management, was characteristic of firms at the extremes.[25]

Other differences in organization also became apparent when the firms were classified by technology.[26] For example, firms with unit and process technologies made greater use of ad hoc, verbal communications, whereas mass-production firms tended to rely more on formal, written communications. Furthermore, jobs tended to be more specialized in mass-production firms than in either job-order or process firms. And, as mentioned above, the mass-production firms relied heavily on the tra-

TABLE 5-3 Summary of Woodward's Research Findings on the Organizational Structures of Successful Firms

Technological Characteristics	*Unit and Small-Batch Production*	*Large-Batch and Mass Production*	*Process Production*
Lower levels	Informally organized, narrow spans of control	Organized by formal process; wide spans	Organized by technological task demands; narrow spans of control
Higher levels	Informally organized; no distinction between line and staff	Organized by administrative processes with line–staff separation	Informally organized; no distinction between line and staff
General characteristics	Few levels; narrow spans of control, low "organizational consciousness"; no clear chain of command; low ratio of administrative to nonadministrative personnel	More "organizational consciousness"; more clearly defined positions; clear chain of command	Many levels; less "organizational consciousness"; high ratio of administrative to nonadministrative personnel

ditional line–staff type of organization. Line managers in these firms engaged mostly in direct supervision, and technical assistance and advice were provided by special staff personnel. On the other hand, line managers in unit and process firms were expected to have greater technical expertise and to make technical decisions (regarding, say, quality control) themselves. Finally, there were more skilled workers in unit and process firms and fewer in the mass-production firms.

Interpretations Woodward's own explanation for these findings is that the firms differed in the degree of coordination they required. In unit-production firms, for example:

> Direct and speedy channels of communication between one department and another were essential at every level of the hierarchy. Bridge communications were important, for a crisis occurring at any stage in the manufacturing sequence could quickly involve all departments.[27]

On the other hand, in the mass-production firms, the functions were more independent of each other and more self-contained. This, in turn, meant that the end result "did not depend on the establishment of a close operational relationship between the people responsible for development, production, and sales. . . ."[28] Research and development, marketing, and production are even more independent of each other in the process firms, says Woodward.

Alternatively, we can interpret her findings by focusing on the importance and number of contingencies—unexpected events—to which each firm had to adapt. For example, unit firms probably face the greatest number of contingencies, but the nature of their flexible production technologies are such that they can readily adapt to most. At the other extreme, in the process firms, contingencies arise only occasionally, but when they do, they are of major importance. Since these highly automated, continuous-flow facilities depend upon predetermined work flows, exceptions or breakdowns may be quite serious. Therefore, the structure of these organizations remains organic, with highly skilled maintenance specialists standing ready to respond to emergencies or contingencies when they arise.

An underlying question can help put the Woodward findings and interpretations into perspective. It is, How much uncertainty or how many contingencies must each organization cope with? The idea that emerges from the Woodward findings, and from those of the other researchers described in this chapter, is that two different kinds of organizations can be conceived of. One is geared chiefly to performance and one to problem solving, and the appropriateness of each is tied to the number of contingencies to which it must adapt. This possibility was predicted by a number of theorists, including March and Simon;[29] however, it has been only in the past few years that empirical support has been obtained and some of the specific relationships discovered.

• *The Aston Studies*

For several years, the research evidence generally supported Woodward's findings.[30] Within a few years, however, members of the Industrial Administration Research Unit at the University of Aston in Birmingham, England, obtained findings that were strikingly at odds with those of the Woodward team. Specifically, the Aston findings seemed to suggest that an organization's size—not its technology—was the main determinent of its organization structure. Their data came from 52 organizations, 31 of which were manufacturing firms. The Aston team initially presented its research findings in two papers, one relating a number of "contextual" variables (like technology and location) to organization structure, and the second focusing on the relation between technology and organization structure. We'll discuss the findings of each paper in turn, but we should first show what these researchers meant by "contextual variables" and "structure."

The Aston "Contextual Variables"[31] Theorists like Burns and Stalker and Woodward focused on one contextual factor (environment or technology) and described its relation to organizational structure. The Aston group began by assuming that there might be *many* factors that could influence structure, and they defined some of these as follows:

1 *Origin and history.* For example, was the firm started by an entrepreneur, or by an existing organization? How old was the firm?

2 *Ownership and control.* For example, how much public accountability was the firm responsible for? What was the relation of the ownership to the management of the firm?
3 *Size.* In terms of the number of employees and amount of net assets of the firm.
4 *Charter.* "Charter" meant the purpose and goals of the firm, and particularly the multiplicity and diversity of its products and services.
5 *Technology.* This basically related to how rigid and automated the work flow was, and how interdependent its segments were.
6 *Location.* Primarily, the number of operating sites the firm had. (The last three contextual variables—charter/technology/location—were found to be highly interrelated.)
7 *Dependence.* For example, how dependent was the firm on a parent firm for its resources, or on a particular supplier?

The Aston Definition of Organization Structure To the Aston group, *organization structure* had three components:

1 *Structuring of activities.* This reflected things like the degree to which jobs were specified in detail, and the degree to which rules and procedures were formalized and documented.
2 *Concentration of authority.* This reflected three factors: the overall degree to which decisions in the organization were centralized, how much autonomy the organization had in relation to its parent firm, and the degree to which selection and promotion procedures were standardized.
3 *Line control of work flow.* This reflected the degree to which supervisors (rather than impersonal rules) controlled the work flow in the firm.

Findings: How Context Influenced Structure Table 5-4 summarizes how the Aston group found context and structure to be related. Their findings suggest that as organization size increases, there is more structuring of activities in terms of documentation of rules, functional specialization, and specification of jobs. Furthermore, the more dependent the organization is on some outside organization (a parent firm or large supplier), the more authority tends to be concentrated at the top of the hierarchy. Operating variability—the extent to which nonstandard products must be produced—is related to "line control of work flow": Here it would seem that the more "nonstandard" the firm's products are, the more it has to depend on direct supervisory control rather than formal rules and procedures.

In summary, size, dependence, and the interrelated charter/technology/location factors largely determine organization structure, according to this study. These findings contradict Woodward's, since she found little or no relation between size and structure and found that technology was the dominant determinant of structure. The Aston group's second paper therefore turns specifically to the question of the technology–structure relationship.

TABLE 5-4 Salient Elements of Context*

Elements of Context	*Structuring of Activities*	*Concentration of Authority*	*Line Control of Work-flow*
Age	—	−0.38	—
Size of organization†	0.69	—	—
Size of parent organization†	0.39	0.39	—
Operating variability	—	—	0.57
Diversity of products	—	−0.30	—
Work-flow integration (technology)	0.34	−0.30	−0.46
Number of operating sites	—	0.39	0.39
Dependence	—	0.66	—

*Significant product-moment correlations.
†Logarithm of number of employees.
Source: Pugh et al., "The Context of Organization Structures," *Administrative Science Quarterly*, Vol. 14 (1969), 110.

Measuring Technology In their research, the Aston group focused on what they called *operations* technology, which consisted of four factors:[32]

1 *Automaticity,* the degree to which the production process is automated.
2 *Work-flow rigidity,* how rigid (versus adaptable) the work-flow process is. For example, in the event of a breakdown, does all work flow stop immediately?
3 *Specificity of evaluations,* or how precisely performance could be measured against formal criteria.
4 Finally, the Aston group also measured technology using a production "continuity" scale similar to Woodward's unit-mass-process production continuum.

Findings: Technology and Structure Findings of this follow-up study again suggested that organizational size, not technology, is a main determinant of organizational structure.[33] In 46 randomly selected firms, for example, technology correlated slightly with structure, but its effects were usually overwhelmed by those of organization size. Similar results were obtained with a separate test on the 31 manufacturing firms.

• *The New Jersey Studies*

How could the Aston group's findings be so different from those of Woodward (who found that technology, not size, determined structure)?[34] A recent study of production plants in New Jersey by sociologist Peter Blau and his associates provides the latest and perhaps clearest answers to this question.[35]

This study consisted of interviews with the "chief executive," plant managers, and so on, in 110 New Jersey manufacturing plants. Blau and his associates sought to determine, among other things, how technology (as measured by both the Aston and Woodward groups) influenced organization structure.

Initial Findings Blau and his team first measured the degree of relationship between technology and organization structure in a manner similar to that used by the Aston group. Specifically, they computed "correlation coefficients" in order to test the degree of (linear) relationship between technology and each dimension of organization structure. Here they found that Woodward's conclusion concerning a broad "technological imperative" was not confirmed. For example, little or no relationship was found between technology and various structural features like number of levels, span of control, and the proportion of management and supervisory personnel. On the other hand, *organization size* seemed to influence organization structure, as the Aston group had found. And the Blau group found that technology had no stronger relation to structure in those departments that were closer to the production floor or in smaller-sized firms in general.

The Blau Group's Additional Findings The researchers thought it was odd that technology seemed to have so little effect on the structures of the manufacturing plants. They therefore carried out an additional study. Here, they categorized firms into Woodward's three production categories—unit, mass and process. They also statistically tested the degree of *curvilinear* relation between technology and organization structure.

Now their findings were much closer to Woodward's. They found curvilinear (∩-shaped) relationships between technology and dimensions of structure like number of levels and supervisory spans of control, for instance. (In other words, the average span of control increases as we move from unit- to mass-production firms, and decreases as we move on from mass to process firms.) Apparently, testing for the *linear* relationship between technology and structure (as the Aston and Blau groups had done initially) hid these Woodward-like curvilinear results.

Interpretations Therefore, both Woodward and Blau found that structures in unit- and process-production firms were similar, and that they differed from those in the middle, mass-production firms. According to Blau and his associates, this is because:

> As one moves from small batch to mass production, the nature of manufacturing tasks becomes more uniform, which is reflected in an increase in routine work, a lower skill level of the labor force, and reductions in support components. The data indicate that these trends are reversed in advanced production technologies (process firms). Thus, production jobs are least standardized in process plants, since they generally involve maintenance of complex equipment or responsible monitoring functions there. Process plants usually have not only the most highly skilled blue-collar work force, but also the largest proportion of white-collar jobs requiring specialized skills.[36]

In summary, the New Jersey studies thus help explain the Woodward and Aston findings and put them in perspective. Woodward's initial conclusion that technology and structure are linearly related is invalidated by the Blau findings, as it was by those of the Aston group. However, both the Woodward and Aston groups found certain curvilinear relations between technology and structure that they generally did not emphasize in their reports. (Woodward, for example, found that organic management systems predominated in unit and process firms, and both groups found the narrowest first-line-supervisor spans of control in unit and process firms.) The Blau findings explicitly tested for curvilinear relations between technology and structure. They suggest that technology and structure are curvilinearly related, and that structures at the extremes—unit and process—tend to be more organic.[37] On the other hand, it is the firm in the middle—the mass-production firm that the classicists studied—that is organized mechanistically long the lines of the classical management principles. Thus, a firm's technology, like its environment, influences its structure.

• *Toward a Broader View of Technology*

The Woodward team focused on familiar, production-oriented types of technology like assembly lines. Therefore, a shortcoming of Woodward's research is that her idea of technology really applies only to manufacturing firms. What we need is a more widely applicable concept of technology.

Sociologist Charles Perrow has developed such a concept. Perrow says that all organizations are designed to get work done, and to do this work, they need "technologies"—a process for acquiring raw materials and transforming them into marketable products.[38] It doesn't matter, says Perrow, whether the product is reformed delinquents, TV programs, government decisions, or steel. In any organization, some technology is required, "not only in the actual production process, but also for procuring the input of materials, capital, and labor and disposing of the output to some other organization or consumer. . . ."[39]

Perrow argues that the way to think about or conceptualize technology is in terms of what he calls its basic dimensions, *analyzability of search* and *number of exceptions*. To understand why these two dimensions are so important, says Perrow, consider the individual who is assigned to do a specific task. This person receives stimuli (orders, signals) to which he must respond. If the stimulus is familiar and the person has learned in the past what to do in the face of it, little search behavior is required. The problem, in other words is "analyzable," and "he may respond automatically or after a moment's thought." The response itself may be to turn to a procedures manual or to another clerk, but in any case, the problem is analyzable and there is a known technology for solving it. Little reflection or judgment or creative problem solving is thus required.

On the other hand, if the stimulus is unfamiliar, it is not immediately analyzable, and a search for the solution must take place without standardized decision rules. Here, says Perrow, the individual must rely upon a "technology" that involves primarily intuitive sorts of processes like experience, judgment, knack, and wisdom.

Thus, one way to think of the sort of technology this person must apply is in terms of whether it involves analyzable or unanalyzable search.

The other dimension of technology, says Perrow, is the variability or "number of exceptions" that the stimuli present to the individual. Sometimes, "the variety is great and every task seems to be a new one demanding the institution of search behavior of some magnitude (whether analyzable or unanalyzable)."[40] Sometimes, on the other hand, the stimuli are not very varied, and the person is confronted chiefly with familiar situations and few new exceptions.

In summary, Perrow argues that any technology (the process the individual will use to react to the stimuli and get his or her task done) has two basic dimensions—degree of variability of stimuli (number of exceptions) and the degree to which search procedures are analyzable. He further argues that one can think of technologies in the form of a matrix (as in Figure 5-1), with four basic types of technology, *each demanding a different type of organization*. For example, one technology characterized by analyzable search and few exceptions is assembly-line manufacturing; and here, says Perrow, the organization structure will be mechanistic. At the other extreme, some organizations perform tasks that require a technology characterized by analyzable search and many exceptions. Here, the technology itself must be flexible, in order to rapidly process information on unexpected problems (exceptions) and to quickly marshal the resources needed to discover how to best react to the stimulus (unanalyzable search). Here, says Perrow, we find R&D firms, firms that are structured organically. Thus, every enterprise has a technology, says Perrow,

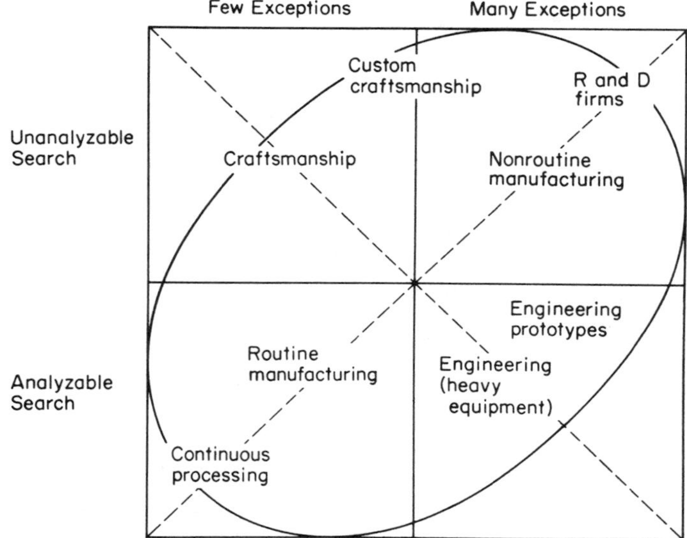

FIGURE 5-1 Technology Matrix. *Source:* Perrow, Organizational Analysis: A Sociological View. © 1970 by Wadsworth. Reprinted by permission of Brooks/Cole.

and the nature of this technology affects the type of organization structure that is required.

ORGANIZATION SIZE AND STRUCTURE

The proposition that size is related to structure seems self-evident. For example, imagine how your organization would evolve as it grew from a handful of employees to 50, 100, or more. At the beginning, you probably wouldn't need an organization structure and could simply have all employees reporting directly to you. But as the number of employees increased, this "structure" would become unwieldy. Eventually you would have to delegate authority to certain of your subordinates, establish separate departments (like production and marketing), and develop more elaborate control systems for monitoring performance and taking corrective action. Although such a scenario seems reasonable, the research findings on the relationship between size and structure are actually quite inconsistent. Few researchers would argue that the two are unrelated, but the prevailing evidence suggests that the effects of size on structure are unclear and are moderated by factors like technology.

• *Positive Findings*

In a study carried out for the American Management Association, Ernest Dale used a questionnaire to survey 100 large (5,000 or more employees) and 66 medium-sized (500 to 5,000 employees) firms.[41] The questionnaire was used to obtain information on topics like type of division of labor, degree of centralization, and number of levels in the company.

Dale found a tendency for organizational size and decentralization to be related. However, he found that certain large corporations retained their functional, centralized organizational structures. His findings support those of Alfred Chandler, who found that even the largest companies in the steel, mining, and paper industries retain the functional, centralized organization structure.[42] Other researchers have come to similar conclusions. The Aston group for example, concluded that:

> The correlation between [size] and structuring of activities leads strong support to descriptive studies of the effects of size on bureaucratization. . . . Larger organizations tend to have more specialization, more standardization and more formalization than smaller organizations. . . .

In a replication of the Aston study, John Child came to similar conclusions. His data were based on 82 British organizations, and he found that for those firms, size "remains the major predictor of decentralization."[43] In their study, the Blau group found that size (in terms of number of employees) was related to some organization-structure features, including the number of levels and divisions.

• *Negative Findings*

On the other hand, Woodward found little or no relationship between organization size and structure. And in a major study of the influence of organizational size, a group of researchers concluded that:

> In general, the findings of this study in regard to size are similar to those in previous research which utilize size as a major variable; that is, the relationships between size and other structural components are inconsistent. . . . There is a slight tendency for larger organizations to be both more complex and more formalized, but only on a few variables does the relationship prove to be strong. On others, there is little, if any, established relationship.

• *Research Problems*

Kimberly, in a recent review of some 80 empirical studies of size and organization structure, identified several problems that may help to explain the inconsistent findings concerning size and structure.[44] First, he says, researchers have generally not provided any theoretical explanations for the proposed relation between size and structure; in other words, why should size affect organization structure at all? Second, his review suggests that there is little agreement on what "size" is, or on how to measure it. For example, some researchers use number of employees; other use the logarithm of number of employees; some use total net assets; and some include part-time and volunteer help, while others do not. Third, Kimberly says, there is not enough evidence concerning the effects (if any) of size on different types of organizations—those in different industries, with different technologies, and so on.

Finally, he says, it is difficult to ascertain whether size "causes" structure, or structure "causes" size. Most studies of size and structure have focused on one or more organizations at one point in time rather than on several organizations over time. Thus it is difficult to determine whether size has influenced structure, or whether, for example, a manager's decision to structure his firm in a particular way (say, to decentralize it) has resulted in duplication of certain services and an increase in number of employees.

• *Discussion*

Given these inconsistent findings, what can we conclude about the size/structure relation? First, certain structural features—like number of levels, number of divisions, and number of job titles—generally *do* increase with organization size. This seems to make sense, since the larger the "task," the more levels, divisions, and job titles you would expect to have.

On the other hand, conclusions concerning the relation between organizational size and *decentralization* apparently cannot be made without considering the technology of the organization. Process-production firms (such as paper) and those in industries where production efficiency is traditionally paramount (such as steel) seem to maintain centralized structures even though they are quite large. In other industries, where competition is more keen (electrical appliances, autos), increased size generally results in increased decentralization and a pushing down of decision making to the lowest level possible.

Technology, Size, and Organization Recent findings tend to confirm the fact that both technology and size do affect organization structure, but that they operate on different dimensions of structure. Marsh and Mannari, in a study of 50 Japanese factories, found that only two dimensions of structure—structural differentiation (the types of departments that were established), and formalization (the use of rules and procedures, and so on)—were clearly more a function of size than of technology. Other aspects, including the differentiation of management from ownership and the span of control of the chief executive, seemed to be more a function of technology than of size.[45] Still other dimensions of structure seemed to be relatively unaffected by either the size or the technology of the organization. In brief, then, it seems that environment, technology, and size all affect organization structure, although they may each mainly affect different structural dimensions.

UNCERTAINTY, COMPLEXITY, AND ORGANIZATION

• Uncertainty: A Central Element

If there is a central theme in the studies described in this chapter, it is that the *uncertainty* with which the organization copes helps determine how the organization should be structured.[46] Burns and Stalker, for instance, explain that "extrinsic factors determine which management system is best," and that:

> . . . these extrinsic factors are all, in our view, identifiable as different rates of technical or market change. By change we mean the appearance of novelties; i.e., new scientific discoveries or technical inventions, and requirements for products of a kind not previously available or demanded.[47]

Similarly, Perrow refers to the number of exceptions and the analyzability of the stimuli, and Lawrence and Lorsch explain that in their "dynamic environment,"

> There is generally a great deal of uncertainty about the impact on markets of the new scientific and technological knowledge. Finally, these dynamic market and scientific conditions mean that the dominant competitive issue for firms in these industries is the capacity to innovate in both processes and products.[48]

In a similar vein, Mintzberg refers to the environment's stability, complexity, market diversity, and hostility as major determinants of its structure, pointing out that "it is not the environment per se that counts but the organization's ability to cope with it—to predict it, comprehend it, deal with its diversity, and respond quickly to it—that is important."[49] And Galbraith defines uncertainty as "the difference between the amount of information required to perform the task and the amount of information already possessed by the organization." He argues that:

> . . . the basic proposition is that the greater the uncertainty of the task, the greater the amount of information that has to be processed between decision makers during the execution of the task. If the task is well understood prior to its performance, much of the activity can be preplanned. If it is not understood, then during the actual task execution more knowledge is required, which leads to changes in resource allocations, schedules, and priorities; all these changes require information processing *during* task performance. Therefore, *the greater the task uncertainty, the greater the amount of information that must be processed among decision makers during task execution in order to achieve a given level of performance.* The basic effect of the uncertainty is to limit the ability of the organization to preplan or to make decisions about activities in advance of their execution.[50]

The concept of uncertainty thus helps explain why different structures are appropriate for different tasks. At one extreme are organizations for performing predictable, routine tasks such as assembling cars or running a rayon mill. Here, efficiency is emphasized, and successful organizations tend to be mechanistic. They stress adherence to the rules and to the chain of command, are highly centralized, and have a more specialized, functional departmentation and a preplanned set of policies and rules for making decisions. At the other extreme, organizations such as high-tech electronic firms have more unpredictable tasks and are more constantly confronted by the need to create new products and adapt to new competitors' innovations. Here, creativity, responsiveness, and entrepreneurial activities are stressed, and, to encourage such activities, these organizations are organic. They do not urge employees to "play it by the rules" or to abide closely to the formal chain of command. In fact (as Burns and Stalker noted), there is often no formal chain of command; instead, communications take place via a constantly shifting network of committees, project teams, and informal interactions.

SUMMARY

The studies by Burns and Stalker help to illustrate the specific links between environment and organization. They found that efficiency-oriented, mechanistic systems characterized by specialized jobs and centralization were most appropriate for unchanging conditions, whereas organic systems were best for unstable conditions "when problems and requirements for action arise which cannot be broken down and distributed . . . within a clearly defined hierarchy." Similarly, Lawrence and Lorsch found that *departments* within organizations each face their own particular environment and thus have their own unique structure.

In addition to the type of environment in which the organization has to compete, researchers like Woodward suggest that the organization's technology—the basic process it used to produce its good or services—also affects the way it is organized and managed. Woodward concludes that only mass-production firms were characterized by adherence to classical management principles such as specialization of jobs and adherence to the chain of command. Organizations at the extreme of her technological scale were characterized by a more organic approach to management. Similar conclusions were reached by the Aston and New Jersey researchers.

Discussion Questions

1 Discuss the relations among environment, technology, size, and organization.
2 What are some of the basic differences between and similarities of mechanistic and organic organizations?
3 As a short project, choose one very familiar organization that you feel is either organic or mechanistic. Look closely at the management functions in this organization, paying particular attention to such things as adherence to rules and procedures, adherence to chain of command, and the type of leadership style. What makes this organization particularly appropriate for dealing with the types of tasks that it has? If you chose a mechanistic organization, what is it about this organization that you think would make it particularly inappropriate for dealing with entrepreneurial, creative, rapidly changing tasks? If you chose an organic organization, why do you think it would be inappropriate for routine tasks?

APPENDIX TO CHAPTER 5
Human Information Processing and Decision Making: A Psychological Explanation of the Effects of Uncertainty on Structure

Much of what was said in this chapter assumes that people have a *limited capacity for processing information*, and that when the information to be processed becomes excessive, *information overload* occurs and some modification of the system's method of handling information (its structure) is required. We present here several studies from the areas of human information processing and decision making to help illustrate how such structural modifications in fact take place.

HUMAN INFORMATION PROCESSING: THE IOTA RESEARCH

Research findings do suggest that the ability of individuals and organizations to process information—to assimilate it and make decisions on it—increases until some "optimum" amount of information must be processed, and thereafter it declines quickly.[51]

One representative group of studies was carried out by James Miller and his associates, using specially built equipment known as the Iota (Information Overload Testing Aid). This equipment consists of a ground-glass screen about three feet by four feet on which various visual stimuli can be projected, and contains a number of buttons and pedals through which subjects can react to the stimuli and slow down the rate at which the stimuli are projected on the screen. Based on a series of experiments with this apparatus, Miller and his associates have been able to develop a clear picture of how people adjust to overloads of information and of what the "optimum" amount of information is.

These researchers say there are seven means by which people can adjust to overloads of information:

- *Omission*—not processing some of the information
- *Errors*—incorrectly identifying some of the information
- *Queuing*—delaying a response during heavy loads, and then catching up during slack periods
- *Filtering*—a systematic omission of certain types of information, usually by some priority system
- *Approximation*—less precise response is given
- *Multiple Channels*—the use of parallel subsystems for processing information—for example, using both audio and visual cues, if available
- *Escape*—leaving the situation, or cutting off the input of information

Miller's subjects were able to use all these adjustment processes; his findings may be summarized as follows: At slow rates of transmission (very little information projected on the screen), subjects used few adjustments. At medium rates, most subjects attempted to use all adjustment processes at one time or another. At higher rates of transmission, subjects switched to filtering—systematically omitting certain types of information, usually using some priority system. Finally, as Miller's subjects reached their "maximum channel capacity"—the absolute limit of their ability to assimilate and process information—they began adjusting primarily by using omission; they simply ceased processing much of the information, omitting information in some random pattern.

The researchers found that subjects' ability to process information reflected a "∩ curve" pattern. Specifically, the subjects' ability to process information actually increased somewhat as the amount of information they had to process increased. It reached a maximum level at some "optimum" amount of information, and then diminished quickly.

Causes of Information Overload

Does this kind of information overload occur in real organizations? Katz and Kahn point out that for managers working in real situations, information overload is a very real problem.[52] Managers, they say, are decision makers and coordinators and thus occupy spots in the organization that require them to assimilate information from sources like subordinates, peers, superiors, and outside vendors. They must then interpret this information and make decisions that result in a coordinated effort, while meeting some "deadline."

The problem of overload arises because organizations do not exist in a constant, unchanging environment. Potential sources of supply may diminish, requiring additional search for new ones. Markets for products grow and decline. Competitors introduce new products, initiate advertising campaigns, change pricing strategies, and buy new, more efficient equipment. The labor market fluctuates, and personnel leave the organization. Thus, managers are almost continually faced with the dilemma of (1) having to coordinate activities within a given time period, while at the same time (2) having to deal with unpredictable, changing environments and frequent floods of information.

Summary: Information Processing and Organization

There is little reason to believe that a manager's reactions to this dilemma are different from those of Miller's subjects. As managers are faced with more and more information—with more uncertain information, more complex information, or more types of information—they reach their capacity for processing it and making decisions, and information overload occurs. And, one would assume, it is at this point that the manager ends up using some adjustment mechanism like filtering or omitting information, and making poorer decisions. In any event, it seems likely that effective managers must take some action before such relatively imperfect adjustments are necessary; and these actions generally involve redesigning the organizations so they can handle more information; this generally means making them more organic.

DECISION MAKING

Economic Man

The idea that individuals' information-processing abilities are limited and that decision makers therefore cannot exercise a complete control of all the information they need is of relatively recent origin. Most classical theorists assumed that the decision maker is operating in a routine, predictable environment in which all possible alternatives, and the outcome for each, are known with certainty. This decision maker, known as Economic Man, has complete information on all matters pertaining to his consumption decisions. He knows the full range of goods and services available on the market and the capacity of each good or service to satisfy his wants. He also knows the exact price of each good or service and that these prices will not be changed by his actions in the market, since (it is assumed) he is an inconsequentially small part of that market. This person also knows precisely what his monthly income will be during the planning period and is able to order his preferences for different bundles (or budgets) of products or services. He can thus choose whichever combination best satisfies his needs (or "maximizes his utility"). Under this theory, business people are concerned mostly with profits, and employees only with maximizing their wages. With spreading industrialization, this theory provided a rationale for industry's embracing of the centralized, specialized, and autocratic structures of the military and religious organizations of previous centuries, and their emphasis on financial incentives. It was out of such an environment that classical organization theory and the scientific-management movement grew.

• *Administrative Man*

In contrast to Economic Man, Herbert Simon and his associates propose an alternate type of decision maker: Administrative Man. Administrative Man, they say, does not have complete knowledge, and although his decisions may be "rational," they are only so given the person's unique values, capabilities, and needs. Simon and his associates therefore substitute the concept of subjective rationality for that of objective rationality. The behavior of any single individual, they say, cannot reach any high degree of rationality because *people have a limited capacity for processing information*.

> The number of alternatives he must explore is so great, the information he would need to evaluate them so vast, that even an approximation to objective rationality is hard to conceive. Individual choice takes place in an environment of "givens"—premises that are accepted by the subject as bases for his choice; and behavior is adaptive only within the limits set by these "givens."[53]

Because of these "cognitive limits on rationality," Administrative Man "satisfices" rather than maximizes. According to March and Simon, "Most human decision making, whether individual or organizational, is concerned with the discovery and selection of satisfactory alternatives; only in exceptional cases is it concerned with the discovery and selection of optimal alternatives."[54] If Simon is correct, then in most instances a centralized, mechanistic structure with one all-knowing chief would be unrealistic, as would a preoccupation with maximizing incentives.

Many studies have been carried out to determine if classical-man or administrative-man assumptions are accurate. In one study, Clarkson developed a computer program that successfully duplicated the investment decisions of a bank investment trust officer. The program, which Clarkson developed based on his observations of the officer, generated about the same portfolio of stock-market investments as did the officer when provided with the same inputs in terms of total value of the portfolio and level of risk. The study supports assumptions underlying the administrative-man proposition, in that it suggests that decision makers apply rules of thumb, or heuristics, in order to make satisfactory decisions in the face of an often overwhelming number of alternatives.

A Contingency View of Organizational Decision Making Based on research like that described above, Grandori has proposed a contingency view of organizational decision making. She basically proposes that the decision-making strategy used depends on the amount of uncertainty surrounding the decision.

In her theory, Grandori relies on five "decision strategies"—five approaches to making a decision—*optimizing, satisficing, incremental, cybernetic,* and *random.* An *optimizing* strategy, in which the decision maker reviews all alternatives, comparing each to the other, is applicable in those situations where uncertainty is at a minimum and where the decision maker understands all options and the pros and cons of each. A *satisficing* or heuristic decision strategy means that when an acceptable alternative is found, the search process stops and that alternative is retained; this approach is appropriate in all those conditions where there is too much uncertainty to apply an optimizing strategy. An *incremental* strategy means that you apply linear-choice rules, such as, "Make the same investment as in the last period plus 10 percent," or, "Buy a machine with the same characteristics as the last one, except that it's faster," without calculating any specific outcome.[55] Incremental decision strategy, she says, is applicable in those situations where not even a satisficing strategy can be applied, such as where "not only is the set of all relevant alternatives undefinable, but the consequences of each alternative with respect to some relevant aspiration level are also unpredictable." With a *cybernetic* decision strategy, the decision maker can only adopt a blind trial-and-error procedure and observe when a trial succeeds. This approach is applicable where even more uncertainty exists, so that the organization "is not even able to perform limited comparisons between the existing solutions and an incremental alternative."[56] Finally, a *random* decision-making strategy means that the decision maker adopts a completely random search-and-choice rule; actions are extracted from a pool, and the choice is then a function of the order in which the organization encounters possible courses of action. This, of course, is the most extreme approach to organizational decision making and is appropriate under the most uncertain conditions, where virtually everything about the choice and courses of action is unknown.

FOOTNOTES

[1]Tom Burns and G.M. Stalker, *The Management of Innovation* (London, Tavistock, 1961).

[2]*Ibid.*, p. 83.

[3]As occurred with the watch industry around 1970, for instance.

[4]Emery and Trist, two other British researchers, referred to this innovative environment as a "turbulent field" environment because change often comes not from a firm's traditional competitor but from "out of the blue;" often, in fact, the changes seem to "arise from the field itself"—from interactions between parts of the environment. They describe an example in which a food-canning company with a hitherto stable demand was almost put out of business by a complex sequence of events. The invention of the quick-freezing process resulted in the availability of low-priced vegetables, which were in turn purchased by new, small canning firms that themselves emerged as a result of the availability of cheaper tin cans. At the same time, the growth of food chains provided a growing market for the products of these small canners, which produced their items with a retailer's own brand name on them. As a result, the varied "texture" of the firm's environment changed, in that previously unrelated or (from the point of view of the canning firm) irrelevant elements in its environment become interconnected. F.E. Emery and E.C. Trist, "The Causal Texture of Organizational Environments," *Human Relations,* Vol. 18 (August 1965), 20–26. As another example, after 1970 (when digital watches were introduced), calculator firms like Texas Instruments suddenly and unexpectedly became competitors in the watch industry.

[5]This is based on "The Mega-Battle for Micro Chip Market Shares," *The Economist,* November 8, 1980, pp. 93–96.

[6]*Ibid.,* p. 94.

[7]Similarly, organizational structure effects many proposals made by managers. Michael Aiken, Samuel Bacharach, and J. Lawrence French, "Organizational Structure, Work Process, and Proposal Making in Administrator Bureaucracies," *Academy of Management Journal,* Vol. 23, No. 4 (December 1980), 631–43.

[8]Burns and Stalker, *Management of Innovation,* p. 92.

[9]Ibid., p. 94.

[10]Ibid., p. 92.

[11]Ibid., pp. 119–22.

[12]Paul R. Lawrence and Jay W. Lorsch, "Organization and Environment" (Boston: Division of Research, Graduate School of Business Administration, Harvard University, 1967). For a discussion of the dimensions of organizational task environments, see Gregory Dess and Donald Beard, "Dimensions of Organizational Task Environments," *Administrative Science Quarterly,* Vol. 29, No. 1 (March 1984), 52–73.

[13]For an extension of this idea to multibusiness companies, see Robert Pitts, "Toward a Contingency Theory of Multi-Business Organization Design," *Academy of Management Review,* Vol. 5, No. 2 (April 1980), 203–10.

[14]Paul R. Lawrence and J.W. Lorsch, "Differentiation and Integration in Complex Organizations," *Administrative Science Quarterly,* Vol. 12, No. 1 (June 1967), 1–47.

[15]*Ibid.*

[16]Although this conclusion about how to measure environment is intuitively attractive, there is debate over (1) how to operationally define "environment," and (2) how adequate the Lawrence and Lorsch environmental-uncertainty questionnaire was. For example, see Henry Tosi, Ramon Aldag, and Ronald Storey, "The Measurement of the Environment: An Assessment of the Lawrence and Lorsch Environmental Uncertainty Scale," *Administrative Science Quarterly,* March 1973, pp. 27–36; and Robert Duncan, "Characteristics of Organizational Environments and Perceived Environmental Uncertainty," *Administrative Science Quarterly,* September 1972, pp. 313–36; also Richard Osborn and James Hunt, "Environment and Organizational Effectiveness," *Administrative Science Quarterly,* June 1974, pp. 231–46.

[17]Lawrence and Lorsch, "Differentiation," For a description of how both environment and strategy also influence the power of a top management, see Donald Hambrick, "Environment, Strategy, and Power within Tough Management Teams," *Administrative Science Quarterly,* Vol. 26, No. 2 (June 1981), 253–75.

[18]See also Michael Dubick, "The Organizational Structure of Newspapers in Relation to Their Metropolitan Environment," *Administrative Science Quarterly,* Vol. 23 (September 1978), 418–33.

[19]F.E. Emery and E.C. Trist, "The Causal Texture of Organizational Environment," *Human Relations,* Vol. 18 (August 1965), 20–26. For a recent discussion of how managements respond to changing environments, see Alan Meyer, "Adapting to Environmental Jolts," *Administrative Science Quarterly,* Vol. 27, No. 4 (December 1982), 515–37; and Sara Kiesler and Lee Sproull, "Managerial Response to Changing Environments: Perspectives on Problem Sensing from Social Cognition," *Administrative Science Quarterly,* Vol. 27, No. 4 (December 1982), 548–70.

[20]Joan Woodward, *Industrial Organization: Theory and Practice* (London: Oxford University Press, 1965).

[21]*For other discussions of the relationship between technology and structure (some contradictory), see W.H. Zwerman, New Perspectives on Organization Theory* (Westport, Conn.: Greenwood Press, 1970); David Gillespie and Dennis Mileti, "Technology and the Study of Organizations: An Overview and Appraisal," *Academy of Management Review,* Vol. 2, No. 1 (January 1977), 7–16; and Robert Sutton and Denise Rousseau, "Structure, Technology, and Dependence on a Parent Organization: Organizational and Environmental Correlates of Individual Responses," *Journal of Applied Psychology,* Vol. 64 (December 1979), 675–87.

[22]Woodward, *Industrial Organization,* p. 24; see also B.C. Reimann, "Organization Structure and Technology in Manufacturing: System vs. Work Flow Perspectives," *Academy of Management Journal* Vol. 23, No. 1 (March 1980), 61–77.

[23]Woodward, *Industrial Organization,* p. 33.

[24]See also Denise Rousseau, "Assessment of Technology in Organizations: Closed vs. Open Systems Approaches," *The Academy of Management Review,* Vol. 4, No. 4 (October 1979), 531–42.

[25]Woodward, *Industrial Organization,* p. 64. Some more recent findings provide support for this assertion. See Robert Keller, John Slocum, Jr., and Gerald Sussman, "Management Systems, Uncertainty, and Continuous Process Technology," Proceedings of the Academy of Management, 33rd Annual Meeting, August 1973, Thad Green and Dennis Ray, ed., pp. 507–8.

[26]More recently, it has also been found that technology affects management's use of intermediate "buffers" between the technology and the organization. See, for example, Daniel G. Kopp and Robert J. Litschert, "A Buffering Response in Light of Variation in Core Technology, Perceived Environmental Uncertainty and Size," *Academy of Management Journal,* Vol. 23, No. 2 (June 1980), pp. 252–66.

[27]Woodward, *Industrial Organization,* p. 134.

[28]*Ibid.,* p. 137.

[29]James March and Herbert Simon, *Organizations* (New York: John Wiley, 1958).

[30]W.H. Zwerman, *New Perspectives on Organization Theory* (Westport, Conn.: Greenwood Press, 1970).

[31]D.S. Pugh, D.J. Hickson, C.R. Hinings, and C. Turner, "The Context of Organizations," *Administrative Science Quarterly,* Vol. 14 (1969), 19–114.

[32]The Aston researchers actually distinguish among three kinds of technology: *operations* (the techniques used in its work-flow activities); *materials* (the actions a person performs on an object); and *knowledge* (how many exceptional cases are there).

[33]The Aston group's findings concerning the dominance of size (as opposed to technology) as a determinant of structure were later confirmed in a study by Child and Mansfield on the "national" group of British firms, and by a study by Hickson et al. of U.S. firms. See John Child and Roger Mansfield, "Technology, Size, and Organization Structure," *Sociology,* Vol. 6 (1972), 369–93; and David Hickson, C.R. Hinings, C.J. McMillan, and J.P. Schwitter, "The Culture-Free Context of Organization Structure: A Trinational Comparison," *Sociology,* Vol. 8 (1974), 59–80.

[34]See, for example, Martin Evans and Will McQuillan, "A Longitudinal Analysis of the Context and Structure of a Large British Financial Institution." *The Journal of Management Studies,* May 1977, for one of a number of studies that suggested that the Aston findings refute those of Woodward.

[35]Peter M. Blau, Cecilia McHugh Falbe, William McKinley, and Phelps K. Tracy, "Technology and Organization in Manufacturing," *Administrative Science Quarterly,* Vol. 21 (March 1976), 20–40.

[36]Blau et al., "Technology and Organization," p. 30.

[37]The Blau group also found that "a process technology in production and the automation of the support functions by on-site computers also exert numerous parallel influences on the administrative structure."

[38]Charles Perrow, *Organizational Analysis: A Sociological View* (Belmont, Calif.: Wadsworth, 1970), pp. 75–78.

[39]*Ibid.,* p. 75. For a scale that can be used to measure Perrow's work-unit technology, see Michael Withey, Richard Daft, and William Cooper, "Measures of Perrow's Work Unit Technology: An Empirical Assessment and a New Scale," *Academy of Management Journal,* Vol. 26, No. 1 (March 1983), 45–63.

[40]Perrow, *Organizational Analysis,* page 77. Fry, in findings that support Perrow's theory, found in his own study that it was the routine-nonroutine dimension of technology that seemed to be most consistently powerful in predicting how organizations would be structured. See Louis Fry, "Technology–Structure Research: Three Critical Issues," *Academy of Management Journal,* Vol. 25, No. 3 (September 1982), 532–52.

[41]This section, except as noted, is based on Richard Hall, *Organizations: Structure and Process* (Englewood Cliffs, N.J.: Prentice-Hall, 1972), pp. 112–39; and Gary Dessler, *Organization and Management: A Contingency Approach* (Englewood Cliffs, N.J.: Prentice-Hall, 1976), p. 111.

[42]Ernest Dale, *Organization* (New York: American Management Association, 1967), p. 110; Alfred Chandler, *Strategy and Structure* (Cambridge, Mass.: M.I.T. Press, 1962).

[43]John Child, "Predicting and Understanding Organization Structure," *Administrative Science Quarterly,* June 1973, pp. 168–85.

[44]John R. Kimberly, "Organizational Size and the Structuralist Perspective: A Review, Critique, and Proposal," *Administrative Science Quarterly,* Vol. 21 (December 1976), 571; Guy Geerarts, "The Effect of Ownership on the Organization Structure in Small Firms," *Administrative Science Quarterly,* Vol. 29, No. 2 (June 1984), 232–37. Geerarts contends that the relation between the size of an organization and its structure is modified by the status of the management of the firm, and that these findings may explain erratic intersample behavioral correlations between size and structure.

[45]Robert Marsh and Hiroshi Mannari, "Technology and Size as Determinants of the Organizational Structure of Japanese Factories," *Administrative Science Quarterly,* Vol. 26, No. 1 (March 1981) 33–57.

[46]For another perspective on this, see Denise Rousseau, "Assessment of Technology in Organizations: Closed versus Open System Approaches," *Academy of Management Review,* 1979, Vol. 4, No. 4 (1979), 531–42.

[47]Burns and Stalker, *Management of Innovation,* p. 96.

[48]Lawrence and Lorsch, "*Differentiation,*" p. 23.

[49]Henry Mintzberg, *Structure in Fives: Designing Effective Organizations* (Englewood Cliffs, N.J.: Prentice-Hall, 1983), pp. 136–37.

[50]Jay Galbraith, *Organization Design* (Reading, Mass.: Addison-Wesley, 1977), pp. 36–37.

[51]Information in this section is based on James G. Miller, "Adjusting to Overloads of Information," in Joseph A. Litterer, *Organizations: Structure and Behavior* (New York: John Wiley, 1969), pp. 313–22. See also Harold Schroder, Michael Driver, and Siegfried Streufert, *Human Information Processing* (New York: Holt, Rinehart & Winston, 1967).

[52]Daniel Katz and Robert Kahn, *The Social Psychology of Organization* (New York: John Wiley, 1966), p. 61. See also Huseyin Leblebici and Gerald Salancik, "Effect of Environmental Uncertainty on Information and Decision Processes in Banks," *Administrative Science Quarterly,* vol. 26, no. 4, December 1981, pp. 578–596.

[53]Herbert Simon, *Administrative Behavior* (New York: Free Press, 1976).

[54]James March and Herbert Simon, *Organizations* (New York: John Wiley, 1958), pp. 140–41.

[55]This is based on Anna Grandori, "A Prescriptive Contingency View of Organization Decision Making," *Administrative Science Quarterly*, Vol. 29, No. 2 (June 1984).
[56]*Ibid.*, p. 199.

CASE FOR CHAPTER 5
CHANGING A CORPORATE CULTURE
Can Johnson & Johnson Go from Band-Aids to High Tech?*

On Albany Street in gritty New Brunswick, N.J., stands Johnson & Johnson's sleek new headquarters. The modernistic aluminum-and-glass structure designed by I.M. Pei stands in marked contrast to Kilmer House, the undistinguished brick building nearby that was its home from the late 1890s until last year. The new architectural face is richly symbolic, for it mirrors the more subtle changes under way within one of the most consistently successful companies in the world.

Best known to consumers for such brands as Band-Aids and Baby Shampoo, J&J has embarked on an accelerated move into far more sophisticated medical technologies. The shift poses big risks, since success depends on whether J&J can manage businesses very different from those it has dominated. And to achieve his goals, Chairman James E. Burke is tinkering in subtle but important ways with a management style and corporate culture that have long been central to the company's success.

• *Marketing Prowess*

A good deal is at stake: In addition to its consumer brands, J&J holds powerful and profitable franchises in hospital supplies and prescription drugs. For years, these product lines have flourished under a marketing-dominated, decentralized management structure. While scores of companies are struggling to eliminate corporate bureaucracies and give power back to operations, J&J is already there.

The people running its 170 "companies" enjoy autonomy unheard of in most corporations. Most divisions have their own boards. Corporate headquarters staff is a scant 750 people. And only one management layer separates division presidents from the 14-member executive committee to whom they report.

It is obvious why J&J is held up as an example of decentralization's virtues. Its earnings growth in the last ten years has averaged 13% annually. The company says

*Reprinted from *Business Week*, May 14, 1984.

55% of 1983's $6 billion in sales and much of its $489 million in earnings came from products that are No. 1 in their markets. And the resuscitation of its Tylenol pain reliever after the 1982 deaths of seven people who had taken cyanide-laced capsules, its repositioning of Baby Shampoo for the adult market, and its come-from-nowhere move to No. 2 in infants' toys demonstrate its legendary marketing prowess.

But while J&J's core businesses remain solidly profitable, Burke believes that maturing markets limit long-term growth potential. Moreover, scientific and technological advances promise to revolutionize health care. Thus, the push into technology "is absolutely critical to the future and to the present," he states flatly. Without it "we would be heading toward being just another company."

So since 1980, J&J has acquired 25 companies, many in promising, high-tech markets. Burke, who became CEO in 1976, has positioned J&J in products ranging from intraocular lenses and surgical lasers to magnetic-resonance scanners for diagnostic imaging.

Now, however, the longtime dominance of marketing and sales executives and the insularity of J&J's units could seriously impede the company's ability to push successfully into these new businesses and to react swiftly to changing competitive conditions in health care. Burke himself recognizes that the company's success will require greater cooperation among corporate units. And he has found that such cooperation can be hard to obtain. Former J&J executives assert, for example, that at least two key managers of J&J's Ethicon Inc., the world's largest maker of sutures, left during a struggle to persuade the unit to go along with a centralized ordering-and-distribution effort deemed critical to maintaining J&J's leading position in hospital supplies.

Learning to manage new businesses is also a major task, as evidenced by the management problems that have plagued the push into medical equipment, where losses have been heavy. One big reason for the red ink is the investment made to position companies such as Technicare Corp.—a maker of diagnostic-imaging equipment, purchased in 1979—for the long haul. The money was spent mainly to develop new products, including magnetic-resonance (MR) machines that provide strikingly clear images of the body's tissue without using radiation.

Dollars alone, however, will not solve the problems at these business:

- *Extracorporeal Inc.* Product-development problems at Extracorporeal, bought in 1978, left its dialysis equipment business with outmoded offerings when the market changed. J&J took a $38 million write-off last year and put the dialysis business on the block.
- *Ortho Diagnostic Systems Inc.* Organizational turmoil has hurt this maker of blood-analysis equipment and reagents. From 1977 to 1981, the marginally profitable Ortho went through four presidents. Long a leader in the field, Ortho failed to latch on to hot new technologies in the 1970s. "It was a general management and research management failure," admits executive committee member Verne M. Willaman. As a result, Ortho has been forced into an ex-

pensive catch-up effort. And although J&J denies them, rumors persist that Ortho, too, will be sold.

- *Technicare Corp.* Customer relations problems stemming from reportedly over-engineered products that were hard to use have hurt Technicare. ITR has lost $110 million since 1979, according to Larry N. Feinberg, an analyst at Dean Witter Reynolds Inc. In computer-assisted-tomography (CAT) scanners, these difficulties helped General Electric Co. to snatch the top spot away from Technicare. Some outsiders predict the same thing could happen with MR machines, which GE just started selling.

Burke acknowledges that his company's record in medical equipment is undistinguished, grading the efforts anywhere "from E-minus to A-plus." But he says: "One of the things we insist on here is that everybody understands part of their job is to fail. You don't move forward unless you make mistakes." The willingness to admit problems and try to learn from them is a J&J strength. The key question, however, is whether the company can apply the lessons to its new businesses.

More than one successful CEO has found that changing his company's mix of businesses is a lot easier than changing manager's attitudes. William T. Ylvisaker succeeded in transforming Gould Inc. into an electronics company only by replacing dozens of key managers. At Emerson Electric Co., a corporate culture that made a religion of cost-cutting and the bottom line threatens Charles F. Knight's ambitions in high tech. And Ruben F. Mettler has experienced some problems getting TRW Inc.'s divisions to share their expertise so the company can make maximum use of its considerable technological strengths.

J&J is discovering that developing and marketing high-tech equipment requires markedly different management skills than selling the products that generated its rapid growth. J&J was founded in 1885 by three Johnson brothers. But the next generation—in the person of "the General," Robert Wood Johnson—is most responsible for shaping the company into its present form. Under the General's rule from 1938 to 1963, the decentralized structure that is J&J's hallmark took shape, and the company introduced many of its most dominant products.

• *Pills vs. Hardware*

The General also wrote the corporate credo, which states that J&J's first responsibility is not to shareholders or employees but to "the doctors, nurses, patients, to mothers, and all others" who use its products. While many high-minded statements of corporate purpose are written and forgotten, J&J's is not.

That tradition may also explain why, despite Burke's ambitions in new technologies, virtually all of the 14 members of J&J's executive committee have consumer-marketing or pharmaceutical backgrounds. And all have been at the company at least 11 years.

After a stint at Procter & Gamble Co., Burke joined J&J in 1953 and rose through the marketing ranks to become chairman in 1976. Initially, Burke ran the

Band-Aid, dental-floss, and first-aid-kit businesses. As chairman, he personally led the marketing campaign to revive Tylenol. And colleagues say Burke foresaw the shift of emphasis in health care to early detection and prevention of illness.

Because its strength is in making and marketing consumer products, some competitors and J&J alumni doubt the company can become a leader in medical equipment. "What pill people have done well in hardware, and what hardware people have done well in pills?" asks GE's chairman, John F. Welch, Jr. "The road is strewn with people who have gone far afield [from the businesses they really know]."

The lack of experience in medical equipment probably helps explain why, Burke has moved cautiously in the field. At $74 million, J&J's acquisition of Technicare is its largest. And even though research-and-development spending has doubled since 1979, and will continue to rise, there is a limit to J&J's daring.

In MR scanners, for instance, GE's Welch makes no bones about his willingness to spend whatever it takes to be the leader. Technicare President Joseph G. Teague, however, says: "We don't have it as a realistic strategy to be No. 1" in the U.S. in several years. Matching GE's expenditures dollar for dollar, he adds, could be "frivolous and very expensive."

The questions of J&J's ability to make it in medical equipment go far beyond its financial commitment. More important is whether it has the management talent. The company's only clear high-tech success is Iolab Corp., the $50 million maker of lenses that are implanted after the surgical removal of cataracts.

Although J&J installed its own man, John R. Gilbert, as president about a year after buying Iolab, he has demonstrated a willingness to use new management aproaches. He spent considerable time learning the manufacturing process, talking to physicians, and questioning the company's founders, who had left—on amicable terms. Iolab's results have been impressive: Sales have jumped nearly fivefold since the acquisition. If J&J had tried to manage Iolab like one of its more established companies, "we would have failed," concedes Herbert G. Stolzer, Gilbert's boss on J&J's executive committee.

J&J's attempts to manage other medical-equipment acquisitions have not been similarly successful. Like many big companies, it has had trouble keeping the entrepreneurs who build the acquired companies. "The thinking is, perhaps understandably, 'Follow us, we have the keys to the kingdom,' " says one alumnus. J&J's financial systems and controls so bothered some managers at Extracorporeal, for instance, that they left, former J&Jers say. "That drives a lot of entrepreneurs crazy," concedes Burke.

Nothing better illustrates that the J&J system does not always contain the keys to the kingdom than its experience with Extracorporeal's dialysis business. Soon after J&J bought the company in 1978, prices for dialyzers—the filters used to clean blood—plunged as the government limited medicare reimbursements. When cost-conscious customers began reusing dialyzers, J&J found itself at a disadvantage, because competitors' products could be prepared for reuse more easily.

• *"Sea Change"*

J&J failed to adapt. As Burke explains it, J&J is so accustomed to selling products used once—often in sterile environments—"that it was appalling to us to think that those things would become reusable."

The kind of cooperation and communication that Burke deems essential for all J&J companies also has been alien to its culture. Burke believes that sharing R&D and marketing resources is a key to speeding product development. That, he says, will enable J&J to regain share in such traditional markets as hospital supplies and to exploit new opportunities created by the movement toward preventive health care. For example, he says, combining J&J's expertise in magnetic resonance and biotechnology could revolutionize diagnostics.

But even Burke acknowledges that persuading divisions to work together has required "a sea change in attitude" for J&J managers so used to independence. One J&J unit, notes J&J President David R. Clare, even refused to take managers from other J&J companies.

Burke and Clare have moved to break down the walls. They have increased the movement of managers between companies and placed more importance on corporate-level communities whose function is to facilitate the exchange of information between companies.

But mixed signals from the top have left some divisional managers confused about just how committed to togetherness their leaders are. A case in point: Johnson & Johnson Products, which sells bandages and splints; Surgikos, a maker of surgical gowns and disinfectants; and Ethicon the suture division, recently proposed that the three package their products in a customized surgical kit. But to their frustration, the divisions' managers have yet to secure New Brunwick's approval.

So it is no surprise that as J&J top managers preach the gospel of cooperation, some in their congregation react with more skepticism than faith. Nowhere is this more evident than in New Brunswick's tribulations in inducing its hospital-supply companies to work together—an effort one former J&J executive dubs "the company's single biggest move away from decentralization."

In a belated attempt to respond to increasing hospital cost-consciousness and the inroads American Hospital Supply Corp. has made into its business, J&J created its Hospital Services Co., which is giving volume discounts to some 24 hospitals on products from seven J&J companies. Crucial to making the plan pay off will be the likely development of a central, computerized ordering system that should considerably reduce customer paperwork, and, finally, match what its competition created in 1976.

• *Less Grumbling*

Some J&J managers have resisted the effort long past a sensible point. "People got fired for not supporting [Hospital Services]," says a former J&Jer who did stints in three of the companies involved. Although J&J denies this, it concedes that managers at Ethicon were resistant to change. Edward J. Hartnett, a company group chairman in New Brunswick, says, "The feeling was, 'I don't really need it.' "

Perhaps because centralization is such a sensitive issue at J&J, Burke and Clare sharply deny that Hospital Services is even a baby step in that direction. The companies involved in the effort will maintain separate sales forces—an indication that the two executives understand that instilling a cooperative spirit will take patience and time. Clare points to J&J's Absorbent Technology Group—a four-company effort to develop products for several markets—as an example of how hostility fades once a payback is evident. Clare himself had to muscle the companies into participating. But now that the group has three products under development, grumbling has diminished.

Burke and Clare have plenty of time. While some consumer markets, such as Band-Aids, are maturing, they are still solidly profitable. Indeed, J&J's 1981 withdrawal from the U.S. disposable-diaper market is the exception rather than the rule. In the last year, J&J rolled out a record six consumer products, ranging from a shampoo for the more brittle hair of women over 40 to a disposable dust cloth that eliminates the need for sprays.

J&J's record in pharmaceuticals demonstrates that there are areas of high science and technology that it indisputably knows how to manage. The $1.2 billion combined sales of its four pharmaceutical divisions make J&J the fifth-largest drug company in the U.S. More than 40% of its R&D spending, which last year totaled $405 million, or 6.8% of sales, went to pharmaceuticals. Such investments already appear to be bearing fruit: J&J now has twice as many new drugs undergoing animal testing as it did five years ago.

Indeed, as significant as the internal challenges at J&J are, another important one comes from without—namely, government efforts to curtail hospital expenditures on sophisticated medical hardware. Burke argues that such hardware can identify health problems before they become catastrophic—and catastrophically expensive to treat.

But given uncerainties clouding the medical technology markets, GE's Welch cautions that the wisest strategy is simply to have "the best. There's no room for the third-best machine. In hardware, Welch scoffs that J&J's no match for GE. His advice to Burke: People who go afar from what they know run into some ground holes." Burke's challenge is to prove J&J can climb out of them.

QUESTIONS

1 In terms of the Burns and Stalker study, how would you describe the changes in J&J's environment?

2 How might "the long-time dominance of marketing and sales executives and the insularity of J&J's units" seriously impede the firm's ability to push successfully into the new high-tech businesses it has acquired? What organizational changes do you think will be required?

3 How does J&J illustrate the fact that "environment and technology influence organizational structure" ?

6

Departmentation and Coordination

OVERVIEW

In this chapter, we discuss how to organize and coordinate departments. We explain the advantages and disadvantages of the basic methods that can be used to organize departments and the conditions under which each is recommended. And we explain how to coordinate departments, describing the main techniques that are used and the conditions under which each is appropriate.

The outline of this chapter is as follows:

- **A** Departmentation
  - **1** By function
  - **2** By product divisions
  - **3** By customer
  - **4** By marketing channel
  - **5** By territory
  - **6** Matrix departmentation
  - **7** Departmentation in practice: a hybrid
  - **8** Research findings: divisional vs. functional departmentation
  - **9** Implications
- **B** Line–staff structure
  - **1** Introduction
  - **2** Factors determining the use of staff
- **C** Achieving coordination in organizations
  - **1** The nature and purpose of coordination
  - **2** Historical perspective on coordination

3 Coordination and task routineness
4 Techniques for achieving coordination
5 Research findings: Achieving effective coordination
6 Implications

DEPARTMENTATION

Every enterprise has to carry out certain activities in order to accomplish its goals. In a company, these might include manufacturing, selling, and accounting. In a city, they might include activities like fire, police, and health protection. In a hospital, they include nursing, medical services, and radiology. In a bank, they include lending, bookkeeping, and security. Departmentation is the process through which these activities are grouped logically and assigned to managers. It is the organizationwide division of work. It results in departments—logical groupings of activities—which also often go by the name of divisions, branches, units, or sections.

The basic question in departmentation is, Around what activities should we organize departments? For example, should departments be established for sales and manufacturing? Or should there be separate departments for industrial and retail customers, each of which has its own sales and manufacturing units? As explained next, many options are available; these include:

1 Functional departmentation:
- **a** Business functions
- **b** Managerial functions
- **c** Technological functions

2 Divisional departmentation:
- **a** Products or product lines
- **b** Customers
- **c** Marketing channels
- **d** Territories

With functional departmentation, departments are built around basic processes like sales or manufacturing. With divisional departmentation, departments are built around "purposes" like particular products, customers, marketing channels, or territories.

• *By function*

Departmentation of an enterprise by function involves grouping activities around essential functions such as production, marketing, and finance. This is depicted in Figure 6–1. Departmentation by business function is typically the basis on which a new business is organized. The head of a new company might ask, "What basic functions will have to be performed if the business is to succeed?" As illustrated in Figure 6-1,

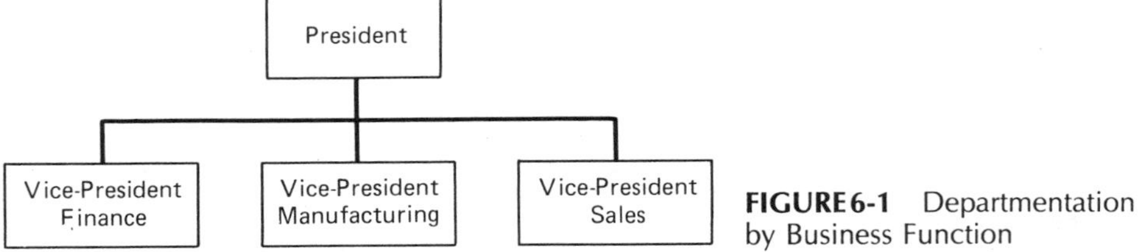

FIGURE 6-1 Departmentation by Business Function

in a manufacturing firm these usually include (at least) manufacturing, sales, and finance.

It is not necessary for the enterprise to be a manufacturing business or for its departments to be built around business functions. The basic business functions around which banks are often departmentalized include operations, control, and loans. Similarly, in a hospital, the basic "business functions" might include nursing, medical services, and radiology. In a university, the basic functions include admissions and registration, maintenance, and teaching.

Closely associated with this form of departmentation are two others: departmentation by managerial functions and departmentation by technological functions. Building departments around managerial functions involves putting managers in charge of departments for functions like planning, control, and administration. As illustrated in Figure 6-2, departmentation based on technological functions is the grouping of such activities as plating, welding, or assembling. Again, the basic idea of any sort of functional departmentation is to group activities around the elemental functions that the organization must carry out. For a manufacturing company, these functions typically include production, marketing, and finance. Within the production department, they might include assembling, welding, and plating. In a school, these elemental functions might include counseling, scheduling, admissions, and budgeting.

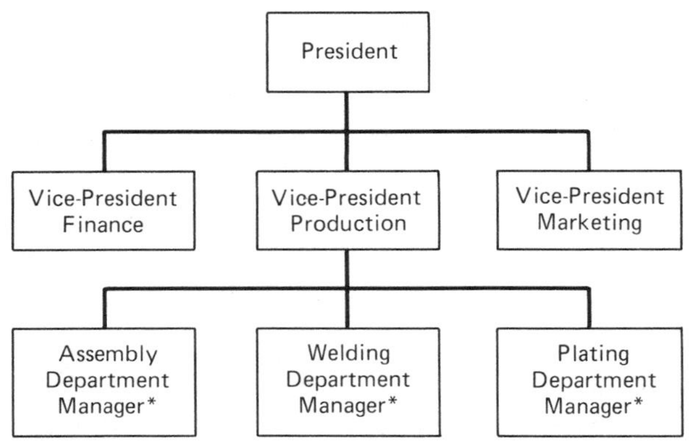

FIGURE 6-2 Process Departmentation Based on Technology

Advantages and Disadvantages Departmentation around functions (either business, managerial, or technical) has several advantages. It is a simple, straightforward, and logical way to organize, since it makes sense to build departments around the basic functions the enterprise must engage in. Functional organizations also usually have single large departments like sales, production, and finance that serve all the company's products. As a result, the volume of business done in each department is relatively high, and with this volume typically come increasing returns to scale—employees become more proficient (from doing the same job over and over again), and the company can afford larger plants and equipment, for instance. There also tends to be less duplication of effort in functional organizations. This is because the same production, sales, and personnel departments typically serve all the firm's products instead of having separate production, sales, and personnel departments for each product. As a result of these advantages, functional organizations are associated with greater efficiency. They are therefore more appropriate in mechanistic situations like production plants, and in efficiency-oriented companies like those in the steel industry, where efficiency rather than flexibility is paramount.

There are also several other advantages. Since managers' duties tend to be more specialized (they specialize in finance, or production, or welding, or planning, and so on), the organization need not seek out or train general managers—those with the breadth of experience to administer several functions. This can simplify both recruiting and training. Department managers in functional organizations also tend to get information on only part of the "big picture" of the company, that which concerns their own specialized function. This can make it easier for top management to exercise tight control over the activities of department managers.

Functional types of departmentation also have disadvantages. Responsibility for overall performance lies squarely on the shoulders of one person, usually the president. This may not be a serious problem when the firm is small, or where there is no diversity of products. But as size and diversity of products increase, the job of coordinating, say, production, sales, and finance for many different products may prove too great for one person, and the enterprise could then lose its responsiveness. Functional departments also tend to result in specialized managers (finance experts, production experts, sales experts, and so forth). Although this may increase their proficiency, it also makes it more difficult to develop managers with the breadth of experience necessary to promote them to executive jobs like that of president.

These advantages and disadvantages are summarized below in Table 6-1.

• *By Product Divisions*

With "divisional" departmentation, department heads are typically responsible for both producing and marketing a product or family of products. This is illustrated in Figure 6-3, which presents part of the organization chart of the General Motors Corporation. Notice how, at the operating-division level, the car and truck group was organized around product lines. Each product division had its own general manager,

TABLE 6-1 Advantages and Disadvantages of Functional Departmentation

Advantages	*Disadvantages*
Managers are functionally specialized and therefore more efficient.	Responsibility for overall performance lies with chief executive only.
Less duplication of effort.	Can overburden chief executive.
Increased returns to scale.	Reduces the attention paid to specific products, customers, markets, or areas.
Training is simplified.	Results in functionally specialized managers rather than "general" managers.
Simple and proven over time.	
Facilitates tight control by chief executive.	

and there were separate product divisions for Buick, Cadillac, Oldsmobile, Pontiac, Chevrolet, and GMC trucks.

Arranging departments around products is often referred to as divisionalization. This emphasizes the fact that the division heads are often in charge of what amounts to self-contained companies, since they manage all the activities needed to develop, manufacture, and sell the product or product line. Notice that the head of such a division therefore has functional departments—say, for production, sales, and development—reporting to him or her.

Advantages and Disadvantages This system has several advantages, most of which stem from the fact that a single manager and department is charged with

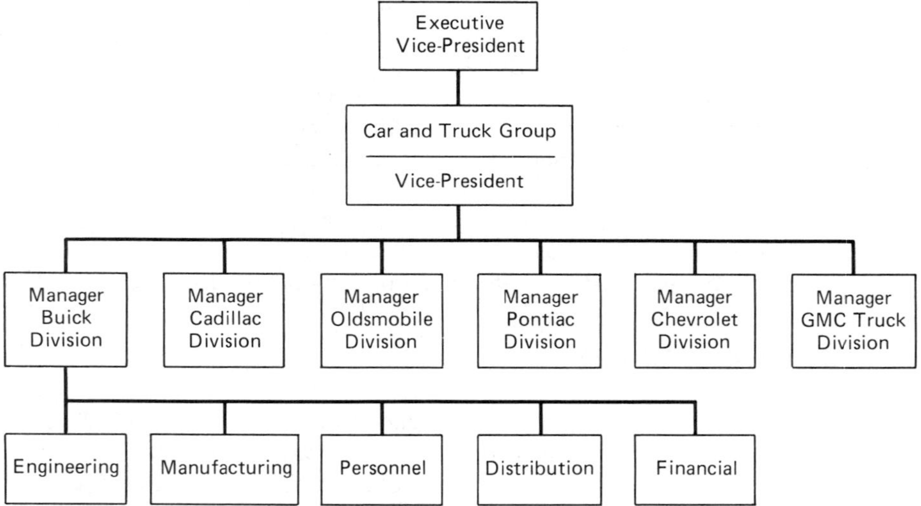

Note: The GM Car and Truck Group was departmentalized by product, and there are separate divisions for Buick, Cadillac, etc.

FIGURE 6-3 Product Departmentation at General Motors

overseeing all the functions needed to produce and market each product. As a result, these product divisions tend to be more sensitive and responsive to the needs of their particular product or product line. Thus, a publisher might set up separate divisions for textbooks, video tapes, and films. The manager in charge of the textbook division might then have his or her own textbook editing, manufacturing, and distribution departments. As a result, the division could usually respond quickly when, say, a competitor brings out a new and innovative textbook, since the manager in charge does not have to rely on (or seek the approval of) editing, manufacturing, or distribution managers who are not in his or her own division. Product departmentation is therefore more appropriate in organic situations where quick, responsive decisions and flexibility (rather than efficiency) are paramount.

There are also four other advantages. First, performance is more easily judged. In other words, if a division is not doing well, it is usually clear who is responsible, since one manager is in charge of the entire division. Related to this, being put in charge of the "whole ball game"—even if it is just one product line—can help motivate the manager to better performance. Furthermore, these self-contained divisions can be good training grounds for an organization's future executives. This is because they come in contact with a wider range of problems, such as production, sales, and finance. Finally, setting up product divisions can help lift some of the management burden from the shoulders of the organization's top management. For example, imagine if the president of GM had to coordinate the tasks of designing, producing, and marketing each of GM's different products. The diversity of problems he or she would face—from overseeing spark-plug production to marketing Cadillacs—would clearly be enormous. Therefore, virtually all large companies that have diverse products and customers have opted for some type of divisionalization.[1]

Departmentation around product divisions also has some serious disadvantages. For one thing, you can see from Figure 6-3 that these divisions breed duplication of effort. The very fact that each product division is self-contained implies that there are several production plants instead of one, several sales forces instead of one, and so on. This kind of duplication not only is very expensive but can create other problems. For example, the company's customers may become annoyed at being visited by salesmen representing different divisions.

Divisionalization can also lead to a loss of top-management control. The heads of the divisions often have considerable autonomy, since they are in charge of all phases of producing and marketing their product. Top management therefore tends to have less control over the day-to-day activities in each division and runs the risk of losing control; a division might run up huge expenses before top management discovers them, for instance. In fact, striking a balance between providing each division head with enough autonomy to run the division and still maintaining top-management control can be a ticklish business.

Finally, these product divisions also require more managers with general management abilities. This is because each product division is in a sense a miniature company, often with its own production plant, sales force, personnel department, and so forth; the managers thus cannot just be sales, production, or personnel specialists.

Advantages and disadvantages of product (division) departmentation are summarized in Table 6-2.

• *By Customer*

This type of divisional departmentation involves organizing departments to serve the needs of particular customers. Figure 6-4, for instance, shows the General Electric Company organization chart. Notice how the company is organized to serve as a supplier for many different customers, including aerospace customers, construction customers, consumer-products customers, and power-generation-customers.

Advantages and Disadvantages This method has several advantages. First, a manager is charged with giving his or her continuous, undivided attention to a customer or a group of customers. This can result in faster, more satisfactory service to each of the organization's customers, particularly when their needs are substantially different. Thus, universities distinguish between the graduate and undergraduate schools, and banks often establish separate departments for personal and commercial customers.

As with product departmentation, the main disadvantage here is duplication of effort: The company may have several production plants instead of one, several sales managers instead of one, and so on. This can reduce overall efficiency.

• *By Marketing Channel*

A marketing channel is the conduit (wholesaler, drugstore, grocery, or the like) through which a manufacturer distributes its products to its ultimate customers. With

TABLE 6-2 Advantages and Disadvantages of Departmentation by Divisions

Advantages	*Disadvantages*
One unit is responsible for giving continuous, undivided attention to the product, so unit is more sensitive and responsive to unique needs of the product.	Duplication of effort, perhaps reduced efficiency. In some situations, customers may also be bothered by representatives of more than one division.
Lifts part of the coordinating from shoulders of top manager.	Finding and training people to head each division is a more difficult job.
Performance more easily identified and judged; this in turn may motivate performance.	Since division heads now do their own coordinating without checking with top manager, the latter could begin to lose control. He or she no longer coordinates and oversees the day-to-day means by which employees do their jobs, just the ends—like whether or not the division makes a profit at the end of the year.
Provides good training ground for future top executives.	

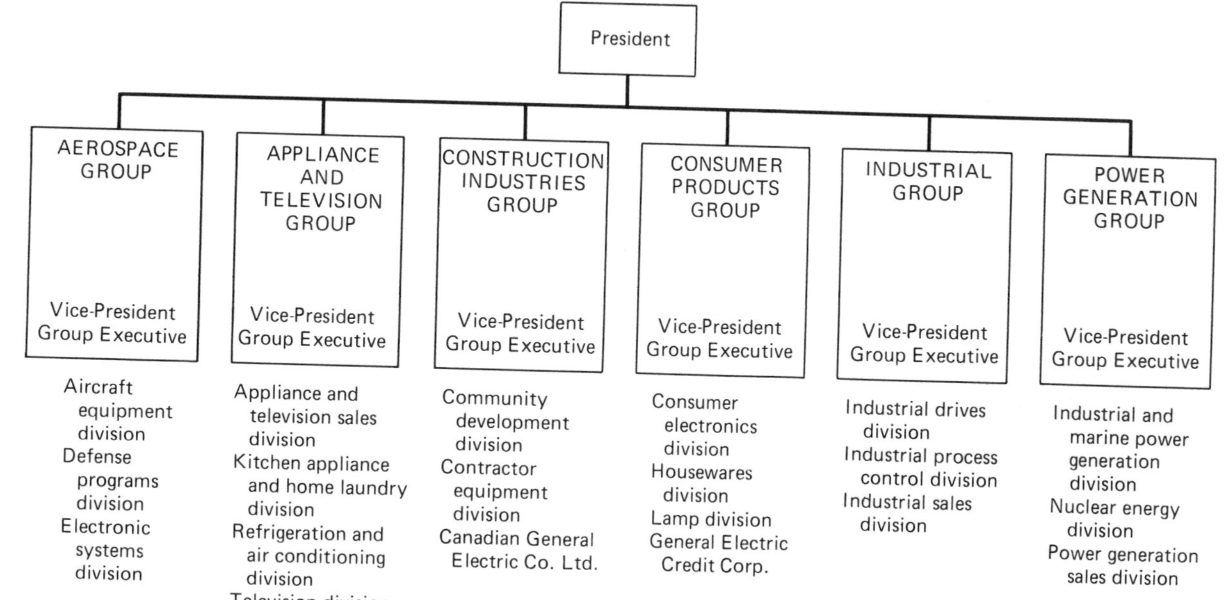

Note: Departments are built around such "customers" as aerospace, appliances and television, and construction.

FIGURE 6–4 Customer Departmentation at General Electric. This chart does not necessarily represent the current organization chart at General Electric. *Source:* Adapted from *Corporate Organization Structures*, National Industrial Conference Board, Inc., No. 210 (1968), p. 59. Reproduced in James Gibson, John Ivancevich, and James Donnelly, Jr., *Organizations* (Dallas: Business Publications, Inc., 1973), p. 139.

marketing-channel departmentation, major departments are arranged around each of the organization's marketing channels. This is a third type of divisional departmentation.

Marketing-channel departmentation is illustrated in Figure 6-5. As you can see, it is similar to customer departmentation, but there are several differences. In customer departmentation, each customer-oriented department is usually responsible for both manufacturing and selling its own product to its own customers. In marketing-channel departmentation, the same product (such as a brand of facial soap) is typically marketed through two or more different channels. Thus, a decision is usually made as to which department will manufacture the product for all the other marketing-channel departments.

Advantages and Disadvantages Organizing around marketing channels usually assumes that it is the unique needs of each marketing channel (rather than the firm's ultimate customers) that must be catered to. In selling its perfumes to its final customers, for instance, Revlon may sell through both department stores and discount drugstores. Yet the demands of these two marketing channels are quite different: The department stores may want the perfume company to supply specially trained salespeople to run concessions in their stores, whereas the discount druggists want quick delivery and a minimum inventory. Putting a manager and department in charge of each marketing channel can help ensure that such diverse needs are met quickly and satifactorily.

As with product and customer departmentation, the resulting duplication—of sales forces, for instance—is a main disadvantage here.

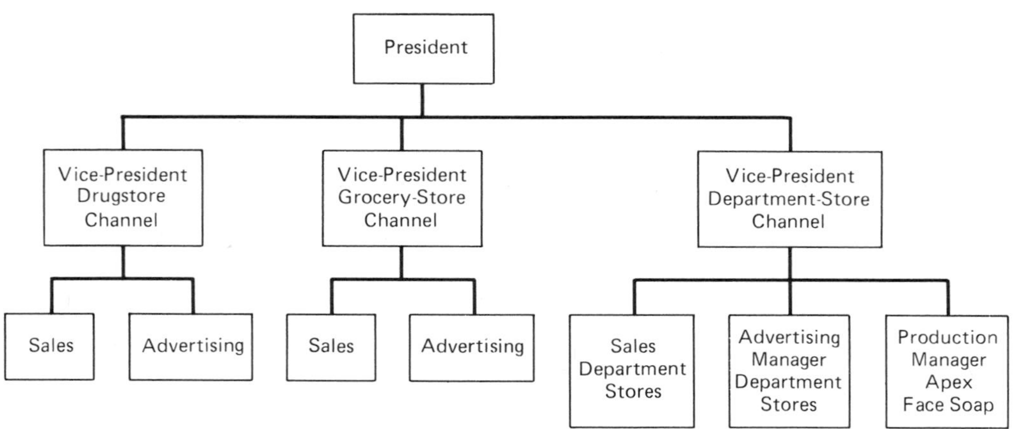

Note: Only the department-store channel produces the soap, and each channel may sell to the same *ultimate* consumers.

FIGURE 6-5 Marketing-Channel Departmentation at Apex Face Soap Co.

• *By Territory*

With this fourth type of divisional departmentation, separate departments are organized for each of the territories in which the enterprise does business. For example, the U.S. Federal Reserve System is divided into twelve geographic areas, centered in cities like Boston, New York, and San Francisco.

Advantages and Disadvantages The main advantage of territorial departmentation is that there is coordination at the point of sale, which can lead to speedier, more satisfactory service. Thus, a department-store chain might organize territorially so that the tastes and needs of customers in each geographic area can be better catered to. Like product, customer, and market-channel departmentation, territorial departmentation is therefore advantageous insofar as it ensures quick, responsive reaction to the needs of the company's clients. Also like these other three forms of departmentation, however, territorial departmentation may suffer from duplication of effort, and from the need to train and hire general managers capable of managing several business functions (like production, sales, and finance).

• *Matrix Departmentation*

With matrix departmentation, a group of product departments is superimposed over a functional departmentation. This is illustrated in Figure 6-6. This company's aerospace-products division is functionally organized, with departments for functions like production, engineering, and personnel. But superimposed over this functional organization are three product groups, for the Venus project, Mars project, and Saturn project. Each of these product groups has its own product manager (or project leader). And one or more representatives from each functional department (like production and engineering) are temporarily assigned to each project.

This is a typical matrix organization. A manager is put in charge of each project and is given the authority and responsibility for completing the project. He or she is assigned a number of personnel from the various functional departments. The manager has the authority for relieving these employees from their regular functional-department assignments and for rewarding them with promotions, salary increases, and so on. This is a temporary kind of departmentation. On completion of the project, the personnel return to their functional departments for reassignment.

Advantages and Disadvantages Matrix departmentation has some important advantages. It ensures a self-contained department that can devote its continuous and undivided attention to the needs of its own project; yet the entire organization need not be permanently organized around what are in fact temporary projects. Management avoids having to set up duplicate functional departments for each of several projects.

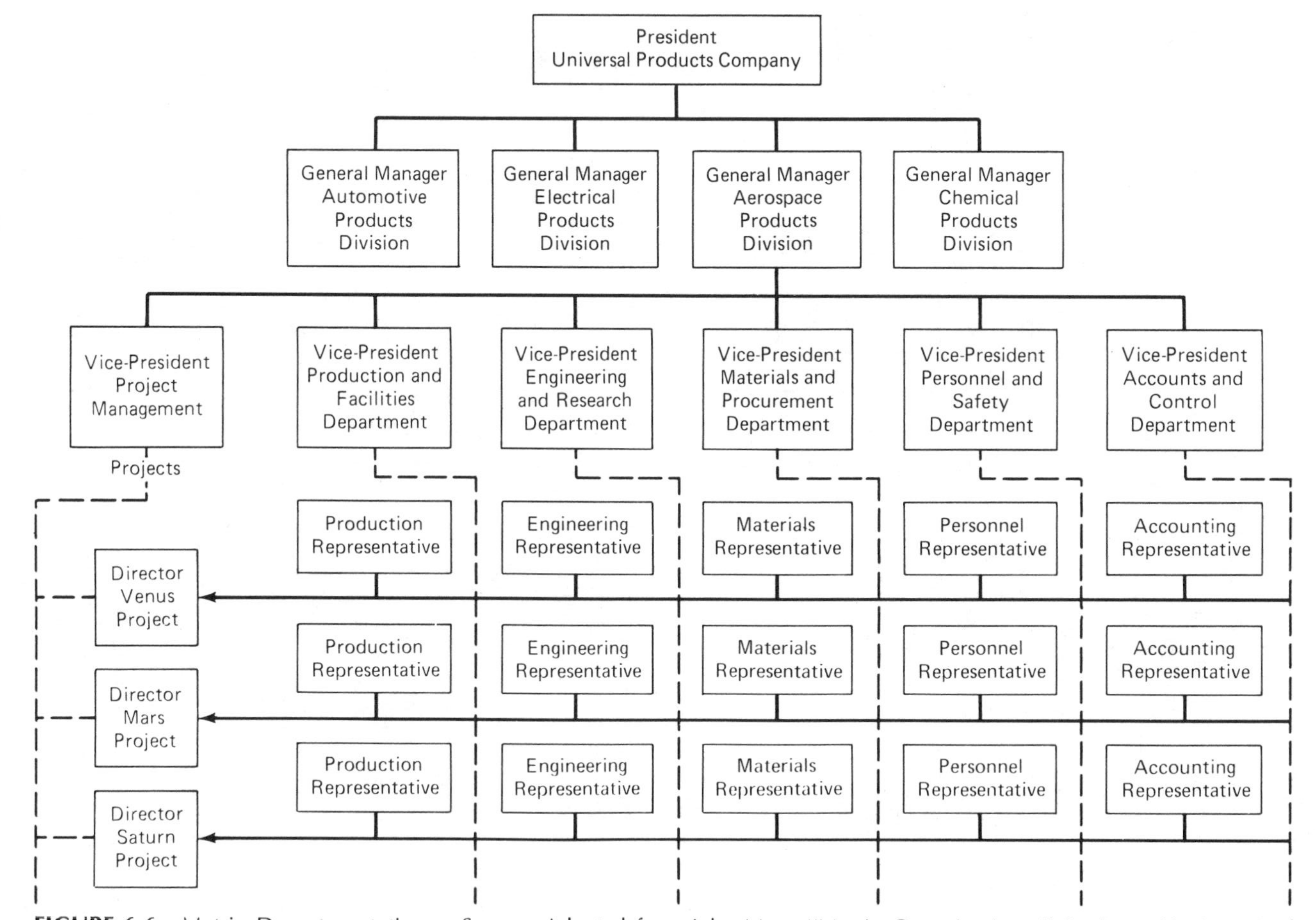

FIGURE 6-6 Matrix Departmentation. *Source:* Adapted from John Mee, "Matrix Organizations," *Business Horizons* Vol. VII (1964), pp. 70–72; reprinted in David Hampton, *Modern Management Issues and Ideas* (Belmont, Calif.: Dickenson, 1969), pp. 92–95.

Matrix organizations have proved quite successful. They have been used successfully by a wide range of companies, including Citicorp Bank, TRW Systems, NASA and many of its subcontractors, UNICEF, and various CPA, law, and security firms, to name just a few.[2]

However, they are also subject to a number of problems that, although avoidable, are potentially serious. These can be summarized as follows:

- *Power struggles and conflict.* The potential exists for power struggles and conflict between managers who head the functional and the product groups. Since authority tends to be more ambiguous and "up for grabs" in a matrix organization, such struggles may be more commonplace in matrix than in traditional organizations.
- *Time consuming.* Matrix organizations tend to result in more intragroup meetings and therefore often seem to be indecisive and time consuming.
- *Excessive overhead.* Research indicates that matrix organizations tend to raise costs as the administrative overhead caused by hiring more managers and secretaries increases. Davis and Lawrence argue that once the matrix is operational, these extra costs disappear.
- *Collapse during economic crunch.* Matrix structures tend to blossom during boom periods and to get phased out during periods of economic recession. In part, this is because top managers, during these recessions, want to reduce the ambiguity, endless meetings, and extra overhead that sometimes attend the matrix form.

• Departmentation in Practice: A Hybrid

In practice, most organizations use several forms of departmentation; they are hybrids, in other words. For example, top management might decide to establish functional departments and then to departmentalize the sales department territorially, with separate sales managers for the North, East, South, and West.

A main advantage of mixing forms of departmentation is that it can help reduce the duplication that is inherent in departmentation around products, customers, market channels, or territory. For example, see Figure 6-7. ABC Publishing's top management might decide to establish one central printing and production department to produce all the publisher's books. However, the other main departments are organized around customers, since there are separate departments for high school books, college books, and general books. In turn, the heads of each of these customer-oriented departments are in charge of subsidiary market research, editing, and sales departments. In this way, the publisher gains the advantage of having a department devoted to reacting responsively to each of its main customer groups. At the same time, it does not have to absorb the expense of having three separate plants.

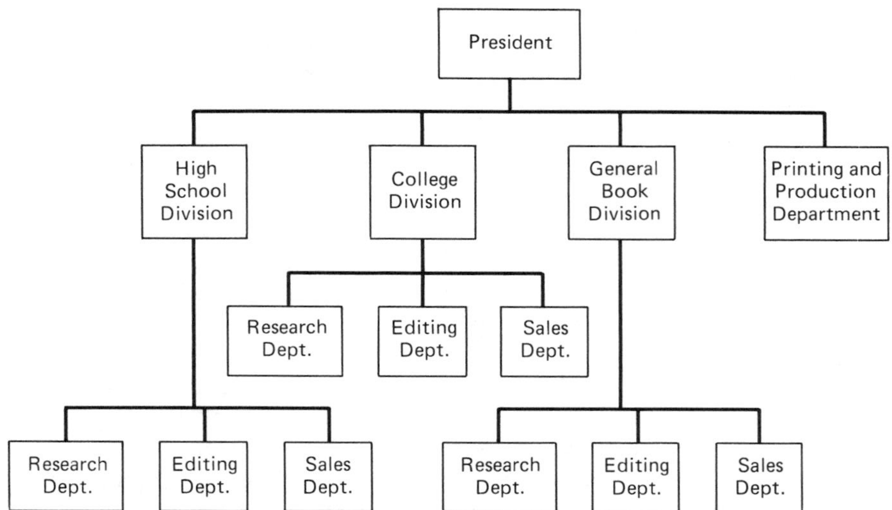

Note: Reducing duplication of effort by "mixing" functional and customer departmentation at the top level.

FIGURE 6-7 Organization Chart of ABC Publishing Co.

• *Research Findings: Divisional vs. Functional Departmentation*

The research findings concerning the relative merits of divisional versus functional departmentation suggest two conclusions: (1) that divisional organizations facilitate coordination, and (2) that top managers tend to install divisional organizations where the products, customers, market channels, or locations the organization serves are very diverse, or where their organizations have grown so large that the problems involved with coordinating the various functions have become insurmountable.

Conclusion 1 Divisional departmentation facilitates coordination, according to the Walker and Lorsch study.[3] Walker and Lorsch studied two manufacturing plants—one, F, organized by function, and the other, P, organized in a divisional way by product. Although they had different organizational structures, the two plants were otherwise similar. Both were making the same product, and their markets, technology, and raw materials were identical. Furthermore, the parent companies were similar, in that both were large national corporations that developed, manufactured, and marketed many consumer products. Management philosophies were also similar; they stressed a desire to foster employee initiative and autonomy, and placed great reliance on selection of well-qualified heads.

The organization structures of the plants are depicted in Figures 6-8 and 6-9. As shown on the charts, there were identical functional specialists for manufacturing, packing, quality control, planning and scheduling, warehousing, industrial engineering, and plant engineering in each plant. However, in plant F, which used functional departmentation,

> Only the manufacturing departments and the planning and scheduling function reported to the plant manager who is responsible for the product. All other functional specialists reported to the staff of the divisional manufacturing manager, who is also responsible for the plants manufacturing other products. At plant P (using the product basis of departmentation), all functional specialists with the exception of plant engineering reported to the plant manager.[4]

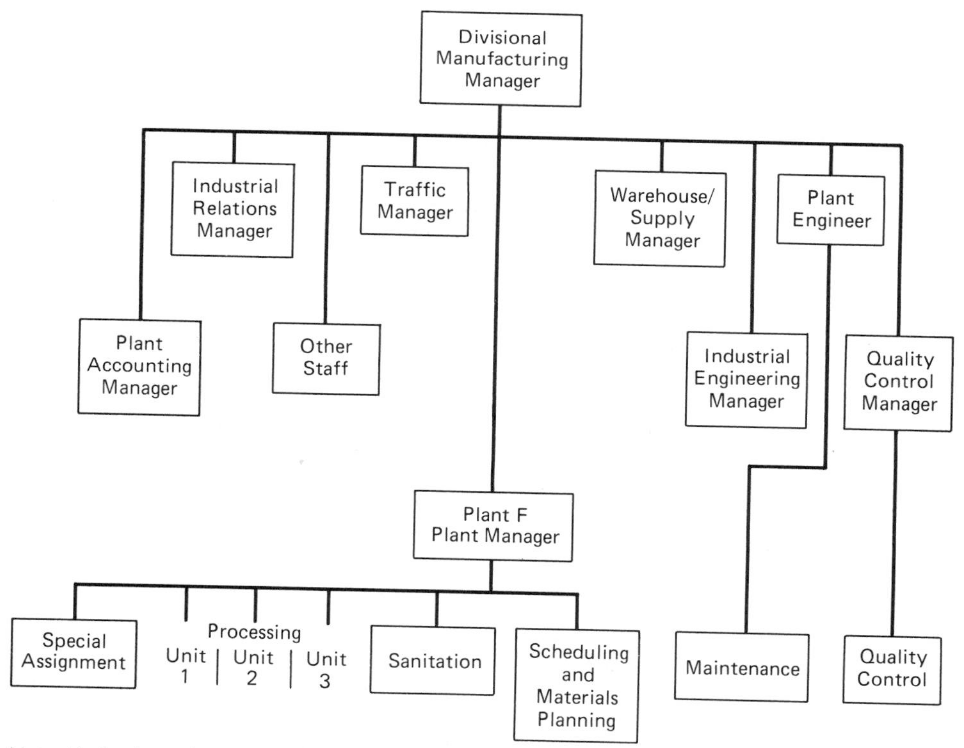

Note: Notice how, from the point of view of the division manufacturing manager, this is a *functional* departmentation. Basically, the plant manager is in charge of only a specialized manufacturing function.

FIGURE 6-8 Organization Chart of Plant F. *Source:* Arthur H. Walker and Jay W. Lorsch, "Organizational Choice: Product vs. Function," *Harvard Business Review,* 46, no. 6 (1968), 133–34.

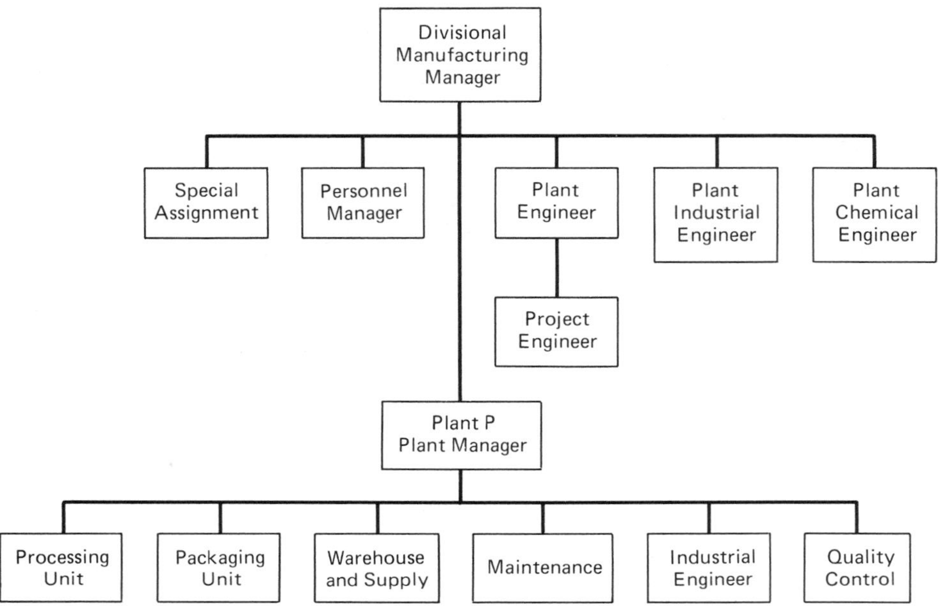

Note: Notice how, from the point of view of the division manufacturing manager, this is a more product (purpose)-oriented departmentation. The plant manager is in charge, basically, of a more complete, self-contained unit. Unlike the case at plant F, he has managers for packaging, warehouse and supply, maintenance, industrial engineering, and quality control reporting to him.

FIGURE 6-9 Organization Chart of Plant P. *Source:* Arthur H. Walker and Jay W. Lorsch, "Organizational Choice: Product vs. Function," *Harvard Business Review,* 46, no. 6 (1968), 133–34.

Plant F, therefore, was considered functionally organized, since the plant manager was primarily responsible for manufacturing and reported to the divisional manufacturing manager. The latter also had the other functional managers—for maintenance, quality control, warehousing, and industrial engineering—reporting to him. On the other hand, plant P was considered to be organized divisionally, by product, since the plant manager had most of the functional managers (such as the industrial engineer and the maintenance manager) reporting directly to him. Plant P was more self-contained and autonomous, whereas Plant F depended on the coordinative efforts of the divisional manufacturing manager for supplying necessary maintenance, quality control, warehousing, industrial engineering, and other advice and resources.

Walker and Lorsch found that plant P was better coordinated than plant F. In plant F, for example, "collaboration between maintenance and production personnel and between production and scheduling was a problem." On the other hand, the only coordination problem in plant P was between production and quality control. Furthermore, communication among employees in plant P was more frequent, less formal, and more often of a face-to-face nature than in plant F.

Conclusion 2 Top managers tend to use divisional organizations where the products, customers, channels, or areas their organizations serve are very diverse, or where the time involved in coordinating separate functions like production, sales, and finance for all products is becoming too burdensome for the top manager. One investigation that illustrates this conclusion was carried out by Alfred Chandler.[5] In his study of American companies, he found that firms in the electronics, automobile, and chemical industries had generally opted for product-oriented divisions at the level just below the president. Part of the reason, Chandler found, was that companies in these three industries all placed an emphasis on research and development and on a strategy of expansion through product diversification.

Other Evidence A case study by Kover supports the idea that divisionalization stimulates and facilitates attention to the needs of the product or customer. His subject was a large advertising agency that had previously been organized primarily along functional lines.[6] Interdepartmental coordination was carried out at that time by account executives. The agency was reorganized to make it product-oriented, and heterogeneous project teams consisting of different specialists were formed to serve a few clients each, with the aim of more tightly integrating client service.

The two pertinent organizational charts are shown in Figures 6-10 and 6-11. Kover found that although client–agency communication improved after the reorganization, communication between specialists was severely reduced. Furthermore, communication between the relatively autonomous departments was reduced and, in effect, the advertising agency became a group of small mini-agencies. The reorganization resulted in a significant shift from dual evaluation of work, in terms of both profession and client, toward an emphasis on client-satisfaction criteria. In other words, the purpose organization seemed to stimulate and facilitate an emphasis upon serving the needs of the client rather than those of a specialized, functional area.

• *Implications*

We can summarize this discussion with the following implications: Arrange departments around functions where:

1 Efficiency is more important than responsiveness.
2 Products, customers, or areas are not very diverse, so that one person (probably the president) can adequately coordinate the basic functions for all products, customers, or areas. (The more diverse the problems and needs of the company's customers, the more difficult it would be for the president to coordinate production, sales, and finance for all the customers.)

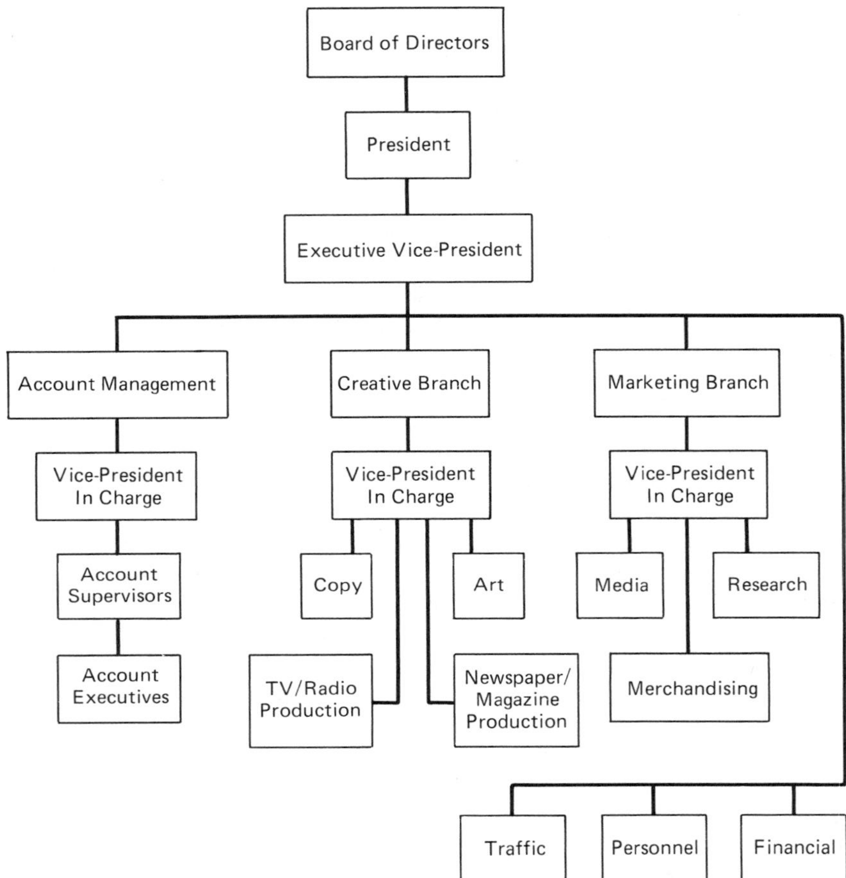

FIGURE 6-10 Organization Chart for the Paragon Advertising Agency (Before Reorganization). *Source:* Society for Applied Anthropology, *Human Organization*, Vol. 22, No. 1 (1963), pp. 252–259.

3 The situation is stable and unchanging, so that the top manager is not confronted with a constant flow of new problems. Many unexpected problems make it more difficult for the president to coordinate production, sales, and finance for several different products. A functional departmentation therefore works best under stable conditions.

Arrange departments around products (or customers, marketing channels, or territories) where:

1 The enterprise is so large and its products (or customers, market channels, or territories) so diverse that one person can no longer alone coordinate the func-

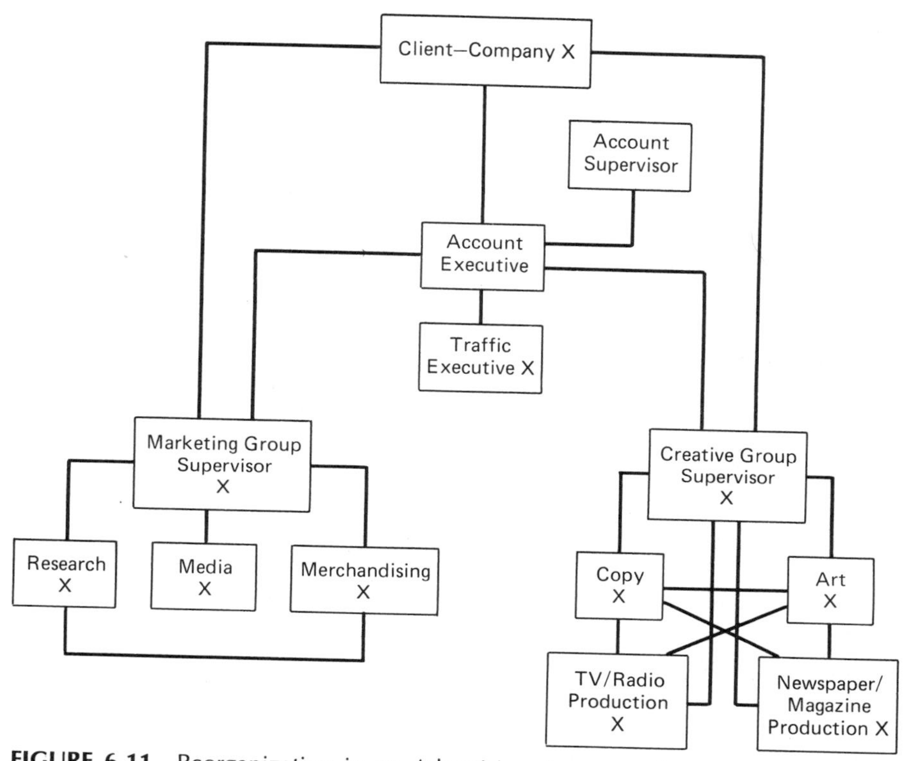

FIGURE 6-11 Reorganization in an Advertising Agency. *Source:* Society for Applied Anthropology, *Human Organization*, Vol. 22, No. 1 (1963), pp. 252–259.

tions (production, marketing, etc.), for all products (customers, market channels, or areas).

2 Being sensitive and responsive to the unique needs of the products (customers, market channels, or areas) is more important than being efficient. Functional vs. product (divisional) departmentation is basically a tradeoff between efficiency and responsiveness. Functional departmentation is superior from the point of view of efficiency. Divisional departmentation is superior from the point of view of responsiveness.

3 Adequate controls can be implemented by top management so that the activity of the product division (or customer, market channel, or geographic department) can be monitored and controlled.

4 Developing general managers is a major consideration.

5 The product (customer, market channel, or area) produces enough volume to warrant a separate general manager and department to oversee the functions (production, finance, sales, etc.) necessary to serve the product (customer, market channel, or area).

LINE–STAFF STRUCTURE

• Introduction

Another familiar way to distinguish between departments is to view them as either *line* or *staff* units. Most writers consider *line functions* to be those that have direct responsibility for accomplishing the objectives of the enterprise, and *staff functions* as those that assist and advise the line manager in accomplishing these objectives. However, keep in mind that staff is not necessarily less important than line, and that many essential activities—including personnel, purchasing, quality control, and plant maintenance—would fall into the staff category.

Frederick Taylor was one of the first organization theorists to see the need for distinguishing between line and staff (or advisory) functions. His solution was a "functional foreman organization" (Figure 6-12) in which each employee reports to *a number of* formal supervisors, each of whom is a specialist in one area. For example, an assembly-line employee might have four bosses, one each for planning, production control, quality control, and inspection.

One of the problems with this type of organization is that the employees are frequently put in a position in which the orders of one boss conflict with those of another. Because of this problem and others, few organizations have adopted the functional foreman form of organization.[7]

The line-and-staff organization is the more usual way of obtaining the specialized advice that Taylor accurately saw was necessary while avoiding the disadvantages of having an employee with more than one boss. Using staff has also been proposed as one means by which a manager can increase his information-handling capacity. The staff unit can compile, analyze, and advise on various matters, so that the manager's ability to process information is, in effect, extended.

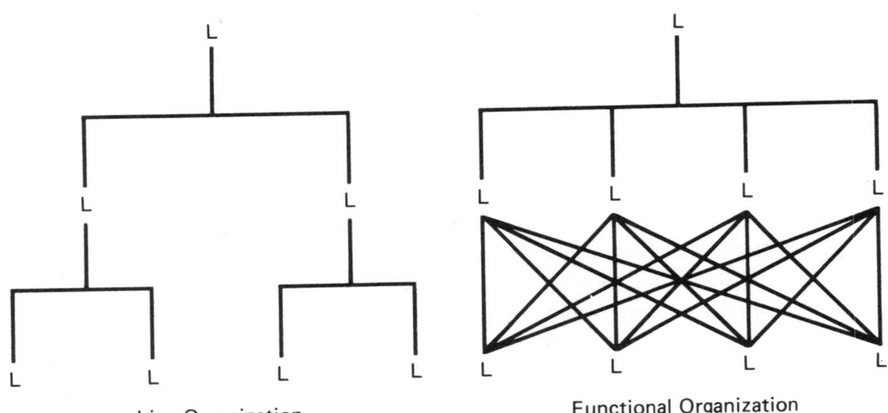

FIGURE 6-12 Line vs. Functional Organization

Types of Staff There are two basic types of staff, as illustrated in Figure 6-13. Personal (or general) staff reports to the executive it serves. One familiar example is the "assistant-to," a person whose responsibility is to assist his or her superior in a variety of problems. Another example is the general staff, whose purpose is to absorb, analyze, and synthesize information and advise top management; an army commander's general staff is an example of this.

Specialist staff is a second type of staff. Here, managers—for personnel, industrial engineering, or quality control, for instance—assist and advise the line managers in the organization by providing expert advice in their specialized areas. For example, the personnel manager helps all managers recruit, screen, and train employees.

Note that a main difference between line and staff managers is that the former can issue orders down the chain of command, whereas the latter can usually just

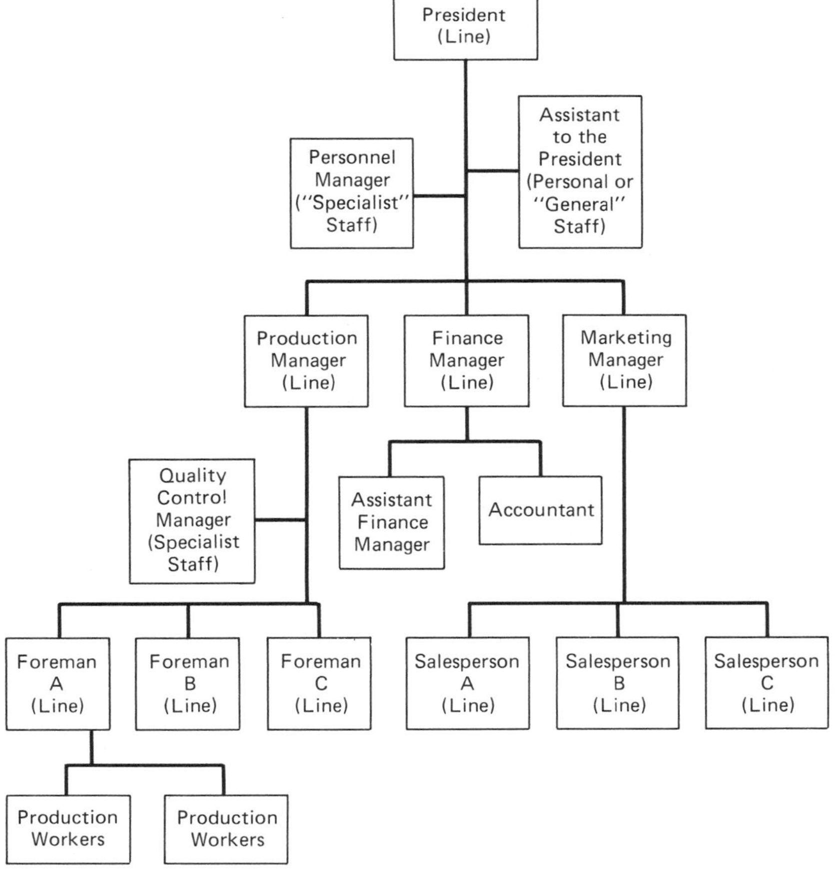

FIGURE 6-13 Line and Staff Authority

assist and advise. Staff units are therefore usually (but not always) shown on the organization chart in a manner that distinguishes them from the "line" chain of command. In Figure 6-13, for instance, the president's assistant, the personnel manager, and the quality control manager are all shown in outlying boxes that separate them from the chain of command. In the case of personal staff, this arrangement indicates that the person or department can assist or advise a superior but cannot issue orders to managers lower in the hierarchy. In the case of specialist staff (like personnel managers), it indicates that the staff manager or department can assist or advise other managers above or below them on the chart, but they cannot order other managers to take particular action, even if those managers are shown lower in the hierarchy.

There are three exceptions to these rules. First, a staff person—say, a personnel manager—will often have his or her own subordinates, and within this department, the manager can, of course, exert line authority by issuing orders to subordinates. Second, a chief executive will sometimes authorize a staff manager to issue orders to other managers in some specific area: A personnel manager may be authorized to issue orders to production and sales managers regarding the personnel test they can use for selecting employees, for instance. (In such a case, the personnel manager is said to have functional authority, in this case with respect to personnel testing.) Finally, a staff person may get line authority just through the power of his or her personality, or because he or she has easy access to the president; in such a case, a staff person could issue orders to other managers even though not authorized to do so by the formal organization chart.

• *Factors Determining the Use of Staff*

The Woodward Studies: Technology and Staff Under what conditions is the use of "staff" appropriate? Technology is one of the factors that have been found to influence the appropriateness of the line–staff structure. Woodward and her team carried out an analysis of the relationship between technology and the use of staff in various English manufacturing firms. They concluded that the line–staff structure was particularly appropriate in large-batch and mass-production firms.[8]

The Woodward team found the simple line organization depicted in Figure 6-14 to be characteristic of successful firms at the extremes of her technological scale—"either small unit production firms or large process production firms of a single-purpose plant type."[9]

If these firms did not have formal staff units, how were the specialized staff functions—such as production control—carried out? The answer apparently is that in the unit production firms, the necessary technical expertise was held by the line managers themselves. In the process firms, on the other hand, the line–staff distinction had become so blurred that it had simply ceased to exist. Specifically, the highly automated and complex nature of the production process in these firms led to a situation in which units that have normally been considered "staff"—such as plant

FIGURE 6-14 Line Specialization. *Source:* Joan Woodward, *Industrial Organization* (London: Oxford University Press, 1965, p. 101.

maintenance—had in fact taken on direct-command authority over the line manager in some areas.

Although the line–staff structure did not exist at the extremes of Woodward's technological scale, it predominated in the middle. In the mass-production firms, "line managers were held accountable for end results, while staff managers were formally responsible for giving advice and guidance to line managers."[10]

Woodward found that three main types of line–staff structures had emerged. The first of these is depicted in Figure 6-15. In these firms, the only managers recognized to have line authority were those with direct responsibility for the production

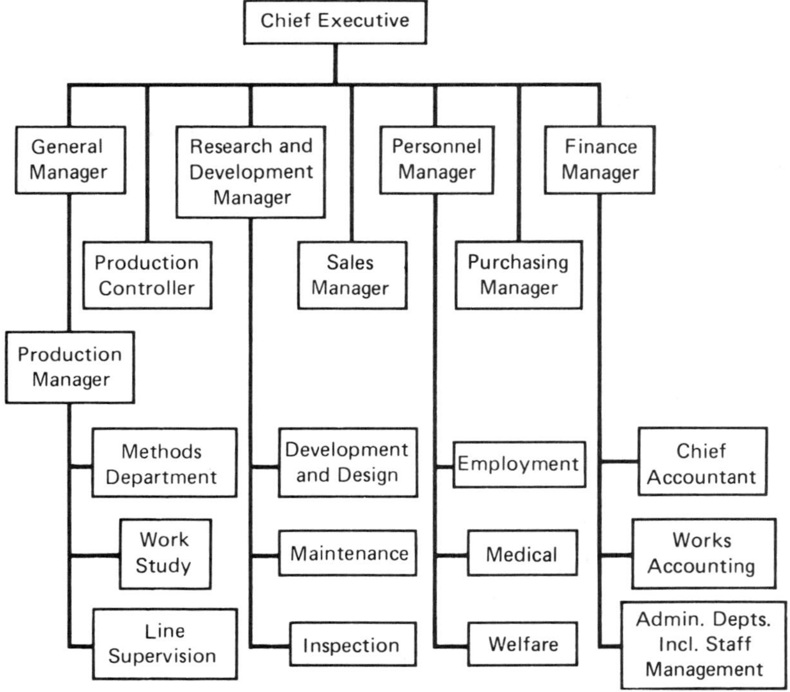

Note: Only the production-related managers were considered line managers.

FIGURE 6-15 Line–Staff Organization. *Source:* Joan Woodward, *Industrial Organization* (London: Oxford University Press, 1965), p. 105.

operations. All the other managers, including personnel, sales, research and development, and finance, were considered staff, and advisory to the chief executive.

The second type of line–staff organization is illustrated in Figure 6-16. In this type of organization, extensive staff specialization had been carried out within the production department, which had its own personnel, accounting, and purchasing units. These staff units, however, had no responsibility for anything outside production management. For example, the personnel manager was not responsible for the personnel function in either the research or sales department.

The third kind of organization is illustrated in Figure 6-17. This kind was referred to by those interviewed as "divisionalized organization," and is a good example of an application of the general-staff concept, which we discussed above. The organization was divisionalized to the extent that separate production divisions were established for each product. Each of these product divisions had, in addition to its own line manager, a variety of staff specialists, including those for personnel, accounting, and inspection. In addition, however, a "general staff," a small group of specialists of senior status, had been appointed to advise the chief executive and board on the formulation of policy relating to their own areas of specialization. These included quality control, personnel, and research and development. These staff specialists, however, had no line authority over the managers of the production divisions.

Staff and Organization Size The *size* of an organization also influences the extent to which it uses staff units.[11] In one representative study, researchers found that staff employment represented a consistent 75 percent of line employment at all size

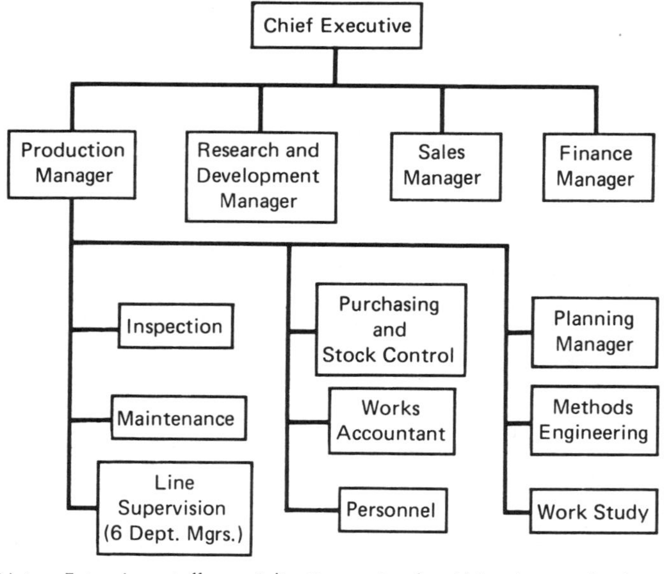

Note: Extensive staff specialization existed within the production department.

FIGURE 6-16 Line–Staff Organization Inside Production. *Source:* Joan Woodward, *Industrial Organization* (London: Oxford University Press, 1965), p. 106.

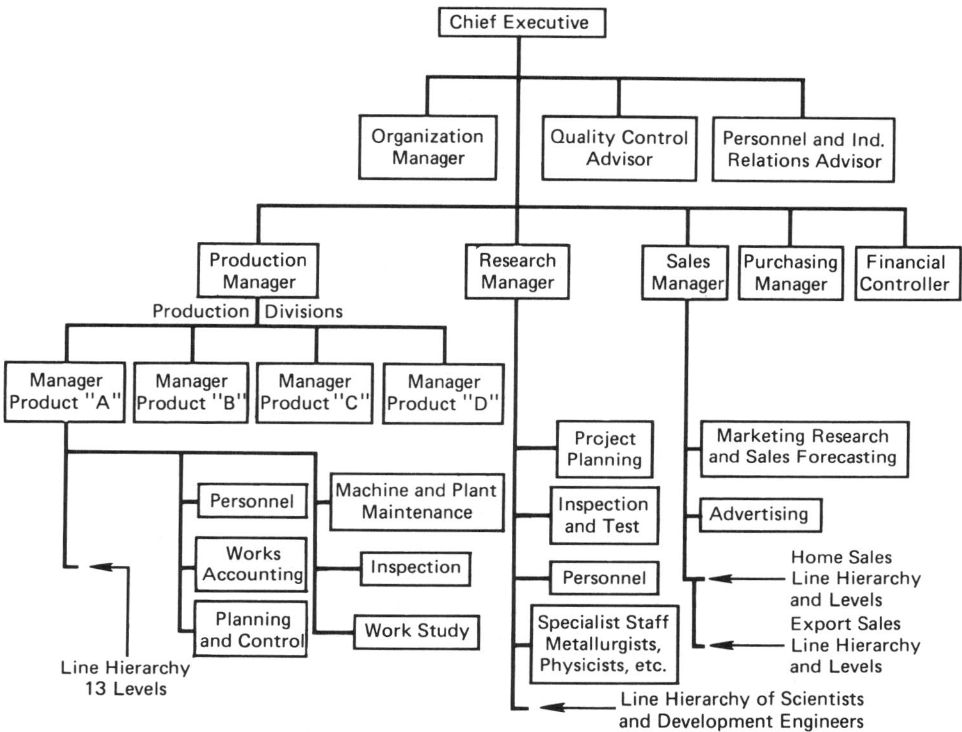

Note: This shows the "general staff" concept. The head office has senior staff managers for advising the chief executive and board in the areas of research, quality control, and personnel.

FIGURE 6-17 Product-Centered Line–Staff Organization. *Source:* Joan Woodward, *Industrial Organization* (London: Oxford University Press, 1965), p. 108.

levels.[12] A similar study focused on line–staff ratios in 155 automotive-parts manufacturers. Here it was found that staff as a percentage of line increased rapidly until the firm had about 550 direct-production employees. Beyond this point, the ratio declined slowly from about 57 to 51 percent.[13]

Haire studied the relative growth of staff employment in four firms and at four levels of employment: 200, 275, 300, and 2,000 employees. His results indicated that the utilization of staff increased rapidly during the early growth of all firms, and then stabilized at about 25 percent of total employment in two firms and at about 50 percent in the other two.[14] Filley used a similar approach to determine the increase in staff in five firms with total employments of 37, 59, 70, 378, and 450 employees. He found that in three of the firms, staff increased quickly, with two stabilizing at about 20 percent of total employment and the third at 40 percent. In the other two firms, however, the ratio of staff to total employment remained relatively constant, at about 20 and 10 percent.[15]

Based on this information, it appears that the proportion of staff usually increases relatively quickly in the earlier stages of an organization's growth, then stabilizes at a certain proportion of total employment. In addition, the proportion of staff, once the organization has reached a certain size, does not increase any more rapidly than total employment in general. Finally, the stabilized ratio between staff and total employment seems to vary markedly between different organizations. In the examples above, for instance, the ratio of staff to total employment ranged from about 10 percent to as high as 75 percent. This, in turn, is compatible with Woodward's findings. If, as Woodward found, technology is an important determinant of the use of staff, then we would expect to find a wide variation in staff utilization, where the studies focus only upon the relation between organizational size and the use of staff and do not "control" for technology.

ACHIEVING COORDINATION IN ORGANIZATIONS

• The Nature and Purpose of Coordination

Coordination is the process of achieving unity of action among interdependent activities.

Coordination is essential whenever two or more interdependent individuals, groups, or departments seek to achieve a common goal. Thus, if two people want to lift a big log, their actions are interdependent, since one person could not lift the log alone, and coordination is required because both people must lift in unison. Coordination here might be achieved by their agreeing to count to five and then lift the log. In a restaurant, the waiters, cooks, bussers, and cashiers are interdependent, since to serve the customers, each must make his or her unique contribution. Because they are interdependent, their work must be coordinated by a store manager who ensures, for instance, that the chef cooks the meal the way the customer ordered it.

Some departments are more interdependent than others, and so the difficulty of achieving coordination varies from situation to situation.[16] Some departments are highly interdependent. In a restaurant, for instance, the waiters and cooks are highly interdependent and a store manager has to spend considerable time ensuring that their efforts are coordinated. At the other extreme, the work of some departments in some organizations involves almost no interdependence. For instance, a president might decide to set up separate divisions for each product line, each of which is then managed as an independent, autonomous business. Here, the job of achieving coordination between the autonomous businesses would be relatively simple, since it's not really necessary for the departments to work in unison.

• Historical Perspective on Coordination

Early management theorists recognized the importance of coordination, and indeed considered it one of the primary functions of management. Fayol viewed it as the binding together of individual efforts to accomplish a common objective, and identified coordination as one of the five major management functions. Mooney and Reilly defined coordination as "the orderly arrangement of group effort, to provide unity of action in the pursuit of a common purpose" and called it the "first principle of management in that it expresses the principles of organization in toto: nothing less."[17] Most assumed that coordination could best be accomplished by just adhering to the chain of command.[18]

Although these early theorists saw that other forms of coordination might sometimes be required, these were viewed as exceptions to the rule and as indications of a poorly designed organization. As Gulick pointed out:

> In discussions thus far, it has been assumed that the normal method of interdepartmental coordination is hierarchical in its operation. . . . In actual practice, there are also other means of interdepartmental coordination which must be regarded as part of the organization as such. Among these must be included planning boards and committees, interdepartmental committees, coordinators, and officially arranged regional meetings, etc. . . . coordination of this type is essential. It greatly lessens the military stiffness and red tape of the strictly hierarchical structure. It greatly increases the consultative process in administration. It must be recognized, however, that it is to be used only to deal with abnormal situations or where matters of policy are involved, as in planning. The organization itself should be set up so that it can dispose of the routine work without such devices, because these devices are too dilatory, irresponsible, and time-consuming for normal administration. Wherever an organization needs continual resort to special coordinating devices in the discharge of its regular work, this is proof that the organization is bad. . . .[19]

Prescriptions such as these worked fairly well, of course, as long as "abnormal situations" were not the rule. As long as an organization could be viewed as operating in a stable environment in which novel, unexpected occurrences were the exception to the rule, hierarchical coordination through the chain of command did not seem to cause many problems and was probably an efficient way of doing things. But, as we have seen in the last few chapters, the environments of organizations are no longer stable. The problems that organizations must cope with have become increasingly complex and diverse, and this change has resulted in a shift in emphasis to coordination through special devices.

• Coordination and Task Routineness

The emphasis placed by classical theorists on using rules, procedures, and the organizational hierarchy for coordination was prompted in part by the predictable nature of the tasks these organizations had to accomplish. In line with this, March and Simon have suggested that the type of coordination used is directly related to the stability of the situation. Where the problems are recurring and routine, *coordination by plan* can be utilized. Here, coordination can be carried on by preestablished programs that specify what activities are to be performed and when.[20]

On the other hand, in situations that are rapidly changing and in which novel problems are the rule, *coordination by feedback* is more appropriate. Here, a specific capacity for perceiving deviations and relaying word to all interested parties is built into the coordination system. As we will see, there are many ways to achieve such coordination, including the use of committees and special "integrating departments." As March and Simon point out:

> The type of coordination used in the organization is a function of the extent to which the situation is standardized. To the extent that contingencies arise, not anticipated in the schedule, coordination required communications to give notice of deviations from planned or predicted conditions, or to give instructions for changes in activities to adjust to those deviations. . . .[21]

• *Techniques for Achieving Coordination*

Galbraith[22] and Mintzberg,[23] working independently, have developed useful descriptions of the techniques managers use to achieve coordination. As explained next, they both conclude that where the problems to be dealt with are routine, managers can rely on simple coordinating techniques like "mutual adjustment," and on more mechanical coordination devices like rules and procedures and the chain of command. But where situations change rapidly, other techniques, like standardizing the skills and knowledge of employees ("professionalizing" them), are required for achieving coordination.

Coordination through Mutual Adjustment According to Mintzberg, *mutual adjustment* achieves coordination through informal communication. This is a simple coordinating approach and is thus used in the simplest of organizations—for example, by two people moving a heavy log. Here, coordination could be achieved by just having one person count "one, two, three, lift," at which time both people lift the object in unison.

Paradoxically, says Mintzberg, mutual adjustment is also used in the most complex of situations, where the situation changes so quickly and where the work to be done is so unpredictable that standard procedures and organizations will not suffice. When a platoon of marines is planning their attack, for instance, they may follow formal procedures and stick to the chain of command. But when they hit the beach, it's more likely that most coordination will take place through an ongoing process of mutual adjustment as the group attempts to adapt to situations as they arise.

Coordination by Rules or Procedures: Standardization of Work Processes If the work is to be done is predictable and can be planned for in advance, you can specify ahead of time what actions your subordinates should take. *Rules and procedures* are thus useful for coordinating routine, recurring activities. They specify in detail, ahead of time, what course of action each subordinate should take if some situation should arise. Thus, the restaurant manager could have a rule that "bussers will bus tables as soon as customers are finished eating." This helps ensure that the table is clear before the next course is served, and that the work of the waiters and bussers is coordinated.

Coordination through Direct Supervision: Using the Hierarchy *Direct supervision* achieves coordination by having one person take responsibility for the work of others, issuing instructions to them and monitoring their results.[24]

In addition to using rules and mutual adjustment, all managers use the chain of command to achieve coordination. Thus, when situations arise that are not covered by rules or targets, subordinates are trained to bring the problem to the manager. Using the hierarchy to achieve coordination—having two or more subordinates come to their supervisor for a decision—works well only while the number of exceptions or problems to be brought to the boss is not too great. If there are too many problems or disagreements brought to the boss, he or she will become overloaded and unable to function effectively. Then the following coordination techniques become necessary.

Coordination through Organization: Departmentation First, some forms of departmentation facilitate coordination better than do others. For instance, suppose a company is organized functionally, with separate departments for production, finance, and sales. These departments are interdependent, which means the president must work hard to coordinate production, finance, and sales for all the company's products. Now suppose the company switches to a product type of departmentation. Now there are separate managers for each of the company's products, each of whom has his or her own production, finance, and sales group. The president does not have to work as hard coordinating the work of the product divisions, because they are not as interdependent as were the production, finance, and sales departments that previously reported to him. On the other hand, having a single manager and department for each product (or customer, market channel, or area) helps ensure that all the work needed to produce, finance, and sell *each product* is tightly coordinated. As a rule, functional departmentation creates additional demands for coordination, since the functional departments are interdependent. Product (or customer, market channel, or area) departmentation reduces the interdependence, and the need for coordination.

Switching to a *matrix departmentation* can also improve coordination. This is because the matrix approach means each project has the continuous and undivided attention of its own product manager and project team.

Coordination through Organization: Using a Staff Assistant Some managers hire an assistant to make the manager's job of coordinating his or her subordinates easier. When subordinates bring a problem to the manager, the assistant can compile information on the problem, research the problem, and advise on what alternatives are available. This effectively *increases the manager's ability to handle problems* and coordinate the work of his or her subordinates.

Coordination through Organization: Using a Liaison When the volume of contacts between two departments (like production and sales) grows, some managers appoint special liaisons to facilitate coordination. For example, the sales department might appoint a salesperson to be its liaison with the production department. This person would be based in the sales department but would travel frequently to the production line to learn as much as possible about the plant's production schedule. Then when an order came in to the sales department, the sales manager could quickly determine from this liaison person what the production schedules were, and whether the order could be accepted and delivered when promised.

Coordination through Organization: Using Committees Many managers achieve coordination by using interdepartmental committees, task forces, or teams. These are usually composed of representatives of five or six interdependent departments, and they meet periodically to discuss common problems and ensure interdepartmental coordination.

Coordination through Organization: Using Independent Integrators[25] An independent integrator's job is to coordinate the activities of several interdependent departments. Integrators differ from liaison personnel in that integrators are independent of (not attached to) the departments they coordinate. Instead, they report to the manager that the departments they coordinate report to. Independent integrators may be either individuals or departments.

As explained below, this coordination technique has proved useful in high-tech companies where work of several interdependent departments must be coordinated under rapidly changing conditions. In the plastics industry, for instance, developing new products involves close coordination between research, engineering, sales, and production departments in a situation where competitors are always introducing new and innovative products. Here, a successful plastics firm might decide to establish a new-product-development department. This department's role is to coordinate (or "integrate") the research, marketing analysis, sales, and production activities that are necessary for developing and introducing a new product.

Achieving Coordination by Standardizing Outputs or Targets Outputs are "standardized" when the results of the work are specified. For example, taxi drivers are not told how to drive or what route to take, says Mintzberg; they are merely told where their fares want to be delivered.

Much the same kind of coordination through standardized targets or outputs occurs in organizations. For example, a president might tell the sales vice-president to sell 10,000 units next year, the production vice-president to produce 10,000 units, and the finance vice-president to finance 10,000 units next year. Then, if each vice-president achieves his or her goal, their efforts should be coordinated, so that the company will sell, produce, and be ready to finance 10,000 units.

Coordination through Standardization of Skills and Knowledge Perhaps the most powerful way of achieving coordination is to standardize *the workers* who do the work, by providing them with the knowledge, skills, and values that will ensure that their work is coordinated with that of their peers. For example, when an anesthesiologist and a surgeon meet in the operating room to remove an appendix, they need hardly communicate; by virtue of their training, they know exactly what to expect of each other, and how to proceed. Their standardized skills thus take care of much of the coordination.[26]

But it is not just by standardizing skills and knowledge that companies like IBM ensure that their workers are "standardized." Instead, as we'll see, it is by carefully screening and socializing their employees, and by establishing a set of values and a philosophy—a "culture" that permeates and guides what employees do. Thus at IBM, the value "IBM means service" underscores the company's devotion to the individual customer, in such a way that everyone from clerks on up is prodded to do whatever he or she can think of to ensure that the individual customer gets taken care of.[27] And to that extent, the president of IBM can be sure that the work of the salespeople is consistent with—is coordinated with—the company's basic goals.

Summary From this you can see that some of the most powerful techniques used for achieving organizational coordination are not really "organizational" at all, but behavioral. In the simplest situations (and in the most complex), *mutual adjustment* is used by individuals who try to adapt to their changing surroundings by watching each other's behavior and making mutual adjustments as needed. And, more to the point, we'll see that the most excellent companies hardly use formal organizational coordination techniques (like independent integrators, or the chain of command) at all, compared to how they depend on creating a pervasive culture throughout the organization, one that helps make each employee's values consistent with the values of the firm. The employees' zealous adherence to these values then provides the self-control that helps ensure coordinated effort.

• *Research Findings: Achieving Effective Coordination*

How do effective organizations achieve coordination? What determines whether liaison personnel, committees, or integrators are appropriate? We turn to these questions in this section.

The Lawrence and Lorsch Studies We discussed some of Lawrence and Lorsch's general findings in Chapter 5. Now we review these findings in more detail, focusing especially on their "coordination" findings.[28]

You may recall that Lawrence and Lorsch's main objective was to answer the question, What kind of organization does it take to deal with various economic and market conditions? The researchers pursued this question by focusing upon two basic concepts, which they called differentiation and integration. *Differentiation* was defined as the "segmentation of the organizational system into subsystems, each of which tends to develop particular attributes in relation to the requirements posed by its relevant external environment." They expected to find interdepartmental differences in the formal structure of the departments, in the interpersonal orientations of department members, and in the goal and time orientation of department members.

Lawrence and Lorsch used the term *integration* synonymously with *coordination*, and defined it as the process of achieving unity of effort among the various subsystems in accomplishing the organization's tasks.[29] They predicted that seven factors would influence whether coordination (integration) was effectively achieved:

1 The type of coordinating unit used
2 Whether the unit was "intermediate" between the units it was coordinating
3 The influence the coordinator had
4 How the coordinator was rewarded
5 The total level of influence in the organization
6 Whether most influence was centered at the right organizational level
7 How conflicts were resolved

Lawrence and Lorsch studied effective and ineffective firms in the plastics, food, and container industries. They obtained three basic sets of findings, concerning (1) uncertainty, (2) differentiation, and (3) integration (coordination).

Their findings concerning the uncertainty facing each department were as follows. The total level of uncertainty—in terms of how clear job requirements are, how long it takes to get results on job performance, and so on—was considerably higher in the plastics and food firms than in the container firms. Furthermore, as shown in Figure 6-18, virtually every department in the plastics and foods firms had to cope with more uncertainty than did any of the three departments in the container industry. And in the container firms, all the departments faced about the same level of uncertainty. In the plastics and foods firms, the research departments faced highly uncertain environments, while the other departments faced predictable environments.[30]

In turn, the departments in the plastics and foods industries were more differentiated than those in the container firms in terms of how structured they were, and in their goal, time, and interpersonal orientations.

In terms of how the firms achieved integration or coordination, Lawrence and Lorsch found the following.[31] First (see Table 6-3), there are some striking differences in the methods used by each of the firms to achieve coordination. Both successful firms in the relatively uncertain plastics and foods industries utilized special integrating units. In the plastics firm, a special integrating department had been established, as well as permanent cross-functional committees at various managerial levels. The successful foods company utilized one person as an integrator and maintained temporary cross-functional teams.

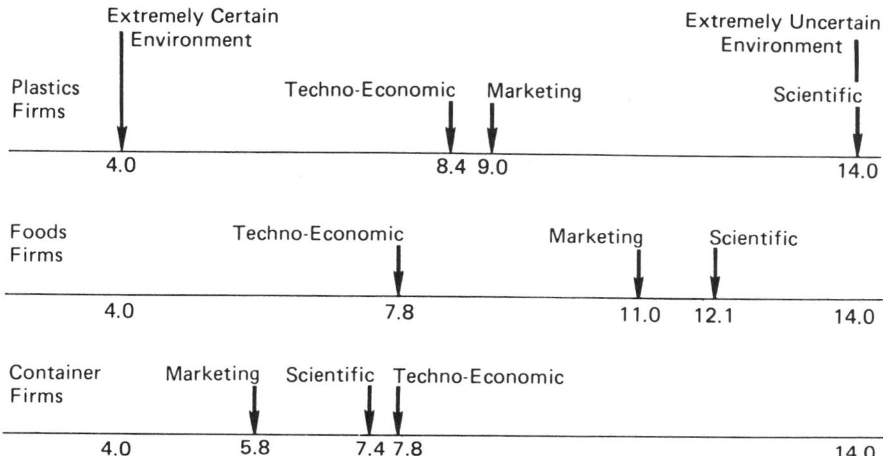

FIGURE 6-18 Average Uncertainty Facing Different Departments in Three Industries. *Source:* Adapted from Paul R. Lawrence and Jay W. Lorsch, *Organization and Environment* (Boston: Division of Research, Graduate School of Business Administration, Harvard University, 1967), p. 95.

The high-performing container firm, which was operating in a more stable environment, achieved coordination through the organizational hierarchy.[32]

On the other hand, managers in the *low*-performing container firm were trying to achieve coordination through a formal integrating department. This department, which reported to the general manager of the firm, had the assigned function of integrating sales requirements and production capacity. However, such a special integrating unit, which had worked so successfully in the more uncertain and rapidly changing plastics and foods industries, seemed inappropriate and ineffective in the more stable container environment. As a matter of fact, it led to "considerable confusion about where conflicts were to be resolved," and this contributed to the poor performance of this firm.

Finally, as shown in Table 6-3, the six other "coordination" factors also influenced whether coordination was achieved, and whether conflicts were dealt with effectively. Coordination was more effective when:

1 The integrating person or group was hierarchically about midway between the departments being coordinated
2 The integrator had a good deal of influence
3 The integrators were rewarded for doing a good job of coordinating
4 The amount of authority or influence lower-level employees had was high (plastics and food firms) or low (container firms)
5 The firm was centralized (container firms) or decentralized (plastics and food firms)[33]

TABLE 6-3 How High- and Low-Performing Firms in Three Industries Achieved Integration and Conflict Resolution

	*Average Level of Differentiation**	*Average Level of Integration***	*Integrating Device*	*Intermediate Position of Integrators*
PLASTICS				
High Perf.	10.7	5.6	Special department	Yes
Low Perf.	9.0	5.1	Special department	Sometimes
FOODS				
High Perf.	8.0	5.3	Special Individuals	Yes
Low Perf.	6.5	5.0	Special departments	No
CONTAINERS				
High Perf.	5.7	5.7	Hierarchy	N.A.
Low Perf.	5.7	4.8	Special department	N.A.

*Reflects how different departments were from each other in terms of such factors as formality of structure, time and goal orientation, and interpersonal relationships. Higher number reflects greater differentiation between departments.
**Reflects such factors as the quality of relations between departments. Higher number reflects higher integration.
Source: Gary Dessler, *Organization and Management* (Englewood Cliffs, N.J.: Prentice-Hall, 1976), pp. 146–47.

In addition, all the successful firms utilized open confrontation and a problem-solving approach to resolve conflicts to a much greater extent than did the low-performing firms.

The Van de Ven, Delbecq, Koenig Studies[34] Subjects here included supervisors and personnel in offices of the administrative headquarters of a large state employment agency. The sample consisted of 197 formal work units, with each work unit "consisting of a supervisor and all nonsupervisory personnel immediately reporting to a supervisor."

As one aspect of their study, the researchers sought to determine the relation between the "task uncertainty" facing a work unit and how the unit achieved coordination. Six methods for achieving coordination were considered: rules, plans, "vertical channels" (referral of problems by the subordinates to their supervisor),

TABLE 6-3 How High- and Low-Performing Firms in Three Industries Achieved Integration and Conflict Resolution (*cont.*)

Influence of Integrating Departments	*Reward System for Integrators*	*Total Level of Organizational Influence*	*Influence at Required Level*	*Mode of Conflict Resolution*
Integrators very high	Overall product group stressed	High	Yes Decentralized	Almost all confrontation; problem-solving
Integrators very high	Integrators' solo performance in functional area stresed	Low	No Centralized	Little confrontation; some forcing and smoothing
Integrators high	Overall product group stressed	High	Yes Decentralized	Confrontation; problem-solving
All units about the same	Overall product group stressed	Low	No Centralized	Confrontation; problem-solving
All functional departments about same	N.A.	Low	Yes Centralized	Confrontation; problem-solving
Sales high	N.A.	High	No Decentralized	Less confrontation

"horizontal channels" (designated work coordinators or informal contact between unit members), unscheduled meetings, and scheduled meetings.

Research findings, presented in Figure 6-19, suggest the following: As the uncertainty of the tasks undertaken by a work unit increases, the use of *impersonal* coordination techniques like rules and plans decreases significantly, and the use of personal and group coordination increases significantly. According to the researchers, as task uncertainty increased from low to high, there were substantial decreases in the use of impersonal rules and plans for work coordination, and large increases in the use of horizontal communication channels and both scheduled and unscheduled group meetings. However, the use of "vertical channels"—the hierarchy, where the supervisor is used to coordinate work activities within the unit—remained quite stable regardless of how uncertain the task. The researchers conclude that as task uncertainty increases, horizontal channels and group meetings are substituted for and replace impersonal modes of coordination like rules and plans, and the hierarchy.

Increased uncertainty seems to result in the increased use of "unprogrammed," personal types of coordination mechanisms like unscheduled and sched-

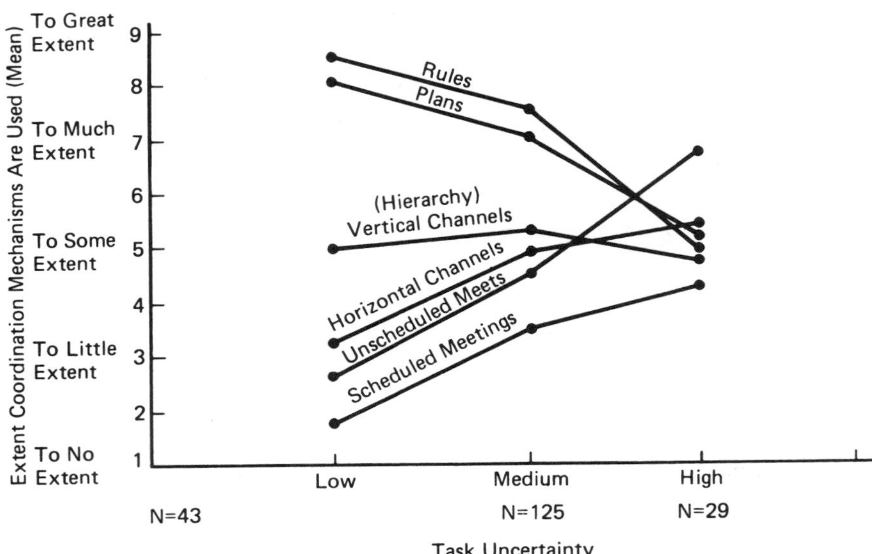

FIGURE 6-19 Coordination Mechanisms Used by Level of Task Uncertainty. *Source:* Andrew H. Van de Ven, Andre L. Delbecq, and Richard Koenig, Jr., "Determinants of Coordination Modes within Organizations," *American Sociological Review,* Vol. 41 (April 1976), 330.

uled meetings. It is true, though, that organizations that rely on such impersonal mechanisms for dealing with uncertainty are also more effective?

The evidence here suggests that the answer is "yes." In a study conducted in 30 hospital emergency units in six midwestern states, Argote measured uncertainty, coordination, and organizational effectiveness and concluded that "programmed means of coordination made a greater contribution to organizational effectiveness under conditions of low uncertainty than under conditions of high uncertainty." Conversely, she found that "non-programmed means of coordination made a greater contribution to organizational effectiveness when uncertainty was high than when it was low."[35] At least in this study of hospital emergency rooms, then, fitting the coordination mechanism to the uncertainty of the task resulted in improved effectiveness, where effectiveness was measured in terms of such criteria as the efficiency with which patients are processed and the quality of nursing and medical care they receive.

• *Implications*

1 The first coordination techniques a manager should implement are mutual adjustment, rules, targets, and a hierarchy. These are the simplest and most basic

facilitators or coordination. Managers typically turn to other methods only when these are no longer effective at achieving coordination.

2 The more interdependent the departments are, the more difficult is the task of coordinating them and the more complicated the coordinative mechanism may be. As a rule, functional departmentation results in higher interdependence. Divisional departmentation results in less interdependence. One way to reduce your role as a coordinator is thus to put each subordinate in charge of a product division. You increase your coordinative job by putting each subordinate in charge of separate functions like production, sales, and finance.

3 The more diverse the interests, values, and goals of the departments to be coordinated, the more difficult is the job of coordinating them. For instance, departments like engineering and production tend to have employees whose backgrounds and values (such as an emphasis on efficiency) are similar. Disagreements here are thus less likely to occur, and achieving coordination is not too difficult. On the other hand, the backgrounds and values of employees in some departments (like basic research and production) tend to be quite dissimilar. Production people might have a short-run, efficiency orientation while research scientists have a long-run orientation and tend toward inefficiency. Here, problems and disagreements are more likely to arise, and coordination is hampered and made more difficult to achieve. Special committees, liaisons, and integrators are thus required.

4 As the number of unexpected problems increases, you should rely less on rules and targets for coordination, and more on scheduled and unscheduled committee meetings, liaisons, and integrators. Mechanistic organizations, therefore, rely more on rules, targets, and the hierarchy for achieving coordination. Organic organizations rely more on committees, liaisons, mutual adjustment, and integrators.

SUMMARY

In this chapter, we explained the basic approaches to organizing departments. Departmentalizing an enterprise by function involves grouping activities around the central functions, like production, marketing, and finance. This is a simple and efficient method of organizing, one that minimizes duplication of effort. Disadvantages include a reduction in responsiveness when the organization gets so large that the person responsible for coordinating the departments becomes overloaded.

The other basic approach to organizing departments is to organize them around product divisions. These organizations can be more sensitive and responsive to the needs of their product or product lines, and performances can be more easily judged. On the other hand, divisionalization often results in duplication of effort and could lead to a loss of top-management control. Other popular approaches to departmentation include departmentation by customer, marketing channel, and territory, and matrix departmentation.

As a rule, departments are arranged around functions where efficiency is more important than responsiveness; products, customers, or area are not diverse; and the situation is stable and unchanging. Arrange departments around products (or customers, market channels, or geographic areas) where the enterprise is so large and its services so diverse that one person alone can no longer coordinate the required functions; being sensitive and responsive to the unique needs of the product is paramount; adequate controls can be implemented by top management; developing general managers is important; and the product (customer, market channel, or area) produces enough volume to warrant a separate general manager and department.

Departments and their managers can also be identified as either line or staff units. Line managers are authorized to issue orders down the chain of command. Staff managers, on the other hand, are authorized to assist and advise line managers. Personal staff report to the executive each serves—compiling data for that person, analyzing problems, and giving advice. Specialist staff advises all the other managers in the organization—for instance, in areas like quality control and industrial engineering. Most small enterprises tend to opt for the pure line form of organization. As the organization grows, however, the manager needs some means of providing the sort of specialized assistance the staff unit can provide. The use of staff is a function of the size of the organization and its technology.

Coordination is the process of achieving unity of action among interdependent activities. It is essential whenever two or more interdependent individuals, groups, or departments seek to achieve a common goal. Techniques for achieving coordination include mutual adjustment, rules or procedures, divisional or matrix departmentation, a staff assistant, liaisons, committees and task forces, and independent integrators.

DISCUSSION QUESTIONS

1 Explain the basic advantages and disadvantages of divisional and functional departmentation.

2 Exlain why and under what circumstances you would use a divisional or a functional approach to departmentation.

3 Assume you are a president and have four functional vice-presidents (for production, sales, finance, and personnel) reporting directly to you. Your company manufactures and sells cleaning products (soaps, detergents, etc.) to industrial, consumer, and government customers. Consumer products (face soaps, etc.) are sold through drugstores and supermarkets, and sales to all other customers are handled directly by your company's salespersons. Develop an organization chart showing what you think would be a logical way to organize your company, assuming that you want to maintain a functional departmentation at the vice-presidential level. Now, assume you find yourself overburdened and want to reorganize completely. Draw a new or-

ganization chart, making sure you are prepared to explain how divisional departmentalization, staff, and coordination could all be used to obtain the advantages you desire (mainly, reducing the burden on you).

4 Explain when and under what circumstances you would use each of the coordination techniques we explained in this chapter.

FOOTNOTES

[1]Ernest Dale, *Organization* (New York: AMA, 1967), p. 109.

[2]For a discussion of this type of organization and its problems, see Stanley Davis and Paul Lawrence, *Matrix* (Reading, Mass.: Addison-Wesley, 1967); and Davis and Lawrence, "Problems of Matrix Organizations," *Harvard Business Review,* May–June 1978, pp. 131–42. For an explanation of how matrix organizations evolve, see Harvey F. Kolodny, "Evolution to a matrix organization," *Academy of Management Review,* Vol. 4, No. 4 (October 1979), 543–53. For a discussion of the sociological and psychological impact of matrix departmentation, see H.R. Smith, "A Socio-Biological Look at Matrix," *Academy of Management Review,* Vol. 3, No. 4 (October 1978), 922–26.

[3]Arthur Walker and Jay Lorsch, "Organizational Choice: Product vs. Function," *Harvard Business Review,* Vol. 46, No. 6 (1968), 133–34.

[4]*Ibid.*

[5]Alfred Chandler, *Strategy and Structure* (Cambridge, Mass.: M.I.T. Press, 1962), p. 362.

[6]Arthur Jay Kover, "Reorganization in an Advertising Agency: A Case Study of a Decrease in Integration," *Human Organization,* Vol. 22 (Winter 1963), 252–59.

[7]Some researchers have found organizations that successfully implemented the functional organization. For an example of this, see Joan Woodward, *Industrial Organization: Theory and Practice* (London: Oxford University Press, 1965). Woodward discovered two firms in the process industry with such an organization.

[8]Woodward, *Industrial Organization.*

[9]*Ibid.,* p. 101.

[10]*Ibid.,* pp. 102–3.

[11]Woodward, however, found that the size and use of staff were *not* related. See *Ibid.,* p. 31.

[12]A.W. Baker and R.C. Davis, "Ratios of Staff to Line Employees and Stages of Differentiation of Staff Functions," *Research Monograph No. 72,* Bureau of Business Research, The Ohio State University, 1954. Also, see John Child, "Parkinson's Progress: Accounting for the Number of Specialists in Organizations," *Administrative Science Quarterly,* September 1973, pp. 328–48.

[13]B. DeSpelder, "Ratios of Staff to Line Personnel," *Research Monograph No. 106,* Bureau of Business Research, The Ohio State University, 1962.

[14]Mason Haire, "Biological Models and Empirical Models and Empirical Histories of the Growth of Organizations," in *Modern Organization Theory,* ed. Mason Haire (New York: John Wiley, 1959), pp. 272–306.

[15]Allen C. Filley, "Decisions and Research in Staff Utilizations," *Academy of Management Journal,* September 1963, pp. 220–31.

[16]For a discussion of this, see James Thompson, *Organizations in Action* (New York: McGraw-Hill, 1967).

[17]James D. Mooney and Allen C. Reilley, *The Principles of Organization* (New York: Harper & Row, 1939), p. 5.

[18]Mary Parker Follett, *Dynamic Administration,* eds. Henry C. Metcalf and L. Urwick (New York: Harper, 1942). Sherman Krupp, *Pattern in Organization Analysis* (New York: Holt, Rinehart & Winston, 1961).

[19]Luther Gulick, "Notes on the Theory of Organization," in papers of the *Science of Administration* by L. Gulick and L. Urwick (The Institute of Public Administration, 1972), pp. 31–37.

[20]James J. March and Herbert A. Simon, *Organizations* (New York: John Wiley, 1958), pp. 158–61.

[21]*Ibid.,* p. 160. Note also that the need for coordination presumes the existence of interdependence and that as the interdependence among organizational units increases, the need for coordination does as well. See, for example, Joseph Cheng, "Interdependence and Coordination in Organizations: A Role-System Analysis," *Academy of Management Journal,* Vol. 26, No. 1 (March 1983), 156–62.

[22]Jay Galbraith, "Organizational Design: An Information Processing View," *Interfaces,* Vol. 4, No. 3 (1974) 28–36, and *Organizational Design* (Reading, Mass.: Addison-Wesley, 1977).

[23]Henry Mintzberg, *Structure in Fives: Designing Effective Organizations* (Englewood Cliffs, N.J.: Prentice-Hall, 1983), pp. 4–9.

[24]Mintzberg, *Structure in Fives,* p. 4.

[25]Paul Lawrence and Jay Lorsch, *Organization and Environment* (Cambridge, Mass.: Harvard University Press, 1967).

[26]*Ibid.,* p. 6.

[27]Thomas Peters and Robert Waterman, Jr., *In Search of Excellence* (New York: Harper & Row, 1982), p. 105.

[28]Paul Lawrence and Jay Lorsch, *Organization and Environment* (Boston: Division of Research, Graduate School of Business Administration, Harvard University, 1967), p. 1. Note that *inter*organizational coordination also occurs, and that the effectiveness of such "boundary spanning" activities affects the performance of the organization. See, for example, Marc Dollinger, "Environmental Boundary Spanning and Information Processing Effects on Organizational Performance," *Academy of Management Journal,* Vol. 27, No. 2 (June 1984), 351–68.

[29]Paul R. Lawrence and Jay W. Lorsch, "Differentiation and Integration in Complex Organizations," *Administrative Science Quarterly,* Vol. 12, No. 1 (June 1967), 1–47.

[30]Lawrence and Lorsch, *Organization and Environment,* p. 93.

[31]*Ibid.,* pp. 95–96.

[32]*Ibid.,* p. 138.

[33]*Ibid.,* pp. 140–51.

[34]Andrew H. Van de Ven, Andre L. Delbecq, and Richard Koenig, Jr., "Determinants of Coordination Modes within Organizations," *American Sociological Review,* Vol. 41 (April 1976), 322–38.

[35]Linda Argote, "Input Uncertainty and Organizational Coordination in Hospital Emergency Units," *Administrative Science Quarterly,* Vol. 27, No. 3 (September 1982), 420–34.

CASE FOR CHAPTER 6
HOW XEROX SPEEDS UP THE BIRTH OF NEW PRODUCTS
Three Promising Copiers Are the Result of Gutting a Stagnant Bureaucracy and Slashing Costs*

After 18 years with Xerox Corp., the only corporate memento Wayland R. Hicks displays on his office wall is the 1983 Grand Prize for Good Design in Business Machines awarded by Japan's Ministry of International Trade & Industry. Xerox's 1075

*Reprinted from *Business Week,* March 19, 1984.

copier, whose stellar performance last year helped halt the company's profit slide, is the first U.S. product to win this honor. But for Hicks, head of the Reprographics Business Group, the award brought more than the usual satisfaction—it was Japanese competitors who just three years ago threatened to drive Xerox out of the copier business.

Now, Hicks is hoping for another triumph. On Mar. 6, Xerox rolled out three copiers that pick up where the 1075 left off. They are the first machines to emerge from a radically new product development process that Xerox began fashioning three years ago when the 1075 and other early machines in the 10 Series were already in the works. For Xerox, once the quintessential innovator that pioneered and dominated the worldwide market for plain-paper copiers—and then lost more than half of it—the future of its backbone copier business may well rest on its new approach to product development.

• *Trimming Paperwork*

To get the machines to market quickly and at lower cost, Xerox gutted an overgrown bureaucratic structure that had weighed the company down with staggering design and manufacturing costs. First it established touch benchmarks. It compared itself in extraordinary detail with the best of its rivals, including its own affiliate, Fuji Xerox Co. It studied how many drawings an average Japanese engineer makes in a year, and compared how much space workers take on the factory floor. Then it collapsed its cumbersome decision-making hierarchy, shifting power from the president's office to the project engineer's desk. And it laid off 17,000 people and cut manufacturing costs more than 50%.

In all, "we cut in half the resources and the time we used to require to develop comparable products three years ago," says Hicks. " 'Benchmarking' is driving our whole business today."

Something had to. Although Xerox created the plain-paper copier business, it ignored the low end of the market that ignited when the Japanese introduced reliable—and inexpensive—machines in the mid-1970s. By 1982, Xerox's market share had sunk to less than 45% from 96% in 1970. From a 1981 high of $8.5 billion, Xerox's sales slipped two years in a row. Last year, the company had to rely on diversification into financial services to mask a continued drop in profits from its basic businesses. Net income fell 22% from a 1981 high of $598 million, and the Crum & Forster Inc. insurance group Xerox bought in January 1983 supplied one-forth of its net income.

Xerox had once hoped to guarantee growth in the 1980s by supplying the exploding office automation market. The company still has two bright spots in its electronic Memorywriter typewriter and electronic printing products, but some observers see its pounce on financial services as an admission that troubles in the office unit are beyond repair.

• *Staying Competitive*

But in its copier business, which still accounts for an estimated 75% of sales, Xerox seems determined to correct its problems. The product development changes it has made range from rethinking basic principles to massive capital spending. President David T. Kearns insists: "We will do what is necessary to remain competitive."

One key change involves decision making. Xerox executives now freely admit that the company had strangled itself with a matrix organization. The heads of groups such as product planning, design, service, and manufacturing were based in Rochester, N.Y., but reported to separate executives at corporate headquarters in Stamford, Conn. Each group worked products through its own hierarchy, then handed them off to the next one. The groups had endless debates over features and design tradeoffs, and "no one had the priority for getting products out," Hicks recalls. Disagreements often reached all the way to the president's office in Stamford.

Now four strategic business units (SBUs) run the copier business. General managers, who each set long-range strategy and oversee product development, report to the 41-year-old Hicks. He in turn answers to one executive at headquarters. This has resulted in an immediate 10% productivity gain, Hicks says. Engineering cycles for some products have been shortened by 50%.

Development of one of the new copiers—the 9900—took three years. That compares with more than five years for a comparable earlier product, says Eric L. Steenburgh, general manager of the High Volume Business Unit. The 9900, a costly ($130,000) copier meant to compete with offset printing machines, has a video monitor that displays instructions and allows the user to program the machine. Last August the team working on software for the machine encountered programming troubles that threatened a major delay. The software codes were failing to trigger the automatic stapler and were not getting messages up on the screen fast enough. In the old days, says chief engineer Daniel W. Cholish, the software designers would have worked alone to sole the problem. This time, a "crisis team" including software designers and manufacturing engineers worked through the Labor Day weekend. "We figured out the bugs and didn't slip the schedule," says Cholish. "To get that commitment would have been impossible in the past."

These days, the development process at Xerox usually begins with ideas generated by an SBU. (An SBU or Strategic Business Unit is a "super division," which is composed of several product divisions. A large company like Xerox may be departmentalized into several SBUs at its highest levels.) These are immediately tested for feasibility by small "product-synthesis" teams that quickly weed out the losers. Several competing teams of designers produce a prototype, sometimes taking up to six months. If the model cannot meet pre-set goals, the project is killed. "We've learned not to fear failure," says Hicks. The old system tended to prevent early mercy killing. "We used to have 200 or 300 people working on a project and sometimes ended up killing it," recalls Hicks.

If a "go" decision is reached, a product "delivery" team headed by a chief engineer takes the prototype through to manufacturing. Meanwhile, market research and benchmarking will have sketched out performance requirements as well as boundaries for development and manufacturing costs. The chief engineer also takes charge of developing a manufacturing process in a pilot plant housed near the design team—a practice borrowed from Japanese rivals.

Nowhere was the value of elevating the role of the chief engineer more evident than in a mid-term design crisis with one of the first 10 Series copiers, the 1045. The machine was in pilot manufacturing when William A. Drawe, then chief engineer, discovered that the wire harness—a device holding some 40 wires connecting internal components—did not meet quality standards. The automatic equipment designed to make the harness required large-gauge wire that eased assembly but caused electrical problems because of its rigidity.

The engineers quickly redesigned the harness to include finer wires. That solved the quality problems. But the supplier's equipment could not connect the wires automatically—a necessary step for Xerox to meet its cost goal. Drawe boldly decided to scrap the $1 million investment in the old automated equipment. Within three months he found another vendor who could supply the gear. Under the old setup, he says, "no one would have stood up and said 'We blew $1 million!' We would have fought to make the original equipment work and probably would have ended up with a high-priced harness."

The episode also was a learning experience in the company's efforts to involve suppliers earlier in the design process. "When we first started getting our suppliers involved early, we were telling them what to do," says Drawe, adding that Xerox had largely dictated design to the first wire harness machine maker. "We were successful the second time because we explained the problem, presented a new design, and let the supplier decide how to design the equipment."

Xerox combined these changes in product development with draconian cost-cutting in manufacturing. It spent $45 million to automate materials-handling and some assembly operations and to computerize inventory tracking systems. These investments, in turn cut the labor force by 34%. Also, vendors now are required to ship materials as they are needed in the factory. Since 1980, this has saved Xerox $240 million in inventory costs. Another 21% savings was realized by ordering larger quantities initially and giving longer contracts.

To improve quality, Xerox asked suppliers to adopt statistical quality control—a type of continuous monitoring common in Japan but not the U.S. If they resisted, "we stopped doing business with them," says Charles F. Christ, president of the Reprographics Manufacturing Group. Christ cut the number of vendors to 400 from 5,000 and last year slashed the defect rate on incoming parts to one-tenth of its 1980 level.

The cumulative effect of such efforts shows throughout the 10 Series. Xerox says it can now build these copiers for 35% to 75% less than the ones they replaced, and claims quality has improved as well. At $10,500, the existing 1045 now costs 42% less than its predecessor, the 3450, did in 1979. Xerox says back orders and multiple orders are at record levels. One aerospace customer, who had dropped the Xerox in 1981 but recently leased 200 of the 1045s, says the machines "will keep Xerox's customers from going to someone else."

Experts also applaud the two new additions of the 10 Series. Both the 1048, costing $7,995, and the 1055, at $14,500, can automatically copy two-sided originals; the 1055 also can reduce, enlarge, and fold to an extent not available on competing copiers. Xerox, says Monica H. Camahort, an associate director at consultants Dataquest Inc., has "added strong products at good prices which bring new sophistication to the market."

Still, Xerox has yet to prove itself in the low end of the copier market, where its share last year slipped to 10.4% from 12.3% in 1982. The hot new entry in that segment is Canon Inc.'s $995 personal copier, a product Xerox will try to match within four months, according to insiders. At the same time, the Japanese are moving into the medium- and high-performance end of the market, Xerox's breadbasket. By midyear, Ricoh Co. will unveil its mid-range 6680 in the U.S.

Meanwhile, the increased electronic content of copiers continues to drive prices down, further squeezing profits. Thus some analysts wonder if Xerox can improve margins, which have fallen since 1979, even with its productivity gains. "The ability to turn a profit remains to be seen," says Eugene G. Glazer of Dean Witter Reynolds Inc.

• *A Winning Hand*

Xerox faces an even more formidable challenge in office systems. The company reorganized this group last June, and it decided to make its products compatible with standards set by International Business Machines Corp. and American Telephone & Telegraph Co. But observers are unmoved. "I see nothing that tells me they have their act together," says a competitor.

The company could regain a winning hand if it plays its strong suit wisely. As some see it, computers, coupled with electronic printers, may supplant copiers by the end of this decade. This trend could work wonders for Xerox, since the company now holds a preeminent position in electronic printing—itself a burgeoning market. Indeed, its position is similar to the one it held at the start of the copier boom, but there are signs of *déjà vu*. IBM, for instance, is investing millions to dominate the high end of electronic printing while Ricoh and Canon have jumped into the low end.

Xerox believes it will not make the same mistakes again. "The Japanese did not make the cost/quality trade-off; they found you can have both. We did, too," says Kearns. "We will never again make the error of underestimating the competition." With its new product development structure in place, Xerox at least has a chance to prove that is true.

Questions

1 Draw, to the best of your ability, the current organization chart of Xerox. What type of departmentation do they have? How do they achieve coordination for product development?

2 What do you think it was about the firm's "matrix organization" that made it inappropriate for Xerox?

7

Organizational Hierarchy and Delegation

OVERVIEW

The purpose of this chapter is to explain the nature of *decentralization,* which can be defined as delegating authority to subordinates for most decisions while maintaining control over essential companywide matters. Included is an explanation of the nature of decentralization and of the factors that determine the extent to which it can and should take place.

The outline of this chapter is as follows:

A. Decentralization
  1 The process of delegation
  2 Decentralization defined
  3 Decentralization and control
  4 Decentralization, communication, and delegation
  5 Divisionalization and decentralization
  6 Situational determinants of decentralization
  7 Implications
B Hierarchical levels and the span of control
  1 Flat vs. tall organizations
  2 Spans of control

DECENTRALIZATION

• The Process of Delegation

Organizing departments and jobs would be impossible without *delegation,* which we can define as the pushing down of the authority from superior to subordinate. This is because the assignment of responsibility for some department or job usually goes hand in hand with the delegation of adequate authority to get the job done. For example, it would be inappropriate to assign a subordinate the responsibility for designing a new product and then tell her she hasn't the authority to hire designers or choose the best design.

But although *authority* can be delegated, *responsibility* cannot. You can *assign* responsibility to a subordinate. However, most managers and management writers would agree that you are still ultimately responsible for ensuring that the job gets done properly. Since you retain the ultimate responsibility for the performance of the job, delegation of authority always entails the creation of *accountability.* Thus, your subordinates automatically become accountable to you for the performance of the tasks assigned to them.

• Decentralization Defined

Decentralizing means *delegating authority to subordinates for most decisions while maintaining control over essential companywide matters.* At General Motors, for instance, the executives in charge of each car line (Buick, Chevrolet, and so on) can make a wide range of production, sales, and design decisions regarding their cars, but the president of GM retains tight *centralized* control over essential organization-wide matters like allocating money for new plants and managing the cash that flows in from consumers. As at GM, "decentralized" companies are usually those organized around product divisions. This is because product-division managers usually have wide-ranging authority and considerable autonomy.

Notice that although they are often used interchangeably, *delegation* and *decentralization* do not mean the same thing. Delegation simply means pushing authority down to subordinates. Decentralization involves (1) determining *what* authority to push down to subordinates (for instance, giving a manager the authority to manage a large plant); (2) developing policies and rules to guide subordinates who have this authority delegated to them (for instance, by telling the manager that all expenditures over $100,000 must be approved by you); and (3) implementing selective but adequate controls for monitoring performance (for instance, by having the auditors check the plant manager's expenditures periodically). When an organization is highly *centralized,* most decisions must be channeled up the chain of command to the president. When an organization is highly *decentralized,* most decisions can be made lower in the organization, and the president need be contacted only regarding selected major decisions.

Example The General Motors Corporation provides a good example of decentralization in practice.[1]

When former president Alfred Sloan first developed GM's decentralized structure, his approach was based on two principles:

1 First, he said that the responsibility attached to the top manager of each car division should in no way be limited. Each division was to be headed by a top manager and be complete "in every necessary function" so that it could exercise "its full initiative" and logical development.

2 However, "certain central organization functions are absolutely essential for the logical development and proper control of the corporation's activities."

In other words, Sloan believed that each of his division managers (like those for the Buick, Chevrolet, and Cadillac divisions) should have complete, self-contained divisions, each of which would do its own manufacturing, marketing, hiring, and so forth.

But Sloan knew that delegating this much authority to his top managers could result in matters drifting out of control. He therefore said that certain "essential functions" would have to be controlled *centrally*. To implement this, Sloan expanded the company's central staff and created (or expanded) many special staff functions for monitoring and controlling the firm's operating divisions. For example, he expanded the finance committee and made it responsible for authorizing dividend rates, top-management salaries, and major appropriations. In this way, GM's central-office staff ended up controlling such things as:

- *Capital appropriations.* For example, all projects requiring capital expenditures had to be submitted to an appropriate committee functioning under the finance and executive committees. All requests were given uniform treatment, and funds were approved for projects on the basis of their relative value to the corporation.
- *Cash.* A system was set up whereby all incoming cash receipts were deposited in certain specified banks. The operating divisions (Buick, Cadillac, etc.) had no control over cash withdrawals or transfers, and all cash accounts were administered by the headquarters financial staff.
- *Inventory.* A new inventory control system was established that was tied to division managers' forecasts of the number of cars and trucks to be produced. These forecasts were submitted to corporate headquarters for approval on a monthly basis, and inventory levels had to be kept within the quantities required by the approved forecast.
- *Division profitability.* A system of interlocking financial ratios was established whereby each division was measured in terms of profits relative to invested capital. Each division, in other words, was evaluated in terms of its overall profitability, on the assumption that, as Sloan put it, "if we had the means to review and judge the effectiveness of operations, we could safely leave the prosecution of those operations to the men in charge of them."

Decentralization at GM therefore represented a shrewd balance between delegated authority and centralized control. On the one hand, division managers had considerable autonomy and the means for designing, producing, and marketing their cars. On the other hand, Sloan was able to maintain control of this far-flung company by centralizing—retaining control over—major decisions regarding capital appropriations, cash allocations, and inventory levels. Thus, decentralization is an approach to organizing and managing that involves *both* selective delegation of authority *and* centralized control over essential matters.

• *Decentralization and Control*

Finding the right balance between autonomy and control is the crucial issue in the art of decentralizing.

An example can illustrate this.[2] Capital budgeting decisions are among the most important that managers make. They involve questions of how, and how much, money is to be spent on capital items like machinery, trucks, and computers. At one extreme, a president could fully *centralize* all capital budgeting decisions by insisting that he or she personally approve, ahead of time, all capital expenditures. Thus, all requests must first go to the president for approval. At the other extreme, the president could fully *decentralize* all these decisions by giving managers the autonomy—by delegating to them the authority—to make capital expenditures without checking with him, or even advising him that the expenditure has been made.

The pros and cons of these two extremes are as follows. With full *centralization,* the volume of work the president has to cope with might be enormous, since he personally has to review every request. Furthermore, delays could be so high (since managers have to wait for the review and decisions) that good opportunities—say, for a bargain on a new truck—might be missed. And the cost of duplicating and transmitting all the necessary documents to the president could be very high. On the other hand, full *decentralization* could lead to a loss of control. If all managers are permitted to spend as they like, they may purchase duplicating equipment inefficiently, for example.

As a result, most actual attempts at decentralization fall between these two extremes. For example, the president might declare that (1) he need be asked for approval only on expenditures over $5,000; (2) the managers can make their own decision on items costing less than $5,000, up to a total of $80,000; and (3) the president must be *informed* within three months after *any* purchase. Decisions regarding capital expenditures are thus effectively decentralized: Managers are delegated the authority to make most capital expenditure decisions themselves, and the president retains control over essential (major) expenditure decisions.

• *Decentralization, Communication, and Delegation*

For a clearer picture of how to decentralize, it is useful to understand that there is both a *communication* and a *delegation* aspect to decentralizing.[3]

The Communication Aspect First, "decentralization" refers to the extent to which employees must channel all their communications *directly* through the head or "hub" of the organization. For example, must the finance, production, and sales managers communicate with one another *only* through the president, or are they permitted to communicate directly in arriving at a joint decision? The more that *all* communications must be channeled through the president, the more centralized the firm is. The more that the managers can communicate directly with each other, the more *decentralized* the firm is.

There are two important things to remember about the communication aspect of decentralization. First, it reflects the extent to which *all* communication *must* be channeled through the president. The more that communication can bypass the president, the more decentralized the structure. Second, notice that to decentralize (in a communication sense), the president must alter the organization structure itself—must, in other words, change the pattern of permissible interactions so that fewer communications need be channeled through the president. He or she must *either* have fewer subordinates reporting directly to him or her, or permit more direct communication between the subordinates (or both). Thus, one way to decentralize is to let subordinates communicate on more matters directly; a second way is to reorganize so that some of your current subordinates report not to you, but to a new "middle layer" of managers between you and those subordinates. This is summarized in Figure 7-1.

The Delegation Aspect of Decentralization The communication aspect of decentralization is not by itself sufficient to explain what most *managers* mean by decentralization. In management jargon, a manager can decentralize but still retain the same organizational structure. What does change is the content—the activities that each subordinate carries out. Specifically, *delegation* takes place, subordinates are given more autonomy, and as a result, the organization is more "decentralized" (from a managerial point of view). The words *delegation* and *decentralization* are therefore inseparable; in fact, many writers equate the two, although to do so is not quite accurate.[4]

There are usually several dimensions along which boss and subordinate interact. For example, the dean of business and his or her chairpersons in a university may have to interact along several dimensions—say, on matters of budget, curriculum, staffing, and travel. When delegation takes place, it means that one or more of these dimensions are cut completely, or that, at least, the volume of required interactions has been reduced. Thus, if the chairperson has to get prior approval before making *any* budget, curriculum, staffing, or travel decision, the organization is highly centralized and delegation is at a minimum. If a chairperson is told that he or she no longer has to inform the dean at all of the budget decisions, then some delegation has taken place—the budget dimension has been cut. If the chairperson is told to get prior approval only for budget expenditures in excess of $10,000, then some delegation has also taken place, since the volume of required interactions (along the

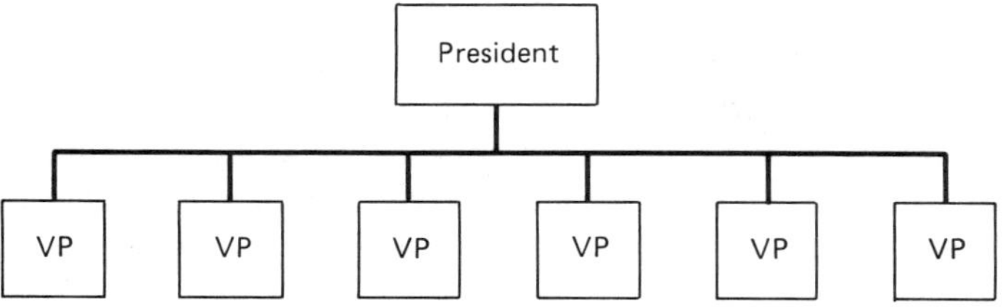

1. Let your vice-presidents communicate directly, rather than through you, as below:

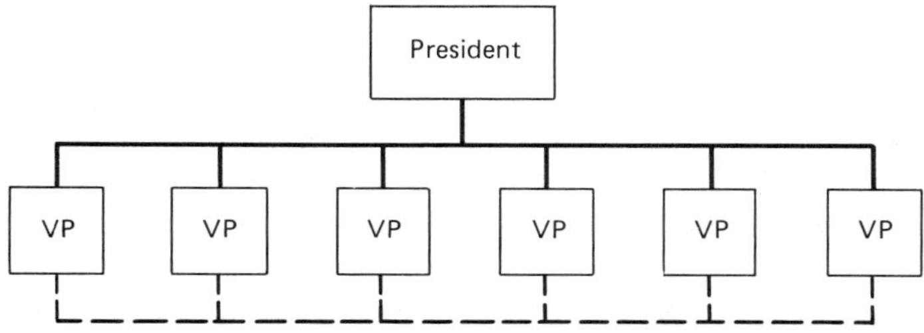

2. Or reorganize, so that fewer vice-presidents report to you, and so more communication takes place below your level.

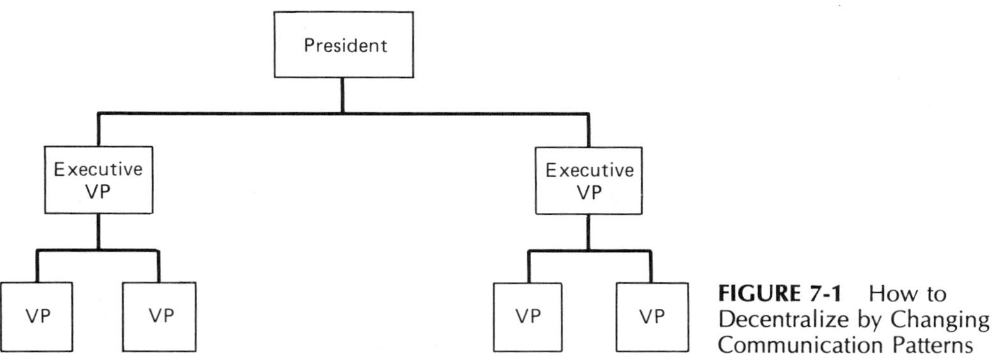

FIGURE 7-1 How to Decentralize by Changing Communication Patterns

budget dimension) will have been reduced. Delegation always means that the subordinate has more autonomy—that he or she can act with more independence.

In terms of the delegation aspect, decentralization can thus range from "abdication" (total decentralization) to total centralization. Total decentralization occurs when all the required links between subordinate and superior are broken—when for instance, a chairperson no longer has to check at all with a dean before making budget, travel, schedule, or curriculum decisions. At the other extreme, total centralization implies an absence of delegation. Here, for instance, a chairperson cannot make *any* budget, travel, schedule or curriculum decisions without first checking with the dean. (As you might imagine, this can be very time-consuming for the dean, which explains a main disadvantage of centralization, as we discuss below.) In practice, the degree of delegation usually falls between these two extremes: For example, the dean might tell the chairpersons that the latter can make most budget decisions themselves but must get the dean's approval for all expenditures over $10,000. In fact, the art of obtaining just this right balance between delegation ("Make most budget decisions yourself") and control ("I have to approve all expenditures over $10,000") is what many managers believe constitutes "decentralization" in the truest sense.[5]

In summary, there are two basic ways to increase the degree of decentralization in an organization. First, you can reduce your span of control and have subordinates who previously reported directly to you now report instead to your remaining subordinates. Another communication change would be to allow more direct communication between your subordinates (perhaps by forming a special interdepartmental committee), so that they no longer have to communicate with one another only through you. Second, you can leave the organization structure as it is and change the *content* of your interactions with your subordinates. Specifically, you can *delegate*—give them more autonomy—so that they no longer have to check with you so often (or at all) on certain matters. Finally, you could, of course, do both—change the communication pattern (perhaps by reducing your span of control or setting up interdepartmental committees) and also give your subordinates more autonomy to design, produce, and market their products.

• *Divisionalization and Decentralization*

There is usually (but not necessarily) a relation between the degree to which an organization is decentralized and the type of organization (whether it is organized divisionally or functionally); and in most cases, a *divisionalized* organization is also a *decentralized* one.

The reason for this—and this is very important—*is that the authority for making a decision can and should be delegated to the level at which the effect of the decision is local.*[6] In an organization departmentalized by business functions, the president could delegate sales-related decisions to the sales manager and production-related decisions to the production manager. The decisions each of these managers would be making would be localized to their own departments. On the other hand, decisions having a *companywide* effect—such as those concerning companywide union agreements—would have to be centralized in the president's office, and so all communications regarding these matters would necessarily have to flow from the vice-presidents up through the president.

This is where product departmentalization or divisionalization comes in. We saw that the managers of product-oriented divisions are often in charge of what amount to their own miniature companies, as in Figure 7–2. All or most of the decisions that have anything to do with their product (whether production, sales, de-

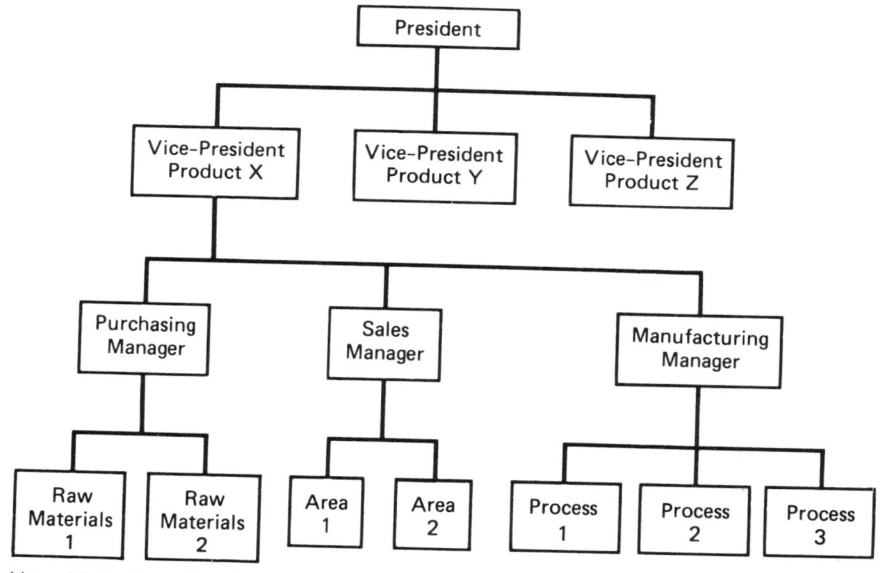

Note: Notice how the vice-president for product X (and for Y and Z, although not shown) has managers for purchasing, sales, and manufacturing reporting to him. His division is "self-contained" in that it can manufacture and sell product X with little or no help from other divisions.

FIGURE 7-2 The "Self-Contained" Aspect of Product-Oriented Departments

sign, or personnel) are "local"—concerned only with their own unit—as far as their product managers are concerned. As a result, the communications flow in a divisionalized organization is literally decentralized, so that there is an increased flow of communications below the presidential level and a reduced flow of communications between the president and the vice-presidents. Recall that one of the advantages of the divisionalized form is that it reduces the information flowing to the president and thus the chance he or she will be overloaded with information. In fact, it is this very overload of information that often leads managers to decentralize.

• *Situational Determinants of Decentralization*

Practicing managers and management consultants are usually in agreement about the advantages of decentralization. Drucker, in an early analysis of decentralization at the General Motors Corporation, found that decentralization led to speedier, more responsive decisions, improved management development, and increased motivation on the part of the managers to do a good job and be rewarded for it.[7] Similarly, Stieglitz states that the advantages of decentralization include quicker and better decisions, better manager development, fewer levels of organization, and the freeing of supervisors to concentrate on broader responsibilities.[8]

Furthermore, decentralization is usually associated with purpose-oriented units. Such units are more self-contained, and their managers can more completely focus on the problems of their "purposes." Also, decentralization usually results in "enlarged," more meaningful (and motivating) jobs for managers.

In summary, decentralization can be effective. By giving subordinates wide-ranging authority while still centrally controlling certain specific activities, you help ensure a more responsive, adaptive organization.

Yet we know that in many cases, decentralization has failed. Decentralization, to be effective, has to be appropriate, and there are many situations and conditions that simply do not lend themselves to the increased autonomy and duplication of effort that are usually associated with decentralization. With this in mind, let us review some of the research studies concerning the situational determinants of decentralization.

The Influence of Diversity: The Chandler Study Historian Alfred Chandler studied the relationship between a firm's strategy, its environment, and its structure, and he has concluded that "structure follows strategy." Specifically, his findings suggest that a strategy of diversification typically leads to the need for a firm to decentralize.

As explained in Chapter 4, among the industries that widely accepted the new, decentralized structure were the electrical and electronics, power-machinery (including automobiles), and chemical industries, with all but two of the twenty leading companies in these industries managed in 1960 through a multidivisional administrative structure.

Because these firms' products were so diverse, and because new products were introduced so often, an organization in which the *same* production department, sales department, and so on served *all* products became unresponsive. As a result, these firms *decentralized* by setting up self-contained product divisions. At Westinghouse, merchandise divisions were established for various electric appliances. These allowed division executives to make most of the sales, engineering, and manufacturing decisions for products in their divisions. Similarly, General Electric established a decentralized organization with vice-presidents for such divisional groups as consumer products, aerospace, and construction materials.

The Influence of Organization Size In a study carried out for the American Management Association, Dale utilized a questionnaire survey of 100 large (5,000 or more employees) and 66 medium-sized (500 to 5,000 employees) companies. The questionnaire was used to obtain information on such topics as type of division of labor, degree of centralization, and number of levels in the company.

Dale found a tendency for organization size and decentralization to be related. However, he found (as did Chandler) that certain large corporations retain their functional, centralized organization structures.[9] His findings support those of Chandler, in that even the largest companies in the steel, mining,and paper industries retained the functional, centralized organization structure.

Dale's findings on the relation between size and decentralization were supported in a later study by Child.[10] His main source of data was 82 British business organizations, and he found that for those firms, size "remains the major predictor of decentralization."

The Influence of Technology and Environment In her study, Woodward found that centralization was most evident in the mass-production firms. At the extremes of her technological scale (where production was either unit or continuous), she found that a more decentralized, organic structure was closely related to success. The Aston researchers found that production technology was related to decentralization in small firms (where the technology impinged on most managerial activities), but that other factors appeared to be more closely related to decentralization in larger firms.[11] These factors included the size of the organization and whether it was highly dependent on other organizations in its environment for survival. Where a company was dependent on a single environmental force—such as a large purchaser or a powerful corporate headquarters—it tended to retain a highly centralized structure. On the other hand, where a company was less dependent upon stable outside forces (and where the environment was thus less predictable), the firm was likely to be more decentralized. These findings are summarized in Table 7-1.

• *Implications*

What sorts of factors determine the extent to which a manager should decentralize? The answer to this lies largely in the fact that *centralization* is usually a much more

TABLE 7-1 Situational Factors That Influence Decentralization

Factor Influencing Degree of Decentralization	*Tendency Toward Centralization*	*Tendency Toward Decentralization*
Uncertainty: rate of change; appearance of novelties (Chandler, Lawrence and Lorsch, Burns and Stalker, Hall)	Low Uncertainty	High Uncertainty
Differentiation of customers, etc.; diversity (Dill, Chandler)	Little Differentiation	Much Differentiation
Organizational size (Dale, Child, Woodward, Pugh et al., Hall)	Small Size	Large Size
Dependence on stable outside factors—large purchaser, etc. (Pugh et al., Dill)	Much Dependence	Little Dependence
Production technology (Woodward, Pugh et al.)	Mass Production	Unit or Continuous Production

time-consuming state of affairs for the boss than is decentralization. With centralization, the boss necessarily gets involved in approving all or most of the subordinates' decisions. With *decentralization*, the person is freed of most of this workload but retains control over major, essential matters. As a result, the decision to decentralize hinges largely on the nature of the task the manager and subordinates face. Specifically, *anything that increases the top manager's workload seems to cause a pressure for decentralization.* Thus, larger organizations, those in industries (like biotechnology) that are undergoing rapid change, and those (like General Electric) that have a wide diversity of products and customers are more likely candidates for decentralization.

In summary, there are two main advantages to decentralizing. First, communications in decentralized structures are less restricted. Employees can communicate with whoever they believe can solve their problems fastest, without going through their boss (or "hub"). Similarly, subordinates have more autonomy and can make more decisions themselves, without getting the approval of the boss. As a result, decision making can be more responsive (since there is less time wasted "checking with the boss"), and this can be very advantageous when (as in the electronics industry) a rapid rate of new-product innovation makes responsiveness a requirement for survival.

A second, related benefit of decentralization is that the potential for overloading the boss is reduced. He or she is no longer involved with the daily details of subordinates' tasks and can concentrate on controlling certain strategic, major decisions, such as very large capital investments. This becomes more important as the manager's workload increases—as products become more numerous and diverse, and as the organization increases in size, for instance. Some implications for management thus include:

1 *The greater the diversity of products, the greater the decentralization.* Recall that Chandler has found that decentralized structures are most often found in companies that market a diverse, wide range of products. Here, product divisions are typically set up, and decision making is decentralized. The reason, he says, is that the problems of doing business in many diverse markets are so varied that a single manager cannot handle them all. Thus, companies like Westinghouse and General Electric opted for a divisionalized, decentralized structure.

2 In general, *the larger the size of the organization, the more the decentralization.* Studies of both American[12] and British[13] firms indicate that larger organizations are usually more decentralized than smaller ones.

There are some notable exceptions to this rule, however. In the case of the largest companies in the steel and paper industries, departments are still built around business functions, and most important decisions remain centralized.[14] For these companies, having efficient manufacturing is of overriding importance, and flexibility is not a key concern. They have thus retained the more efficient functional, centralized organization structures.

3. *The more rapidly changing the environment, the more decentralized is decision making.* For example, where companies depend on a single, predictable customer (as does a Sears, Roebuck supplier), most decisions remain centralized. Where environments are less predictable, decision making is usually more decentralized. Here, intense competition, new-product developments, and similar unexpected changes require a more responsive organization, one where lower-level managers are authorized to make quick, on-the-spot decisions.[15] *Organic* organizations therefore tend to be more decentralized.
4 *Developing adequate, timely controls is the essence of decentralizing.* Simply delegating authority to subordinates without instituting timely controls is more "abdication" than "decentralization." In the capital budgeting example above, for instance, the president had the wisdom to draw clear limits around the size of the capital expenditures his subordinates could make. And he ensured that he would be informed on a timely basis if the decisions his subordinates made were poor ones. As at GM, decentralizing usually requires establishing special "home office" staff units to monitor essential centralized matters like capital expenditures.
5 *Managers should delegate those decisions that involve large amounts of time but minimal erosions of their power and control.*[16] At General Motors, for instance, the president created decentralized divisions that could make most day-to-day production and sales decisions themselves. However, the president retained tight control over power-laden activities like cash management, budgeting, overall division profitability, and capital investments.

The point is worth repeating. Whenever you decentralize, you reduce the power and control you can wield over subordinates. Since subordinates no longer have to get, say, your approval for most capital decisions, your power over them—the extent to which you influence them—is reduced. For instance, you can no longer control what specific capital investments they make. As subordinates are given more autonomy, the best you can hope for is that you will be able to intelligently choose the most critical decisions to control, such as all investments over $10,000; you can no longer personally approve and control *all* expenditures, as you did before. Therefore, managers should delegate those decisions that involve large amounts of time but minimal erosions of their power and control (like making day-to-day production-schedule decisions). Power-laden decisions (regarding, for instance, major capital expenditures) should remain centralized.

HIERARCHICAL LEVELS AND THE SPAN OF CONTROL

The number of hierarchical levels and the span of control are two other dimensions of organization structure. We discuss these dimensions in this section.[17]

There is a close relation between the number of people reporting to a manager and the number of management *levels* in an organization. For example, if an organization with 64 workers to be supervised contains a span of control of 8, there will be 8 supervisors directing the workers and one manager directing the supervisors (a "flat" organization). If, on the other hand, the span of control were 4, the same number of workers would require 16 supervisors, who would in turn be directed by 4 managers. These 4 managers would in turn be directed by one manager (a "tall" organization).

Classical theorists such as Graicunas and Fayol felt that tall organizational structures improved performance by requiring small spans and close supervision.[18] The superiority of tall organizations has not been supported by researchers, however.

• *Flat vs. Tall Organizations*

There are two related categories of findings concerning flat versus tall organizations. One involves the effect of each type of organization on the morale of the employees. The second concerns the relative efficiency of each type of organization.

Effects on Morale One of the first and most extensive empirical studies on the effect of flat and tall organizations on morale was carried out by Worthy in the Sears, Roebuck company.[19] He found that the merchandising vice-president and store managers each had over 40 managers reporting directly to them. Because of this wide span, managers "cannot be running constantly to superiors for approval of their actions," so that this broad, flat type of structure encouraged manager development and increased employee morale.

Worthy's views have gained wide acceptance, but findings of a number of other studies cast some doubt on their validity. Two researchers surveyed over 700 scientists working in organizations in the United States to determine what if any relationship existed between their satisfaction with their jobs and the tallness or flatness of the organizations in which they were working.[20] Most of the organizations they studied were quite small; yet the fact that they found generally insignificant relationships between tallness or flatness and satisfaction cast some doubt on the generality of the Worthy findings. Porter and Lawler surveyed over 1,500 managers in an effort to determine the nature of the relationship between tall or flat organizations and manager satisfaction.[21] Although they did not find any clear general superiority of flat over tall organizations, they did find that in companies employing fewer than 5,000 people, managerial satisfaction was greater in flat than in tall organizations. On the other hand, in companies with 5,000 or more employees, the tall type of organization seemed related to greater satisfaction. In one recent study of nearly 300 salesmen in three organizations, salesmen whose managers had wide spans reported that they were more satisfied, under less stress, and also performed better than salesmen whose managers had narrow spans.[22]

On the whole, the findings suggest that employees whose managers have wide spans of control (which would be associated with flat organizations) tend to have higher morale. However, this is not always the case, and several factors, including the size of the organization and personality of the employee, help determine the emergent morale.[23]

Which Is More Efficient? Carzo and Yanouzas set up a laboratory experiment to test the relative efficiency of flat and tall structures under controlled conditions.[24] Their two experimental organizations are shown in Figure 7-3. Each organization had 15 members, with the tall structure having four levels and the flat having two. Each position had a specialized task and title, and a definite hierarchy existed, with the president's office as the central position at the top of it. Each president was responsible for coordinating all tasks and for making final decisions on the assigned problem, and each of the subordinates to the president was responsible for decision making in particular market areas.

The experimental task was for each organization to arrive at decisions about the quantity of goods to order from its suppliers. To do this, organization members had to estimate demand, analyze inventories from the previous period, and consider

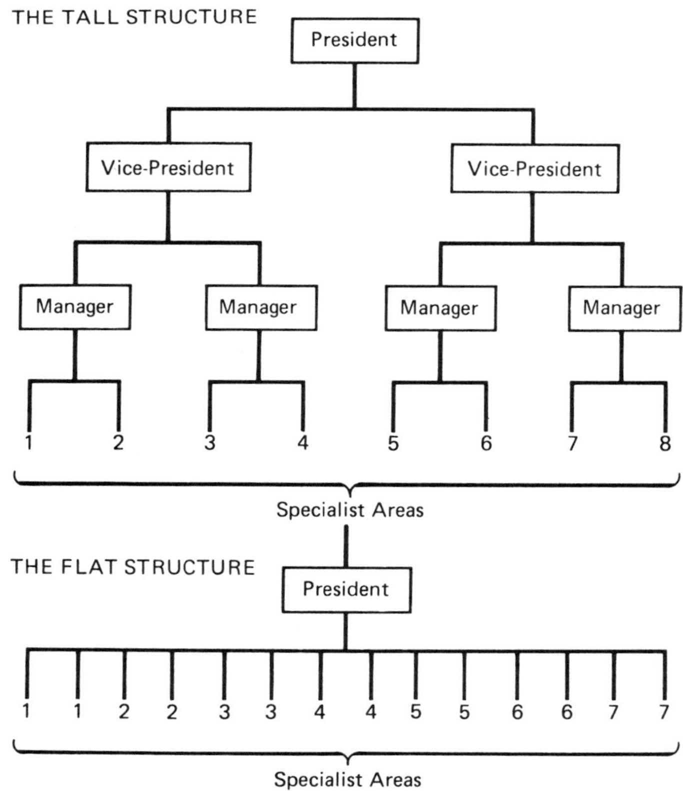

FIGURE 7-3 Tall and Flat Structures *Source:* Rocco Carzo, Jr., and John N. Yanouzas, "Effects of Flat and Tall Organization Structure," *Administrative Science Quarterly*, Vol. 14, No. 2 (June 1969), 181.

back orders from the previous period and restrictions on the amounts that could be ordered.

Although experience at the task improved performance, "organization structure had no significant effect on the time taken to make decisions or on the pattern of improvement." Carzo and Yanouzas suggest:

> This may be partly because coordination time in the flat structure off-set the greater time required for decisions to pass through several levels of a tall structure.[25]

The researchers found that the tall structure was associated with higher profits and rate of return—at least, once the groups had learned their tasks.

> [This] seemed to be partly because in these organizations decisions were subjected to more analysis, and because the narrow span of supervision in a tall structure permitted a more orderly decision and communication process.[26]

• *Span of Control*

Early theorists favored a narrow span of control. Fayol, for example, stated:

> Whatever his rank, a man has only to command a very small number of direct subordinates, usually less than 6, except that a foreman, who is dealing with quite a simple operation, is in direct command of 20 or 30 men.[27]

However, most of these writers were experienced enough to know that the span of control at any level could deviate from these optimums in response to factors such as interdependence of subordinates and the company's rate of growth.

In 1933, Graicunas made an interesting attempt at explaining the disadvantages of large spans of control.[28] He pointed out that arithmetical increases in the number of subordinates reporting directly to a manager are accompanied by potentially geometric increases in the number of possible contacts within the manager's work group. Graicunas expressed this relationship in the formula:

$$C = N\,(2N/2 + N - 1)$$

where C represents the total possible contacts and N the number of subordinates reporting directly to the manager. His formula assumes that all possible relationships are used and that the manager must be involved in supervising all his subordinates. In practice, however, many interrelationships never take place, and many subordinates need little or no supervision from their managers. Furthermore, his formula does not consider such factors as interdependence of subordinates or the nature of their jobs, and the research evidence indicates that these have an important influence on the span of control.

It is therefore not surprising that spans that deviate considerably from those recommended by the classicists are found in current practice. Dale, for example, found that in 100 companies with more than 5,000 employees, the number of executives reporting to the chief executive varied from 1 to 24, with a median of 9. In fact, as seen in Table 7-2, there were only 26 companies in which the span was as narrow as 6. In 46 companies with fewer than 5,000 employees, the chief executives had from 1 to 17 immediate subordinates, and the median was about 7.

TABLE 7–2 Number of Executives Reporting to the President in 100 Large Companies

Number of Executives Reporting to the President	*Number of Companies*
1	6
2	—
3	1
4	3
5	7
6	9
7	11
8	8
	Median
9	8
10	6
11	7
12	10
13	8
14	4
15	1
16	5
17	—
18	1
19	—
20	1
21	1
22	—
23	2
24	1
Total	100

Source: Reprinted by permission of the publisher, from Ernest Dale, *Planning and Developing the Company Organization Structure*, Research Report #20 (New York: American Management Association, 1952), p. 77.

Determinants of Span: Research Findings Research attempts to account for these variations in spans provide some useful insights.[29] They indicate that factors such as *technology, task routineness,* and *employee professionalism* influence what is an "optimal" span for a situation. Woodward presents evidence (Table 7-3) that indicates three things: First, supervisory spans varied widely. Second, both unit (span = 23) and process (span = 13) firms had smaller supervisory spans than had mass-production firms (span = 49). Finally, within each type of technology, successful firms had spans at or near the median, whereas those that were less successful had spans that were either too low or too high for their production systems.

Lawrence and Lorsch measured average span of control as one dimension of their measure of organizational structure. They considered spans of 10 to 11 persons as indicative of low structure, and spans of 3 to 5 as indicative of high structure. Their findings suggest that spans tend to increase with increasing task uncertainty.[30]

The Lockheed Company has developed a weighted-index system as an aid in organization design and planning.[31] Based upon experience and the prescriptions of classical theory, Lockheed pinpointed several factors that it felt should be weighed in determining the span of control:

- Similarity of subordinates' functions
- Geographic closeness of subordinates
- Complexity of subordinates' functions
- Direction and control required by subordinates
- Coordination of subordinates required
- Planning importance, complexity, and time required

TABLE 7–3 Average Span of Control of First-Line Supervisors, Analyzed by the Level of Success

	Span of Control					
Production System	*Up to 20*	*21 to 40*	*41 to 60*	*61 to 80*	*81 to 90*	*Median*
Unit and Small-Batch						
All firms	7	12	4			23
Above-average success		5				
Below-average success	2		3			
Large-Batch and Mass						
All firms	1	7	13	6	3	49
Above-average success			5			
Below-average success	1	2		1	2	
Process						
All firms	18	7				13
Above-average success	6					
Below-average success	1	3				

Source: Adapted from Joan Woodward, *Industrial Organization; Theory and Practice* (London: Oxford University Press, 1965), p. 69.

The Lockheed weighting system is shown in Table 7-4. Each management position is evaluated for each of the six span factors (such as similarity of functions and coordination). Then the point values for each manager's position are added up to provide a "supervisory index," which reflects how much difficulty he should have managing the work of his subordinates. As shown in Table 7-5; the higher the supervisory index, the lower the suggested span of control.

The company had some success with this approach. One of its units expanded its average span from 3.8 to 4.2, and thus reduced supervisory levels from 5 to 4. Another unit extended the average span of managers from 3.0 to 4.2 and thus cut levels from 6 to 5. All told, the savings in managerial and supervisory payrolls were reported as "substantial."

How valid is the Lockheed system? Udell carried out a study to determine whether the Lockheed span factors corresponded to differences in span of control for marketing and sales executives in 67 Midwest manufacturing companies.[32] He found a positive relation between span of control and geographical separation of

TABLE 7–4 The Lockheed Weighting System

Span Factor	*Point Value for Each Factor*				
Similarity of functions	Identical	Essentially alike	Similar	Inherently different	Fundamentally distinct
	1	2	3	4	5
Geographic closeness	All together	All in one building	Separate building, 1 plant location	Separate locations, 1 geographic area	Dispersed geographic areas
	1	2	3	4	5
Complexity of functions	Simple, repetitive	Routine	Some complexity	Complex, varied	Highly complex, varied
	2	4	6	8	10
Direction and control	Minimum supervision and training	Limited supervision	Moderate, periodic supervision	Frequent, continuing supervision	Constant, close supervision
	3	6	9	12	15
Coordination	Minimum relationships with others	Relationships limited to defined courses	Moderate relationships easily controlled	Considerable close relationships	Extensive mutual nonrecruiting relationships
	2	4	6	8	10
Planning	Minimum scope and complexity	Limited scope and complexity	Moderate scope and complexity	Considerable effort required; guided only by broad policies	Extensive effort required; areas and policies not chartered
	2	4	6	8	10

Source: Harold Stieglitz, "Optimizing Span of Control," *Management Record,* Vol. 24 (September 1962), 27.

TABLE 7–5 Middle-Management Index and Suggested Span of Control

Supervisory Index	*Suggested Standard Span*
40–42	4–5
37–39	4–6
34–36	4–7
31–33	5–8
28–30	6–9
25–27	7–10
22–24	8–11

Source: Harold Stieglitz, "Optimizing Span of Control," *Management Record,* Vol. 24 (September 1962), 29. © 1962 National Industrial Conference Board.

subordinates. He also found positive (but not very significant) relations between span and:

1 Similarity of functions supervised
2 Subordinate's experience on the job
3 The use of personal assistants by the supervisor
4 The amount of supervision subordinates received from others in the firm

Determinants of Span of Control: Summary What contextual factors determine span of control? In what way is organizational effectiveness determined by the appropriateness of the span of control to the situation? These questions can now be addressed.

The evidence concerning appropriate spans of control is conflicting. On the one hand, the prescriptions of classical theorists and the work done by Lockheed suggest that the more complicated subordinates' jobs are, the narrower must be the manager's span of control. Intuitively this makes sense, since it should be more difficult for a manager to supervise the work of subordinates whose jobs are complex than of subordinates whose jobs are simple.

Yet the research findings (of Woodward, for example) suggest that this "common-sense" solution doesn't always apply. Generally, instead, where subordinates' jobs are complex and unpredictable, we often find wider—not narrower—spans of control.

There are several reasons for this. We know, for example, that where a person's task is nonroutine, that person is usually given more autonomy;[33] and such increased autonomy would seem to be related to wider rather than narrower spans of control. Furthermore, it seems likely that complex, unpredictable work tasks are associated with people who have more experience and professionalism and who can therefore be expected to exhibit a greater degree of self-control. In conclusion, it appears that complex, uncertain tasks are usually associated with wide spans of control but that this probably assumes a high degree of professionalism and self-control on the part of subordinates.

SUMMARY

In effective organizations, decentralization usually increases as the demands on the president increase. For example, the determinants of degree of decentralization include uncertainty and rate of change, differentiation and diversity of customers, organization size, dependence on a stable outside factor, and production technology. Generally, high uncertainty, much diversity, large size, little dependence, and unit or continuous technologies are associated with more decentralization. On the other hand, low uncertainty, little differentiation, small size, much dependence, and a mass-production technology are associated with centralization. One can view these situational factors in terms of the problem solving, decision making, and overall information processing that they require management to engage in. For example, a more changing or diverse environment, or a relatively large organization, would necessarily give rise to the need of upper-level managers to handle greater quantities of problems. Since there is a limit to how much information a person can effectively handle, the manager must transfer some of the problem solving and decision making to subordinates, by delegating more decision making to them or by setting up self-contained decentralized divisions.

DISCUSSION QUESTIONS

1 Discuss the relationships between delegation, decentralization, and centralization. Why are decentralization, divisionalization, and departmentation by purpose closely associated?
2 What were the factors that Chandler found had led many organizations to adopt the divisionalized organization structure? What is some of the other evidence in support of Chandler's findings?
3 What are some of the advantages and disadvantages of flat and tall organizations? What are some of the factors that influence what span of control is most appropriate?
4 What do we mean when we say, "the authority for making a decision can and should be delegated to the level at which the effect of the decision is local"?

FOOTNOTES

[1]This section based on Thomas J. McNichols, *Executive Policy and Strategic Planning,* (New York: McGraw-Hill, 1977), pp. 38–43.

[2]Kenneth Mackenzie, *Organizational Structure* (Arlington Heights: Ohio, AHM, 1978).

[3]*Ibid.*, pp. 198–230.

[4]See, for example, Joseph Litterer, *The Analysis of Organizations* (New York: John Wiley, 1965), p. 379.

[5]For example, Koontz and O'Donnell argue that decentralization is a philosophy of organization and management—one that implies both selective dispersal and concentration of authority. Harold Koontz and C. O'Donnell, *Management* (New York, McGraw-Hill, 1976), p. 375.

[6]Harold Stieglitz, *Organizational Planning* (New York: The National Industrial Conference Board, Inc., 1962).

[7]Peter Drucker, *Concept of the Corporation* (New York: John Day, 1946), pp. 47–48.

[8]Harold Stieglitz, *Organizational Planning* (New York: The National Industrial Conference Board, Inc., 1962).

[9]Ernest Dale, *Organization* (New York: AMA, 1967), p. 110.

[10]John Child, "Predicting and Understanding Organization Structure," *Administrative Science Quarterly,* June 1973, pp. 168–85. Also see Daniel Robey, M.M. Bakr, and Thomas S. Miller, "Organizational Size and Management Autonomy: Some Structural Discontinuities," *Academy of Management Journal,* Vol. 20, No. 3 (1977), 378–97.

[11]D.S. Pugh, D.J. Hickson, C.R. Hinigs, and C. Turner, "Dimensions of Organization Structure," *Administrative Science Quarterly,* Vol. 13 (1968), 65–105; see also "The Context of Organization Structures," *Administrative Science Quarterly,* Vol. 14 (1969), 91–114. Sergio Mindlin and Howard Albrich present a good review of this in "Interorganizational Dependence: A Review of the Concept and a Re-Examination of the Findings of the Aston Group," *Administrative Science Quarterly,* Vol. 20 (September 1975), 382–91.

[12]Dale, *Organization,* p. 110.

[13]Child, "Predicting and Understanding Organization Structure"; and Robey et al., "Organizational Size and Management Autonomy."

[14]Dale, *Organization,* p. 10; Chandler, *Strategy and Structure,* p. 325.

[15]Sergio Mindlin and Howard Albrich present a good review of this in "Interorganizational Dependence: A Review of the Concept and a Reexamination of the Findings of the Aston Group," *Administrative Science Quarterly,* Vol. 20 (September 1975), 382–91.

[16]Mackenzie, *Organizational Structure,* pp. 195–243.

[17]Robert L. Kahn and Daniel Katz, "Leadership Practices in Relation to Productivity and Morale," in D. Cartwright and A. Zander, *Group Dynamics, Research and Theory* (Evanston, Ill.: Row, Peterson and Company, 1960), pp. 554–70.

[18]A. Graicunas, "Relationship in Organization," in Luther Gulick and L. Urwick, *Papers on the Science of Administration* (New York: Institute of Public Administration, 1937), pp. 181–88; Henri Fayol, *General and Industrial Management,* trans. Constance Storrs (London: Sir Isaac Pittman, 1949).

[19]James Worthy, "Organization Structures and Employee Morale," *American Sociological Review,* Vol. 15 (1950), 169–79.

[20]L. Meltzer and Jay Salter, "Organizational Structure and the Performance of Job Satisfaction of Physiologists," *American Sociological Review,* Vol. 27 (1962), 351–62.

[21]Lyman W. Porter and Edward E. Lawler III, "The Effects of Tall versus Flat Organization Structures on Managerial Job Satisfaction," *Personnel Psychology,* Vol. 17 (1964), 135–48; Lyman Porter and Jay Siegel, "The Effects of Tall versus Flat Organizations Structures on Managerial Satisfactions in Foreign Countries," unpublished manuscript, University of California, Berkeley, 1964.

[22]John Ivancevich and James Donnelly, Jr., "Relation of Organizational Structure to Job Satisfaction, Anxiety, Stress, and Performance," *Administrative Science Quarterly,* June 1975, pp. 272–80.

[23]Edwin E. Ghiselli and Jacob P. Siegel, "Leadership and Managerial Success in Tall and Flat Organization Structures," *Personnel Psychology,* Vol. 25 (September 1972), 617–24.

[24]Rocco Carzo, Jr., and John N. Yanouzas, "Effects of Flat and Tall Organization Structure," *Administrative Science Quarterly,* Vol. 14, No. 2 (June 1969), 178–91.

[25]*Ibid.,* p. 189.

[26]*Ibid.,* p. 190. The experimental control and statistical analyses of the Carzo-Yanouzas experiment have been criticized by Hummon and justified by Carzo and Yanouzas. See Norman P. Hummon, "Criticism of Effects of Flat and Tall Organization Structure," *Administrative Science Quarterly,* Vol. 15, No. 2 (June 1970), 230–40; and Rocco Carzo, Jr., and John Yanouzas, "Justification for the Carzo-Yanouzas Experiment on Flat and Tall Structures," *Administrative Science Quarterly,* Vol. 15, No. 2 (June 1970).

[27]Fayol, *General and Industrial Management;* see also R.C. Davis, *Fundamentals of Top Management* (New York: Harper & Row, 1951).

[28]Graicunas, "Relationship in Organization."

[29]Some writers have noted that the problem of measuring the span of control is more complicated than it might first appear. They say that although most researchers use "raw span"—total subordinates divided by total superiors—other, adjusted measures, including such factors as the number of "helpers" the supervisor has, may better reflect span of control and total supervisory effort. See, for example, William G. Ouchi and John B. Dowling, "Defining the Span of Control," *Administrative Science Quarterly,* September 1974, pp. 357–65. For a second view of this problem, see Kenneth D. MacKenzie, "Measuring a Person's Capacity for Interaction in a Problem Solving Group," *Organizational Behavior and Human Performance,* Vol. 12 (1974), 149–69.

[30]Joan Woodward, *Industrial Organization: Theory and Practice* (London: Oxford University Press, 1965), p. 69. See also Paul K. Lawrence and Jay W. Lorsch, *Organization and Environment* (Boston: Division of Research, Graduate School of Business Administration, Harvard University, 1967), p. 32.

[31]Reported by Harold Stieglitz, "Optimizing Span of Control," *Management Record,* Vol. 24 (September 1962), 25–29. See also James Gibson, John Ivancevich, and James Donnelly, Jr., *Organizations* (Dallas: B.P.J., 1973), pp. 133–35.

[32]J.G. Udell, "An Empirical Test of Hypotheses Relating to Span of Control," *Administrative Science Quarterly,* Vol. 12 (1967), 420–39.

[33]See Gerald Bell, "The Influence of Technological Components of Work upon Management Control," *Journal of the Academy of Management,* Vol. 8, No. 2 (1965), 127–32. Other researchers agree. Dewar and Simet, and Van Fleet, for example, suggest that the factors (such as size, routineness, and number of different specialties supervised) that affect the span of control are level-specific: Dewar and Simet found that size has little effect at lower levels but a positive one at middle levels, and Van Fleet concludes that "the span itself may not be as important as are [factors like organizational level]." The prevailing evidence, though, seems to suggest that task routineness does influence the appropriate span of control. R.D. Dewar and D.P. Simet, "A Level Specific Prediction of Spans of Control, Examining the Effect of Size, Technology, and Specialization," *Academy of Management Journal,* Vol. 24 (1981), 5–24; David Van Fleet, "Span of Management Research and Issues," *Academy of Management Journal,* Vol. 26, No. 3 (September 1983), 546–52.

CASE FOR CHAPTER 7
THE VALUE OF DECENTRALIZING LINE OF BUSINESS STRATEGY IN DIVERSIFIED COMPANIES: THE APPROACH AT CML GROUP*

Christopher G. Risanti

"Street smarts," says Charles M. Leighton, "will beat the hell out of analytical smarts any time."

He once taught management at Harvard Business School, but Charlie Leighton doesn't believe in ponderous corporation procedures. As chairman of the holding company called CML Group, he lets the managers of the 11 subsidiaries operate by "gut feeling," he says.

The managers like being left alone, and CML does fine. Last year, the group

*Reprinted by permission of *The Wall Street Journal,* © Dow Jones & Company, Inc. (July 12, 1982). All rights reserved. Christopher G. Risanti is a staff reporter for *The Wall Street Journal.*

of leisure-product companies recorded profits of $2.7 million on sales of $108.5 million. CML has posted annual profit increases averaging 18.2 percent during the last nine years.

It's an interesting case study in decentralized management. Headquarters consists of nine people, including three secretaries (one of whom Mr. Leighton shares with a colleague). His office is on the second floor of an old railroad depot, and trains noisily rattle past.

• *The Leisure Game*

Mr. Leighton, a slight and relaxed man of 47, ran Bangor Punta Corporation's leisure-time group for four years. In 1969, he decided to strike out on his own and test his management theories. Closely held CML says it has acquired only elite companies specializing in "ego-intensive products."

They include Boston Whaler, Inc., a maker of small, expensive boats; Carroll Reed Ski Shops, Inc., a sportswear retailer; Ericson Yachts, Inc.; Sierra Designs, a California maker of camping equipment; Gokeys, which makes hunting boots and camping equipment; Hoyt Archery Company; The Outdoorsman, Inc., a sporting-goods retailer; Mason & Sullivan, a manufacturer of do-it-yourself clock kits; and Country Store of Concord, Inc., a sportswear retailer.

Business consultants say many holding companies exert too much control when they acquire a number of concerns. "They feel they should be managing, but they don't know much about the individual businesses," says Robert H. Waterman, a director of McKinsey & Co., a New York–based management consulting firm. "What they're really doing is interfering."

CML tries to avoid that. Heads of subsidiaries set financial goals, handle internal differences, and even start new product lines without CML's approval if substantial capital outlays aren't required.

When a CML director asked a sales manager at Mother Karen's, a skiwear designer, what she did for market research, she replied that she "skis the slopes every weekend." And Boston Whaler executives say they received no intervention from CML while settling a strike at Whaler's main plant in Rockland, Massachusetts, last year.

Hands-off is the CML strategy, but CML isn't a passive parent and Mr. Leighton gets his message across. At a Carroll Reed store, for example, he was annoyed by cigarette butts littering the doorway. After his suggestions that a receptacle be placed outside were ignored, he took a broom, swept the stoop, and emptied the butts into a container. A pail was outside the next day, he says.

One reason CML can loosen the reins of its subsidiaries is that it selects experienced managers to instill modern business techniques into the small companies. The original entrepreneurs developed loyal customers and reputations in their field for such items as an Olympic-winning archery bow, $800 miniature replicas of characters from *The Wizard of Oz,* and build-it-yourself grandfather clocks. But CML's handpicked managers must install computers, chart three-year plans, and expand sales.

Some of the entrepreneurs and managers, however, say even CML doesn't offer enough freedom.

David Loveless, president of Boston Whaler, has supervised a growth in sales to $25 million from $5 million since the CML takeover in 1969. He says the only disadvantage of doing business with CML is that CML is "relatively risk adverse."

And John Riddle, president of Yankee Sturbridge Workshop, Inc., retailer of Early American furniture, agrees. "The presidents want to be more aggressive" than CML will allow, he says. Ted Hood, founder of Hood Sailmakers, Inc., eventually bought his company back from CML when CML refused to underwrite Hood's America's Cup entry—an expensive venture that conservative CML managers vetoed.

Mr. Leighton says he owns about 10 percent of the shares of CML and is its second-biggest stockholder, behind the Reader's Digest Association, Inc., which Mr. Leighton says holds between 20 percent and 30 percent.

• *Solid Backing*

Mr. Leighton and G. Robert Tod, CML president, got their initial capital for the holding company—$2 million—from various venture capitalists and foundations, including the Ford Foundation and First National Bank of Boston. "They were interested in our style," says Mr. Tod.

With that cash, Mr. Leighton approached Carroll P. Reed, who had founded his skiwear business in 1936. Mr. Reed initially wasn't interested. But Mr. Leighton, anticipating Mr. Reed's desire for retirement and underscoring CML's low-profile management style, persuaded him to sell for up to $2.5 million in deferred cash payments and earnouts.

CML has "been first class all the way," says Mr. Reed, who left the company in 1974. But he seems disappointed over the transformation of his "mom and pop store" into a company with annual sales of $35 million and a mailing list 10 times its original size. "They try to keep it personal, but you can't with a million customers; they're in it for business, we did it for people," he says. Mr. Leighton's brother, Frederick, is president of Carroll Reed.

Within a week of the Reed acquisition, CML purchased Boston Whaler for an undisclosed price. The boat maker had run into cash problems as a result of dabbling in the capital-intensive industry of engine manufacturing. Since then, CML has acquired companies at the rate of about one a year.

Questions

1 With so much decentralization at CML, how does Mr. Leighton maintain control?
2 What, if anything, has Mr. Leighton centralized at his company?
3 Do you think CML is an example of effective decentralization?

Formalization and Communication

OVERVIEW

In this chapter we explain the nature, determinants, and effects of organizational *formalization*—the extent to which rules, procedures, instructions, and communications are written; and we discuss organizational communication and the degree to which it too is formalized.

The outline of this chapter is as follows:

- A The nature of formalization
  - 1 What is formalization?
  - 2 Why behavior is formalized
  - 3 Some dysfunctions of formalization
  - 4 Determinants of formalization
- B The nature of organizational communication
  - 1 Introduction
  - 2 Communication and organization structure
- C Communications in the effective organization
  - 1 Communication and innovation

THE NATURE OF FORMALIZATION

• What Is Formalization?

In an organization, *formalization* "denotes the extent to which rules, procedures, instructions, and communications are written."[1] For example, are there written job descriptions? Is the use of interoffice memos for stating positions encouraged? Is there a policies and procedures manual?

There are many ways to formalize behavior in organizations. Mintzberg, for example, lists these:[2]

1 *Formalization by job.* First, the organization can formally specify the nature of the job, typically documenting it in a formal *job description.* In addition, the worker may also be told what specific steps to take in his or her work; for instance: First, turn on the press, then adjust the gears, then place the tube on the rack, and then cut the tube.
2 *Formalization by work flow.* On a broader scale, the organization can also formalize or specify the behavior expected by *formalizing the work flow;* in other words, specifying what specific work is to occur at each step of the process. For example, manufacturing facilities often use job-order tickets that specify in writing what work is to be performed at each work station as a particular order proceeds through the plant. As another example, orchestra musicians usually work from written arrangements that specify each of their roles in a given symphony.
3 *Formalization by rules. Rules* are probably the most familiar examples of formalization. At work, behavior is formalized with rules such as, "No smoking on the job," and "All male employees must wear their light-blue or white dress shirts when dealing with the public."
4 *Formalization by structure.* Finally, you can formalize *organizational communications* by specifying whom each employee can or cannot communicate with in the organizational chain of command.

• Why Behavior Is Formalized

Formalization represents the organization's way of prescribing the discretion of its members by telling them in writing what to do, how to do it, and when to do it.

There are several reasons why organizations try to formalize behavior. They do it first to *reduce variability;* in other words, to ensure that every task is performed in a consistent manner. This helps to ensure that the organization's product is produced consistently and cost-effectively. (This is why ice-cream stores have written procedures showing how much of what ingredient should be put in malteds, for instance.) Formalization in the form of written procedures also helps to ensure *coordinated effort;* thus, when the fire truck arrives at a fire, each firefighter's job (unrolling the hose, hooking it to the hydrant, turning on the pumps) is formally prescribed, helping to ensure that the work of the fire team is coordinated once it arrives at the fire. Formalization also helps ensure *fair treatment,* both to the organization's employees and to its clients. In an organization run by rules, unacceptable behavior is clearly defined, and employees can predict how infractions will be dealt with. And they also know that all employees will be treated about the same, "according to the rules."

• *Some Dysfunctions of Formalization*

The advantages of formalization are clear, but so are the drawbacks. There are, first, behavioral drawbacks. The basic point behavioralists like Argyris, Likert, and McGregor make is that people need autonomy and freedom, and that this need is strangled by a network of organizational rules. The result, they say, is that tight rules are imposed, workers resist, dysfunctional consequences (like absenteeism and tardiness) arise, and then more rules are applied to control the resistance. The ultimate result, say behavioralists, is that employees are treated more like children than like mature adults. They then respond like children, by refusing to show the initiative expected of adults. Such resistance can be a serious problem even where the task is highly routinized, as on an assembly line. And for tasks that demand a larger dose of initiative, such resistance can be fatal.

Related to this, formalization can also reduce an organization's responsiveness, such as its ability to move quickly when introducing new products or responding to competitive pressures. For example, Peters and Waterman found a formal procedure to be used by a new-venture department manager in a "moderately high technology business" as diagrammed in Figure 8-1. The circles in the diagram represent organizational units—for example, the one containing "MSD" is the Management Sciences Division—and the straight lines depict the formal linkages (such as standing

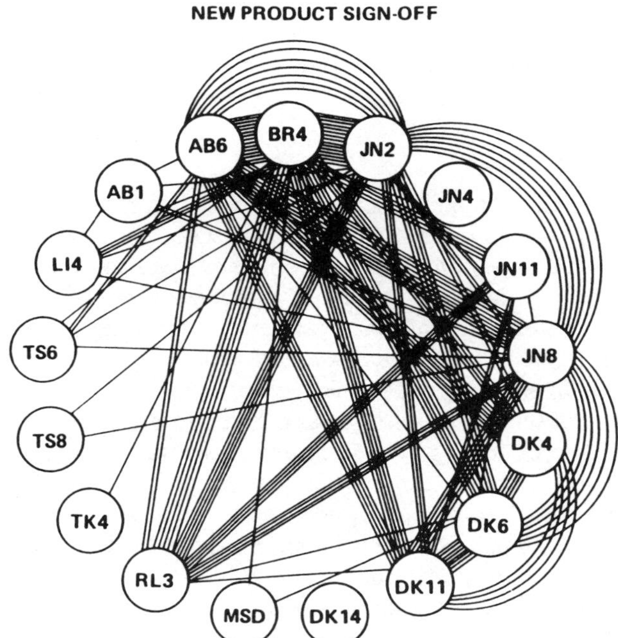

FIGURE 8-1 New-Product Sign-Off Procedure

committees) that are involved in launching a new product. In this organization there are 223 such formal linkages between departments, and as many groups and committees that have to sign off on the company's formal new-product-authorization form. Each formal linkage, say Peters and Waterman, was instituted for a sensible reason, such as to ensure coordinated effort between sales and production. But the effect of the product sign-off procedure is to "capture action like a fly in a spider's web and drain the life out of it."[3]

Yet although formalization can certainly have such adverse effects, remember that its net effect may be favorable on balance. This is illustrated by a recent study of 247 senior scientists and engineers employed in the research, development, and engineering divisions of three firms.[4] In this study, the researchers found that formalization had opposing effects on the alienation of the professionals studied. (Alienation, they say, primarily reflects the extent of self-estrangement from work and results from the sorts of powerlessness, meaninglessness, and isolation that a multitude of formal rules may cause.) On the one hand, they agree that formalization had fostered alienation by inhibiting identification with the organization and reducing the scope of each professional's job.

But on the other hand, they found that formalization can actually reduce alienation and thus improve the professional's lot. They note, for example, that although professionals do seek a measure of autonomy and discretion at work, they can nonetheless suffer from lack of clarity, and that formalization can reduce such ambiguity. Formalization also tends, according to the study, to provide a basis for identification with the organization, perhaps by crystallizing the organization's basic goals and values.

Furthermore, conclude these researchers, formalization can operate in other ways to reduce employee alienation. By facilitating access to a resource and knowledge base, it can reduce employees' sense of powerlessness and can actually decrease their sense of meaninglessness by providing a framework within which to view their contributions to the organization and the organization's contributions to their professional goals. Similarly, by providing the professional with a greater scope and clearer context for self-expression at work, formalization may prevent self-estrangement and thereby reduce alienation as well.

In summary, finding the "right" amount of formalization is part of the art of management: Formalization's dysfunctional effects (including alienation and organizational paralysis) can certainly occur, but without adequate formalization, the results can be as severe. Thus, as these researchers conclude, formalization up to some optimal point can be beneficial, although, obviously, it can be overdone.

• *Determinants of Formalization*

Several factors affect the degree to which an organization will be formalized. In a research project known as the Aston studies, a British group found that the *size of the organization* was the factor most strongly correlated with "structuring of activities'' (a catchall phrase that included degree of job specialization, standardization, and formalization).[5] It was found that large organizations exhibited proportionally more formalization and ''structuring of activities'' than did smaller ones. Other factors that were associated with increased formalization included *size of the organization's parent organization, work-flow integration* (a composite measure of how rigid and automated the production technology is), and the degree to which the organization is *unionized.* Generally speaking, says Khandwalla, the larger the organization, the more unionized it is, and the more integrated and automated its work flow is, the more structured—formalized—its activities are likely to be.[6]

The *variability and predictability of the task* also influence the degree of formalization. Hall, for example, studied departments in ten organizations and concluded that those that performed uniform, easily routinized tasks were more bureaucratic and formalized than those that did not.[7] Similarly, Van de Ven and Delbecq found that examples of formalization (such as many rules and detailed work steps) were more prevalent where the work in the organization was low in variability.[8]

The relationship between predictability and formalization is perhaps clearest in Burns and Stalker's descriptions of their rayon and electronics firms. In the ''predictable'' rayon mill, ''technical and market conditions approximated very closely to stability [and] at all levels, decision making occurred within the framework of familiar expectations and beliefs.'' Unpredictable fluctuations in demand did occur, say Burns and Stalker, but these were treated as deviations from normality, and ''part of the task of management was to constrain the sales office in London to avoid such deviations.''[9] And this organization was correspondingly highly formalized, in that there was a ''clearly defined program [and] the normative character of everybody's work is quite explicit in the factory.''[10] For Example, there was a set of permitted tolerances, bound together in a book, set down for all production stages. This book was called the ''factory bible,'' and it was in the hands of every department head. Most of the skilled work in the factory, and a good deal of the work of foremen and heads of departments, focused on controlling production processes so that they were in accordance with the norms laid down in the ''factory bible.''

At the other extreme, ''all electronics firms encountered much higher rates of technical and other change,''[11] and here, written communication inside the factory was actively discouraged. ''Most important of all, however, was the need of each individual manager for interaction with others, in order to get his own tasks and functions defined, in the absence of specifications from above.''[12] However:

> . . . this process of ''finding-out'' about one's job proved to be unending. Their roles were continually defined and redefined in connection with specific tasks and as members of specific cooperative groups.[13]

For the firms in this rapidly changing environment, in other words, formal written policies and procedures—in fact, formal communications in general—were kept to a minimum.

THE NATURE OF ORGANIZATIONAL COMMUNICATION

• Introduction

Organizational communication is the subject that deals with the exchange of information and transmission of meaning throughout the organization. Communication can take many forms, including written policies, procedures, and rules, and oral communications. In some organizations, as we've seen, communications are written and highly formalized, whereas in others, they are unwritten and informal.

Even though most organizations establish formal communication flows and documents like procedures and rules, they all rely first and foremost on their organization structures for ensuring effective communication among employees. Here, too, the permitted communication flows in some organizations are formalized and rigidly adhered to, while in others, there are virtually no required communication channels at all, and anyone can speak with anyone else, quite informally.

• Communication and Organization Structure

The organization structure (as depicted in an organization chart) *restricts most communication to certain formally sanctioned routes.* Thus in Figure 8–2, the production manager is formally authorized to communicate with the production supervisor and with the vice-president for production. However, the production manager would generally *not* be expected to communicate directly with a sales manager. Instead, if the production manager thought an order was going to be delayed, he should, strictly speaking, relay this information to the production vice-president, who in turn would relay it to the sales vice-president, who would relay it to the sales manager.

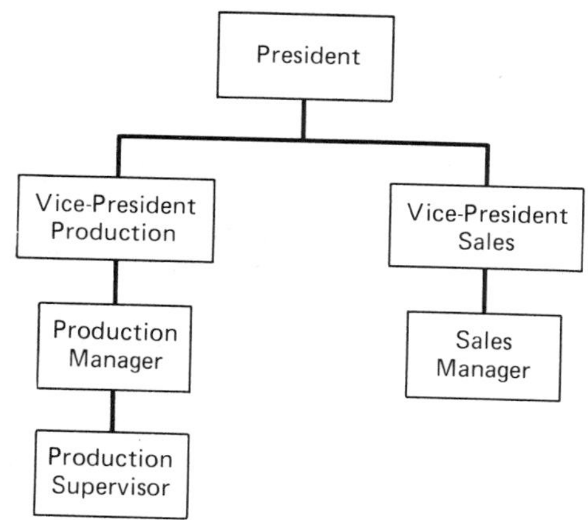

FIGURE 8–2 Formal Communication Sanctioned by Organization Structure

Thus, *organization structure restricts communications to relatively few, formally accepted channels.*

This restriction serves several purposes, according to classical theorists. Without it, everyone could potentially talk with everyone else whenever a problem arose, and the number of messages would soon become distracting. Furthermore, if communication were *not* more or less restricted to formal channels, interdepartmental coordination could suffer. Thus, suppose our supervisor spoke with a sales manager and obtained the latter's approval to delay a particular order for one month. Not knowing of this delay, however, the supervisor boss might have already scheduled other production jobs for the following month, jobs that would now have to be postponed.

Informal Organizational Communication This helps illustrate one of the most serious communications problems that plague organizations: Restricting communication to formally acceptable channels can lead to a lack of responsiveness. Thus (in the example above), it could take several days for the message from the production manager to make its way through the chain of command to the sales manager and for the latter's response to be returned; in this time, the customer might be lost. This is the main reason why there is always some informal communication in organizations—for example, between the sales and production managers. Informal communications like these seemingly defy the pattern of communication that is required by the organization chart. Yet without some informal communication, things might soon run out of control, as they might if the sales manager had to wait for a response from the production manager. Sometimes, managers formalize these informal communications. For example, the president might authorize the sales manager and production supervisor to communicate directly and make schedule changes, but with the stipulation that the production manager and vice-presidents for sales and production must be informed of any such changes within 24 hours.

The Communication Network Study What pattern best facilitates communication? A study by Leavitt addressed this question.[14] In this study, 20 groups of five persons each were arranged in one of the four "communication networks" shown in Figure 8–3. Each person was placed in a compartment at a table in such a way that his or her communication was restricted. For example, each subject in the "all-channel" network could communicate with any other subject. However, subjects in the wheel network could communicate only with the subject in the central position (hub) of the network, but this central person could communicate with the four remaining subjects in his network. (The lines all show two-way linkages.) All each person knew was to whom he could send messages and from whom he could receive them.

At first glance, the networks may seem unrealistic, but they are representative of actual organization structures.[15] For example, the wheel network is similar to the centralized structure shown in Figure 8–4, in which there is a president to whom all vice-presidents report. The vice-presidents can communicate only with their subor-

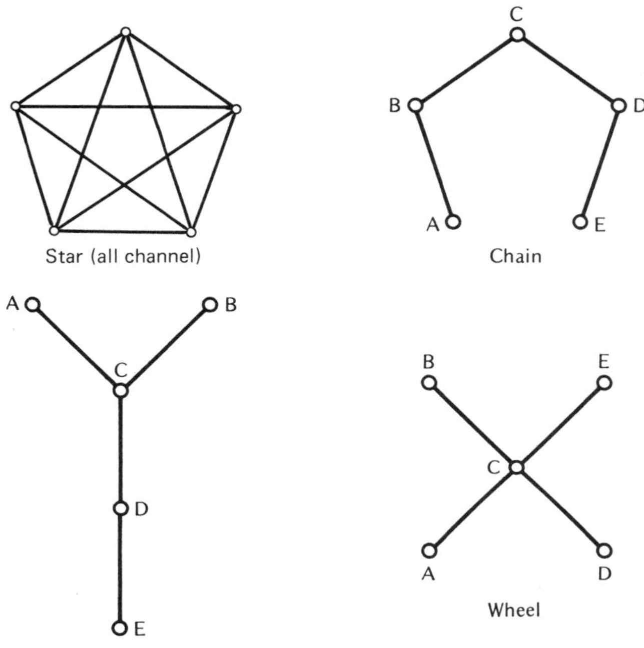

FIGURE 8–3 Four Communication Networks Used in Leavitt Experiments

Note: Each person (A, B, C, D, and E) could communicate only with the person or persons he was linked to *directly*. Thus, in the "wheel" network, C could communicate with all four people, but E could communicate *only* with C.

dinates and with the president, and the latter makes all interdepartmental decisions. On the other hand, the all-channel network is similar to the more "open," decentralized structure also shown in Figure 8–4. In this case, there is a president and two vice-presidents, one for production and one for marketing. Each vice-president in turn can communicate either with the president or with his or her own subordinate—the production manager and sales manager, respectively—or with the manager in the other department. Interdepartmental communication in this organization is thus more open, in that everyone can speak with everyone else.

As summarized in Table 8–1, the researchers found that the best communication pattern depended on the nature of the problem that had to be solved. Where the problem was simple and straightforward, the wheel network was best. (Here, for instance, each person held a card bearing five symbols, only one of which was common to the cards of all members. The job of the person in the middle was simply to get individual inputs from each person, identify commonalities, and report which symbol all had in common.) But for complex problems, the more decentralized all-channel network was best. (Here, for instance, each person was given marbles that were difficult to describe. Two people looking at identical marbles could describe

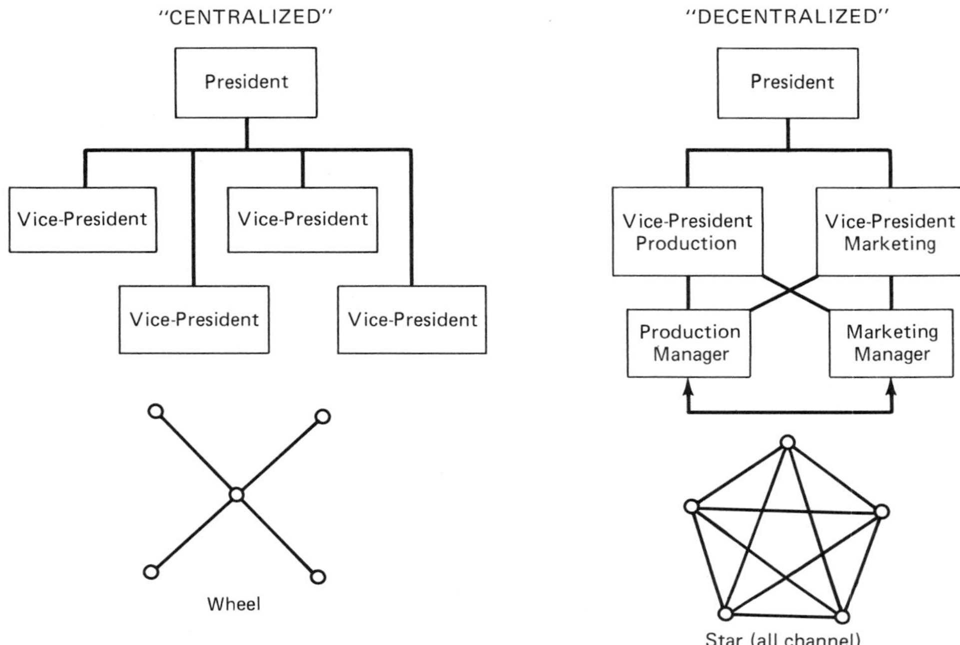

Note: This organization chart shows how communications are restricted in the organization and how these restrictions make the organization on the left similar to a "wheel," and that on the right similar to a "star."

FIGURE 8–4 How Networks Are Similar to Actual Organizations

them quite differently. For instance, what one might view as "greenish-yellow," another might call "aqua.") Here, the person in the middle of the wheel network could not quickly arrive at a decision regarding what color was common to all the models. Instead, the all-channel network in which communications could flow freely from person to person arrived at the fastest decision. The implication is that in organic-type situations that call for responsiveness and a lot of give and take, an all-channel network in which interdepartmental communication is encouraged is best. For making routine, programmed decisions, a more centralized hierarchy is best.

Organizational Communications Networks A few studies of communications networks have been carried out in large organizations. One study involved personnel from divisions in a large aerospace firm and took place in connection with a reorganization.[16] The initial organization is presented in Figure 8–5. According to the researcher, the communications system of this group "was primarily an all-channel network. Everyone in the group was free to use whatever channels of communication he desired, with the result that most of the group's time was spent in discussion, and very little work was accomplished." However the morale of this group was high,

TABLE 8–1 Relative Performance of Centralized (Wheel, Chain, Y) and Decentralized (All-Channel) Networks for Simple and Complex Tasks

	*Simple Problems**	*Complex Problems†*
Time		
Centralized faster	X	
Decentralized faster		X
Messages		
Centralized sent more		
Decentralized sent more	X	X
Errors		
Centralized made more		X
Decentralized made more	X	
Satisfaction		
Centralized higher		
Decentralized higher	X	X

*Simple problems: symbol-, letter-, number-, and color-identification tasks.
†Complex problems: arithmetic, word arrangement, sentence construction, and discussion problems.
Source: Reprinted from M.E. Shaw, "Communication Networks," in L. Berkowitz, ed., *Advances in Experimental Social Psychology, Vol. 1* (New York: Academic Press, 1964), pp. 111–47.

each person's advice was appreciated and carefully evaluated, and individual group members were therefore very involved in their tasks.

The group was reorganized by management into a wheel network (see Figure 8–6). Whereas communications had formerly been unrestricted, they were now very restricted, and this restriction (concerning who would communicate with whom) was formalized by a strongly worded directive from management. Employees eventually reacted by following this directive exactly and protecting their own interests by com-

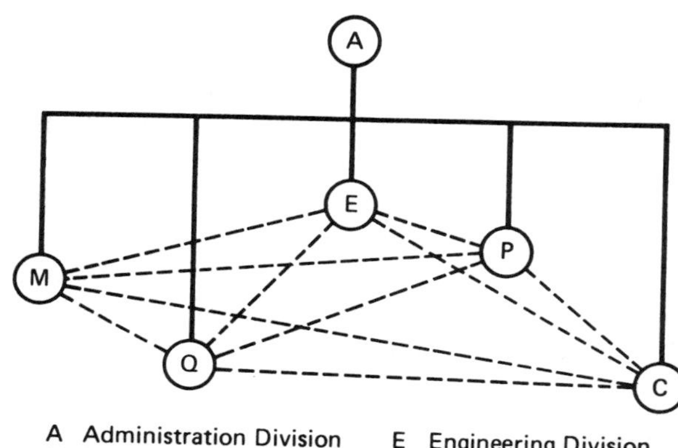

FIGURE 8–5 The Initial Organization: An All-Channel Network. *Source:* Peter Mears, "Structuring Communication in a Working Group," *The Journal of Communication,* Vol. 24, No. 1 (1975), 73.

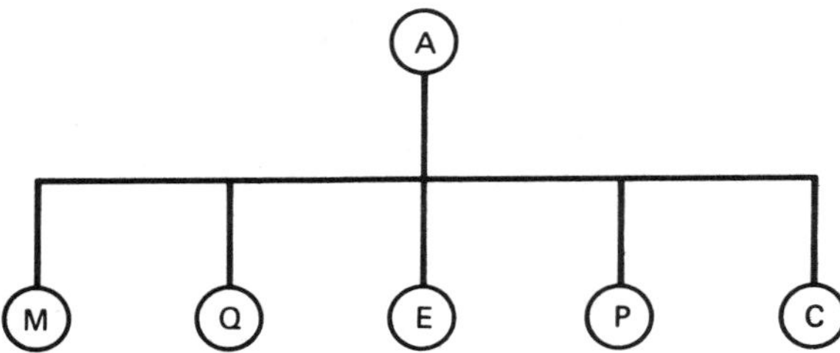

FIGURE 8–6 New "Wheel Network" Organization. *Source:* Peter Mears, "Structuring Communication in a Working Group," *The Journal of Communication,* Vol. 24, No. 1 (1975), 74.

menting only on what affected them; as a result, the number of errors grew tremendously.

The researcher found that part of the reason for the eventual breakdown in the wheel network was the "overload" on the central, coordinating group member:

> The task was complex, and the individuals refused to accept the dictates of the central person without sufficient information. This forced the central person to handle more and more messages until he could do only one of two things: either state that he could not handle the job or try to circumvent the group entirely by pointing out to management that the group was uncooperative. Management ultimately allowed the structure to return to a network somewhat closer to what it had been originally. Morale in this group even after several months had not returned to its previous levels. These findings may support the notion that more decentralized free-flowing communications networks are appropriate for solving complex problems for which employee participation is required, and also that such networks, on the whole, are associated with higher employee morale.[17]

Summary In summary, these results indicate that different types of tasks demand different types of communication patterns. For example, a centralized, wheel-type network was shown to be especially useful for handling clear-cut, routine problems. On the other hand, wheel networks tend to break down where problems required more analysis. Here, the amount of data the hub had to handle was often so excessive that the person became overloaded and activities ground to a halt; errors were made more frequently, responses were delayed, and some data were simply ignored.[18] For these kinds of problems, it was shown that decentralized all-channel networks solve the problems best. Here, communications were relatively free-flowing, others (besides the hub) could make decisions, and decisions were quickly arrived at.

COMMUNICATIONS IN THE EFFECTIVE ORGANIZATION

• Communication and Innovation

In their study of "excellent" innovative companies, Peters and Waterman found that these companies used very informal—almost unorthodox—means of communicating.[19]

Excellent Companies' Use of Information Communication Peters and Waterman found that the nature and uses of communication in the excellent companies was remarkably different from those of their nonexcellent peers. Specifically:

> The excellent companies are a vast network of informal, open communications. The patterns and intensity cultivate the right people getting into contact with each other, regularly, and the chaotic/anarchic properties of a system are kept well under control simply because of the regularity of contact and its nature.[20]

In these outstanding and innovative companies, "the name of the success game" is rich, informal communication:

> The astonishing byproduct is the ability to have your cake and eat it, too; that is, rich informal communication leads to more action, more experiments, more learning, and simultaneously to the ability to stay better in touch and on top of things.[21]

How Companies Encourage Effective Informal Communication In the excellent companies, say Peters and Waterman, the intensity and sheer volume of communications are unmistakable, and usually start with a stress on informality.[22] Specifically, they found that several techniques were used to encourage informal communication:

1 *Communications systems are informal.* At Walt Disney Productions, for instance, everyone from the president down wears a name tag with just his or her first name on it. At 3M there are endless meetings, few of which are scheduled; most, instead, are characterized by the casual getting together of people from different disciplines to talk about problems in a campuslike, shirtsleeves atmosphere.

2 *Communication intensity is extraordinary.* At the more successful companies, meetings and presentations are held in which "the questions are unabashed; the flow is free; everyone is involved. Nobody hesitates to cut off the chairman, the president, or board member."[23] What is encouraged, in other words, is an open confrontation of ideas in which people go after issues bluntly and straightforwardly. Meetings in these excellent companies are thus not highly formal and politicized affairs but rather open, information discussions in which all points of view can safely be aired.

3 *Communication is given physical support.* In the more effective companies, "physical supports" like blackboards and open offices facilitate and encourage frequent informal interaction. In one high-tech firm, for instance, all employees from president down work not in offices, but in 6-foot-high doorless cubicles that encourage openness and interaction among employees. Corning Glass installed escalators (rather than elevators) in its new engineering building to increase the chance of face-to-face contact.[24] Similarly, another company got rid of its small, four-person round tables in its dining room, substituting instead long, rectangular ones that encourage strangers to come in contact, often across departmental lines. Similarly, managers are encouraged to get out of

their offices, walk around, and strike up conversations with those both in and outside their own departments.

What this all adds up to, say Peters and Waterman, is "lots of communication." In the most excellent of their excellent companies, they say, you can't wander around long without "seeing lots of people sitting together in rooms with blackboards working casually on problems."[25]

How do excellent companies maintain control and coordination with so little formally constrained communication? According to Peters and Waterman, "the intense informal communication system acts as a remarkably tight control system." As one manager at 3M put it, "Of course we are under control. No team can spend more than a few thousand dollars without a whole bunch of people looking over their shoulders, not kicking them around, but being genuinely interested in how it's going."[26] In other words, lots of people in the most excellent firms are so involved with each other's work that almost everyone knows how projects are going, so things can never get too far out of control. In summary, then, in these innovative companies, formalization is held to a minimum and "all-channel" communications are encouraged, aided by constantly shifting informal meetings (even at lunch) among employees from different departments and levels in the firms.

Mechanistic and Organic Management Systems Peters and Waterman's findings regarding the degree of formal communication in innovative companies is consistent with the findings of Burns and Stalker. Recall that they, too, found that communication in organic organizations was relatively unplanned and informal, with a "lateral rather than a vertical direction of communication in the organization, and communication between people of different rank, resembling consultation rather than command."[27] And there was "a content of communication which consists of information and advice rather than instructions and decisions."[28] Even at lower management levels, say Burns and Stalker, "the same free and frequent contact between individuals was maintained as prevailed among the directors." You go to the person who is most concerned with the problem in hand, "whether foreman or director."[29]

In mechanistic organizations, on the other hand, there was "a tendency for interaction between members of the concern to be vertical, i.e., between superior and subordinate."[30] In the mechanistic organization, each employee's rights and obligations are precisely defined, formal procedures tell him what to do and how and when to do it, and employees are encouraged to pursue their own narrow specialization and to refer questions to their immediate superiors.

SUMMARY

Formalization denotes the extent to which rules, procedures, instructions, and communications are written. Among the ways a manager can formalize behavior in organizations are formalization by job, by work flow, by rules, and by structure.

Behavior is formalized for many reasons, including to reduce variability, coordinate effort, and ensure fair treatment. However, formalization can also have dysfunctional effects—for instance, when it reduces employee morale.

Several factors affect the degree to which an organization will be formalized. These include the size of the organization, work-flow integration, and (primarily) the variability and predictability of the task.

Organizational communication can take many forms, among them policies, procedures, rules, and oral communications. The organization structure restricts most communication to certain formally sanctioned routes and, to that extent, serves to formalize communication (and therefore behavior) in the organization. In some organizations, the structure is such that communications are highly formalized and mechanistic; in others, they are much less so. Research findings indicate that complex, innovative tasks generally demand less formal communications networks, whereas predictable, routine tasks are associated with highly formalized and structured communication flows. In the most effective innovative companies, there is extensive use of informal communication.

Discussion Questions

1 Explain four ways in which behavior in organizations can be formalized.
2 Discuss the determinants of formalization.
3 According to the textbook, what is the purpose of restricting communication to a relatively few formal channels?
4 Explain what you think are the organizational implications of the Leavitt communication network studies.

Footnotes

[1]D.S. Pugh, D.F.Hickson, C.R. Hinings, and C. Turner, "Dimensions of Organization Structure," *Administrative Science Quarterly,* Vol. 13 (1968), 65–91.

[2]Numbers 1–3 based on Henry Mintzberg, *The Structuring of Organizations* (Englewood Cliffs, N.J.: Prentice-Hall, 1979), pp. 81–82.

[3]Thomas Peters and Robert Waterman, Jr., *In Search of Excellence* (New York: Harper & Row, 1982), pp. 18–19.

[4]Dennis Organ and Charles Greene, "The Effects of Formalization on Professional Involvement: A Compensatory Process Approach," *Administrative Science Quarterly,* Vol. 26, No. 2 (June 1981), 237–52.

[5]See, for example, D.J. Hickson, D.S. Pugh, and D.C. Pheysey, "Operations Technology and Organizational Structure: An Empirical Reappraisal," *Administrative Science Quarterly* Vol. 14 (1969), 370–97.

[6]Pradip Khandwalla, *The Design of Organizations* (New York: Harcourt Brace Jovanovich, 1977), p. 514.

[7]R.H. Hall, "Intraorganizational and Structural Variation: Application of the Bureaucratic Mode," *Administrative Science Quarterly,* 1962, pp. 295–308.

[8]Andrew Van de Ven and André Delbecq, "A Task Contingent Model of Work Unit Structure," *Administrative Science Quarterly* Vol. 19 (1974), 183–97.

[9]Tom Burns and G.M. Stalker, *The Management of Innovation* (London: Tavistock, 1961), p. 93.
[10]*Ibid.*, p. 80.
[11]*Ibid.*, p. 90.
[12]*Ibid.*
[13]*Ibid.*, pp. 92–93.
[14]Harold Leavitt, "Some Effects of Certain Communication Patterns on a Group Performance," *Journal of Abnormal and Social Psychology,* Vol. 46 (1972), 38–50.
[15]Keep in mind, though, that the networks differ only in the degree to which communication is centralized. Remember that in "real" organizations, *delegation* can take place (it could not here), and furthermore, the problems to be solved generally have more dimension than the simple ones considered by these subjects.
[16]Peter Mears, "Structuring Communication in a Working Group," *The Journal of Communication,* Vol. 24, No. 1 (1975); 71–79; Keith Davis, *Organizational Behavior: A Book of Readings* (New York: McGraw-Hill, 1977), 128–32.
[17]Mears, "Structuring Communication."
[18]*Ibid.*
[19]This is based on Peters and Waterman, *In Search of Excellence* (Harper & Row), pp. 119–218.
[20]*Ibid.*, p. 122.
[21]*Ibid.*, p. 124.
[22]*Ibid.*, pp. 218–20, 122–23.
[23]*Ibid.*, p. 219.
[24]*Ibid.*, p. 122.
[25]*Ibid.*, pp. 122–123.
[26]*Ibid.*, p. 223.
[27]Burns and Stalker, *Management of Innovation,* p. 121.
[28]*Ibid.*
[29]*Ibid.*, p. 91.
[30]*Ibid.*, p. 120.

CASE FOR CHAPTER 8
A SLIMMED-DOWN BRUNSWICK IS PROVING WALL STREET WRONG
Critics Said Dump Sports Gear. Instead, Brunswick Dumped a Stodgy Bureaucracy*

In 1982, Brunswick Corp. had to decide what kind of company it should be. To thwart a hostile takeover, it had just sold its promising medical-equipment business. And investment bankers, pessimistic about management's ability to do much with its mature, cyclical businesses, were telling the company that the only hope for salvation lay in a major redeployment of assets.

The message: Get out of the recreation business that had made Brunswick a hot property in the 1960s. Sell off bowling, sell off billiards, sell off outboard motors. Use the money to develop the Skokie (Ill.) company's budding defense and tech-

*Reprinted from *Business Week,* May 28, 1984.

nical businesses (now 30% of sales), whose products range from camouflage netting to filtration systems.

But to Brunswick Chief Executive Jack F. Reichert, Wall Street's assessment was a personal affront. "I was so angered that I stayed up until 3 A.M., wrote my goals on a yellow legal pad, and vowed we would focus on our present businesses and not try to be something we aren't," he recalls. Ever since then, the ordained Presbyterian elder has been crusading to prove that the fault lay not in the product line but in past management approaches. And the dramatic changes Reichert has made have convinced line managers that his credo—"wealth is created at the operating division level, not at the corporate level"—is rooted in real faith.

• *Shock Therapy*

Brunswick's financial performance is now making believers of investors as well. Brunswick's stock is hovering around 28, up from 9 one year ago—and for good reason. Extensive cost-cutting, a 59% reduction in corporate staff, and efficiencies wrought through decentralization have put Brunswick in its best shape in years. Its debt has fallen from 39.4% of capital in 1981 to 26.6% today. And its earnings rebounded from a $19.7 million loss in 1982 to a $66.1 million profit in 1983, when sales rose 14%, to $1.2 billion. That performance is only $628,000 shy of the earnings record set in 1981—when Brunswick still had highly profitable Sherwood Medical Industries.

The shock of selling Sherwood to American Home Products Corp.—to ward off Whittaker Corp.'s takeover bid—gave Reichert the chance to pump some life into his slow-moving, bureaucratic company. With Chairman K. Brooks Abernathy, a finance man who became chairman in 1976 and retired last September, yielding his power, Reichert was free to move. "All along Jack was champing at the bit to make big changes," a former insider says. "But without the trauma of losing Sherwood, he wouldn't have been able to do it in such an aggressive manner."

Reichert eliminated the chief operating officer's job (his previous title) and four group executive positions. He consolidated 11 divisions into 8. Gone, too, are two of three corporate planes, the executive dining room, and $20 million worth of administrative overhead. And by renting out two-thirds of the company's sprawling headquarters, he is saving $2 million a year in real estate costs.

• *Quick Answers*

But Reichert, 53, is proudest of how he reduced Brunswick's corporate staff from 560 to 230 and streamlined reporting lines. Only five layers of management stand between him and the lowest-ranking employee.

Reichert's decisiveness and no-nonsense style contrast sharply with that of his predecessor. Abernathy, a General Electric Co. alumnus, delighted in big staff and reams of analysis. "In the past, we had to justify everything we did," says Richard

J. Jordan, general manager of Brunswick's Mercury Marine Div., which has about a third of the U.S. outboard-motor market. "Now we are more concerned with running a business." Adds a former manager: "When you go to talk to Jack about a proposition, you don't have to have 14 pages of financial data to back it up."

Because the divisions' general managers now report directly to the chairman, decisions that once took weeks or months now take hours or days. For instance, when James G. Buick, general manager of Brunswick's 200 bowling centers, needed a next-day answer on whether he could spend $400,000 to install automatic scorers to ward off a regional competitor, he called Reichert. "We discussed it, and he said, 'Fine, go ahead.' That wouldn't have happened in the earlier environment," Buick says.

Outsiders give Reichert—a 26-year Brunswick veteran who rose through the sales ranks to become president in 1977—high marks for implementing his master plan with little turnover in the upper operating ranks. He has also improved morale throughout the company, insiders maintain. One key tool Reichert has used: compensation. Last December he spent $875,000 after taxes to double the 3½ shares awarded to each employee under a federally sponsored payroll-related stock-ownership plan. And he has expanded the corporate incentive program fourfold to include the top 500 managers. Bonus size depends heavily on the financial performance of each manager's division. But success in meeting other targets—ranging from product quality to two "personal" goals specifically related to the manager's job—is taken into account. "As soon as you've tasted the fruit," says Mercury Marine's Jordan, "you see this is the way to go."

• *Turf Battles*

Indeed, Mercury Marine's sales soared 27% last year, and its earnings tripled. The improved economy certainly helped. But just as important were dramatic operational improvements in manufacturing and inventory management. The biggest savings came from consolidating the four product lines—Mercury and Mariner outboard motors, MerCruiser stern drives, and Quicksilver boating parts—under one management. That move cut $5 million in overhead and reduced the breakeven point by $100 million in annual sales.

Previously, each unit had its own manager, credit department, and controller. And because the divisions shared manufacturing facilities, turf battles abounded. "If you were short an item," one insider says, "you were at the mercy of who controlled the production line."

Now a single manufacturing operation allots production according to sales forecasts. Those forecasts have been sharpened by closer contact with Mercury Marine's dealers, who are given rebates if they agree to set and then meet annual sales goals. Another benefit of the rebate program: Brunswick's relations with dealers are on the mend. In the past, notes Oak Lawn (Ill.) dealer Harry A. Wood, dealers resented Brunswick's rigid refusal to discount prices in the face of competition. The improvement in relations comes at a critical time. Japan's Yamaha Motor Corp.

USA, which has supplied low-power boat engines to Brunswick, is becoming a competitor: In September, Yamaha began selling engines in the U.S. under its own name.

Reichert still faces the challenge of changing a corporate culture that focuses on avoiding failure rather than taking risks for a potential payoff. To help turn the tide, he is establishing venture-capital groups within the divisions. The groups, consisting of small management teams dedicated to nurturing new products, are funded from corporate coffers. Managers, therefore, do not have to choose between sacrificing their bonuses or their profits to get the ventures off the ground. Already, Brunswick has five projects, ranging from a 30% interest in a fledgling software company to Witec, a company that has developed an injection-molding process for making intricate parts from powdered metal.

• *Earning Their Spurs*

Reichert is counting on Witec, which will ship its first products this summer, to generate sales of $4 million this year and "hundreds of millions of dollars someday." But he stresses that he is making sure that managers realize some failures are both expected and acceptable. "Look, I know I'm not going to go 5 for 5," he says. "But I don't think I'll go 0 for 5 either."

Even with Brunswick's strong earnings and its $500 million defense backlog, some observers still insist that Reichert must make a big acquisition. "At some point the cyclical nature of the marine business will catch up with them," warns Joseph T. Fitzgerald, an analyst at Bankers Trust Co. Reichert is willing to spend $50 million to $75 million for some small acquisitions—possibly to supplement Brunswick's fishing tackle, defense, and technical businesses. His real goal, however, is to convince investors that good management—and not just a strong economy—is responsible for his company's revival. As Reichert himself acknowledges, though, only the next recession will determine whether Brunswick's managers have truly earned their spurs.

Questions

1 In what specific ways has Mr. Reichert reduced formalization at Brunswick?
2 What role does goal setting play in the new, less-formalized Brunswick?
3 How has the reduced formalization led to improved communications at Brunswick?

9

Organization Design

OVERVIEW

In this chapter we will discuss how to design an organization structure by focusing on five ideal or "pure" structural configurations: simple structure, machine bureaucracy, professional bureaucracy, divisionalized form, and adhocracy. Most organizations, as we'll see, are structured as one of these forms, so that by identifying the nature of the environment and task of the organization, it should be possible to fit the appropriate configuration to the demands of its task.

The outline of this chapter is as follows:

INTRODUCTION TO ORGANIZATION DESIGN

• Where We Are Now

We have discussed the basic elements of organization design—departmentation, coordination, decentralization, and formalization—and contextual determinants of structure, like environment, technology, and size. We can now turn to the task of pulling together these elements and address the question of how to actually design an organization structure.[1]

We already have a clue as to how to do this from findings like those of Burns and Stalker. These experts, you may recall, concluded that standard or ideal types of organizational configurations are appropriate for different tasks. For example, Burns and Stalker's mechanistic organizations (with their high degree of formalization, functional division of work, and hierarchical coordination) are appropriate for simple, unchanging environments, whereas organic organizations are appropriate for instability and change. Similarly, Woodward concluded that the classical, bureaucratic type of structure is best for the mass-production type of firms, and the more organic, flexible, professional type of organization was best for automated firms. Perhaps, then, organization design can be facilitated by identifying several standard organization structures (or "configurations") and then deciding which is more appropriate for the particular situation you are designing the organization for. Henry Mintzberg has developed such an approach to organization design.

Mintzberg builds his approach around five basic elements, which are presented in Figure 9-1; they are the *strategic apex, middle line, operating core, technostructure,* and *support staff.* At the base of the organization are its operators, the people who actually perform the basic work of producing the product and rendering services; they constitute the *operating core.* Here are workers like assemblers, salespersons, and shippers.

As the organization grows, the need for supervision increases, so even a small company will have a full-time manager who sits at the *strategic apex.* In a corporation, the strategic apex includes the board of directors, president, president's staff,

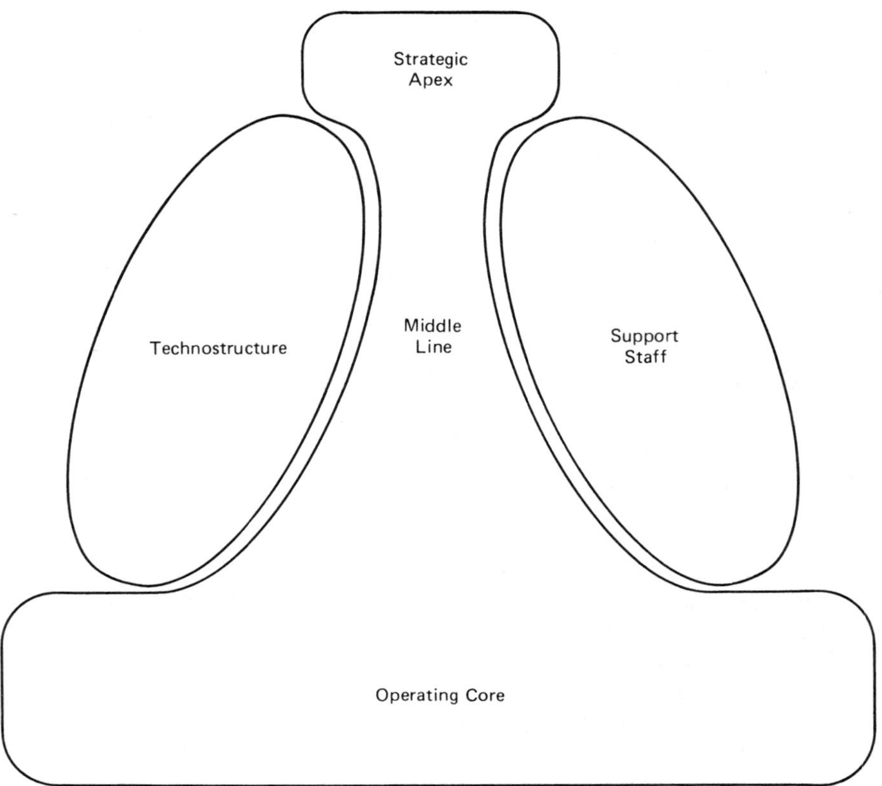

FIGURE 9-1 The Five Basic Parts of the Organization

and executive committee of the board of directors. Most organizations also create a *middle line,* a hierarchy of managers between the operating core and strategic apex; this is the familiar chain of command, including vice-presidents for operations and marketing, plant managers, regional sales managers, and (between the middle line and operating core) foremen and district sales managers.

As the organization grows, it may turn increasingly to standardization as a means of coordinating its work—for example, by standardizing work processes, products, and employee skills and knowledge. The responsibility for such standardization falls mostly on a group of analysts Mintzberg calls the *technostructure,* a group usually referred to as "staff." Employees in the technostructure include specialists for strategic planning, personnel training, production scheduling, and work study. Finally, says Mintzberg, an organization may add staff units of a different kind, *not to improve standardization but to actually service itself* by providing special services like a cafeteria or mailroom or legal counsel. Mintzberg calls these employees and the part of the organization they form the *support staff,* and they include legal counsel, public relations, payroll, mailroom, and cafeteria. Figure 9-2 summarizes the types of positions you might expect to find in Mintzberg's strategic apex, middle line, operating core, technostructure, and support staff.[2]

Five Basic Configurations Mintzberg contends that most organization structures can be classified as belonging to one of five ideal or "pure" structural configurations, which he calls *simple structure, machine bureaucracy, professional bureaucracy, divisionalized form,* and *adhocracy.*[3] Many hybrids are possible, says Mintzberg, and in reality other types of structures may exist. Nevertheless, he says, "there are times when we need to caricature, or stereotype, reality in order to sharpen differences and so to better understand it," and the use of these five basic structures can vastly improve an ability to analyze and design organization structures.[4] We will explain each of these five basic structures or configurations in turn.

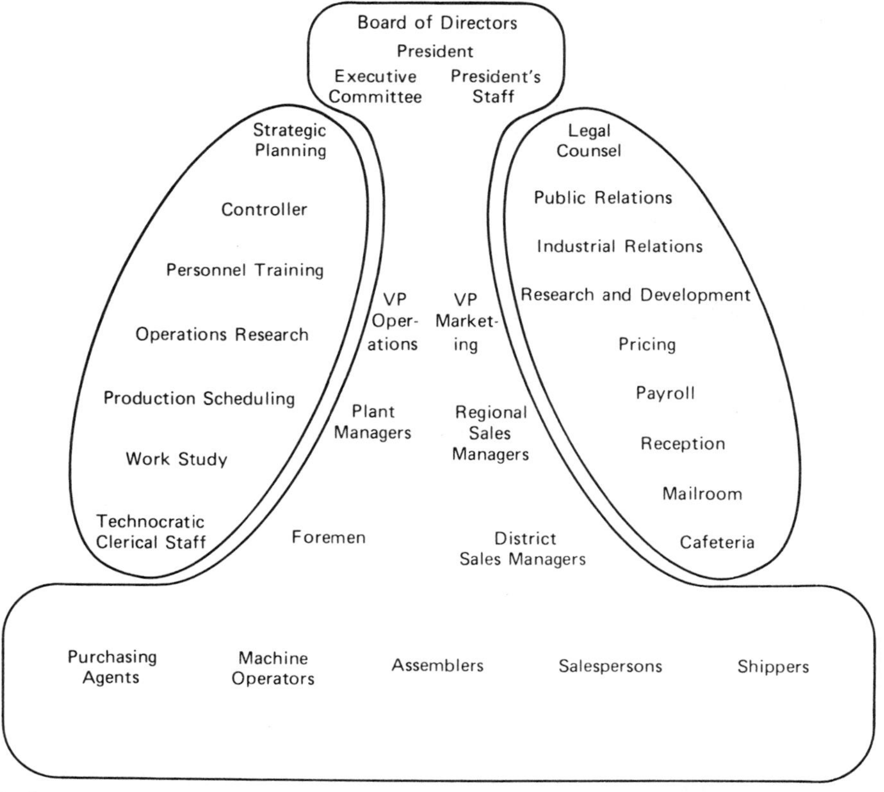

FIGURE 9-2 Some Members and Units of the Parts of the Manufacturing Firm

THE SIMPLE STRUCTURE

• *The Nature of the Simple Structure*

An automobile dealership with a flamboyant owner, a middle-sized retail store, and a corporation run by a strong, aggressive entrepreneur exemplify Mintzberg's simple structure.

The simple structure is more than anything a nonstructure, in that it avoids using all the formal devices of structure like division of work and decentralization. It usually has little or no technostructure (controllers, industrial engineers, and so on), few support staffers (mailroom, cafeteria, and the like), and a small or nonexistent management hierarchy. This is basically a structure in which a strong entrepreneur/manager singlehandedly controls all employees and manages the organization with the power over all major decisions in his or her hands. The strategic apex is thus the key point of this structure, and the manager's ability to directly supervise all the workers makes the structure a very organic one. Grouping into organizational units—if it exists at all—is usually on a loose functional basis, with the coordination between units left to the chief executive. An example, showing the organization of a small chain of retail stores, is presented in Figure 9-3. Note that all the employees report directly to the owners, and that there is no middle line (middle management), or technostructure, (like industrial engineers), and virtually no support staff. In the simple structure, the prime coordinating mechanism is direct supervision, the key part of the organization is the strategic apex, and the main design characteristics are centralization and a highly organic structure.

• *Factors Influencing the Emergence of the Simple Structure*

Companies that are organized as simple structures tend to be young and small, and to have nonsophisticated technologies, a simple, dynamic environment, and (possibly) a very hostile environment and/or a top manager with strong power needs.

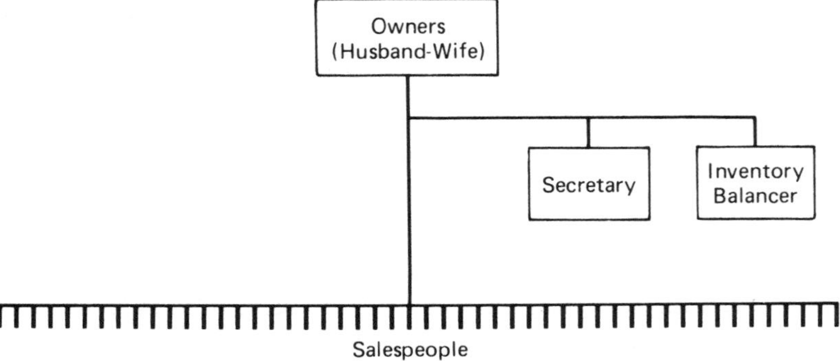

FIGURE 9-3 Chez Lutin—The Typical Simple Structure

Above all, contends Mintzberg, the environment of the simple structure tends to be both simple and dynamic.[5] The environment is *simple* insofar as the organization typically focuses on a narrow line of products, and it is *dynamic* insofar as the environment itself (in terms of technological change, or new-product introduction by competitors, for instance) changes rapidly and unexpectedly. The simplicity of the environment permits one central manager to easily grasp all the details of the environment, and its dynamic aspects demand the responsiveness provided by the organic, simple structure.

Age is an important factor leading to the simple structure, since virtually all new organizations start out with this form. And under crisis conditions—such as when a takeover bid forces management to centralize—even large corporations may slip back to the simple form. In fact, one advantage of this form is its sense of mission; this is essential when the company is new, and also when it confronts a crisis.[6]

THE MACHINE BUREAUCRACY

• Introduction

A national post office, a steel company, and a giant automobile company are all examples of machine bureaucracies. In all these, most of the operating work is repetitive, so that the organization's work processes can be standardized. The machine bureaucracy is the bureaucracy of Max Weber with its standardized assignments of duties, training, communication channels, and work rules, and its clearly defined hierarchy of authority. It is the structure Joan Woodward found in the mass-production firms, that Burns and Stalker found in the rayon-textile mill, and that Lawrence and Lorsch found in their container firm.

• Description of the Basic Structure

According to Mintzberg, the basic structure of a machine bureaucracy can be summarized as follows. It has:

> . . . highly specialized, routine operating tasks, very formalized procedures in the operating core, a proliferation of rules, regulations, and formalized communications throughout the organization, large-sized units at the operating level, reliance on the functional basis for grouping tasks, relatively centralized power for decision making, and an elaborate administrative structure with a sharp distinction between line and staff.[7]

The Operating Core In the operating core (say, on an auto assembly line), the tasks are simple and repetitive and tend to require minimal skills and training. As a result, there is a clear division of labor, and formalization of behavior emerges as the key organizational concern. Because the workers are left with little discretion, coordination usually can't be achieved through mutual adjustment. Therefore, *direct supervision by first-line managers* and *standardization of work processes* handle most of the coordination.

The Middle Line Because it's essential to seal off the operating core from disruptive environmental influences, an elaborate administrative structure (or "middle management") exists in machine bureaucracies. In keeping with the drive toward specialization, managers in the middle line are usually divided into functional departments, and the managers themselves have three main tasks. One is to handle the disturbances that arise among the highly specialized workers of the operating core (since, even with standardized operating procedures, conflicts are bound to arise). A second is to act as liaison between the analysts of the technostructure (like industrial engineers) and the workers in the operating core. The third task is to "support the vertical flows in the structure—the aggregation of the feedback information up the hierarchy and the elaboration of the action plans that come back down."[8]

The Rest of the Structure Because the machine bureaucracy depends on the standardization of work processes for coordination, the technostructure—which houses analysts like industrial engineers—emerges as the key part of the structure. Although there is a sharp distinction between line and staff authority in machine bureaucracies, the standardizers in the technostructure—work analysts, job-description designers, schedulers, quality control engineers, and accountants—retain considerable informal power and have the job of standardizing everyone else's work. There is also a well-developed support staff, containing specialized units for activities like pricing and payroll. At the *strategic apex*, managers are largely concerned with what Mintzberg calls "fine tuning of their bureaucratic machines"—in other words, with ensuring that the organization runs smoothly and efficiently. Throughout the machine bureaucracy, in fact, there is an "obsession with control," which reflects (1) the drive to eliminate all possible uncertainty (so that the machine can run smoothly, without interruption), and (2) the fact that machine bureaucracies are structures riddled with conflict, because of the functional differentiation of departments and the rigid distinction between line and staff. The control systems themselves are thus devoted partly to managing the interunit squabbles that inevitably occur.

• *Determinants of the Machine Bureaucracy*

The main condition driving organizations toward machine bureaucracies is an environment that is simple and stable: The focus is on just one or two products or a very narrow product line, and technological innovation and competitive pressures for change are minimal. The machine bureaucracy also tends to be found in mature organizations, ones that are large enough to have the volume of operating work needed for repetition and standardization, and old enough to have been able to settle on the standards they wish to use.[9] Mass-production firms are the most familiar machine bureaucracies.

Examples of machine bureaucracies are presented in Figures 9-4 and 9-5. The first figure shows the machine bureaucracies as represented by Mintzberg's machine-bureaucracy configuration, and the second shows the structure of a large steel company that is organized as a machine bureaucracy. Notice the division of the *operating core* into an operations division and a marketing division, as well as the *strategic apex* (president and board of directors), *technostructure* (engineering, facilities planning), and *support staff* (personnel division, industrial relations).

THE PROFESSIONAL BUREAUCRACY

• Introduction

Many organizations are bureaucratic without being highly centralized like the machine bureaucracies. In these organizations—which include universities, general hospitals, and public accounting firms—the work is stable, so that behavior can be standardized, predetermined, and predictable, while at the same time complex, so that it must be controlled directly by the operators who do it. Professional bureaucracies thus rely on the skills and knowledge of their operating professionals to function; they all produce standard products or services.

• The Basic Structure

In professional bureaucracies like public accounting firms, highly trained and indoctrinated specialists—professionals—are hired for the operating core and given con-

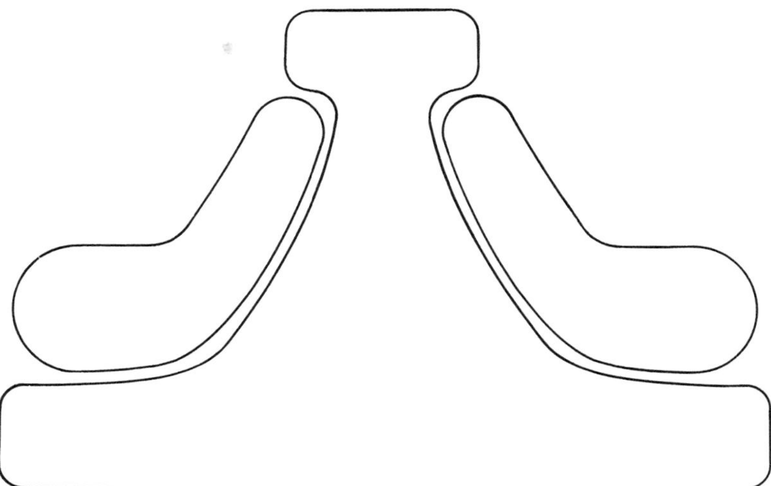

FIGURE 9-4 The Machine Bureaucracy

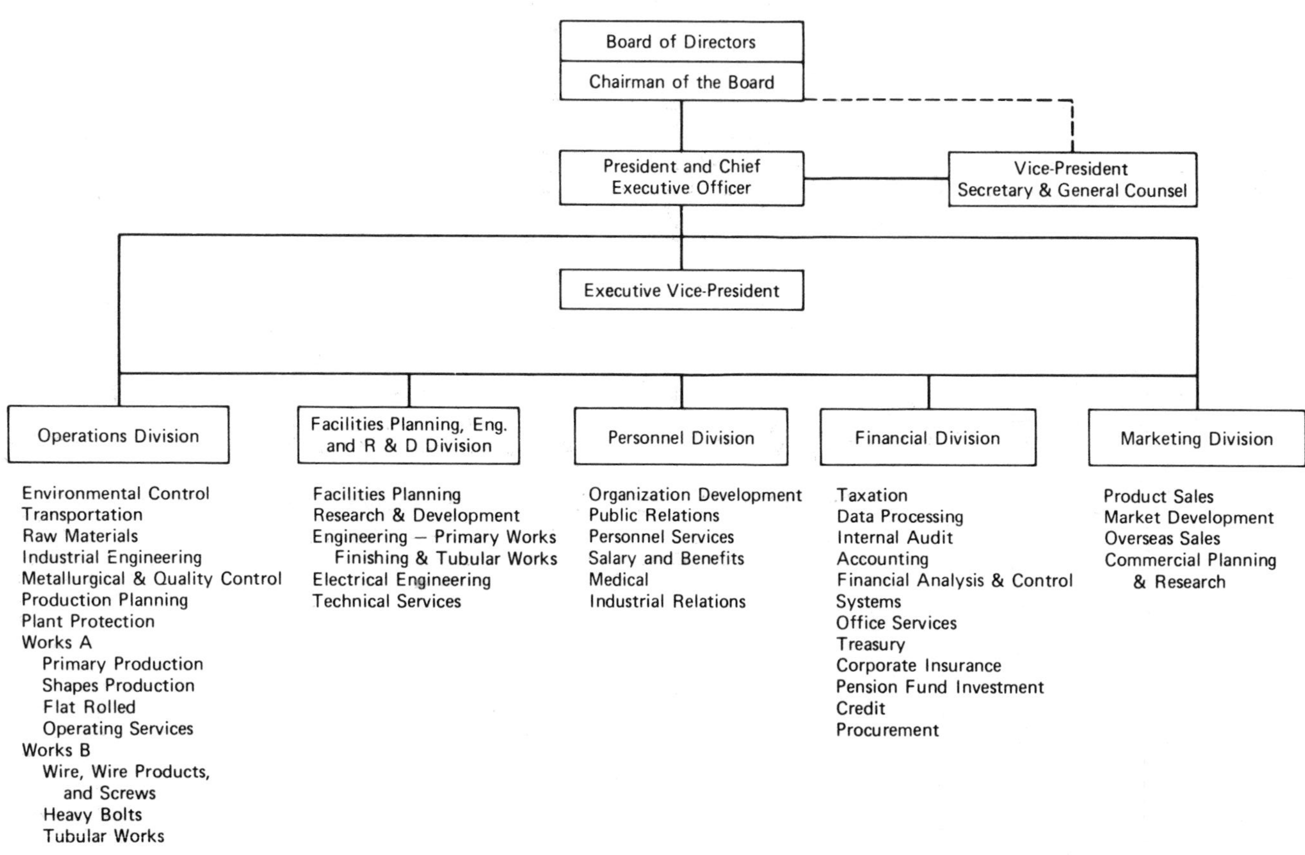
Board of Directors
Chairman of the Board
President and Chief Executive Officer
Vice-President Secretary & General Counsel
Executive Vice-President
Operations Division
Facilities Planning, Eng. and R & D Division
Personnel Division
Financial Division
Marketing Division
Environmental Control
Transportation
Raw Materials
Industrial Engineering
Metallurgical & Quality Control
Production Planning
Plant Protection
Works A
Primary Production
Shapes Production
Flat Rolled
Operating Services
Works B
Wire, Wire Products, and Screws
Heavy Bolts
Tubular Works
Facilities Planning
Research & Development
Engineering – Primary Works
Finishing & Tubular Works
Electrical Engineering
Technical Services
Organization Development
Public Relations
Personnel Services
Salary and Benefits
Medical
Industrial Relations
Taxation
Data Processing
Internal Audit
Accounting
Financial Analysis & Control
Systems
Office Services
Treasury
Corporate Insurance
Pension Fund Investment
Credit
Procurement
Product Sales
Market Development
Overseas Sales
Commercial Planning & Research

FIGURE 9-5 Organigram of a Large Steel Company

siderable control over their own work. Professional bureaucracies thus rely for coordination on the *standardization of skills* of professionals, so that, for instance, the managing partner of a public accounting firm can be reasonably sure that his field staff's work will be accomplished effectively even without his active involvement. For example, he can be reasonably sure that one of his accountants, when at a client's for an audit, will collect all the required information and analyze it fully, so that the resulting audit meets the standards of the firm and national association of CPAs. Since the professionals in such a firm exert considerable control over their own work, the implication is that they also work relatively independently of their colleagues but closely with the clients they serve.

The "professionalization" of the employees in such a firm usually begins with a long period of college study. Most such organizations also have well-developed training and indoctrination programs, although it is also common to have a long period of on-the-job training, such as an internship in medicine.

All this training is geared to one goal, says Mintzberg—the internalization of standards that serve the client and coordinate the professional work. In other words, the structure of these organizations is essentially bureaucratic, in that its coordination, like that of the machine bureaucracy, is achieved by design, by standards that predetermine what is to be done.[10] However, machine and professional bureaucracies generate their own standards, in terms of work standards designed and imposed by the technostructure on the operators and line managers. In the professional bureaucracy, on the other hand, standardization (and compliance) comes more from within the operators themselves, at least insofar as the operators, in joining their profession, are committed to the values and standards of the professional group (like the American Medical Association) that they've chosen to join.[11]

• *An Example*

An example of a professional bureaucracy is depicted in Figures 9-6 and 9-7. In the professional bureaucracy, the *operating core* (with its highly trained professionals) is the key component. In most such firms, the only other part that is fully elaborated

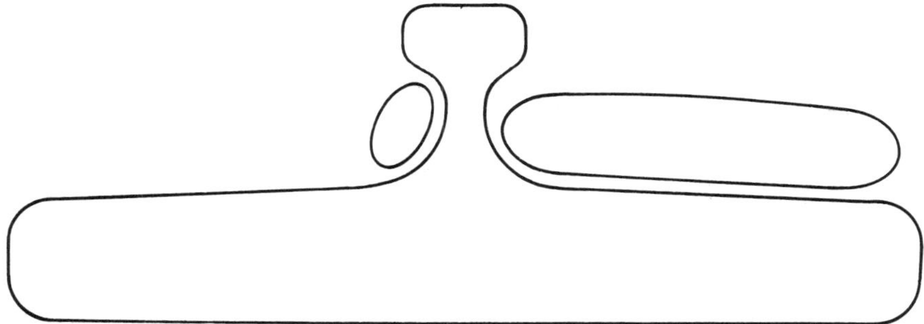

FIGURE 9-6 The Professional Bureaucracy

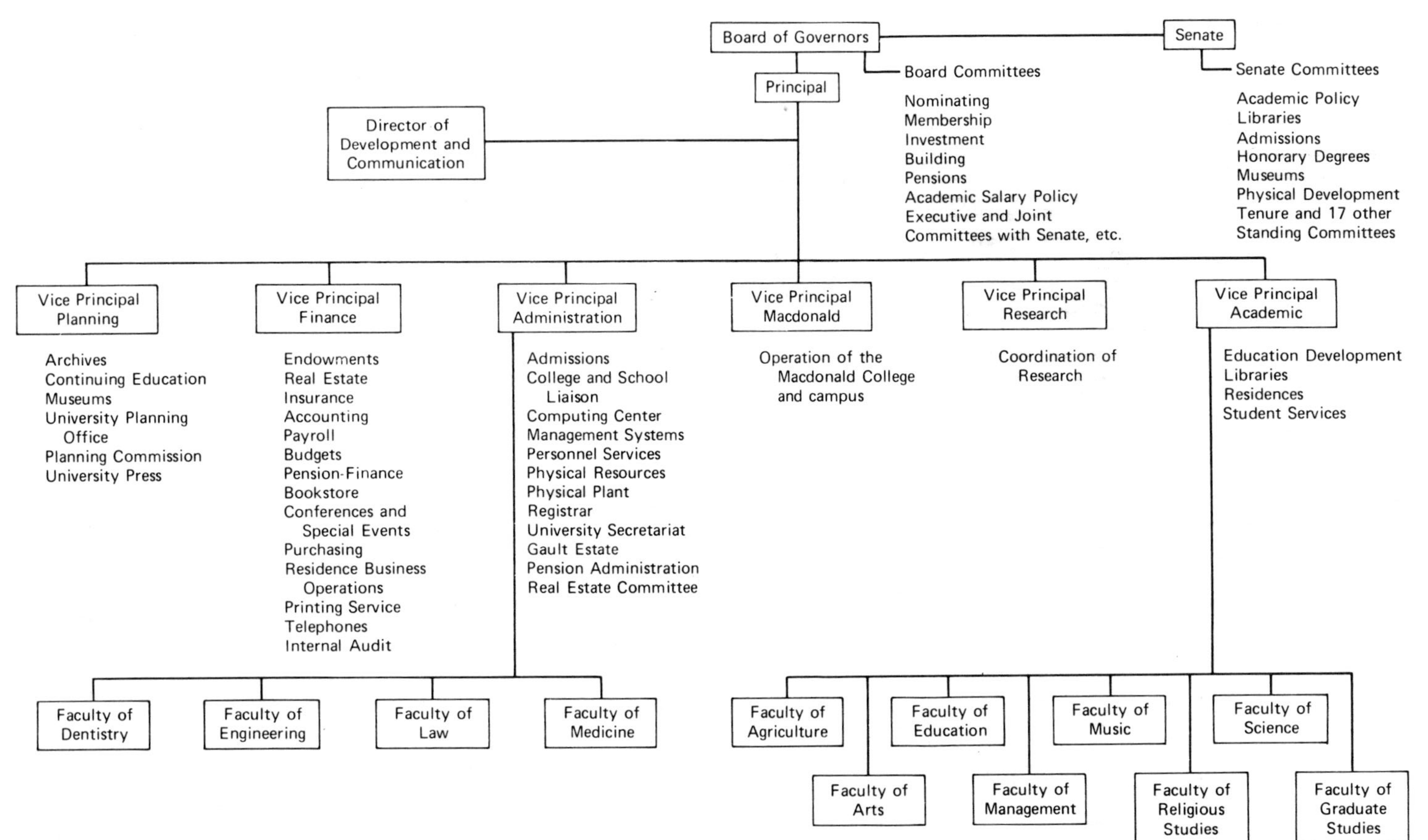

Board of Governors
Senate
Board Committees
Nominating
Membership
Investment
Building
Pensions
Academic Salary Policy
Executive and Joint
Committees with Senate, etc.
Senate Committees
Academic Policy
Libraries
Admissions
Honorary Degrees
Museums
Physical Development
Tenure and 17 other
Standing Committees
Principal
Director of Development and Communication
Vice Principal Planning
Archives
Continuing Education
Museums
University Planning Office
Planning Commission
University Press
Vice Principal Finance
Endowments
Real Estate
Insurance
Accounting
Payroll
Budgets
Pension-Finance
Bookstore
Conferences and Special Events
Purchasing
Residence Business Operations
Printing Service
Telephones
Internal Audit
Vice Principal Administration
Admissions
College and School Liaison
Computing Center
Management Systems
Personnel Services
Physical Resources
Physical Plant
Registrar
University Secretariat
Gault Estate
Pension Administration
Real Estate Committee
Vice Principal Macdonald
Operation of the Macdonald College and campus
Vice Principal Research
Coordination of Research
Vice Principal Academic
Education Development
Libraries
Residences
Student Services
Faculty of Dentistry
Faculty of Engineering
Faculty of Law
Faculty of Medicine
Faculty of Agriculture
Faculty of Arts
Faculty of Education
Faculty of Management
Faculty of Music
Faculty of Religious Studies
Faculty of Science
Faculty of Graduate Studies

Note: This unofficial organigram was drawn by Henry Mintzberg based upon university documents.

FIGURE 9-7 Organigram of McGill University (circa 1978)

is the *support staff,* because "given the high cost of the professionals, it makes sense to back them up with as much support as possible, to aid them and have others do whatever routine work can be formalized."[12] Thus, universities have printing facilities, faculty clubs, and other such support units. At the same time, the technostructure tends *not* to be highly elaborated (since there is little need for or possibility of forcing the professionals to adhere to company-generated work standards), and there tends to be minimal use of a middle line of management, since the professionals mostly coordinate and control themselves. In other words, there is relatively little need for direct supervision of these professionals, who in effect supervise themselves. The professional bureaucracy is of course highly decentralized, with decision making delegated down the chain of command and the professionals—nonmanagers—having considerable authority.

• *Determinants of the Professional Bureaucracy*

Professional bureaucracies exist wherever the operating core of an organization is dominated by professionals who use procedures that are difficult to learn yet are well defined.[13] According to Mintzberg, "this means an environment that is both complex and stable—complex enough to require the use of difficult procedures that can be learned only in extensive formal training programs, yet stable enough to enable these skills to become well defined, in effect, standardized."[14] The environment is thus the major factor leading to the use of the professional bureaucracy. The most familiar example of the professional bureaucracy is the *personal-service organization,* such as universities, accounting firms, and law and consulting firms.

THE DIVISIONALIZED FORM

• *Introduction*

According to Mintzberg:

> Like the professional bureaucracy, the divisionalized form is not so much an integrated organization as a set of quasi-autonomous entities coupled together by a central administrative structure. But whereas those "loosely coupled" entities in the professional bureaucracy are individuals—professionals in the operating core—in the divisionalized form they are units in the middle line. These units are generally called *divisions,* and the central administration, the headquarters.[15]

The divisionalized form is widely used among America's largest corporations, the vast majority of which have taken the divisionalized form. Note, though, that the divisionalized form is not a complete structure from the strategic apex to the operating core as were the other configurations we discussed. Instead, the divisionalized form is more a structure superimposed on others, in that *each division has its own structure;* the divisionalized-form configuration itself focues on the structural relationship between the headquarters and the divisions—in effect, between the strategic apex and the top of the middle line.[16]

• *The Basic Structure*

Perhaps the most familiar characteristic of the divisionalized form is the fact that the units (divisions) at the top of the middle line are grouped around markets (usually, products or customer groups). As we explained in Chapter 6, divisions are created according to the market served and are then given control of the operating functions (production, sales, finance, and so forth) required to serve these markets. This dispersal and duplication of the operating functions minimizes the interdependence between divisions, so that each can operate essentially as a quasi-autonomous entity, free of the need to coordinate with the others. At the same time, the structural arrangement leads to pronounced decentralization from headquarters, but, as we discussed, this decentralization tends to be highly circumscribed: The top managers of the divisions are given considerable authority, but certain essential companywide decisions (regarding matters like cash management and major capital outlays) are usually centralized. Furthermore, there is generally little decentralization *within* the divisions, which themselves tend to be functionally organized. As a rule, the prime coordinating mechanism in the divisionalized form is the *standardization of outputs,* in that specific financial targets are set for the divisions and then monitored by a central planning staff at headquarters. The divisionalized figuration is depicted in Figure 9-8.

• *Determinants of the Divisionalized Form*

As we explained in our discussion of Chandler's "structure-follows-strategy" findings, the main contingency factor driving the organization to become divisionalized is *market diversity.* An organization faced with disparate markets has an incentive to

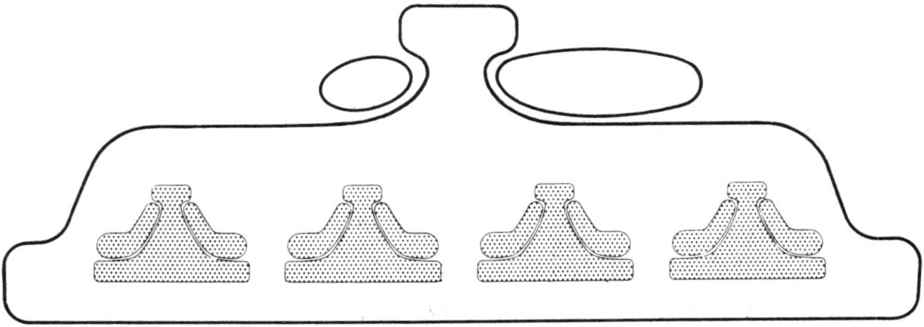

FIGURE 9-8 The Divisionalized Form

create a unit to deal with each one, whereas the organization faced with a single integrated market simply can't split itself into autonomous divisions.

Several other determinants are associated with the divisionalized form. Divisionalization is, first, only possible when the organization's technological system can be efficiently separated into segments, one for each division. Thus, an aluminum company with a single expensive smelter may be unable to set up several divisions, since it can't duplicate its smelters, but a company like General Electric may be able to build several assembly plants for its various product lines.[17]

The divisionalized form works best in environments that are neither very complex nor very dynamic, the same environment that leads to the machine bureaucracy.[18] In fact, divisionalized forms often start out as machine bureaucracies, (recall Westinghouse, for instance); they operate in simple, stable environments but then "graduate" to divisionalized forms when the company diversifies its product lines. Similarly, age and size often lead to divisionalization, since, as organizations grow larger and older, they often divisionalize, partly to diversify (and thus reduce the risk of putting all their eggs in one basket) and partly to maintain their growth after expansion in their traditional lines becomes more difficult.

THE ADHOCRACY

• Introduction: The Need for Adhocracy

In their study of the management of innovation, Burns and Stalker found that the electronics firms encountered very high rates of technical and other change and, as a result, were forced to continually innovate new and varied products. Innovation to these firms was vital, since without it, they could not survive in their rapidly changing and turbulent environment.

These firms, you may recall, were organized very differently from those that were geared to exist under more stable conditions. For example, in these innovative firms, a deliberate attempt was made to avoid specifying individual tasks and to forbid any dependence on the management hierarchy. The head of one of the firms the researchers talked to, for instance, attacked the idea of the organization chart as inapplicable in his concern and as a "dangerous method of thinking about the working of industrial management."[19] In these firms, *employees' roles were continually defined and redefined in connection with specific projects and as members of specific cooperative groups or task forces.* These firms were, in other words, networks of continually shifting groups and individuals, always working on developing new products. And although this caused some ambiguity and concern for some employees, a set of common beliefs and a sense of common purpose helped to hold the employees together and to ensure that the work of the organization was done effectively.

Recent studies also support the fact that innovation demands this sort of organic, free-flowing management system. In their search of excellent (and highly innovative) corporations, for instance, Peters and Waterman found that the most effective firms were organized loosely around venture product teams, informal communications, voluntary assignment of team members, and a pervasive culture that supported the occasional failures while encouraging continued creativity and innovation. Similarly, Toffler, in his book *Future Shock,* notes that what he calls adhocracies "now change their internal shape with a frequency—and sometimes a rashness—that makes the head swim. Titles change from week to week. Jobs are transformed. Responsibilities shift. Vast organizational structures are taken apart, bolted together again in new forms, then rearranged again. Departments and divisions spring up overnight only to vanish in another, and yet another, reorganization."[20]

Similarly, says Mintzberg, none of the structural configurations so far discussed in this chapter is capable of sophisticated innovation, the kind required of a space agency or a sophisticated defense/electronics firm like Hewlett Packard.

> The simple structure can certainly innovate, but only in a relatively simple way. Both the machine and professional bureaucracies are performance, not problem-solving, structures. They are designed to perfect standard programs, not to invent new ones. And while the divisionalized form resolves the problem of strategic flexibility in the machine bureaucracy, . . . it, too, is not truly innovative. A focus on control by standardizing outputs does not encourage innovation.[21]

Instead, to repeat, innovation requires a different configuration, "one that is able to fuse experts drawn from different disciplines into smoothly functioning ad hoc project teams."[22] The resulting structure may be termed the adhocracy.

• *The Basic Structure*

The adhocracy is, first, an organic, free-flowing structure, one with little formalization of behavior; a free-flowing network of communications; a tendency to group specialists in functional units for housekeeping purposes but to deploy them in small, market-based project teams to do their work; and a reliance on mutual adjustment and liaisons to achieve coordination within and between these teams. Innovation demands breaking established patterns, so adhocracies cannot rely on standardization to achieve coordination, nor on highly formalized behaviors, nor on an overemphasis on formal planning and control.[23] Instead, the adhocracy must be designed for spontaneity.

In the adhocracy, there is a need to achieve a continual intermingling of highly specialized professionals like solid-state physicists, systems designers, and engineers. Adhocracies, like professional bureaucracies, are usually staffed with highly trained professionals with the skills to develop the firm's new product. But unlike the professional bureaucracy, the adhocracy can't rely on the standardized skills of these experts to achieve coordination, because that would lead to standardizaion (as it does in accounting firms) instead of innovation. "Rather, it must treat existing knowledge and skills merely as bases on which to build new ones."[24] Furthermore (unlike in, say, an accounting firm, where one expects the professional to apply a standard set of skills to a more or less standard set of auditing problems), the skills of the adhocracy's professionals must be combined and intermingled in order to create the technical breakthroughs that mean innovation. In the adhocracy, in other words, the professionals must amalgamate their efforts, and the main function of the adhocracy must be to encourage this kind of cross-breeding. The adhocracy does this by minimizing the importance of traditional structural elements like the chain of command, substituting instead an organization built around small, market-based project teams and a highly organic structure and system of free-flowing communications. Coordination in the adhocracy must be achieved by those with the knowledge—that is, by the experts (say, the engineers on the project teams) who actually do the project work. This means that in the adhocracy, *mutual adjustment* again becomes the prime coordinating mechanism, as it is in the simple structure. But whereas in the simple structure, it is often a strong central manager who provides an integrating sense of purpose for the organization, in the adhocracy it is more often a pervasive company culture that facilitates tight coordination, a culture that embodies the basic philosophy and values of the enterprise and to which all its employees become committed through a long period of careful scanning and socialization.

The Matrix Mintzberg contends that in practice, the matrix structure is most representative of the adhocracy, in that adhocracies also tend to use both functional and project bases for grouping concurrently. In other words, the experts are grouped in functional units for housekeeping purposes—for hiring, for professional communication, and the like—but are employed in project teams to carry out their basic work.[25] As a result, says Mintzberg, managers abound in the adhocracy. There are *functional managers* responsible for their functional specialties (like engineering), *project managers* responsible for accomplishing the missions of their project teams, and *integrating managers* and other liaison positions to coordinate the efforts among the functional units and project teams.

Yet based on their study of excellent companies, Peters and Waterman raised a warning about the use of matrix structures. The most effective corporate innovators, they say, maintain "simple form, and lean staff" and keep their structures as simple as possible. Therefore, say Peters and Waterman, "our favorite candidate for the wrong kind of complex response, of course, is the matrix organization structure,"[26] since the matrix, as used today, often breeds confusion and complexity by making it unclear who reports to whom and what each employee's priorities really are (for example, is he or she primarily committed to a functional group, or to a project team?). In their efforts to deal with the ensuing confusion, say Peters and Waterman, many matrix-based firms react by appointing a cadre of staffers (Mintzberg's "liaison managers") who, they say, "gain and retain substantial power by ensuring that everything stays complex and unclear"; that is, the staff becomes the umpire at the matrix cross-over points, where, say, project and function clash.[27]

In the best-run companies, say these authors, something very different is meant by *matrix management*. In these organizations (like Boeing and NASA), "people operate in a binary way: They are *either* a part of a project team and responsible to that team for getting some task accomplished, *or* they are part of a technical discipline, in which they spend some time making sure their technical department is keeping up with the state of the art. When they are on a project, there is no day in, day out confusion about whether they are really responsible to the project or not. They are."[28]

The Operating Adhocracy Mintzberg distinguishes between two types of adhocracies—operating and administrative. The operating adhocracy contains multidisciplinary teams that innovate and solve problems directly on behalf of its clients. Examples here include think-tank consulting firms, creative advertising agencies, and manufacturers of engineering prototypes. The operating adhocracy is similar in some respects to a professional bureaucracy, but with one major difference: "Faced with a client problem, the operating adhocracy engages in creative effort to find the novel solution; the professional bureaucracy pigeonholes it into a known contingency to which it can apply a standard program. One engages in divergent thinking aimed at innovation; the other in convergent thinking aimed at perfection."[29]

A distinguishing feature of an operating adhocracy is that its administrative and operating work tend to blend into a single effort. That is, in an operating adhocracy, such as a creative advertising agency, it is difficult to differentiate the planning and design of the work from its actual execution, since both require the same specialized skills on a project-by-project basis. As a result, "the operating adhocracy may not even bother to distinguish its middle line from its operating core." Middle managers, support staff (like market researchers), and operating employees (like artists) work together on project teams.

The Administrative Adhocracy Like the operating adhocracy, the administrative adhocracy also depends on project teams. But unlike the operating adhocracy, it does make a sharp distinction between its administrative component and its operating core, and the operating core is usually cut right off from the rest of the organization, with the administrative component that remains continuing to be structured as a project-oriented adhocracy. One way to accomplish this is to do away with the operating core altogether, perhaps by contracting the operating work out to private companies, as NASA did in the 1960s.

Management in the Adhocracy In both types of adhocracy, the relation between the operating core and the administrative component is unlike that of any other structural configuration. In the operating adhocracy, management merges with the operating core into a single entity; in the administrative adhocracy, the operating core becomes a relatively unimportant and often separate part of the organization. In both cases, *line managers need exercise little direct supervision over the operating employees;* instead, the managers become functioning members of the project teams, with special responsibility to effect coordination between them.[30] But in this capacity, the managers act more as peers than as supervisors, and their influence derives from their expertise and interpersonal skills rather than from their formal positions. One side effect of this is that the distinction between line and staff blurs in the adhocracy.

• *Determinants of the Adhocracy*

Adhocracy is primarily a response to an environment that is both dynamic and complex. A dynamic, rapidly changing environment (like that confronting high-technology companies) calls for an organic structure, whereas the complex environment calls for a differentiated, decentralized one. *Adhocracy is the only configuration that is both organic and relatively decentralized,* in that the work is decentralized selectively to differentiated, self-contained work constellations or project teams.[31]

• *Specific Attributes of Adhocracies*

In their study, Peters and Waterman found that eight attributes seemed to set apart the most excellent, innovative companies. In most cases, these companies were organized as adhocracies, so a brief description of each attribute can help illustrate what real-life adhocracies (and other excellent organizations) are like.[32]

A Bias for Action *A bias for action* pervades Peters and Waterman's excellent companies. While less effective firms "are ensnared in massive reports that have been massaged by various staffs and sometimes, quite literally, hundreds of staffers and interlocking committees and task forces," life in most excellent companies is dramatically different. Task forces do exist but for only several days or weeks, and they have just a few employees working on a clear and specific mission. Communication (as we explained in Chapter 8) flows freely, and numerous techniques are used to spur informal communication and get everyone talking. Small groups are usually the basic organizational building blocks for excellent companies, and firms like 3M often have several hundred four- to ten-person venture teams working on projects at the same time. Membership in these project groups tends to be voluntary and limited to ten or less, and the task forces are usually pulled together rapidly, when needed, and usually not accompanied by a formal chartering process. Documentation is usually informal, and no staff are assigned as executive directors, "assistant-tos" or full-time report writers. *Experimentation,* often in the form of getting the project to the market on a small, limited basis, is encouraged. Pervading the whole innovative firm is thus a basic action orientation, fostered through the use of ad hoc task forces, small groups, and temporary structures. There isn't the preoccupation with doing things by the rules that one finds in the machine bureaucracy.

Close to the Customers "Stay close to the customer" is a central value in the excellent firms. To make sure it stays in touch, for instance, IBM measures customer satisfaction on a monthly basis, and corporate officers still make sales calls with great regularity.

Autonomy and Entrepreneurship Perhaps the most important element of these companies' enviable track records is an ability to be big and yet act small at the same time, thereby encouraging the entrepreneurial spirit among their people. Small, market-oriented groups predominate in the adhocracy-type structures of the excellent firms, with hundreds of "venture teams" at 3M, more than 90 product customers-centers at Texas Instruments, and more than 150 product divisions (called "companies"), each with its own chairman, at Johnson & Johnson. This may seem duplicative and inefficient, but:

> . . . it eventually became clear that all of these companies were making a purposeful tradeoff. They were creating almost radical decentralization and autonomy, with its attendant overlap, messiness around the edges, lack of coordination, internal competition, and somewhat chaotic conditions, in order to breed the entrepreneurial spirit. They had forsworn a measure of tidiness in order to achieve regular innovation.[33]

Even in multibillion-dollar companies like Hewlett Packard and Johnson & Johnson, divisions are intentionally kept small ($70 million at Hewlett Packard and $30 million at Johnson & Johnson) and limited to about 1,000 employees. When the divisions approach 2,000 people, they are reorganized into smaller units, each, as usual, with full product-development capability.[34] In these excellent firms, autonomy and entrepreneurship are thus encouraged, and the structural implication of this is that the organization is designed as an adhocracy with numerous interdisciplinary project groupings accomplishing the company's work.

Productivity through People Executives in the excellent firms express an abiding belief in getting productivity through people—in other words, the capabilities of their employees to do a great job. Structurally, this translates into the absence of a rigidly adhered-to chain of command, less "organization consciousness" (to use Burns and Stalker's term), and a flatter organization, one with fewer layers between the president and first-line operators. And, to repeat, the excellent firms find a way to keep their operating units small. They do this because:

> . . . the point of smallness is that it induces manageability and, above all, commitment. A manager really can understand something that is small and in which one central discipline prevails. More important, even in institutions that employ hundreds of thousands of people, if the divisions are small enough, or if there are other ways of simulating autonomy, the individual still counts and can stand out.[35]

In firm after firm, therefore, operating units are kept small. At Johnson & Johnson, Hewlett Packard, and 3M (as already noted), operating divisions are kept to $30 to $40 million per division on average. At Emerson Electric, few plants employ more than 600 workers, a size at which the chairman feels that management can maintain personal contact with individual employees. Similarly, at Blue Bell manufacturing, units are kept at about 300 people. As a result, there is increased face-to-face contact; supervisors get to know the families, concerns, and day-to-day problems of each of their people; and the operators themselves can more closely identify with the goals of their unit. The conclusion that Peters and Waterman draw from their research is that, regardless of industry, "it seems that more than 500 or so people under one roof causes substantial and unanticipated problems. More significant, even for the cost-oriented companies, small is not only more innovative but also more productive."[36]

Hands-on, Value-driven As we've already seen, virtually all the successful organic/adhocracy companies (including Burns and Stalker's, Woodward's, and Peters and Waterman's) had a clear set of guiding beliefs and values that were internalized by all employees and that helped to guide them as they made their day-to-day decisions at work. These values (like a belief in being the best, a belief in superior quality and services, and a belief that most members of the organization should be innovators) were usually stated in qualitative terms and spread not through policies and procedures manuals but through a socialization process in which all managers and employees gradually internalized the stories and myths that were always the carriers of the values present in these firms. In most of these firms, dominant leaders (like Thomas Watson, Sr., at IBM, and Ray Kroc at McDonald's) viewed their major role as setting the tone of their firms; that is, as establishing a simple guiding set of principles or values that would percolate throughout the organization and act as guiding beacons for all their employees.

Stick to the Knitting Another attribute of excellent firms is that organizations that branch out into other products or services (whether by acquisition or internal diversification) usually "stick very close to their knitting." Ideally, they diversify around a single skill, the way 3M diversified around the coating and bonding technology, for instance.[37] The second best alternative is to branch out into related fields, such as General Electric's move from electric power-generation turbines to jet engines (another turbine). The least successful companies, say Peters and Waterman, diversified into a wide variety of fields and must now contend with businesses they know little about.

Simple Form, Lean Staff Excellent companies generally don't have complex, ambiguous matrix structures and overburdening staffs; instead, "underpinning most of the excellent companies we find a fairly stable, unchanging form—perhaps the product division—that provides the essential touchstone which everybody understands, and from which the complexities of day-to-day life can be approached."[38] The most common simple form that Peters and Waterman found was the product division, although many other companies had maintained something close to a basic functional form. In these companies, "simplicity in the basic structural arrangement actually facilitates organizational flexibility. It seems that because the basic form is clear, flexibility around the basic structure is made easy. The excellent companies, as we've seen, do make better use of task forces, project centers, and other ad hoc devices to make things happen. The excellent companies also *appear* to be reorganizing all the time. They are; but most of the reorganization takes place around the edges. The fundamental form rarely changes that much."[39] Similarly, the headquarters staffs of these corporations are held to a minimum: Emerson Electric has 54,000 employees and fewer than 100 in corporate headquarters, Dana employs 35,000 people and fewer than 100 in corporate headquarters, and Schlumberger, the $6-billion diversified oil service company, runs its worldwide empire with a corporate staff of 90.[40]

Related to this, spans of control tend to be very wide in these organizations, since the employees, all of whom are committed to the organization's basic unifying values, generally require less supervision. What emerges, say Peters and Waterman, is an organization chart that looks much like an hourglass, with a corporate headquarters, a minimal middle management, and a large network of operating employees. Their findings are quite consistent with Mintzberg's adhocracy configurations.

Simultaneous Loose-Tight Properties Finally, and in summary, the most effective organizations exhibit simultaneously both loose and tight traits. On the loose side, Peters and Waterman found:

> . . . clubby, campus-like environments, flexible organizational structures (hiving off new divisions, regular reorganizations), volunteers, zealous project champions, maximized autonomy for individuals, teams, and divisions, regular and extensive experimentation, positive reinforcement, (such as quickly introducing new products on a prototype basis), and strong social networks and a spirit of camaradarie. All of these traits focus on the positive, the excitement of trying things out in a slightly disorderly (loose) fashion.[41]

But at the same time, these excellent companies exhibited a remarkably tight, culturally driven set of properties that enabled them to stay on target. For example, most had rigidly shared values—in other words, an organizational culture that emphasized values such as an action orientation, regular informal communications, quick feedback, and quality and service. In these organizations, nothing gets very far out of line, because each employee is a committed employee, and each knows what the organization expects. And, of course, the process of constant interaction and communication ensures that everyone knows what everyone else is up to. In these excellent companies, therefore, *autonomy is a product of discipline.* The discipline (a few shared values) provides the framework. "It gives people confidence (to experiment, for instance) stemming from stable expectations about what really counts."[42] Thus, as we will see in our discussion of organizational leadership and culture in Chapter 13, *organizational culture*—a set of shared values—provides the framework in which autonomy can safely prevail. There is, in other words, a pervasive self-discipline in these firms, a self-discipline born of commitment to a set of common, shared values that is in turn bred through a careful process of selection and socialization. Quality, innovativeness, informality, customer service, and people; these are the central values that guide adhocracies and that constitute the guiding framework within which their employees exercise self-control.

SUMMARY

Mintzberg contends that most organization structures can be classified as belonging to one of five ideal structural configurations, which he calls simple structure, machine bureaucracy, professional bureaucracy, divisionalized form, and adhocracy. The simple structure is more than anything a nonstructure, in that it avoids using all the formal devices of structure like division of work and decentralization. It is best for simple, dynamic environments. The machine bureaucracy is the typical mechanistic organization and is ideal for simple, unchanging tasks. The professional bureaucracy (such as an accounting firm) consists of highly trained professionals who are given a great deal of discretion, so that its operating core is the key component. This type of structure exists wherever the operating core of an organization is dominated by professionals who use procedures that are difficult to learn yet are well defined. The divisionalized form is unique, in that each division typically has its own structure; the main contingency factor driving such organizations is market diversity.

Finally, in the adhocracy, we find a deliberate avoidance of specifying individual tasks and the forbidding of any dependence on the management hierarchy. Typically, adhocracies use informal communication devices (like those we discussed in Chapter 8) and techniques like project teams and innovation-oriented values to maintain "tight" control while ensuring "looseness" for innovation.

Discussion Questions

1. Explain each of Mintzberg's "five basic elements," relating them to traditional organizatonal components like staff and middle management.
2. Explain the nature and determinants of the simple structure, machine bureaucracy, professional bureaucracy, divisionalized form, and adhocracy.
3. Explain the difference and similarities between the machine bureaucracy and the professional bureaucracy.
4. As a project, examine the organization chart of your college and explain which of Mintzberg's five structural configurations it most nearly matches.
5. Explain each of the specific attributes of adhocracies.

FOOTNOTES

[1]Material in this chapter is based largely on Henry Mintzberg, *The Structuring of Organizations* (Englewood Cliffs, N.J.: Prentice-Hall, 1979); and Henry Mintzberg. *Structure in Fives: Designing Effective Organizations* (Englewood Cliffs, N.J.: Prentice-Hall, 1983).

[2]Mintzberg, *Structure in Fives,* pp. 99–101.

[3]*Ibid.,* p. 105.

[4]*Ibid.,* p. 156.

[5]Mintzberg, *The Structuring of Organizations,* p. 308.

[6]*Ibid.,* p. 310.

[7]*Ibid.,* p. 315.

[8]*Ibid.,* p. 316.

[9]*Ibid.,* p. 325.

[10]*Ibid.,* p. 351.

[11]*Ibid.,* p. 351.

[12]*Ibid.,* p. 355.

[13]*Ibid.,* p. 366.

[14]*Ibid.*

[15]*Ibid.,* p. 380.

[16]*Ibid.,* p. 381.

[17]Recall, though, that some companies, like General Motors, have got around this problem by setting up decentralized divisions while at the same time maintaining large centralized production facilities. This may be treated as a hybrid—combining aspects of both the divisionalized form and the machine bureaucracy.

[18]Mintzberg, *The Structuring of Organizations,* p. 399.

[19]Tom Burns and G. M. Stalker, *The Management of Innovation* (London: Tavistock, 1969), p. 92.

[20]Alvin Toffler, *Future Shock* (New York: Bantam Books, 1970), p. 128.

[21]Mintzberg, *The Structuring of Organizations,* p. 432.

[22]*Ibid.*

[23]Note that the simple structure is also organic and therefore capable of innovation, but innovation is restricted to simple environments that can be easily comprehended and controlled by a central leader.

[24]Mintzberg, *The Structuring of Organizations,* p. 434.

[25]*Ibid.,* p. 435.

[26]Thomas Peters and Robert Waterman, Jr., *In Search of Excellence* (New York: Harper & Row, 1982), p. 306.

[27]*Ibid.,* p. 308.

[28]*Ibid.,* p. 307.

[29]Mintzberg, *The Structuring of Organizations,* p. 436.

[30]*Ibid.,* p. 440.

[31]Note that the divisionalized form is not a highly organic one and that, furthermore, the operating cores of the divisions are often organized as matching bureaucracies.

[32]This section is based on Peters and Waterman, *In Search of Excellence,* pp. 119–325.

[33]Peters and Waterman, *In Search of Excellence,* p. 201.

[34]*Ibid.,* p. 215.

[35]*Ibid.,* pp. 271–72.

[36]*Ibid.,* p. 275.

[37]*Ibid.,* p. 293.

[38]*Ibid.,* p. 308.

[39]*Ibid.,* p. 311.

[40]*Ibid.,* p. 311.

[41]*Ibid.,* p. 320.

[42]*Ibid.,* p. 322.

CASE FOR CHAPTER 9
THE SHAPE OF THINGS TO COME*

W. Brooke Tunstall

> This is not the end. It is not even the beginning of the end. But it is perhaps the end of the beginning.
>
> Winston Churchill

Ten short years ago, the organizational structure of the Bell System reflected more than half a century of stability and success. A structure ideally suited for a "steady state" regulated environment, it had stood the test of time so well that, to at least one highly placed AT&T corporate officer, discussion of organization change was "out of bounds" in his presence.

But the extended calm was deceptive. In the past decade, we have undertaken two reorganizations, each lasting five years—and now we are on the brink of a third and far more drastic restructuring. In 1973, AT&T and the operating companies moved from the highly efficient functional structure of plant/traffic/commercial to a customer services/operator services/network services structure. The new structure was responsive to the reality of existing service needs, and at the same time, it positioned the company to move forward in an era of gradually increasing competition.

Even as the new structure was being implemented, however, further evolution was being anticipated. In the early fall of 1973, John D. deButts, then AT&T chairman of the board, predicted, "The competitive structure—one focused on markets and requiring the segmentation of business and residence accounts—is about five years down the road." His was an uncanny forecast. As if measured with the accuracy of sidereal time, the market-oriented business/residence/network structure was implemented at AT&T in the fall of 1978, exactly five years later, and in the operating companies a few months after that.

At the time, it was hoped that we could settle down with our new structure, "fine-tuning" it as we came to understand the marketplace better. But dramatic events in the industry—to include most prominently the FCC's Computer Inquiry II Order (CI-2) and the Modification of Final Judgment (MFJ) signed by Judge Harold H. Greene in August—helped decide matters to the contrary. We now face the third and by far the most transforming structural change. Moreover, more change looms ahead. As the competitive world of telecommunications shakes down in 1984 and beyond, succeeding generations of managers can count on continual modifications

*This article is reprinted from *Bell Telephone Magazine,* No. 34 (1982), pp. 14–19. W. Brooke Tunstall is an assistant vice-president and director of corporate planning at AT&T.

to the structure. Forged by new products, new services, and above all, new management strategies, organization forms will adapt constantly in the years ahead.

• *Where We Are*

Organization theory holds that in a competitive environment, structure follows strategy; that is, the organizational forms are our means of focusing resources—people and dollars—on the strategic aims of the corporation. However, for the Bell System, organizational form also will be dramatically altered by mandates from arenas that are external to the corporation. CI-2 and the MFJ are larger-than-life examples.

In fact, whatever the yardsticks with which they are measured, the dislocations associated with both mandates are staggering. The divestiture of the 22 Bell operating companies ordered in the MFJ represents a "spinning off" of about 90 billion dollars of assets—unprecedented in all of corporate history. Such a breach leaves a multitude of structural rearrangements. For example, we are faced with the task of identifying tens of thousands of operating company business, residence, and interexchange people and transferring them to AT&T; of redeploying thousands more General Departments employees to the operating companies' central and regional staffs, to the interexchange organizations, and to the AT&T corporate management staff.

We do not have the luxury of focusing on divestiture issues alone, because a full year earlier we must meet the enormous restructuring challenges associated with CI-2. (The necessity of identifying and reassigning more than 70,000 employees to the fully separated subsidiary only hints at the size of *this* undertaking.)

By itself, either the CI-2 Order or the MFJ would have affected the Bell System's organizational structure dramatically. Taken together, however, they necessitate an organizational jigsaw puzzle that must be fitted together a piece at a time if it is to be comprehended. The following paragraphs attempt to escort the reader through the puzzle-solving process—first stating facts, then setting forth organizational solutions, and finally presenting as yet unasnswered questions about structure.

• *CI-2—Facts*

The Computer Inquiry II Order culminated a decade of effort by the FCC to introduce competition into the telecommunications industry. Essentially, the Order requires the formation of a fully separated subsidiary (FSS) to market all *new* customer premises equipment (CPE) and enhanced services. The split between the existing equipment and new equipment was dubbed—uneuphoniously—"bifurcation."

CI-2 also requires separate incorporation of the FSS, with neither officers nor books of account in common with AT&T carriers or their affiliates. Further, it stipulates that marketing, ordering, billing, and accounting must be *fully* separate; that product-specific (nongeneric) software must be developed within the corporate boundaries of the FSS or obtained from nonaffiliates; and that any information

AT&T provides the FSS on the network standards and related technical information must be made available to other interested parties. Finally, it orders that tariff regulation by the FCC or new CPE products and enhanced services will no longer exist after January 1, 1983.

Clearly, the Order was designed to place the FSS on an equal competitive footing with other vendors, with no cross-subsidy, in the form of dollars or knowledge, from other affiliates of AT&T. Bifurcation was designed to prevent the existing customer base from being used in the marketing and sale of new equipment.

• *CI-2—Organizational Response*

In response to CI-2, American Bell Inc. (ABI)—the beginnings of the FSS—has been formed and is beginning to offer certain elements of an enhanced service, AIS/Net 1000. On January 1, 1983, ABI will begin to offer new customer premises equipment; and some 27,000 operating company, Bell Labs, Western Electric, and AT&T employees will be transferred to ABI to form its initial corporate employee body. This group includes some 4,000 people from Bell Labs and Western Electric to perform hardware and software development and engineering/design functions.

Throughout 1983, each operating company will provide installation and maintenance for new business-systems CPE under contract. However, on January 1, 1984, the I&M force—another 45,000 employees—will be transferred from the operating companies to American Bell.

The final complement of ABI is currently put at approximately 76,000. (All the figures cited here represent plans as this article goes to press and are, of course, subject to modification as restructuring plans unfold.)

• *CI-2—Remaining Structural Questions*

ABI, which will be offering CPE and enhanced services, will meet all the externally imposed imperatives of CI-2. However, a number of internal managerial considerations are yet to be resolved. For example:

- How do we organize and operate the embedded base organization (EBO)—the in-place CPE left behind after ABI begins to offer new CPE on January 1, 1983?
- Would it be more effective for ABI to have its own manufacturing capability or to continue the current matrix arrangement with Western Electric?
- What should be the boundaries of the emerging lines of business (LOBs) within ABI?
- What is the most efficient deployment of staffs within ABI subtending units?

These are only several of the critical structural questions still under study. These kinds of questions—perhaps, in their ultimate effect, more profound than the external mandates—will have to be answered over time, after due consideration of all financial, operational, and service criteria.

Of course, the task of answering each such question is complicated dramatically by even larger structural changes looming just beyond—changes associated with the MFJ order to divest the exchange and exchange access parts of the business. It is, in fact, difficult to exaggerate the scope and complexity of this undertaking. One Bell operating company officer said of it: "It's much more like pulling taffy apart than like cutting a ribbon."

But why—given daily business-page accounts of mergers, acquisitions, divestitures, and joint ventures of other giant industrial corporations—is the Bell System's divestiture job *so* complex and wrenching?

There *are* explanations. One is that for the major part of this century, all Bell System elements have strived for the greatest possible integration of organizational forms and of operational and administrative systems. Driven by Theodore Vail's philosophy of "One System, One Policy, Universal Service," the nationwide network has been designed with integration as a constant goal. All internal administrative and operational support systems were designed as unified systems. Pricing structures have always tried to recover the full cost, based on "value of service" tenets. Physical assets (such as office space and motor vehicles) did not recognize exchange and interexchange boundaries. Jobs were not designed discretely between CPE, exchange, and interexchange. Finally, and profoundly, the corporate culture reflected the values of a vast and indivisible family, united by the concept of universal service.

There is no analogy to this experience in any other industry; there is no similar divestiture model to follow. In fact, the Bell System's horizontal divestiture is a one-time, one-industry happening—one in which thousands of Bell System people are tackling the arduous task of "pulling the taffy apart."

• *MFJ—Facts*

The basic thrust of the Modification of Final Judgment was to promote competition in the telecommunications industry by separating the "monopoly" exchange and exchange access services from the "competitive" services. Many other far-reaching provisions and stipulations are embedded in the MFJ as well. Major elements in the MFJ include the following:

- Exchange boundaries, referred to by AT&T as local access and transport areas (LATAs), are based on standard metropolitan statistical areas (SMSAs). Transport services (excluding, however, information services) within the LATA exchanges (i.e., intra-LATA services, which comprise the majority of the operating companies' assets) remain with the operating companies.
- Services between LATAs within each state—inter-LATA, intrastate—currently provided by the operating companies will be transferred to AT&T.
- Printed directory operations, both White and Yellow Pages, remain with the

operating companies. Certain limitations are placed on AT&T in the area of electronic publishing after divestiture.

- Cellular mobile telephone services to end-users (scheduled for late 1983) will belong to the divested operating companies. Design and development of cellular systems will remain with AT&T, in support of the operating companies.
- All existing ("embedded") customer premises equipment in the operating companies will be assigned to AT&T at divestiture.
- The operating companies will be permitted to market (but not to manufacture) new CPE after divestiture.
- Technical and operations support for the divested companies may be supplied by a central staff maintained by the divested companies.

• *MFJ—Organizational Response (AT&T)*

The basic job of restructuring post-divestiture AT&T is one of moving from a geographical profit-center orientation with a large General Departments central staff to a market-based national line-of-business profit-center orientation with a relatively small policy/strategy/financial management corporate staff. Such a rearrangement calls for the redeployment of the nearly 15,000 employees currently in the General Departments to the prospective post-divestiture entity staffs. These include the operating companies' central staff, operating company regional staffs, the new AT&T corporate staff, AT&T interexchange staff, ABI, information planning services allowed under the MFJ, and the embedded base organization.

The process by which this redeployment will be accomplished, dubbed functional realignment, is well under way, and the unbundling of the General Departments begins in the fourth quarter of this year.

By mid-1983, divestiture "shadow" organizations should be in place, ready to assume their new roles on the first day of 1984. (The early formation of post-divestiture structures is necessary because of the complexity of the task. In fact, a "flush cut" scenario is patently impractical, if not impossible.) A 6- to 12-month in-place "get ready" organizational plan is needed to assure a smooth transition.

AT&T's new building at 550 Madison Avenue in New York City, scheduled for completion in mid-1983, will serve as the new post-divestiture AT&T Headquarters. The roles, functions, and structure of the new headquarters operation will be considerably different from the aggregate General Departments of today. In contrast, it will be limited to corporatewide administration, strategic planning, financial management, policy formulation, and broad monitoring of key operational indicators. Following the pattern of most other large corporations, operational methods, practices, and decisions will be delegated to the profit-center-oriented lines of business—an arrangement representing a radical departure from former General Department's roles.

The AT&T interexchange entity (ATTIX), a combination of portions of the current Long Lines organization and the General Departments, plus the interexchange portion of the operating companies, will comprise the regulated sector after divestiture. The embedded CPE base, which is currently under regulation, will be managed by the embedded base organization. Its final positioning in the structure will unfold over the coming months.

ABI, AT&T International, AMPS, and those directory-like services allowed under the MFJ, in combination with Western Electric and Bell Laboratories, will make up the detariffed/unregulated sector's operational units. Western Electric and Bell Labs, freed by the MFJ from many constraints of the 1956 Consent Decree, will be unrestricted in their product and service offerings.

This new AT&T structure will, of course, reflect the separation of the detariffed portion of the business from the remaining portions in keeping with CI-2 mandates. In addition, other CI-2 requirements, such as the separation of books of account and boards of directors and the full distribution of technical information by AT&T to the FSS and all other vendors, will be put into effect.

• *MFJ—Remaining Structural Questions (AT&T)*

Both the limitations and the freedoms embodied in the MFJ present critically important internal questions with regard to structure. For example:

- To what degree should the LOBs be vertically integrated?
- What distribution channels should be used for the sale of telephones—and for the sale or lease of business systems?
- What should be the marketing strategy and structure for the embodied base organization?
- How should AT&T redeploy the General Departments staff units among the LOBs?
- How will ATTIX organizationally merge the interstate operations with the intrastate, inter-LATA units?

These questions are not trivial. In fact, the ways in which these questions are answered may have a profound impact on AT&T's future service and earnings performance for years to come.

• *MFJ—Organizational Response (Regional Companies)*

In preparing for divestiture, the regional company management teams have a different, albeit an equally challenging, set of strategic and structural decisions. In contrast to AT&T's job of redefining geographic profit centers into lines-of-business profit centers, the basic restructuring task for the regional companies (except for the Southwestern and Pacific companies) will be to combine and unify multiple geographic profit centers—formerly the operating companies—into a single, cohesive regional corporation. Fundamental to this unification will be the degree to which line and staff units are centralized within the region. Four alternative organization models present themselves on a spectrum ranging from highly decentralized to highly centralized:

- **Model 1—Highly Decentralized** Current operating company line and staff unit would remain decentralized and in place. A small regional planning and financial staff would be formed as a regional headquarters to guide, direct, and coordinate activities within the region.
- **Model 2—Partial Centralization of Staffs** "Corporate" staff functions (finance, planning, legal, regulatory, public relations/public affairs) would be regionally centralized, leaving operational staffs decentralized.
- **Model 3—Complete Centralization of Staffs** All staffs would be regionally centralized, leaving line units reporting to local operating companies.
- **Model 4—Highly Centralized** All line and staff units would be regionally centralized.

Judging from the organizational direction in recent years, one could expect the general trend among the regional companies to be toward the highly centralized model. However, the degree of centralization sought by each region will be influenced by a complex of factors, ranging from the chief executive's style of management and the size and makeup of current staff groups to geography, earnings requirements, and the degree of standardization of current administrative and operational support systems.

Another organizational requirement will be the replacement of staff functions—ranging from financial and technical planning to supplying central administrative services—formerly supplied by the General Departments under the License Contract. Some of these support functions will be assumed by the regional staffs, while others will be delegated to the operating companies' central staff unit.

• *MFJ—Remaining Structural Questions (Regional Companies)*

Not surprisingly, there are corollary strategic and structural questions that require answers, most appropriately by the regional chief executive officer. For example:

- What exchange and exchange access strategies and structures should be employed in the post-divestiture environment?
- What CPE strategies and structures offer the best opportunities?
- Should directory be combined into one regional organization?

Each region has set up steady teams to pursue answers to these and other such significant questions. Fortunately, the operating companies have accumulated a great deal of experience and intelligence in dealing with such questions since the

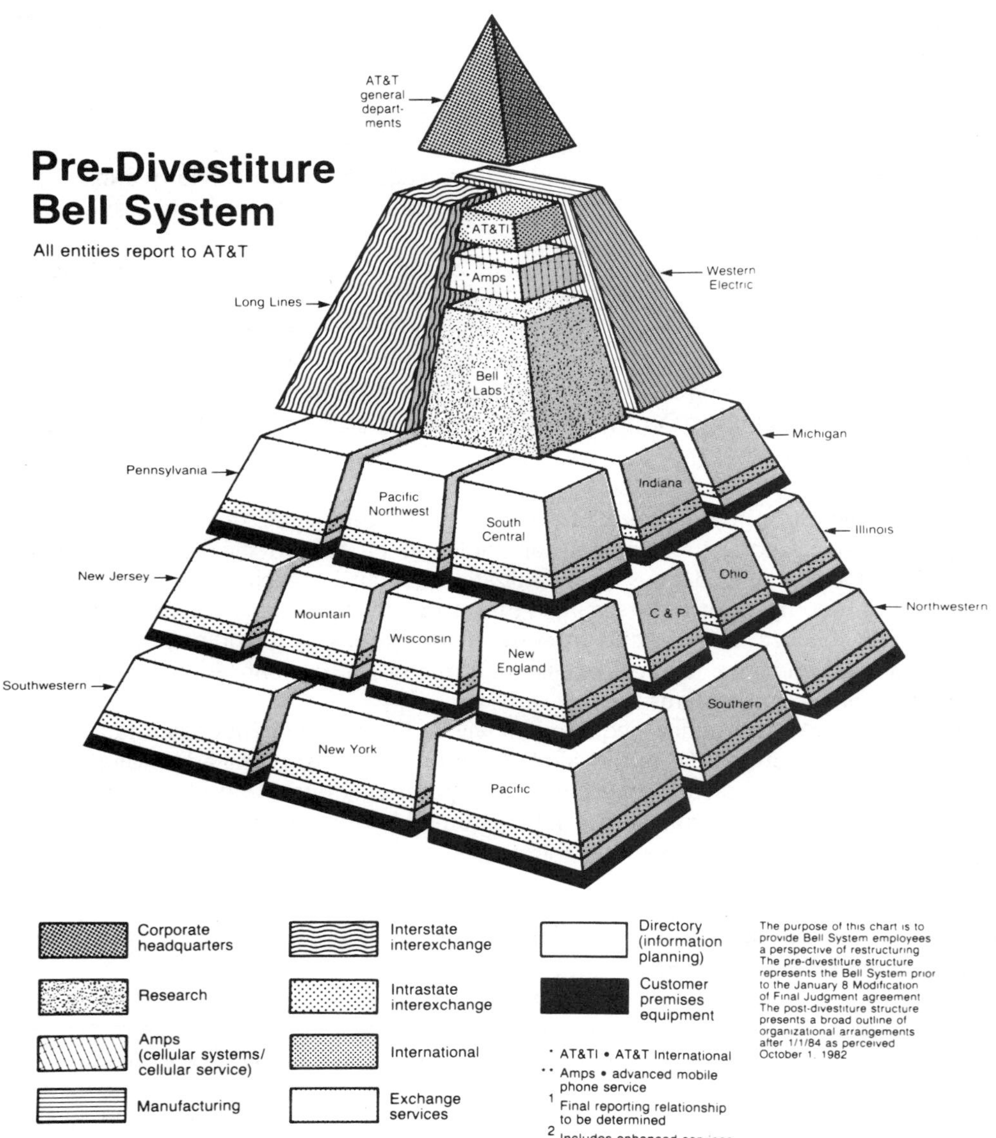
Pre-Divestiture
Bell System
All entities report to AT&T
AT&T general depart- ments
Long Lines
AT&TI
*Amps
Western Electric
Bell Labs
Michigan
Pennsylvania
Pacific Northwest
South Central
Indiana
Illinois
New Jersey
Ohio
Mountain
C & P
Northwestern
Wisconsin
New England
Southwestern
Southern
New York
Pacific
Corporate headquarters
Research
Amps (cellular systems/ cellular service)
Manufacturing
Interstate interexchange
Intrastate interexchange
International
Exchange services
Directory (information planning)
Customer premises equipment
* AT&TI • AT&T International
** Amps • advanced mobile phone service
1 Final reporting relationship to be determined
2 Includes enhanced services
The purpose of this chart is to provide Bell System employees a perspective of restructuring The pre-divestiture structure represents the Bell System prior to the January 8 Modification of Final Judgment agreement The post-divestiture structure presents a broad outline of organizational arrangements after 1/1/84 as perceived October 1. 1982

FIGURE 9A

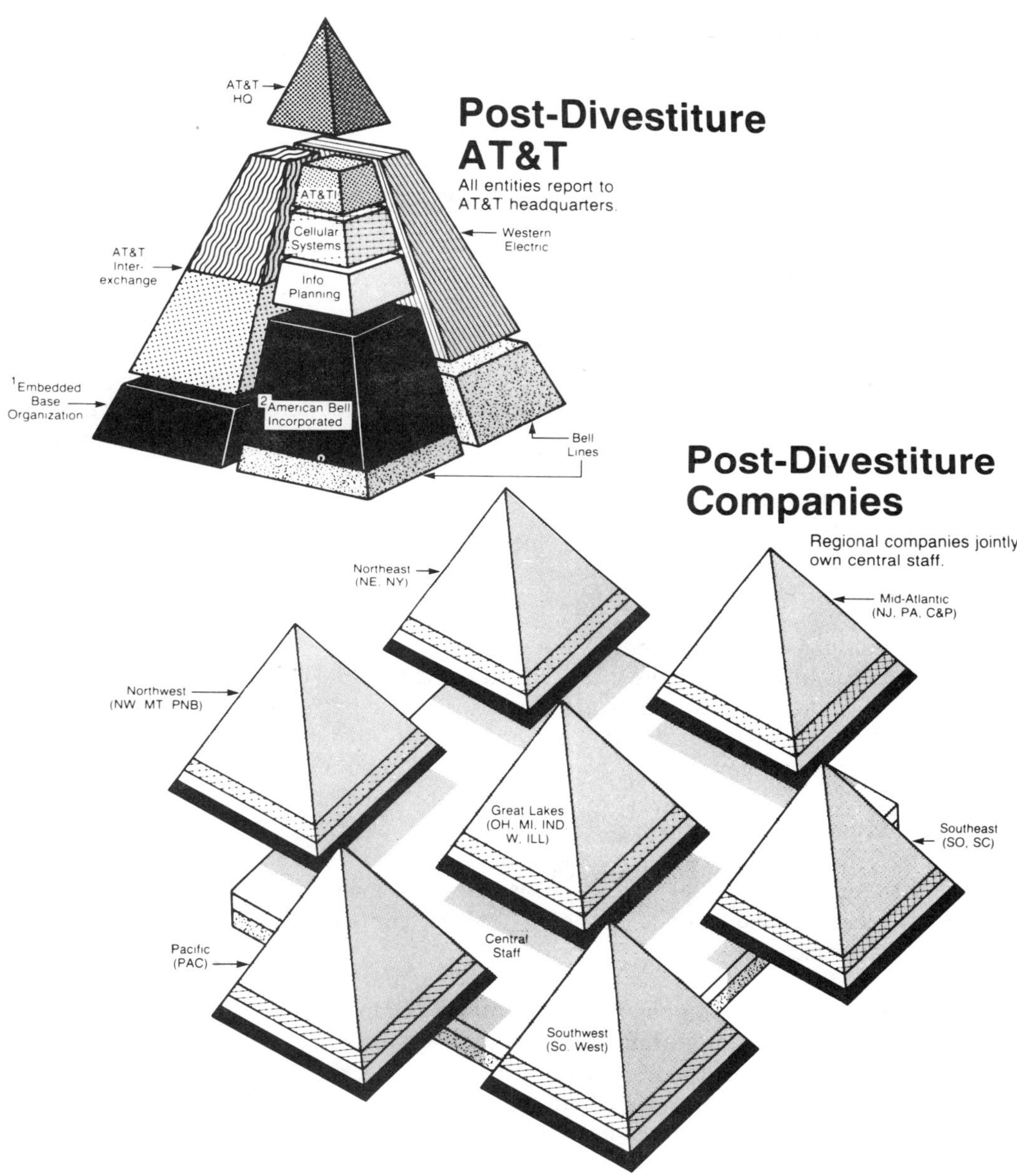
Post-Divestiture AT&T
All entities report to AT&T headquarters.
AT&T HQ
AT&TI
Cellular Systems
Info Planning
Western Electric
AT&T Inter-exchange
[1]Embedded Base Organization
[2]American Bell Incorporated
Bell Lines
Post-Divestiture Companies
Regional companies jointly own central staff.
Northeast (NE, NY)
Mid-Atlantic (NJ, PA, C&P)
Northwest (NW MT PNB)
Great Lakes (OH, MI, IND W. ILL)
Southeast (SO, SC)
Pacific (PAC)
Central Staff
Southwest (So. West)

FIGURE 9A *(continued)*

1978 restructuring. Both will serve them well in confronting the challenges posed by divestiture.

• *Where We Are Going*

For some, it might be comforting to imagine that, when the dust settles in 1984, both AT&T and the divested companies could anticipate once again the advantages of a stable, unchanging organization—with the decade from 1973 to 1983 having been an aberration, a discontinuity between two steadfast, unwavering organizational forms. This, as asserted earlier, is not to be.

Fundamental assumptions underlying this prediction are: (1) that the telecommunictions/information industry in the United States will remain on its high-growth trajectory through the remainder of this century; (2) that deregulation of the industry will continue; and (3) that a worldwide perspective of telecommunications/information equipment and systems will become more prevalent.

Based on these premises, we can speculate about the direction of structural changes and thus about where we are going. At AT&T:

- The corporate headquarters staff will become increasingly focused—and sophisticated—in strategic and financial matters, including voluntary spin-offs, acquisitions, mergers, and joint ventures.
- LOBs based on products and markets will multiply considerably.
- LOBs will become increasingly vertically integrated with their own product-specific hardware/software development and manufacturing capabilities.
- Common-technology research and development will remain centralized in order to take advantage of economies of scale and to provide the "critical mass" necessary for scientific and high-technology work.
- AT&T will become increasingly diversified in its businesses—moving first into strongly related businesses. (This does not mean that the company will become a conglomerate. It means that the company will move toward greater diversification.)

Each regional company also will unfold organizationally in its own way. The direction will depend upon the answers to the strategic questions and structural options outlined earlier and upon the evolution of local regulation and competition.

Clearly and undeniably, there will be changes—perhaps traumatic changes—not only in our corporate culture but also in regard to our assumptions about our mission and our place in the telecommunications industry. However, no characteristic of our "pathway to the future" is more prominent or more significant than profound change. Yet we must take care—at least to the degree possible—to assure that certain heritages from our past are not changed. It would, for example, be a signal loss if, in the turmoil created by divestiture, AT&T or any of the regional companies lost sight of the importance of balancing constituency interests—the "three-legged stool" representing investors, customers, and employees that has served Bell so well throughout successive generations of managers. It would be no less a loss if other positive aspects of our corporate culture were tossed aside for new values and perceptions. However, the dedication and energy with which thousands of people are tackling the job of divestiture is a positive sign.

I suspect that the strength of 100 years of cultural heritage will continue to influence and motivate us—in every one of the post-divestiture entities in which we are called together to serve. If that happens, we should transcend all the dislocations, the tough questions, and the hard work that characterizes the "end of the beginning" we have reached.

QUESTIONS

1 In terms of Mintzberg's five types of organizations, what did AT&T start out as, before divestiture? What did it end up as, after divestiture?
2 To what extent has "structure followed strategy" at AT&T?
3 What do you think would be the ideal structure for AT&T today?
4 What reorganizational problems do the regional phone companies face as of the end of this article?

CASE 1 FOR PART II (Chapters 4-9)
THE FOOD CANNING COMPANY

The following case history helps illustrate several important features of organizational environments. It shows for example, how such environments evolve and become complex, and how these complexities influence the organization's functioning. This actual example is excerpted from a paper by British researchers Emery and Trist.[1]

The company concerned was the foremost in its particular market in the food-canning industry in the U.K. and belonged to a large parent group. Its main product—a canned vegetable—had some 65 percent of this market, a situation that had been relatively stable since before the war. Believing it would continue to hold this position, the company persuaded the group board to invest several million pounds sterling in erecting a new, automated factory, which, however, based its economies on a built-in rigidity—it was set up exclusively for the long run expected from the traditional market.

The character of the environment, however, began to change while the factory was being built. A number of small canning firms appeared, not dealing with this product or indeed with others in the company's range, but with imported fruits. These firms arose because the last of the postwar controls had been removed from steel strip and tin, and cheaper cans could now be obtained in any numbers—while at the same time, a larger market was developing in imported fruits. This trade being seasonal, these firms were anxious to find a way of using their machinery and retaining their labor in winter. They became able to do so through a curious side effect of the development of quick-frozen foods.

The quick-freezing process demanded great constancy at the growing end. It was not possible to control this beyond a certain point, so that quite large crops unsuitable for quick freezing but suitable for canning became available—originally from another country (the United States), where a large market for quick-frozen foods had been established. These surplus crops had been sold at a very low price for animal feed. They were now imported by the small canners, at a better but still comparatively low price, and additional cheap supplies soon began to be procurable from underdeveloped countries.

Before the introduction of the quick-frozen form, the company's own canned product—whose raw material had been specially grown at additional cost—had been the premier brand, superior to other varieties and priced higher. But its position in the product spectrum now changed. With the increasing affluence of the society, more people were able to afford the quick-frozen form. Moreover, there was competition from a great many other vegetable products that could substitute for the staple, and people preferred this greater variety. The advantage of being the premier line among canned forms diminished, and demand increased both for the not-so-expensive varieties among them and for the quick-frozen forms. At the same time, major changes were taking place in retailing; supermarkets were developing, and more and more large grocery chains were coming into existence. These establishments wanted to sell certain types of goods under their own house names and began to place bulk orders with the small canners for their own varieties of the company's staple that fell within this class. As the small canners provided an extremely cheap article (having no marketing expenses and a cheaper raw material), they could undercut the manufacturers' branded product, and within three years they captured over 50 percent of the market. Previously, retailers' varieties had accounted for less than 1 percent.

The new automatic factory could not be adapted to the new situation until alternative products with a big sales volume could be developed, and the scale of research and development, based on the type of market analysis required to identify these, was beyond the scope of the existing resources of the company either in people or in funds.

The changed texture of the environment was not recognized by the able but traditional managers until it was too late. They failed entirely to appreciate that a number of outside events were becoming connected with each other in a way that was leading up to irreversible general change. Their first reaction was to make a herculean effort to defend the traditional product; then the board split on whether or not to make entry into the cheaper, unbranded market in a supplier role. Group HQ now felt it had no option but to step in, and many upheavals and changes in management took place until a "redefinition of mission" was agreed upon, and slowly and painfully the company reemerged with a very much altered product mix and something of a new identity.

Questions

1 Emery and Trist entitle their paper, "The Causal Texture of Organizational Environments." What do they mean by the term "causal texture"?
2 How, based on this case history, are a company's strategy and its environment related?
3 In what way was this company's problem a result of a poorly chosen strategy?
4 In what way did the firm's technology become part of its "context"?
5 How did an envolving environment create new uncertainties and unpredictable contingencies for this company? What were some of these new, unpredictable events?

Footnote

[1]F.E. Emery and E.C. Trist, "The Causal Texture of Organizational Environments," *Human Relations,* Vol. 18, No. 1 (February 1965), 21–32; reprinted in John Maurer, ed., *Readings in Organization Theory* (New York: Random House, 1971), pp. 46–57.

CASE 2 FOR PART II (Chapters 4-9) PREBUILT, INC.

• *Situation*

Prebuilt, Inc., supplies large-scale prefabricated shelters to customers for whom time is the essence, and the firm's reputation for meeting deadlines is therefore critical to its survival. The need to respond quickly to the client's needs necessarily results in a number of daily crises, but at Prebuilt, the number and severity of these crises seem to be aggravated by several internal organizational problems that are most likely the result of the rapid growth the firm has had in the past two years. Prebuilt currently meets its deadlines, a fact that seems primarily due to the extraordinary efforts of a group of highly motivated and committed managers. However, the firm does little or no long-range planning, managers are "utility infielders" without the time to give proper attention to their own departments, and profitability is probably affected adversely by the need for rework and by the errors that eventually occur. Furthermore, the firm apparently can't handle as much business as it might otherwise, and it may be approaching its capacity for handling additional projects, deadlines, and crises.

• *Background*

Prebuilt, founded 20 years ago by William Ross, originally manufactured a patented construction panel consisting of a honeycomb core to which two steel faces were laminated. The firm's first customers were door manufacturers, who used the sturdy, lightweight panels to manufacture their products.

Since that time, however, the range of products and services offered by Prebuilt has expanded considerably, and especially rapidly during the last four years. Expansion of the product line began 15 years ago, when the firm developed the capability to manufacture doors. In addition, at about that time, an engineer named Bob Roan became affiliated with the firm and developed a system whereby Prebuilt's panels could be structurally connected into complete shelters (houses and the like).

About four years ago, the firm was approached by a representative of the Egyptian government, who asked if Prebuilt could provide his country with what amounted to a complete town—1,000 homes, a commissary, a small hospital, a school building, and other structures. Prebuilt took the contract and, in doing so, had to add a variety of new services to those already offered, including "buy outs" (buying and providing the electrical equipment, washing machines, and air conditioners needed to complete the houses), transportation of all goods and materials from the United States to Egypt, and on-site supervision and construction (laborers were recruited from Taiwan). Numerous problems, most of which are still in the process of being worked out, were incurred on this project, and whether the firm can win a new, larger contract of the same type is now the question.

Over the past 20 years, the firm has gone through a series of expansions and contractions, but none as drastic as in the past four years. Prior to being awarded the Egyptian contract, the firm had fewer than 50 employees. It now employs almost 600 people, and this rapid growth has amplified the "growing pains" the company might normally be expected to experience. In addition, the nature of its current business—which management defines as "providing 'turnkey,' fully complete and operational towns for foreign governments"—makes meeting deadlines (rather than costs) the primary consideration, and these time pressures have compounded Prebuilt's problems. The difficulty of constructing shelters thousands of miles away from the company's home base (which is Atlanta) and the communication problem involved in doing business in the Middle East (management can plan on making only one phone call per day out of Egypt) has aggravated even further the normal problems that might be expected to arise in the manufacture and distribution of this product.

As a result of the many problems and daily crises that have surfaced over the past four years, Mr. Ross called in a group of consultants to analyze the firm and make recommendations for improving the organization's responsiveness and overall effectiveness. Most of the following has been excerpted from the consultant's report:

Engineering From our preliminary investigation, the main problem is probably a lack of effective project-design input at the sales presentation stage and thereafter. A common occurrence is apparently for Sales and the client to meet and develop a project based on a set of "standard" designs with little or no input from Engineering, and for the Sales Department to then estimate the project's cost. Engineering is brought in after the fact to develop the project, a situation that seems to put the engineers on the defensive and generally results in their identifying required project modifications. Engineering sends a list of required material to Purchasing, often making assumptions about quality of components, etc., without input from Sales. Someone in Engineering finds a mistake (or Sales stumbles on one), and others have to be changed. This entire process is additionally hampered by the fact that Engineering is inadequately staffed. For example, it appears that the lack of sufficient in-house structural and mechanical engineers frequently results in a bottleneck, since it makes the firm more dependent on the schedule of its outside consultants.

Organizational Structure and Coordination Inadequate and informal interdepartmental project coordination is a major problem at Prebuilt, and the lack of effective coordination may in fact lie at the root of many of the firm's other problems. At the present time, there is no formal organization chart. In interviews, we found constant reference to the need for improved coordination between Sales and Engineering, between Engineering and Purchasing, and between Shipping and Purchasing, for example. As a larger issue, it appears that projects are often sold, engineered, purchased, and shipped without any one identifiable person or group of peole having both the authority and responsibility for managing them from start to finish. There also appear to be no regularly scheduled meetings of the department heads to monitor the progress of projects. Formal project schedules that could aid the coordination are apparently inadequate. In addition to the fact that there is no organization chart, there are also no job descriptions or clear lines of authority at Prebuilt, and actions are often seen as "violations of the chain of command," with many managers complaining that they don't know who reports to them. To some extent, this lack of structure may be beneficial: In a firm where responsiveness is essential, a preoccupation with adhering to the chain of command could be deadly. And in the absence of formal coordination devices, such as effective schedules, project managers, and schedules of meetings, top managers must often inject themselves into all departments and at all levels in order to handle crises and perform the missing coordination function. The problem is that at Prebuilt, the organization is not formally structured to be flexible—there is instead no structure at all. Everyone is a "utility infielder"; no one "minds the store"; more crises erupt; formal coordination is adequate; and everyone again becomes a "utility infielder." This cycle is in turn aggravated by the firm's engineering documentation, and communications problems. In addition, several key jobs apparently must be staffed, or restaffed.

Procedures/Documentation/Scheduling Prebuilt needs to thoroughly reevaluate its procedures and documentation on a department-by-department basis. References were constantly made, for example, to material that is "lost in corners" in the warehouse, and to unverifiable "short-shipping" claims by clients. Paperwork, particularly bills of material, sometimes get mislaid, and there is a need for a more complete documentation (an "archive") of past products for sales presentation purposes. Personnel policies and procedures are needed covering basic areas such as job descriptions, performance appraisal, and compensation management. A more effective project-scheduling and reporting system for planning, controlling, and coordinating projects is also needed; projects that management thought were on time have been found to be as much as two months late.

Communications Vertical and horizontal communication throughout the organization is inadequate. For example, there is often inadequate communication between Sales and Engineering. The result is that projects can be designed and engineered that don't entirely meet the expectations of the client, since specific requirements (such as what quality floors to use), although known by Sales, often never reach Engineering, which in turn makes erroneous assumptions about these factors. For its part, the sales group apparently often gets little feedback on the final prices until purchase orders are already filled, and so its input often surfaces too late. In terms of vertical communication, managers refer to the fact that they often "just hear rumors" about what is going on at the corporate level; one such rumor concerned the possible purchase of a construction firm, and another concerned the hiring of a personnel manager.

• *Problems*

These various problems have manifested themselves in what can only be described as an ongoing series of crises. A great deal of the work has to be redone when, for example, it is determined that ceilings don't conform to the customer's specifications, or electrical equipment is not compatible with the voltage available in the client country. Much of the incoming material gets lost in the company's warehouse, with no record kept of its location. No clear records are kept of exactly how much material (how many panels, say) is shipped to the customer, and the firm usually cannot prove its case when the customer complains that it hasn't received all the necessary material. In order to fight these ongoing critics, middle- and top-level managers often find themselves in the shipping area in the dead of night, loading trucks to expedite orders. The net effect is that costs are so much higher than anticipated that the profitability of the project (and the firm's cash-flow position) is much lower than it should be. In addition, the firm now finds itself unable to bid for new, larger projects from a position of strength. Unless its major customers are shown that

Prebuilt is eliminating its organizational and managerial problems and can successfully complete its current project, it is doubtful that any additional major contracts will be forthcoming. Without new contracts, the firm would have to lay off virtually all the employees who were hired in the past four years and, in addition, would be left with so much indebtedness that the viability of the firm would be in danger.

Dissussion Questions

In previous chapters, we discussed the context of organizations and the way this context influences organization structure and design. We discussed several organization-design strategies and the fact that under uncertain conditions, mechanistic methods for structuring and coordinating organizations are insufficient. Here, instead, other strategies—like environmental management, or the creation of self-contained tasks—become necessary.

Prebuilt is a good example of a company that operates in a fairly uncertain and unpredictable environment. Customer specifications often change overnight; problems can occur during transportation and in Egypt that require quick, effective reaction; and the firm is constantly working against what often seem impossible deadlines in a situation where meeting deadlines is by far the main criterion of effectiveness.

Given these facts, which of the following organization-design strategies would you suggest if you were Prebuilt's consultants?

- *Mechanistic* (hierarchy, rules and procedures, planning, and goal setting). These are "basic" strategies for ensuring that the work of the different units or departments in the organization is coordinated. Rules, for example, are predetermined decisions that are aimed at ensuring that decisions made in each unit contribute in a coordinated way to the organization's goals; managers in the hierarchy are then supposedly left free to handle only "exceptions." We saw that as situations become more unpredictable, organizations and their managers have to process more information, and these mechanistic devices become inadequate. It is at this point that one or more of the following design strategies become necessary.
- *Environmental management.* The organization can attempt to "manage" its environment—for example, by purchasing suppliers or entering cartels.
- *Creation of slack resources.* The organization can attempt to reduce the number and severity of exceptions by introducing "slack resources" like inventories. Thus, a sudden rush job doesn't create the additional problem of having to find the necessary raw materials.
- *Creation of self-contained tasks.* We also know that creating self-contained departments that can focus all their attention on, say, one specific project facilitates coordination.
- *Invest in vertical information systems.* Another technique the organization can

use to handle overloads of information is the establishment of "vertical information systems," like staff assistants who analyze and summarize problems for line managers, thereby, in effect, increasing the managers' ability to process information and make decisions.

- *Create lateral relations.* Finally, the organization can encourage "lateral relations" in order to reduce the information that must be relayed up the chain of command. This might involve simply direct contact between lower-level managers, or the creation of committees, integrators, or special liaison personnel.

Which of these design strategies would you recommend if you were Prebuilt's consultant? At a minimum, your recommendation should make provision for the following departments: marketing/sales; accounting/finance; engineering; manufacturing; purchasing; and shipping, warehousing, receiving. Develop an organization structure, and present *specific* examples of how you would implement the other design strategies you choose to recommend. (Please do not read any further until you have completed this project.)

• *Recommendations*

The actual recommendations made by the consultants in this case and implemented by Prebuilt utilized all the design strategies we discussed.

Mechanistic First, an organization structure was designed (see Figure II-1). This clarified responsibilities and reporting relationships, provided a chain of command through which decisions could be made, and furnished job descriptions that answered the question, "Who does what?" In order to provide for more effective project coordination, a matrix structure was implemented in which a project manager was identified and project teams developed for each of the company's major projects. The organization structure, in other words, provided for the self-containment of tasks (projects).

In addition, all procedures, documentation, and forms were evaluated department by department, and the flow of written information between departments was tracked to determine what changes in procedures were necessary. A policy and procedures manual was developed that specified, for example, the procedure to be used in determining customer requirements and communicating these requirements between the sales and engineering departments. A more effective project scheduling and reporting system was set up to indicate planned milestones and provide for daily feedback to top management as to the status of each component of each project. Every department (production, sales, purchasing, and so on) involved in a project participated in developing the project's schedule and then concentrated on meeting its deadlines (as detailed in the schedule) and thereby the overall project deadline.

Environmental Management "Environmental management" was a second design strategy used. Long-term contracts were entered into between the company

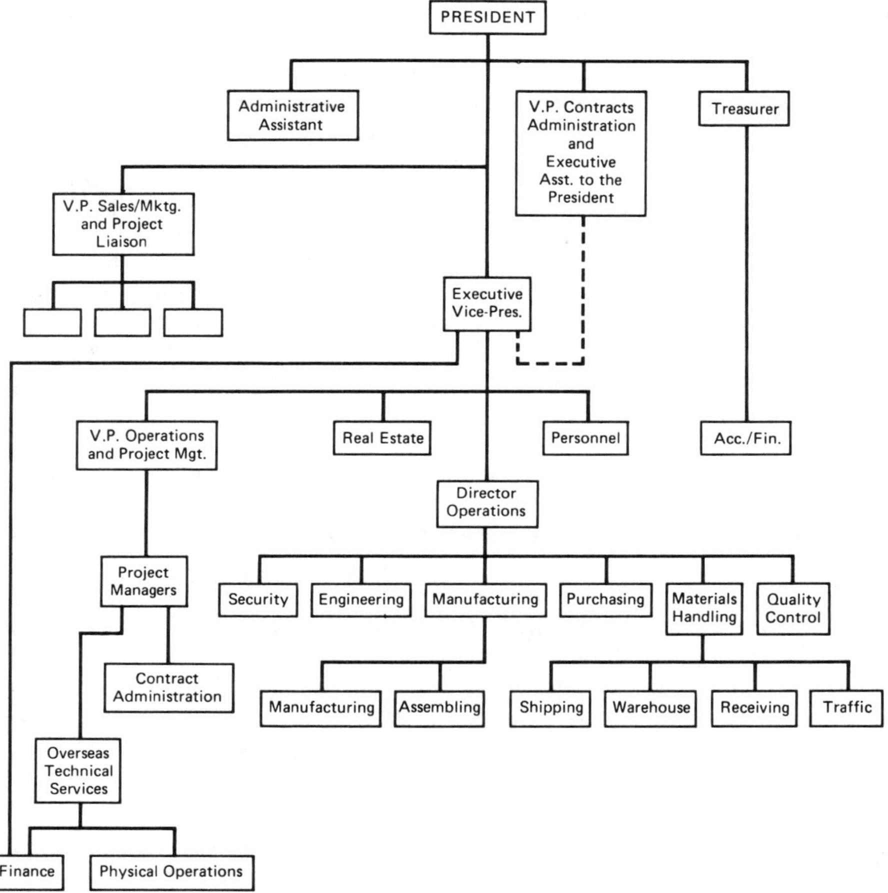

FIGURE II-1 Prebuilt, Inc., Corporate Organization Chart

and a construction firm in Taiwan to reduce the uncertainties involved in recruiting, hiring, and supervising the construction teams in Egypt. The company also began manufacturing more of the basic components of its products; for example, whereas it had formerly purchased the honeycomb cores for its panels, it now set up assembly lines for manufacturing its own cores. A set of "standard" shelters was designed from which the sales team developed orders; this further reduced the number of "exceptions" the firm had to deal with. A long-range-planning committee was established to determine what markets the firm should pursue over the next five to ten years. It was felt that this type of planning would reduce the "knee-jerk" reactions the firm was currently making to new and unexpected market possibilities.

Create Slack Resources Several specific actions that were undertaken to reduce the number of exceptions that could arise might be considered creation of slack resources. The company's basic "house" was redesigned so that more of the actual assembly could take place at the Atlanta factory. For example, roof trusses that were formerly shipped in pieces to the foreign country and then constructed on the site were not bolted together at the factory. The net result was a reduction in the number of separate parts that had to be transported, warehoused in Egypt, and constructed on-site. Furthermore (particularly since costs were of secondary importance to the customer), substantial increases were made in inventory levels, and intentional overshipping of parts to Egypt was begun in order to ensure that no part shortages occurred there. To further reduce uncertainties, full prototypes of each house and shelter to be built overseas were first constructed at the firm's Atlanta facility, in order to ensure that the "bugs" were designed out of each before the materials for thousands of them were shipped overseas.

Create Self-Contained Tasks As noted above, a matrix structure was developed for each project. A manager and team for each project were assigned, thus ensuring that each project received the continuous and undivided attention of one group.

Create Vertical Information System Several vertical information systems were also developed. A computer system was installed that provided project managers and top managers with "on-line" feedback concerning the progress of each project, inventory levels, and so on. Each project manager was assigned a "project control officer" whose function was to carefully monitor each step of each project and keep the manager advised of project progress.

Create Lateral Relations Finally, several steps were taken in the way of lateral relations to reduce the number of exceptions and amount of information being channeled up the chain of command: An "engineering liaison officer" was assigned to the sales department. His function was to attend sales presentations and generally ensure (1) that customer requirements were communicated to the engineering department, and (2) that engineering had an opportunity to provide early input in the early stages of the development of the project. Project teams met weekly to discuss problems, and the president, executive vice-president, and director of operations met weekly with the managers for engineering, manufacturing, purchasing, material handling, sales, and project management to discuss matters of concern.

10

Job Redesign and Enrichment

OVERVIEW

In the preceding part of this book, we discussed organization structure and design, but we have seen that providing an organization structure is only half the problem facing the organization theorist or manager. The basic assumption one makes in structuring an organization and giving each worker a task is that those tasks *will in fact be carried out* in some dependable, predictable fashion; in this third part of the book we thus shift our focus to *motivation and compliance* in organizations.

This chapter, on Job Redesign, provides a bridge between the topics of organization design and motivation. In it we explain how to design the specific jobs that comprise the overall organization structure to ensure the emergence of self control. In the following three chapters, we turn to the topics of Imposed Control, Self-Control, and Leadership.

The outline of this chapter is as follows:

A Introduction: intrinsic rewards and motivation
B Basic approaches to job design
  1 The argument for specialization
  2 Toward less-specialized jobs
C Arguments for and against job enrichment
  1 The case for job enrichment
  2 Arguments against job enrichment
  3 How successful has job enrichment been?
D Characteristics of enriched jobs
  1 A technology for enriching jobs

E Descriptions of actual job-redesign programs
  1 The stockholder-correspondent job at AT&T
  2 Job "nesting" at AT&T
  3 Production teams at Volvo
  4 Job redesign at Saab-Scania
F Implications: conditions under which job enrichment is most effective
  1 The two main barriers in job enrichment
G Appendix: Individual and situational factors in job design

INTRODUCTION: INTRINSIC REWARDS AND MOTIVATION

Few rewards are as powerful as the sense of accomplishment and achievement that come from doing a job that one genuinely wants to do, and doing it well. Thus, the person who collects stamps, builds a ham radio, or volunteers time at the hospital generally doesn't have to be coerced or prodded into doing the job well, since these "jobs" carry their own intrinsic rewards in terms of challenge, achievement, and so on. These sorts of jobs, in other words, are "designed"—in terms of their content, functions, and specific duties—so that performing them contributes to and satisfies people's higher-order needs for achievement, recognition, and self-actualization. Needless to say, designing jobs in organizations so that they provide such intrinsic rewards should substantially increase employee moral and performance, since, in the words of psychologists Katz and Kahn:

> . . . motivation is so internalized that performance is autonomous. The supervisor does not have to be present to wave a stick or offer candy. The activities carry their own rewards; they are so much a pattern of motive satisfaction that they need no additional incentives.[1]

THE BASIC APPROACHES TO JOB DESIGN

The basic issue in job design is whether jobs should be highly specialized and routine or highly "enriched" and nonroutine. Those who advocate specialization argue for making jobs as simple as possible, so that each worker performs the same highly specialized task over and over again, many times a day, thus bringing about certain production efficiencies. Advocates of job enrichment, on the other hand, claim that such highly specialized jobs lead to unanticipated problems like boredom and animosity, and that tasks should actually be recombined into more "enriched" jobs.

• *The Argument for Specialization*

The modern argument for job specialization had its origins in the classical economic theory that developed in the early 1800s. This theory emphasized the advantages of efficiency, and it was (and still is) widely believed that highly specialized jobs are more efficient than less-specialized ones. For example, one writer of the period, engineer Charles Babbage, listed the following reasons for making jobs as specialized as possible:

1 *Less time required for learning.* When the job is highly specialized and involves, say, always turning the same screw, it can be learned quickly, and little training is required. For example, it would probably take only two or three hours to train an assembly-line worker to install a door handle on a car. However, it might take several days to train him to assemble a door, and several years to train a person to assemble an entire car.
2 *Less waste of material during training period.* Some material is usually wasted while a person is learning how to perform a task, but this waste tends to be minimized when the job is simple and easily learned.
3 *Less time lost in switching from task to task.* A short "warm-up" period is usually required when a person starts a new task; as a result, some time is always lost when switching from task to task. When a person can habitually perform the same task over and over again, no changeover time is lost.
4 *Proficiency increases with practice.* When people perform the same task over and over, they acquire a skill or proficiency that enables them to perform the job relatively efficiently. In other words, "practice makes perfect."
5 *Hiring made more efficient.* By dividing work into specialized jobs, the organization can hire and pay for a person who has exactly the skill level called for. Where the job is not specialized and requires the worker to perform several tasks, that person has to have enough skill to perform the most difficult task, and this skill is wasted on the simpler tasks the person also has to perform.
6 *Parts become uniform and interchangeable.* Since each person is making the same part over and over again, the parts become more uniform and, as a result, more interchangeable.[2]

Scientific Management These somewhat theoretical arguments were expanded upon and applied by advocates of the scientific-management school of thought. Scientific managers like Frederick Winslow Taylor and Frank and Lillian Gilbreth developed principles and practices for "scientifically" analyzing tasks. In addition to using stopwatches to improve production efficiency, these experts developed various tools, including "motion-study principles," "therbligs," and "micromotion study," to assist them in their quest for efficiency. Many of these tools are still used effectively today. *Motion-study principles* include, for example, the following:

1 The two hands should begin as well as complete their motions at the same time.
2 The two hands should not be idle at the same time except during rest periods.
3 Motions of the arms should be made at opposite and symmetrical directions and should be made simultaneously.[3]

Therbligs, another example of the tools used by those in the scientific-management school to analyze jobs,[4] consist of elemental motions like "search," "grab," "hold," and "transport." Just as the 26 letters of the alphabet can be used to construct a multitude of words, any task, it was assumed, could be analyzed in terms of about 20 therbligs. It was believed that by observing and analyzing jobs, one could identify redundant or unnecessary therbligs, eliminate these, and thereby increase the worker's productivity.

Micromotion study represents a similar approach to job design. It involves taking motion pictures of the worker doing his or her job, and then analyzing the film by running it forward and backward at different speeds so that various details of the job can be examined and reexamined. Used in conjunction with timing devices, it was (and is) possible to determine precisely how long each component activity of a task takes a worker, and to improve the worker's performance by modifying or eliminating one or more of these activities.

The Drawbacks to Specialization Scientific-management theorists took a purely "rational" approach to job design and pursued technical efficiency single-mindedly. The result was highly simplified, short-cycle jobs that consisted of performing the same activity over and over again, hundreds of times a day. The worker in this system was relegated to little more than a cog in the machine; he or she was studied, analyzed, and prodded in a manner that many found increasingly demeaning and unacceptable. Workers' responses were as completely programmed and beyond personal control as they could be.

Almost from the onset of industrialization, however, workers have rebelled against being kept in a tight harness and dragged away from the challenge that craft work provides; this rebelliousness has manifested itself in a number of ways.[5] These ranged from relatively harmless actions like daydreaming[6] to more serious problems like excessive absences[7] and antimanagement activities like wildcat strikes and sabotage.[8] In summary, as psychologists Sayles and Strauss point out:

> . . . management pays a price for the work simplification, routinization, and ease of supervision inherent in mass-production work. The cost is largely in terms of apathy and boredom, as positive satisfactions are engineered out of the jobs. Being confined physically and limited socially to contacting his own immediate supervisor, the factory worker sees very little of the total organization and even less of the total product being manufactured. It is hardly surprising that there is frequently little pride in work or identification with a job.[9]

• *Toward Less-Specialized Jobs*

Job Enlargement and Rotation Management's initial response to problems like these was often to redesign jobs, through either job enlargement or job rotation. *Job enlargement* involves assigning workers additional same-level tasks in order to increase the variety of tasks they have to perform.[10] For example, if the work involved assembling chairs, the worker who previously only bolted the seat to the legs might take on the additional task of assembling the legs and attaching the back as well. *Job rotation* involves systematically moving workers from one job to another. Thus, on an auto assembly line, a worker may spend an hour fitting doors, the next hour installing headlamps, the next hour fitting bumpers, and so on.

Job enlargement and job rotation are similar in two ways: First, they both represent the antithesis of job specialization. With job specialization, the objective is to reduce the job to its fundamental components and to assign each component to a worker who will then perform it routinely. Job enlargement and rotation involve *recombining* simple jobs, assigning several to a worker so as to increase the variety of tasks he or she performs. Second, job enlargement and job rotation are similar in that they are not primarily aimed at injecting "challenge" or a sense of accomplishment into jobs. Instead, they are aimed at reducing the monotony and boredom that may be inherent in highly specialized jobs, by increasing the number and variety of simple tasks that are assigned to the worker.

Job Enrichment Job enrichment is an approach aimed at building into the job "motivators" such as challenge. It involves redesigning jobs—for example, by letting the person schedule her or his own work in order to experience a feeling of responsibility, achievement, growth, and recognition by doing the job well. Job enrichment is always concerned with changing the content—the specific duties and functions—of the job rather than with external "hygiene factors" such as salary and working conditions.

An example of what Frederick Herzberg calls "a highly successful job enrichment experiment" is illustrated in Table 10-1. In this case, the jobs were those of

TABLE 10-1 Outline of a Successful Job-Enrichment Project

Specific Changes Aimed at Enriching Jobs	*"Motivators" These Changes Are Aimed at Increasing*
A. Removing some controls while retaining accountability	Responsibility and personal achievement
B. Increasing the accountability of individuals for own work	Responsibility and recognition
C. Giving a person a complete natural unit of work (module, division, area, and so on)	Responsibility, achievement, and recognition
D. Granting additional authority to an employee in his activity; job freedom	Responsibility, achievement, and recognition
E. Making periodic reports directly available to the worker himself rather than to the supervisor	Internal recognition
F. Introducing new and more difficult tasks not previously handled	Growth and learning
G. Assigning individuals specific or specialized tasks, enabling them to become expert	Responsibility, growth, and advancement

Source: Frederick Herzberg, "One More Time: How Do You Motivate Employees?" *Harvard Business Review* (Jan./Feb. 1968). Copyright © 1968 by the President and Fellows of Harvard College; all rights reserved.

people responsible for corresponding with a large corporation's stockholders—answering their questions, and so on. On the left of the table are listed some of the changes that were aimed at enriching the job, such as "removing some controls while retaining accountability." On the right are listed the "motivators"—such as for recognition—that those job changes were aimed at satisfying.

Even though the terms are sometimes used interchangeably, job enlargement and job enrichment are not exactly the same thing. Job enlargement usually involves a *horizontal* expansion of the worker's job by increasing the number and variety of similar tasks he or she is assigned. Job enrichment, on the other hand, usually involves a *vertical* expansion of the worker's job, in that tasks formerly carried out by the supervisor are not assigned to the worker. For example, the person may be given more discretion to *schedule* the day's work, *communicate* directly with clients, and *inspect* the work that is produced.

ARGUMENTS FOR AND AGAINST JOB ENRICHMENT

• The Case for Job Enrichment

The case for job enrichment may be summarized as follows: By increasing the duties and responsibilities of a job, job enrichment replaces the sense of achievement, challenge, and accomplishment that specialization removes and, in doing so, leads to better employee morale and performance. Job enrichment builds "motivators" into the job, motivators like challenge and responsibility, which can satisfy needs for psychological growth, achievement, recognition, and advancement.[11] Job specialization, on the other hand, results in routine, short-cycle jobs that in turn can lead to monotony, boredom, dissatisfaction, and various behavioral consequences such as absenteeism and reduced performance.

The case for job enrichment is an appealing one for several reasons. It is, first of all, intuitively appealing, since it just seems to make more sense to assume that people prefer interesting jobs to uninteresting ones. Related to this, job enrichment reflects what many believe is a more positive view of the nature of man, a view that emphasizes the importance of employees' achievement and self-actualization. Finally, much research evidence supports the usefulness of job enrichment. For reasons like these, the job-enrichment technique has spawned an unusal number of zealots. Their gospel was summarized as follows in the study *Work in America,* which was written for the Department of Health, Education and Welfare:

> Significant numbers of American workers are dissatisfied with the quality of their working lives. Dull, repetitive, seemingly meaningless tasks, offering little challenge or autonomy, are causing discontent among workers at all occupational levels. . . . The redesign of jobs is the keystone of this report.[12]

• *Arguments Against Job Enrichment*

The arguments against job enrichment can be summarized within the following categories:

High Expense First, job enrichment *increases* costs for exactly the reasons that specialization *reduces* them. Specifically, it involves higher training and production costs, and whether the benefits derived can compensate for these higher costs is something that has to be evaluated for each situation. As two writers put it:

> At some point, suggestions for enlarging jobs, increasing skills, lengthening job cycles, and rotating tasks bump into the logic which dictated the division of labor in the first place. . . . The return to craft production may be humanly desirable but is impractical. Every addition to jobs which requires workers to spend more time learning the job, or alternating tools, or which entails greater inventories or duplication of tools, is likely to raise unit costs.[13]

Inadequate Theoretical Basis Others argue that job enrichment's theoretical underpinnings are shaky on two counts. First, job enrichment is based largely on the theory that only challenging jobs can motivate high performance in the long run, and many believe this is not so. Some experts argue that nonjob factors like pay and working conditions are as (or more) important, for instance.[14] Second, we believe now that routine, short-cycle jobs are not automatically viewed as boring, demoralizing, or counterproductive by many (or most) workers. In some instances, researchers have found that workers with low "need-to-achieve" might actually *prefer* the more routine jobs. The question of how various individual and situational factors affect the way workers respond to enriched jobs is discussed at length in the appendix to this chapter.

Natural Selection: Workers Get What They Want One writer argues that job enrichment often fails because workers in apparently routine, "boring" jobs have intentionally chosen these types of jobs and are therefore put off by attempts to complicate them.[15] Similarly, Giles recently found that a "self-selection" process (that is, allowing employees to decide whether or not they will be placed in an enriched job) may be a useful selection technique for job enrichment. Specifically, he found that it was the employees who seemed best suited for job enrichment—for instance, those who were strongly motivated by a need to achieve—that volunteered to participate in the job-enrichment program.[16]

• *How Successful Has Job Enrichment Been?*

These arguments notwithstanding, the bottom line is whether or not job enrichment is effective at improving performance; this, unfortunately, is not an easy question to answer. The main problem is that most of the studies in this area have been "uncontrolled," since, in addition to the job-enrichment program, other changes were also taking place in the companies studied.

Thus, it is impossible to say for sure whether the improvements that occurred during the enrichment program resulted from the enrichment or from some other change such as a pay raise, friendlier managers, or a tighter job market.[17] As a result, the research findings are sketchy; but on the whole, they indicate that job enrichment can improve employee attitudes and performance (especially quality of output) if the enrichment program is implemented properly.

Herzberg reports the results of one relatively well controlled experiment that involved the stockholder correspondents of a large corporation.[18] There, "almost all indexes of performance and job attitudes were low, and exit interviewing confirmed that the challenge of the job existed merely as words"; therefore, a job enrichment program was implemented. Among other things, this involved removing some supervisory controls, increasing employees' accountability for their work, granting employees additional authority, and adding new and more difficult tasks to those previously handled. The enrichment program was implemented in one "achieving" group, while a "control" group continued to do the job in the traditional way. (There were also two "uncommitted" groups of correspondents to ensure that attitudes in the achieving and control groups hadn't changed merely because employees knew that they were part of an experiment.) The change in performance for each group is displayed in Figure 10–1. Performance (in terms of quality and speed of response to stockholders' letters of inquiry) improved markedly in the achieving group; attitudes improved as well.

As another example, from 1965 to 1968, a group of researchers at AT&T conducted 19 formal field experiments in job enrichment.[19] According to Robert Ford, a job enrichment advocate, "of the nineteen studies, nine were rated 'outstandingly successful,' one was a complete 'flop,' and the remaining nine were 'moderately successful.' "[20]

In another experiment, a group of researchers investigated the effects of both job enrichment and goal setting on employee productivity and satisfaction. They found that job enrichment improved satisfaction but had little effect on productivity. Goal setting, on the other hand (having a supervisor and the employee jointly set specific, difficult goals for the latter), had a major effect on productivity and a less substantial effect on satisfaction. These researchers therefore suggest using job enrichment in conjunction with goal setting.[21]

Psychologist Edwin Locke and his associates introduced a job-enrichment program in three clerical work units of a federal agency. In this case, job enrichment apparently had no effect on attitudes. Productivity did rise, but on the basis of interviews and observations, the researchers concluded that these changes could be attributed mainly to a more efficient use of manpower and elimination of unnecessary operations, rather than the job-enrichment program.[22]

Summary On the whole, job enrichment does seem to result in improved attitudes and performance, but two caveats are in order.[23] First, detractors have argued that most studies of enrichment have been uncontrolled, have used unrepresentative

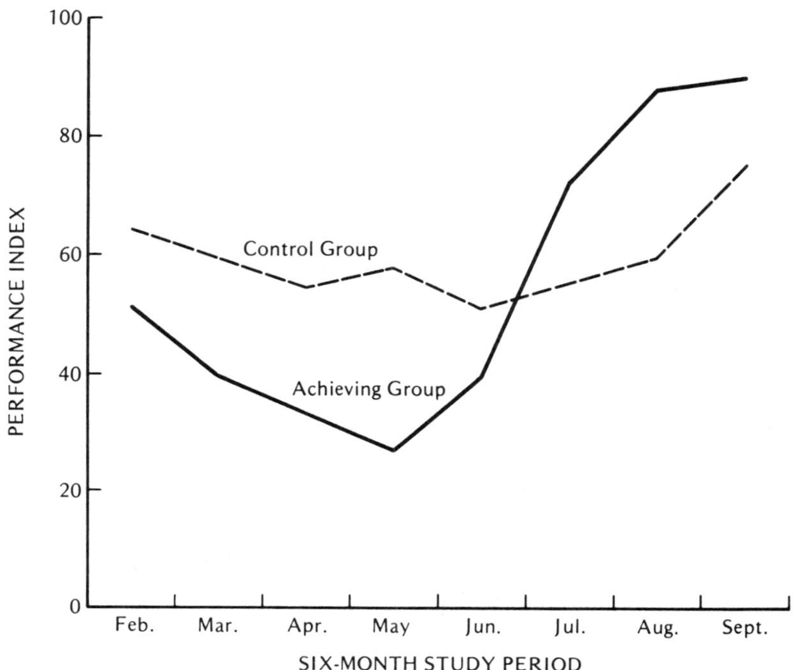

FIGURE 10-1 Effect of Job Enrichment in Stockholder-Correspondent Study. *Source:* Frederick Herzberg, "One More Time: How Do You Motivate Employees?" *Harvard Business Review* (Jan./Feb. 1968). Copyright © 1968 by the President and Fellows of Harvard College; all rights reserved.

groups of employees, and have reflected the overoptimism of the researchers themselves.[24] Many of these arguments are valid, and enrichment advocates will have to try to deal with them. (However, from a practical point of view, it may be impossible to implement an effective enrichment program without simultaneously making other improvements in the organization—such as better pay, improved staffing, and more attention to goal setting. Moreover, unscrambling the effects of all these changes may not be feasible or particularly useful.) Second, it is apparent that the way the enrichment is implemented will determine its effectiveness: Do employees want the program? Is it economically feasible in this case? and so on. We should, therefore, turn to the question of how to implement a job-enrichment program.

CHARACTERISTICS OF ENRICHED JOBS

According to Frederick Herzberg, the ingredients of an enriched job are as follows:

- *Direct feedback.* The employee should get timely, direct feedback concerning his or her performance.

- *Client relationships.* The worker should have a customer or client to serve, either external to the organization or inside it. For example, instead of typing memos for everyone on a first-come-first-served basis, each secretary in the typing pool is assigned to a specific department.
- *New learning.* According to Herzberg, an essential ingredient of a good job is the opportunity for individuals to feel that they are growing psychologically. In one case, for example, laboratory technicians were previously responsible only for setting up the laboratory equipment for the research scientists. With job enrichment, they were given additional responsibility for the research reports, which created the opportunity for them to analyze and evaluate data and to learn to write scientific reports.
- *Scheduling.* Another ingredient is the opportunity to schedule one's own work. In one plant, for example, workers had previously been told when they could take the coffee, rest, and lunch breaks. After enrichment, workers were held accountable for meeting quotas and could schedule their own breaks.
- *Unique experience.* Herzberg says that "in this day of homogenization and assembly-line intelligence, when everyone is judged on sameness, there exists a countervailing need for some personal uniqueness at work—for providing aspects of jobs that the worker can consider 'doing his own thing.' "[25]
- *Control over resources.* Herzberg recommends giving employees or groups of employees their own "mini-budgets," and pushing cost and profit centers down as low as is organizationally feasible.
- *Direct communications authority.* The worker should have direct access to his or her customer or client.
- *Personal accountability.* For example, eliminate separate inspectors, and allow the employee to both assemble and inspect his or her own product.[26]

• A Technology for Enriching Jobs

A group of researchers has developed a new technology for implementing job-enrichment programs.[27] They say that people "get turned on to"—are motivated to peform—their work if (1) the activity is *meaningful* to the person, (2) the person knows he or she is solely *responsible* for its completion, and (3) he or she has *knowledge of results* within a few seconds.

As illustrated in Figure 10-2, the researchers assume there are five "core job dimensions" that determine whether the person will in fact experience this meaningfulness, responsibility, and knowledge of results.

- *Skill variety.* The degree to which the job requires the worker to perform activities that challenge his or her skills and abilities.
- *Task identity.* The degree to which the job requires completion of a whole identifiable piece of work.
- *Task significance.* The degree to which the job has a substantial and perceivable effect on the lives of other people, in the organization or in the world at large.

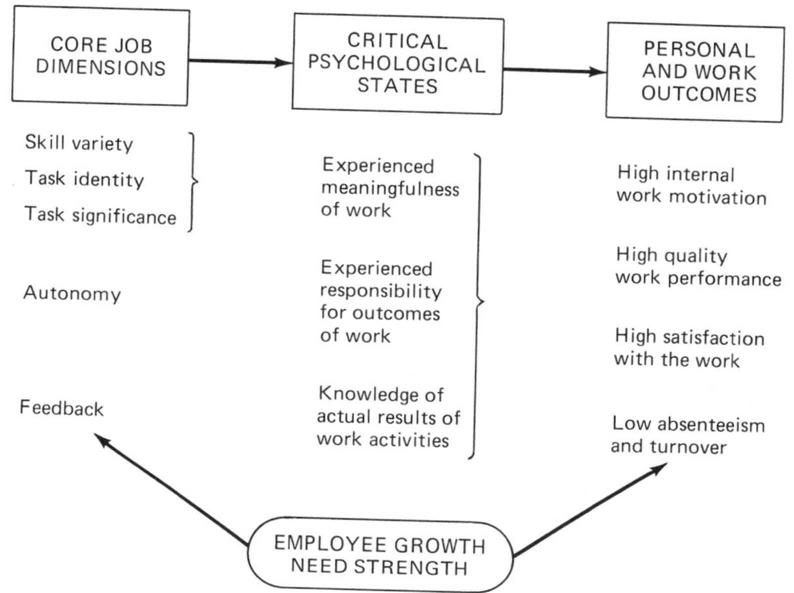

FIGURE 10-2 Relationships Among Core Job Dimensions, Critical Psychological States, and On-the-Job Outcomes. *Source:* J. Richard Hackman, Greg Oldham, Robert Janson, and Kenneth Purdy, "A New Strategy for Job Enrichment," *California Management Review*, Vol. 17, No. 4.

- *Autonomy.* The degree to which the job gives the worker the freedom and independence.
- *Knowledge of results.* The degree to which the worker gets information about the effectiveness of his or her job efforts.

Step 1—Diagnosis The first step in developing a job-enrichment program, according to these researchers, is to diagnose the problem to determine whether or not the job is amenable to job enrichment. This process consists of answering four questions (the researchers have questionnaires to formalize this process):

1. *Are motivation and satisfaction central to the problem?* Or is there some other problem—a poorly designed production system, etc.?
2. *Is the job low in motivating potential?* Is the *job* the source of the motivation problem identified in question 1?
3. *What specific aspects of the jobs are causing the difficulty?* Here the job is examined in terms of the five "core dimensions" discussed above.
4. *How "ready" are the employees for change?* As we discussed above, not everyone is motivated by job enrichment. The extent to which job enrichment is effective depends on the workers' needs for self-actualization, achievement, and so on.

Step 2—Implementation After diagnosis of the problem, the next step is implementation. Here, as summarized in Figure 10-3, one takes specific action to enrich the jobs. For example:

1 *Form natural work groups.* Here, the job is changed to make each person responsible, so that he or she "owns" an identifiable body of work. For example, instead of having the typist in a typing pool do work for all departments, we might make the work of one or two departments the continuing responsibility of each typist.
2 *Combine tasks.* For example, let one person assemble a product from start to finish, instead of having it go through several separate operations that are performed by different people.
3 *Establish client relationships.* Let the worker have contact, as often as possible, with the consumer of the product.
4 *Establish vertical loading.* Let the worker plan and control his or her own job, instead of having it controlled by outsiders. For example, let the worker set his or her own schedule, do his or her troubleshooting, decide when to start and stop working, etc.
5 *Open feedback channels.* Finally, find more and better ways for the workers to get quick feedback on their performance.

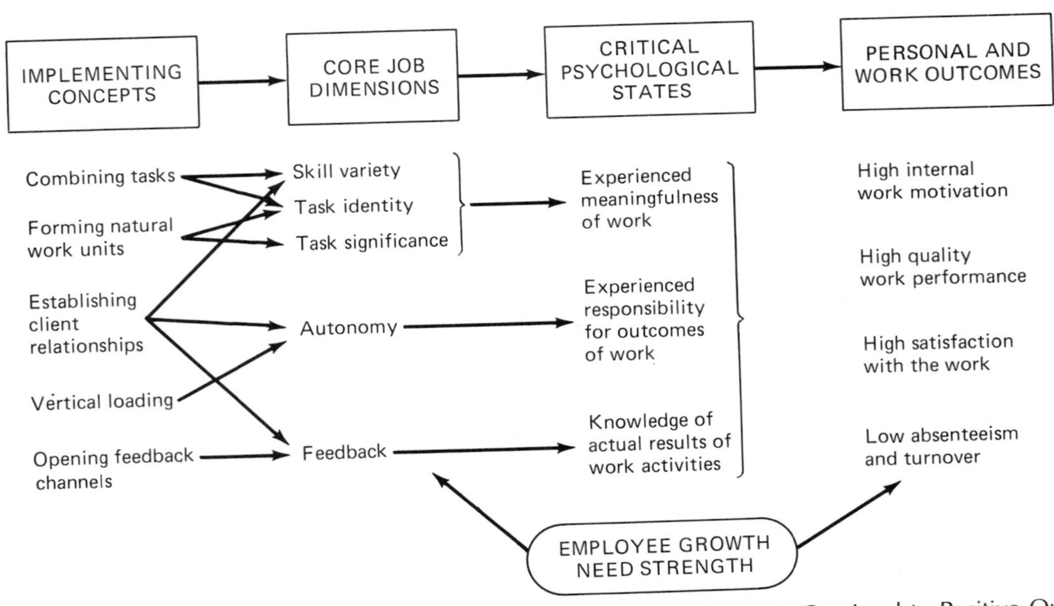

FIGURE 10-3 The Full Model: How Use of the Implementing Concepts Can Lead to Positive Outcomes. *Source:* J. Richard Hackman, Greg Oldham, Robert Janson, and Kenneth Purdy, "A New Strategy for Job Enrichment," *California Management Review,* Vol. 17, No. 4.

Research Results The researchers tested their job-enrichment approach at the Travelers Insurance Company and found it to be effective. The work group chosen was a keypunching operation. Here, the employees' function was to transfer the information from printed or written documents onto punched cards for computer input. Work output was inadequate, error rates were high, schedules were often missed, and absenteeism and turnover were higher than average. The researchers first carried out a diagnosis based on the steps summarized above, and determined that there was a need for job enrichment. As a result, they took the following steps:

- *Natural work groups.* Each keypunch operator was assigned continuing responsibility for certain accounts—for example, each worked only for particular departments.
- *Task combination.* Keypunchers began doing more of their own planning and inspecting.
- *Client relationships.* Each operator was given several channels of direct contact with clients. The operators, not their assignment clerks, now inspect the documents for correctness and legibility. When problems arise, the operators, not the supervisors, take them up with the client.
- *Vertical loading.* Here, for example, operators may now set their own schedules and plan their daily work as long as they meet the schedules.
- *Feedback.* In addition to feedback from client contact, other channels of feedback were installed. For example, the computer operator now returns incorrect cards to the operators who punched them, and operators correct their own errors.

According to the researchers, the results of this experiment were dramatic. The number of operators declined from 98 to 60. In the group whose jobs were enriched, quantity of work increased by almost 40 percent, as compared with only about 8 percent in the control, no-change group. Absenteeism in the enrichment group decreased by 24 percent after jobs were enriched, while in the control group, absenteeism actually increased by almost 30 percent. Turnover attitudes toward the job increased by over 16 percent in the enrichment group while remaining about the same in the controlled group. Actual savings in salary and machine rental charges during the first year totaled $64,305. Thus, the application of this particular job-enrichment technology apparently resulted in substantial increases in employee morale and productivity.[28]

DESCRIPTIONS OF ACTUAL JOB-REDESIGN PROGRAMS

In practice, job enrichment is usually carried out in conjunction with other redesign efforts, including job enlargement, job rotation, and the instituting of self-contained work teams. Furthermore, as we will see, job-enrichment programs are often associated with increased employee participation and with an improvement in such things as pay and working conditions. Several examples of actual job-redesign programs follow.

• *The Stockholder-Correspondent Job at AT&T*

The enrichment of the stockholder-correspondents' job at AT&T (which we mentioned briefly earlier) is one good example of job enrichment in practice.[29] Stockholder correspondents are responsible for corresponding with stockholders of the company by answering the latter's questions and informing them about such things as stockholders' meetings. This would seem to be a relatively complex and challenging job, but in this case, "performance and attitudes were found to be low" and, according to Herzberg, "the challenge of the job existed merely as words."[30]

As a result, a controlled job-enrichment experiment was carried out that, as we have seen, proved quite successful. It involved "vertical loading" of the correspondents' jobs, as follows:

- "Subject-matter experts" were appointed within each group of correspondents for other members to consult with before seeking supervisory help. (The supervisor had been answering all specialized and difficult questions.)
- Correspondents now sign their own names on letters. (The supervisor had been signing all letters.)
- The work of the more experienced correspondents was proofread less frequently by supervisors and was done at the correspondent's desk, dropping verification from 100 percent to 10 percent. (Previously, all correspondents' letters had been checked by the supervisor.)
- Production was discussed, but only in terms such as, "A full day's work is expected." As time went on, this was no longer mentioned. (Before, the group had been constantly reminded of the number of letters that needed to be answered.)
- Outgoing mail went directly to the mailroom without going over supervisors' desks. (The letters had always been routed to the supervisors.)
- Correspondents were encouraged to answer letters in a more personalized way. (Reliance on the form-letter approach had been standard practice.)
- Each correspondent was held personally responsible for the quality and accuracy of letters. (This had been the responsibility of the supervisor and the verifier.)[31]

• *Job "Nesting" at AT&T*

The American Telephone & Telegraph Company has carried out numerous job-enrichment programs; according to Robert Ford, who was responsible for these changes, they demonstrate that productivity and morale rise when a worker can claim "a job of my own."[32] The general strategy behind job enrichment at AT&T is summarized in Figure 10-4. As you can see, improving a job involves pulling down

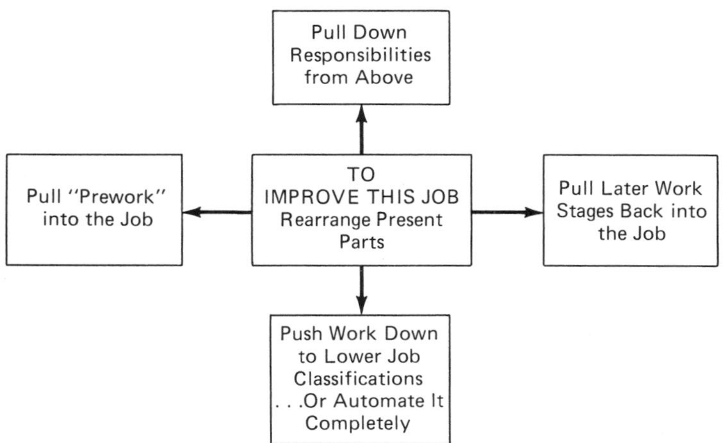

FIGURE 10-4 Steps in Enriching a Job at AT&T. *Source:* Robert Ford, "Job Enrichment Lessons from AT&T," *Harvard Business Review,* January–February 1973. Copyright © 1973 by the President and Fellows of Harvard College; all rights reserved.

responsibilities from above (for example, by letting employees schedule their own work and deal directly with clients); pulling "prework" and later work stages into the job (for example, by letting keypunch operators verify their own work); and pushing work down to lower job classifications (for example, having the supervisor delegate more responsibility to subordinates).

At the former Indiana Bell Telephone Company, before enrichment, 33 clerical employees compiled all telephone directories for the state. The processing from clerk to clerk was laid out in 21 steps, many of which were for verification. The steps included manuscript reception, manuscript verification, keypunch, keypunch verification, and so on, in what amounted to an assembly-line operation. Morale was low, turnover was unacceptable, and a job-enrichment program was instituted in order to alleviate these problems. Supervisors and employees were consulted, and all agreed that employees could do error-free work; consequently, most "verification" steps were eliminated. Next, employees agreed that they could "own" their own phone books and perform all remaining steps themselves. For example, new entries to all directories had previously been made by a succession of clerks; now, *all* paperwork connected with the book belonging to a clerk stayed with that clerk. According to Ford, "owning" her or his own book, combined with the increased responsibility and range of tasks each clerk performed, has increased morale and performance at Indiana Bell.

Based on successes like this, AT&T has been investigating ways of going beyond enrichment of individual jobs. One way it is doing this is by "nesting" several jobs to improve morale and upgrade performance. Basically, job nesting involves rearranging the physical layout of offices in order to reinforce the fact that each group of employees has its own particular client to serve.

For example, the former Southwestern Bell Telephone Company was able to substantially improve the morale and productivity of a group of its service representatives through a combination of job enrichment and job nesting. Before the job enrichment started, the service representatives' office was laid out as it appears in Figure 10-5. Desks were lined up in a standard, "in-line" arrangement, facing the desks of the supervisors, who exercised close control of the service representatives.

As part of the enrichment effort, each service-representative group was assigned a geographical locality of its own, rather than just "the next customer who calls in from anywhere in the district"; this added an "enriched" element to their jobs. At the same time, each geographical-location group was "nested" by moving the workers' desks and those of their supervisors to form a sort of wagon-train layout. As seen in Figure 10-6, they were gathered into a more or less circular shape and were no longer directly facing the desks of the business-office supervisors and unit managers. (The district manager's office was further removed, too.) In total, this nesting, as well as the fact that the workers were not as closely supervised as before, helped to reinforce the unique identity of each service group.

• *Production Teams at Volvo*

As is often the case, job redesign at Volvo Auto in Sweden began as a reaction to a number of severe personnel problems facing the company.[33] Wildcat strikes, turnover, absenteeism, and dependence on foreign workers had become such acute problems that management was willing to experiment with the relatively "ineffi-

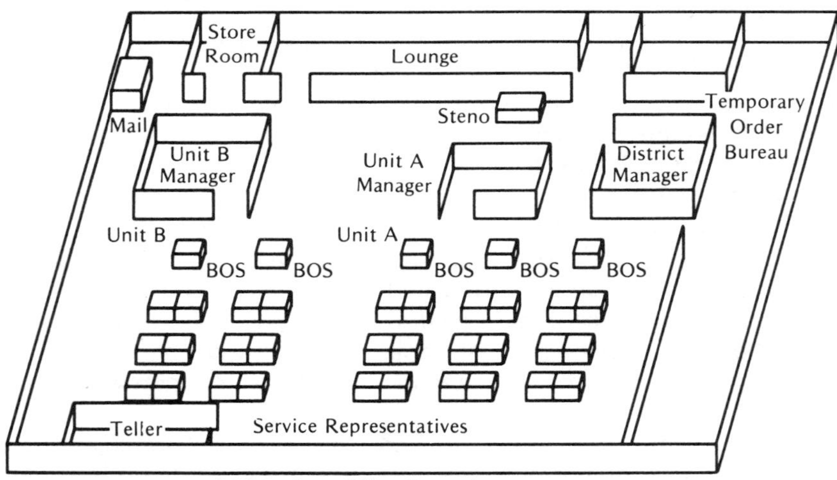

Note: Desks lined up in standard "in-line" arrangement, facing supervisors.

FIGURE 10-5 District Service Representatives' Office Layout Before Job Enrichment. *Source:* Robert Ford, "Job Enrichment Lessons from AT&T," *Harvard Business Review,* January–February 1973. Copyright © 1973 by the President and Fellows of Harvard College; all rights reserved.

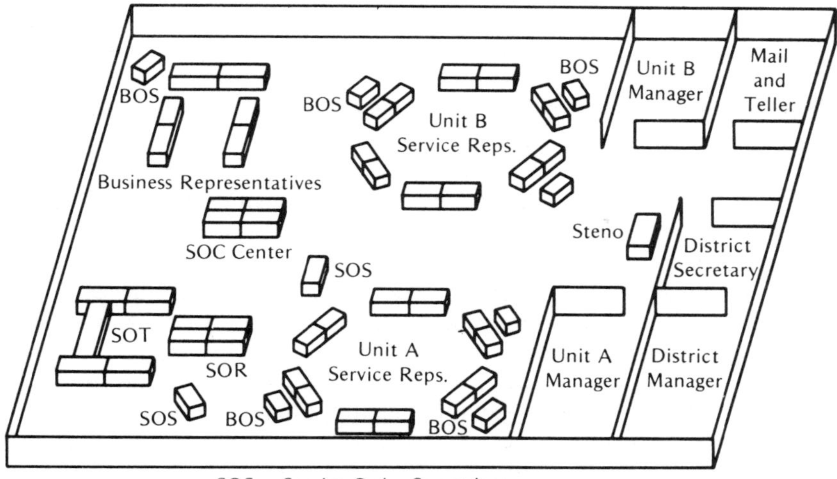

SOS — Service Order Supervisor
SOC — Service Order Control
SOR — Service Order Reviewers
SOT — Service Order Typists

Note: Desks for each area are moved into "wagon-train" circles, with reps no longer facing supervisors directly.

FIGURE 10-6 Job Nesting: Service Representatives' Office Layout After Job Enrichment Program Was Implemented. *Source:* Robert Ford, "Job Enrichment Lessons from AT&T," *Harvard Business Review,* January–February 1973. Copyright © 1973 by the President and Fellows of Harvard College; all rights reserved.

cient," less-specialized jobs in order to reinstate some semblance of continuity in its production lines.

Job redesign at Volvo included job rotation, job enlargement, and an enrichment of employees' jobs that involved forming them into production teams. *Job rotation* was instituted on the production line that was responsible for sealing car bodies. The internal-sealing job is an especially uncomfortable one, since employees have to work in a cramped position inside the car body. In this case, jobs were rotated every other hour. The remaining jobs on the line were rotated daily. *Job enlargement* was instituted on an assembly line. Here, employees follow the same car body for seven or eight stations along the line for a total period of 20 minutes, performing each of the jobs that a separate worker previously would have carried out at each station. This results in a job for each worker that takes seven or eight times longer than his previous, specialized job. Job rotation and enlargement is strictly voluntary at Volvo, and about 20 percent of the employees have volunteered for these programs.

Several Volvo plants have also instituted job enrichment by means of production-team programs. At one truck-assembly plant, for example, production teams of five to twelve men together assemble entire engines. Each group elects its own "charge hand" (supervisor), schedules its own output, distributes work among its members, and does its own quality control. The team is paid on a group (rather than individual) piecework basis, and everyone in the group except the charge hand therefore earns the same amount.

So far, the effectiveness of job redesign at Volvo is unclear. At a truck-assembly plant, the introduction of the production teams has apparently reduced turnover and absenteeism and improved product quality. At the auto plant, where job rotation and enlargement were introduced, turnover has dropped from 40 to 25 percent. However, the introduction of job redesign coincided with an economic slowdown that may have accounted for much of this reduction. And when Volvo surveyed its employees to probe for the causes of turnover and absenteeism, most of the causes turned out to be external—child care, long-distance traveling to the plant, and so on. As a result, Volvo instituted other changes (including extending the bus fleet and lending money to employees to purchase apartments), and these changes probably contributed to the reduction in turnover and absenteeism.

Regardless of this, Volvo's new assembly plant at Kalmar, Sweden, has been especially designed to accommodate the production-team approach. The plant is shaped like a star, and in each point of the star there is a work group finishing a big share of the whole automobile—the electrical system, the safety system, the interior, and so on. Each work team of 15 to 25 people distributes the work among themselves, and the employees determine their own work rhythm, subject to meeting overall production standards. Thus, if they decide to work hard in the morning and relax in the afternoon, the decision is theirs. As with the truck-assembly plant, each team chooses its own boss and can change this selection if that person does poorly. Architecturally, the building has been designed to preserve the atmosphere of a small workshop. For example, each work team has its own entrance, dressing room, restroom, and so on. Furthermore, each team is physically shielded from a view of the other teams by special walls and buffers.

• *Job Redesign at Saab-Scania*

One of the best-known job-enrichment programs was instituted at the Scania division of the Saab automobile company in Sweden. As in the case of Volvo, employee turnover had been running (in 1969) about 45 percent annually, and the personnel situation was described by one expert as "horrendous";[34] it was becoming impossible to fill jobs on the shop floor and therefore to maintain an even flow of production.

As a result of these problems, several job-redesign programs were initiated at Saab. For example, one plant instituted small-group assembly of auto engines. As shown in Figure 10-7, this plant is laid out so that all the basic components for an engine—cylinder heads, engine block, spark plugs, and so on—are supplied to one of seven production teams (in the upper left of the figure). Each team plans its own work, makes its own assignments, and assembles its own engine; the engines are

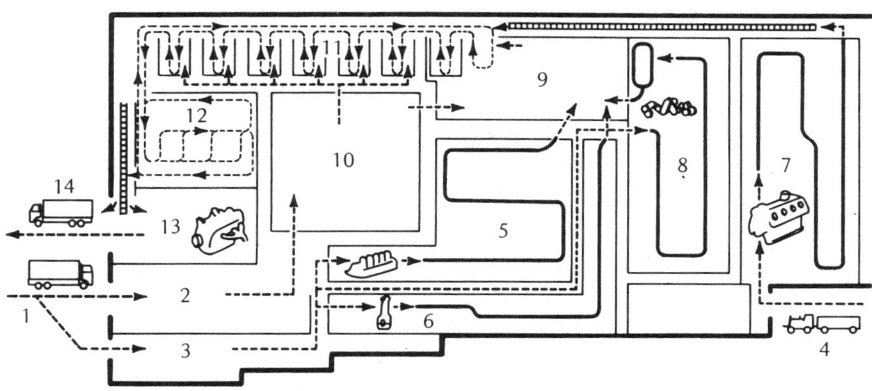

1. Goods Reception
2. Arrival Inspection Purchased Factory Parts
3. Raw Material Store
4. Engine Blocks (Material from Own Foundry)
5. Machining Cylinder heads
6. Machining Connecting Rods
7. Machining Engine Blocks
8. Machining Crankshafts
9. Preassembly
10. Parts Store
11. Group Assembyly
12. Engine Testing
13. Ready Stock
14. Engines to Trollhattan and Uusikaupunki

FIGURE 10-7 Diagram of Engine Plant, Saab-Scania. *Source:* "Job Redesign on the Assembly Line," Organizational Dynamics, autumn 1973, p. 57. © 1973 by AMACOM, a division of American Management Associations.

then sent to testing and shipping.[35] A similar program was instituted in a truck-chassis assembly plant. Here, production groups of five to twelve workers with related job duties decide among themselves how they will do their jobs. For instance, they can rotate job assignments, do many jobs or fewer, and vary their pace. Furthermore, other tasks have been "pulled into" and made a part of each truck-chassis-assembly group's job. For example, certain "housekeeping," simple service and maintenance, and quality control activities previously performed by staff personnel were made an integral part of the production teams' tasks.

As at Volvo, the effectiveness of job redesign at Saab is not entirely clear, although (again, as at Volvo) management thinks enough of the programs to be planning to continue and expand them. On the positive side, the production-team approach means that each worker is less specialized and able to do more jobs, which makes the plant more flexible. Automation has, in a sense, been reversed, so there is less investment in complex, automated machine tools. Productivity is apparently higher than it would have been with the conventional (but troubled) assembly line, although at this point there is no absolute proof. Each engine now takes longer to assemble and training costs have increased, but on the other hand, quality has improved and turnover has decreased. Yet an economic downturn and other changes make it difficult to assess the extent to which improvements are a result of job redesign.

IMPLICATIONS: CONDITIONS UNDER WHICH JOB ENRICHMENT IS MOST EFFECTIVE

• *The Two Main Barriers in Job Enrichment*

Numerous barriers to effectively implementing job enrichment have been identified,[36] but these barriers usually fall into one of two categories. First, there is often insufficient *diagnosis* of the job involved, of the situation surrounding these jobs, and of the need for using job redesign to raise morale and performance. As a result, job enrichment (or some other job-redesign program) is often initiated even though employees do not want it, or when the job itself is not amenable to enrichment, or when the "motivational" problem is caused not by the job but by some other problems, like low pay, poor working conditions, unclear performance standards, or inadequate training. The second barrier is that the redesign is often attempted in a vacuum, rather than as a concerted effort—one entailing improved training and appraisal, better pay, and various other associated improvements. As a result, employees (subordinates, supervisors, and managers alike), lacking in sufficient training, education, and "priming," may resist the "improvements" and further cripple the program.[37]

We have already touched on some of the problems that arise when these barriers are not met and the job redesign is not effectively accomplished. Perhaps most seriously, of course, productivity may be reduced with no corresponding increase in quality (or other benefits), so that the net effect of the redesign on the company's "bottom line" is negative.

Diagnosis: Conditions under Which Job Enrichment Will More Likely Be Effective Given the need to accurately diagnose the situation before proceeding with job enrichment (or some other job-redesign program), it would be useful to summarize some "guidelines for diagnosis," and these follow. In order to diagnose the need for job redesign, one can ask the following questions:[38]

- *Is motivation central to the problem?* We have seen that job enrichment has the potential for increasing morale and performance, but this is important only when the problem (such as high turnover, low quality, or poor productivity) stems from dissatisfaction or low motivation. In many cases, employees couldn't do the job even if they wanted to, because they live too far from the plant, their tools are inadequate, there is interdepartmental conflict, or for some other "nonmotivational" reason.
- *Is there an easier way?* Related to the first question, it is usually a good idea to ask if there is an easier way to improve the situation in question. Sometimes, for example, improved personnel testing and training might eliminate the problem.

- *Are the "hygienes" adequate?* One thing most job-enrichment experts agree on is that enrichment will not reduce problems caused by inadequate "hygienes" like low pay, poor working conditions, or unacceptable leadership practices. Employees usually have to be at least adequately satisfied with these hygienes—in other words, their lower-level needs must be fairly well satisfied—in order for job enrichment (with its appeal to higher-level needs) to be effective.[39]
- *Is the job low in motivating potential?* Is it low, for example, in terms of the skill variety, task identity, task significance, autonomy, and knowledge of results that were part of the job-enrichment technology we discussed earlier in this chapter?
- *Is it technically and economically feasible to enrich the jobs?* In some cases, there are simply too many costs involved in "de-automating" to make job enrichment ever pay for itself. At Saab, for example, the complexity of assembling an entire diesel-truck engine was so great that the employees themselves asked to have the experiment aborted. Frederick Herzberg suggests zeroing in on those jobs in which "the investment in industrial engineering does not make changes too costly."[40] Richard Walton says that the particular technology in the manufacturing process must provide significant room for human attitudes and motivation to affect costs, and furthermore, it has to be technically and economically feasible to eliminate some (but not all) of the routinized, inherently boring work.[41]
- *Is quality important?* There seems to be little doubt that as far as the final product is concerned, it is its *quality* rather than its *quantity* that is usually the main "performance" beneficiary of job enrichment. An important question, then, concerns whether quality—or an increase in quality—is necessary.
- *Are workers ready for the change—and do they want it?* Experts also agree that the workers that seem to benefit most from job enrichment are those whose "psychological growth" needs—their higher-level needs for self-actualization, achievement, and challenge—are aroused. Remember, as we discussed earlier in this chapter, that for many employees (and for many different reasons), *apparently* boring jobs may be neither boring nor dissatisfying to the workers; instead, these workers may simply "get turned on" by various *non*-work interests.

Job Enrichment as Part of a Concerted Effort It is also apparent that job enrichment is usually not effective unless it is part of a broader effort within the organization. Specifically, it should coincide with coordinated changes in pay, performance appraisal, training, and similar factors. As one expert has stated:

> Job design may generate into a mere gimmick if it is not part of both a comprehensive new policy concerning the use and development of human resources and a comprehensive new philosophy of management.[42]

Often, many nonjob factors have to be reappraised and possibly changed when implementing a job-enrichment program.[43] These include:

- *Managerial assumptions and supervisor/subordinate relationships.* For example, supervisors and managers have to understand that the employees can function effectively with their new autonomy.
- *Organization structure.* For example, enriched jobs often permit wider "spans of control" as the tasks normally carried out by the supervisors are absorbed by their subordinates.
- *Pay.* Job enrichment leads to increased responsibility and often to a production-team approach to assembly. Changes like these demand commensurate changes in how employees are paid—for example, there may be a shift from individual incentive to group incentive plans, and to higher pay in general.
- *Performance appraisal.* As jobs become more responsible and less routine, there may have to be a shift from a more "mechanical" approach to appraisal (e.g., graphic rating forms) to a more professional approach involving mutual goal setting. In fact, some researchers have found that goal setting is a natural complement to job enrichment.[44] In general, this often entails a deemphasis on closely monitoring the *means* by which employees get their tasks done, and a corresponding emphasis on periodically checking the *end results.*
- *Communications.* Job enrichment (like any organizational change) requires open, effective communications in order to be implemented properly. This usually involves a good deal of two-way communication between supervisors and production workers about schedules, production problems, and quality.[45]
- *Selection, placement, and training.* The new responsibility, decision making, and involvement associated with job enrichment generally demand corresponding changes in the organization's selection, placement, and training procedures. Workers who have the ability to learn the new techniques have to be trained in their proper execution, new selection criteria have to be developed, and more care has to be taken in placing employees in the more demanding jobs.

SUMMARY

The basic issue in job design is whether the job should be highly specialized and routine or enriched and nonroutine. Those who advocate specialization argue that specialized jobs are more efficient—there is less time required for learning, less wasted materials, and so on. Those who argue for job enrichment claim that by increasing the duties and functions of a job, job enrichment replaces the sense of achievement, challenge, and accomplishment that job specialization removes.

The technology for enriching jobs assumes that there are five core dimensions that determine whether the person will experience the necessary job meaningfulness: skill variety, task identity, task significance, autonomy, and knowledge of results. Actual job-redesign programs at companies like AT&T suggest that job enrichment can be effective, although it is not entirely clear that job enrichment is effective without associated factors like changes in pay.

DISCUSSION QUESTIONS

1. Is job enrichment useful for improving performance?
2. Would you recommend job enrichment for workers who are dissatisfied because of low pay? Why, or why not?
3. Discuss the conditions under which job enrichment will more likely result in increased motivation.
4. Explain how you would diagnose the need for a job enrichment program.

APPENDIX TO CHAPTER 10
Individual and Situational Factors in Job Design

INTRODUCTION AND BACKGROUND

Some experts argue that individuals vary so widely in their values and needs that one cannot generalize about the effectiveness of job enrichment. Proponents of this view generally do not argue that job enrichment is ineffective; they argue, instead, that for many employees and situations, it is simply inappropriate.

The origins of this argument can be traced back to several early studies that seemed to indicate that employees do not respond in any consistent way to either boring or enriched jobs. Smith, for example, surveyed 72 women performing repetitive work in a knitwear mill.[46] She found that repetitive work was not necessarily related to boredom on the job and that the extent to which a worker was bored with her job was a function of such personal factors as age. In another study of the effects of routine jobs on women workers, researchers reviewed 115 assembly-line operators over a two-year period.[47] They found that fewer than 20 percent felt their work was monotonous or boring; furthermore, monotony and boredom were not necessarily related to dissatisfaction or frustration. The researchers emphasized that repetitive work need not be dissatisfying, particularly when it has *traction*—a smooth process that is not interrupted by outsiders, problems, or excess pressure for quantity.[48]

In summary, studies like these suggested that not all employees and situations are amenable to job enrichment and that it would be useful to identify the "individual difference" factors that influence whether or not a person responds favorably to a more enriched job.

ALIENATION FROM MIDDLE-CLASS VALUES

The first "individual difference" factor researchers turned to was employees' adherence to (or alienation from) "middle-class values." The basic thinking here was that employees who did not have middle-class values would not seek out or prefer jobs with increased responsibility, higher status, or more autonomy, and that for these employees at least, job enrichment would be a failure.[49]

This line of research originated with and was based upon three main studies. In 1965, Turner and Lawrence reported the results of a study in which they found that workers from factories in small rural towns seemed to react well to enriched jobs, but those from urban cities did not. Turner and Lawrence concluded that workers in large urban cities tend to be "normless," since they are so heterogeneous in their values and backgrounds that a consistent pattern of middle-class values is lacking.[50]

Two years later, Blood and Hulin took issue with Turner and Lawrence's conclusions, arguing that workers in cities were not necessarily normless but might simply have different values from those of the middle class. In their paper, Blood and Hulin analyzed data from 1,900 male workers in 21 plants in the eastern United States. The researchers were particularly interested in determining whether workers' adherence to or alientation from "middle-class values" had any effect on how they responded to enriched jobs. They therefore classified these 21 plants geographically along six dimensions, such as "slum conditions" and "prosperity and cost of living," since they assumed that workers in certain plants—such as in slum areas—would most likely be alienated from middle-class values. They found that alienated workers (actually, workers who they *assumed* were alienated, based on their plant's location) did not respond favorably to enriched jobs (jobs with more variety, responsibility, and autonomy). Workers from "non-alienated" plants did respond favorably to enriched jobs.[51] In a follow-up study the next year, Hulin and Blood expanded on their findings. Basically, they argued that white-collar workers in general and blue-collar workers from small rural towns would respond favorably to enriched jobs, since they generally share middle-class values. Blue-collar workers from cities, they argued, are generally alienated from middle-class values and will therefore respond negatively to enriched jobs.[52]

The Turner-Lawernce/Hulin-Blood findings have stimulated a great deal of research, but the prevailing evidence suggests that these researchers' conclusions (concerning the effects of "alienation") are unfounded. Stone and Porter, for example, studied 593 predominantly blue-collar workers in urban areas and concluded that job variety and autonomy were in fact positively correlated with job satisfaction. (These findings are at odds with Blood and Hulin's conclusions that urban blue-collar workers would not respond well to enriched jobs, since they are likely to be alienated from the middle-class values.) Other studies that have used plant location as a substitute or surrogate measure of worker alienation have come to similar conclusions.[53]

Actually, although Hulin and Blood initially argued that plant location (rural versus urban) could be used as an indicator of whether workers in the plant were or were not alienated, they have subsequently altered their position. Hulin, for example, noted that it was unfortunate that plant location was receiving so much attention by researchers, rather than workers' actual alienation or nonalienation from middle-class values. As a result, recent studies have measured employee values and alienation directly.[54]

Yet most of these findings continue to cast doubt on the Turner-Lawrence/Hulin-Blood conclusions.[55] In one study, for example, Stone obtained data from 594 subjects working in a variety of jobs and organizations in the southern California area. Specifically, he obtained data on job scope (such as variety and autonomy), on employee satisfaction (for example, with pay, promotions, and supervision), and on the extent to which employees adhere to Protestant-ethic values (such as whether they have pride in their work, are involved in the job, and prefer to strive to better themselves). Stone concludes that:

> On the basis of the present study's findings and those of numerous other researchers, it would appear that efforts aimed at increasing the scope of worker's jobs [e.g., job enrichment] will be reacted to no less positively by alienated than by [nonalienated] workers. The application of techniques such as job enrichment should not, therefore, be restricted to individuals who have internalized the work norms and values of the "middle class" [i.e., the Protestant ethic], as has been suggested by Hulin and Blood. This should not be interpreted as meaning that individual differences (with respect to preferences for job enrichment) should be neglected by either the researcher or the practitioner. What is suggested, however, is that the Protestant ethic is probably *not* an important individual differences variable to consider when the researcher or practitioner is concerned with how satisfaction with the work itself will be influenced by changes in job scope.[56]

THE EFFECTS OF "HIGHER-ORDER-NEED" STRENGTH

Research efforts have recently turned to the question of whether employees' psychological *needs* influence how they react to enriched jobs. For example, many experts believe that it is only those employees who have strong "higher-order needs"—needs for personal growth, esteem, and autonomy, for instance—that react favorably to enriched jobs.

They argue that enriched jobs are by definition jobs with more variety, responsibility, and challenge and that such jobs should be more attractive (or, perhaps attractive *only*) to employees who covet responsibility, challenge, and autonomy.

Although their position seems logical enough, the research evidence does not provide any clear-cut answers one way or another. In one study, Hackman and Lawler found a more positive relation between employee satisfaction and job scope (such as how much skill variety and autonomy the job provided) for employees with strong higher-order needs. However, there are two problems with their reported findings. First, Hackman and Lawler measure higher-order-need strength *indirectly,* with a questionnaire that asks employees what sort of jobs they prefer. For example, employees have to choose between "a job which offers little or no challenge," and "a job which requires you to be completely isolated from co-workers"; similarly, employees have to choose between "a job where the pay is very good," and "a job where there is considerable opportunity to be creative and innovative."[57] Yet some argue that it is questionable whether asking employees what sort of jobs they prefer is equivalent to measuring their "higher-order-needs strength."[58] In other words, employees with stronger higher-order needs (as measured by Hackman and Lawler's questionnaire) are only slightly more "turned on" by the enriched jobs than are employees with weaker higher-order needs. Some recent studies that have attempted to measure higher-order-needs strength directly (rather than by inferring it from the jobs employees say they would choose) have found no real differences between how employees with strong and weak higher-order-needs strengths react to enriched jobs.[59] Perhaps the clearest conclusion we can draw from this research is that employees with strong higher-order needs—strong needs for personal growth and development, autonomy, esteem, and achievement—will usually react *slightly* better to enriched jobs than will employees whose needs for these things are not so strong. From a practical point of view, however, the difference is only slight, and it would therefore seem to be unwise to elect not to proceed with an enrichment program if the only drawback seems to be that employees do not have strong higher-order needs.

THE EFFECTS OF NEED FOR ACHIEVEMENT

A more promising line of research focuses on the role of "need for achievement" in job enrichment. People who have high needs for achievement derive their satisfaction from accomplishing challenging tasks. They therefore seek out challenging jobs, try to assume personal responsibility for problem solving, and prefer situations where they receive clear feedback on task performance. (Conversely, people who do not have this high need to achieve do not seek out challenging jobs and prefer situations where the responsibilities for the job are shared with others.)

Steers and Spencer believe that the reason the findings concerning higher-order-need strength are inconclusive is that there are simply too many needs scrambled together under the umbrella of "higher-order-needs." That is, higher-order needs include needs people have for esteem, personal growth and development, autonomy, and achievement; and the consensus is building that treating all these needs as one broad higher-need category is not sound.[60] As a result, some researchers (like Steers and Spencer) argue that research efforts should focus on only one of these higher-order needs at a time, and in particular on need for achievement.

There are several reasons for focusing on need for achievement and its influence on how employees react to enriched jobs. The most important reason is that need for achievement specifically focuses on the task as the primary vehicle for satisfying people's needs to achieve. In other words, people with high needs to achieve *by definition* derive their satisfaction from accomplishing challenging tasks. A second reason is that need for achievement, being but one component of a person's higher-order needs, is an easier factor to measure and manipulate in an experiment.

One recent study using need for achievement involved 115 managers in various departments of a major manufacturing firm.[61] The researchers predicted that managers with high needs to achieve would react better to enriched jobs; specifically, they hypothesized that enriching the jobs of these managers would make them more committed and would result in higher performance than would enriching the jobs of managers with relatively low needs to achieve.

The findings in this study were as follows: First, as far as organizational commitment was concerned, it seemed to make no difference whether the employees whose jobs were enriched were high or low achievers. In other words, whether the managers had high or low needs to achieve, enriching their jobs seemed to lead to higher commitment. On the other hand, whether or not the person had a high need to achieve did seem to have a clear effect on how he or she *performed* the new enriched job. The job performance of "high-need-to-achieve" employees was clearly and directly related to how enriched their jobs were (in terms of variety, autonomy, and so on). Similarly, job enrichment had no effect on the performance of employees who had low needs to achieve. As the researchers summarize:

> . . . increasing the job scope of employees' work activities by providing greater amounts of variety, autonomy, feedback, and so forth, should serve to enhance employee commitment for *most* employees and employee performance for *some* (those with high needs for achievement).[62]

THE EFFECTS OF PERCEPTION

Different people perceive the same task differently, and so perceptions play a role in job design. Thus, an employee who is new to the task, or who has a relatively low education level, might perceive the task as much more challenging than would a veteran employee with a college degree, for instance.

One study illustrates this point well. Stone had students perform a simple task and then fill out questionnaires concerning their perceptions of the task and satisfaction with it.[63] Stone found that even though the task was identical for all students, there were significant differences in how the students perceived their task—in terms of how much variety and autonomy it provided and how challenging it was, for instance. Aldag and Brief came to a similar conclusion. They studied a group of hospital employees and found that employees with relatively little education viewed apparently routine jobs as being relatively enriched.[64] The implication seems to be that a manager who is considering implementing a job-enrichment program should first ascertain how the affected employees perceive their jobs now; many employees seem to perceive apparently "routine" jobs as already quite enriched.

THE EFFECTS OF SITUATIONAL FACTORS

Researchers have identified two important situational factors that influence the appropriateness of job enrichment. First, many researchers now believe that job enrichment has positive effects only up to a point, and that beyond this point it becomes dysfunctional. Therefore, how enriched the job is *at present* is one important situational factor: Very unenriched, routine jobs are most amenable to enrichment, but it is also possible to enrich a job too much. Beyond a point, additional increases in the job's variety and complexity can and often will result in confusion and feelings of incompetence on the part of employees.[65]

How *satisfied* employees are with extrinsic job factors is another important situational factor. Researchers have found that employees who are satisfied with extrinsic factors (pay, job security, supervision, and coworkers) respond well to job enrichment—their performance goes up, and they are more satisfied. On the other hand, employees who were dissatisfied with extrinsic factors did not respond as well to job enrichment.[66]

INDIVIDUAL AND SITUATIONAL FACTORS: SUMMARY AND IMPLICATIONS

Many studies have been carried out to determine which employees and situations are most appropriate for job enrichment. On the whole, the findings indicate that enriched jobs are usually positively related to employee satisfaction, and also to employee performance, *regardless of individual differences in employees.*[67] Generally speaking, for instance, job enrichment can be expected to be as effective for rural workers as for city workers, for blue-collar workers as for white-collar workers, for workers with strong Protestant-work-ethic values as for those with weak ones, and for those with weak higher-order-need strength as for those with strong. However, employees with high needs to achieve seem to respond consistently *more* favorably to enriched jobs than do those with low needs for achievement. The way the employees perceive the task is also important. Different employees perceive ev the same task differently, and for those who already perceive the job as complex and challenging, job enrichment could backfire. (The converse is also true: Those who perceive even complex jobs as routine and boring might respond well to job enrichment.)

Two situational factors are also important. First, the degree to which the job is already enriched (or perceived as enriched) is important. Perhaps the most crucial finding here is that jobs can be enriched only up to a point; beyond that point, employees may be so confused by the variety and complexity of the job that the enrichment becomes dysfunctional. Job enrichment also seems to work best in those situations where employees are already fairly satisfied with extrinsic factors like pay, working conditions, and supervision. Job enrichment apparently will not compensate for inadequacies in extrinsic factors like these.

One implication of all this is that job enrichment is most attractive when employees with high needs for achievement perceive their jobs as routine, and when they are already reasonably well satisfied with factors like pay and working conditions. Related to this, it would probably be unwise to implement a job-enrichment program without ensuring that employees are already fairly well satisfied with pay, supervision, and working conditions. It is also important to keep in mind that it is not the objective features of the job—its apparent complexity, routineness, or variety—that workers seem to respond to, but instead their perceptions of the job, and these perceptions are obviously influenced by things like employee ability background and educational level.[68]

Footnotes

[1]David Katz and Robert Kahn, *The Social Psychology of Organizations* (New York: John Wiley, 1966), p. 345.

[2]Charles Babbage, *On the Economy of the Machinery and Manufacturers* (London: Charles Knight, 1832), pp. 169–76; reprinted in Joseph Litterer, *The Analysis of Organizations* (New York: John Wiley, 1965), pp. 73–75.

[3]Richard Hopeman, *Production* (Columbus, O.: Charles E. Merrilll, 1965), pp. 478–85.

[4]The notion of a therblig was developed by Frank and Lillian Gilbreth, using their last name spelled backwards to come up with the name for their tool.

[5]See Leonard Sayles and George Strauss, *Human Behavior in Organizations* (Englewood Cliffs, N.J.: Prentice-Hall, 1966), pp. 42–50.

[6]Daniel Bell, "Work in the Life of an American," in William Haber et al., *Man in Power in the United States* (New York: Harper & Row, 1948), p. 15.

[7]Arthur Turner and Paul Lawrence, *Industrial Jobs and the Worker* (Cambridge, Mass.: Harvard University, Graduate School of Business Administration, 1965), pp. 35–48; also Charles Walker and Robert Guest, *The Man on the Assembly Line* (Cambridge, Mass.: Harvard University Press, 1952), p. 120.

[8]Leonard Sayles, "Wildcat Strikes," *Harvard Business Review*, Vol. 32, No. 6 (November 1954), 42–52.

[9]Sayles and Strauss, *Human Behavior in Organizations,* p. 47; see also J.W. Gooding, *The Job Revolution* (New York: Walker, 1972); and *Work in America*, Report of a Special Task Force to the Secretary of Health, Education and Welfare (Cambridge, Mass.: M.I.T. Press, 1973). One recent study suggests that there may also be a significant relationship between technology and grievance rates. See Nels E. Nelson, "Grievance Rates and Technology," *Academy of Management Journal,* Vol. 22, No. 4 (December 1979), 810–14. And Runcie argues that an essential aspect of understanding the drawbacks of a highly specialized job must begin with "a recognition of the humanness of individual workers," since when you work on a production-line job, performing the same task on a car 385 times a day, "you have to do something to stop feeling like a machine yourself." John Runcie, "By Days I Make the Cars," *Harvard Business Review,* May–June 1980, pp. 106–15.

[10]See, for example, Chris Argyris, *Integrating the Individual and the Organization* (New York: John Wiley, 1964).

[11]Frederick Herzberg, "The Wise Old Turk," *Harvard Business Review,* September–October 1974, pp. 70–80.

[12]*Work in America.*

[13]Sar Levitan and William Johnston, "Job Redesign, Reform, Enrichment—Exploring the Limitations," *Monthly Labor Review,* 96 (July 1973).

[14]For discussion of this, see Chapter 12.

[15]See Mitchell Fein, "Job Enrichment: A Re-evaluation," *Sloan Management Review,* Winter 1974, p. 124; reprinted in Jerome Schnee, E. Kirby Warren, and Harold Lazarus, *The Progress of Management* (Englewood Cliffs, N.J.: Prentice-Hall, 1977), p. 132.

[16]William Giles, "Volunteering for Job Enrichment: A Test of Expectancy Theory Predictions," *Personnel Psychology,* Vol. 30 (Autumn 1977), 427–35.

[17]See, for example, Albert King, "Expectation Effects in Organization Change," *Administrative Science Quarterly,* June 1974, pp. 221–30.

[18]Frederick Herzberg, "One More Time: How do you Motivate Employees?" *Harvard Business Review,* Motivation Series, 1970, pp. 54–63.

[19]Robert Ford, "Job Enrichment Lessons from AT&T," *Harvard Business Review,* January–February 1973, pp. 96–106.

[20]Robert Ford, *Motivation Theory through the Work Itself* (New York: American Management Association, Inc., 1969), p. 188. Also William Reif and Fred Luthans, "Does Job Enrichment Really Pay Off?" *California Management Review,* Vol. 15, No. 1, 30–37. Reif and Luthans point out that no claim is made that these 19 trials cover a representative sample of jobs and people within the Bell System: There are more than 1,000 different jobs in the Bell System, not just the nine of these studies.

[21]Dennis Umstot, Cecil Bell, Jr., and Terrence Mitchell, "Effects of Job Enrichment and Task Goals on Satisfaction and Productivity: Implications for Job Design," *Journal of Applied Psychology,* Vol. 61, No. 4 (August 1976), 379–94.

[22]Edwin Locke, David Sirota, and Alan Wolfson, "An Experimental Case Study of the Successes and Failures of Job Enrichment in a Government Agency," *Journal of Applied Psychology,* Vol. 61, No.6 (December 1976), 701.

[23]Note, first, that most studies of the moderating effects of factors like higher-order needs conclude that job scope and satisfaction are directly related, regardless of individual employee differences like plant location or higher-order-need strength. For a review of studies that show that enriched jobs are *usually* related to improved attitudes and *often* to performance, see A.P. Brief and R.J. Aldag, "Employee Reactions to Job Characteristics: A Constructive Replication," *Journal of Applied Psychology,* Vol. 60 (1975), 182–86; J.R. Hackman and E.E. Lawler, "Employee Reactions to Job Characteristics," *Journal of Applied Psychology,* Vol. 55, (1971), 259–86; J.R. Hackman and G.R. Oldham, "Development of the Job Diagnostic Survey," *Journal of Applied Psychology,* Vol. 60 (1975), 159–70; J.R. Hackman and G.R. Oldham, "Motivation through the Design of Work: Test of a Theory," *Organizational Behavior and Human Performance,* Vol. 16, No. 2 (August 1976), 250–79; L.W. Porter and R.M. Steers, "Organizational Work and Personal Factors in Employee Turnover and Absenteeism," *Psychological Bulletin,* Vol. 80 (1973), 151–76; R.D. Pritchard and L.H. Peters, "Job Duties and Job Interests as Predictors of Intrinsic and Extrinsic Satisfaction," *Organizational Behavior and Human Performance,* Vol. 12 (1974), 315–30; B.M. Staw, *Intrinsic and Extrinsic Motivation* (Morristown, N.J.: General Learning Press, 1976); E.F. Stone, "The Moderating Effect of Work-Related Values on the Job Scope–Job Satisfaction Relationship," *Organizational Behavior and Human Performance,* Vol. 15 (1976), 147–67; Umstot, Bell, and Mitchell, "Effects of Job Enrichment and Task Goals"; and J.P. Wanous, "Individual Differences and Reactions to Job Characteristics," *Journal of Applied Psychology,* Vol. 59, (1974), 616–22.

[24]See M. Fein, "Motivation for Work," in *Handbook of Work, Organization, and Society,* ed. R. Dubin (Chicago: Rand McNally, 1973); Fein, "Job Enrichment: A Re-evaluation"; and F.K. Foulkes, *Creating More Meaningful Work* (New York: American Management Association, 1969).

[25]Herzberg, "The Wise Old Turk."

[26]*Ibid.,* pp. 70–80.

[27]J. Richard Hackman, Greg Oldham, Robert Johnson, and Kenneth Purdy, "A New Strategy for Job Enrichment," *California Management Review,* Vol. 17, No. 1 (1975), 51–71, reprinted in H. Kirk Downey, Dan Hellreigel, and John Slocum, Jr., *Organizational Behavior* (St. Paul: West, 1977), pp. 304–

32. For discussions of some of the work that led up to this development, see Arthur Turner and Paul R. Lawrence, *Industrial Jobs and the Worker* (Cambridge, Mass.: Harvard University, Graduate School of Business Administration, 1965), discussed in Raymond Aldag and Arthur Brief, *Task Design and Employee Motivation* (Glenview, Ill.: Scott Foresman, 1979), pp. 45–48; see also Hackman and Lawler, "Employee Reactions to Job Characteristics"; and Wayne Cascio, *Applied Psychology in Personnel Management* (Reston, Va.: Reston, 1978), p. 355. For other studies in this area, see R.J. Aldag and A.P. Brief, "Some Correlates of Work Values," *Journal of Applied Psychology,* Vol. 60 (1975), 757–70; and A.P. Brief, M. Wallace, and R.J. Aldag, "Linear vs. Non-Linear Models of the Formation of Effective Responses: The Case of Job Enlargement," *Decision Sciences,* Vol. 7 (1976), 1–9.

[28]See also Hackman and Oldham, "Motivation Through the Design of Work."

[29]This example is based on Frederick Herzberg, "One More Time."

[30]*Ibid.,* p. 60.

[31]*Ibid.,* p. 62.

[32]This section is based on Ford, "Job Enrichment Lessons from AT&T."

[33]See Charles Gibson, "Volvo Increased Productivity through Job Enrichment," *California Management Review,* Vol. 15, No. 4 (Summer 1973), 64–66; Editor of *Organizational Dynamics,* "Job Redesign on the Assembly Line: Farewell to Blue Collar Blues?" *Organizational Dynamics,* Vol. 2, No. 2 (1973), 51–67, reprinted in Dennis Organ, *The Applied Psychology of Work Behavior* (Dallas: BPI, 1978).

[34]Organ, *Applied Psychology of Work Behavior,* p. 269.

[35]Although this approach worked well enough with small auto engines, it proved impossible with larger truck diesel engines. The latter was a six-hour undertaking involving 1,500 parts, and the approach was abandoned at the employees' request.

[36]See, for example, J. Richard Hackman, "Is Job Enrichment Just a Fad?" *Harvard Business Review,* September–October 1975, pp. 129–38; and Cascio, *Applied Psychology in Personnel Management,* pp. 358–60.

[37]See Richard E. Walton, "How to Counter Alienation in the Plant," *Harvard Business Review,* November–December 1972, p. 77.

[38]Except where noted, these are based on the research findings discussed previously in this chapter. See also James Shaw, "An Information-Processing Approach to the Study of Job Design," *Academy of Management Review,* Vol. 5, No. 1 (January 1980), 41–48.

[39]Rollin Simmons and John Oriff, "Worker Behavior vs. Enrichment Theory," *Administrative Science Quarterly,* Vol. 20 (1975), 606; G.R. Oldham, J.R. Hackman, and J.L. Pearce, "Conditions under Which Employees Respond Positively to Enriched Work," *Journal of Applied Psychology,* Vol. 61 (1976), 395–403.

[40]Herzberg, "One More Time," p. 62.

[41]Walton, "How to Counter Alienation," p. 79.

[42]Einar Thorsrud, "Job Design in the Wider Context," in Lewis Davis and James Taylor, eds., *Design of Jobs* (Baltimore: Penguin, 1972).

[43]The list following is based on Cascio, *Applied Psychology in Personnel Management,* pp. 363–67.

[44]Umstot, Bell, and Mitchell, "Effects of Job Enrichment."

[45]M. Beer and E.F. Huse, "A Systems Approach to Organizational Development," *Journal of Applied Behavior Science,* Vol. 8 (1972), 79–101.

[46]P.C. Smith, "The Prediction of Individual Differences and Susceptibility to an Industrial Monotony," *Journal of Applied Psychology,* Vol. 43 (August 1959). See also Edward O'Connor, Cathy Rudoff, and Lawrence Peters, "Individual Differences and Job Design Reconsidered: Where Do We Go From Here?" *Academy of Management Review,* Vol. 5, No. 2 (April 1980), 249–54.

[47]A.N. Turner and A.L. Michlette, "Sources of Satisfaction in Repetitive Work," *Occupational Psychology,* Vol. 36 (June 1962), 215–31.

[48]M.D. Kilbridge, "Turnover, Absence, and Transfer as Indicators of Employee Dissatisfaction with any Repetitive Work," *Industrial and Labor Relations Review,* Vol. 15 (1961), 22.

[49]C.L. Hulin and M.R. Blood, "Job Enlargement, Individual Differences, and Worker Responses," *Psychological Bulletin,* Vol. 69 (1968), 41–55.

[50]Turner and Lawrence, *Industrial Jobs and the Worker.*

[51]M.R. Blood and C.L. Hulin, "Alienation, Environmental Characteristics, and Worker Responses," *Journal of Applied Psychology,* Vol. 51 (1967), 284–90.

[52]Hulin and Blood, "Job Enlargement"; see also Oscar Martinson and E.A. Wilkening, "Rural-Urban Differences in Job Satisfaction: Further Evidence," *Academy of Management Journal,* Vol. 27, No. 1 (1984), 199–206.

[53]E.F. Stone and L.W. Porter, *Job Scope and Job Satisfaction: A Study of Urban Workers* (Technical Report No. 22), Graduate School of Administration, University of California, Irvine, November 1973.

[54]J.M. Shepard, "Functional Specialization, Alienation, and Job Satisfaction," *Industrial and Labor Relations Review,* Vol. 26 (1973), 851–53; R.J. Aldag and A.P. Brief, "Impact of Individual Differences on Employee Effective Responses to Task Characteristics," *Journal of Business Research,* Vol. 3 (1975), 311–22.

[55]C.L.Hulin, "Reply," *Industrial and Labor Relations Review,* Vol. 26 (1973), 853–55. In addition to the studies described herein, see, for example, E.F. Stone, "Job Scope, Job Satisfaction, and the Protestant Ethic: A Study of Enlisted Men in the U.S. Navy," *Journal of Occupational Behavior,* Vol. 7 (1975), 215–24.

[56]Stone, "The Moderating Effect of Work Related Values." Wanous reports some findings that indicate some modest support for the Turner-Lawrence/Hulin-Blood position. See Wanous, "Individual Differences"; see also J.S. Kim, "Relationships of Personality to Perceptual and Behavioral Responses in Stimulating and Nonstimulating Tasks," *Academy of Management Journal,* Vol. 23, No. 2, (June 1980), 307–19.

[57]Hackman and Lawler, "Employee Reactions to Job Characteristics." For replications of this study, see Brief and Aldag, "Employee Reactions to Job Characteristics"; D. Robey, "Task Design, Work Values, and Worker Response: An Experimental Test," *Organizational Behavior and Human Performance,* Vol. 12 (1974), 264–73; H.P. Sims and A.D. Szilagyi, "Job Characteristics Relationships: Individual and Structural Moderators," *Organizational Behavior and Human Performance,* Vol. 17 (1976), 211–30; Hackman and Oldham, "Motivating Through the Design of Work."

[58]J.R. Hackman and G.R. Oldham, "The Job Diagnostic Survey: An Instrument for the Diagnosis of Jobs and the Evaluation of Job Redesign Projects," Technical Report No. 4, Department of Administrative Services, Yale University, May 1974.

[59]For discussion of this, see Richard Steers and Daniel Spencer, "The Role of Achievement Motivation and Job Design," *Journal of Applied Psychology,* Vol. 62 (August 1977), 473; and Eugene Stone, Richard Mowday, and Lyman Porter, "Higher Order Need Strengths as Moderators of the Job Scope–Job Satisfaction Relationship," *Journal of Applied Psychology,* Vol. 62 (August 1977), 466–71.

[60]See, for example, J.B. Miner and H.P. Dachler, "Personal Attitudes and Motivation," *Annual Review of Psychology,* Vol. 25 (1973), 379–402; R.M. Steers and D.M. Braunstein, "A Behaviorally Based Measure of Manifest Needs and Work Settings," *Journal of Occupational Behavior,* Vol. 9 (1976), 251–66; Stone, Mowday, and Porter, "Higher Order Need Strengths"; and Steers and Spencer, "The Role of Achievement Motivation in Job Design."

[61]Steers and Spencer, "The Role of Achievement Motivation in Job Design."

[62]Steers and Spencer, "The Role of Achievement Motivation in Job Design." In one study, the moderating effects of the Protestant ethic, growth-need strength, and need for achievement may actually have been opposite to those hypothesized. Daniel G. Ganster, "Individual Differences and Task Design: A Laboratory Experiment," *Organizational Behavior and Human Performance,* Vol. 26, No. 1 (August 1980), 131–48.

[63]E.F. Stone, "Some Personality Correlates of Perceptions of and Reactions to Task Characteristics," Working Paper, Purdue University, 1977; Aldag and Brief, *Task Design and Employee Motivation,* pp. 93–94.

[64]R.J. Aldag and A.P. Brief, "Moderators of Relationships of Job Behaviors to Perceptions of Core Task Dimensions," Proceedings of the 8th Annual Midwest Conference of the American Institute for Decision Sciences, 1977, pp. 327–29.

[65]H.P. Sims and A.D. Szilagyi, "Job Characteristics Relationships"; Aldag and Brief, "Moderators of Relationships of Job Behaviors"; and Aldag and Brief, *Task Design and Employee Motivation,* p. 94.

[66]Oldham et al., "Conditions under Which Employees Respond Positively."

[67]For discussion, see Robert P. Vecchio, "Individual Differences as a Moderator of the Job Quality–Job Satisfaction Relationship: Evidence from a National Sample," *Organizational Behavior and Human Performance,* Vol. 26, No. 3 (December 1980), 305–25; O'Connor, Rudoff, and L.H. Peters, "Individual Differences and Job Design Reconsidered."

[68]Actually, the person's *desire* for job enrichment has been found to have more of an effect on how that person responds to job enrichment than do other moderators, like urban-rural influences. David J. Cherrington and J. Lynne England, "The Desire for an Enriched Job as a Moderator of the Enrichment–Satisfaction Relationship," *Organizational Behavior and Human Performance,* Vol. 25, No. 1 (February 1980), 139–59.

CASE FOR CHAPTER 10
MEMO FROM THE GENERAL MANAGER

Cal Johnson, general manager of the assembly department of TMC's refrigeration division, was perplexed. For several months, a number of men working on mechanical assembly had been grumbling about their jobs. Mostly they mentioned things like the monotony of the assembly work, long hours at the conveyor, low pay, and noisy working conditions.

The comments of two of the older and more experienced employees were typical. Sam Campanella told Johnson that he was ready to ask for a transfer if something wasn't done about his job: "A guy can go crazy just screwing on doors and fitting gaskets all day with no variety!" Harry Kranz threatened to quit outright at the end of the month if things didn't get better. "Why can't we be given more different things to do? Any Lincoln Zoo monkey could do what I can do! Why can't you give us bigger jobs, like putting together a whole compressor assembly, or even a whole refrigerator? We'd be a lot happier and turn out more and better units than we're doing now!"

As Cal Johnson reflected on these reactions from his workers, he opened a memorandum he had just received from the vice president:

March 12, 1982

To: Production Managers and General Foremen
From: John Garrison
Subj: Work Specialization Program

Our industrial engineers tell me that we can both cut costs and speed up production through further specialization of assembly-line jobs. I have scheduled a meeting on this subject Thursday, March 25, for all concerned. Jim Carpenter of Industrial Engineering will be there to present his views.

John Garrison

QUESTIONS

1. How would you go about analyzing whether there is a need for job enrichment here, based on our discussions in this chapter?
2. If you were Johnson, would you discuss the situation with your production manager and/or with Garrison before the meeting? If so, what would you plan to say? Would you explore the problem with your assemblers?
3. What would you plan to say at the March 25 meeting? Would you be willing to compromise with industrial engineering?
4. Suggest some practical approaches to this potentially serious conflict between the needs of the company and those of the assemblers.
5. Do you think you would recommend job enrichment here? Why, or why not?

11

Power and Control in Organizations

OVERVIEW

This chapter deals with the nature of the techniques managers use to impose compliance on employees—in other words how they use power, authority, and control to ensure that employees perform as expected. *Imposed control,* as we will see in this chapter is an effective enough technique when the jobs to be done are routine and predictable; however, we'll see in the following chapter that innovative and creative jobs require a different approach to control, *self-control.*

The outline of this chapter is as follows:

- **A** Imposed vs. self-control in organization theory
  - **1** Katz and Kahn's theory
  - **2** Imposed vs. self-control: other views
  - **3** Situational determinants of imposed control vs. self-control
- **B** Power and authority in organizations
  - **1** Power and authority defined
  - **2** The sources of power and authority
  - **3** Obedience to authority: why people comply
- **C** Control systems
  - **1** Process of control
  - **2** How employees evade controls
  - **3** The effectiveness of "legal compliance"
  - **4** Participation and control: the Tannenbaum studies

IMPOSED VS. SELF-CONTROL IN ORGANIZATION THEORY

We have already touched on the distinction between imposed control and self-control—for example, in Chapters 2 and 3. In this first section we address this subject more completely, beginning with a discussion of how theorists have distinguished between imposed and self-control.

• *Katz and Kahn's Theory*

According to Katz and Kahn, there are three main types of behaviors that organizations must elicit to survive—attracting employees, ensuring dependable behavior, and evoking innovative behavior—and different "motivational patterns" are required for producing these behaviors.[1] They say there are four such motivational patterns (see Table 11-1), and that these can be viewed as forming a continuum from imposed, legal compliance through self-control.

Type A is legal or imposed compliance. Here, employees comply with rules or directives because they consider them legitimate job demands, or because of a fear of sanctions. This, according to Katz and Kahn, is the basic pattern of motivation in classical organization theory. Motivation and the desire to comply bear no relation to the task itself; instead, any rule or directive from the proper authority must be obeyed because it is the law of the organization, and acceptance of these laws is part of the "contract" the employee enters into when joining the organization. Katz and Kahn say the problem with legal compliance "lies in its inability to motivate people for anything but routine compliance with role requirements." The classicists' solution to this problem was the use of rewards.

TABLE 11-1 Motivational Patterns for Producing Various Types of Required Behaviors

A Legal compliance. Securing acceptance of role prescriptions and organizational controls on the basis of the fact that they derive from *legitimate authority*. The rule-enforcement approach of simple machine theory.

B The use of rewards or instrumental satisfactions for inducing required behaviors. The approach of modified machine theory.

- **1** System rewards, earned through membership or seniority in system, such as fringe benefits, cost-of-living raises, or other benefits across the board.
- **2** Individual rewards, such as pay incentives and promotion, on the basis of individual merit
- **3** Instrumental identification with organizational leaders, in which followers are motivated to secure the approval of leaders
- **4** Affiliation with peers, to secure social approval from one's own group

C Internalized pattern of self-determination and self-expression. The satisfactions from accomplishment and the expressions of talents and abilities.

D Internalized values and the self-concept. The incorporation of organizational goals or subgoals as reflecting values or self-concept.

Source: Adapted from Daniel Katz and Robert L. Kahn, *The Social Psychology of Organizations* (New York: John Wiley, 1966), p. 341.

Katz and Kahn's second (type B) pattern involves the use of rewards for inducing required behavior. In other words, the employees' actions become instrumental in the achieving of specific desired rewards. Such rewards include pay, promotion, benefits, achievement, and approval from supervisors or from one's own group.

Katz and Kahn's third and fourth types differ conceptually from these first two. Both A and B rely on the use of external reminders, like rules and rewards, and on the imposition of legitimate authority. Types C and D, on the other hand, are aimed at encouraging self-control, and in both these types, employees derive satisfaction directly from the job itself. Here, "motivation is so internalized that performance is autonomous. The supervisor does not have to be present to wave a stick or offer candy. The activities carry their own rewards. . . ."[2] Type C entails *job identification.* Here, the job is sufficiently challenging and interesting that it provides an opportunity for self-expression and achievement for the employee. He or she thus derives satisfaction directly from performing the task, just as a scientist does from scientific inquiry and a composer from creating a symphony. Employees comply—carry out the job assigned—not because rules or supervision is imposed on them, but because they identify with the job and receive satisfaction from accomplishing it.

Katz and Kahn's final type, D, is based on employees' internalization of the organization's goals, and as we've seen, this is a crucial factor in adhocracy-type organizations. Here, the employee adopts the organization's goals as his or her own. People comply or are motivated because by doing so and contributing to the organization's goals, they are also contributing to their own. The wave of nationalism that compelled young men to join the army during World War II is one example of this. Some firms' "profit-sharing" plans are another. The willingness of young engineers at Apple Computer to work 18-hour days developing their firm's new products is yet another.

According to Katz and Kahn, each of these four patterns is appropriate for tapping a different type of behavior. For example, legal compliance (type A) is usually not effective for attracting people into a system or holding them there, except in such instances as military service. However, it can bring about acceptable levels of individual performance in both quantity and quality, and the more routine the activity, the more likely this is to be true.

Classical theorists recognized this and added rewards (type B) to ensure compliance above minimum standards. But although organizationwide and individual rewards can be useful for attracting people to the organization and ensuring dependable behavior, they are not as useful for invoking the strong motivation necessary for calling forth innovative and spontaneous behavior.

For evoking innovative behavior, managers have to depend more on the employee's self-control. Katz and Kahn say that type C (job identification) is an excellent device for ensuring dependable and innovative behavior, since it affords intrinsic job satisfaction. Type D (the internalization of organizational goals) is also useful for ensuring both dependable and innovative behavior, since here, various techniques are used to synchronize organizational and individual goals. In both cases, employees perform their jobs because they *want* to. Types C and D (and to a lesser extent, type B) are thus essential in the adhocracy.

• *Imposed vs. Self-Control: Other Views*

Other theorists have also distinguished between imposed and self-control. For example, McGregor's Theory X, which we discussed in Chapter 3, seems to emphasize control of people by rewards and punishments. His Theory Y "emphasizes the ability of people to exercise self-control and their desire to perform effectively."[3] Similarly, Blau distinguishes between "behavior control" and "output control" and says that evaluating a person on the basis of his output makes him want to discipline himself, rendering close, imposed supervision of the person's day-to-day behavior superfluous.[4]

Another writer says that in controlling the work of people, only two phenomena can be observed—monitored and controlled behavior, and the outputs that result from behavior.[5] He says that in order to apply behavior control, the organization must possess at least agreement, if not true knowledge, about means and relationships. In other words, one must understand how the behavior is related to the actual output—the product or service—that the organization is ultimately interested in. Whether control is based on monitoring behavior or output, he says, thus depends upon the accuracy with which each can be measured, and the technological or task characteristics of the work will play an important role in this determination. For example:

> Except at the extremes, the dean of the school of business cannot control his faculty research by observing the behavior of faculty members. At best, he can control the quantity of output, but certainly not the quality through these means. On the other hand, the manager of a tin can plant can observe the behavior of his employees, and, if they behave as he knows they should, he can be certain that the expected tin cans are being produced. . . . The business school dean, wanting the research produced by his faculty to be well regarded by their peer group, can simply survey that peer group for their evaluations.[6]

• *Situational Determinants of Imposed vs. Self-Control*

Is imposed, "behavior" control more appropriate where tasks are routine? Is self-control (where just output is monitored) more appropriate where tasks are unpredictable?

There has not been a great deal of research on these questions. In their study, Lawrence and Lorsch found that in the more uncertain plastic firms, even low-level managers made many important decisions. In the more predictable container firms, decision making was centralized, and so lower-level managers' behavior was more circumscribed than that of those in the plastics firms.[7] However, perhaps a better illustration of when imposed (versus self-) control is appropriate is contained in a study by Bell.

The Bell Studies Bell carried out a study to test the following hypothesis:[8]

> The more unpredictable the work demands of a subordinate's job, the more distant the supervision will be . . . the more predictable the work demands, the closer the supervision.

To test this hypothesis, Bell developed questions for measuring task predictability and closeness of supervision. Predictability was measured by asking respondents two questions:

1. If you listed the exact activities you would be confronted with on an average workday, what percentage of these activities do you think would be interrupted by unexpected events?
2. Everyone is confronted with certain routine and repetitive activities. What percentage of the activities or work demands connected with your job would you consider to be of a routine nature?

Closeness of supervision was measured by asking the respondents the following two questions:

1. How often does your supervisor keep a close check on what you are doing and closely observe your work?
2. To what extent does your immediate supervisor influence what you do in a particular workweek?

The findings supported Bell's hypothesis. In those jobs in which the work tasks were very predictable, the supervisors exerted relatively close control over the subordinates. Jobs containing unpredictable activities evidenced a lack of close supervision. Bell also found that worker discretion (the extent to which the worker exercised self-control), as measured by questions such as, "To what extent do you control your job and the general pace of your work?" was related to the predictability of work demands. The more unpredictable the work demands confronting the employee, the greater the likelihood that he or she will exert a high degree of discretion. Bell also found that the more professional training an employee has, the more self-control he or she exerts in carrying out duties. Taken as a whole, Bell's findings suggest that imposed control—perhaps in the form of budgets and formalization—would be most appropriate in mechanistic organizations. In adhocracies, as expected, employees require more autonomy, so that techniques for eliciting self-control become more important.

POWER AND AUTHORITY IN ORGANIZATIONS

Techniques for imposing control include *power and authority* (discussed in this section) and *control systems (discussed next). Self control* is addressed in the following chapter.

• Power and Authority Defined

Authority may be thought of as the "fuel" of organization, since without a distribution of authority, the organization structure is merely a shell. Authority is the right each position holder has to influence or command thought, opinion, or behavior. It gives managers the right to carry out their tasks by giving orders to their subordinates, and it gives them the right to expect compliance. It lies at the core of what Katz and Kahn call legal compliance.

The words *authority, power,* and *influence* are interrelated. Influence is usually defined as the act of producing an effect—of somehow getting someone or something to take some action. Power, on the other hand, is usually viewed as the possession of the potential for influencing others, or the ability to act or produce some effect. To Weber, "Power is the probability that one actor within a social relationship will be in a position to carry out his own will despite resistance, regardless of the basis on which this probability rests."[9]

Similarly, Etzioni defines power as "an actor's ability to induce or influence another actor to carry out his directives or any other norms he supports."[10] He distinguishes among three types of power, which he calls coercive, remunerative, and normative. Coercive power involves the application (or threat of application) of physical sanctions. Remunerative power is control over incentives and rewards. Normative power derives from the person's esteem or prestige. Thiebault and Kelley say that all types of power derive from one person's dependence on another: "The power of A over B is equal to, and based upon, the dependence of B on A."[11] A person's power can (but need not) stem from "illegitimate" sources, sources that violate prevailing norms of acceptability. For example, a thief might have power over a victim because of the gun he holds.

Authority, like power, refers to a person's potential for influencing others, but the word *authority* "has implict in it the notion of legitimacy or ethical sanctification."[12] In line with this, Weber says there are three legitimate bases of authority: charismatic, traditional, and legal.[13] Charismatic authority derives from some "extraordinary" quality of the person that makes others wish to do his bidding. Traditional authority is based on "piety for what actually, allegedly, or personally has always existed"; the authority of a monarch would be one example. With legal authority, submission does not rest upon devotion to charismatic persons, or upon some sacred tradition:

> Rather, submission under legal authority is based upon an *impersonal* bond to the generally defined and functional "duty of office." The official duty—like the corresponding right to exercise authority . . . is fixed by *rationally established* norms, by enactments, decrees, and regulations, in such a manner that the legitimacy of the authority becomes the legality of the general rule, which is purposely thought out, enacted, and announced with formal correctness.[14]

In modern organizations, what Weber calls "legal authority" is probably most widely used for exacting obedience. Each person in the organizational hierarchy is delegated authority to make certain decisions and take certain actions. *Subordinates who are hired and who elect to remain with the organization generally do so with the understanding that they accept this authority as legal;* as Simon points out, "The most striking characteristic of the 'suborindate' role is that it establishes an area of acceptance in behavior within which the subordinate is willing to accept the decisions made for him by his superior."[15] Simon views authority not from the point of view of the authority holder, but from the point of view of the subordinate. He says:

> An individual accepts authority when he sets himself a general rule that permits the communicated decision of another to guide his own choice (i.e. to serve as a premise of that choice) independently of his judgment of the correctness or acceptability of the premise.[16]

In other words, according to Simon, for authority (as he defines it) to be exercised, each subordinate must obey almost mechanically, without particularly examining the merits of the order and carrying it out on its merits. To the extent that a subordinate *does* examine the merits of each order and carry it out on its merits, types of influence other than authority (such as persuasion) must have been used. According to Simon, therefore, authority, strictly speaking, is exercised only when an order is carried out and the subordinate does not examine its merits (or hardly does so), or when he carries it out even though he thinks it is wrong.

• *The Sources of Power and Authority*

In investigating the sources of power and authority, we will see that two basic factors—dependence, and the acceptance of legal authority that is a natural consequence of the subordinate's role—together help explain the sources of power and authority in organizations.

The Bases of Social Power French and Raven distinguish among five bases of power that to them "seem especially common and important."[17] They call these reward power, coercive power, legitimate power, referent power, and expert power.

Reward power is defined as power whose basis is the ability to reward. According to French and Raven, the strength of the reward power one person holds over another increases with the magnitude of the rewards the latter perceives the former can mediate for him. A person has power over another to the extent that he or she can significantly influence the positive rewards (such as money) accruing to the other person and can significantly reduce the "negative" rewards (such as poor working conditions) the other person might otherwise have to endure.

Coercive power is similar to reward power in that it also involves one person's ability to manipulate the attainment by another of positive (or negative) rewards. The coercive power of one person over another stems from the real or imagined expectation on the part of the latter that he will be punished if he fails to conform to the influence attempt. In organizations, coercive power is a familiar ingredient in group pressure. Groups are famous, for example, for keeping "rate busters" in line by coercing them with fears of ostracism or physical violence.

French and Raven's *legitimate power* is similar to Weber's "legitimate authority" (which, remember, may be based on charisma, tradition, or legality) and is characterized by the feeling of "oughtness" on the part of a person. Legitimate power is defined as stemming from internalized values in a person that dictate that another has a legitimate right to influence him and that he has an obligation to accept this influence. The actual source of this legitimate power, and the reason subordinates feel they ought to obey, might be tradition (as in the case of a monarch) or may derive from the office the superior holds. For example, on agreeing to join an organization its salespeople accept the right of the sales manager to assign them work, since this is a legitimate right of the office of "sales manager" in the organization structure. Similarly, "a judge has a right to levy fines, a foreman should assign work, a priest is justified in prescribing religious beliefs, and it is the management's prerogative to make certain decisions."[18]

The *referent power* one person has over another is similar to Weber's "charismatic authority" (which is based on the "extraordinary" characteristics of the person in power) but goes a step further: Referent power is based on the fact that one person identifies with and is highly attracted to another. A verbalization of such power might be, "I want to be like that person, and therefore I shall behave or believe as he does."

Finally, *expert power* derives from the fact that one person is viewed as an expert in some area and others must therefore depend on him for advice and counsel. Expert power in an organization often stems from a person's position in the communications network and from that person's ability to control access to coveted information. Thus, even an organization's president may find herself deferring to one of her firm's research scientists in those cases where the scientist has the knowledge and expertise to solve some critical problem with one of the firm's products.

Sources of Power of Lower Participants in Organizations David Mechanic points out that it is not unusual for lower participants "to assume and wield considerable power and influence not associated with their formally defined positions." He says that the source of this power is other people's dependence on these "lower participants."[19] In essence, he says, these low-ranking employees have a considerable personal power but no delegated authority, and this power stems not so much from their personal traits as from particular aspects of their location within their organizations.

Mechanic says that power stems from dependence, and that when a person is dependent on another, he or she is potentially subject to the other person's power. Within organizations, he says, one makes others dependent by controlling access to *information, persons,* or *instrumentalities.* Thus, a scientist might have power because others depend on the information she has about an important production process. The president's secretary might have power because she controls access to an important person—the president. An air-base commander may find himself partly at the mercy of the maintenance clerk whose years of experience have given him access to and control over sources of airplane parts.

Several factors contribute to such dependence, and therefore to the power of lower participants. One is their expertise—the knowledge they have for which others must depend on them. Another is the person's effort and interest—his or her willingness to take on a task that others are unwilling to do. Another attribute is attractiveness, charisma, or "personality." The person's location in the organization is also important, as exemplified by the president's secretary. Other "participants" have power that derives from coalitions they have formed—for example, with suppliers, allowing them to control access to critical supplies.

Conclusion We will assume that there are two basic sources of power and authority in organizations. One stems from dependence. This can result from the power holder's access to people, information, or instrumentalities, or, to use French and Raven's terms, from his ability to reward, coerce, or act as referent or expert to another.

The second source of power and authority might be termed *legality.* It derives from the feeling of a person that another person has a legitimate right to command obedience. Traditional authority (like that of a monarch) is one example of this. In organizations, one familiar example is the acceptance by a subordinate of the authority of a superior, an authority legally sanctioned by the organization and accepted by the subordinate as one of the conditions of continued employment. This is the "legitimate" base of French and Raven's analysis of social power, and it manifests itself in (in Simon's words, quoted earlier) "an area of acceptance and behavior within which the subordinate is willing to accept the decisions made for him by his superior."

• *Obedience to Authority: Why People Comply*

Predictability is an essential ingredient of organizations. For an organization to be able to function with any degree of effectiveness, each position holder must be able to assume that the people he or she directs will comply with orders and carry out their tasks. The president who directs the vice-presidents to increase efficiency, the shipping manager who directs the truckers to make certain deliveries, and the production foreman who directs an employee to tighten a bolt all issue orders on the assumption that these orders will be carried out. To the extent that orders are carried out, tasks can be accomplished in such a way that they contribute in an integrated way to the organization's goals. To the extent that orders are not obeyed, there is no way to ensure that the logic of the organization's departmentation and coordination will function effectively. Having discussed sources of power and authority in organizations, we should now therefore turn to a more detailed discussion of obedience to authority: *why people obey.*

Simon and the Zone of Acceptance Prof. Herbert Simon has developed one of the most complete explanations of authority and obedience in organizations. He says there are two basic ways in which behavior of employees can be influenced: One is to establish *in the employees* the attitudes and habits that will lead them to the "right" decision; the second is to *impose* the necessary decisions on them.[20]

The first approach (getting the person to want to do the task) is accomplished by developing loyalty, commitment, and self-control in the employee—for example, through training and indoctrination. The second approach (imposing the decision on the person) relies, according to Simon, on the exercise of authority. *Authority* to Simon means "the power to make decisions which govern the actions of another," and, in accepting authority, a subordinate suspends his or her own judgment. Technically, as we saw earlier, authority as defined by Simon is exercised only when one person carries out the orders of another without particularly evaluating the merits of the orders; that is, when subordinates suspend their judgment and simply and mechanically "follow orders." When they do this, authority has been exercised; but when they must be persuaded (or must persuade themselves) to carry out the orders, some other mode of influence, like indoctrination must be used.

A critical question, then, is, When and under what conditions will a person suspend his own judgment and acquiesce to authority? According to Simon, a person will suspend judgment and mechanically follow orders as long as those orders fall within the person's "zone of acceptance." If the superior attempts to carry authority beyond a certain point (beyond the persron's "zone of acceptance"), disobedience will follow, and the person will no longer mechanically do what is "right" from the point of view of the organization:

> Once the system of values which is to govern in an organization has been specified, there is one and only one "best" decision. Yet there is an area of acceptance within which the individual will behave "organizationally." When the organizational demands fall outside this area, personal motives reassert themselves and the organization, to that extent, ceases to exist. When a person is behaving impersonally, then, an organizational scale is substituted for his personal value scale as the criterion of "correctness" in his decisions.[21]

Why do people permit themselves to be influenced by the organization? Why, that is, does a person join an organization and then submit to its authority by following those orders that fall within his or her zone of acceptance? According to Simon, the answer lies in the fact that "individuals will do what is required when their behavior contributes indirectly or directly to their own personal goals." Thus, they will join and remain useful members of an organization (they will have a zone of acceptance within which orders will be carried out) as long as, from their point of view, the inducements (like money) provided by the organization equal or exceed the contributions (like the effort) that must be provided in return.

The "width" of the zone of acceptance will vary from person to person and organization to organization. In a voluntary organization, for example, each person's zone of acceptance might be quite narrow, since the organization controls few important rewards or sanctions. But on a military parade ground, the zone of acceptance of each marcher might be quite wide, and each might be willing to unthinkingly carry out orders that cover his behavior down to the smallest detail.

Simon cites several things that affect the width of a person's zone of acceptance. First is the factor of legality: In joining and remaining with an organization, a person agrees to a greater or lesser extent to "follow orders" and to exhibit "an area of acceptance in behavior within which he will follow orders." Beyond this, the width of a person's zone of acceptance is also affected by the quality and quantity of inducements the organization can provide, as well as by the employee's personality. Size of financial rewards, fear of losing a job, and a "follower" mentality are some other factors.

Let us summarize our discussion of Simon's theory of authority. He says the organization can influence employees either by establishing in them the attitudes and desire to do the job, or by imposing on them its decisions. The former involves the use of *influence* modes like persuasion, suggestion, and building of loyalty to the organization—for example, through careful training and selection. The latter involves exercising authority, and in this case, the employee "holds in abeyance his own critical faculties," doing so as long as the order falls within his "zone of acceptance." The former involves tapping the employee's self-control; the latter can be viewed as imposed control.

Simon points out that these forms of influence are interchangeable. For example, as employees become familiar with their jobs through training, they are usually given more discretion and are not as closely supervised. Furthermore:

> Administrators have increasingly recognized in recent years that authority unless buttressed by other forms of influence is relatively impotent to control the decision in any but a negative way. The elements entering into all but the most routine decisions are so numerous and so complex that it is impossible to control positively more than a few. Unless the subordinate is himself able to supply most of the premises of decision, and to synthesize them adequately, the task of supervision becomes hopelessly burdensome.[22]

Thus, says Simon, reliance on the exercise of authority (in which employees mechanically obey those orders that fall within their zone of acceptance) is of limited usefulness unless it is buttressed by the self-control of the employee. In modern organizations, the tasks are often so complex and the contingencies so widespread that it is simply not feasible to rely entirely on an employee's mechanical compliance or a perpetually present supervisor. Instead, the subordinates themselves have to "supply most of the premises of decision" by exhibiting initiative in evaluating different courses of action and choosing the best one. This is why, according to Simon, effectively staffing the organization is so important, since hiring people who can exercise such self-control can greatly reduce the need to rely on their mechanical compliance with imposed authority.

A Study of Obedience Yet it is obvious that an employee's willingness to "follow orders" and to substitute, in Simon's words, an "organizational scale for his personal value scale as the criteria of 'correctness' in his decisions" is still a major factor in compliance.[23] To what extent do subordinates obey authority—"substitute an organizational scale for their own value scale"—because they view that authority as legitimate, and obeying as part of their job? Stanley Milgram carried out a study that shed some startling light on this question.[24]

Milgram's experiments, originally conducted at Yale in 1962–63, set out to answer the following question: In a laboratory situation, if an experimenter tells a subject to act with increasing severity against another person, under what conditions will the subject comply, and under what conditions will he disobey? The design of his study was as follows:

> Two people come to a psychology laboratory to take part in a study of memory and learning. One of them is designated as a "teacher" and the other a "learner." The experimenter explains that the study is concerned with the effects of punishment on learning. The learner is conducted into a room, seated in a chair, his arms strapped to prevent excessive movement, and an electrode attached to his wrist. He is told that he is to learn a list of words; whenever he makes an error, he will receive electric shocks of increasing intensity. (The "learner" is actually one of the researchers, and no electrical shocks are actually given.)
>
> The real focus of the experiment is the teacher. After watching the "learner" being strapped into place, he is taken into the main experimental room and seated before an impressive shock generator. Its main feature is a horizontal line of 30 switches, ranging from 15 volts to 450 volts, in 15-volt increments. There are also verbal designations which range from "slight shock" to "danger—severe shock." The teacher is told that he is to administer the learning test to the man in the other room. When the learner responds correctly, the teacher moves on to the next item; when the other man gives an incorrect answer, the teacher is to give him an electric shock. He is to start at the lowest level (15 volts) and to increase the level each time the man makes an error, going to 30 volts, 45 volts, and so on.
>
> The "teacher" is a genuinely naive subject who has come to the laboratory to participate in the experiment. The learner, or victim, actually receives no shock at all. The point of the experiment is to see how far a person will proceed in a concrete

and measurable situation in which he is ordered to inflict increasing pain on a protesting victim. At what point will the subject refuse to obey the experimenters?

Conflict arises when the man receiving the shock begins to indicate that he is experiencing discomfort. At 75 volts, the "learner" grunts. At 120 volts he complains verbally; at 150 he demands to be released from the experiment. His protests continue as the shocks escalate, growing increasingly vehement and emotional. At 285 volts his response can only be described as an agonized scream.

Observers of the experiment agree that its gripping quality is somewhat obscured in print; for the subject (the "teacher") the situation is not a game, and conflict is intense and obvious. On the one hand, the manifest suffering of the learner presses him to quit. On the other, the experimenter, a legitimate authority to whom the subject feels some commitment, enjoins him to continue. Each time the subject hesitates to administer shock, the experimenter orders him to continue. To extricate himself from the situation, the subject must make a clear break with authority. The aim of this investigation was to find when and how people would defy authority in the face of a clear moral imperative.

There are, of course, enormous differences between carrying out the orders of a commanding officer during times of war and carrying out the orders of an experimenter. Yet the essence of certain relationships remains, for one may ask in a general way: How does a man behave when he is told by a legitimate authority to act against a third individual? If anything, we may expect the experimenter's power to be considerably less than that of the general, since he has no power to enforce his imperatives, and participation in a psychological experiment scarcely evokes the sense of urgency and dedication engendered by participation in war.[25]

Findings, Interpretations, Implications According to Milgram, the results of his study "are both surprising and dismaying." Although many of his subject "teachers" experienced stress and protested to the experimenter, a substantial portion of them—almost two-thirds—fell into the category of obedient subjects, continuing to the last shock on the generator. These subjects, remember, were not some "sadistic fringe of society," but "ordinary people drawn from working, managerial, and professional classes." Milgram found that "the ordinary person who shocked the victim did so out of a sense of obligation—a conception of his duties as a subject—and not from any peculiarly aggressive tendencies."

What keeps the subject obeying the experimenter?

> First, there is a set of "binding factors" that lock the subject into the situation. They include such factors as politeness on his part, his desire to uphold his initial promise of aid to the experimenter, and the awkwardness of withdrawal. Second, a number of adjustments in the subject's thinking occur that undermine his resolve to break with the authority. The adjustments helped the subject maintain his relationship with the experimenter, while at the same time reducing the strain brought about by the experimental conflict. They are typical of thinking that comes about in obedient persons when they are instructed by authority to act against helpless individuals.[26]

Milgram's findings paint a vivid picture of the adjustments through which obedience to legitimate authority takes place. The subjects, he found, became so absorbed in the "narrow technical aspects" of the task that they lost sight of its broader consequences. (One is reminded of the Watergate affair, which was to follow these studies by ten years.)[27] Furthermore, the obedient subject begins to see himself as not responsible for his own actions, as he "divests himself of responsibility by attributing all initiative to the experimenter, a legitimate authority." Obedient subjects saw themselves not as people acting in a morally accountable way, but as the agents of external authority: When asked after the experiment why they had gone on, the typical reply was, "I wouldn't have done it by myself. I was just doing what I was told." And, Milgram believes, this was not just a "thin alibi concocted for the occasion":

> Rather, it is a fundamental mode of thinking for a great many people once they are locked into a subordinate position in a structure of authority. The disappearance of a sense of responsibility is the far-reaching consequence of submission to authority.[28]

It further appeared that people working under authority did not lose their "moral sense," but instead shifted it to a consideration of how well they were living up to the expectations that *the authority* had for them. Most subjects also saw their behavior in a larger context—the pursuit of scientific truth. Some devalued the victim as a consequence of acting against him, making comments like, "He was so stupid and stubborn he deserved to get shocked."

What Milgram found, therefore, was that people were much more willing than one might have imagined to "just follow orders" and to substitute, in Simon's terms, an organizational scale for their personal value scale. Even in this laboratory setting, where the available rewards and sanctions were few, each subject's zone of acceptance—the zone in which orders were mechanically complied with because they emanated from a legitimate authority—was quite wide. People obeyed simply because they had elected to join the organization (the experiment) and viewed following legitimate orders as part of their jobs. And this phenomenon of obedience, says Milgram, may be largely a result of the process of division of work:

> There was a time, perhaps, when men were able to give a fully human response to any situation because they were fully absorbed in it as human beings. But as soon as there was a division of labor among men, things changed. Beyond a certain point, the breaking up of society into people carrying out narrow and very special jobs takes away from the human quality of work and life. A person does not get to see the whole situation but only a small part of it, and is thus unable to act without some kind of overall direction. He yields to authority but in doing so is alienated from his own actions.[29]

Conclusion There are many ways an organization can influence its members' behavior. It can build organizational loyalty through various indoctrination techniques and use training, selection, persuasion, and incentives to encourage initiative and self-control. An organization can also impose its authority on its members, by manipulating the dependence of the members on the organization, or by relying on the members' obedience to legitimate authority. In practice, these modes of influence are interchangeable, in that authority, for example, is not relied on to the exclusion of persuasion. Yet it appears that the range of orders with which employees will mechanically comply may be wider than originally thought, and that this wide "zone of acceptance" is the most striking characteristic of the "subordinate" role in organizations.

CONTROL SYSTEMS

• Process of Control

Every organization has to ensure that its workers are performing as expected, and *control* is the task of ensuring that activities are providing the desired results. All control systems collect, store, and transmit information on profits, sales, or some other factor. And all control systems are aimed at influencing behavior, which is one reason why "controlling someone" often has negative overtones. Control also requires that targets, standards, or goals be set, and this is why the word *planning* is always used with the word *control*.

Control systems are similar to rules (and close supervision), in that they are imposed on employees for the purpose of ensuring compliance. However, whereas rules can be thought of as simply standards of acceptable behavior, control systems include not only standards but also means (such as budget reports) for *monitoring* compliance with those standards as well as means for taking *corrective action*.

The Control Process Control is the task of ensuring that activities are providing the desired results. Control involves setting a target, measuring performance, and taking corrective action.

Whether the "controller" is the supervisor on an assembly line or the mayor of New York, the control process remains essentially the same and involves three steps:

1. Establish a standard, goal, or target.
2. Measure actual performance against this standard.
3. Identify deviations and take corrective action.

Establish Standards Control begins by setting standards; these standards are typically expressed in terms of money, time, quantity, or quality (or some combination of these). Often these standards are expressed in *monetary* terms. Thus, a salesperson might be told that his or her quota is to sell $8,000 worth of products per month; or a production supervisor may be told to cut costs by $2,000 per week. Standards of performance are also expressed in terms of *time*—such as having to meet a certain sales quota in a week, or complete a report by May 1.

Other standards are *quantitative*. Thus, production supervisors are usually responsible for producing a specified number of units of product per week. The number of labor hours used per unit of time is another example of a quantity standard. Still other standards are expressed in terms of quality. These are often expressed in terms of reject rates in quality control, in grades of products sold (such as "grade A"), or in terms of the quality of a requested report or forecast. For each area (quantity, quality, or whatever), the usual procedure is to *choose a yardstick* and then set a standard, as is illustrated in Table 11-2.

Choosing yardsticks (like "cars sold") is a crucial step in the standards-setting process, and there are a multitude of yardsticks from which to choose. In terms of quantity, for instance, yardsticks include units produced per shift and grievances submitted per quarter. For quality, yardsticks might include rejection ratio and programming errors. In terms of timeliness, yardsticks include percentage of on-time departures and processing time. In terms of cost, possible yardsticks might include processing costs and percentage of deviation from budget. These yardsticks and some others are presented in Table 11-2.

Once a decision is made as to which yardsticks are to be used to measure performance, they can be converted into specific, measurable standards or goals. Thus, "units produced per shift" might be converted into this goal for the supervisor: "Produce ten units per shift." Similarly, "programming errors" can be converted to the goal for the computer programmer: "Make no more than five programming errors."

Measure Actual Performance Against Standards The second control step is measuring actual performance against the standards and determining whether or not there are any deviations.

In organizations, monitoring performance is accomplished through both personal and impersonal means.[30] The simplest and most commonly used way of measuring actual performance against the standard is by personal observation. For example, a new employee might get on-the-job training, with his or her performance personally observed by a supervisor. Sales managers typically make sales calls with their salespeople once or twice a year in order to observe their performance. Or a production supervisor may personally observe each of his or her subordinates' performance on an assembly line.

Although there is no substitute for the personal, on-line information provided by this sort of personal supervision, monitoring performance in this way is subject to two limitations. First, supervision that is perceived by employees as "too close" can

TABLE 11-2 Examples of Control Standards

Area	*Yardstick*	*Standard/Goal*
Quantity	Number of products produced	Produce 14 units per month.
Quality	Number of rejects	No more than 10 rejects per day.
Timeliness	Percent sales reports in on time	Return 90% of sales reports on time.
Dollars	Percent deviation from budget	Do not exceed budgeted expenses by more than 5% during year.

result in aggressive, hostile reactions on the part of the employees,[31] and at the other extreme, the laissez-faire leader—one who does not monitor performance at all—necessarily has to rely entirely on the employees' good intentions for maintaining control. Therefore, finding the golden mean that represents just the right amount of personal supervision is one ever-present problem with this approach.

A second difficulty with relying on personal observation is that it becomes more difficult as the manager assumes more responsibilities. Other things being equal, where there are only three or four subordinates to be supervised, personal observation may suffice; but where the workers' jobs are complex or where their number is too high, it becomes difficult or impossible to directly observe each subordinate's performance.

When the job gets too big for one person to handle, two things usually occur. First, as we explained earlier, a division of work takes place. For example, a hospital director might hire two assistant directors to observe employees on different floors; or a production supervisor might hire two assistants to manage the plant's two assembly lines. But even with this extra help, the manager still needs some way of controlling performance, since having two assistants does not guarantee that the workers will perform satisfactorily. It is at this point that formal, impersonal, written control reports become more important. Budget control reports, quality control reports, and inventory control reports are three examples of impersonal techniques used for monitoring performance and identifying deviations. A fourth is the computerized management information system.

Identify Deviations from Standards and Take Corrective Action Once the manager has compared actual with planned performance, the next step is to identify important deviations and take corrective action. This in turn requires applying many of the concepts and techniques discussed in previous chapters. In terms of decision making, for instance, it is important to clearly identify the central problem. Inadequate performance is usually just a symptom, and so the manager has to find out why performance is not up to par. For example, ask, "Are the plans themselves in need of revision?"; "Is training and development called for?"; "Is the deviation due to poor staffing?"; and so forth. Finally, taking remedial action will require applying many of the concepts we have discussed—on how to communicate with and motivate subordinates, for instance, as well as the *organizational change and development* techniques explained in Chapter 16.

• *How Employees Evade Controls*

Managers and employees have found many ingenious ways through which to evade controls. In one study, departmental efficiency ratings were raised by transferring personnel "on paper" from departments with low efficiencies to those with high ratings. Efficiency ratings then appeared much more consistent from department to department than they actually were. The opposite type of falsification also occurs: Managers have knowingly falsified production records in order not to exceed the quota by too great an amount.[32] The list of ways in which employees try to "get around" controls could be expanded. Edward Lawler and John Rhode say, however, that there are three basic ways in which employees resist and evade control systems; they call these "rigid bureaucratic behavior," "strategic behavior," and "invalid data reporting."[33]

Rigid Bureaucratic Behavior This refers to the tendency of people to try to look good in terms of the control standards. They concentrate their efforts where results are measured, often disregarding the organization's more important goals. The problem stems mostly from incomplete standards. For example, in one state employment agency, employees found that they were measured on the number of job seekers they *interviewed* rather than on the number they placed in jobs. The number of interviews soared, but little attention was focused on adequately counseling applicants. When it became apparent what was happening, several new standards (such as the ratio of placements to interviews) were devised. These were aimed at providing a more complete—and acceptable—set of standards for the counselors.[34]

Strategic Behavior "Strategic behavior" refers to the tendency of people to provide information in such a way that they look good for a certain period. As an example, many government agencies assign budgets to departments with the stipulation that any funds not spent by the end of the year be returned. What often happens is that at the end of the year, employees rush to spend all their available funds—often for unnecessary "frills." They look good (they've spent their yearly allocation), but their expenditures are often frivolous. However, you do not have to be in a government agency to incur this problem. It can happen whenever a project you assign must be completed within a certain time.

Invalid Data Reporting Perhaps the easiest way to evade control systems is simply to report back erroneous, invalid data. In one company, for example, salesmen's activity was "controlled" by requiring them to send in reports listing clients contacted. Management never screened these lists, however, and the salesmen evaded control by listing clients that actually hadn't been seen yet.

• *The Effectiveness of "Legal Compliance"*

Legal compliance is at one extreme of Katz and Kahn's continuum and represents a situation in which organization members obey orders, rules, or control standards because they are perceived as stemming from legitimate sources of authority and because they are enforced by legal sanctions.[35] As you may recall, Katz and Kahn suggest that legal compliance can be used to reduce absenteeism and to bring about acceptable levels of individual performance, particularly where the activity is routine.

Two researchers carried out a study to test this hyothesis.[36] They say that a crucial factor in the success of a strategy to control attendance through legal compliance is recognition and acceptance of the legitimacy of the policy and the policy-making process by the organizational members, and that once the worker knows and accepts the rules of the system, then attendance should be fairly predictable. However, as we have seen, such controls often have unanticipated consequences. The question, therefore, is this: What is the effect of an undeniably legal control system on absenteeism and on performance and satisfaction?

Subjects in this study were 297 undergraduates who had enrolled in an intermediate accounting course at Purdue University. Each student was provided a course syllabus indicating that class attendance was expected, but the specific aspects of the attendance policy were left deliberately vague. In the "compulsory attendance" condition, the instructors announced to one of their two classes that the university regulations stated that attendance was compulsory and that the instructor was required to enforce the policy; consequently, attendance would be taken and included in the computation of the final grade for the course. In the second, "noncompulsory attendance" condition, each instructor acknowledged to his other class the existence of an attendance policy established by the university. These students, however, were informed that the university delegated considerable latitude to instructors to design and enforce an operational attendance policy, that it was the instructor's policy to treat attendance as a voluntary matter, and that it would not be a factor in the determination of the final grade in the course.[37]

The researchers found that absenteeism was substantially reduced by utilizing the compulsory, "legal compliance" control strategy. Furthermore, this strategy not only lowered absenteeism but also increased performance of the accounting students, and it did not result in reduced satisfaction with the instructor or the course. The researchers conclude:

> Since a legalistic control strategy is relatively easy to administer and offers lower initial cost to managers, it may be the most effective control strategy in many organizational settings. It is an empirical question whether similar (or superior) results can be accomplished with the other motivational patterns suggested by Katz and Kahn.[38]

• *Participation and Control: The Tannenbaum Studies*

Arnold Tannenbaum and his associates have carried out many studies aimed at measuring control in organizations and the interplay of employee participation and organizational control.

Tannenbaum defines control as "any process in which a group of persons or organization of persons determines, that is, intentionally affects, the behavior of another person, group, or organization."[39] To Tannenbaum, in other words, control is synonymous with *influence* and may be considered in terms of either the *total amount of control* in the organization or the *distribution of control* among members at various hierarchical levels. In organizations characterized by a high amount of *to-*

tal control, says Tannenbaum, members engage in more frequent attempts to influence behavior than do members of "low-control" organizations. In organizations where there is relatively equal *distribution of control,* members at all levels have about the same influence on others, whereas in organizations with an unequal distribution, members of certain organizational levels (usually, the top) exert more influence. Tannenbaum's control concept is tied to that of employee participation, since participative organizations would normally be expected to be characterized by a relatively equal distribution of control among levels, whereas autocratic organizations would be characterized by very high levels of control at the top of the hierarchy and very low control at the lower levels.

Studies carried out in several countries lend support to Tannenbaum's contention that participative organizations are characterized by a more egalitarian distribution of control and, in fact, a greater total amount of control than are less-participative organizations, and this is illustrated by a recent study in Germany.[40]

Figure 11-1 presents the results of this study in graphic form, using a device developed by Tannenbaum that he calls the *control graph.* The control graph shows the amount of control exercised at each hierarchical level in the organization—in this case, the top or plant-management level, the middle, "all other managers" level,

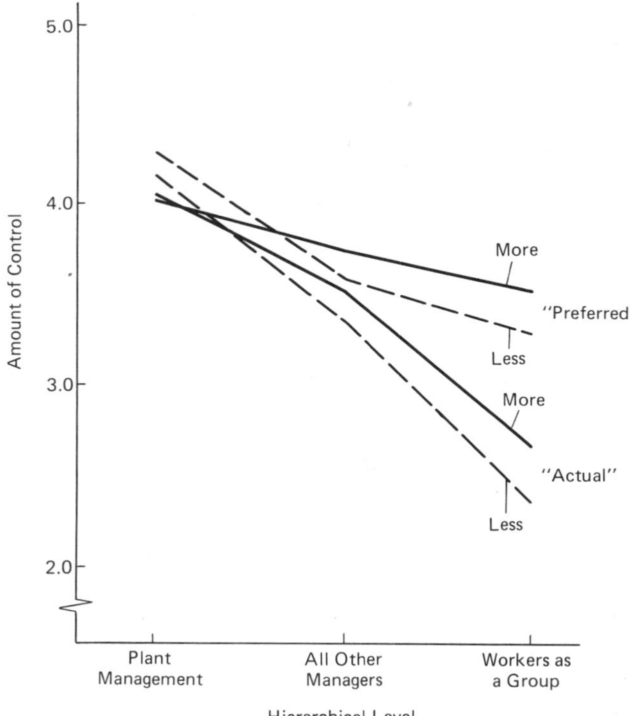

Note: Distribution of "actual" and "preferred" control as reported by organization members in *more* and *less* participative plants.

FIGURE 11-1 Distribution of Actual and Preferred Control. *Source:* Klaus Bartolke et al.,[1] Worker Participation and The Distribution of Control as Perceived by Members of Ten German Companies," *Administrative Science Quarterly,* Vol. 27, No. 3 (September 1982), 380–97.

and the bottom, "workers as a group" level. This particular control graph shows the "actual" and "preferred" level of control reported by employees at each level and demonstrates that the total control is higher and the distribution control more egalitarian in the more-participative companies than in the less-participative ones. Here, in other words, the participative systems seem to enhance the control of workers at the bottom without decreasing the control exercised by managers and supervisors.

According to these researchers, the data of their study of ten German plants illustrate three important phenomena about control. First, the hierarchical distribution of control occurs in all plants, whether relatively more participative or not, and it is reported by all groups of respondents—managers, supervisors, and workers. Second, the distribution of control that members prefer implies a greater total amount of control as well as a more equalized distribution than that which they perceive to exist, since employees report wanting to increase the control of those of the lower level without decreasing that exercised by managers. The preference, furthermore, stops short of complete equality, "with all groups indicating the managers *should* have more control than workers."[41]

Finally, the distribution of control as reported by members of the relatively more participative companies appeared to differ from that reported in the less-participative companies. Participation, according to the employees in all these companies, appeared to have the effect of increasing the control exercised by workers without decreasing that of managers. In fact, managers in the more-participative companies actually perceived themselves as exercising more influence than did managers in the less-participative ones. Encouraging employee participation may thus actually enhance organizational control by increasing the total amount of control in the organization, as well as making the distribution of control more equitable while still maintaining its hierarchical nature. Possibly, in fact, as these researchers conclude, control in the participative organization is different from that in the traditional, nonparticipative organization:

> In theory, it is more mutual (rather than exclusively hierarchical and unilateral), and it is supposed to be less coercive than in the traditional organization. Ideally, this control arises from mutual esteem, respect, and the acceptance of others as equals with needs and interests of their own. Real participation does not eliminate control, but changes its quality.[42]

Thus, intrinsic motivation-eliciting techniques like those discussed in the next chapter may actually help to enhance imposed control by equalizing the distribution of organizational control and reducing its coercive nature.

SUMMARY

In this chapter, we discussed techniques that are aimed at ensuring compliance through the use of imposed means like power, authority, and formal controls. We explained several views of authority and said that the concept of legal authority as applied to organizations implies that subordinates who are hired and elect to remain with the organization generally do so with the understanding that they accept this authority as legal; following orders (at least, up to a point) is thus "part of their jobs." Several things determine the width of an employee's "zone of acceptance," including inducements like wages and, most important, the factor of "legality." In particular, in joining and remaining with an organization, a person agrees to a greater or lesser extent to follow orders and to exhibit, in Simon's words, "an area of acceptance in behavior within which he will follow orders." Milgram's study suggests that a person's willingness to follow orders and to substitute an organizational scale for his personal-values scale as a criteria of "correctness" in his decisions may be greater than originally thought, and in fact the major element in compliance.

Formal control systems like budgets are another means for imposing control. Such systems can be dysfunctional, and we discussed some specific human problems with controls. The results of at least one study suggest that legal-compliance techniques like rules can be effective, at least for ensuring attendance and minimally dependable behavior.

Discussion Questions

1 Compare and contrast Weber's concept of authority with that of Simon and Barnard.

2 What does Simon mean by "zone of acceptance"? What role does it play in determining whether or not an employee obeys orders?

3 According to Simon, one of the reasons most employees willingly follow orders is simply that, as subordinates, they have agreed to view superiors' authority as legitimate—at least up to a point. Does this actually seem to be the case in organizations? What did you base your decision on?

4 "Employees have devised many ingenious ways of evading control systems, and these problems can be especially hard to deal with where jobs require originality and judgment." Discuss whether you agree or disagree with this statement and why.

Footnotes

[1]Daniel Katz and Robert L. Kahn, *The Social Psychology of Organizations* (New York: John Wiley, 1966), p. 336.

[2]*Ibid.*, p. 345.

[3]Edward Lawler III and John Grant Rhode, *Information and Control in Organizations* (Pacific Palisades, Calif.: Goodyear, 1976).

[4]Peter Blau, *Bureaucracy in Modern Society* (New York: Random House, 1956), p. 82. See also Peter Blau and W. Richard Scott, *Formal Organizations* (San Francisco: Chandler, 1962).

[5]William G. Ouchi, "The Relationship between Organizational Structure and Organizational Control," *Administrative Science Quarterly*, March 1977, p. 99.

[6]*Ibid., p. 97.*

[7]*Paul R. Lawrence and Jay W. Lorsch, Organization and Environment* (Boston: Division of Research, Graduate School of Business Administration, Harvard University, 1967).

[8]Gerald D. Bell, "The Influence of Technological Components of Work upon Management Control," *Journal of the Academy of Management,* Vol. 8, No. 2 (1965), 127–32. See also Bell, "Predictability of Work Demands and Professionalism as Determinants of Workers' Discretion," *Journal of the Academy of Management,* Vol. 9, No. 1 (March 1966), 20–28.

[9]Quoted in Sanford Dornbusch and W. Richard Scott, *Evaluation and the Exercise of Authority* (San Francisco: Jossey Bass, 1975), p. 31.

[10]Amitai Etzioni, *Complex Organizations* (New York: Free Press, 1961), pp. 3–22.

[11]Dornbusch and Scott, *Evaluation and the Exercise of Authority,* p. 31.

[12]Robert Peabody, "Perceptions of Organizational Authority: A Comparative Analysis," *Administrative Science Quarterly,* Vol. 6, No. 4 (1962), 514.

[13]Max Weber, *Essays in Sociology* (New York: Oxford University Press, 1946), pp. 294–301.

[14]Weber, *Essays in Sociology,* p. 299.

[15]Herbert Simon, *Administrative Behavior* (New York: Free Press, 1976), p. 133.

[16]Herbert Simon, "Authority, Power, and Influence," in *Studies in Managerial Process and Organizational Behavior,* eds. John Turner, Alan Filley, and Robert J. House (Glenview, Ill.: Scott-Foresman, 1972), pp. 59–64.

[17]John R.P. French, Jr., and Bertram Raven, *Studies in Social Power* (Ann Arbor, Mich.: Institute for Social Research, 1959); reprinted in Henry Tosi and W. Clay Hamner, *Organizational Behavior and Management* (Chicago: St. Clair Press, 1977), pp. 442–56.

[18]*Ibid.,* p. 450.

[19]David Mechanic, "The Sources of Power of Lower Participants in Complex Organizations," *Administrative Science Quarterly* Vol. 7, No. 3 (December 1962), 349–64; reprinted in Robert Doktor and Michael Moses, *Managerial Insights* (Englewood Cliffs, N.J.: Prentice-Hall, 1973), pp. 357–67. See also Peabody, "Perceptions of Organizational Authority," p. 512.

[20]Simon, *Administrative Behavior.*

[21]Simon, *Administrative Behavior,* p. 204.

[22]Simon, *Administrative Behavior,* p. 227.

[23]*Ibid.,* p. 204.

[24]Stanley Milgram, *Obedience to Authority: An Experimental View* (New York: Harper & Row, 1974), pp. 1–12. Copyright © 1974 by Stanley Milgram. Reprinted by permission of Harper & Row, Publishers, Inc. Reprinted by Jerome E. Schnee, E. Kirby Warren, and Harold Lazarus, *The Progress of Management* (Englewood Cliffs, N.J.: Prentice-Hall, 1977), pp. 427–36.

[25]*Ibid.,* pp. 429–30.

[26]*Ibid.,* p. 432.

[27]From the *Miami Herald,* Wednesday, October 5, 1977: "John Ehrlichman, 52, in a prison camp in Sanford, Ariz., said he got into trouble because 'I had an exaggerated sense of my obligation to do as I was bidden without exercising my independent judgment.' He told of how he began to rationalize that 'things will get better' and eventually saw himself in the White House 'as the better of angels.' 'Looking back, there were all kinds of red flags,' he said, 'and had I been wiser, I certainly would have checked out when I realized I was in a moral dilemma.' But instead, 'I abdicated my moral judgments and turned them over to someone else.' 'I am guilty in law and in fact and in these months in prison I've come to accept this reality.' "

[28]Milgram, *Obedience to Authority,* p. 433.

[29]*Ibid.,* pp. 435–36.

[30]For a discussion, see Joan Woodward, *Indusrial Organization: Behavior and Control* (London: Oxford, 1970), pp. 37–56.

[31]Robert Day and Robert Hamblin, "Some Effects of Some Close and Punitive Styles of Leadership," *American Journal of Sociology,* Vol. 69 (1964), 499–510.

[32]Fred Jasinski, "Use and Misuse of Efficiency Controls," *Harvard Business Review,* Vol. 34, No. 4 (July–August 1956), 105–12; Joseph Berliner, *Factory and Manager in the USSR* (Cambridge, Mass.: Harvard University Press, 1957).

[33]Lawler and Rhode, *Information and Control in Organizations.*

[34]P.M. Blau, *The Dynamics of Bureaucracy* (Chicago: University of Chicago Press, 1955), in Lawler and Rhode, *Information and Control in Organizations,* pp. 83–84. V.F. Ridgway, "Dysfunctional Consequences of Performance Measurements," *Administrative Science Quarterly,* Vol. 1, No. 2 (September 1956), 240–47; reprinted in Turner, Filley, and House, *Studies in Managerial Process and Organizational Behavior,* pp. 190–91.

[35]See John Baum and Stewart Youngblood, "Impact of an Organizational Control Policy on Absenteeism, Performance, and Satisfction," *Journal of Applied Psychology,* Vol. 60, No. 6 (1975), 688–94. See also John Baum, "Effectiveness of an Attendance Control Policy in Reducing Chronic Absenteeism," *Personnel Psychology,* Vol. 31, No. 1 (Spring 1978).

[36]Baum and Youngblood, "Impact of an Organizational Control Policy."

[37]*Ibid.,* p. 690.

[38]*Ibid.,* p. 693.

[39]Arnold S. Tannenbaum, *Control in Organizations* (New York: McGraw-Hill, 1968), p. 5.

[40]Klaus Bartolke, Walter Eschweiler, Peter Flechsemberger, and Arnold Tannenbaum, "Worker Participation and the Distribution of Control as Perceived by Members of Ten German Companies," *Administrative Science Quarterly,* Vol. 27, No. 3 (September 1982), 380–97.

[41]Bartolke et al., "Worker Participation," p. 393.

[42]*Ibid.,* p. 395.

CASE FOR CHAPTER 11
CONTROL PROBLEMS

Chase Manhattan Bank recently sustained a loan loss of $20 million, a loss that some feel may have been tied at least partly to inadequacies in the bank's financial control and auditing procedures. At Chase, as at some other banks, officers have authority to disburse $3 million per loan without anyone's approval. Bankers reportedly insist that such latitude is necessary for the business to run smoothly and profitably. As one Chase officer put it, "If you have a bank the size of this bank and you don't give people independent lending judgment, the bank would slow to a halt." Yet in this instance, effective financial control measures aimed at preventing misuse of such authority apparently failed to operate effectively.

The trouble apparently started when a bank officer decided to make a loan to a former college colleague. As another bank office now points out, the lending officer may have precipitated his problems by his willingness to do favors for friends—"with a friend you just don't ask the hard questions," he says. In any event, the loan (for a recreation complex in the Florida Keys) led to other loans, some to borrowers who had already been turned down by other banks, and some to borrowers who had previously pleaded guilty to charges of securities fraud in Federal Court.

By late 1979, some of the loans the officer had made were coming due but weren't being paid off. At this point, the loan officer, already in a panic, began what one affidavit refers to as "an ingenious scenario of high finance," by his utilization of a clever book-juggling act involving the basic principle of borrowing from Peter to pay Paul. When the loan officer's superiors were due to examine the branch's accounts, for instance, he had one borrower sign a blank Chase check that was later filled in in the amount of $500,000. The check was then allegedly used to reduce the borrower's own overdrafts.

According to *The Wall Street Journal,* Chase may have lacked effective control measures to prevent such loans. They report that the bank's "credit policy guide" stipulates that new borrowers must submit detailed financial statements, including unqualified opinions from an accountant. Yet this documentation wasn't furnished when a $2.96 million loan was made. Chase also had a credit-review policy whereby a credit-review committee reviewed prospective loans. But individual loans weren't reviewed unless the officer involved brought the loan to the committee's attention—the equivalent, according to *The Wall Street Journal,* of blowing a whistle on oneself. (At Citibank, in comparison, at least three officers must approve any loan.)

The Brooklyn branch office from which these loans were made has meanwhile been staffed with all new managers. And although Chase still refuses to discuss the case or identify its principals, it defends its auditing procedures. "Hypothetically," says a Chase spokesman, "if one or more officers were to violate established procedures, they may be able to circumvent the system, but eventually those violations will be exposed through the audit process." Nevertheless, the spokesman adds, "As a result of all this, we have made some minor enhancements in the credit procedures."

Questions

1 What do you think were the main inadequacies in Chase's control system?

2 To what extent do you think behavioral factors like company culture and improved employee selection and training could have helped Chase avoid this problem?

CASE FOR CHAPTER 11
CLEVER CASH MANAGEMENT REVS FIAT'S FINANCES
Minimizing Exchange Risk and Interest Costs Pays Off So Well It Is a Corporate Priority*

Last year an astounding $54 billion in cash—payments, receivables, and other items—flowed through the giant auto maker Fiat's Italian operations. Careful yet innovative management of this cash flow was a key reason Fiat survived a flood of

*Reprinted from *Business Week,* April 30, 1984.

red ink that swamped earnings through the late 1970s and early 1980s. Now, the same tight controls and centralized financing are enabling the company to make new investments at a rate of about $1 billion a year, even while reducing debt from $5 billion in 1980 to $3.5 billion today. "We operate as a central bank," explains Gian Luigi Garrino, director of corporate finance and control, "and we think it works."

Guido Vitale, managing director of Milan-based investment bank Euromobiliare, praises Fiat's cash management system for being "as sophisticated as any worldwide." To keep a tight rein on its 421 companies in 55 countries, Fiat has opted for a high degree of centralized financial control. Executives at company headquarters in Turin set financial strategy and manage operations for the worldwide group. The head office also does most of the negotiating for new lines of credit and international loans, and it oversees all Fiat's foreign exchange operations.

To keep track of everything, Fiat has put in place a complicated reporting system that allows it to check the exact income and outflow positions of its companies over successive 10-day periods and to estimate the company's financial position over the following four months. That allows the central finance operation in Turin to exploit expected cash surpluses by investing the money or to cover potential shortfalls. "Without that," says Garrino, "we would have no cash management."

• *Hedging by Telex*

Because Fiat must use the lira, a weak currency, for much of its operations, controlling foreign exchange exposure is especially important. Punctually every Friday afternoon, the central finance department sends telexes to its operating companies throughout Italy, where 60% of Fiat's sales and the bulk of its exports are generated. The telexes give strict guidelines to be used in foreign exchange transactions for the following week.

Generally, Fiat bills all exports in the buyer's currency, and the company tries to minimize its exchange risk by borrowing in local currencies. "In this way, none of our operating companies run risks. Only we do in central finance," says Garrino. To cover that risk, every 10 days Garrino checks the foreign exchange exposure of 40 companies in the Fiat group that together account for 80% of the company's total foreign exchange operations. "We find where the long and short positions are and balance them out," says Fiat's 37-year old finance manager, Gabriele Galateri di Genola, who holds an MBA from New York's Columbia University.

This close attention to foreign exchange exposure and local cash management can translate into significant savings. When Fiat recently decided to transform some short-term debt into medium-term, it elected to borrow in dollars to cover simultaneously a long dollar position it held in the foreign exchange market. So on Mar. 5 it issued $100 million in variable-rate notes priced at ¼% over the London interbank offered rate (LIBOR), thereby solving two problems at the same time.

In another example, Fiat found that its U.S. operation had an excess of $10 million and that its Swiss-based company, International Holding Fiat (IHF), had a $10 million debt for which it was paying ¼% over LIBOR. If the U.S. company had put its money on deposit, it would have earned LIBOR minus 1/8%. So Fiat had the U.S. operation lend its excess cash to IHF at LIBOR. The American company earned more than it would have from a bank, and IHF had its interest payments cut. In all, the company saved 3/8% on the deal.

• *Doing a Service*

Despite its success with a centralized treasury, Fiat has not made cash management a profit center. "Cash management at Fiat is a service for the members of the group, and our job is to ensure that they get the lowest-cost money they can," says Garrino. "If we allow our Fiat auto operating company, with sales of $7.1 billion, to go to the market on its own, it will get better terms than our Sorin Biomedica, with sales of $63.8 million. But if we send them together under the Fiat name, they both benefit."

By aggregating the borrowing needs of the group's individual companies into a lump sum and arranging a single big loan, Fiat has more negotiating clout with banks anxious to get the business. In Italy, where the company borrowed $1.5 billion last year, Fiat managed to win favorable terms—at least 1% below the prime rate, now at 17.5%.

Even in its foreign borrowings, Fiat takes the package approach, negotiating for all under the Fiat name and saving as much as 1/2% on the spread over LIBOR by doing so. Using this method, Fiat has a $1.8 billion "umbrella line of credit" with major international lenders, among them Citibank, Deutsche Bank, and Banque Paribas. The cost varies from 1/4% over LIBOR for money borrowed for six months to 3/8% over LIBOR for up to two-year funds. "It gives us tremendous flexibility, and it is nice to know it is there," says Galateri di Genola of the credit line.

Although it was born to combat lean times, centralized cash management is now at Fiat to stay. The company plans to invest an average of $1 billion a year through most of the 1980s, and it wants to do that while shrinking its debt further. Fiat executives hope that continuing with tight cash and financial management practices will be a big help in meeting that goal.

QUESTIONS

1 How do Fiat's centralized financial controls help the firm to achieve coordinated actions among its subsidiaries?
2 Do finance chief Garrino and his department exercise only "staff" authority? Explain your answer.

12

Motivation and Innovation

OVERVIEW

In this chapter we explain how to elicit *intrinsic motivation,* motivation that comes from within the person and derives from his or her ability to satisfy higher-order needs for competence, self-determination, and self-actualization. Self-control and innovation of the sort required in organic, adhocracy-type organizations generally tend not to be as much required in mechanistic organizations, since here you can use formalization, close supervision, or imposed controls to gain compliance. Indeed, as we've seen, the whole tenor of adhocracies reflects a looseness of structure that will be effective only when a "tight" system of values and self-controls keeps all employees in line. In this chapter, then, we begin to look more closely at the techniques managers use to elicit such self-control.

The outline of this chapter is as follows:

- **A** Intrinsic motivation in organization theory
  - **1** Introduction
  - **2** The classicists
  - **3** Herbert Simon
  - **4** Behavioral-systems writers
  - **5** Contingency theorists
- **B** Building commitment
  - **1** Introduction
  - **2** Building loyalty and commitment
  - **3** Participation, "ownership" of organizational goals, and self-control
  - **4** Staffing and orientation

- C Reward systems
    - 1 Salary and wages
    - 2 Incentive plans
- D Motivation and innovation in organizations
    - 1 Rewards and reinforcement
    - 2 Trust and innovation
    - 3 A respect for the individual
    - 4 The extended family
    - 5 Socialization
- E Appendix: brief survey of motivation theories

INTRINSIC MOTIVATION IN ORGANIZATION THEORY

• Introduction

The techniques presented in this chapter all aim at eliciting *intrinsic motivation,* motivation that comes from within the person and is derived from his or her ability to satisfy higher-order needs for competence, self-determination, and self-actualization.[1]

The superiority of intrinsic motivation—of getting employees to genuinely *want* to do their jobs—has, of course, been known for ages; John Stuart Mill, for example, in commenting over 100 years ago on "close supervision," contended, "Nor are the greatest outward precautions comparable in efficacy to the monitor within."[2] But though the superiority of intrinsic motivation was understood, its use until the 1930s was rather limited; instead, managers and organization theorists generally emphasized the use of punishment, close supervision, and rewards. Several factors helped account for this, including the assumption by managers that workers disliked work and were lazy (McGregor's "Theory X" argument), the fact that jobs tended to be of the routine variety and therefore lent themselves to legal-compliance techniques, and, more recently, the assumption that man as an economic, rational entity sought simply to maximize his income and so could be motivated through sole reliance on external rewards (Taylor's incentive-pay-plan argument). We can get a useful perspective on the importance of *intrinsic* motivation in organization theory by briefly reviewing what some organization theorists had to say about it.

• The Classicists

Classical theorists generally prescribed using legal compliance and rewards for motivating employees. Taylor, for example, sought almost single-mindedly to develop tools and techniques for scientifically analyzing work and developing fair incentive plans. Similarly, Fayol's work is filled with references to using "sanctions" and "constant supervision" for ensuring "discipline."

However, although the classicists emphasized legal compliance and rewards, it would be inaccurate to assume that they didn't understand the usefulness of intrinsic motivation. Fayol, for example, talked in terms of the importance of "subordination of individual interests to general interests," and of "devotion and loyalty"; yet almost every such reference was paired with the fact that such motivation must be developed through legal compliance and rewards. For instance, he wrote of the importance of "respect for authority and discipline" in developing initiative. Furthermore, subordination of individual interests to general interests is important, he said, but the means of effecting it are "firmness and good example on the part of superiors; agreements as far as is possible; constant supervision."[3]

It is probably not that these men didn't understand the value of intrinsic motivation, but rather that, given the values to which they subscribed, they simply assumed that all behavior in organizations necessarily grows out of economic motives. They assumed, in other words, that workers and entrepreneurs are all rational, economic beings who seek to maximize their benefits, and that these benefits are almost always described in economic terms.

Thus, motivation to the classicists was synonymous with rewards and legal compliance, not so much because they did not appreciate the value of intrinsic motivation but rather because they assumed that man was motivated primarily by economic gain.

• *Herbert Simon*

Herbert Simon was one of the first theorists to address the importance of intrinsic motivation. Simon saw that there were two basic ways in which the "behavior of the operative employee" could be influenced:

> These influences fall roughly into two categories: (1) establishing *in the operative employee himself* attitudes, habits, and the state of mind which lead him to reach that decision that is advantageous to the organization, and (2) *imposing* on the operative employee decisions reached elsewhere in the organization. The first type of influence operates by inculcating in the employee organizational loyalties and a concern with efficiency, and more generally by training him. The second type of influence depends primarily upon authority and upon advisory and informational services. It is not insisted that these categories are either exhaustive or mutually exclusive. . . .[4]

Simon feels that three factors contribute to the development of self-control. One is the development of organizational loyalty or identification. Here, the person identifies with the organization, and its goals become his or her own. The second is inculcation in employees of (or the hiring of those who believe in) "the criterion of efficiency." As a result, the employee is motivated "to take the shortest path, the cheapest means, toward the attainment of the desired goals." Training is a third method for developing self-control, according to Simon; it "prepares the organization member to reach satisfactory decisions himself, without the need for the constant exercise of authority or advice."

• *Behavioral-Systems Writers*

Other writers, like McGregor, clearly saw the need for intrinsic motivation and, in fact, were often as extreme in their position as were the classicists in theirs. McGregor, you will recall, distinguished between two sets of management assumptions, which he called Theory X and Theory Y. Theory X assumed that man works as little as possible, lacks ambition and responsibility, is inherently self-centered, and requires close supervision to perform adequately. Theory Y, on the other hand, assumes that people are not by nature passive or resistant to organizational needs, that motivation and the capacity for assuming responsibility are present in all people, and that the essential task of management is to arrange "organizational conditions" so that people can achieve their own goals best by directing their own efforts toward organizational objects. According to McGregor:

> . . . Theory X places exclusive reliance upon external control of human behavior, while Theory Y relies heavily on self-control and self-direction.[5]

McGregor says that Theory X assumptions manifest themselves in management's attempts to direct and control behavior through a "carrot and stick theory of motivation." Legal compliance through rules, close supervision, and their associated sanctions would in this case be the "sticks," with rewards representing the "carrots." In either case, says McGregor, the carrot-and-stick approach is no longer adequate, because it satisfies only people's lower-level needs, and these needs are already fairly well satisfied in modern societies:

> The philosophy of management by direction and control . . . is inadequate to motivate because the human needs on which this approach relies are today unimportant motivators of behavior. Direction and control are essentially useless to motivating people whose important needs are social and egoistic.[6]

Instead of using "carrots and sticks," says McGregor, managers should concentrate on building self-control to ensure compliance. They can do this, he says, by making employees' jobs more challenging (through job enlargement), and through participation and management by objectives.

Other behavioral-systems writers have come to similar conclusions. Herzberg, for example, prescribes making jobs more challenging and interesting. Katz and Kahn prescribe "craftsmanship" (job enrichment), letting employees participate in decision making, and the selection of employees whose values and goals are the same as or similar to those of the organization.

• *Contingency Theorists*

Contingency theorists like Woodward, Lawrence and Lorsch, and Burns and Stalker also accept the necessity for intrinsic motivation, but they usually tie its use to the nature of the employee's task. Findings here suggest that tapping employees' intrinsic motivation, although perhaps always laudable, is particularly appropriate in more creative, entrepreneurial, organic situations where greater reliance necessarily has to be placed on eliciting self-control and creativity. In more routine, mechanical types of jobs, legal compliance and incentive rewards at least function effectively. As Burns and Stalker put it:

> The distinctive feature of the second, organic system is the pervasiveness of the working organization as an institution. In concrete terms, this makes itself felt in a preparedness to combine with others in serving the general aims of the concern. Proportionately to the rate and extent of change, the less can the omniscience appropriate to command organizations be ascribed to the head of the organization; for executives, and even operatives, in a changing firm it is always theirs to reason why.[7]

And in another place they state:

> The emptying out of significance from the hierarchic command system, by which cooperation is insured and which serves to monitor the working organization under a mechanistic system, is countered by the development of *shared beliefs* about the values and goals of the concern (in the organic system). The growth and accretion of institutionalized values, beliefs, and conduct, in the form of *commitments,* ideology, and manners, around an image of the concern in its industrial and commercial setting make good the loss of formal structure.[8]

In summary, most theorists recognize the advantages of eliciting intrinsic motivation and self-control, and they have prescribed some specific techniques for doing so. We will discuss several in this chapter, including building commitment, and employee selection and orientation.

BUILDING COMMITMENT

• *Introduction*

Few would argue with the fact that the most powerful way to ensure compliance is to synchronize the organization's goals with those of its employees; to ensure, in other words, that the two sets of goals are essentially identical, and that by pursuing his or her own goals, the person pursues the organization's goals as well.

Early theorists understood this but mistakenly assumed that goals could be described solely in economic terms. As a result, a series of plans was (and still is) proposed in which the "one best way" to carry out a task is determined, and in which incentive plans are relied upon for employee motivation. As a result of such a plan, the theory goes, the individual worker, by pursuing his or her maximum economic gains, pursues the organization's goal as well, that goal being the maximization of profits. Today, we know that such extrinsic rewards are not usually sufficient for synchronizing the individual's and organization's goals. Instead, other techniques, like building commitment, participation, management by objectives, and employee selection, are required. In this section we discuss the first of these, building commitment.

• *Building Loyalty and Commitment*

Developing loyalty and commitment among organizational members has occupied theorists from the time of Plato, when writers were concerned with forging the allegiance of citizens to the state.[9] Steers says that organizational commitment can be defined as the relative strength of an individual's identification with and involvement in a particular organization, and that it can be characterized by at least three factors: (1) a strong belief in and acceptance of the organization's goals and values; (2) a willingness to exert considerable effort on behalf of the organization; and (3) a strong desire to maintain membership in the organization.[10] Similarly, Buchanan says that commitment embodies three separate but closely related component attitudes: (1) a sense of identification with the organizational mission; (2) a feeling of involvement or psychological immersion in organizational duties; and (3) a feeling of loyalty and affection for the organization as a place to live and work, quite apart from the merits of its mission or its purely instrumental value to the individual. Furthermore, he says, identification implies the alignment of individual and organizational goals: The employee comes to think of the aims of his organization in personal terms and to incorporate them into his own goal system.[11]

Studies suggest that commitment does result in valuable outcomes to the organization. Commitment is inversely related to employee turnover, and sometimes positively related to employee performance as well.[12] Buchanan asserts that committed people require less supervision and that "the most significant attribute of commitment is its capacity for fusing individual and organizational goals."[13] Two studies shed light on the antecedents and outcomes of organizational commitment.

The Buchanan Study Subjects in this study were 279 managers from eight large organizations in the United States. Buchanan administered questionnaires that measured what he considers the "three component attitudes" of commitment—identification, involvement, and loyalty; they also measured "experiences that fostered commitment among all 279 managers."

He found that the following five "organization experiences" had a significant effect on the employees' commitment:

- *Personal importance.* The experience of being treated as a productive and valuable member of the organization was far and away the most influential of the five.
- *Work-group experiences.* In general, the more cohesive (that is, friendly and close-knit) the group, and the more positive the group's overall feeling toward the organization, the more likely was the manager to report strong commitment.
- *Realization of expectations.* This scale asked managers to evaluate their organizations in terms of such questions as, "Has my organization fulfilled its promises to me and otherwise met my expectations in areas I care about?"
- *Organization commitment norms.* Commitment, Buchanan found, is part of a largely implicit network of norms, values, and beliefs that constitute the culture of an organization and that its members are expected to accept as a condition of membership. Those who sensed that their organizations expected them to be committed were more committed than those who did not perceive such an expectation.
- *First-year job challenge.* This result suggests that the first job assignment may be of extraordinary importance in setting the tone of a manager's relationship with his organization for years to come.

The Steers Study A study by Steers expands on Buchanan's findings.[14] Steers developed a model that we present in Figure 12-1. As you can see, the model consists of two parts: (1) antecedents of commitment, and (2) outcomes of commitment. According to Steers, there are three basic antecedents of commitment: personal

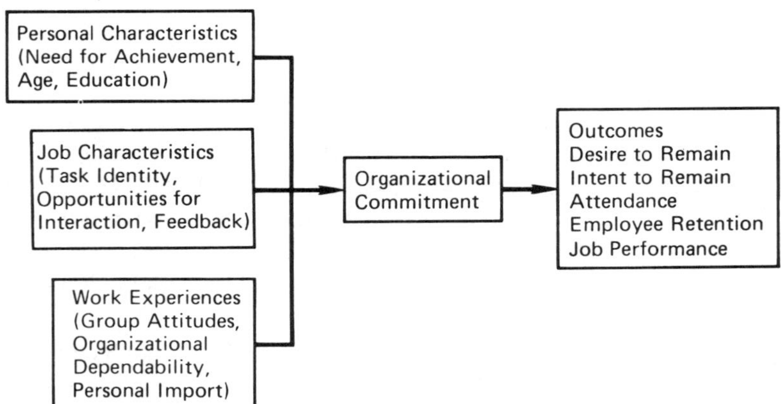

FIGURE 12-1 Hypothesized Antecedents and Outcomes of Organizational Commitment. *Source:* Richard M. Steers, "Antecedents and Outcomes of Organizational Commitment," *Administrative Science Quarterly,* Vol. 22, No. 1 (March 1977), 47.

characteristics (like need for achievement); job characteristics (how interesting the job is); and work experiences (such as group attitudes). He says these antecedents combine in molding an employee's commitment, which in turn leads to outcomes such as desire to remain with the organization, attendance, and job performance. The purpose of Steers's study was to determine the usefulness of this model.

Subjects came from two organizations. The first was a midwestern hospital; here, subjects were 382 employees, including administrators, nurses, service workers, and clerical employees. The second sample consisted of 119 scientists and engineers employed by a research laboratory. Questionnaires were used to collect the data.

Steers found that six variables were significantly related to an employee's commitment: the person's *need for achievement,* his *group's attitude* toward the organization, his *education* (inversely), *organizational dependability* (how dependably the organization was seen to carry out its commitments to employees), the person's *perceived personal importance* to the organization, and "*task identity* (the existence of challenging tasks)."[15] At least one of the variables fit into each of Steers's three basic "antecedent" categories, and he says this supports his prediction that all three antecedent categories (personal characteristics, job characteristics, and work experiences) influence commitment.

Steers also found that several *outcomes* were related to commitment in both organizations. These included the employees' *desire to remain* with the organization, *intent to remain* with the organization, *attendance* (for the scientists and engineers), and *turnover* (for the hospital employees). *Quantity of work* and the employees' *readiness for promotion* were moderately related to commitment for the hospital employees, but not for the scientists. Commitment thus seems to be strongly related to the desire and intent of employees to stay with an organization, but its effects on job performance are inconclusive. One explanation for this, Steers says, may be that performance is a function of not just commitment and motivation, but the employee's skills and expectations that he or she can accomplish the task.[16] In any case, says Steers, developing commitment is still a crucial task for management and involves ensuring that employees' highest level needs are satisfied:

> Individuals come to organizations with certain needs, desires, skills, and so forth and expect to find a work environment where they can utilize their abilities and satisfy many of their basic needs. When the organization provides such a vehicle (for example, where it makes effective use of its employees, is dependable, and so forth), the likelihood of increasing commitment is apparently enhanced. When the organization is not dependable, however, or where it fails to provide employees with challenging and meaningful tasks, commitment levels tend to diminish.[17]

Summary Commitment is a person's identification with, involvement in, and loyalty to the organization. It is elicited by feelings of importance the person receives on the job, work-group experiences, realization of expectations, first-year job challenge, the organization's dependability in carrying out its commitment to the individual, and the person's perceived personal importance to the organization. Outcomes of commitment include desire and intent to remain with the organization, reduced turnover, and (sometimes) higher-quality work and readiness for promotion.

Participation, "Ownership" of Organizational Goals, and Self-Control

The use of "participation" (encouraging employees to participate actively in developing and implementing decisions directly affecting their jobs) has been popular as a commitment-building device since the time of the Hawthorne studies. Many writers contend that participation is more effective than autocratic management, since when people become personally involved with their tasks, the execution of those tasks becomes a means for satisfying their own needs, such as for achievement.[18] In theory, deriving such satisfaction reinforces successful performance, thus providing a further impetus. On the other hand, autocratic management supposedly makes work simply the carrying out of the supervisors' will, does not satisfy subordinates' needs, and should thus have a negative effect on performance.

Others feel that participation is effective because employees who participate in decision making become "ego-involved" with the resulting decisions and develop a sense of ownership of the decisions that emerge from the decision-making process. In other words, participation can increase the degree to which group members "own" their work practices—and therefore the likelihood that the group will develop a norm of support for those practices.[19]

The prevailing evidence does suggest that employees who participate in decision making develop an ownership of their work practices, and therefore self-control. In one study, for example, participation in the development of an incentive plan for office maintenance workers changed the communication among workers from initial "shared warnings" about management to "helping members (especially new members) come to understand and believe in our plan."[20]

Because of findings like these, participation has been widely used in the implementation of organizational changes: Participants feel they have a sense of ownership of the changes, and are therefore motivated to see these changes put into effect. A classic study of this was carried out by Coch and French.[21] The researchers hypothesized that allowing employees to participate in planning and implementing the necessary procedural change would make a significant difference in their acceptance of the change. The researchers set up four experimental groups. In group I (the control, or "no participation" group), employees went through the usual factory routine. Here, the production department modified the job, a new piece rate was set, and the operators were called in to a meeting and told about the job change. Their questions were answered, and then they went back to work.

Group II was the "participation through representation" group. Here, before any changes took place, a group meeting was held and the need for change was presented dramatically. Management then presented a plan to institute the new work method, and a few representatives of the group were selected to help management work it out.

Groups III and IV were the "total participation" groups. All these employees met with management, and the need for a cost reduction was presented. All the employees in each group discussed the current methods and how they might be improved. When the new methods were agreed on, the operators were trained in them and returned to work.

The results of this study, which appear quite definitive, are presented in Figure 12-2. In group I ("no participation"), resistance developed almost immediately, and according to the researchers, 17 percent quit in the first 40 days. Grievances were filed about the piece rate and, as you can see, productivity dropped.

At the other extreme, employees in groups III and IV ("total participation") showed no such signs of resistance. Productivity climbed immediately, and there were no quits during the experiment.[22]

Other studies can also be cited; in summarizing the evidence, Lawler concludes that participation is effective because:

> . . . people become "ego involved" in decisions in which they have had an influence. The decisions become their decisions and they develop expectancies to the effect that when the decisions are successfully implemented they will experience such intrinsic rewards as feelings of competence and self esteem. Because of this, they work to implement the decision even though no extrinsic rewards are involved.[23]

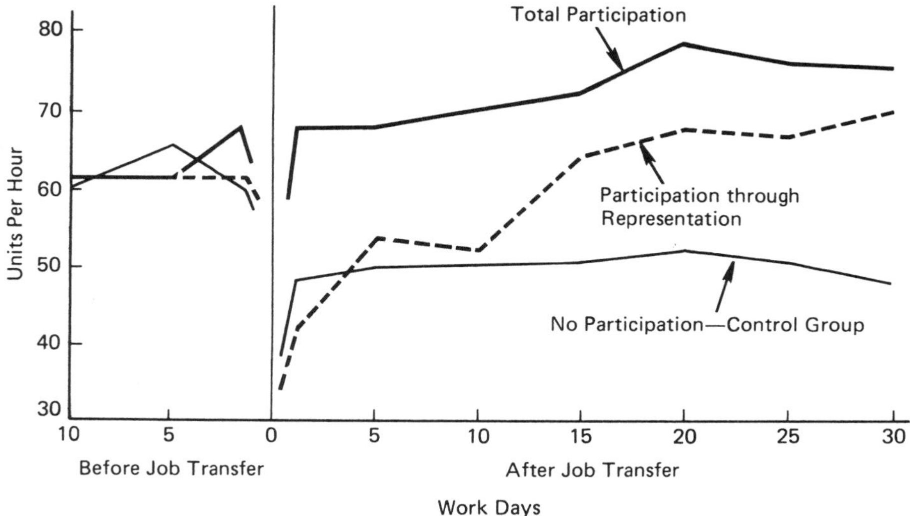

FIGURE 12-2 Effects of Participation. *Source:* Lester Coch and J.R. French, Jr., "Overcoming Resistance to Change," *Human Relations,* Vol. 1, No. 4 (1948); reprinted in Paul Lawrence and John Seiler, *Organizational Behavior and Administration* (Homewood, Ill.: Irwin/Dorsey, 1965), pp. 931–32.

• *Staffing and Orientation*

Effectively staffing the organization—recruiting, selecting, placing, and socializing new employees—affects the level of motivation and performance in the organization in several ways. First, performance depends not only on the employee's motivation but on his abilities as well, and it is through staffing that employees with the right abilities are matched with the right jobs. Furthermore, the staffing process includes orientation and socialization activities, and these play an important role in inculcating in the employee an appreciation for and identification with the goals of the organization. And it is also through staffing that people are selected whose values are compatible with those of the organization; through staffing, for example, the civil-rights crusader is matched with the Civil Liberties Union and the arbiters of social injustice are drawn to social work.

Staffing involves placing the right person in the right job. It entails several steps, including (1) job analysis—determining what the job entails and what traits and skills are needed to perform it; (2) personnel planning and recruiting; (3) employee selection—using, for example, application blanks, interviews, and personnel tests; and (4) orientation and training. The combined effect of these activities should be to ensure that employees with the right abilities are placed in the right jobs. And these activities ensure (or should ensure) that employees whose values are compatible with those of the organization are selected, and that employees develop an appreciation for and identification with the organization's goals.

Work Values and "Central Life Commitment" Selecting employees whose values are compatible with those of the organization is a crucial element in synchronizing the goals of the organization with those of the individual. A missionary hospital in Africa could hardly expect to keep an income-conscious doctor motivated, and a college devoted to open admissions and maximizing enrollment would find a research-minded professor rapidly becoming demoralized.

Similarly, Simon contends that hiring employees who believe in the "criterion of efficiency" can help ensure that employees will do their best for the organization, and the evidence suggests that such people can be identified, and therefore hired.[24] In one such study, it was found that job enrichment might not be effective among urban, blue-collar workers, who were found to be alienated from Protestant-work-ethic values. In a later study, researchers found that workers from factories located in small towns responded very differently from workers who came from urban factory settings: Workers from the small town tended to be more inclined toward the challenging jobs, a fact the authors contend derives from the fact that the small-town workers have a strong work ethic.[25] Therefore, although there is some debate over what causes some workers to be less alienated from work-ethic values, it does seem apparent that there are significant differences in the values workers bring to their jobs and that these differences affect the way they perform their jobs.

Other studies have focused on whether work, for some people, represents a stronger "central life interest" than it does for others.[26] In one study here, 24 percent of the industrial workers in the sample reported work as a central life interest. In studies since then, lower percentages of blue-collar workers in a variety of settings have been found to have a central life interest in work—11 percent of lumber workers, and 12 percent of long-distance truck drivers, for example.[27] There was also a wide range among business executives and supervisors, although most tend to have a high central life interest in work. For example, 84 percent of American executives, 82 percent of Japanese middle managers, and 54 percent of industrial supervisors were found to have such a central life interest.[28]

Subjects in a recent study included 409 employees in 37 branches of a bank and 605 employees from one division of a telephone company. Workers with a central life interest in work had a higher level of commitment to their work organization and also a higher level of attraction to individual features of their organization (such as supervision, immediate work colleagues, and the like) than did workers with other, nonwork central-life-interest orientations. Workers with a nonwork central life interest were found to have a low level of orgnaizational commitment.

Orientation and Socialization Katz and Kahn point out that "the adult socialization process in the organization can build upon the personal values of its members and integrate them around attractive organizational models. People can thus identify with the organizational mission."[29]

Personnel managers have long understood the usefulness of orientation in easing the entry of new employees into the organization. In one study at the Texas Instruments Company, for example, researchers discovered that short orientation programs helped to ease the entry of new employees and thereby to reduce their initial anxiety and significantly reduce their turnover.[30] Orientation programs have also been found to minimize what might be called the "reality shock" some new employees undergo. This reality shock, according to Hall, is caused by the incompatibility between what employees expect in their new job and the realities they are confronted with.[31] Orientation, says Hall, can help overcome this problem by providing for more realistic expectations on the part of new employees. In this way, the organization ensures not only that it hires those whose values are compatible with its own, but also that the assimilation and socialization of the employee into the organization is as smooth as possible.

Several orientation and selection techniques have proved successful as far as boosting loyalty and employee commitment is concerned. Formal and planned socialization aids like on-site orientation sessions and off-site residential training sessions did foster loyalty to and commitment to the organization. Off-site residential training programs, where available, were also strongly correlated with positive newcomer job attitudes (in terms of job satisfaction, commitment, and tenure intention, for instance), possibly because selection for participation in these programs may signal that a new employee has "been noticed," or "paid his or her dues." In one recent study, though, by far the most important activity involved in socializing employees was not a formal training session at all, but instead was "daily interactions with peers while working."[32]

REWARD SYSTEMS

Even with modern motivation techniques like job enrichment, there is no doubt that money is still a most important motivator. As three experts put it:

> Pay, in one form or another, is certainly one of the mainsprings of motivation in our society . . . the most evangelical human relationist insists it is important, while protesting that other things are too (and perhaps in his view, nobler). . . . As it is, it must be repeated: Pay is the most important single motivator used in our organized society.[33]

• *Salary and Wages*

Most employees are paid on the basis of the time they put in on the job. For example, blue-collar workers are usually paid hourly or daily *wages;* this is often called daywork. Some employees—managerial, professional, and usually secretarial and clerical—are *salaried.* They are compensated on the basis of a set period of time (like a week, month, or a year) rather than hourly or daily.

Job Evaluation Determining the rate at which to pay an employee is accomplished through *job evaluation.* The overall purpose of job evaluation is to determine the relative worth of each job. Basically, it involves comparing jobs to one another based on their content, with this content usually defined in terms of "compensable factors" like skills, effort, responsibility, and working conditions. The basic assumption of job evaluation is that all jobs that are similar (say, in terms of skills, effort, responsibility, and working conditions) should be paid at the same rate. In the federal government, for instance, a fire chief, an army major, and a chief computer programmer may all be graded GS-12 under the government evaluation system, and therefore paid at the same rate. If the job evaluation is implemented properly, the pay system in your firm should be an equitable one, because jobs of about the same level of difficulty would all be paid at about the same rate.

Should You Keep Pay Rates a Secret? There are two opposing points of view with respect to the question, Should employees know what other employees in the organization are being paid? The basic argument *for* making pay rates known is that it improves employee motivation. This point of view assumes that an employee has to see the link between his effort and rewards in order to be motivated; that with an open pay system, an employee can see that effort is rewarded and will therefore be motivated to perform better.

The problem, though, is that in many companies, there are inequities in the pay scale, perhaps because someone had to be hired in a hurry, or because of the superior salesmanship of a particular applicant. As a result (say opponents of "open pay"), letting everyone know what everyone else's pay is simply underscores these inequities and actually demotivates rather than motivates employees. (Remember that according to equity theory, if a person believes he is inequitably paid, he may well reduce his effort in order to reduce the perceived inequity.)

The implication is that open pay systems should be used only with the greatest caution. Under the best of conditions, letting everyone know what everyone else is making *may* improve performance. But if conditions are not right, and especially if there are any lingering inequities in the pay structure, publicizing salaries will cause more trouble than it's worth.

• *Incentive Plans*

There are many types of incentive plans, but they are all similar in that they tie the person's pay to the amount he or she produces. Linking effort and pay in this way should motivate performance and boost commitment by synchronizing the employees' and employer's goals: Employees see that the harder they work, the more they are paid. The most popular incentive pay plans are piecework, the Scanlon plan, and bonuses and commissions.

Piecework This is the oldest type of incentive plan, and the most commonly used. Earnings are tied directly to what the worker produces, by paying the person a piece rate for each unit produced. Thus, if Smith gets 20 cents a piece for stamping out knobs, he would make $20 for stamping out 100 for the day, and $40 for stamping out 200.

Piecework incentive plans have a number of advantages. They are simple to calculate and easily understood by employees, and rewards are directly tied to performance. Thus, these plans should and do motivate performance.

Piecework also has some disadvantages. The production standards become tied (in workers' minds) irrevocably with the amount of money earned. Thus, when industrial engineers attempt to analyze or reanalyze production standards, they meet considerable worker resistance. Piece rates are also still associated with past shady practices of employers. For example, it was common for employers to arbitrarily raise production standards if they found their workers earning what they felt were excessive wages. Because of its checkered history, the use of piecework seems to be diminishing, although this is still the most widely used incentive plan.

The Scanlon Plan The Scanlon plan is an organizationwide incentive plan in which all (or virtually all) employees in the plant or organization can participate.

The Scanlon plan has three basic features.[34] The first is the philosophy of cooperation on which it is based. It assumes that managers and workers have to rid themselves of the "us" and "them" attitudes that normally inhibit employees from developing a sense of ownership in the company, substituting instead a climate in which everyone cooperates because each understands that economic rewards are contingent on honest cooperation. Management's attitudes are largely the key to the success or failure of a Scanlon plan. Where key executives and supervisors have a genuine respect for each employee, implementing a Scanlon plan can improve performance. On the other hand, when such positive attitudes are lacking, it is doubtful that the plan can succeed. Therefore, for a Scanlon plan to succeed, there must be a pervasive *philosophy of cooperation* throughout the organization, and this cooperation, in turn, demands that management have or develop a genuine respect for each person and his or her abililties.

The second feature of the plan is the *involvement system*. This takes the form of two levels of committees: the departmental level and the executive level. Productivity-improving suggestions are presented by employees to the appropriate department-level committees, which then selectively transmit viable suggestions to the executive-level committee. The latter then decides whether to implement the suggestion. These committees are all superimposed on the regular organization structure and thus become a new mechanism for communicating productivity-improving suggestions to management.

The third element of the plan is the *sharing-of-benefits formula*. The Scanlon plan assumes that employees should share directly in any extra profits resulting from their productivity-improving suggestions. Basically, the formula shows the historical relationship between labor costs and the value of production, and assumes that a reduction of labor costs (assuming production stays the same) or an increase in production (assuming labor costs stay the same) will generate extra profits for the business, part of which should be shared with the workers.

The Scanlon plan has been quite successful. Employees make many suggestions, they accept the need for technological changes, and, perhaps most important, a work climate hostile to loafing results. The plan tends to encourage a sense of partnership and sharing among workers, one in which the organization's goals become synchronized with those of its employees.

Commissions Financial rewards for salespeople have traditionally relied heavily on incentives in the form of sales commissions, although in most cases some minimum salary is also guaranteed.

The widespread use of incentives for salespeople is due to three things: tradition, the unsupervised nature of most sales work, and the assumption that incentives are needed to motivate salespeople. And, in fact, salespeople seem to clearly prefer being paid on an incentive basis: Over 95 percent of the respondents in one study said they preferred to be paid thus.

As mentioned, most companies pay their sales force a combination of salary and commissions, and the widespread use of such plans has several advantages. Salespeople have a floor to their earnings, so that they need not worry about their families' security. Furthermore, with the salary component in the compensation plan, the company has more control over its sales force; for example, it can direct its salespeople's activities by pinpointing what services the salary component is being paid for. The commission component then provides a built-in incentive for superior sales performance.

Improving the Incentive Plan When an incentive plan fails, it is generally for one of four reasons. *Unfair standards* are the major reason: In order for employees to be motivated, the production standard must be viewed as fair and attainable, and to the extent that it is not, motivation will not take place. *Fear of a rate cut or raising of standards* is another persistent problem, and employees must be fairly well convinced that increased efforts (and earnings) on their part will not simply result in the raising of standards. *Group restrictions* are another problem, one that was first identified by the original human-relations researchers during their Hawthorne studies. If for any reason the group views the plan as not in its best interest, it will —through education, ostracism, or punishment—see that the production level of group members is held to a minimum. Other employees simply resent any plan that seems to degrade their desire to work by making it appear that they are only "in it for the money."

MOTIVATION AND INNOVATION IN ORGANIZATIONS

The innovative organization (Burns and Stalker's organic organization, or Mintzberg's adhocracy, for instance) depends above all on the self-control of its employees, a self-control that manifests itself in a willingness to exhibit initiative—that "something extra" that's required of employees when compliance can't be ensured through close supervision or formal rules and procedures. We have discussed some of the general ways in which employers elicit self-control, including staffing, participation, and rewards; we turn now to a discussion of some specific examples of how innovative organizations elicit intrinsic motivation and self-control.

• *Rewards and Reinforcement*

According to Peters and Waterman, there is, first, a pervasive feeling in innovative companies that employees are all winners, and the reward system reinforces this.[35] At IBM, for instance, the company ensures that 70 to 80 percent of its salespeople meet quotas, whereas less-successful companies arrange that only 40 percent of the sales force does this. In the less-successful firms, then, 60 percent of the salespeople necessarily think of themselves as losers.

The problem with this, say Peters and Waterman, is that when you label someone a loser, he soon starts acting like one, a phenomenon known in management as the *Pygmalion effect.* (Pygmalion was a sculptor in Greek mythology who carved a statue of a beautiful woman that was subsequently brought to life. George Bernard Shaw's play *Pygmalion,* the basis of the musical hit, *My Fair Lady,* had the theme that how you treat people will influence how they behave. Studies do consistently show that expecting the best from your subordinates generally boosts performance.)[36] Peters and Waterman found that control and reward systems in many ineffective firms were built on the "apparent assumption that 90% of the people are lazy ne'er-do-wells, just waiting to lie, cheat, or steal. . . ."[37] The excellent companies, on the other hand, build control and reward systems that say, "I know you can do a good job, I expect you to do a good job, and you'll be rewarded for doing a good job."

Related to this, Peters and Waterman "were struck by the wealth of nonmonetary incentives used by the excellent companies." In these companies, "the volume of contrived opportunities for showering pins, buttons, badges, and medals on people is staggering. . . ."[38] These firms, in other words, actively seek out and pursue endless excuses to give out rewards. (Remember, though, that these small incentives work only because they are part of a more comprehensive program; they are not in themselves a substitute for the sort of supportive management that permeates the excellent companies.)

• *Trust and Innovation*

The word *trust* comes up repeatedly among managers of excellent companies. "Treat people as adults," say Peters and Waterman, "treat them as partners. . . . Treat *them*—not capital spending and automation—as the primary source of productivity gains. These are the fundamental lessons from the excellent companies' research."[39] In other words, if you want productivity and the financial rewards that go with it, you must treat your workers as your most important asset. Similarly, Ouchi, in his study of Japanese management, contends that "the first lesson . . . is trust. Productivity and trust go hand in hard, strange as it may seem."[40] Another writer, summing up a main reason for the extraordinary results Japanese managers have achieved, puts it this way:

> Japanese managers trust not only their workers but also their peers and superiors. Because Japanese companies assume that personnel at all levels are competent—and, above all, trustworthy to have the company's best interest in mind—they do not employ highly paid executives whose only jobs are to review and pass on the work of other highly paid executives. They do not write job descriptions giving managers authority for specific fiefdoms and putting them into conflict with managers of rival fiefdoms. Instead, their operations are lean at the staff level and rich on the line level—where profits are made.[41]

• *A Respect for the Individual*

There is also, in most innovative firms, a deep sense of respect for the individual. For example, Thomas J. Watson, Jr., former chairman of IBM, says that "IBM's philosophy is largely contained in three simple beliefs. I want to begin with what I think is the most important: *our respect for the individual.* This is a simple concept, but in IBM it occupies a major portion of management time. We devote more effort to it than anything else."[42]

In fact, say Peters and Waterman, there was hardly a more pervasive theme in their excellent companies than *respect for the individual.* This respect manifested itself not just in concrete policies (in terms of appeal processes for disciplinary matters, for instance). It also manifested itself in small ways, such as a people-oriented language that served to upgrade the status of individuals, as in calling McDonald's employees "crew members," and Wal-Marts' "associates."[43]

• *The Extended Family*

Many of the most successful companies also view themselves as "extended families," and although paternalism still carries negative overtones in the United States, it is apparent that the most excellent firms have struck a balance between the strictly businesslike relationship now found between most employers and employees and the deep paternalism that characterizes many Japanese firms. Thus, companies like 3M and IBM have become "community centers" for employees rather than just places to work. They have clubs, choral groups, and intramural sports, in addition to the more traditional annual picnics, and these activities help to cultivate the idea that the employees' futures and those of their families are intimately linked to those of the firm. Many people find such intermingling of personal and business activities distasteful. Therefore, this intermingling also acts as a self-selection tool, quickly screening out those who wouldn't "fit" in these firms in the first place.

• *Socialization*

Related to this, successful firms, as noted above, spend a lot of time socializing incoming managers and employees—carefully screening them and then infusing them with the company's basic values. Potential management recruits are often brought back seven or eight times in order to make sure that the company knows whom it is hiring and that the recruit knows what he or she is getting into. Once the person is hired, the long process of socialization begins, a process aimed at infusing the employee with the values of the firm and of melding his or her goals with those of the company until the two are one; we pursue this point at length in the following chapter.

SUMMARY

In this chapter we discussed techniques for eliciting intrinsic motivation and self-control. These techniques include loyalty and commitment, participation, rewards, and staffing and orientation. Unlike the compliance techniques discussed in the preceding chapter, these involve getting the employee to identify with his or her job or with the goals of the organization, and thereby to be motivated; techniques like legal compliance, on the other hand, are based on the use of extrinsic procedures in maintaining control.

Classical theorists understood the advantages of getting employees to want to do their jobs and to exhibit self-control. But motivation to the classicists was synonymous with rewards and legal compliance, a fact that reflected the prevailing values and tasks of the day. The intrinsic-motivation techniques we discussed in this chapter can be quite effective. *Commitment* was found to be inversely related to employee turnover and sometimes positively related to employee performance as well. *Participation* facilitates organizational changes, raises employee morale, and can boost employee performance. Similarly, staffing and orientation techniques can be used to effectively recruit, hire, and place people whose values and skills are appropriate to the organization.

DISCUSSION QUESTIONS

1 Herbert Simon says that techniques that are aimed at eliciting self-control and imposed-control techniques like close supervision can be substituted for one another, at least up to a point. Do you think this is true? Do you think his statement is more true for some jobs than for others? Why?
2 Explain how you would go about building loyalty and commitment in your department.
3 Explain why it is important to place the right person in the right job.
4 Explain the relationship between motivation and innovation in organizations.

APPENDIX TO CHAPTER 12
Brief Survey of Motivation Theories

HUMAN NEEDS AND MOTIVATION

Most psychologists believe that all motivation is ultimately derived from a tension that results when one or more of our important needs are unsatisfied. Thus, a person who is hungry is motivated to find food; a person who needs security is motivated to find it; and a person with a compelling need to accomplish challenging tasks might try to conquer a mountain. The work of three psychologists—Abraham Maslow, John Atkinson, and Frederick Herzberg—is closely associated with human needs and motivation.

• *Abraham Maslow and the Needs Hierarchy*

Maslow says that man has five basic categories of needs: physiological, safety, social, ego, and self-actualization needs.[44] He says these needs form a hierarchy or ladder (as in Figure 12-3) and that each need becomes active or aroused only when the next lower need is reasonably satisfied.

Physiological Needs The lowest level in Maslow's hierarchy contains the physiological needs. These are the most basic needs everyone has, for food, drink, shelter, and rest.

Safety Needs When the physiological needs are reasonably satisfied—when one is no longer thirsty, has enough to eat, has a roof overhead, and so forth—then the safety needs become activated. They become the needs that the person tries to satisfy, the needs that motivate him. These are the needs for protection against danger or deprivation and the need for security.

Social Needs Once a person's physiological and safety needs are satisfied, according to Maslow, they no longer motivate behavior. Now the social needs become the active motivators of behavior—needs such as for affiliation, for giving and receiving affection, and for friendship.

Ego Needs Next in the hierarchy are the ego needs, which McGregor has interpreted as:

1 Those needs that relate to one's self-esteem—needs for self confidence, for independence, for achievement, for confidence, for knowledge

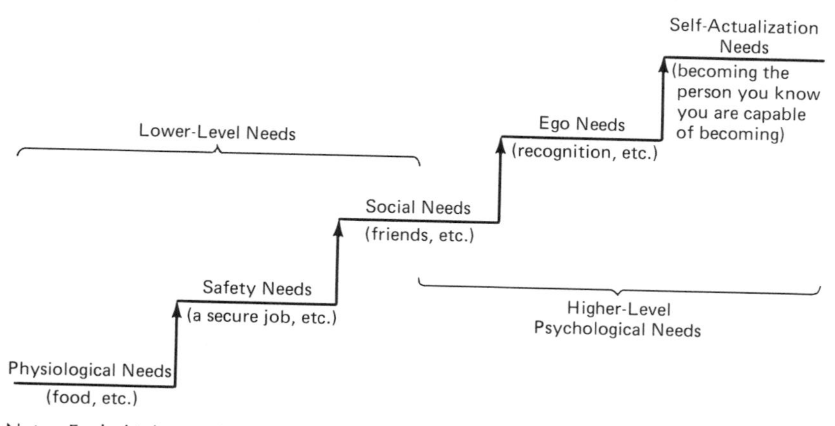

Note: Each higher order needs become active only when succeedingly lower-level needs are fairly well satisfied.

FIGURE 12-3 Maslow's Needs Hierarchy

2 Those needs that relate to one's reputation—needs for status, for recognition, for appreciation, for the deserved respect of one's fellows

One of the big differences between these ego needs and the physiological, safety, and social needs is that the ego needs (and the self-actualization needs discussed next) are rarely satisfied. Thus, according to Maslow, people have a constant, infinite need for more achievement, more knowledge, and more recognition. On the other hand, the physiological, safety, and social needs are finite; they can be and often are fairly well satisfied. As with all needs, ego needs motivate behavior, says Maslow, only when the lower-level needs are reasonably satisfied.

Self-Actualization Finally, the highest-order need begins to dominate a person's behavior, once all lower-level needs are reasonably satisfied. This is the need for self-actualization or fulfillment, the need we all have to become the person we feel we have the potential for becoming. This is the need that drives an artist to express herself on canvas, the need that motivates a student to work all day and then take a college degree in night school. This need, as with the ego needs, is rarely if ever satisfied.

• *Atkinson and Need Achievement Theory*

Need achievement theory focuses on one of Maslow's "esteem" needs—the need to achieve—and aims at predicting the behavior of those who rank high or low in the need to achieve. Atkinson says people who are high in achievement need have a predisposition to strive for success.[45] They are highly motivated to obtain the satisfaction that comes from accomplishing or achieving some challenging task or goal. They prefer tasks for which there is a reasonable chance for success and avoid those that are either too easy or too difficult. Relatedly, such people prefer getting specific, timely criticism and feedback about their performance. Studies show that people with a high need to achieve do perform better, especially on entrepreneurial tasks like starting a new business.[46] And one of the interesting aspects of achievement motivation is that people can apparently be trained to be more achievement-oriented, a fact to which we now turn.

• *Frederick Herzberg and the Motivator-Hygiene Theory*

The Theory Herzberg says that man has a lower- and a higher-level set of needs, and that the best way to motivate someone is to offer to satisfy the higher-level needs. Offering a person a raise or better working conditions, says Herzberg, is no way to motivate someone, since lower-level needs are quickly satisfied. And once they are satisfied (once the person has enough income, for instance), the only way to motivate the person is by offering even more money, or even better working conditions, in an endlessly escalating process. The right way to motivate someone, says

Herzberg, is to arrange the job in such a way that the person gets a "charge" out of doing it. Then, by performing the job, the person is motivated to keep trying to satisfy his or her *infinite craving* to satisfy higher-level needs for things like achievement and recognition.

Hygienes and Motivators Based on his studies, Herzberg believes that the factors (which he calls *hygienes*) that can satisfy lower-level needs are different from those (which he call *motivators*) that can satisfy (or partially satisfy) a person's higher-level needs. He says that if hygiene factors (like better working conditions, salary, and supervision) are inadequate, employees will become dissatisfied. But — and this is extremely important—adding more of these hygiene factors (like salary) to the job is not the way to try to motivate someone, since once the lower-level needs are satisfied, you will have to escalate your offer to further motivate the person. Hygienes like salary and working conditions, says Herzberg, will only prevent dissatisfaction (as when an employee thinks his or her salary is too low). Offering more hygienes is a very inefficient way to encourage motivation.

On the other hand, says Herzberg, "job content" or "motivator" factors (like opportunities for achievement, recognition, responsibility, and more challenging jobs) *can* motivate employees, because they appeal to employees' higher-level needs for achievement and self-esteem. These *are needs that are never completely satisfied* and for which most people have an infinite craving. Thus, according to Herzberg, the best way to motivate employees is to build challenge and opportunities for achievement into their jobs. The method Herzberg recommends for applying his theory is called *job enrichment* and was explained in Chapter 10.

EQUITABLE REWARDS AND HUMAN MOTIVATION

• Equity Theory

The equity theory of motivation assumes that people are strongly motivated to maintain a balance between what they perceive as their inputs, or contributions, and their rewards. Basically, equity theory states that if a person perceives an inequity, a tension or drive will develop in the person's mind, and the person will be motivated to reduce or eliminate the tension and perceived inequity.

Most managers recognize that inequitable treatment does have profound effects on employee behavior. Mike might be happy with his $10,000 salary and work hard to earn it, until he learns that Joe down the hall earns $800 more for the same job. Mike's first reaction will very likely be to get a quick raise, but if that fails, his performance will probably diminish as he tries to reduce what he sees as an inequity, by reducing his contribution to the firm.

One of the tricky aspects of these inequities is that most people have an inflated view of their own performance and also tend to overestimate what other peo-

	Employee thinks he is underpaid	Employee thinks he is overpaid
Piece-rate Basis	Quality down Quantity the same or up	Quantity the same or down Quality up
Salary Basis	Quantity or quality should go down	Quantity or quality should go up

FIGURE 12-4 The Effects of a Perceived Inequity on Performance

ple are earning. Most people, in other words, have a sort of built-in predisposition toward viewing situations as inequitable.

Effect on Performance According to equity theory, exactly *how* the person goes about reducing what is perceived as an inequity depends on whether he or she is paid on a piece-rate basis (by the piece) or on a straight salary basis (say, by the week):

1 If a person is paid on a *piece-rate* basis and thinks he is *overpaid*, the quantity the person produces should stay the same or may decrease, since producing *more* would simply increase the financial rewards to the person and therefore increase his perceived inequity even more. However, quality should increase, since this should allow an increase in the inputs a person sees himself as providing, thus reducing his perceived inequity.
2 On the other hand, if the person is paid per piece and views himself as *underpaid,* the quality of his work should go down, and the quantity he produces will probably increase, depending on how much the person is paid per piece he produces.
3 If the person is paid a *salary* (regardless of his output), and views himself as *overpaid,* then either the quantity or quality of his work should increase, since this will reduce the perceived inequity.
4 However, if the person is paid a salary and believes he is *underpaid,* then his quality and quantity should both decrease. This is summarized in Figure 12-4.

BEHAVIOR MODIFICATION AND POSITIVE REINFORCEMENT AT WORK

Behavior modification (a term that is often used synonymously with *operant conditioning*) involves changing (modifying) behavior through the use of rewards or punishment. Behavior modification is built on two principles: (1) Behavior that appears to lead to a positive consequence (reward) tends to be repeated, whereas behavior that appears to lead to a negative consequence tends not to be repeated[47] and (2) therefore, by providing the properly scheduled rewards, it is possible to change a person's motivation and behavior. The two important concepts in behavior modification are *the types of reinforcement* and *the schedules of reinforcement.*

• *Types of Reinforcement*

Assume you are a manager whose employees are chronically late for work. You want to use behavior modification to train them to come in on time. There are four types of reinforcement you could use: positive reinforcement, negative reinforcement, extinction, and punishment.

First, you could focus on reinforcing the *desired* behavior (which in this case is coming to work on time). To do this, you could use either positive or negative reinforcement. *Positive* reinforcement might involve giving rewards like praise or raises each time the person comes to work on time. *Negative* reinforcement also focuses on reinforcing the desired behavior—coming to work on time; but instead of your providing a positive reward, the "reward" is that the employee avoids some negative consequence, such as being harassed or reprimanded for coming in late. The "reward" is thus a negative one: Employees come in on time to avoid some negative consequence like harassment or a reprimand.

Alternatively, you might focus on reducing the *un*desired behavior (coming in late) rather than on rewarding the desired behavior. With behavior modification, there are two types of reinforcement you can use to reduce undesired behavior: *extinction* and *punishment.* People tend to repeat behavior that they have learned leads to positive consequences; with *extinction,* reinforcement is withheld, so that over time, the undesired behavior (coming in late) disappears. For example, suppose an employee learns from experience that coming to work late invariably leads to a scolding by the foreman, which in turns leads to much laughter and attention from the worker's peers. That laughter represents a positive reinforcement to the worker for coming in late. Extinction would involve the foreman's ignoring the employee, thus removing the attention and laughter—the reinforcement—from the worker's friends as well.

Punishment is a second way to reduce undesired behavior. Here, for instance, you might reprimand or harass late employees. Punishment is the most controversial method of modifying behavior, and Skinner (who did much of the work in this area) recommends extinction rather than punishment for decreasing the frequency of undesired behavior at work.[48] In fact, whenever possible, managers are advised to use *positive reinforcement,* since this focuses on improving the *desired* behavior, rather than reducing the undesired behavior.

The four types of reinforcement—positive reinforcement, negative reinforcement, extinction, and punishment—are summarized in Table 12-1.

TABLE 12-1 Types of Reinforcement

Stimulus	*Work Behavior*	*Possible Supervisory Action*	*Type of Reinforcement*
Supervisor's instruction to arrive on time	1. Consistently arrives on time	1. Praise employee and recommend a high increase in pay	*Positive Reinforcement*
		2. Avoid harassing the employee and do not reprimand	*Negative Reinforcement (Avoidance)*
	2. Consistently arrives late	3. Withhold reprimand (and laughter)	*Extinction*
		4. Reprimand and harass employee	*Punishment*

Source: Adapted from John Ivancevich, Andrew Szilagyi, Jr., and Marc Wallace, Jr., *Organizational Behavior and Performance* © 1977 by Scott, Foresman and Company. Reprinted by permission.

• *Schedules of Positive Reinforcement*

The *schedule* with which positive reinforcement is applied is as important as the type of reinforcement used.[49] Basically, there are four schedules you could use:

Fixed-Interval Schedule A fixed-interval schedule is based on time. Here, the person gets reinforcement (a reward) only when the desired response occurs and *only after the passage of a specified fixed period of time* since the preceding reinforcement. For example, at the end of each week, you might go around and praise each employee who came to work on time every day that week.

Variable-Interval Schedule Variable-interval schedules are also based on time. However, the person is reinforced at some *variable* interval around some average. For example, suppose you want to provide reinforcement on the average of once a day for all employees who come to work on time. You can visit them on average once a day—once on Tuesday, skip Wednesday, three times on Thursday, and so on—in such a way that the praise averages out to about once a day.

Fixed-Ratio Schedule A fixed-ratio schedule is based on units of *output* rather than on time. With a fixed-ratio schedule, rewards are delivered only when a fixed number of desired responses occur. Most piece-rate incentive pay plans are on a fixed-ratio schedule. The worker is rewarded every time he or she produces a fixed number of pieces.

Variable-Ratio Schedule Variable-ratio schedules are also based on units of output, but the number of desired outcomes necessary to elicit a reward changes around some average. The Las Vegas–type slot machines are good examples of rewards administered according to variable-ratio schedules. The number of times you can expect to hit a jackpot with such machines, *on the average* over the long term, is predictable. Yet the jackpots come randomly on a variable-interval schedule. Thus, you might get no jackpots for five times and then hit two in a row; you might go 50 times without a jackpot and then you get one.

Which ratio schedule is most effective?

1. In general, the fastest way to get people to learn is to *not put them on schedule at all.* Instead, reinforce the desired outcome *continuously,* each and every time it occurs. The drawback is that the desired behavior also diminishes very rapidly once you stop reinforcing it.
2. Variable-ratio reinforcement (the Las Vegas type) is the most powerful at *sustaining* behavior. With this schedule, people will continue producing the desired response for a long time even without reinforcement, since they are always expecting to "hit the jackpot" on the next try.
3. Fixed- and variable-ratio schedules are both better at sustaining behavior than are either of the interval schedules, which are based on time.

MOTIVATION: AN OVERVIEW

• An Expectancy Approach

It would be useful to summarize and integrate these motivation theories, and to do so we can draw on what is called the *expectancy theory of motivation.* This theory assumes that a person's motivation to exert effort is based on his or her expectations of success.[50] Expectancy theory as formulated by psychologist Victor Vroom assumes that to motivate someone, it is not enough to offer the person something to satisfy his or her important needs. The reason for this, says Vroom, is that in order for the person to be motivated, he must also be reasonably sure that he has the *ability* to obtain the reward. For example, telling a man you will appoint him sales manager if he increases sales in his district will probably not motivate him if he knows the task is virtually impossible.

Basically, Vroom contends that for motivation to take place, two things must occur:

1 The "valence" or value of the particular outcome (such as becoming sales manager) must be high for the person.
2 The person must feel he or she has a reasonably good chance of accomplishing the task and obtaining the outcome. That is, the person must be convinced that effort will be *instrumental* in obtaining the reward.

A Model of Motivation As illustrated in Figure 12-5, motivating someone can be thought of within an expectancy framework. Expectancy theory states that motivation will occur (1) if the incentive is of value to the person, and (2) if the person is reasonably sure that effort on his or her part will result in accomplishing the task and obtaining the incentive.

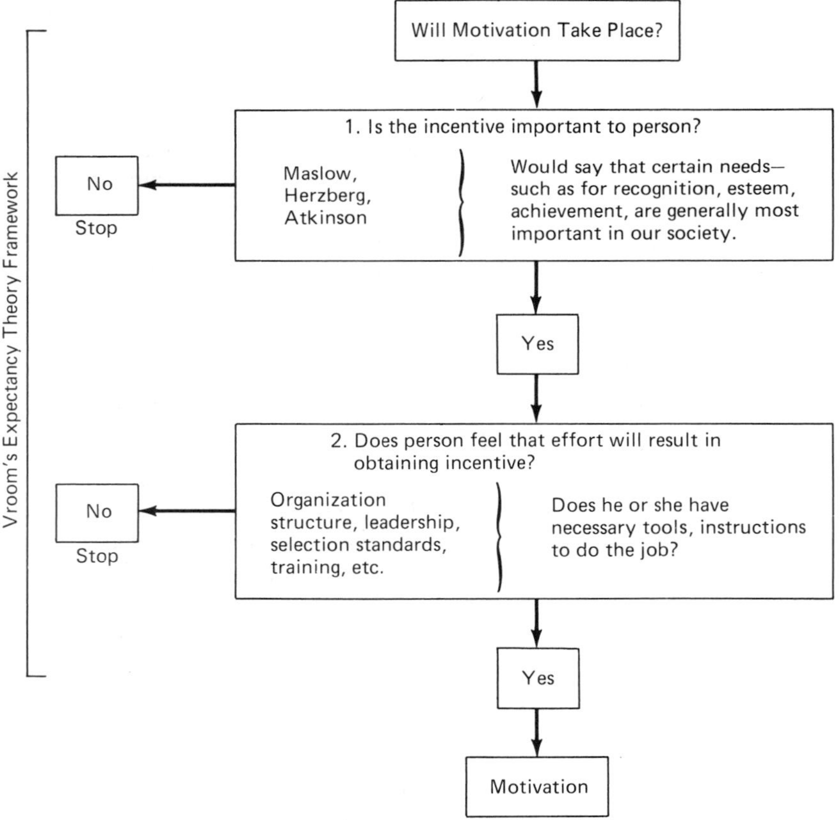

FIGURE 12-5 A Model of Motivation

Therefore, as shown in the model, for motivation to take place, several things must occur. First, the incentive must be important to the person. (Theorists like Maslow, Herzberg, and Atkinson would suggest that certain needs—like those for recognition, esteem, and achievement—are the most important in our society.) Related to this, the incentive cannot just be important but must also be viewed as equitable if it is to elicit the desired motivation. (An *in*equitable reward can also elicit motivation if, for instance, a person paid a salary believes he or she is overpaid.) Second, the person must feel that effort *will in fact lead* to rewards. Here, other, nonmotivational matters (including human factors like skills and work groups, and organizational factors like adequate plans, organization charts, and training) must be addressed, to ensure that there are no impediments to performing. All the management functions—planning, organizing, staffing, controlling, *and* leading—thus influence motivation.

• *Principles of Motivation*

- *Rewards should be tied to performance.* Theories we studied show that motivation is greatest when obtaining the reward depends on performance. For those tasks for which and people for whom pay is the most obvious reward, this suggests an emphasis on incentive bonuses and piece-rate plans. For all jobs, it suggests tying *nonfinancial* rewards (like advancement, recognition, and praise) to performance.
- *Rewards should be equitable.* For example, salaried employees who feel they are underpaid will reduce the quality or quantity of their performance, whereas those who believe they are overpaid will improve their performance.
- *A person should have the ability to accomplish the task to be motivated to do so.* If a person believes there is little or no chance of successfully completing a task (and therefore obtaining the reward), that person would probably not be motivated to accomplish it. Thus, always ask, *"Could the employee do the job if he or she wanted to?"*
- *Distinguish between low-level needs and higher-level needs.* Low-level needs are those for food, clothing, shelter, and security. High-level needs are those for recognition, achievement, and self-actualization. Wherever possible, try to elicit motivation by appealing to the relatively infinite higher-level needs. Before doing so, however, make sure the lower-level needs are adequately satisfied.

FOOTNOTES

[1]There is debate as to just what "intrinsic motivation" means. Deci, Cascio, and Krussell say it is a difficult concept to operationalize. Scott implies that it may be motivation that emerges in the absence of external rewards. Deci says that "intrinsically motivated behaviors are ones that are involved with the human need for being competent and self-determining." E.L. Deci, Wayne Cascio, and J. Krussell, "Cognitive Evaluation Theory and Some Comments on the Calder-Staw Critique," *Journal of Personality and*

Social Psychology, Vol. 31 (1975), 81–85; W.E. Scott, Jr., "The Effects of Extrinsic Rewards on Intrinsic Motivation: A Critique," *Organizational Behavior and Human Performance,* Vol. 15 (1975), 117–29; E.L. Deci, *Intrinsic Motivation* (New York: Plenum Publishing Corp., 1975); and E.L. Deci, "Notes on the Theory and Metatheory of Intrinsic Motivation," *Organizational Behavior and Human Performance,* Vol. 15 (1976), 130–45.

[2]John Stuart Mill, quoted in Alvin Gouldner, "About the Functions of Bureaucratic Rules," in Joseph Literer, *Organizations* (New York: John Wiley, 1966), p. 379.

[3]Henri Fayol, *General and Industrial Management,* trans. Constance Storrs (London: Sir Isaac Pitman, 1949).

[4]Herbert Simon, *Administrative Behavior* (New York: Free Press, 1976), p. 11.

[5]Douglas McGregor, "The Human Side of Enterprise," *Management Review,* November 1957, pp. 22–28, 88–92; reprinted in Fred Luthans, *Contemporary Readings in Organizational Behavior* (New York: McGraw-Hill, 1972), pp. 38–40.

[6]*Ibid.,* p. 24.

[7]Tom Burns and G.M. Stalker, *The Management of Innovation* London: Tavistock, 1961), p. 125.

[8]*Ibid.,* p. 122.

[9]Bruce Buchanan, "To Walk an Extra Mile: The Whats, Whens, and Whys of Organizational Commitment," *Organizational Dynamics,* Spring 1975, pp. 67–80; and Jerome Schnee, Harold Lazarus, and E. Kirby Warren, *The Progress of Management* (Englewood Cliffs, N.J.: Prentice-Hall, 1977).

[10]Richard M. Steers, "Antecedents and Outcomes of Organizational Commitment," *Administrative Science Quarterly,* Vol. 22 (March 1977); Lyman Porter, Richard Steers, Richard Mowday, and Paul Boulian, "Organizational Commitment, Job Satisfaction, and Turnover among Psychiatric Technicians," *Journal of Applied Psychology,* Vol. 59 (November 1974), 603–9.

[11]Buchanan, "To Walk an Extra Mile."

[12]James Poch and Richard Steers, "Job Attachment, Satisfaction, and Turnover among Public Employees," Technical Report No. 6, Office of Naval Research, University of Oregon, 1976; Porter et al., "Organizational Commitment"; and Richard Mowday, Lyman Porter, and Robert Dubin, "Unit Performance, Situational Factors, and Employee Attitudes In Spatially Separated Work Units," *Organizational Behavior and Human Performance,* Vol. 12 (1974), 231–48. The findings generally suggest that organizational commitment is associated with organizational adaptability, turnover, and tardiness but not with organizational performance per se. See, for example, Harold Angle and James Perry, "An Empirical Assessment of Organizational Commitment and Organizational Effectiveness," *Administrative Science Quarterly,* Vol. 26, No. 1 (March 1981), 1–14.

[13]Buchanan, "To Walk an Extra Mile"; see also Bruce Buchanan, "Building Organizational Commitment: The Socialization of Managers in Work Organizations," *Administrative Science Quarterly,* Vol. 19 (1974), 533–46; and Charles A. O'Reilly III and David Caldwell, "The Commitment and Job Tenure of New Employees: Some Evidence Opposed to Decisional Justification," *Administrative Science Quarterly,* December 1981, pp. 597–616.

[14]Steers, "Antecedents and Outcomes."

[15]See J. Richard Hackman and Edward E. Lawler III, "Employee Reactions to Job Characteristics," *Journal of Applied Psychology,* Vol. 55 (1971), for task identity scale.

[16]For additional studies in this area, see Samuel Rabinowitz, Douglas Hall, and James Goodale, "Job Scope and Individual Differences as Predictors of Job Involvement: Independent or Interactive?" *Academy of Management Journal,* Vol. 20, No. 2 (1977), 273–81; Bill McKelvey and Yuma Sekaran, "Toward a Career Based Theory of Job Involvement: A Study of Scientists and Engineers," *Administrative Science Quarterly,* Vol. 22, No. 2 (June 1977), 280–305.

[17]Steers, "Antecedents and Outcomes," p. 53. Bateman and Strasser, in a recent longitudinal analysis of the antecedents of organizational commitment, found that eight potential nondemographic causal predictors, including leader reward behavior and job characteristics, did not predict organizational commitment in a following time period, a finding that "runs counter to what previous researchers have believed to be the causal priorities among these variables. . . ." See Thomas Bateman and Stephen Strasser,

"A Longitudinal Analysis of the Antecedents of Organizational Commitment," *Academy of Management Journal,* Vol. 27, No. 1 (March 1984), 95–112.

[18]Steven Sales, "Supervisory Style and Productivity: Review and Theory," *Personnel Psychology,* Vol. 19, No. 3 (1966), 275–86; Ahmed Abdel-Halim, "Effects of Task and Personality Characteristics of Subordinate Responses to Participative Decision-Making," *Academy of Management Journal,* Vol. 26, No. 3 (September 1983), 477–84.

[19]J. Richard Hackman, Edward E. Lawler III, and Lyman Porter, *Behavior in Organizations* (New York: McGraw-Hill, 1975), p. 419.

[20]See Kenneth Scheflen, Edward E. Lawler III, and J. Richard Hackman, "Long Term Impact of Employee Participation in the Development of Pay Incentive Plans: A Field Experiment Revisited," *Journal of Applied Psychology,* Vol. 55 (1971), 182–86; and Edward E. Lawler III and J. Richard Hackman, "Impact of Employee Participation in the Development of Pay Incentive Plans: A Field Experiment," *Journal of Applied Psychology,* Vol. 53 (1969), 467–71.

[21]See "Participation and Decision Making in Work Group Activity," in Paul Lawrence and John Seiler, *Organizational Behavior and Administration* (Homewood, Ill.: Richard D. Irwin, 1965), pp. 931–32.

[22]See also Nancy Morse and Evert Reimer, "The Experimental Change of a Major Organizational Variable," *Journal of Abnormal and Social Psychology,* Vol. 52, No. 1 (January 1956), 120–39.

[23]Edward Lawler III, "Control Systems in Organizations," in Marvin Dunnette, *Handbook of Industrial and Organizational Psychology* (Chicago: Rand McNally, 19976), p. 1281. See Also Joseph Alutto and Donald Redenburgh, "Characteristics of Decisional Participation by Nurses," *Academy of Management Journal,* Vol. 20, No. 2 (1977), 341–47.

[24]Herbert Simon, *Administrative Behavior.*

[25]See John Castellano, "Rural and Urban Differences: One More Time," *Academy of Management Journal,* Vol. 19, No. 3 (1976); A.N. Turner and P.R. Lawrence, *Industrial Jobs and the Worker* (Boston: Harvard University Press, 1965).

[26]See, for example, Robert Dubin, "Industrial Workers' Worlds: A Study of the Central Life Interests of Industrial Workers," *Social Problems,* Vol. 3 (1956), 130–42.

[27]Kenji Ima, "Central Life Interests of Industrial Workers: A Replication among Lumber Workers," unpublished master's thesis, University of Oregon, cited in Robert Dubin, Joseph Champous, and Lyman Porter, "Central Life Interests and Organizational Commitment of Blue Collar and Clerical Workers," *Administrative Science Quarterly,* Vol. 20 (September 1975), 411–21.

[28]Walter Corrie, Jr., "Work as a 'Central Life Interest': A Comparison of the Amana Coloney Worker with the Nonamana Coloney Worker in a Given Industrial Setting," unpublished doctoral dissertation, University of Iowa, 1957; Calvin Endo, "Career Anchorage Points and Central Life Interests of Japanese Middle Managers," unpublished doctoral dissertation, University of Oregon, 1970; John Mauere, "Work as a Central Life Interest of Industrial Supervisors," *Academy of Management Journal,* Vol. II (1968), 329–39.

[29]Daniel Katz and Robert Kahn, *The Social Psychology of Organizations* (New York: John Wiley, 1966), p. 366.

[30]Earl Gomersall and M. Scott Myers, "Breakthrough in On-The-Job Training," *Harvard Business Review,* Vol. 44 (July–August 1966), 62–72.

[31]Douglas Hall, *Careers in Organizations* (Pacific Palisades, Calif.: Goodyear, 1977).

[32]Meryl Louis, Barry Posner, and Gary Towell, "The Availability and Helpfulness of Socialization Practices," *Personnel Psychology,* Vol. 36, No. 4 (Winter 1983), 857–66.

[33]Orlando Behling and Chester Schriesheim, *Organizational Behavior* (Boston: Allyn & Bacon, 1976), p. 33.

[34]Brian Moore and Timothy Ross, *The Scanlon Way to Improved Profits* (New York: John Wiley, 1978).

[35]Thomas Peters and Robert Waterman, Jr., *In Search of Excellence* (New York: Harper & Row, 1982), p. 57.

[36]Robert Rosenthal and Lenore Jacobson, *Pygmalion in the Classroom* (New York: Holt, Rinehart & Winston, 1968).

[37]Peters and Waterman, *In Search of Excellence,* p. 58.

[38]*Ibid.,* p. 269.

[39]*Ibid.,* p. 238.

[40]William Ouchi, *Theory Z* (New York: Avon, 1981), p. 5.

[41]*Business Week,* "Trust, the New Ingredient in Management," July 6, 1981, pp. 104–5.

[42]Peters and Waterman, *In Search of Excellence,* p. 238.

[43]*Ibid.,* p. 260.

[44]This section is based on Douglas McGregor, "The Human Side of Enterprise," *The Management Review* November 1962, pp. 22–28, 88–92. Reprinted in M. Richard and W. Neilander, *Readings in Management* (Cincinnati, O.: Southwestern, 1974), pp. 433–41.

[45]John Campbell and Robert Pritchard, "Motivation Theory in Industrial and Organizational Psychology," in M. Dunnette, *Handbook of Industrial and Organizational Psychology* (New York: Rand McNally, 1976), pp. 63–130.

[46]David McClelland, *The Achieving Society* (New York: Van Nostrand Reinhold, 1961); Edwin Cornelius III and Frank Lane, "The Power Motive and Managerial Success in a Professionally Oriented Service Industry Organization," *Journal of Applied Psychology,* Vol. 69 (February 1984), 32–39.

[47]W. Clay Hamner, "Reinforcement Theory and Management in Organizational Settings," in Henry Tosi and W. Clay Hamner, *Organizational Behavior and Management: A Contingency Approach* (Chicago: St. Clair, 1974), pp. 86–112. This principle is also known as the *law of effect.*

[48]Hamner, "Reinforcement Theory," p. 95.

[49]*Ibid.,* pp. 99–103.

[50]David Nadler and Edward Lawler III, "Motivation: A Diagnostic Approach," in J. Richard Hackman, Edward Lawler III, and Lyman Porter, *Perspectives on Behavior in Organizations* (New York: McGraw-Hill, 1977), pp. 26–38.

CASE FOR CHAPTER 12
HOW THE PC PROJECT CHANGED THE WAY IBM THINKS*

Even the most astute observer would never recognize the nondescript single-story building in Boca Raton, Fla., as a product development laboratory of International Business Machines Corp., the world's premier computer maker. The converted warehouse has a leaky roof, few windows, and a malfunctioning air conditioner. Yet a small team of IBM engineers began working here in 1980 and managed to design the computer that has ended up significantly changing the entire personal computer business—and IBM as well.

The design team was not expecting such grandiose results that first summer. They were not developing a computer to fit IBM's traditional product lines but creating instead a product that would enable the computer giant to enter the already exploding personal computer market.

*Reprinted from *Business Week,* October 3, 1983.

• *Free Rein*

The task force responsible for what was to become IBM's Personal Computer was set up as an independent business unit, separate from the Armonk (N.Y.) giant's bureaucratic tangle and granite-set rules. Taking that unconventional—for IBM—approach was the key to the PC's phenomenal success. "We were allowed to develop like a startup company," says Philip D. "Don" Estridge, the project leader, whose personal star in IBM has risen just as fast as the Personal Computer. "IBM acted as a venture capitalist," he explains. "It gave us management guidance, money, and allowed us to operate on our own."

Their triumph is dramatically changing the entire corporation. "The PC has reinvigorated the company," declares Stephen T. McClellan, who has long followed IBM for Salomon Bros. "If 5% of your business is growing at a huge rate, it stimulates revenue growth and adds an element of dynamic creativity,"he explains. A runaway best-seller, the PC will account for as much as $2.5 billion in worldwide revenues this year—more than any other single computer in IBM's product line. The PC and its associated products will represent 5% or more of IBM's estimated 1983 revenues of $41 billion, predicts William D. Easterbrook, computer industry analyst for Kidder, Peabody & Co. The Boca Raton development lab is now surrounded by a mass of new IBM construction. In the past two years the company has added 1 million sq. ft. of space and 2,500 people at its Boca Raton facility.

Although Estridge hopes that size and success will not change the entrepreneurial feeling remaining in the PC operation, IBM is bringing the group into the corporate fold. Today, Estridge says, "we want to fit into IBM, because it is the right thing for our customers." He is no longer just one of several executives reporting to one of the company's six manufacturing divisions. In August, Estridge was appointed president of a new seventh production unit, Entry Systems Div., and was given complete responsibililty for the Personal computer and several other small computers.

• *Proof of the Pudding*

The unexpectedly rapid success of the PC also is enabling IBM to keep up with another major industry trend that neither the computer giant nor its competition had expected. Personal computers in general, and the PC in particular, are becoming the most popular method for professionals and executives alike to tap into information processing. "We did not anticipate in August, 1981, that microcomputers would become the work stations of the future," acknowledges Douglas R. LeGrande, the new vice-president for operations at Entry Systems Div. But today, he says, the PC is "viewed [by IBM] as a strategic product."

The rocketing triumph of the Personal Computer also provides the most visible confirmation yet of the aggressive strategy that IBM put in place in 1979 and 1980. During the 1970s, the computer giant was unable to establish a strong position in such high-growth markets as distributed data processing and office automation. As a result, its overall market share slipped from 60% to about 32% of the broadly defined information processing market. To ensure that IBM did not continue to miss market opportunities, then-Chairman Frank T. Cary radically changed the company's operations.

Management was encouraged to explore new high-growth markets such as the personal computer and to experiment with new distribution channels, such as independent retailers. And in a broad effort to lower production costs, IBM invested many millions of dollars in automated production facilities. "The success of the PC justifies the grand strategy that IBM put in place in 1979," says Kidder Peabody's Easterbrook.

• *Spartan Setting*

IBM certainly developed the PC in an uncharacteristic manner for a large, structured company. Unlike most of its product design teams, which must account for their every move,the Boca Raton group was on its own, except for quarterly corporate reviews. Like hundreds of entrepreneurs in the personal computer business outside the company, the IBM designers worked 80 to 100 hours per week under spartan conditions for a year to bring the machine to life. "If you're going to compete with five men in a garage, you have to do something different" than what IBM usually does, says David J. Bradley, one of the designers of the PC.

This autonomy was largely responsible for the Personal Computer's quick penetration of the market. For example, instead of using proprietary electronic circuitry, as IBM usually does, Estridge's team got the go-ahead to use a microprocessor designed by Intel Corp. for the heart of the computer. "We used readily available components," says designer Bradley. "To get it done quickly, we relied on our management to run interference with [the rest of IBM's] management."

• *Going for Results*

IBM's decision to go to outside software suppliers also played a key role in the quick launching of the PC. IBM usually prefers to write its own software for a new computer, but this product strategy seriously delayed the introduction of another IBM small computer, the System/23 Datamaster. The design of this product was completed before the PC was even started, yet the two machines came out at the same time. "The Datamaster took too long to develop because the software was written internally," says William L. Sydnes, a former employee who worked on both the Datamaster and the PC projects.

IBM has extended the same autonomy that it gave the PC organization to other groups. It has set up a total of 15 of what it calls Special Business Units and Independent Business Units to work in such areas as robotics, telecommunications, and new data displays. "The idea is to have a small group of people with a single result orientation,'' Estridge explains. In the Entry Systems Div., such independent teams are believed to be working on a home computer, code-named Peanut; a portable version of the IBM PC; and a more powerful model that can also run several work stations.

IBM's Joyce Wrenn, for example, manages a software publishing operation that writes manuals, organizes software production, and selects PC programs for IBM to publish. "We have everything in Boca Raton that we need to get the product out," Wrenn points out. "That means we can move very quickly," she says, unlike typical company operations that "do not have everything needed in one location."

Current IBM product designers, however, will never be given as much freedom as was the original Personal Computer team, according to some observers. "In the beginning, [IBM] designed one product for one market. No one argued over the product overlap," says William H. Gates, the 27-year-old Microsoft chairman who worked closely with the design team. Estridge agrees that if working with other IBM computers "had been a major consideration, I think we would have designed [the PC] differently."

To ensure that customer software will not become obsolete, any new IBM personal computer will have to be compatible with the current PC. The PCs will also have to operate with IBM's large mainframe computers, so that customers can gain access to large databases. A major problem that needs to be resolved is the overlap between the PC and such existing IBM computers as the Datamaster desktop and the Displaywriter word processor. IBM "can't continue to support different [designs]," says industry analyst Robert T. Fertig, president of Enterprise Information Systems Inc. So, he adds, "some will fall by the wayside."

Putting Estridge in charge of all IBM small computers was a signal from management that the PC line is the most likely to survive. But it is not clear that the free spirit of the PC will survive. "They won't be able to make a move without corporate's O.K.," says a former regional sales manager for the IBM PC. Adds another former member of the team: "They will become more cumbersome. It will be hard to keep the entrepreneurial spirit alive."

Most of the original design team has already left the Boca Raton facility. Several have joined smaller companies, and others requested transfers within IBM. "It was a very demanding environment that required a lot of personal sacrifice," comments Sydnes. But unlike a small startup company, he says, "IBM has a problem in terms of rewarding individual contributors." After more than 18 years at IBM, Sydnes has resigned to join Franklin Computer Corp. as vice-president for research and development—a title that is harder to come by at a multibillion-dollar corporation. "Going from a total unknown to a vice-president," he says, "feels pretty good."

• *A Nicer Giant*

While IBM's PC operation may not remain as entrepreneurial as its personal computer competitors, the lessons that IBM learned from the PC are like a breath of fresh air throughout the vast corporation. "The PC has promoted a change in the climate of thinking at IBM," says David N. Martin, president of National Advanced Systems, an IBM competitor in computers. Perhaps most noticeable, he says, is IBM's willingness to deal with outside suppliers.

"The whole product line has gotten behind the PC," says Thomas J. Crotty, who follows the computer industry for Gartner Group Inc. For example, on Sept. 15, IBM introduced new programs for its 4300 line of mainframe computers that make it easier and less expensive to attach PCs to the mainframe. "It's done wonders for morale at IBM," says Crotty. PC operations manager LeGrand agrees. "There is a rekindling of the positive attitude that lapsed at IBM in the 1970s," he says. "There is a feeling [within the company] that if IBM can do this, we can do anything."

QUESTIONS

1 How do you think IBM's "venture capital" approach to developing the PC contributed to the project group's motivation and the innovation they achieved?

2 Why do you think several of the project group's original members requested transfers or left the company once the project was completed? Do you think that would have happened in a smaller company?

13

Leadership, Values, and Culture

OVERVIEW

This chapter explains the determinants of *organizational culture,* and in particular, leadership and how the leader's actions mold the organizational culture. An organization's culture reflects the prevailing values of the organization, and these values are set first and foremost by the organization's leader. Culture, as we'll see in this chapter, plays a crucial role in maintaining compliance in the organic structure, since it is in part through company culture that management ensures that all employees' values are consistent with those of the commpany at large.

The outline of this chapter is as follows:

A Introduction
B Survey of leadership theories
  1 Trait theory
  2 Behavioral theories: styles of leadership
  3 Fiedler's contingency theory of leadership
C Leadership findings and organization theory
  1 The functions of leadership in organization theory
  2 The leader's "structuring" function
  3 The leader's motivation/compliance function
  4 Leadership and culture: establishing the values of the enterprise
D Role of culture in organization design
  1 Culture and innovation
E Culture and organization design
  1 Burns and Stalker: the organic organization

INTRODUCTION

If you were to visit New York, Paris, Rome, and Tokyo, you would not be surprised to find cultural differences between the people of each city. In New York, business-people might want to "get right down to business," but in Tokyo, you might spend a maddening half hour on social pleasantries before being able to broach your subject to a Japanese manager. Similarly, in Japan, the desire to produce high-quality products seems an ingrained cultural value that helps explain the Japanese product-quality mystique.

Just as societies have different cultures, so do companies and departments within them. Some banks are conservative, for instance, whereas others are aggressive and risk-oriented. Some airlines suffer through years of labor conflict; others, like Delta, have cultures that encourage management and labor to pull together in a nonadversary relationship. Similarly, some departments are oppressive to work in, and some are pleasant. In other words, companies have different cultures just as societies do. And just as society's culture helps influence how its members behave, so does a company's culture influence the opinions and behavior of its employees.

An organization's culture can be defined as the prevailing values of the organization, and as such, it always constitutes more than its constituent parts. Employees pick up cues about their organization—from the behavior they see rewarded, and from how they are appraised, or (primarily) from the actions of their leader—and from these cues they form a composite picture or pattern concerning the organization in which they are working, its overall value set or *company culture.* We start with a review of leader-effectiveness theories and then explain the factors, including leadership, that combine to influence the company's culture.

SURVEY OF LEADERSHIP THEORIES

Leadership effectiveness theories fall into three categories: the trait, behavioral, and contingency theories. We begin with trait theory, which assumes that effective leaders have a finite number of identifiable traits or characteristics that distinguish them from ineffective leaders.

• *Trait Theory*

Most of the early research on leadership traits was inconclusive: Specific traits were found to be related to leader effectiveness, but none were found to be so related in a variety of different studies and situations. For example, traits classified as physical, social background, intelligence and ability, and personality were found to differentiate leaders from followers and effective leaders from ineffective leaders in specific studies. However, most reviewers were in agreement that the use of various traits had not proved very useful for the selection of leaders.[1] More recently, Palmer concluded that his own investigation "showed no support for the hypothesis that management effectiveness, as evaluated by subordinate managers, is a function of the personality characteristics of the individual. . . ."[2]

The Ghiselli Research More recently, a number of researchers, most notably Edwin Ghiselli,[3] have carried out multicompany studies that suggest it may be possible to identify traits that distinguish effective from ineffective leaders in a variety of settings.

Ghiselli's subjects included 306 middle managers, ranging in age from 26 to 42. They were employed by 90 different businesses and industrial organizations throughout the United States; an average of three to four men were drawn from each firm. The firms were in the transportation, finance, insurance, manufacturing, utilities, and communication industries. About 90 percent of the subjects were college graduates; all had had at least some college.

Ghiselli's findings are summarized in Figure 13-1, which presents the relative importance of his 13 traits to managerial talent. First, you can see that supervisory ability—the capacity to direct the work of others, and to organize and integrate their activities so that the goal of the work group can be attained—seems to be the most powerful trait for predicting leader effectiveness. According to Ghiselli, "it is the trait which plays the most important role, and stands out clearly and is apart from all of the other traits."

Next in importance is a cluster of five traits: the need for occupational achievement, intelligence, the need for self-actualization, self-assurance, and decisiveness. According to Ghiselli, "the traits in this cluster are just about equally important, and can be said to play a major role in managerial talent."

Below these, and fairly well spread out, are a number of traits that can be characterized as playing a minor role in managerial talent. These include the need for security, working-class affinity, initiative, need for high financial reward, need for power, maturity, and masculinity/femininity.

Trait Theory: Discussion Ghiselli found that six traits (supervisory ability, occupational achievement, intelligence, self-actualization need, self-assurance need, and decisiveness) characterized effective managers, and it is probably reasonable to assume that these traits characterize, more narrowly, effective leaders as well. These

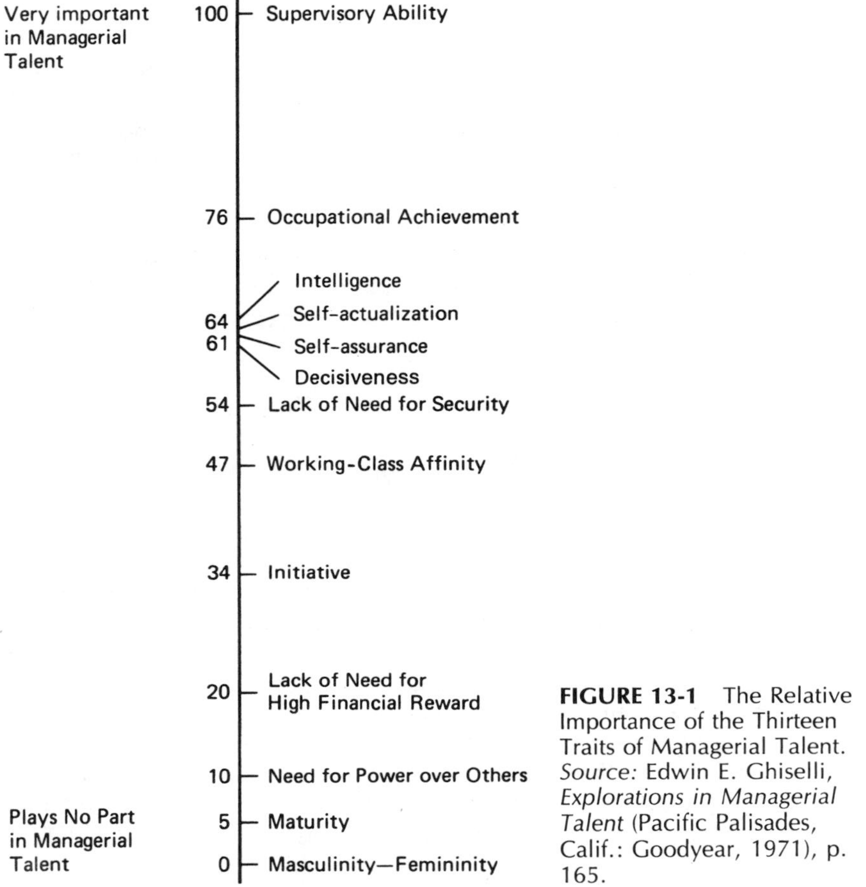

FIGURE 13-1 The Relative Importance of the Thirteen Traits of Managerial Talent. *Source:* Edwin E. Ghiselli, *Explorations in Managerial Talent* (Pacific Palisades, Calif.: Goodyear, 1971), p. 165.

findings suggest that trait theory is probably of some use in predicting leader effectiveness, but several caveats are in order. First, many studies of leader effectiveness have been carried out in formal organizations where screening processes have already acted to ensure that leaders are similar to each other. Furthermore, even though Ghiselli's research tapped a wide range of firms and subjects, more work is needed before we can generalize his findings in regard to other, specific organizations. In summary, the trait approach is useful, but at this point it is necessary to identify traits that predict leader effectiveness within specific organizations (perhaps using Ghiselli's findings as a starting point). These traits can then be used to screen leader candidates.

• Behavioral Theories: Styles of Leadership

Behavioral leadership theories focus on what leaders do and how they behave in carrying out their leadership functions, rather than on traits like intelligence or initiative. Trait theory attempts to explain leadership on the basis of what the leader *is*, behavioral theory on the basis of what the leader *does*.

Structuring and Considerate Styles *Initiating structure* and *consideration* are two frequently used descriptions of leader behavior. These two factors were developed out of research begun in 1945 at Ohio State University that was aimed at constructing an instrument for describing various leadership styles.[4] On the basis of conversations with various specialists, researchers developed a list of nine dimensions or categories of leadership behavior. Descriptive items were then written for each, and a final instrument, known as the Leader Behavior Description Questionnaire (LBDQ), was produced, which included a total of 150 of these descriptive items.

Findings: Leader Consideration Leader consideration is generally found to be positively related to employee satisfaction, but its effects on employee performance are still unclear. In one major study, Stogdill surveyed over 1,000 managers in 27 organizations, including those in the metals, chemicals, textiles, aircraft, and retail-store industries, and in government agencies. Although few relationships (between leadership and morale or performance) were found that characterized *all* the organizations of a given type, leader consideration was generally related to the employee's satisfaction, and especially to how satisfied he or she was with freedom on the job.[5] No consistent relation was found between consideration and employee performance.

Findings: Initiating Structure The effects of *initiating structure* on subordinate satisfaction or performance, however, are inconsistent. In their study, Fleishman and Harris found structure and grievance rates to be directly related, but *where consideration was high,* leader structure and grievances were unrelated. Most researchers have failed to find any consistent relation between initiating structure and satisfaction or performance.[6]

In summary, we will conclude that (1) leader consideration is positively related to employee satisfaction, although its effects on employee performance are unclear; and (2) one cannot generalize about the effects of initiating structure, except to say that its relation to employee satisfaction and performance may be positive, negative, or nonexistent, depending on the situation.[7]

Production-Centered and Employee-Centered Leadership Styles At about the same time that researchers at Ohio State were undertaking the construction of their LBDQ, a similar program was being instituted at the University of Michigan's

Survey Research Center.[8] This line of research led to the identification of two dimensions of leader behavior, which were called *employee orientation* and *production (job) orientation.* The former was described as behavior by a leader indicating that he views his employees as human beings of intrinsic importance and accepts their individuality and personal needs. Production orientation is behavior that stresses production and the technical aspects of the job and reflects an assumption that employees are simply means to an end.

This line of research was developed by Rensis Likert of the University of Michigan. Likert and his associates have carried out many studies to determine which leadership style appears most effective. He concludes:

> Supervisors with the best record of performance focus their primary attention on the human aspects of their subordinates' problems and on endeavoring to build effective work groups with high performance goals.[9]

Although Likert and his associates have claimed that the employee-centered leader is the most effective one, even their own data suggest that at times a production-centered one is best. For example, he has found a number of instances in which employee-centered leadership was associated with low productivity;[10] and in at least one instance, the production-centered supervisor had a high-producing unit.[11]

Close and General Styles of Leadership These styles of leadership were originally defined and studied by researchers at the University of Michigan.[12] They developed their leadership styles on the work previously carried out at the Survey Research Center. *Close supervision* was conceptualized as "one end of a continuum that describes the degree to which a supervisor specifies the roles of the subordinates and checks up to see that they comply with the specifications."[13] The *laissez-faire* leader, who takes a completely hands-off policy with his subordinates, would be at the other extreme, with the *general* leader somewhere in the middle of the continuum.

Most of the early research findings suggested that close leadership was associated with lower subordinate satisfaction. For example, Morse obtained data from female workers in a large metropolitan insurance firm and found that workers subjected to close supervision were usually less satisfied with the reasonableness of the supervisor's expectations and with the rules she enforced.[14] Similarly, Katz and Kahn reported finding a relation between closeness of supervision and aggressive feelings of workers in a tractor plant.[15] However, the results are far from definitive. Katz and his associates found no relation at all between close or general supervision and worker aggression.[16] In another study, researchers attempted to ascertain the effects of close versus general styles of leadership.[17] They found that close supervision was related to employee aggressiveness, but that the specific effects of close supervision depended largely on the self-esteem of the subordinate, with increases in aggressive feelings occurring only in those with low self-esteem.

• *Fiedler's Contingency Theory of Leadership*

Behavioral scientists have long recognized the importance of situational factors in explaining leader effectiveness. Stogdill, after reviewing a large number of leadership studies, concluded that the traits or skills required in a leader are largely determined by the situation in which he is to exercise leadership.[18] Similarly, as we have seen, no one style of leadership has been found to be universally effective—a fact that led Tannenbaum and Schmidt to conclude that "effective leadership depends on the leader, his followers, the situation, and interrelationships between them."[19]

The contingency model of leadership effectiveness grew out of a comprehensive program of research begun at the University of Illinois by Fred E. Fiedler in 1951. Although Fiedler's work has recently been subjected to some rather sharp criticism, he and his colleagues have answered many of their critics' questions, and the debate appears to be a continuing one.

The Theory Fiedler originally sought to determine whether a leader who was very lenient in evaluating his associates was more or less likely to have a high-producing group than the leader who was highly demanding and discriminating. At the core of this research program is the "esteem for the least preferred coworker," or LPC scale, a measure of leader orientation. The person who fills it out is asked to think of all the people with whom he has ever worked and to focus on the one person with whom he "had the most difficult time in getting a job done"—that is, his least-preferred co-worker. The rater is then asked to describe this person on a series of bipolar, 8-point, descriptive adjective scales whose extremes are labeled in the following fashion:

Pleasant . . . . Unpleasant
Intelligent . . . . Stupid

Although Fielder originally felt that the LPC was measuring a personality trait, some of his recent papers suggest that the LPC is actually measuring a style of leadership, ranging from considerate leadership (high LPC) to structuring leadership (low LPC).

At the base of Fiedler's theory are three situational dimensions that he feels influence and determine whether considerate or structuring leader styles are called for:

1 *Position power.* "The degree to which the position itself enables the leader to get his group members to comply with and accept his direction and leadership."
2 *Task structure.* How routine and predictable the work group's task is.
3 *Leader–member relations.* The extent to which the leader "gets along" with his men, and the extent to which they have confidence in him and are loyal to him.

Findings Fiedler claims to have found that "the appropriateness of the leadership style for maximizing group peformance is contingent upon the favorableness of the group-task situation."[20] As shown in Figure 13-2, Fiedler feels that where the situation is either favorable or unfavorable to the leader (where leader–member relations, task structure, and leader position power are either very high or very low), a more task-oriented, structuring leader is appropriate. On the other hand, in the mid-range, where these factors are more mixed and the task is not as clear-cut, a more considerate, relationship-oriented leader is appropriate. To explain these findings, Fiedler says:

> In the very favorable conditions in which the leader has power, informal backing, and a relatively well-structured task, the group is ready to be directed, and the group members expect to be told what to do. . . . In the relatively unfavorable situation, we would again expect that the task-oriented leader will be more effective than will the considerate leader who is concerned with interpersonal relations (the group will fall apart without the leader's active intervention and control). . . . In situations which are only moderately favorable (or moderately unfavorable) for the leader, a considerate, relationship-oriented attitude seems to be most effective. . . . Here the leader must provide a nonthreatening, permissive environment if members are to feel free to make suggestions and to contribute to discussions. . . .[21]

Criticisms The results of recent studies cast some doubt on the validity of Fiedler's findings and theory. Graen and his associates carried out laboratory experiments in which they obtained results strongly contradicting the Fiedler model.[22] Others have found that task structure seems to be the only important situational factor.[23] A number of writers, including Fiedler, have pointed out fundamental deficiencies in the contingency model.[24] For example, a situation of high position power in one study might be considered one of low position power in another.

Other criticisms attack the measure of leadership style, the LPC. Fiedler suggested that high LPC reflected a considerate, relationship-oriented leader and low LPC a task-oriented leader.[25] However, a number of studies in which a leader's style and behavior on the LPC were compared with the consideration and initiating-structure scales of the Ohio State LBDQ do not support this assertion.[26] Furthermore, it has been found that the LPC is not a very reliable scale; indeed, the same person may obtain significantly different LPC scores on different days.[27] This may result from some fundamental flaw in the scale, or it may occur because the characteristics themselves, measured by the LPC, vary with the task. Thus, Fiedler found that the high-LPC leader, as the situation becomes more threatening, tends to become both more considerate *and* more critical, task-oriented, and structuring.[28]

In summary, the Fiedler theory has generated a great deal of interest and research and has contributed to our knowledge of leader effectiveness. However, it has several flaws, and it is doubtful that the theory, by itself, can consistently predict leader effectiveness.[29] There is little doubt that other factors like the leader's super-

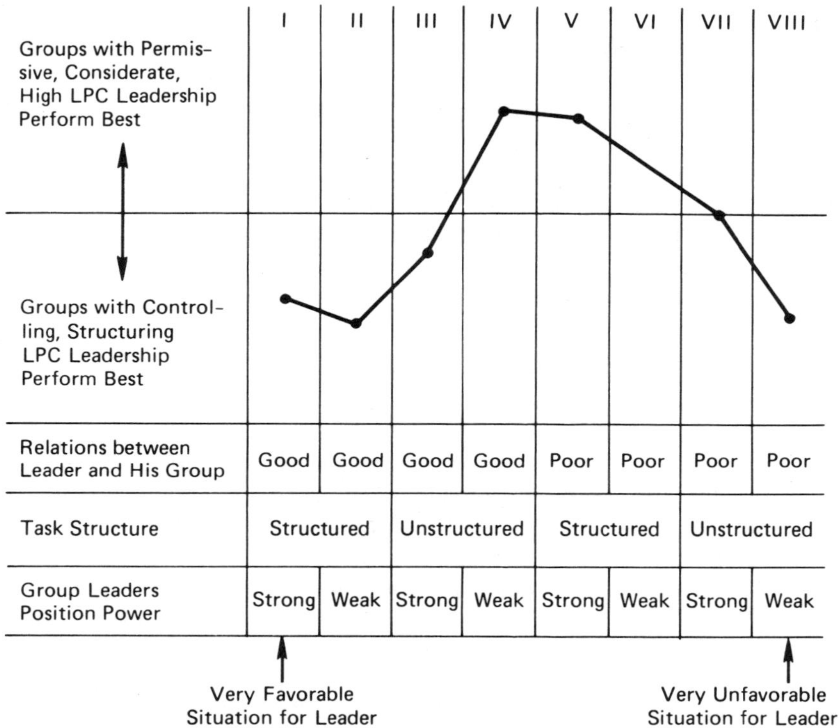

FIGURE 13-2 Fiedler's Findings on How Leadership Effectiveness Varies with the Situation. *Source:* Adapted from Frederick E. Fiedler, *A Theory of Leadership Effectiveness* (New York: McGraw-Hill, 1967), p. 146. Used by permission of McGraw-Hill Book Company.

visory ability and intelligence also influence his effectiveness; furthermore, the effects of *combinations* of considerate and structuring leadership must be considered.

LEADERSHIP FINDINGS AND ORGANIZATION THEORY

• The Functions of Leadership in Organization Theory

Writers have long pondered the role played by the leaders in organizations, and many theories of what the leader's functions are have been proposed. These range from purely technical functions like developing procedures and rules to more subjective functions like developing the culture of the firm. In keeping with the thrust of this book, we will focus on two main leadership functions, *providing structure* and *ensuring motivation and compliance.*

• *The Leader's "Structuring" Function*

Katz and Kahn have pointed out that no organization chart or set of rules and procedures can ever be totally complete, and where there are gaps, it is the leader's job to provide the necessary "incremental" structure, instructions, tools, and procedures.

This seems to suggest that a leader's structuring behavior might be more successful when there are such "gaps," and when he is thus *required* to clarify duties, provide instructions, and so forth. Perhaps, then, this is why styles like "initiating structure" have been found to be positively, negatively, and not related to employee satisfaction and performance.

The House Path-Goal Theory of Leadership Robert J. House has proposed a theory of leadership that helps explain the "situational" nature of the leader's structuring function. His theory states that the functions of a leader consist largely of increasing personal rewards for subordinates for goal attainment and of making the path to these rewards easier to follow—by clarifying it, reducing roadblocks and pitfalls, and increasing the opportunities for personal satisfaction en route. This theory is based on the expectancy theory of motivation as proposed by Vroom. Recall that the central concept of expectancy theory states that motivation is a function of both the person's ability to accomplish the task and his or her desire to do so.[30] House says that a leader can increase an employee's motivation by ensuring that the person has the ability to accomplish the task, and that the leader can do this by providing "structure" (in terms of instruction and so forth) when needed.

House's basic thesis is as follows. He says that ambiguous, uncertain situations have the potential for being frustrating and that, in such situations, the structure provided by the leader will be viewed as legitimate and satsifactory by subordinates. On the other hand, in routine situations, such as might be encountered on assembly-line tasks, the additional structure provided by a production-oriented leader might be viewed as illegitimate and redundant by the subordinates, who might therefore become dissatisfied. House's view of leader structure is therefore quite similar to Katz and Kahn's "incremental structure" view of the leader's functions.

House and his associates have carried out a number of studies to determine the usefulness of his model. One study found some modest support for his hypothesis,[31] but two others found that the effect of leader structure on employee satisfaction was influenced by a variety of factors, including how considerate the leader was and to what extent the subordinate disliked unstructured, ambiguous tasks.[32]

Others have found that "Expectancy Theory has the capacity to predict and explain leader behavior," a finding that provides some indirect support for the path-goal theory.[33] Evans found that a path-goal theory was more useful in predicting the behavior of subordinates who were more "rational."[34] Two researchers collected data from a total of 1,161 hospital employees, and their findings supported the path-goal theory as it applied to the relationship between leader behavior and subordinate satisfaction, but not as it applied to subordinate performance.[35]

In total, the findings suggest that this theory of leader effectiveness is useful. The ideas that the appropriate level of leader structure depends on how ambiguous the task is and that the necessary level of leader consideration varies with the intrinsic satisfaction of the task have both received support.

• *The Leader's Motivation/Compliance Function*

What can a leader do to ensure that subordinates carry out their tasks? House's path-goal theory aims at providing at least part of the answer: By structuring the task as needed, the leader increases the subordinates' ability to do the task and thus their motivation to do so.

Many other suggestions have been made concerning how a leader should behave in order to best ensure employee compliance. The classical theorists, for example, prescribed close supervision, the human-relations theorists supportive leadership, and Katz and Kahn participative leadership. Let us briefly review the "compliance" prescriptions of these theorists.

The Classicists' Prescription: Close Supervision In Chapter 2, we saw that when classicists like Fayol addressed the problem of motivation and compliance, they usually prescribed the use of sanctions, constant supervision, and a subordination of individual interests to those of the firm, rather than trying to make the two compatible. For example, about the only explicit statement Fayol makes in regard to using something other than sanctions or close supervision in motivating workers is his mention of managers "setting a good example," and also letting subordinates make more decisions in order to tap their initiative.

How effective is close supervision as a compliance tool? Most of the research on close supervision as a leadership style has focused on its effect on employee satisfaction, rather than performance. These findings (as we discussed above) suggest that closely supervised subordinates are less satisfied and more aggressive toward their leaders than are employees who are not closely supervised. In terms of *performance,* findings like those of Bell suggest that close supervision can increase compliance on routine tasks, but on nonroutine tasks a more general type of supervision is best.[36]

The Human-Relations Prescription: Supportive Leadership The essence of the human-relations movement that grew out of the Hawthorne studies was that leaders could increase productivity by increasing the morale of their employees.[37] The human-relations solution for ensuring compliance therefore calls for leaders to be more considerate and supportive, on the assumption that this will increase satisfaction and thereby increase performance.

Katz and Kahn's Prescription: Participative Leadership Katz and Kahn say that "the most consistent and thoroughly demonstrated difference between successful and unsuccessful leadership . . . has to do with the distribution or sharing of the leadership function."[38] They say that participative leadership results in more-motivated employees because employees "have greater feelings of commitment to decisions in which they have a part, or in which they act autonomously."[39]

• *Leadership and Culture: Establishing the Values of the Enterprise*

There is a related "motivational" function that leaders must carry out, one not often mentioned by behavioral scientists but very necessary nonetheless: The leader, more than any other person in the firm, must promulgate the basic values, beliefs, and expectations that will drive the organization; in other words, he or she must mold the company's *culture*.

Chester Barnard is one who stressed this aspect of the leader's job. He says, for example, that "executive responsibility, then, is that capacity of leaders by which, reflecting attitudes, ideals, hopes, derived largely from without themselves, they are compelled to bind the wills of men to the accomplishment of purposes beyond their immediate ends, beyond their times."[40]

The Mercer Study A recent study involving 305 chief executive officers in a cross-section of industries left no doubt about the role leaders play in forming company culture.[41] For example, 97 percent agreed that "strong corporate values—the beliefs and attitudes the company and its employees and managers live by—are important to our company's success," and 94 percent agreed that the organization's corporate values "are shaped by top management." How does top management shape the corporate culture? Not so much through written edicts and rules as though unwritten, "softer" means like setting examples.

In the Mercer study, for instance, the question was asked, "Which of the following would you say are the most important ways your company reinforces its corporate values? (1 representing the most important, 2 the next most important, etc.)"

The results are presented in Table 13-1. Notice that "examples set by top management" is by far the most important way in which the company reinforces its corporate values. One hundred eighty-three (out of 305) of the chief executives ranked this method first, and a total of 249 ranked it first, second, or third. Less than half the executives believed that hard means of communication, like corporate communication practices and customer-relation policies, are important ways that companies use for reinforcing their corporate values.

Leadership, Culture, and Excellence Peters and Waterman similarly conclude that "clarifying the value system and breathing life into it are the greatest contributions a leader can make."[42] They contend that the leader does this by example and

TABLE 13-1 Which of the Following Would You Say Are the Most Important Ways Your Company Reinforces Its Corporate Values? (#1 representing the most important, #2 the next most important, etc.)

Rank Order		*Ranked #1*	*Ranked #2*	*Ranked #3*	*Aggregate Ranking*
1	Example set by top management	183	33	33	249
2	Example set by middle management	10	83	29	122
3	Corporate communications practices	29	39	50	118
4	Customer relations policies	31	42	37	110
5	Compensation/benefit policies	12	45	45	102
6	Company relations with the community	13	29	34	76
7	Employee performance reviews	23	19	37	72
8	Employee relations with unions	5	3	17	25
9	Other	3	4	5	12

by creating symbols, rituals, and myths. "What is tricky about values," says one consultant,

> . . . is that often we cannot see ourselves objectively. If management says "the customer is always right," then punishes an employee for continuing to serve a customer a few minutes after closing time, we would say that the real value there is not "the customer is first"; the real value—and the one being expressed to the employee in that situation—is "store hours first, the customer second."[43]

The excellent companies, says Peters and Waterman, were therefore "vast tapestries" of stories and legends, all of which served to reinforce how the owners of the business (and their predecessors) had on various occasions engaged in actions that typified the company's basic values—stories about how a salesman drove through the night to deliver a needed product to a customer, or how a project team worked nonstop for a month to get a new product out ahead of the competition.

In summary, one of the leader's main roles in organization theory is to set the tone of the organization—to establish its culture in terms of the basic values and beliefs the firm and its employees will live by. Once the culture is institutionalized, it provides a guiding beacon for all employees, so that wherever they are and whatever they do, they will be able to use the values that they have internalized to guide them, with values like "quality first" making it quite clear to them what behaviors their firms expect of them.

Poorer-performing companies can have strong cultures too. But in such companies, the basic values will more often stress company politics and basic beliefs like, "Above all else, protect your position in the organization," and, "Don't share important information with others." Other less-effective firms try to substitute various financial goals and budgets for values like customer satisfaction and product quality. In these companies, then, top management makes it clear through word and deed what values it really cherishes, and these are the values that the employees adopt as well.[44]

ROLE OF CULTURE IN ORGANIZATION DESIGN

• Culture and Innovation

Innovative, organic "adhocracies"—with their shifting job assignments, lack of formalization, and flexible formal chain of command—have what might at first appear to be an almost insurmountable problem: namely, how to maintain control over a widespread group of employees, none of whom fits into a neat organizational niche. In a mechanistic organization, close supervision, formal policies and rules, and strict adherence to the chain of command help ensure that top management effectively controls employees. In adhocracies, though, these kinds of formal, imposed control devices are minimal, so the problem is to ensure that employees use their initiative—be motivated to use self-control and make decisions that are best not just for themselves, but for the company as well.

In trying to elicit such self-control, employers use, as we have seen, many techniques, including participation, socialization, and rewards (as explained in the preceding chapter). But they also do more: "Without exception," Peters and Waterman note, "the dominance and coherence of culture proved to be an essential quality of the excellent companies."[45] It is, in fact, a tight set of commonly shared values—a company culture—that helps ensure that in every work-related decision they make, employees understand what the company wants them to do, and do it. Thus, the typical young manager or engineer at Hewlett-Packard or Apple Computer doesn't have to be forced to work late or to go that extra mile to get out the new product. They do it in part because the culture of their firm demands it and because they have accepted the sorts of values that their culture reflects.

Apple Computer, Inc., is an example. Its success is due to "more than just having the right product at the right time. It is also the result of the company's homespun, entrepreneurial corporate culture."[46] According to one report, Steven Jobs, the company's chairman and cofounder, brought to Apple "a blunt style of communication, a dislike of hierarchy and rules, and a bias in favor of a small madcap group of brilliant guys producing something in a corner on a very tight deadline."[47] At Apple, this philosophy translates into a lack of bureaucracy and rules, and an informal attire that "reflects an underlying attitude that gives far more weight in doing an interesting, important job than to possessing the trappings of power."[48] In turn, Apple has been able to attract a band of highly motivated young professionals whose enthusiasm is typified by the T-shirts worn by the members of one project team, "working 90 hours a week and loving every minute of it." At Apple, most experts agree, the company's culture—its basic values—have had a major influence on the company's success.

CULTURE AND ORGANIZATION DESIGN

The shared values that underlie a company's culture help determine how its organization structure can and will be designed. This is because these values serve as a framework, one that helps provide each employee with direction and a sense of purpose, even without a rule book or chain of command; this role is illustrated by the findings of Burns and Stalker, Ouchi, and Peters and Waterman.

• Burns and Stalker: The Organic Organization

Burns and Stalker were among the first experts to stress the importance of company culture, and their findings help to show the role this concept plays in organization design.[49] Organic—highly innovative—organizations, say Burns and Stalker, to achieve coordinated action in the absence of formal rules and chain of command must:

> . . . rely on the development of a common culture, of a dependable constant system of shared beliefs about the common interest of the working community and about the standards and criteria used in it to judge achievement, individual contributions, expertise, and other matters by which a person or a combination of people are evaluated. A system of shared beliefs of this kind is expressed and visible in a code of conduct, a way of dealing with other people. This code of conduct is, in fact, the first sign to the outsider of the presence of a management system appropriate to changing conditions.[50]

Furthermore, "The distinctive feature of the organic system is the pervasiveness of the working organization as an institution. In concrete terms, this makes itself felt in a preparedness to combine with others in serving the general aims of the concern."[51]

• Ouchi and Theory Z

William Ouchi's studies of Japanese corporations help to illustrate the techniques these companies use to maintain their high productivity. The excellent Japanese companies, he says, subscribe to an approach he calls "Theory Z," an approach characterized by a concern for people, participative decision making, and lifetime employment. Above all, though, there is a set of values—a culture—that all employees share.

Ouchi points out that the basic mechanism of control in a Japanese company is embodied in these shared values.[52] Those who grasp and become committed to these values and beliefs, says Ouchi,

> . . . can deduce from the general statement an almost limitless number of specific rules or targets to suit the changing conditions. Moreover, the specific rules or targets will be consistent between individuals. Two individuals who both understand the underlying theory will derive the same specific rule to deal with a particular situation. Thus the theory provides both control over the ways people respond to problems and coordination between them, so solutions will match with one another.[53]

• *Peters and Waterman: The Excellent Company*

Like Burns and Stalker and Ouchi, Peters and Waterman also found that company culture played a central part in their "excellent" companies. Specifically, they found that the existence of such a culture reduced the need for policy manuals, organization charts, and detailed procedures and rules, since in these companies, "people way down the line know what they are supposed to do in most situations because the handful of guiding values is crystal clear."[54] In these companies, the culture—the basic values and beliefs all employees share, like, "IBM means service," and, "It's the customer that counts"—provide a constant, ever-present guiding framework. But within this framework, employees are able to improvise—for instance, by doing whatever they can to see that the customer is serviced.

This results in what Peters and Waterman call the *loose/tight phenomenon*, the "co-existence of firm central direction and maximum individual autonomy. . . ."[55] Autonomy, say Peters and Waterman, "is a product of discipline. The discipline (a few shared values) provides the framework. It gives people confidence (to experiment, for instance) stemming from stable expectations about really what counts."[56] So in a company like 3M, control is in some respects "loose"; for instance, small groups of employees are always meeting and developing projects with little supervision from above. Yet this apparently loose approach is effective here (and at other such firms) because it is matched by a "tight" commitment to shared values that encourage regular communication, customer-oriented problem solving, and engineering excellence.

• *Summary*

Company culture affects organization design. A strong positive culture—a set of values and beliefs such as, "The customer is always right," and "Quality counts"—provides the basic touchstone that enables innovative organizations (adhocracies) to organize loosely, with few detailed procedures and rules and a flexible chain of command. Perhaps mechanistic organizations, with their tight formal control systems, can get by without such a culture. But in the innovative organization, a set of shared values is essential, since they provide the framework within which flexibility and creativity can flourish.

CREATING THE COMPANY CULTURE

Although creating the company culture is, as we have seen, largely a leadership issue, there are also other concrete actions management can take to foster employee commitment to and identification with its fundamental beliefs and values.

• *Values and Culture: The Mercer Study*

Defining corporate culture as "an expression of the combined influence of the company's basic beliefs, values, expectations and typical patterns of action," the study by William M. Mercer, Inc., a management consulting firm, helps to illustrate some of the actions managers take to foster employees' commitment to and identification with the company's fundamental beliefs and values.[57] The findings of this study can be summarized as follows.

Extent to Which Companies Have Addressed Corporate Values According to the survey, a majority of employers say their companies have addressed the issue of corporate values, with over 40 percent reporting that the issue has received "a great deal" of attention in their firms, and a total of 86 percent reporting that they had addressed the issue of corporate values at least "to some extent." Only 13 percent said that corporate values have been addressed "hardly at all."

Question: Broadly speaking, to what extent would you say your company has addressed the issue of corporate values?

A great deal	41%
To some extent	45%
Hardly at all	13%
Not sure	1%

Origin of Corporate Values The chief executives (the subjects of this survey) say that their companies' corporate values originate from themselves and from their top management far more often then they do from "all levels of the company." In total, 51 percent reported that their organizations' corporate values stem at least in part from the corporate founder, 93 percent that they "flow principally from the chief executive," and 94 percent that their organization's corporate values "are shared by top management."

Importance of Corporate Values to Success Nearly all the employers also agreed that corporate values are important to their own companies' success. That is, virtually all agreed that "strong corporate values are important to our company's success"; 92 percent disagreed with the statement, "The importance of corporate values has been overstated."

Most Important Corporate Values In this study, the executives were presented with a list of ten values and asked to rank them from most important (1) to least important (10). The results were as follows:

Rank	*Values*
1	Performance
2	Fairness
3	Competitiveness
4	Team spirit
5	Corporate family spirit
6	Innovation
7	Entrepreneurship
8	Individual achievement
9	Loyalty
10	Tradition

Compensation and Corporate Values Well over half—63 percent—of the chief executives reported that their companies' compensation and benefit practices were designed to reinforce corporate values. Cash and noncash incentives were clearly the most important financial tools used to reinforce corporate values, and 77 percent of the executives anticipated that "pay for performance" in one form or another would become a more important tool for reinforcing values in the future.

• *The Predominant Values*

We can get another perspective on creating the company culture by looking more closely at the predominant values that the excellent companies espouse. In its study, the Mercer Company found that "performance" was ranked most important, and "fairness," "competitiveness," and "team spirit" were ranked second, third, and fourth. But here the executives had to choose from a closed list of values. In an open-ended question ("How do you anticipate that your company's values might change in the light of emerging business conditions over the next five years?"), most cited as emerging values an *increased emphasis on performance, entrepreneurship, teamwork,* and *competitive spirit and innovation.*

Interestingly, the Peters and Waterman study (which focused only on innovative, "excellent" companies) unearthed a somewhat different set of dominant beliefs and values:

1 A belief in being "the best"
2 A belief in the importance of the details of execution, the nuts and bolts of doing the job well

3 A belief in the importance of people as individuals
4 A belief in superior quality and service
5 A belief that most members of the organization should be innovators, and in its corollary, the willingness to support failure
6 A belief in the importance of informality to enhance communication
7 Explicit belief in and recognition of the importance of economic growth and profits

These then are the values that underlie the cultures in the most innovative of companies.

• *Creating the Company Culture: Examples*

Introduction Of the many factors that combine to create a company's culture, Peters and Waterman concluded that three were dominant: *leadership, myths,* and *reinforcement*. The *leader* decides what the dominant values will be. Then, through the examples he or she sets and the decisions he or she makes (the subordinates hired, the compensation system, and so on), the leader creates a set of shared values, beliefs, and expectations—a company culture.

Next, *stories and myths* usually play an important role in spreading the president's gospel. As Peters and Waterman point out, values are usually not transmitted through written rules; instead, they are diffused by softer means, specifically through "stories, myths, legends, and metaphors."[58] Thus in the excellent companies, stories, legends, and myths abound that support the company's basic beliefs; for example, "innovation" stories abound at 3M, and "quality" stories at Johnson & Johnson. Partly because these stories exist, everyone at these firms knows what is important. Thus, at Johnson & Johnson, every employee from chairman of the board to assembly worker knows that product quality is essential, and at Hewlett-Packard, all employees know they must be innovative.

Finally, *positive reinforcement* and rewards also play a big role in company culture. In excellent companies, great pains are taken to reinforce those employee actions that support the company's basic values. At Tupperware, rallies are held every Monday night; each person marches up on stage, in the reverse order of last week's sales, while their peers celebrate them by rising and joining in applause; almost everyone, according to Peters and Waterman, receives a pin or badge. In most excellent companies, then, a multitude of rewards (ranging from commissions to badges, pins, and applause for a job well done) are used to reinforce the "right" behavior, where "right" means behavior that is consistent with the basic values of the firm. We can close this chapter with examples of how two famous companies have developed two rather different cultures.[59]

Competitive Culture at Pepsi-Cola, Inc. Not too long ago, Pepsi-Cola, Inc., was known as a sleepy little New York–based bottler, one whose lame slogan was, "Twice as much for a nickel, too." Since the 1950s, however, its management has moved decisively and aggressively to make PepsiCo the number 1 marketer of soft drinks. Its efforts illustrate how far a management will go to mold the company culture to the sort required for achieving the company's goals.

To top management at PepsiCo, creating an aggressive and competitive culture is an important part of achieving leadership in the soft-drink industry. In a multitude of ways, therefore, PepsiCo management endeavors to create the sort of competitive culture it believes is required. Severe pressure is put on the managers to show continual improvement in market share, for instance, and careers often ride on tenths of a market-share point, according to one source. "Creative tension" is nurtured at the company by constantly moving managers to new jobs. Because of this tactic, people work long hours and engage in political maneuvering just to keep their jobs from being "reorganized out from under them."

Like Marines, PepsiCo executives are also expected to be physically fit. The company employs physical-fitness instructors out of headquarters, and one former executive claims that to get ahead in the company, a manager must stay in shape. The company also encourages one-on-one sports, as well as interdepartmental games like soccer and basketball.

The pervasive culture of competition at PepsiCo has the effect of screening out less-competitive managers, of course. But the ones that remain have adopted the competitive values to the extent that top management believes they are required if the company is to become number 1.

Supportive Culture at J.C. Penney At retailer J.C. Penney, the foundations of the company's culture were laid more than 70 years ago in what founder James Cash Penney called "The Penney Idea." Penney's idea—the fundamental values on which he built his empire—can be summarized as follows:

1 To serve the public, as nearly as we can, to its complete satisfaction
2 To expect, for the service we render, a fair remuneration and not all the profit the traffic will bear
3 To do all in our power to pack the customer's dollar full of value, quality, and satisfaction
4 To continue to train ourselves and our associates so that the service we give will be more and more intelligently performed
5 To improve constantly the human factor in our business
6 To reward men and women in our organization through participation in what the business produces
7 To test our policy and methods by asking, "Does it square with what is right and just?"

At Penney's, these values boil down to treating everyone the company deals with fairly, and nowhere is this more apparent than in the firm's treatment of its employees. "Everyone is treated as an individual," notes one former executive, and another says that Penney's has "an openness in the organization that many large companies don't seem to achieve."[60] For its part, Penney's does its best to cultivate this culture; for example, it always tries to find new jobs for marginal employees rather than firing them. This has resulted in a tremendously loyal staff, who are always more willing than most retail employees to do that "little bit extra" to satisfy the customer.

SUMMARY

We began by discussing several theories of leadership. Trait-theory research findings show that several traits seem to distinguish leaders from nonleaders in many situations. With respect to behavioral or style theories of leadership, the findings indicate that considerate leaders tend to have more satisfied employees but that production-oriented or structuring leaders often have higher-performing employees (albeit less-satisfied ones).

Fiedler contends that the leader has to fit his or her style to the situation. He says the leader's position power, leader–member relations, and the task structure combine to determine whether a people- or task-oriented leader will be most effective.

In general, the leader has two functions in organization theory: providing direction and ensuring compliance. With respect to the latter, leaders must also *establish values.* The values themselves largely constitute the *culture* of the firm. Organic organizations in particular must have values and a culture that helps the firm maintain control; essential values here include a belief in being the best and in superior quality and service.

DISCUSSION QUESTIONS

1 How would you define the phrase, "failed to exert leadership"?
2 Explain each of the functions of leadership in organization theory.
3 Explain the leader's role in developing an organization's culture.
4 Explain the role of culture in organization design.
5 Describe the specific steps you would take to develop a company culture.

FOOTNOTES

[1]Ruth Nutting, "Characteristics of Leadership," *School and Society,* Vol. 18 (1923), 387–90; C. Bird, *Social Psychology* (New York: Appleton-Century, 1940); W.O. Jenkins, "A Review of Leadership Studies with Particular References to Military Problems," *Psychological Bulletin,* 44 (1947), 54–79; R.M. Stogdill, "Personal Factors Associated with Leadership: A Survey of Literature," *Journal of Psychology,*

25 (1948), 35–71; R.D. Mann, "A Review of the Relationships between Personality and Performance in Small Groups," *Psychological Bulletin,* 56 (1959), 241–70; T.O. Jacobs, *Leadership and Exchange in Formal Organiations* (Alexandria, Va.: Human Resources Research Organizations, 1970); and R.M. Stogdill, *Handbook of Leadership* (New York: Free Press, 1974).

[2]Walter J. Palmer, "Management Effectiveness as a Function of Personality Traits of the Manager," *Personnel Psychology,* Vol. 27 (1974), 283–95; see also Avis Johnson, Fred Luthans, and Harry Hennessey, "The Role of Locus of Control in Leader Influence Behavior," *Personnel Psychology,* Vol. 37, No. 1 (Spring 1984), 61–76; and Robert Rice, Debra Instone, and Jerome Adams, "Leader Sex, Leader Success, and Leadership Process: Two Field Studies," *Journal of Applied Psychology,* Vol. 69, No. 1 (February 1984), 12–31.

[3]Information here is based on Edwin E. Ghiselli, *Explorations in Managerial Talent* (Pacific Palisades, Calif.: Goodyear, 1971).

[4]R.M. Stogdill and A.E. Coons, eds., *Leader Behavior: Its Description and Measure* (Columbus: Bureau of Business Research, Ohio State University, 1957).

[5]Ralph Stogdill, *Managers, Employees, Organizations* (Columbus: Bureau of Business Research, Ohio State University, 1965).

[6]L.L. Cummings and W.E. Scott, *Readings in Organizational Behavior and Human Performance* (Homewood, Ill.: Richard D. Irwin, 1969), p. 462.

[7]See Chester Schriesheim, Robert J. House, and Steven Kerr, "Leader Initiating Structure: A Reconciliation of Discrepant Research Results and Some Empirical Tests," *Organizational Behavior and Human Performance,* Vol. 15, No. 2 (April 1976); and M.N. Petty and Gorden J. Lee, Jr., "Moderating Effects of Sex of Supervisor and Subordinate on Relationships between Supervisory Behavior and Subordinate Satisfaction," *Journal of Applied Psychology,* Vol. 60, No. 5 (October 1975).

[8]Rensis Likert, *New Patterns of Management* (New York: McGraw-Hill, 1961).

[9]*Ibid.,* p. 7.

[10]*Ibid.,* Chap. 2.

[11]This suggests that other situational factors may influence the appropriateness of various leadership styles. See, for example, Henry Sims, Jr., and Charles Manz, "Observing Leader Verbal Behavior: Toward Reciprocal Determinism in Leadership Theory," *Journal of Applied Psychology,* Vol. 69, No. 2 (May 1984), 222–32; Madelyn Heilman, Harvey Hornstein, Jack Cage, and Judy Herschlag, "Reactions to Prescribe Leader Behavior as a Function of a Role Perspective: The Case of the Vroom-Yetton Model," *Journal of Applied Psychology,* Vol. 69, No. 1 (February 1984), 50–60.

[12]D. Katz and R.L. Kahn, "Leadership Practices in Relation to Productivity and Morale," in *Group Dynamics,* eds. D. Cartwright and A. Zander (Evanston, Ill.: Row, Peterson, 1960), pp. 554–70.

[13]Robert C. Day and Robert L. Hamblin, "Some Effects of Close and Punitive Styles of Leadership," *American Journal of Sociology,* Vol. 69 (1964), 499–510.

[14]Nancy Morse, *Satisfactions in the White Collar Job* (Ann Arbor: Survey Research Center, University of Michigan, 1953).

[15]Katz and Kahn, "Leadership Practices."

[16]Daniel Katz and Robert Kahn, "Some Recent Findings in Human Relations Research in Industry," in *Readings in Social Psychology,* eds. G.E. Swanson et al. (New York: Holt and Company, 1950), pp. 650–52.

[17]Day and Hamblin, "Some Effects of Close and Punitive Styles of Leadership."

[18]Ralph Stogdill, "Personal Factors Associated with Leadership."

[19]Robert Tannenbaum and Warren Schmidt, "How to Choose a Leadership Pattern," *Harvard Business Review,* Vol. 36 (March–April 1958), 95–101.

[20]Frederick E. Fiedler, *A Theory of Leadership Effectiveness* (New York: McGraw-Hill, 1967), p. 147.

[21]*Ibid.*

[22]G. Graen, K. Alvares, J.B. Orris, and J.A. Martella, "Contingency Model of Leadership Effectiveness: Antecedent and Evidential Results," *Psychological Bulletin,* Vol. 74 (1970), 285–96. See also Graen, Orris, and Alvares, "Contingency Model of Leadership Effectiveness: Some Experimental Results," *Journal of Applied Psychology,* Vol. 55 (1971), 196–201.

[23]J.P. Campbell, M.D. Dunnette, E.E. Lawler, and K.E. Weick, *Managerial Behavior, Performance and Effectiveness* (New York: McGraw-Hill, 1970).

[24]Terence Mitchell, Anthony Biglan, Gerald Oncken, and Frederick Fiedler, "The Contingency Model: Criticisms and Suggestions," *Academy of Management Journal,* Vol. 13, No. 3 (September 1970), 253–67.

[25]Fiedler, *A Theory of Leadership Effectiveness,* p. 45.

[26]For example, see Martin M. Chemers and Robert W. Rice, "A Theoretical and Empirical Examination of Fiedler's Contingency Model of Leadership Effectiveness," in *Contingency Approaches to Leadership,* eds. J.G. Hunt and L. Larson (Carbondale: Southern Illinois University Press, 1974), pp. 91–123.

[27]Mitchell et al, "The Contingency Model"; John Kennedy, Jr., "Middle LPC Leaders and the Contingency Model of Leadership Effectiveness," *Organization Behavior and Human Performance,* Vol. 30, No. 1 (August 1982), 1–14; Claude L. Graeff, "The Situational Leadership Theory: A Critical View," *The Academy of Management Review,* Vol. 8, No. 2 (April 1983), 285–91.

[28]The literature on the LPC is voluminous. In addition to the studies mentioned, see, for example, Martin G. Evans, "A Leader's Ability to Differentiate the Subordinate's Performance," *Personnel Psychology,* Vol. 26 (1973), 385–95; Joe E. Stinson and Lane Tracy, "Some Disturbing Characteristics of the LPC Score," *Personnel Psychology,* Vol. 27 (1974), 477–85; Martin G. Evans and Jerry Dermer, "What Does the Least Preferred Co-worker Scale Really Measure?" *Journal of Applied Psychology,* Vol. 59, No. 2 (1974), 202–6; Lars Larson and Kendrith M. Rowland, "Leadership Style and Cognitive Complexity," *Academy of Management Journal,* Vol. 17, No. 1 (March 1974), 37–45; Marshall Sashkin, F. Carter Taylor, and Rama C. Tripathi, "An Analysis of Situational Moderating Effects on the Relationship between Least Effective Co-worker and Other Psychological Measures," *Journal of Applied Psychology,* Vol. 59, No. 6 (1974), 731–40; Robert Rice and Martin Chemers, "Personality and Situational Determinants of Leader Behavior," *Journal of Applied Psychology,* Vol. 60, No. 1 (February 1975); and William Fox, "Reliabilities, Means, and Standard Deviations, for LPC Scales: Instrument Refinement," *Academy of Management Journal,* Vol. 19, No. 3 (September 1976), 450–61.

[29]This is my conclusion based in the research findings obtained up to this point. For a good summary of the opposing view, see Chemers and Rice, "A Theoretical and Empirical Examination of Fiedler's Contingency Model"; also Steven Green, Delbert Nebeker, and M. Allen Boni, "Personality and Situational Effects on Leader Behavior," *Academy of Management Journal,* Vol. 19, No. 2 (June 1976), 184; Paul Bons and Fred Fiedler, "Changes in Organizational Leadership and the Behavior of Relationship and Task Oriented Leaders," *Administrative Science Quarterly,* Vol. 21, No. 3; and Robert P. Vecchio, "An Empirical Examination of the Validity of Fiedler's Model of Leadership Effectiveness," *Organizational Behavior and Human Performance,* Vol. 19, No. 1 (June 1977), 180–206.

[30]J.W. Atkinson, ed., *Motives in Fantasy, Action, and Society* (New York: Van Nostrand Reinhold, 1958).

[31]Robert J. House, "A Path-Goal Theory of Leader Effectiveness," *Administrative Science Quarterly,* Vol. 16 (1971), 321–38.

[32]Robert J. House and Gary Dessler, "A Path-Goal Theory of Leadership: Some Post-Hoc and A-Priori Tests," in Hunt and Larson, eds., *Contingency Approaches to Leadership;* and Gary Dessler, "Investigation of a Path-Goal Theory of Leadership," unpublished doctoral dissertation, 1973, City University of New York.

[33]Robert M. Nebeker and Terence B. Mitchell, "Leader Behavior: An Expectancy Theory Approach," *Organizational Behavior and Human Performance,* Vol. 11 (1974), 355–67.

[34]Martin G. Evans, "Extensions of a Path-Goal Theory of Motivation," *Journal of Applied Psychology,* Vol. 59, No. 2 (1974), 172–78.

[35]Andrew D. Szilagyi and Henry P. Sims, Jr., "An Exploration of the Path-Goal Theory of Leadership in a Health-Care Facility," *Academy of Management Journal,* Vol. 17, No. 4 (December 1974), 622–34. See also Gary Dessler and Enzo Valenzi, "Initiation of Structure and Subordinate Satisfaction: A Path Analysis of Path-Goal Theory," *Academy of Management Journal,* June 1977.

[36]Gerald D. Bell, "The Influence of Technological Components of Work upon Management Control," *Journal of the Academy of Management,* Vol. 8, No. 2 (1965), 127–32. See also Gerald D. Bell,

"Predictability of Work Demands and Professionalization as Determinants of Workers' Discretion," *Journal of the Academy of Management,* Vol. 9, No. 1 (March 1966), 20–28.

[37]Victor Vroom, *Work and Motivation* (New York: John Wiley, 1964); Cummings and Scott, *Readings in Organizational Behavior,* Chap. 3.

[38]Katz and Kahn, *The Social Psychology of Organizations,* p. 332.

[39]*Ibid.*

[40]Chester Barnard, The Functions of the Executive (Cambridge, Mass.: Harvard University Press, 1938), p. 283.

[41]This is based on "Employer Attitudes Toward Compensation Change and Corporate Values," William M. Mercer, Inc., 1211 Avenue of the Americas, New York, NY 10036, 1983.

[42]Thomas Peters and Robert Waterman, Jr., *In Search of Excellence* (New York: Harper & Row, 1982), p. 291.

[43]Karin Allport, quoted in Commerce Clearing House, *Human Resources Management: Ideas and Trends in Personnel,* December 30, 1983, p. 203.

[44]Peters and Waterman, *In Search of Excellence,* pp. 72–3.

[45]*Ibid.,* p. 75.

[46]"Can Apple's Corporate Counterculture Survive?" *Business Week,* January 16, 1984, p. 82. For a research study that supports the notion that organizational culture can influence innovation, see Augustus Abdey and John Dickson, "RND Work Climate and Innovation in Semi-Conductors," *Academy of Management Journal,* Vol. 26, No. 2 (June 1983), 362–68. These researchers concluded that "the work climate of innovative RND subsystems is characterized, first, by a reward system that recognizes and equitably rewards excellent performance and, second, by a willingness to take risks and experiment with innovative ideas and proposals."

[47]*Ibid.*

[48]*Ibid.*

[49]Specifically, Burns and Stalker define nonprogrammed decision making this way: "In nonprogrammed decisions the alternatives of choice are not given in advance, but must be discovered by a rational process of searching." Tom Burns and G.M. Stalker, *The Management of Innovation* (London: Tavistock, 1961), p. 116.

[50]*Ibid.,* p. 119.

[51]*Ibid.,* p. 25.

[52]William Ouchi, *Theory Z* (New York: Avon, 1982), p. 35. Note that not everyone agrees with Ouchi's Theory Z perspective. See, for example, Jeremiah Sullivan, "A Critique of Theory Z," *The Academy of Management Review,* Vol. 8, No. 1 (January 1983), 132–42.

[53]Ouchi, *Theory Z,* p. 35.

[54]Peters and Waterman, *In Search of Excellence,* p. 76. For a contrasting view, see Daniel Carroll, "A Disappointing Search for Excellence," *Harvard Business Review,* No. 6 (November–December 1983), 78–87.

[55]Peters and Waterman, *In Search of Excellence,* p. 318.

[56]*Ibid.,* p. 322.

[57]"Employer Attitudes," p. 1.

[58]Peters and Waterman, *In Search of Excellence,* p. 282. For explanations regarding the measurement and etiology of organizational culture, see, for example, Benjamin Schneider and Arnon Reichers, "On the Etiology of Climates," *Personnel Psychology,* Vol. 36, No. 1 (Spring 1983), 19–40; Maryan Schall, "A Communication-Rules Approach to Organizational Culture," *Administrative Science Quarterly,* Vol. 28, No. 4 (December 1983), 577–81; and Allan Wilkins and William Ouchi, "Efficient Cultures: Exploring the Relationship between Culture and Organizational Performance," *Administrative Science Quarterly,* Vol. 28 (September 1983), 468–81.

[59]Corporate Culture: The Hard to Change Values that Spell Success or Failure," *Business Week,* October 27, 1980, pp. 154–60.

[60]"Corporate Culture: The Hard to Change Values," p. 158.

CASE FOR CHAPTER 13
THE CORPORATE CULTURE AT IBM: HOW IT REINFORCES STRATEGY*

Susan Chace

When Thomas J. Watson, Sr., died in 1956, some might have thought the IBM spirit of the stiff white collar was destined to die with him. But indications are that the founder's legacy of decorum to International Business Machines Corporation still burns bright. Consider the way an IBM man on a witness stand in San Francisco the other day replied when questioned about an after-hours encounter with a competitor:

Q. "All of you were in the hot tub with the Qyx district manager?"
A. "The party adjourned to the hot tub, yes. Fully clothed, I might add."

That an IBMer invited to a California hot tub should fear that propriety demanded a swimsuit wouldn't surprise many people who have ever worked for the giant company. For, besides its great success with computers, IBM has a reputation in the corporate world for another standout trait: an almost proprietary concern with its employees' behavior, appearances, and attitudes.

What this means to employees is a lot of rules. And these rules, from broad, unwritten ones calling for "tasteful" dress to specific ones setting salemen's quotas, draw their force at IBM from another legacy of the founder: the value placed on loyalty. Mr. Watson believed that joining IBM was an act calling for absolute fidelity to the company in matters big and small.

• *Esprit de Corps*

And just in case an IBM employee isn't a self-starter in the loyalty department, the company has a training regimen geared to instilling it. In brief, this consists of supervising new trainees closely, grading them, repeatedly setting new goals for them, and rewarding them amply for achievement. Suffused in work and pressure to perform, employees often develop a camaraderie, an espirt de corps.

What it all amounts to is a kind of IBM culture, a set of attitudes and approaches shared to a greater or lesser degree by IBMers everywhere. This culture, as gleaned from talks with former as well as current employees, is so pervasive that, as one nine-year (former) employee puts it, leaving the company "was like emigrating."

*Reprinted by permission of *The Wall Street Journal,* Susan Chace is a staff reporter for *The Wall Street Journal.*

To George McQuilken, who left IBM to found his own company, Spartacus Computers, Inc., "the hardest part about being gone was the first few times I tried to make a decision on my own about anything, like what hotel to stay in, or who I wanted to hire."

For those who don't leave, IBM returns the loyalty. It prides itself on being able to reward those who follow its code and meet its expectations with success and security for life. The most valued of these employees are sometimes known within the world of IBM as "sorries"—people the computer company would especially be sorry to lose.

• *Divorce Court*

Virginia Rulon-Miller was once an IBM sorry. A self-described "lifer" at IBM, she got into trouble when her interpretation of IBM's largely unwritten rules clashed with that of her superiors. Unlike most separations from IBM—quiet resignations to pursue other interets—hers was a messy divorce that ended up in court.

Gina Rulon-Miller joined IBM as a receptionist in Philadelphia in 1967 at age 19. After 12 years, five moves, and numerous stints at IBM training schools, she became a marketing manager, in San Francisco, supervising salesmen who sold fancy typewriters and other IBM equipment to such companies as Pacific Telephone & Telegraph and Standard Oil of California.

On a June day in 1979, Miss Rulon-Miller abruptly turned in her keys and her plastic identification card and fled IBM, after her boss confronted her with her relationship with Matt Blum, once an IBM supersalesman and at that time a manager at a competing office-products company. In an emotionally charged interview, her boss said she was being given a nonmanagement post at the same salary. To her, steeped in IBM's get-ahead culture, this was tantamount to being released, and she said so. She sued, charging wrongful dismissal.

• *Inherent Conflict?*

At the trial, IBM conceded that Miss Rulon-Miller was a loyal employee with an outstanding record and that there was no indication she had ever passed company secrets to her boyfriend. But, it argued, the mere existence of a relationship between business rivals was a conflict. "She clearly cared very much for Matt Blum," IBM said. "And she clearly cared for his success. And if that is the case, she had a conflict of interest."

Miss Rulon-Miller's lawyers argued that what really worried IBM was the possibility she would defect to Matt's company, Exxon Corporation's Qyx, encouraging other IBM salesmen to defect as well. The jury sided with her, saying in effect that the company couldn't dicate any employee's off-the-job behavior. If awarded her $300,000 in compensatory and punitive damages. IBM has said it would appeal, but it won't discuss the case with a reporter.

Even though Miss Rulon-Miller has since spent two years wandering around the country, taking four different jobs and losing her boyfriend in the process, she has a typical IBMer's nostalgia for the company she left. She says the company "created me professionally," and her harshest comment about it is, "I'm not as positive about IBM as I was before."

How does IBM inspire positive feelings even in former employees who take it to court? Largely by following Mr. Watson's basic formula: systematic goading toward excellence, combined with constant supervision and frequent rewards. Its more flamboyant aspects are gone; probably no IBMer will ever again be feted as Otto E. Braimayer, an early 40-year employee, once was, with a formal dinner featuring 40 waiters carrying in 40 cakes. But management-by-merit-badge techniques continue to keep employees arriving at 7:30 A.M. to attend meetings before their regular duties begin.

Every year an employee gets a Performance Plan, a written set of very specific goals. The manager neatly lays out the employee's responsibilities. Meeting or exceeding Performance Plan goals leads to promotions and raises.

Tight discipline is also enforced by near-constant observation and grading. At sales training schools, trainees know what can happen if they fail to leave their rooms "broom clean": They may be called back to try again, or their manager may be charged for the cleanup. Vigilance even extends to the evening hours. Instructors take notice of who is burning the midnight oil preparing for the next day's product-demonstration tests and who seems to have a crush on whom. "Report cards" grade trainees on matters ranging from product knowledge and presentations to attitude—enthusiasm, confidence, sincerity, cooperation, work with others, desire to learn.

• *Rising Quotas*

One way to stand out at training school is to finish work in time to help slower classmates. Those who help the most may be elected class officers. Then they may get choice sales territories when they return to the field.

Once out in the field, salesmen get a quota of IBM machines to be placed in their territories. Each year the quota is raised or the territory cut or both, partly to test employees' ingenuity in selling more products to the same people. Customers need to be sold hard; IBM takes back the commission if a customer decides to return rented equipment after a year or so.

The Performance Plan is law. Extensions to deadlines for handing in reports are given for good reasons only. (A broken leg will do.) Employees get an overall rating based on the various points in their plans. A "1" means exceeding expectations; a "5" is unsatisfactory.

Achievement is followed by immediate rewards. Insiders say the most cherished of these isn't money. It's having your name and quota on the bulletin board with a notation saying "100%." It's having a party thrown for you at your branch because you have satisfied a prickly customer. It's a steady flow of letters of commendation. Says one ex-IBMer: "If you burp the right way, they send you a certificate."

• *Thank-You Notes*

Gina Rulon-Miller was a "1" who burped the right way. Her file overflowed with notes. "Dear Gina, thank you . . . for the excellent job you did in setting up our case studies at your branch last month" or "for helping to make this business show a success." Or, "Your performance in purchase and new equipment placements has been tremendous." Congratulations "for qualifying for your third 100% club. . . . May the force be with you."

The notes and the quotes, the training and the praise are very effective. "People work their brains out," says Miss Rulon-Miller's brother Todd, an IBM veteran who now works for an American Express Company unit. The results please IBM, too. Asked whether company officials ever wonder if IBM has too many rules, a spokesman replies: "IBM has an adequate number of rules. We think they are proper and necessary. But we always try to challenge bureaucracy, so that any time we felt a rule was extraneous or unnecessary, we would seek to eliminate it."

The hard work that the IBM atmosphere inspires has another effect, Todd Rulon-Miller believes. "A close clique forms from the pressure everyone feels," he says. "The first thing they want to do at night is go out and have drinks with each other. Then they start blending business and social life. They rent cabins in Tahoe together, buy a sailboat, join a softball team, play golf."

When a member of the clique leaves the office, he may want to keep up his IBM-based social life. So it was that Matt Blum, the IBM salesman, even after his defection to Exxon was playing third base for a softball team of IBMers the night an IBM man showed up dressed as a big typing ball from an IBM Selectric typewriter to cheer the team up. Mr. Blum shared beer and golf with his IBM buddies. He braved San Francisco Bay in a communal sailboat. And he even invited the (clothed) IBMers into his hot tub.

• *Rapid Rise*

Meanwhile, IBM offered Miss Rulon-Miller a management job. She accepted it enthusiastically, even though it meant temporarily lower pay. In quick succession she got a $4,000 raise, joined a group of top IBM salespeople for a week's celebration in Bermuda, and pressured an IBMer who knew the intricacies of Qyx machines to talk to her people at 7:30 A.M. so they would know what they were up against.

Then one day Wayne Fyvie, another IBMer, spotted Miss Rulon-Miller with Mr. Blum. Mary Hrize, also of IBM's San Francisco office, began to worry that Mr. Blum might snoop in Miss Rulon-Miller's briefcase and discover information that would help Qyx and hurt IBM. And Philip Callahan, Miss Rulon-Miller's boss, who was under pressure to stem a tide of salesman defections, hastily told her she was losing her management position.

In California State Supreme Court in San Francisco last December, it became clear that IBM didn't have written rules about the propriety either of golf games with competitors' employees or of close personal relationships with them—to say nothing of hot-tub parties. The company officials who testified couldn't agree about whether moving Miss Rulon-Miller out of management was a disciplinary act, or about how it squared with IBM's code of "respect for the individual." One IBM loyalist said the switch was merely a way to accommodate her personal relationship by removing her from a potential source of conflicts.

The jurors didn't buy that, concluding that IBM had acted with "oppression or actual malice" in its dealing with Miss Rulon-Miller. But their verdict didn't do much to clarify the company's encompassing but unwritten code of behavior, a code that pervades the life of every IBM professional. One former IBMer, reflecting on his years at corporate headquarters in Armonk, New York, describes the way that atmosphere affected him: "In my 15 years there," he says, "I never lost the feeling that I was breaking a rule. But I never knew what the rule was."

Questions

1 Name some specific ways in which IBM absorbs new employees into its corporate culture.
2 List the basic elements (such as loyalty) that you think characterize IBM's culture.
3 What do you think are the advantages and disadvantages of all the rules IBM makes its employees adhere to?

CASE FOR PART III (Chapters 10—13)
THE DON ROSS COMPANY

As his plane sped home to Atlanta from New York, Don Ross stared out the window and wondered what to do next. The companies he had established in New York, Atlanta, and Miami were all failing and his banks were clamoring to be paid. A mortgage payment was three weeks overdue on the 50 acres of land he had bought in New York State for building town homes, while in Miami the ice cream store he had built was losing a $1,000 a week. And, in Atlanta his pride and joy—his ornamental ironworks company—was being sued by disgruntled clients who claimed he wasn't providing the products he had promised.

Don Ross was 28 years old when he moved with his wife and children to Atlanta seven years ago. He had been in the home improvement business with his father in New York, and when he arrived in Atlanta he decided to go into a similar business. After moving his family into a condominium apartment (he moved to Atlanta with about $50,000 cash), he incorporated with the intention of selling wrought iron gates, railings, and window guards in the Atlanta area. He spoke with several ironworks manufacturers who agreed to supply him with the finished products, and he then began placing newspaper ads to attract customers.

At first he got only three or four leads per week, but within several months 50 to 60 leads per week were coming into his office (which was the spare bedroom in his apartment). He was soon earning well over $30,000 a year and in some respects had what some might consider the perfect business: He had no overhead to speak of, no payroll to meet, his suppliers installed all the railings for him, and he could come and go as he pleased without being locked into a 9 to 5 routine. He could have increased his sales considerably either by increasing his advertising, or by hiring another salesperson.

Don decided, however, that he'd never be as successful as he would have liked by simply acting as the middleman between the ironworks suppliers and the customers. He therefore decided to set up his own manufacturing and installing operations.

He rented a small warehouse and hired two experienced iron workers and two others that he could train to install his products. He also bought the necessary iron working machines and tools. This situation was satisfactory for several months, but sales were soon so good that he had to increase the size of his manufacturing and installing operations. He needed more workers and more machinery and tools. Most of all, however, he first needed more space.

He decided (being am ambitious fellow) that it was foolish for him to continue renting space and that the best thing to do was to buy a warehouse. He found what he considered to be a good buy on some warehouse space which, in fact, contained not only a warehouse big enough for his own business, but several connecting rows of warehouses that he could rent out. He bought these with a bank mortgage, purchased (on a time payment basis) the extra machinery he needed, and hired the additional workers. By this time, of course, he was so involved in trying to rent his extra warehouse space, negotiating loans for his equipment, and continuing to sell his products that he didn't have much time to check the references of his new workers, which he said "would have been just a waste of time anyway." He personally supervised all his employees, paying them on a straight-salary basis.

His sales continued to increase, since there was a housing boom at the time, and Don soon needed three more trucks to transport his goods to the job sites. He decided to purchase these, rather than rent them. His thinking in this case was much the same as it had been when he decided to purchase the warehouse: Why split his profits with anyone else?

Also about this time, Don decided to diversify into two new business ventures. With the money that was rolling in from his ironworks business, he purchased land in upper New York State on which he planned to build town homes that city bound "yuppies" could use as vacation retreats. Being an impetuous fellow he did not check very carefully into the intricacies of developing the land but simply jumped at the opportunity to buy it for twenty percent down, with the rest financed by the seller. He hired a local contractor to begin the process of developing the land and in particular to bulldoze it and begin acquiring the necessary permits and zoning variances so he could build the town homes.

At about the same time he decided to invest in an ice cream store in Miami, Florida. Since he wasn't about to share his profits with a franchisor he came up with his own name (Don's Ice Cream) and opened his doors next to a 5-theater movie house. All the while the profits from his ironworks business kept rolling in, since he still directly supervised his ironworks employees, including those who built the products in the factory and the teams that did the actual installation.

As what Don liked to refer to jokingly as his mini-conglomerate began to grow, though, he found he simply couldn't devote any time at all to continue supervising the employees at his ironworks firm. He became what he always swore he would never become, an absentee owner, one who had to rely almost entirely on the good judgment and best intentions of his managers.

And therein lay the problem, because Don was really not very good at choosing managers. He liked to refer to himself as a "bottom line" man and, therefore, perpetually hired the least expensive people he could find.

His problems multiplied. In the ironworks firm he would come in some days and find employees strolling around in back of the factory, smoking, having obviously not worked at all that day. After going through four managers he finally had a good one, but after 6 months on the job the fellow quit to open his own ironworks business and took two of Don's best employees with him. Don was devastated.

At about this time, everything started going wrong. Don thought that he could greatly increase ironworks sales by providing his customers with bank financing. He considered accepting credit cards and letting Visa and Mastercard do the financing for him. He felt, however, that he would be needlessly splitting his profits with a credit card company and that, as he put it, "Sears Roebuck has gotten rich by financing their customers themselves." He therefore arranged to countersign a series of bank loans to ironworks customers. He soon found that he had to spend more and more of his time overseeing the manufacturing operation, getting credit from banks, and renting his warehouses, and sales began to slide. While he tried to get other managers he found himself increasingly ensnared in the day-to-day details of running his ironworks factory, while at the same time trying to keep an eye on his New York and Miami businesses. He found it increasingly difficult to control the installation crews that were out in the field, and customers began complaining about shoddy workmanship: Many refused to pay. Since Don had financed these customers through his business, he was soon short of cash and found himself spending too much time in Small Claims Court trying to collect from his customers.

As Atlanta moved into a construction slump Don's business headed downhill rapidly. Tenants moved out of his warehouses, and he found none to replace them. Sales dropped to 30 percent of their previous levels, and he couldn't make the necessary payments on his warehouses, trucks, or machinery. He had to lay off many of his employees and was slow in paying others. Some threatened physical violence against him and his family. Some of his less violent employees reported him to the Occupational Safety and Health Administration for safety reasons, and he received \$5,000 in fines which he could not pay. He stumbled gamely on, with enormous expenses and diminishing sales.

In New York, the problem grew increasingly worrysome. He had to reduce by half the number of town homes he planned to build, since he couldn't get the zoning variance he desired. His contractor in New York was little help: As he told Don, "Look, I am just an employee and you can't expect me to knock my brains out when you won't even give me a raise." Don was afraid to fire him, though, because he still knew more about the details of the needed rezoning, sewer work, and so forth than anyone else.

The profits at his ice cream store also began to, well, melt. He had opened the store with a big advertising campaign and the store had opened with a "bang." He had clowns in front with balloons, and he gave away free ice cream cones to children; in the first two weeks he made an operating profit of over \$4,000.

Things worked fine, in fact, as long as he was around to keep his eye on the store. As he became dragged into the day-to-day details of his Atlanta business, though, he had to let his employees and store managers run the ice cream store. He made an unexpected trip there to speak to his manager one day and was shocked to find the store filthy and one of his employees sitting on a bench outside while several customers were leaving the store in disgust. Perhaps more bothersome was the fact that his sales revenue was no longer consistent with the amount of ice cream he was buying. He was suffering from what is euphemistically known in retailing as "shrinkage," which means that someone in his store was stealing from him. Either free ice cream cones were being given out, or, more likely, someone was not ringing up sales and was instead pocketing the money.

Don didn't know what to do. Everywhere he turned he was under the gun: His creditors were after him for payment on the land; he was losing thousands on his ice cream store because of sloppy management and theft; and his pride and joy, his ironworks business was failing too. He just did not know what to do, or where to turn.

• *Epilog*

Don held out for another six months, but his expenses were so high that he could no longer stay in business. The ironworks declared bankruptcy three years ago and Don was heard to remark that he couldn't figure out how the other ironworks suppliers stayed in business, although from their advertising they obviously did. He was forced to sell his ice cream store at a loss but was thankful to recoup at least part of his investment, although it wasn't much. His creditors in New York foreclosed on his property: He lost his entire deposit as well as the tens of thousands of dollars he had already spent on developing the land and building roads. Having personally signed for most of the loans on his businesses, he was forced to sell his condominium and move his family to a rental apartment in a slightly run down part of town. This was rough on the parents but even rougher on the children who had to move to a new school district in the middle of the year.

About six months after going out of business, Don was explaining to a friend what sort of business he'd like to get into, considering the harrowing experience he'd just been through. The perfect business said Don would require little or no labor, and customers would pay cash. Furthermore, said Don, there wouldn't be much overhead so a downturn in demand wouldn't affect his firm too adversely. "But, Don," said his friend, "don't you realize that that's pretty much the business you had when you first moved to Atlanta several years ago? You sold the ironworks out of your house, placed small ads, and let your suppliers worry about controlling their employees. You had the perfect business: you just didn't know it."

Discussion Questions

1. What is Don's main problem? Specifically, if you were Don's consultant what would you explain to him before he goes into business again?
2. In the last few chapters we discussed several techniques for ensuring compliance, in other words for ensuring that employees carry out the tasks they are assigned. The techniques included the Scanlon plan, commissions, job enrichment, and socialization. Based upon your knowledge of the motivation and compliance techniques presented in these last four chapters, develop a proposal for each of Don's businesses that could have helped him to motivate his employees to treat his businesses more like their own.

Group Processes and Organization Theory

OVERVIEW

In this fourth part of the book we turn our attention to the topics of organizational groups, intergroup relations, and organizational change.

Groups play a crucial role in organization theory for two reasons, and the purpose of this chapter is to explain the reasons. First, groups affect how their members define their self-interest, and therefore their compliance; as Elton Mayo says:

> If a number of individuals work together to achieve a common purpose, a harmony of interests will develop among them to which individual self-interest will be subordinated. This is a very different doctrine from the claim that individual self-interest is the solitary human motive.[1]

Second, groups influence (and are influenced by) organization structure. Groups, we will see, can add to or detract from the formal organization structure, by filling in the "gaps" in an inadequate structure or short-circuiting an adequate one. Therefore, because groups do exert a powerful influence on both structure and worker compliance, we discuss group processes and their effects on these factors in this chapter.

The outline of this chapter is as follows:

A The effects of groups on individuals: the Hawthorne studies
- **1** Introduction
- **2** The illumination studies

3 The relay assembly test room studies
4 The interviewing program
5 The bank wiring room studies
6 The researchers' theory and conclusions
7 Criticisms of the Hawthorne studies
8 Contributions of the Hawthorne studies: summary

B Theory of group influence
1 The Homans Model
2 Factors that influence group cohesiveness

C Group norms and member compliance
1 What are norms?
2 How groups influence perception and behavior

D Groups and organization structure
1 The organization as a structure of groups
2 How organization structure affects group functioning
3 How groups affect organization structure: the informal organization
4 Team-based organization designs

THE EFFECTS OF GROUPS ON INDIVIDUALS: THE HAWTHORNE STUDIES

The experiments at the Hawthorne works of Western Electric are of tremendous importance in organization theory, for several reasons. First, it was during these studies that organization theorists first became fully cognizant of how employees' work groups, attitudes, and needs affected their motivation and behavior. In addition, the Hawthorne studies remain to this day a classic, one that Blum and Naylor call "the most significant research program undertaken to show the enormous complexity of the problem of production in relation to efficiency." As a work of research, these studies are far from perfect. Still, they provide a fascinating example of the scientific method applied to organizational questions, of the need for hypothesis testing and controlled experimentation, and of the need to maintain an open, inquisitive mind while in the pursuit of truth through science. For these reasons, we will discuss these studies at some length.[2]

• *Introduction*

During the spring of 1927, a series of experimental studies was begun at the Hawthorne works of the Western Electric Company in Chicago. The results of these studies literally changed the course of organization theory, in that they introduced the notion that a person's work group (and attitudes) are important determinants of the person's motivation and compliance. The four Hawthorne studies we will focus on are:

- The illumination studies
- The relay assembly test room studies
- The interviewing program
- The bank wiring observation room studies

• *The Illumination Studies*

Although the illumination studies are often viewed as part of the Hawthorne studies, they actually preceded the main studies and lasted from November 1924 through April 1927. Their importance lies in the fact that their findings provided the stimulus for the later Hawthorne studies.

The illumination experiments began as a straightforward industrial engineering study to determine the relation between level of illumination and worker productivity. The organization theory that prevailed at that time assumed economic rationality on the part of workers and generally assumed that they were "motivated" solely by external factors like pay and the physical conditions of their surroundings. In line with these assumptions, the illumination researchers expected that productivity would increase with increasing levels of illumination, and they set out to determine what the optimum level of illumination was.

Very Taylor-like

There were actually three separate illumination experiments, each aimed at clarifying the somewhat startling findings of the preceding one. In the first experiment, workers in three Western Electric departments were exposed to various levels of illumination. The researchers found that although productivity increased with greater illumination, it did not do so in direct proportion to the increase in illumination. Of more importance, however, production efficiency "did not always fall off with the decrease in illumination."[3]

In the second illumination experiment, the researchers attempted to carry out more of a "controlled" study. Only one of the original three departments was chosen for this study, and its workers were divided into two groups, "each group composed of an equal number of operators of about the same experience":

> One group, called the "test group," was to work under variable illumination intensities; the other group, called the "control group," was to work under an intensity of illumination as nearly constant as possible. The groups were located in different buildings in order to reduce the influence of any spirit of competition. . . . It was thought that by this method the differences in production efficiency could be related directly to differences in illumination intensity.[4]

In this experiment, as in the first, productivity did not vary in direct proportion to level of illumination. Instead:

> This test resulted in very appreciable production increases in both groups and of almost identical magnitude. The difference in efficiency of the two groups was so small as to be less than the probable error of the values. Consequently, we were again unable to determine what definite part of the improvement in performance should be ascribed to improved illumination.[5]

The researchers thought these findings might have resulted from the fact that both groups were exposed to both artificial and natural light and that the latter varied during the day. A third illumination experiment was therefore carried out. Now the control group was provided with a constant level of illumination, and the test group with a carefully controlled series of changes in illumination level. The productivity of the test and control groups both *increased* as illumination *decreased* until the productivity of the control group finally leveled off when the level of illumination in their enclosure became constant. However, the productivity of the test group continued to *increase* with *decreases* in illumination, until the illumination finally got so low that workers protested, "saying that they were hardly able to see what they were doing."[6]

These experiments failed in their basic purpose—determining the relationship between effort and illumination—but probably had a more profound effect on the evolution of organization theory than any other experiments before or since, because they raised important questions that were seized upon by a group of perceptive and open-minded scientists. The illumination experiments suggested, for example, that light was only one factor, and apparently a minor one, among many that affect employee output. And they also suggested that more carefully controlled experiments had to be used in further experimentation with workers. Based upon these implications, the researchers began what have become known as the Hawthorne studies, a series of experiments aimed at determining—under carefully controlled conditions—what factors influence productivity and behavior.

• The Relay Assembly Test Room Studies

From the findings of the illumination studies, "it was decided to isolate a small group of workers in a separate room somewhat removed from the regular working force, where their behavior could be studied carefully and systematically."[7] Researchers felt that this procedure would enable them to study the factors influencing worker productivity while controlling the number of variables "which inevitably creep into a large group situation." For example, "such influences as the amount of work ahead of the operators, changes in type of work, the introduction of inexperienced operators, and the shifting of personnel because of fluctuation in work schedules could be largely eliminated."[8] Experimental conditions could be imposed with less chance of having them disrupted by departmental routines, and finally, "in a small group there was the possibility of establishing a feeling of mutual confidence between investigators and operators, so that the reactions of the operators would not be distorted by general mistrust."[9]

The Job The job finally chosen involved the assembly of telephone relays, an operation performed by women, which consisted of putting together about 35 small parts in an assembly fixture and securing them by four machine screws. The various parts were put in front of the operators in small bins. The selection of the parts was done by the operator, using both hands, and required considerable skill in picking them up and placing them in the pile-up in front of her. The complete operation required about one minute, and the task was therefore highly repetitive; each operator assembled about 500 relays each day. A photo of the relay assembly test room operators, taken during the Hawthorne experiment, is presented in Figure 14-1.

The Subjects The subjects for the relay assembly test room were chosen as follows: Two experienced operators who were known to be friendly with each other were asked to participate in the test and to choose the remaining members of the group. The group selected consisted of six women—five to do the actual assembly operation and a sixth to act as layout operator. The latter's duties "were of a minor supervisory character and consisted of assigning work and procuring parts for each assembler." This arrangement of having a layout operator serve the assemblers was identical with that in the regular relay assembly department, "with the exception that quite frequently in the regular department one layout operator served six or seven girls instead of five as in the test room."

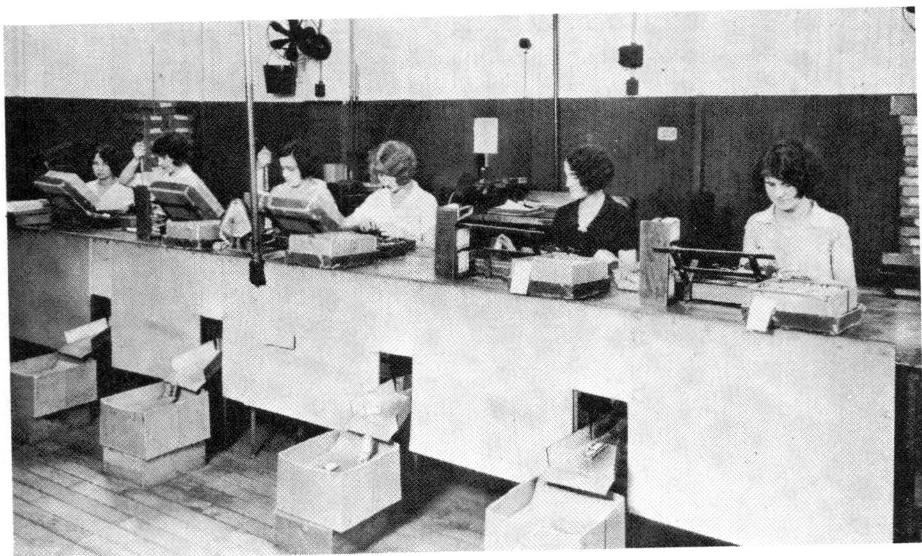

FIGURE 14-1 Photograph of Relay Assembly Test Room. *Source:* F.J. Roethlisberger et al., *Management and the Worker* (Cambridge, Mass.: Harvard University Press, 1939), © 1939, 1967 by the President and Fellows of Harvard College.

In addition, there was a "test room observer" whose function was to keep accurate records of all that happened and to create and maintain a friendly atmosphere in the room. The test room occupied about 560 square feet of floor space in a corner of one of the regular shop rooms and was enclosed by a board partition that extended partway to the ceiling.

The Purpose The relay assembly test room studies have also been called the rest-pause experiments, since they aimed at determining, under carefully controlled conditions, the effects of rest pauses and fatigue on employee productivity. (The topic of fatigue was a controversial one in industrial circles at the time, and the illumination studies had cast some doubt on the accuracy of preceding findings on the effects of rest pauses.) The original relay assembly test room studies therefore set out to answer six questions:

- Do employees actually get tired out?
- Are rest pauses desirable?
- Is a shorter working day desirable?
- What are the attitudes of employees toward their work and toward the company?
- What is the effect of changing the type of working equipment?
- Why does production fall off in the afternoon?

The Study As summarized in Table 14-1, the relay assembly test was organized into 13 periods, each period representing one in which a specific condition of work was enforced. Periods 1–3 constituted an introductory phase, the purpose of which was preparation for experimentation. During period 1, the operators were still in the regular department; period 2 permitted them time to become familiar with their new test room surroundings; and in period 3, a change in wage payment was introduced, "a necessary step before the experiment proper could begin." The researchers' description of their findings during the remaining periods paints a fascinating picture of the problems and potential of organizational research, and of the application of observation, generalization, and experimentation to studying organizational phenomena.

Periods 4–7 In periods 4–7, experiments concerned entirely with rest periods were carried out. In period 4, the investigators began with short rest periods of five minutes each, one during the morning and the other in the afternoon. Because the researchers wanted to place these rest periods where they would be most advantageous, a meeting was called at the superintendent's office. The women were shown their output curves, and the low and high points in the day were pointed out. "When asked at what times they would like to have their rests, they unanimously voted in favor of 10 o'clock in the morning and 2 o'clock in the afternoon." Accordingly, the investigators agreed to institute the rest pauses at these times. (As we will see, the Hawthorne experiments were filled with such attempts by the researchers to maintain the friendly, cooperative attitudes of their subjects.)

TABLE 14-1 Schedule of Test Periods: Relay Assembly Test Room

Period Number	Special Feature	Dates Included	Duration in Weeks	*Times of Rest Pauses* A.M.	P.M.
1	In regular department	4-25-27 to 5-10-27	Approx. 2	None	
2	Introduction to test room	5-10-27 to 6-11-27	5	None	
3	Special group rate	6-13-27 to 8-6-27	8	None	
4	Two 5-min. rests	8-8-27 to 9-10-27	5	10:00	2:00
5	Two 10-min. rests	9-12-27 to 10-8-27	4	10:00	2:00
6	Six 5-min. rests	10-10-27 to 11-5-27	4	8:45, 10:00, 11:20	2:00, 3:15, 4:30
7	15-min. A.M. lunch and 10-min. P.M. rest	11-7-27 to 1-21-28	11	9:30	2:30
8	Same as 7 but 4:30 stop	1-23-28 to 3-10-28	7	9:30	2:30
9	Same as 7 but 4:00 stop	3-12-28 to 4-7-28	4	9:30	2:30
10	Same as 7	4-9-28 to 6-30-28	12	9:30	2:30
11	Same as 7 but Sat. A.M. off	7-2-28 to 9-1-28	9	9:30	2:30
12	Same as 3 (no lunch or rests)	9-3-28 to 11-24-28	12	None	
13	Same as 7 but operators furnish own lunch, company furnishes beverage	11-26-28 to 6-29-29	31	9:30	2:30

Source: F.J. Roethlisberger and William Dickson, *Management and the Worker* (Cambridge, Mass.: Harvard University Press, 1939), © 1939, 1967 by the President and Fellows of Harvard College.

Based on the generally favorable attitude of the operators to these rest pauses, ten-minute rests were instituted in period 5. Here again (as had been the case in period 4), the operators' output rate increased, so that even with the "nonproductive" rest pauses, they were producing—and earning—more than they had previously.

In period 6, the operators were again asked for their opinions concerning the length of the rest periods to be introduced. However, although they expressed a preference for two 15-minute breaks, a series of six 5-minute pauses was instituted. The operators clearly disliked this new situation and expressed their dislike by returning late from work breaks, laughing and talking on the job, and generally acting "troublesome and rebellious."

In period 7, there was a 15-minute rest in the morning and a ten-minute rest in the afternoon. This period was chiefly notable for the emergence of a "personnel problem," in which two of the operators became increasingly hostile toward the researchers. For their part, the researchers sought to keep employee attitudes a "constant" so as to better assess effects of factors like rest pauses on worker activity. Given the researchers' attempts to maintain high employee morale, the attitudes of the two hostile women was viewed as a failure for which the women themselves were held responsible.[10]

The results and conclusions of this portion of the relay assembly test room studies may be summarized as follows: Productivity (average hourly output per week) generally increased for periods 1 through 7, and the researchers concluded that this was due to the introduction of rest pauses. A second, more tentative conclusion was that the operators' attitudes toward one another and toward the group influenced their productivity. (For example, there was a tendency for the output of the two uncooperative operators to vary similarly.) Very soon, this latter conclusion, concerning the effects of employee attitudes and relations on productivity, was to become the pivotal finding of the Hawthorne studies, as the researchers—through a process of observation, generalization, and experimentation—attempted to develop and test new hypotheses for explaining their findings. As the researchers point out:

> In looking back it is clear that two essentially different sorts of changes occurred in the first seven periods of the experiment. There were those changes introduced by the investigators in the form of experimental conditions; these were well noted and recorded. There was another type of change, however, of which the investigators were not so consciously aware. This was manifested in two ways: first, in a gradual change in social interrelations among the operators themselves, which displayed itself in the form of new group loyalties and solidarities; secondly, in a change in the relation between the operators and their supervisors. The test room authorities had taken steps to obtain the girls' cooperation and loyalty and to relieve them of anxieties and apprehensions. From this attempt to set the proper conditions for the experiment, there rose indirectly a change in human relations which came to be of great significance in the next stage of the experiment, when it became necessary to seek a new hypothesis to explain certain unexpected results of the inquiry.[11]

Periods 8–13 Periods 8 through 13 focused on the effects on productivity of shorter working days and weeks. During period 8, the two uncooperative operators were replaced with two new workers who were chosen by the foreman. Also in this period, the working day was shortened by stopping work at 4:30 instead of 5:00, and the rest periods (a 15-minute break in the morning and a 10-minute afternoon break) were continued.

Although the workday had now been shortened considerably, output had still not diminished, and the investigators therefore used period 9 "to find out what would happen to output if the working day was shortened still further, and at what point in this process the total weekly output would begin to fall off."[12] After the approval of the operators was obtained, the daily working hours were therefore reduced by an additional half hour. Although the workers were in favor of this shorter working day, it apparently proved too drastic a cut, and total weekly output and earnings dropped.

In period 10, investigators began a process aimed at lengthening the work week and reducing rest pauses to what they were when the experiments began. At the end of period 10, the situation was identical with period 7—a full 48-hour workweek, with a morning rest of 15 minutes and an afternoon rest of 10 minutes. The operators now complained of fatigue and tiredness, a complaint they had not expressed in period 7.

In period 11, the operators worked only five days, with Saturday mornings off (they normally worked five and a half days). Rest pauses as in period 7 were continued, and weekly working hours were reduced to about 42 hours. The return to the original hours of work (48 hours per week with no rest pauses) commenced on September 3, 1928, during period 12. In preparation for the elimination of rest pauses, the operators were told that it was "just another experimental feature" and that as usual they should work at a "natural pace." It was apparent from the operators' comments, however, that they strongly disliked the return to the full 48-hour week.

In period 13, rest pauses were reinstated and again were 15 minutes in the morning and 10 minutes in the afternoon. This period lasted for seven months, the longest interval for any of the experimental periods, and its length reflected a number of important changes that were noted during it. For example, there was a significant increase in group morale, and this manifested itself in a high degree of group cooperation. Apparently partly as a result of the return of the rest pauses, the operators exhibited new pride in their work and worked hard to beat their former output records. More important, they worked hard to help each other:

> If one girl wished to slack off, another girl, generally her neighbor alongside, would agree to speed up. Instead of antagonistic competition, there was concerted effort toward a common goal.[13]

Researchers' Hypotheses to Explain Major Findings Generally speaking, output had risen regardless of breaks or work hours, and the researchers developed five hypotheses to explain this puzzling upward trend. First, they hypothesized that *im-*

proved conditions and work methods in the test room might account for their findings, but they concluded that the improvements were not significant and that in some respects, working conditions were not as good as in the plant at large. They next hypothesized that the rise in output may have resulted from the *reduction in fatigue* that the rest pauses provided, but concluded (based on later experiments) that fatigue was never a significant problem in the test room. They hypothesized that the rest pauses had been effective not so much in reducing fatigue as in *reducing the monotony* of work; they were never able to discount this hypothesis, pointing out that "monotony in work is primarily a state of mind and cannot be assessed on the basis of output data alone."

Fourth, they hypothesized that the new *incentive wage plan* might account for the improvement in output. However, based on later studies, they concluded that "there was absolutely no evidence in favor of the hypothesis that the continuous increase in output in the relay assembly test room during the first two years could be attributed to the wage incentive factor alone."[14]

Their fifth and final hypothesis was that the increased output and improved attitude in the test room could best be related to the change *in the method of supervision* that had gradually taken place. Proponents of this view felt that the experimental periods "had been essentially carriers of social value."[15] They had been effective as a means of gaining the operators' confidence and of establishing effective working relations between operators and supervisors. In countless ways, for example, the test room observer "had shown his personal interest in the girls and their problems. He had always been sympathetically aware of their hopes and fears. He had granted them more and more privileges."[16] Furthermore:

> No longer were the girls isolated individuals, working together only in the sense of an actual physical proximity. They had become participating members of a working group with all the psychological and social implications peculiar to such a group. . . . In period 13 the girls began to help one another out for the common good of the group. They had become bound together by common sentiments and feelings of loyalty.[17]

As they looked back on their experiment, it became obvious to the researchers that a number of significant differences existed between social conditions in the test room and those in the plant at large. It was obvious to the girls, for example, that they had become the focus of considerable attention from top management. Furthermore, they were exposed to a completely new system of control. Supervision outside the test room "meant upholding all the rules and practices intended to maintain efficiency in the department." For the experimenters, however, control meant a "controlled experiment," and for this they needed willing and cooperative subjects. Toward this end, operators were advised of and consulted about changes to be made and were questioned sympathetically about their reactions to the different conditions of work. Ironically, therefore, the researchers' attempts to maintain a "controlled experiment" had drastically altered the social conditions of work, as well as the attitudes and output of the operators!

Relay Room: Conclusion Thus, "the chief result of the first two years of experimentation in the relay assembly test room, then, had been to demonstrate the importance of employee attitudes and preoccupations." The rest pauses were obviously desirable (and were to be continued throughout the plant), but management—and later, organization theorists—would no longer draw any simple cause-and-effect equations between working conditions and output:

> [Management] began to see that such factors as hours of work and wage incentives were not things in themselves having an independent effect on employee efficiency; rather, these factors were no more than parts of a total situation and their effects could not be predicted apart from that total situation.[18]

The relay assembly test room (and the earlier illumination experiments) thus became the basis of a new organization theory, one in which the social and technical aspects of work were viewed as interrelated and in which the social conditions of work and employee attitudes took on a new importance. To this day, the relay assembly test room studies, although far from a perfect model of scientific investigation, stand out as perhaps the most important example of scientific inquiry and theory building in the social sciences.

● *The Interviewing Program*

Based on the relay assembly test room results, it was apparent that supervisor behavior was an important ingredient in employee morale and productivity. However, little was known at the time about employee complaints or what sorts of supervisor behaviors contributed to high or low employee morale. In order to obtain this information, the researchers decided to interview a group of employees in order to learn more about their opinions with respect to their work, working conditions, and supervision. The interviews began on a small scale in the inspection department, and gradually grew to the point where the likes, dislikes, complaints, and attitudes of more than 21,000 employees were obtained through interviews.

At first, researchers tried to relate employees' comments regarding satisfaction and dissatisfaction to their physical environment. But it was quickly determined that even people working in similar surroundings did not react in the same way to those surroundings; for example, "some expressed satisfaction, some dissatisfaction with similar plant conditions, wages, and working conditions."

Eventually, the researchers began to focus on the *personal situations* of the interviewees as a source of their complaints, and several important conclusions were drawn. For example, in one of the earliest descriptions of the need to build achievement and self-actualization into work, the researchers concluded from the interview data that "the meaning a person assigns to his position depends on whether or not that position is allowing him to fulfill the social demands he is making of his work." They further concluded that psychological factors (and particularly a person's background and "previous social conditioning") help determine whether he or she will be satisfied or dissatisfied in any particular work situation.[19] Finally, the researchers concluded that it was not simply working conditions or a person's personality that determines his attitudes, but also his work group and his relationship to it:

> It became clear that many employee comments which had formerly been interpreted in terms of the interviewees' personal situation could be better understood if they were interpreted in light of the employee's existing social relations within the plant: the social organization of the group with which he worked and his position in that group.[20]

In summary, the interviewing program emphasized the importance of group processes to employee attitudes and productivity, and one symptom of this relation was restriction of output: Specifically, the researchers found that the plant's incentive systems were not working as planned and that work-group pressure for restriction of output appeared to be the main reason.

• *The Bank Wiring Room Studies*

As a result of these observations, it was decided to study more intensively the mechanics of small-group processes—"to obtain more exact information about social groups within the company."[21] This time, however, the researchers took steps to avoid the problems that had confounded the earlier, relay assembly test room studies. For example, although the 14 men chosen as subjects were taken out of their regular department and placed in a special room, no other change was made in their conditions of work except that an investigator was present to observe their behavior.

One of his first observations was that the employees in the test room had a clear notion of a "proper day's work."[22] As soon as these employees felt they could finish what they considered enough for the day, they slacked off, and as a result, the output graph from week to week tended to be a straight line. To facilitate this, the employees also reported more or less output than they actually produced so as to ensure what appeared to be a constant rate of production.

The researchers discovered that the workers were able to do this because they had developed an informal social organization—a cohesive work group. Although friendships sprang up and two cliques formed, the 14 workers shared a common body of sentiments: that a person should not turn out too much work, and that if he did, he was a "rate buster." Ironically, the industrial engineers who had designed the plant's incentive plan had assumed that the work group would pressure slower workers to maintain a high pace of work and therefore ensure high pay for all group members. Instead, it was found that the employees brought pressure to bear *not on the slower workers but on the faster ones,* often through a process called "binging," slapping the errant worker on the arm. The workers never made clear why they wished to hold production even from week to week, although they alleged that "someone" would "get them" by reducing their wage rates if output rose too high.

The researchers also found that the informal organization of the group served both *external* and *internal* purposes. Internally, the informal organization functioned to control and regulate the behavior of its members. Externally, however, it functioned as a protective mechanism. "It served to protect the group from outside interference by manifesting a strong resistance to change, or threat of change, in conditions of work and personal relations."

The workers' behavior was usually not based on their actual experience with Western Electric, since the company's policy was that piece rates would not be changed unless there was a change in manufacturing process. Instead, the researchers found that the group's resistance seemed to derive in some complicated fashion from the position of that group in the total company structure and its consequent relations with other groups within the company. This position usually dictated that this group be on the receiving end of a constant series of technical changes emanating from higher in the organization; they felt they were always getting "dumped on" by "higher-ups."

As a result of the group's perceptions (or misperceptions), the researchers found that otherwise "logical" plans often did not work as intended. Partly because the workers saw themselves as having to accommodate themselves frequently to changes they did not initiate—changes that often seemed to further subordinate them in the company's social structure—and partly because the technical innovations caused changes in the workers' jobs and perceived status, otherwise "logical" changes were often resisted. As the researchers put it:

> The study of the bank wiremen showed that their behavior at work could not be understood without considering the informal organization of the group and the relation of this informal organization to the total social organization of the company. The work activities of this group, together with their satisfactions and dissatisfactions, had to be viewed as manifestations of a complex pattern of interrelations. In short, the work situation of the bank wiring group had to be treated as a social system; moreover, the industrial organization in which this group was a part also had to be treated as a social system.[23]

• *The Researchers' Theory and Conclusions*

The Hawthorne researchers made several important contributions to organization theory, but probably the most basic was their notion of an industrial organization as a *sociotechnical system:*

> The two aspects into which an industrial plant can be roughly divided—the technical organization and the human organization—are interrelated and interdependent. The human organization is constantly molding and re-creating the technical organization either to achieve more effectively the common economic purpose or to secure more satisfaction for its members. Likewise, changes in the technical organization require an adaptation on the part of the human organization.[24]

Relatedly, the researchers concluded that *employee attitudes and morale* appeared to be a major determinant of productivity and that a variety of factors, including the worker's personality and his supervisor's behavior, influenced his attitudes and morale. They concluded that a person's *work group* had a prevailing effect on his or her attitudes and productivity and that the group's attitudes were in turn a complex function of its perceived relationship to the rest of the organization. Later research findings would cast doubt on the notion that morale had determining effects on productivity, but the researchers' basic conclusions concerning the organization as a sociotechnical system and the effects of groups on their members are accepted today.

• *Criticisms of the Hawthorne Studies*

The Hawthorne studies and the human-relations school they spawned have been severely criticized, and our discussion would be incomplete without a brief discussion of these criticisms.

Philosophy The most vehement criticisms relate not so much to the Hawthorne studies themselves, but to the human-relations school and philosophy that Elton Mayo and others built on their interpretations of the Hawthorne findings. The empirical studies themselves, objectively reported in major works like *Management and the Worker,* have generally escaped this criticism. However, later works like Mayo's *Human Problems of Industrial Civilization* are laden with the human-relations writers' one-sided interpretations of the Hawthorne findings, and it is this one-sided interpretation—and the underlying philosophy implicit in it—that has been criticized.[25] Several economists, for example, write that by encouraging workers to develop loyalties to anything but their own self-interests, and by preaching collaboration instead of competition, human relations would eventually lead to reduced efficiency. Others point out that it is difficult to understand Mayo's work "unless one realizes how much he abhors conflict, competition, or disagreement: conflict to him is a social disease and cooperation is a social help."[26] Finally, critics charge that the human-relations movement, built as it is on a philosophy of worker–management harmony, is not only antithetical to a viable capitalistic system but impractical as well.

Methodology Others have attacked the methodology of the Hawthorne studies.[27] With respect to the relay assembly test room studies, for example, Alex Carey points out that there was no attempt to establish sample groups "representative of any larger population than the groups themselves," and that no generalization is therefore legitimate. Furthermore:

> There was no attempt to employ control data from the output records of the girls who were not put under special experimental conditions [and] even if these points had been met, the experiments would still have been of only minor scientific value, since a group of five subjects is too small to yield statistically reliable results.[28]

In his analysis, Carey asserts that the objective evidence obtained from these studies does not support any of the conclusions derived by the Hawthorne investigators and that it is only by "massive and relentless reinterpretation" that the researchers were able to draw the conclusions they did.

Findings Related to this criticism are some concerning the *findings* of the Hawthorne studies. Carey, for example, says that the Hawthorne researchers grossly overstated their case for the importance of employee attitudes and that their findings may well simply reflect "a rather old world view about the value of monetary incentives, driving leadership, and discipline." Others accuse Carey of himself overstating the case; they point out that, far from underrating the importance of financial incentives, the Hawthorne researchers took pains to state that wage incentives *alone* could not account for their findings.[29]

The Hawthorne researchers' conclusions concerning the cause-and-effect relation between employee morale and productivity has also been widely criticized. Here, the prevailing evidence does suggest that there is no simple cause-and-effect relation and that, as often as not, (1) high productivity *leads* to high morale, or (2) the two are unrelated.[30]

Contributions of the Hawthorne Studies: Summary

Criticisms like these are not without merit, and it is probably true that the Hawthorne researchers and their proponents overstated their case.[31] Yet it would be a mistake to disregard the Hawthorne findings, as Carey suggests, as "worthless scientifically." Even though those findings may have been oversimplified and overstated, they were responsible for adding new and essential dimensions to organization theory. They introduced the idea of the organization as an *open system* in which the technical and human segments are closely intertwined. They emphasized the importance of *employee attitudes* in an era when wage incentives and physical work conditions were often viewed as the only requirements for high productivity. Finally, they showed how cohesive *work groups* act to protect their self-interest by restricting output, resisting change, and undermining otherwise "rational" wage-incentive plans. Later research strongly supported the conclusion that groups have an influence on their members, and we will discuss such group processes in the remainder of this chapter.

THEORY OF GROUP INFLUENCE

It was clear from the Hawthorne findings that groups have a profound influence on their members; researchers turned next to determining how—the process and mechanics through which—these group effects emerged.

• *The Homans Model*

George Homans developed one of the earliest theories of group influence, and the so-called Homans Model has become something of a classic. It was developed from the Hawthorne findings and emphasizes the relation between the activities that are *required* of the group, and those that *emerge* from within the group itself.[32]

Three Basic Elements According to Homans, all group behavior consists of one or more "basic elements," which he calls "activities," "interactions," and "sentiments."

- *Activities.* Activities are things that people do, such as planting, cutting, smoking, walking. To be precise, says Homans, all activities "refer in the end to movements of the muscles of men. . . ."
- *Interactions.* Interactions are communications of any sort between individuals. These communications need not be verbal and in fact may be nonverbal: "Perhaps the simplest example of interaction, though we should find it complex enough if we studied it carefully, is two men at opposite ends of a saw, sawing a log. When we say that the two are interacting, we are not referring to the fact that both are sawing—in our language, sawing is an activity—but to the fact that the push of one man on the saw is followed by the push of the other. In this example, the interaction does not involve words."
- *Sentiments.* Sentiments are "internal states of the human body" and include motives, drives, emotions, feelings, effective states, sentiments, and attitudes. Sentiments thus range from fear and hunger to affection. Unlike activities and interactions, sentiments cannot be seen or observed.

External and Internal Systems Homans says group behavior can be observed in terms of an external system and an internal system. Each system contains its own activities, interactions, and sentiments.

The *external* system is composed of those required activities, interactions, and sentiments that the group must carry out to survive. For example, in the bank wiring room at Hawthorne, the required *activities* included wiring equipment and soldering connections. Similarly, "there were the necessary *interactions* between a solderman and the three wiremen he worked for, between an inspector and the wiremen and soldermen whose work he passed judgment on, [and] between the group chief and all the men in the room."[33] Finally, the bank wiremen's external system contained given and required *sentiments*. The given sentiments were those attitudes, values, and motives that the wiremen brought with them to their jobs and that were "generated by the circumstances of their lives outside the plant";[34] the required sentiments were those that were required for adequate job performance—for example, wanting to do a good job.

On the other hand, the Hawthorne researchers discovered that the activities, interactions, and sentiments that *emerged* from the work groups were different (and often at odds with) those of the external system, a phenomenon that Homans comments on as follows:

> When a number of persons have come together to form a group, their behavior never holds to its first pattern. Social life is never wholly utilitarian; it elaborates itself, complicates itself, beyond the demands of the original situation.[35]

What emerges, says Homans, is an *internal* system, "the elaboration of group behavior that simultaneously arises out of the external system and reacts upon it." This system is also composed of activities, interactions, and sentiments, but in this case, these elements *emerge* out of the group's situation rather than being required by it.

> Instead of the motives for getting a job done, we shall have to deal with sentiments developed on the job, such as liking or disliking for others, approval or disapproval of the things other persons do. Instead of activities demanded by the job, we shall have to deal with activities spontaneously evolved that serve to express the attitudes of persons toward one another. And instead of interactions required for the coordination of practical activities, we shall have to deal with interactions elaborated socially—for fun, so to speak.[36]

The Homans model is illustrated in Figure 14-2. According to this model, background factors like technology, job design, and rules combine to determine the required and given behavior (the external system) in terms of required activities, interactions, and sentiments. In turn, an internal system (also composed of activities, interactions, and sentiments) emerges as the group members interact with one another. For example, special sentiments called *norms* develop; these are "laws" governing things like desirable output level. Also, new communications channels and new activities (like restricting output) emerge. As a result, the output of the group, in terms of productivity, satisfaction, and individual development, is often quite different from that expected by management.

• *Factors that Influence Group Cohesiveness*

What determines the extent to which a group can influence the behavior and compliance of its members? To a large extent, it depends on the attraction the group has for its members—on its *cohesiveness*. Therefore, in this section we will discuss some of the factors that influence group cohesiveness.

Group Size The size of the group is one important factor. In one study, Seashore collected data on almost 6,000 people in industry and found that group cohesiveness declined as group size increased, up to about 20 members; beyond this size, cohesiveness leveled off.[37] In fact, group size seemed to have more of an influence on group cohesiveness than did such things as similarity in education or age. Part of

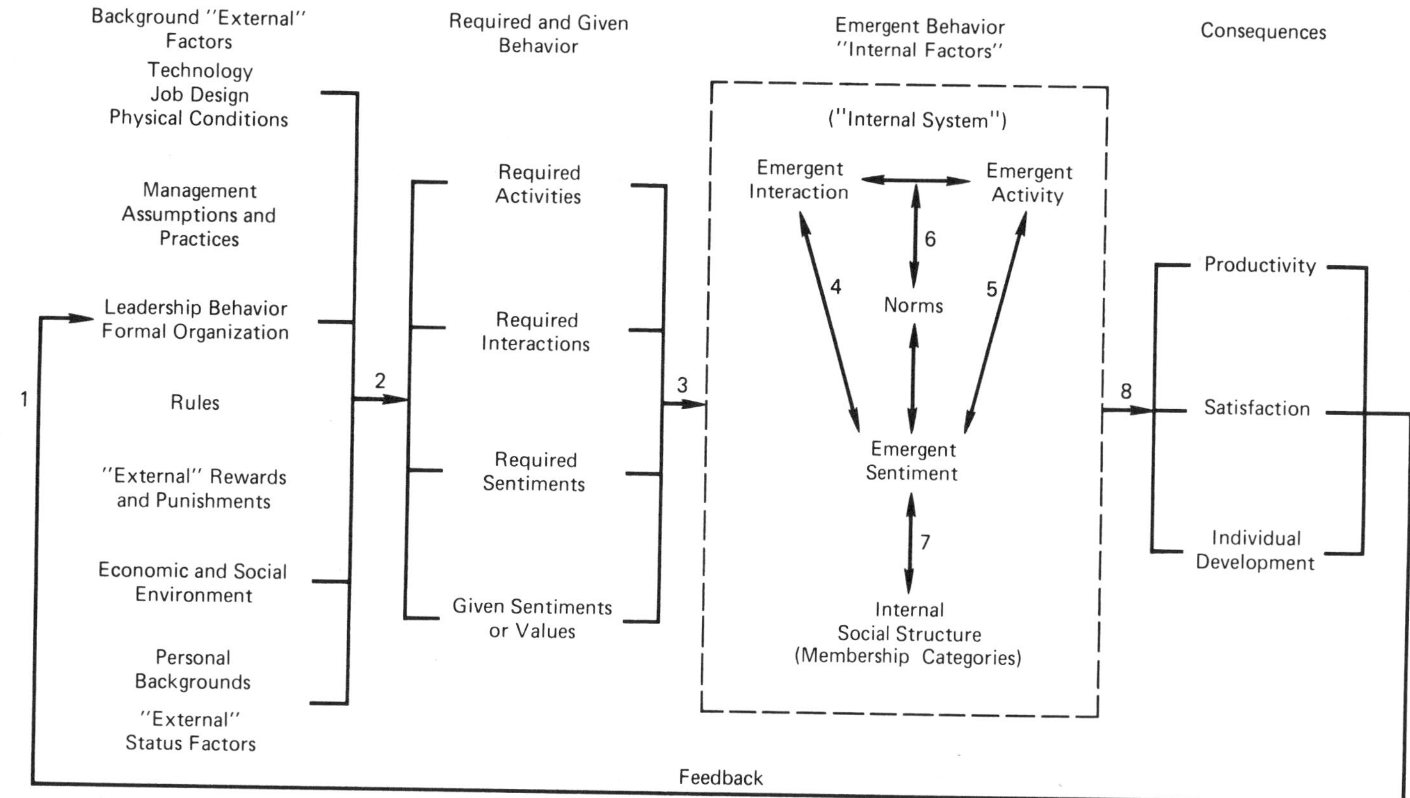

FIGURE 14-2 How Work-Group Behavior Is Related to "External" Factors such as Technology and Environment. *Source:* Arthur Turner, "A Conceptual Scheme for Describing Work-Group Behavior." Copyright © 1961 by the President and Fellows of Harvard College. Reproduced by permission.

the reason for this is that communication and interaction are prerequisites for the existence of a cohesive group; and as group size becomes too large, the number of possible interactions becomes so large that both interaction and communication begin to break down.

Intragroup and Intergroup Competition Intragroup competition undermines group cohesiveness. In one study, management put production supervisors under considerable pressure to minimize departmental costs. Then a situation occurred in which certain goods were damaged at some unknown point in the production process. Normally, the cost of the damage would have been absorbed by the negligent department. In this case, the plant manager called a meeting of his subordinates to determine who was to be charged with the expense. Every department head emphatically denied that his department was responsible, and the meeting ended with the department managers blaming one another for the damaged merchandise. Thus, the competition created by the cost-minimization program resulted in hostilities and ill feeling that drastically reduced the cohesiveness and unity of the foremen group. In the end, the plant manager had to charge the loss against general plant overhead.

Whereas intragroup competition can undermine group cohesiveness, intergroup competition can frequently increase it. In one study, groups were assigned problems and then had to compete with each other in a situation in which only one group could win.[38] The researchers found that the newly created competitive environment increased group cohesiveness. Of equal importance, however, is that whether a group wins or loses has important implications for its cohesiveness. In losing groups, researchers have found that tension emerges that can upset internal relationships and undermine group cohesion.

Status Group cohesiveness is directly related to *group status*.[39] Such status may reflect many things, including differences in organizational level, overall performance, the work that the group is doing, or the amount of discretion extended to the group. However, there are a number of exceptions to this rule. For example, in those low-status groups whose members could not easily leave, the group did exhibit relatively high cohesion. On the other hand, a high-status group that was unsuccessful in carrying out its goals had relatively low cohesiveness.

Goals One reason a person joins a group is his feeling that the group can help him accomplish his goals. Agreement over goals, therefore, increases cohesiveness; differences undermine it.[40] Similarly, major disagreements over how the goal is to be achieved (assuming that all group members agree on the goal) have disruptive effects on cohesiveness.

Environment and Proximity Walker and Guest have found that the noise that often attends an assembly line inhibits verbal interaction and group cohesiveness.[41]

However, a more basic factor inhibiting cohesiveness in such a situation may be the nature of the work itself, which usually requires little or no exchange of tools, or reciprocal or team action.

Stable Relationships The existence of stable relationships is another requisite for a cohesive group. For example, studies of California aircraft factories concluded that groups that were frequently disturbed or rearranged did not become cohesive, but exhibited high rates of absenteeism and turnover.[42]

GROUP NORMS AND MEMBER COMPLIANCE

• What Are Norms?

Groups control their members through the use of norms, which Hare calls "rules of behavior, proper ways of acting, which have been accepted as legitimate by members of a group [and which] specify the kinds of behavior that are expected of group members."[43] Hackman says that norms have these five characteristics:

1 Norms are structural characteristics of groups that summarize and simplify group influence processes. In other words, a norm summarizes and highlights those processes within the group that are intended to regulate and regularize group-member behavior.
2 Norms apply only to behavior, not to private thoughts and feelings. According to Hackman, "behavioral compliance does not necessarily reflect the true private attitudes and beliefs of group members." He says that through the use of norms, a group member can be coerced into agreeing (or saying he agrees) with the group as a whole, but that his or her attitudes and beliefs may continue to conflict with those of the group.
3 Norms are generally developed only for behaviors that are viewed as important by most group members, and only for behaviors that otherwise would have to be controlled by direct and continuous social influence.
4 Norms usually develop gradually, but the process can be short-cut if members want. Hackman says that norms about behavior typically develop gradually and informally as members learn what behaviors are, in fact, important for the group to control, but that "if for some reason group members decide that a particular norm would be desirable or helpful, they simply agree to such a norm suddenly by declaring that 'from now on' the norm exists."
5 Not all norms apply to everyone. For example, high-status members often have more "freedom" to deviate from the letter of the norm than do other people.[44]

• *How Groups Influence Perception and Behavior*

Social Control: Imposed Control vs. Self-Control Hare calls the process through which group members put pressure on the individual "social control." Through social control, "behavior is confined to acceptable limits, limits which maximize the possibilities of survival for the individual and the group."

Social control is sometimes *imposed* on deviant group members. For example, by educating, ostracizing, or on occasion physically punishing the deviant, group members put pressure on him or her. But Hare says that in most cases, social control is *self-control:*

> This is the self-control which takes place during the initial phase of the social act when the individual modifies his behavior as a result of his anticipation of the response of the other person. . . . This process of modification of behavior may range from an individual's conscious attempts to conform to norms to the unconscious acceptance of group or individual directives.[45]

Effects of Groups on Perception and Judgment Groups can influence their members behavior *indirectly* by influencing their perception and judgment. The classic study of this phenomenon was carried out by Asch. The subjects were asked to compare and to match lines of various lengths, and Asch arranged for all but one of the subjects to give erroneous answers so that Asch could study the responses of the naive subject.

Of the 50 naive subjects, about one-fourth reported the true length of the lines, although this contradicted the length reported by the rest of the group. Asch reports that the rest of the subjects "yielded" for one (or more) of three reasons:

- *Distortion of perception.* A small minority of the naive subjects reported that they were unaware that their estimates had been distorted by the majority and that they actually came to perceive the majority estimates as correct.
- *Distortion of judgment.* Most of the subjects who yielded belonged to this category. These subjects lacked confidence in their own perceptions and came to believe that their perceptions were inaccurate and those of the majority were accurate.
- *Distortion of action.* These subjects did not come to view their perceptions as inaccurate, nor did the group distort their true perceptions. Instead, these subjects yielded because of what they felt was an overwhelming need to go along with the group. They were afraid to appear different or as outsiders and therefore willingly parroted the majority position although they knew it was incorrect.[46]

Conditions Determining Compliance with the Majority What are the factors that determine whether the individual will in fact comply with the opinion of the group majority? Research suggests at least interrelated factors:

- *Characteristics of the environment.* First, where the items on which decisions must be made are *ambiguous or unclear,* there tends to be much greater reliance on the group and a greater tendency to go along with the group majority's decision.
- *Characteristics of the perceiver.* Second, individuals who are *insecure,* or who feel poorly qualified to assess the situation, are more apt to go along with the group majority's decision.
- *Characteristics of the group.* Finally, a group that is seen as being highly *credible* will for obvious reasons evoke more compliance than a group that is not. Similarly, where there is a greater *unanimity of views* among group members, individual group members can be expected to comply more with the group majority than where there is not such unanimity.[47]

Effects of Groups on Behavior and Compliance Writers since the time of the Hawthorne studies have recognized the fact that groups influence the behavior and compliance of their members. Exactly what effects do groups have on the productivity of their members? Two representative studies, one by Schachter and one by Seashore, help answer this question.

In a laboratory study, Schachter was able to manipulate two independent variables. First, he was able to categorize the group as either high-cohesive or low-cohesive. He was also able to categorize the group according to whether it had positive or negative norms (that is, whether the group agreed with the performance standards it had to meet).[48]

Schachter's findings are summarized in Table 14-2. They indicate that a highly cohesive group with positive norms can cause a significant increase in group production, whereas a highly cohesive group with negative norms can bring about a significant decrease. On the other hand, there is some indication that a low-cohesive group with positive norms can still result in increased production, but that a low-cohesive group with negative norms has very little effect on production.

Seashore's study was conducted in a heavy-machinery company and focused on the relationship between work-group cohesiveness and various measures of anxiety and productivity.[49] The employees were well educated, mostly married, of various ages, and about 93 percent male. Questionnaires were administered to a total of 5,871 employees, who were the constituents of 228 work groups.

TABLE 14-2 Relationship Between Group Cohesiveness, Production Norms, and Change in Production

	Change in Production for Positive Norm	*Change in Production for Negative Norm*
High-Cohesive Groups	+5.92	−2.16
Low-Cohesive Groups	+5.09	−.42

Source: S. Schachter et al., "An Experimental Study of Cohesiveness and Productivity," *Human Relations* (Fall 1951), p. 233.

To measure group cohesiveness, the researchers constructed an "index of cohesiveness" based upon responses to questions such as, "Do you feel that you are really a part of your work group?" and, "If you had a chance to do the same kind of work for the same pay in another work group, how would you feel about moving?" This index was then correlated with measures of anxiety, perceived company "supportiveness," and productivity.

The researchers found that members of high-cohesive groups were much less anxious and tense than were members of low-cohesive groups. Specifically, they were less likely to report feeling "jumpy" or "nervous" or perceiving a lack of "supportiveness" by the company. Furthermore, members of high-cohesive groups where the production was at least average were less likely to report feeling under pressure for high production.

Cohesiveness also had two effects on group productivity. First, there was less *variability* in actual productivity within high-cohesive groups. Second, the actual *level* of production might be either high or low, depending upon whether the high-cohesive group members had a favorable attitude toward the company.

In summary, high group cohesiveness is associated with low anxiety and tension as well as with a greater ability to withstand complaints, abuse, or pressure emanating from the group's environment. High cohesiveness is also associated with less variability in production; however, whether such a stable, uniform production rate is high or low seems to depend largely upon whether the group views management's goals as acceptable.

Therefore, groups influence their members' perception, judgment, behavior, and compliance. We turn next to an analysis of how groups affect—and are affected by—the organization's structure.

GROUPS AND ORGANIZATION STRUCTURE

• The Organization as a Structure of Groups

According to Rensis Likert, an organization functions best when its personnel function not as individuals but as members of highly effective work groups with high performance goals. Therefore, he says, management should deliberately endeavor to build these effective work groups, linking them into an organization structure by means of people who hold overlapping group membership (as in Figure 14-3). His theory of the organization as a structure of groups is built on his "principle of supportive relationships":

> The leadership and other processes of the organization must be such as to insure a maximum probability that in all interactions and all relationships with the organization each member will, in the light of his background, values, and expectations, view the experience as supportive and one which builds and maintains his sense of personal worth and importance.[50]

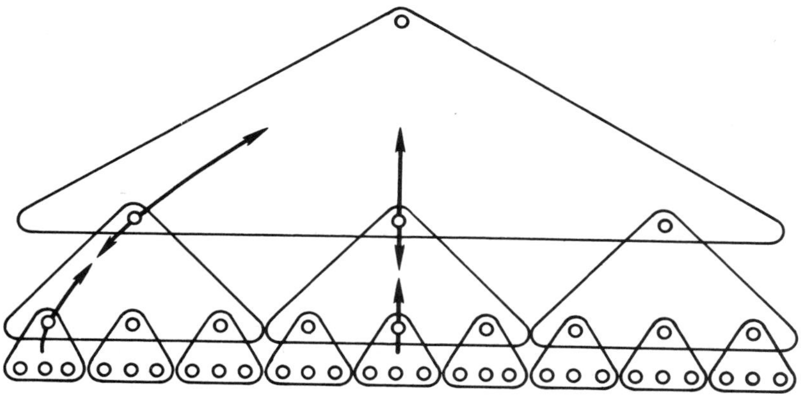

(The Arrows Indicate the Linking Pin Function)

FIGURE 14-3 The Linking Pin and Overlapping Groups. *Source:* Rensis Likert, *New Patterns of Management* (New York: McGraw-Hill, 1961), p. 113.

The desire to achieve and maintain a sense of personal worth is clearly a central concept of this principle. According to Likert, "the most important source of satisfaction for this desire is the response we get from the people we are close to . . . the face-to-face groups with whom we spend the bulk of our time are, consequently, the most important to us." As a result:

> Management will make full use of the potential capacities of its human resources only when each person in an organization is a member of one or more effectively functioning work groups that have a high degree of group loyalty, effective skills of interaction, and high performance goals.[51]

As in Figure 14-3, the supervisors in the most effective organizations function as "linking pins" between their own supervisors and their subordinates. Likert says that to function effectively in this role, the supervisor must have enough influence with his own superior to be able to affect the superior's decisions. To the extent that a supervisor cannot perform this linking-pin function, the effectiveness of the organization as a structure of effective work groups is reduced, since the contributions that the supervisors' group might otherwise have made to problem solving and decision making in the organization are lost or reduced.

• *How Organization Structure Affects Group Functioning*

Structure both affects and is affected by group processes; we first discuss the influence of structure on groups.

Task Structure The design of the task or organization influences group behavior in several ways. First, as we have seen, proximity and the ability to interact are prerequisites to group formation, and in situations where proximity or opportunities for interaction are reduced, group cohesiveness tends to be reduced as well.[52]

Similarly, the work flow implicit in the organization structure determines required interactions and status, which in turn affect group functioning. In a classic study of restaurants, for example, Whyte found that the work flow placed higher-status employees (like cooks) in a position of taking orders from lower-status employees (like waitresses), and as a result, work-group functioning suffered.[53] (Eventually, the problem was partially solved by having the waitresses clip their orders to a revolving clipboard, thus eliminating the interaction between the cook and waitress.)

In another famous study, Trist and his associates investigated the effects of converting from a "short-wall" to a "long-wall" method of mining in British coal mines.[54] In the former, each miner was proficient at all the necessary mining tasks, and the miners, working as a highly cohesive group, took turns carrying out these tasks. This system was replaced by a "long-wall" system, in which miners worked across a long mine face and each worker had a single task. With the long-wall method, the first shift of miners carried out a single task, the second shift carried out a second task, and the third shift carried out the third basic mining task.

The long-wall method was not successful. Ability to face the dangers of deep mining is perhaps the most important characteristic miners must have, and this ability tends to be higher within cohesive work groups. In the case of the long-wall method, these cohesive work groups were broken down by changes in the required activities and interactions of group members. Miners now had specialized jobs to do and no longer shared common tasks (or a common pay rate); and they were now more independent of one another and often worked widely separated from one another. These structural changes undermined group cohesiveness and functioning.

Walker and Guest, in their studies of work groups on assembly lines, made a number of useful observations of the structural and technological factors that undermine group functioning.[55] According to them, "the first and most obvious barrier is noise. In many of the sections along the line, verbal interaction, at least, is difficult or impossible." More important, the technical nature of assembly-line work "neither suggests nor compels interaction," so that groups have less of a formal need to emerge. Furthermore, assembly lines put a good deal of distance between workers (particularly those on opposite ends of the line), and this too reduces interactions and group formation. However, Walker and Guest found that although group formation had usually been hampered by these structural and technological factors, in some cases cohesive groups had emerged. This was generally because more effective foremen took specific action (such as holding periodic meetings with their men) to cultivate cohesive groups. Task structure also affects group functioning in many other ways. For one thing, as we have seen, departmentation results in *differentiation* whereby departments each develop their own goals and point of view. Therefore, where a unit is placed on the organization chart has implications for its functioning. For example, the quality control group that reports to the production manager might develop a very different—and less independent—point of view than one reporting to the president. The placement of groups or work units lower or higher on the organization chart also has implications for each unit's status, and thus for the resulting group and intergroup behavior.

Group Size Organization structure can also influence group functioning more indirectly through its effect on group size. The span of control implicit in an organization structure determines the number of subordinates reporting to a supervisor and therefore the size of each work group. To the extent that group size and cohesiveness are inversely related, smaller groups should foster more satisfaction than large ones, and this seems to be the case. The findings relating group size and performance, however, are mixed. Most have found that small groups produce more, perhaps because coordination is easier. It is likely, though, that the effect of group size depends on how structured the group's task is. Researchers have found that group size was positively related to performance for highly structured tasks, possibly because the leader could watch each man closely. On the other hand, the size–performance relationship was negative where the task was unstructured.[56]

"Ambient Stimuli" Hackman says that ambient stimuli—"stimuli which potentially are available to all group members"—affect group functioning. Among these stimuli are the other people in the group, the materials and task the group is working on, and aspects of the group's workplace.[57] He says that "the ambient stimuli which characterize a given group can strongly affect a group member's behavior-outcome expectancies" (that is, his perceptions of "what leads to what" for that group). For example, the layout that characterizes a traditional elementary-school class—chairs lined up in rows and bolted to the floor, communications routinely passing from teacher to student in one direction, and the like—provide a new group member (student) with a good deal of information about behavior-outcome contingencies, such as that sitting quietly at a desk will result in no unpleasant interactions with the teacher. In summary, says Hackman, "the ambient stimuli present in a group setting often prompt fairly strong inferences by group members regarding what behaviors are likely to be appropriate and inappropriate in that group."

Engineering the Task Hackman says that managers can and should attempt to "engineer" a group's ambient stimuli so as to affect group behavior in specified ways. He says there are three primary "sources" of ambient stimuli that are potentially manipulable: "(A) the particular *people* who compose the group, (B) the *situation or environment* in which the group functions, and (C) the *task* of the group." For example, it is often possible to manipulate the characteristics of the task or situation so as to highlight the availability of certain rewards (or punishments). Similarly, managers can influence group cohesiveness by changing the people who compose the group, and by influencing the proximity and work flow of those people.[58]

• *How Groups Affect Organization Structure: The Informal Organization*

Groups that emerge in an organization can also modify the organization structure. Stieglitz says that "to some people, that mystical entity known as the 'informal' organization is the real organization. It is how things really get done." This informal organization, he says, encompasses all relationships and channels of communication that mature, reasonable people are expected to develop and use in order to meet organizational objectives. This informal organization is informal "only in the sense that nobody has found it necessary to inundate the organization with memorabilia that fully spell out its workings."[59] Katz and Kahn point out that this informal organization (which itself is composed of groups or "role-sets" that emerge spontaneously) is necessary because it is impossible to specify in advance every required task or to plan for every contingency; instead, informal relationships emerge through which the formal organization is expanded and elaborated.

Woodward presents some useful anecdotal findings in this regard. In her study:

> It was found, for example, that organizational objectives were frequently achieved through the informal rather than the formal organization. A dysfunctional formal organization could be compensated by contributive informal relationships. This was particularly noticeable in relation to technical change.[60]

In three of the firms the Woodward team studied, changes in organization structure were planned and put into effect at the same time as the technical change. In the remaining firms, however, technical changes were made without changing the formal organization, "it having been taken for granted that the existing organizational structure would prove adequate for the new technology." However, in every case this proved not to be so:

> The first thing that happened was that informal organization began to respond to the new situational demands imposed upon it. The result was a serious discrepancy between formal and informal organizations, and the achievement of organizational goals almost entirely through an informal network of relationships. In general, senior management were sophisticated enough to be aware that this was happening, and after a varying period of time had elapsed, changes were made in formal organization. Either the existing informal relationships were defined and formalized or mechanisms were introduced to minimize the discrepancy. For example, in one firm a production committee was set up to allow people to establish contact with those to whom they were not related in the formal hierarchy.[61]

• *Team-Based Organization Designs*

Discoveries like those of the Hawthorne researchers—that a cohesive, highly motivated group can have a positive effect on a company's effectiveness—have not gone unnoticed by contemporary organization theorists. As a result, several team-based organization designs are today in use, and, in fact, their use epitomizes much of what is new today in organizational theory.

Quality Circles If there is a single concept that is closely identified with Japan's industrial growth, it is probably the *quality circle,* a group of eight to ten employees that meets once a week to spot and solve problems in their work areas. The idea of using small groups of workers to solve work-related problems was actually popularized by U.S. management consultants and then adopted by the Japanese after World War II. U.S. companies, stunned by dwindling productivity, then borrowed the idea back from the Japanese, who believed that such groups are partly responsible for the spectacular productivity gains that have been made since the war.

At the present time, quality circles are in use at hundreds of U.S. firms, and the number is growing. Companies using them include General Motors, Ford Motor Co., Northrup, Rockwell International, and American Airlines. They were first used in the United States in 1974 by Lockheed's Space and Missile Unit and proved so successful they were soon adopted by other firms.

The basic idea of a quality circle is as follows. A plant steering committee, composed of labor and management, decides which area of a company could benefit from a circle. Then, eight to ten workers from that area are asked to serve on a circle and to meet once a week on company time. In addition to the workers, those attending the meeting include the group's immediate supervisor and a person trained in personnel or industrial relations; the latter instructs the workers in elementary data gathering and statistics. The circle selects and analyzes a problem, develops a solution, and presents its findings to management, which generally accepts the group's recommendations.

Based on the findings to date, quality circles appear to be quite successful, from the point of view of both management and labor. General Motors has about 100 quality circles operating in various plants of its car divisions, and in at least one case, a circle was responsible for saving the company $225,000 annually. A circle at an American Airlines maintenance center in Tulsa came up with a saving of $100,000 a year by simply replacing old hand grinders with more efficient tools. The workers themselves (1) often share in any cost savings (Northrup, for example, pays circle members about 10 percent of any cost savings), and (2) get a feeling of accomplishment from tackling a challenging task; so they, too, gain from the quality circles. At present, the evidence is anecdotal and does not address such questions as whether the cost of the circles warrants the benefits they produce. On the whole, however, the circle idea appears to be an effective one for harnessing the performance-stimulating potential in a work group.

Project Teams Just as Likert concluded that the best organizations are networks of small, motivated work groups, so too have excellent companies found that small groups should be their basic organizational building blocks.[62] This is illustrated by the fact that companies like 3M have hundreds of 4- to 10-person "venture teams" in action at any one time, and Texas Instruments has more than 9,000 teams searching for small productivity improvements. Most of these are ad hoc task forces, small groups that are formed for short-term specific purposes and then quickly disbanded.

In the most effective companies, these task forces are small (ten employees or less), and their duration is usually limited to four months or less. Membership is generally voluntary, and the task force itself is usually pulled together rapidly, when needed, and not accompanied by a formal chartering process; that is, the group receives some quick instructions rather than a formal document enumerating its authority and responsibilities. Similarly, there are usually no "staff" personnel assigned (such as an executive director, "assistant to," or full-time report writer). In fact, documentation is usually informal and often scant; control is maintained instead by the commitment of employees to the value of communication. As a result, members of each group are constantly (if informally) communicating with one another, with management, and with the members of other groups, so that everyone always knows where each project stands. And follow-up is usually swift: within two or three months, top management wants to know specifically what the team has accomplished, and an answer like "we're still working on a report" is usually not satisfactory, since the focus is on action and results.

One characteristic of the group that can undermine its creativity, though, is its longevity.[63] Katz found that project groups (like those described above) become increasingly isolated from key information sources both within and outside the organization as they become more stable over time. As members of the group work together and become more familiar with each other, and as the group and its members, in a sense, age together, group members become less open to new ideas from outsiders, whether members of other project teams within the same organization or other professionals outside the organization. One implication, Katz says, is that periodically injecting new members into these groups can have an energizing and destabilizing function and actually improve the group's openness to new ideas and therefore its technical performance. These findings help to explain why the most successful of Peters and Waterman's excellent companies encourage members of project teams to intermingle—for instance, by reducing physical barriers like walls and by encouraging large groups of employees to sit together in the company cafeteria.

SUMMARY

Groups play a crucial role in organization theory because they influence and are influenced by organization structure, and because they affect their members' behavior and compliance. In this chapter, therefore, we discussed group processes and their relation to organization theory.

It was during the Hawthorne studies that organization theorists first became fully aware of how employees' work groups, attitudes, and needs affect their motivation and behavior. Groups can influence their members' perception, judgement, and behavior, in part because cohesive groups can enable their individual members to better withstand complaints, abuse, or pressure emanating from the groups' environment.

Likert was one of the first to describe the role of groups or teams in the organization structure, explaining that ideally, organizations should be composed of overlapping groups in which supervisors perform "linking-pin" functions. Today, theories like those of Likert find their modern counterpart in team-based organization designs like quality circles and project teams.

Discussion Questions

1 "Supervisors should always strive to have cohesive groups." Discuss whether you agree or disagree with this statement, and why.
2 Discuss the factors that influence group cohesiveness.
3 Describe how the Homans model of work-group behavior underscores the contingency or situational aspects of group behavior.
4 What role did the Hawthorne studies play in changing the direction of organization theory?
5 Do you agree that as a research study, the Hawthorne experiments were "worthless scientifically"? Why, or why not?
6 Describe what Homans means by activities, interactions, and sentiments. How useful do you think his theory is for explaining work-group behavior?
7 Explain specifically how you would go about increasing the cohesiveness of some work group.
8 "One cannot predict the effectiveness of an organization structure or of a leader without understanding the group processes that exist in the situation." Explain whether you agree or disagree with this statement, and why.
9 Under what conditions are group members more likely to comply with the opinion of the group majority?

Footnotes

[1]Elton Mayo, *The Political Problems of an Industrial Civilization* (Boston: Graduate School of Business, Harvard University, 1947), p. 21.

[2]This section is based on F.L. Roethlisberger and William Dickson, *Management and the Worker* (Cambridge, Mass.: Harvard University Press, 1939); and Henry Landsberger, *Hawthorne Revisited* (Ithaca, N.Y.: Cornell University Press, 1958).

[3]Roethlisberger and Dickson, *Management and the Worker,* p. 15.

[4]*Ibid.,* p. 16.

[5]*Ibid.*

[6]*Ibid.,* p. 17.

[7]*Ibid.,* p. 19.

[8]*Ibid.*

[9]*Ibid.,* p. 20.

[10]*Ibid.*, p. 54.
[11]*Ibid.*, pp. 58–59.
[12]*Ibid.*, p. 62.
[13]*Ibid.*, p. 73.
[14]*Ibid.*, p. 160.
[15]*Ibid.*, p. 88.
[16]*Ibid.*, p. 72.
[17]*Ibid.*, p. 72.
[18]*Ibid.*, p. 185.
[19]*Ibid.*, pp. 373–75.
[20]*Ibid.*, p. 374.
[21]*Ibid.*, p. 385.

[22]See George Homans, *Fatigue of Workers: Its Relation to Industrial Production* (New York: Rinehart, 1941), pp. 77–86; reprinted in Paul Lawrence and John Seiler, *Organizational Behavior and Administration* (Homewood, Ill.: Richard D. Irwin, 1965).

[23]Roethlisberger and Dickson, *Management and the Worker,* p. 551.
[24]*Ibid.*, p. 553.
[25]See Landsberger, *Hawthorne Revisited,* Chap. 3.
[26]*Ibid.*, p. 31.

[27]For a discussion of this, see Alex Carey, "The Hawthorne Studies: A Radical Criticism," *American Sociological Review,* June 1967, pp. 403–16.

[28]*Ibid.* See also John Adair, "The Hawthorne Effect: A Reconsideration of a Methodological Artifact," *Journal of Applied Psychology,* Vol. 69, No. 2 (May 1984), 334–45.

[29]See Jon Shepard, "On Alex Carey's Radical Criticism of the Hawthorne Studies," *Academy of Management Journal,* March 1971, 23–31.

[30]See, for example, Dennis Organ, "A Reappraisal and Reinterpretation of the Satisfaction Causes Performance Hypothesis," *Academy of Management Review,* Vol. 2, No. 1 (1977), 46–53; J.E. Sheridan and J.W. Slocum, Jr., "The Direction of the Causal Relationship between Job Satisfaction and Work Performance," *Organizational Behavior and Human Performance,* Vol. 14, No. 2 (October 1975), 159–72.

[31]See, for example, Edwin Locke, "Nature and Causes of Job Satisfaction," in Marvin Dunnette, *Handbook of Industrial and Organizational Psychology* (Chicago: Rand McNally, 1976), p. 1299.

[32]This information is based on George Homans, *The Human Group* (New York: Harcourt Brace Jovanovich, 1950), pp. 25–40, 90–107, 108–13, and 118–19; and Joseph Litterer, *Organizations* (New York: John Wiley, 1969), Vol. I, 167–88.

[33]Litterer, *Organizations,* p. 180.
[34]*Ibid.*, p. 178.
[35]*Ibid.*, p. 185.
[36]*Ibid.*, p. 186.

[37]Stanley F. Seashore, *Group Cohesiveness in the Industrial Work Group* (Ann Arbor: Survey Research Center, University of Michigan, 1954), pp. 90–95. For an excellent discussion of group cohesiveness, see Joseph A. Litterer, *The Analysis of Organizations* (New York: John Wiley, 1965), pp. 91–101.

[38]Robert R. Blake and Jane S. Mouton, "Reactions to Intergroup Competition under Win-Lose Conditions," *Management Science,* Vol. 7 (1961), 432.

[39]John W. Thibaut, "An Experimental Study of Cohesiveness of Underprivileged Groups," *Human Relations,* Vol. 3 (1950), 251–78.

[40]John R.P. French, Jr., "The Disruption and Cohesion of Groups," *The Journal of Abnormal and Social Psychology,* Vol. 36 (1941), 361–77.

[41]C.R. Walker and R.H. Guest, *The Man on the Assembly Line* (Cambridge, Mass.: Harvard University Press, 1952), pp. 135–40.

[42]Elton Mayo and George H. Lombard, "Teamwork and Labor Turnover in the Aircraft Industry of Southern California," Business Research Report #32 (Boston: Graduate School of Business Administration, Harvard University, 1944), p. 8.

[43]A.P. Hare, *Handbook of Small Group Research* (New York: Free Press, 1962), p. 24.

[44]J. Richard Hackman, "Group Influences on Individuals," in Marvin Dunnette, ed., *Handbook of Industrial and Organizational Psychology,* pp. 1494, 1497. Copyright © Rand McNally College Publishing Company, 1976.

[45]Hare, *Handbook of Small Group Research,* p. 25.

[46]S.E. Asch, "Effects of Group Pressure upon the Modification and Distortion of Judgments," in Guy Swanson, Theodore Newcomb, and Eugene Hartley, *Readings in Social Psychology* (New York: Henry Holt and Company, 1952), pp. 6–7; and Michael Olmstead, *The Small Group* (New York: Random House, 1959), pp. 67–81.

[47]For a good review of these findings, see Hare, *Handbook of Small Group Research,* and Hackman, "Group Influences on Individuals."

[48]S. Schachter, N. Ellerston, D. McBridge, and D. Gregory, "An Experimental Study of Cohesiveness and Productivity," *Human Relations,* Fall 1951, 229–38.

[49]Seashore, *Group Cohesiveness in the Industrial Work Group.*

[50]Rensis Likert, *New Patterns of Management* (New York: McGraw-Hill, 1961), p. 103.

[51]*Ibid.,* p. 104.

[52]See, for example, A.K. Rice, "Productivity and Social Organization in an Indian Weaving Shed," *Human Relations,* Vol. 6 (1953), 311; E.L. Trist and K.W. Bamforth, "Some Social and Psychological Consequences of the Long Wall Method of Coal-Getting," *Human Relations,* Vol. 4 (1951), 1–38.

[53]William F. Whyte, *Human Relations in the Restaurant Industry* (New York: McGraw-Hill, 1948).

[54]Trist and Bamforth, "Some Social and Psychological Consequences."

[55]Charles Walker, Robert Guest, and Arthur Turner, *The Foremen on the Assembly Line* (Boston: Harvard University Press, 1956).

[56]Edwin Thomas and Clinton Fink, "Effects of Group Size," *Psychological Bulletin,* Vol. 60, No. 4 (1963), 371–84; A.P. Hare, "A Study of Interaction and Consensus in Different Sized Groups," *American Sociological Review,* Vol. 17 (1952), 261–67; Stanley F. Seashore, *Group Cohesiveness in the Industrial Work Group* (Ann Arbor: Survey Research Center, University of Michigan, 1954), pp. 90–95; and Robert C. Cummins and Donald C. King, "The Interaction of Group Size and Task Structure in an Industrial Organization," *Personnel Psychology,* 1973, pp. 87–94.

[57]J. Richard Hackman, "Group Influences on Individuals," pp. 1455–1526.

[58]*Ibid.,* p. 1471.

[59]Harold Stieglitz, "What's Not on the Organization Chart," *The Conference Board Record,* November 1964, pp. 7–10.

[60]Joan Woodward, *Industrial Organization: Theory and Practice* (London: Oxford University Press, 1965), p. 239.

[61]*Ibid.*

[62]George Munchus III, "Employer-Employee Based Quality Circles in Japan: Human Resource Policy Implication for American Firms," *The Academy of Management Review,* Vol. 8, No. 2 (April 1983), 255–61.

[63]Ralph Katz, "The Effects of Group Longevity on Objective Communities and Performance," *Administrative Science Quarterly,* Vol. 27, No. 1 (March 1982), 81–104.

15

Intergroup Relations and Conflict

OVERVIEW

In this chapter we discuss the origins and management of *intergroup conflict*—conflict, for instance, between line and staff units, or production and sales departments. Intergroup conflict is a familiar aspect of organizations, and one that has important implications for organization structure and theory. The effectivenes of a structure depends on the departments' working together effectively, and although intergroup conflict can be useful when it leads to controlled competition and more creative decisions, it can also undermine the structure's effectiveness by reducing interdepartmental communication and collaboration.

The outline of this chapter is as follows:

A Introduction
B Types of conflict
 1 Functional and dysfunctional conflict
 2 Individual, interpersonal, and organizational conflict
 3 Line–staff conflict
C Sources of intergroup conflict
 1 Interdependencies and shared resources
 2 Intergroup differences in goals, values, or perceptions
 3 Authority imbalances
 4 Ambiguity

INTRODUCTION

Conflict is a familiar characteristic of organization life. One cause is the self-interest of individuals in the organization, which often manifests itself in competing objectives, philosophies, or methods, and in the associated struggles of one or more levels or departments to dominate others. Conflict may be interpersonal in nature and emerge out of the visceral, apparently "irrational" and selfish desires of some individuals to have their own way. Some people seem to be characterized by such tendencies and predisposed to respond to threatening or frustrating situations with aggression, anger, and abrasiveness. This sort of conflict stems from the structure of the organization and results in problems between departments, divisions, or other units in the organization.

Anyone who has ever worked in an organization is aware of the fact that conflict exists and that it can have dysfunctional effects on the organization and the people in it. Opposing parties tend to put their own aims above those of the organization, and the organization's effectiveness suffers as the goals that should be guiding performance become superseded by those of the opposing groups. Time that could have been used productively is instead squandered as the opposing parties hide valuable information from each other and jockey for position, each thereby preventing the other from carrying out assigned tasks; and those involved in the conflict can become so personally wrapped up in the tensions it produces that, if it is left unbridled, their emotional and physical well-being can be drastically undermined.

Perhaps the most insidious effect of organizational conflict is that it doesn't remain organization-bound for long; instead, its effects are observed by customers and stockholders, and it is taken home by the opponents, whose innocent families are often caught in the fallout.

TYPES OF CONFLICT

• *Functional and Dysfunctional Conflict*

Despite the fact that it can have adverse effects, most experts today view conflict as a potentially useful aspect of organizations because, if it is properly channeled, it can be an engine of innovation and change. According to Robbins, the idea that conflicts are inherently destructive has been replaced with what he calls the *interactionist* view.[1] This view recognizes the necessity of conflict and explicitly encourages a certain amount of controlled conflict in organizations. The basic case for this view is that some conflict is necessary if an organization is to avoid stagnation and myopic decision making, and an example often cited is a paper by Janis called "Group-Think." In this paper, Janis describes how potential critics of the abortive Bay of Pigs invasion of Cuba were put under tremendous pressure not to express their opposing viewpoints. For example, then–Attorney General Robert Kennedy at one point took Arthur Schlesinger aside and asked him why he was opposed to the invasion. According to Janis, Kennedy listened coldly and then said, "You may be right or you may be wrong, but the president has made his mind up. Don't push it any further. Now is the time for everyone to help him all they can."[2]

Janis believes that if Kennedy and his staff had encouraged the expression of more criticism, many of their questionable assumptions would have been challenged, and much better decisions would have resulted. As Robbins puts it:

> Constructive conflict is both valuable and necessary. Without conflict there would be few new challenges; there would be no stimulation to think through ideas; organizations would be only apathetic and stagnant.[3]

This generally positive picture of conflict appears to be supported by surveys of current management practice. In one recent survey of top and middle managers, for example, managers rated "conflict management" as of equal (or slightly higher) importance to topics like planning, communication, motivation, and decision making. The managers spent about 20 percent of their time on conflicts; yet they did not consider the conflict level in their organizations to be excessive. Instead, they rated it as about right—that is, at the midpoint of a scale running from "too low" to "too high."[4]

Keep in mind, however, that even though today we view intergroup conflict as an often useful reality in organizations, such a view did not always prevail. To the classicists, for instance, with their mechanical, closed-system view of organizations, conflict simply could not—or should not—arise, since a network of financial incentives and close supervision supposedly ensured unanimity of goals throughout the organization, and a rigid chain of command provided an ever-present vehicle for resolving disagreements. Similarly, although the human-relations theorists were more realistic in their views of conflict, they too viewed it as an aberration; for example, Mayo ". . . abhors conflict, competition, and disagreement; conflict to him is a social disease and cooperation is a social help."[5] The acceptance of conflict as a real and useful aspect of organizations is thus a fairly recent phenomenon.

• *Individual, Interpersonal, and Organizational Conflict*

Three different kinds of organizational conflict can be identified: individual, interpersonal, and intergroup. "Role conflict" is a familiar example of individual conflict. Role conflict occurs when a person is faced with conflicting orders, such that compliance with one would make it difficult or impossible to comply with the other. Sometimes such orders are obviously conflicting, as when a corporal receives orders from a captain that would force him to disobey an order from his sergeant. Sometimes, however, the source of the role conflict is not quite so obvious, as when obeying an order might force a person to violate his or her cherished values and sense of right and wrong. In any case, role conflict is a serious problem in organizations, one that can be stressful to the persons involved and can adversely effect their morale and performance.[6]

Conflict in organizations can also be interpersonal, occurring between individuals, or between individuals and groups. Sometimes, of course, such conflicts arise from "legitimate" sources, as when there are real differences in goals or objectives between the parties involved. Often, however, interpersonal conflicts arise not from legitimate differences but as a result of the personalities involved. Some people are simply more aggressive and conflict-prone than others, and some are so hypersensitive that every comment is viewed as an insult.[7]

Finally, there are intergroup organizational conflicts—for instance, between line and staff units, or between production and sales departments. We will focus on the causes and management of intergroup conflicts in the remainder of this chapter.

• *Line–Staff Conflict*

Creating separate line and staff units—for instance, appointing a personnel manager to do all recruiting in a plant where recruiting was formerly done by foremen—often leads to intergroup conflict (in this case, between the personnel manager and foremen).

Such line–staff conflict helps illustrate the sorts of factors that can cause intergroup conflict. In the example above, the work of the foremen and personnel manager is now *interdependent,* in that the foremen must check with the latter before hiring someone; foremen may respond to this apparent abridgement of their authority with anger and resentment, and conflicts thus arise.

Furthermore, there are sometimes *personality differences* between line and staff managers. Dalton found that staff personnel were usually younger and came from different social backgrounds from those of line managers.[8] He also found that the staff managers were better educated and more embroiled in the politics of the organization. In addition, since staff people had fewer organizational levels to advance to, each frequently tried to enlarge his or her own "empire."

Another problem is that line and staff managers often *differ in their views* of what activities are legitimate for the staff manager. Two researchers carried out a study that sheds some light on the nature of this problem.[9] They collected two types of data from 71 western New York organizations about perceptions of the role of the top-level staff personnel manager in each organization. The first set of data concerned the *extent to which the personnel manager and other staff and line managers agreed* on the current responsibilities of the personnel manager; these responsibilities included supervising subordinates, representing the company, union activities, and so forth. The second set of data concerned *what these groups of managers thought the personnel manager's responsibilities should be.*

The researchers found a consensus among the managers about the personnel manager's current responsibilities, but significant differences in what the three groups thought the legitimate responsibilities of the personnel manager should be. Both personnel administrators and other managers agreed that the former should participate more fully in organizational decisions; however, the personnel manager expressed the much stronger desire, and this seemed to lead to the conflict.[10]

One symptom of line–staff conflict may be the lower levels of satisfaction often found among staff managers. Three studies by the Opinion Research Corporation reported that engineers and scientists in staff positions were less satisfied with their jobs than were engineers and scientists in line positions.[11] Another study surveyed line and staff managers. Line managers reported a greater incidence of desirable conditions of work and seemed to believe that their needs were better satisfied than were those of the staff managers.[12] Similarly, Dalton found that staff managers in three plants had a turnover rate between two and four times that of line managers.[13]

SOURCES OF INTERGROUP CONFLICT

Many factors, including misunderstandings and personality clashes, can lead to conflict. Four main factors are discussed next.

• Interdependencies and Shared Resources

The existence of what March and Simon call a "felt need for joint decision making" is one important antecedent to intergroup conflict. Walton and Dutton define interdependence as "the extent to which two units depend on each other for assistance, information, compliance, or other coordinative acts in the performance of their respective tasks."[14] For obvious reasons, intergroup conflict is unlikely between units that are *not* required to interact with each other. Dutton and Walton have found that although interdependence can provide an incentive for collaboration, it also presents an occasion for conflict, and that interdependence thus tends to heighten the intensity of either antagonism or friendliness between units. It also increases the *consequences* of interunit conflict for organizational performance.

Similarly, conflict potential increases when two units depend upon a common pool of scarce resources, such as capital funds or a typing pool. As Walton and Dutton state:

> If the two units have interdependent tasks, the competition for scarce resources will tend to decrease interunit problem solving and coordination. Also, if competition for scarce resources is not mediated by some third unit and they must agree on their allocation, they will come into direct conflict.[15]

Examples abound of how interdependence or competition for scarce resources leads to conflict. Conflicts are a way of life for members of quality control and production departments, and sales and production departments, for example; these types of departments depend on each other and are interdependent. On the other hand, intergroup conflict is less likely to occur between, say, the finance and quality control departments, since the people in these departments are not too interdependent. Similarly, competition for scarce resources—such as when two or more departments must compete for limited funds, or for the services of a typing pool—generally leads to "office politics," hiding of information, and conflict.

Of course, interdependence does not necessarily have to lead to intergroup conflict. If the situation is managed correctly, or if the groups' overall aims are similar, interdependence can provide an incentive for collaboration rather than conflict; this is one reason that the conflict-management techniques discussed later in this chapter are important.[16]

• *Intergroup Differences in Goals, Values, or Perceptions*

People who are in agreement in terms of their goals, values, or perceptions are less likely to find themselves arguing than are those with fundamental differences.

Differences in Goals Differences in goals are a familiar source of intergroup conflict. Dutton and Walton, for instance, found that the preference of production units for long, economical runs conflicts with the preference of sales units for quick delivery for good customers, and that these differing goals often lead to intergroup conflict.[17]

Similarly, Dalton found that line–staff conflicts often arise because staff units value change, whereas line units value stability.[18]

Other fundamental differences in goals that have been found to lead to conflict include emphasis on flexibility versus stability; emphasis on short-run versus long-run performance; and emphasis on measurable versus societal needs.[19] In summary, when the goals of two groups are similar or identical, there is little chance that serious conflict will arise, but when there is a fundamental difference in goals, it probably will.

Differences in Values and Perceptions Similarly, when two groups differ in terms of their values or in the way they perceive a situation, conflicts are more likely to arise. One good example of this is illustrated in the sorts of differences that lead to line–staff conflict. Dalton's study of line–staff conflict provides some specific examples of how differences in values and perceptions can lead to conflict. He found that conflicts between line and staff managers arose because:

1 Staff personnel tend to be younger, more educated, of a higher social status, and more ambitious and restless than line managers.
2 The older, often more experienced line managers tend to dislike having to take advice from younger staff managers. They fear being "shown up."
3 Line managers tend to view staff as agents on trial, as people who must constantly prove themselves. The staff managers, on the other hand, view themselves as experts.
4 Line managers frequently feel that staff members are encroaching on their duties and prerogatives.
5 Line managers complain that staff members give unsound advice, steal credit, and fail to see the "whole picture."
6 Staff managers, on the other hand, feel that line managers are "bull-headed," do not give staff enough authority, and resist new ideas.

Organizational Differentiation Lawrence and Lorsch believe that "organizational differentiation" is a frequent source of intergroup conflict.[20] They found that as each department in an organization tries to cope with the unique demands of its own environment, it necessarily develops its own types of procedures, cherished values, and points of view. For example, a research department in a chemical firm might be run very democratically, and its personnel might develop a rather long-term time perspective, since most of the things they are working on will not reach fruition for years. On the other hand, the production department might be run more autocratically, and its managers might be expected to put a much greater emphasis on immediate results. Lawrence and Lorsch believe that the greater the differentiation between departments, the more *potential* for conflict there is. However, they found that whether conflict in fact emerges depends on several things, including the way departments settle their differences.

• *Authority Imbalances*

When a department's actual authority is inconsistent with its members' prestige, intergroup conflicts are more likely to develop. Seiler studied several firms and found that intergroup conflicts arise either because points of view are in conflict (the "differences in goals, values, and perceptions" problem we discussed above), or because a department's authority is inconsistent with its prestige. (See Table 15-1.) As an example of the latter, Seiler found that in one company, the production department was in the position of having to accept instructions from a production engineering department composed of employees with skills no greater than (and in fact, quite similar to) those possessed by production employees. As a result, "production managers spent an inordinate amount of time checking for consistency among the various items produced by production engineering."[21]

• *Ambiguity*

Dutton and Walton found that where responsibility for a problem could not clearly be assigned to a department, there was an increase in conflict between units. Similarly, Dalton, in his study of line–staff conflict, found that conflicts often arose when it was difficult to determine whether a contribution had been made by the line or the staff unit. Conflict is also a familiar phenomenon in organizations where departmental responsibilities are not clearly delineated and where "power vacuums" arise and each department fights to fill those vacuums.

TABLE 15-1 Summary of Seiler's Findings on Organizational Conflict

	Where Points of View Are Closely Allied	*Where Points of View Are in Conflict*
Where authority* is consistent with prestige differences	We will tend to find . . . . . . Collaboration and productive conflict.	We will tend to find . . . . . . Energies absorbed by efforts to force points of view on other groups. Relations will be formal and often arbitrated by outsiders.
Where authority is inconsistent with prestige differences	We will tend to find . . . . . . Energies devoted to regaining a "proper" authority relationship. Relations will usually be distant and between low hierarchical levels of the two groups (e.g., messengers).	We will tend to find . . . . . . Energies initially expended on forcing points of view and righting authority relations. But the task will be so patently fruitless that the groups will break off contact rather than expose themselves to further threat.

*As indicated by work flow.

Source: John A. Seiler, "Diagnosing Interdepartmental Conflict," *Harvard Business Review*, September–October 1963, pp. 121–32.

A MODEL OF INTERGROUP CONFLICT

What is the process through which organizational conflicts arise? Do conflicts between departments go through a predictable sequence of stages? We address these questions next.

Several models attempt to explain and describe the emergence and process of intergroup conflict. For example, Lewis Pondy has developed a model that assumes that intergroup conflict is a sequence of interlocking "conflict episodes."[22] He says that whether the conflict involves groups at different levels in the organization or groups at the same level, it usually evolves through five fairly distinct stages.

• *Stage 1: The Latent Conflict Stage*

Pondy says that each conflict episode usually begins with a "latent conflict" stage. At this stage, the basic prerequisites (such as competition for scarce resources, or differences in goals between departments) are present, but the conflict has not yet emerged.

• *Stage 2: The Perceived Conflict Stage*

Whether or not these prerequisites lead to conflict depends in part on the *perceptions* of the people involved. Prerequisites of conflict are always present to some degree between departments, but it is only when the differences are seen as significant that they lead to conflict. For example, if two departments have to share a water cooler, conflicts would probably not arise even if the sharing caused some waiting. On the other hand, if the departments had to share a typing pool and reports were often late because of it, there would probably be more likelihood that conflict would emerge as each department tried to get its work typed first.

Conversely, conflict may be *perceived* even though the basic conditions of conflict—what Pondy calls latent conflict—do not exist. One familiar example of this occurs when there is a "communications breakdown" or misunderstanding between groups with respect to each other's true position. Here, basic sources of conflict like competition for scarce resources and differences in goals do not actually exist. However, owing to misunderstandings, group members misperceive the true positions of the members of the other group, and so conflicts may arise.

• *Stage 3: The Felt Conflict Stage*

The next stage in the evolution of a conflict may be called the "felt conflict" stage. Pondy says that even though people perceive that there is a basis for conflict, it will usually not arise unless the differences become personalized or internalized ("felt"). In other words, for conflicts to emerge, the people in each group usually have to become "ego-involved" in a conflict relationship, in that each of them becomes so intent on "winning" that the best interests of the organization are ignored. Often what results is a feud, in which the people in each department identify so completely with the goals and values of their own groups that they see every action of the competing group personally. Like the hillbilly feuds of years ago, the members of each group may continue trying to "pick off" the opposing group's projects and people, even though to an outsider the conflict seems baseless and irrational.

• *Stage 4: The Manifest Conflict Stage*

The next stage, according to Pondy, is characterized by open conflict. Open, violent aggression is the most extreme example of such behavior, but it would be unusual in work organizations. However, the motivation driving such aggression may remain and may manifest itself in sabotage, defensive coalitions, apathy, or rigid, blind adherence to rules, all of which, of course, reduce the organization's effectiveness.[23]

• *Stage 5: Conflict Aftermath*

Assuming that the conflict does manifest itself, the way it is managed and resolved has important implications for whether it results in a more cooperative relationship or in continued conflict. Pondy says (and many experts would agree) that if the conflict is confronted and resolved to the satisfaction of all participants, the basis for a more cooperative relationship may be laid. On the other hand, "if the conflict is merely suppressed but not resolved, the latent conditions of conflict may be aggravated and explode in more serious forms until they are rectified or until the relationship dissolves." This legacy of conflict, which may be a force for either cooperation or continued conflict, is what Pondy calls "conflict aftermath."

In summary, the aftermath of conflict may be either positive or negative for the organization, depending on how the conflict is confronted and resolved.

• *Walton and Dutton: A General Model of Intergroup Conflict*

Walton and Dutton have developed a "general model" of interunit conflict that they suggest is:

> . . . applicable to all lateral relations between any two organizational units (departments, divisions, sections, and so on) that engage in any type of transaction, including joint decision making, exchanging information, providing expertise or advice, and auditing or inspecting.[24]

Their model includes the following sets of related variables: antecedents to conflict, attributes of the lateral relationship, management of the interface, and consequences of the relationship. The model is presented in Figure 15-1.

Antecedents to Interunit Conflict and Collaboration These writers say that manifest conflict results largely from factors that originate outside the particular relationship or that antedate the relationship. Many of these factors or conditions for conflict are thus "built into" the relationship by those who design the structure and technology of the organization. For example, conflict sources like interdependence, authority–prestige imbalances, rewards, ambiguities, and sharing of common resources are often part of the environment of the groups, and are factors over which the groups have little or no control. Other factors, like communication breakdowns, dissatisfaction, and interunit differences in values and perceptions, are usually at least partly under the control of the group members themselves.

The Interdepartmental Relationship The nature of the interdepartmental relationship is the next important factor in these writers' model of the conflict process. They distinguish between "integrative" and "distributive" lateral relationships. These differ as follows: Decision making in the integrative relationship emphasizes problem solving and free exchange of information, whereas that in the distributive relationship emphasizes bargaining and information distortion. Interactions in the integrative relationship are flexible and open; those in the distributive relationship are rigid and formal. The attitudes toward the other unit when an integrative relationship prevails are positive and friendly; those for the distributive relationship are negative and suspicious. These writers say that developing an integrative relationship is advisable, and that a distributive relationship always results in conflict.

Management of the Interface Walton and Dutton say that even though the conflict potential of a situation is largely determined by the antecedents and nature of the interunit relationship, some organizations are more successful at controlling

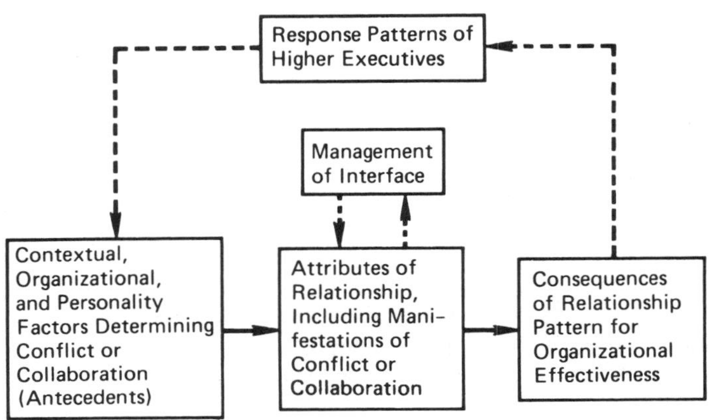

FIGURE 15-1 Walton and Dutton's General Model of Interunit Conflict. *Source:* Richard E. Walton and John M. Dutton, "The Management of Interdepartmental Conflict: A Model and Review," *Administrative Science Quarterly*, Vol. 14, No. 1 (March 1969), 78.

conflict because of the *conflict-management strategies* they use; these strategies are what they mean by "management of the interface." For example, is there an *open confrontation* of conflict, a *problem-solving* orientation, or a "smoothing over" of problems?

Consequences of Interunit Conflicts Intergroup conflicts, say Walton and Dutton, can result in competition, concealment, rigidity, appeals to superiors, and low trust and suspicion. However, they say, whether the conflict results in positive or negative consequences will depend on things such as the personalities of the participants and the conflict-management strategies used.

• Models of Conflict: Summary and Implications

These models have much in common, and their commonalities and differences allow us to combine them into a general model of the conflict process. It is presented in Figure 15-2 and consists of three components: antecedents of conflict, conflict moderators, and actual, manifest conflict.

Pondy and Walton and Dutton conclude that the conflict process begins with certain *antecedents*. For Pondy, these antecedents include, for example, competition for scarce resources, drives for autonomy, and differences of subunit goals. For Walton and Dutton, they include interdependence, authority–prestige imbalances, sharing of common resources, and rewards and ambiguities.

Second, these theorists agree that several factors *moderate* or influence whether conflict in fact occurs. Pondy, for example, says that whether conflict becomes perceived and felt depends on several things, like communications break-

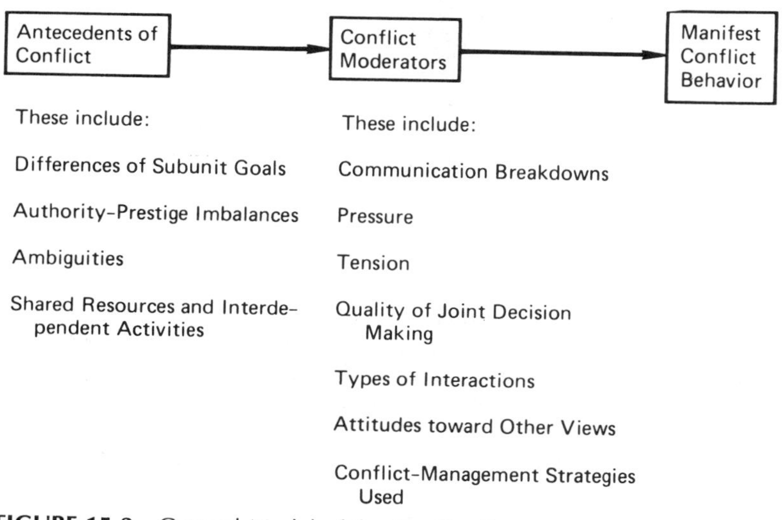

FIGURE 15-2 General Model of the Conflict Process

downs, and pressure and tension. Walton and Dutton talk in terms of the quality of joint decision making, the type of interaction, and the attitudes toward the other units, as well as the conflict-management strategies that are used.

Finally, there is an actual or *manifest* conflict stage, which, says Pondy, is characterized by open conflict.

Some implications of this discussion (and of our previous discussion on the sources of conflict) are these: There are various sources or *antecedents* of conflict, including interdependencies and shared resources; differences in goals, values, or perceptions; authority imbalances; and ambiguities. Furthermore, whether conflict arises depends on such things as the quality of joint decision making and the strategies used to *manage* any conflicts. Therefore, techniques for reducing specific antecedents of conflict and for more effectively *managing* conflicts should be useful, and we turn to such techniques in the next section.

TECHNIQUES FOR MANAGING ORGANIZATIONAL CONFLICT

The many techniques for managing or resolving conflicts generally fall into one of three categories. The first involves setting *superordinate goals* and thus creating an area of commonality between the previously competing groups—for example, by convincing each that they share a common enemy. Second, there are various *structural approaches* that involve, for instance, reducing the interdependencies between the competing groups or referring the disagreement to a common superior. Finally, different *conflict-resolution behaviors* can be used; these include avoiding the problem, confronting the problem, and negotiating a solution.

• Common Goals and Conflict Management

Most of the conflict models we discussed assume that incompatible goals are a necessary antecedent for the development of conflict.[25] Conversely, it is generally acknowledged that the existence of "superordinate" goals—goals "which have a compelling appeal for both [groups] but which neither could achieve without the other"—reduces dysfunctional conflict.[26] Edgar Schein, for example, points out:

> The fundamental problem of intergroup competition is the conflict of goals and the breakdown of interaction and communication between the groups; this breakdown in turn permits and stimulates perceptual distortion and mutual negative stereotyping. The basic strategy of reducing conflict, therefore, is to find goals upon which groups can agree and to reestablish valid communication between the groups. The tactics to employ in implementing this strategy can [include] . . . locating a common enemy [and] locating a superordinate goal.[27]

Therefore, one of the most familiar and sensible ways of shortcircuiting conflicts is to find some common ground that the parties can agree on. In labor–management negotiations, for example, arbitrators generally begin their work by finding some point of agreement. As another example, national leaders use the ploy of claiming that their countries are about to be attacked in order to bring about at least a temporary unification by the opposing factions in their own countries.

In summary, disagreement over goals often leads to conflict. Conversely, the existence of "superordinate" goals—goals "which have a compelling appeal for both [groups] but which neither could achieve without the other"—reduces conflict.

The Sherif Experiments in Group Conflict Sherif carried out a series of experiments in intergroup conflict and common goals using groups of boys in a summer camp.[28] His hypothesis was that "when two groups have conflicting aims—i.e., when one can achieve its end only at the expense of the other—their members will become hostile to each other even though the groups are composed of normal, well-adjusted individuals." To test this hypothesis, his research team produced friction between the groups of boys by arranging a tournament of games, including baseball, touch football, a tug-of-war, and a treasure hunt. They found that although the tournament started in a spirit of good sportsmanship, as it progressed, this good feeling soon evaporated.

Between the groups, there sprang up enmity, as members began calling their rivals "sneaks" and "cheaters." They refused to have anything to do with those in the opposing group, and boys often turned against buddies they had chosen as "best friends" when they first arrived at the camp. The rival groups made threatening posters and planned raids against each other. In one case, a group burned a banner left behind by the opposing team, only to have its own banner seized the next morning. Name-calling, scuffles, and raids were the rule of the day.

Within each group, solidarity increased, and there were other important changes as well. One group deposed its leader because he could not "take it" in the contest with the adversary. Another group made a hero of a boy who had previously been regarded as a bully. Generally speaking, morale and cooperativeness within each group became stronger.

Sherif and his associates then hypothesized that "just as competition generates friction, working in a common endeavor should promote harmony." They therefore set about creating a series of "urgent and natural" situations that would face their competing groups with the need to work together to accomplish superordinate goals. On one occasion, the researchers rigged a breakdown in the pipeline supplying water to the camp. They called the boys together to tell them of the crisis, and both these initially hostile groups promptly volunteered to search the water line for the trouble. The two groups worked together harmoniously, and before the end of that afternoon, they had located and corrected the difficulty.

Another time, the two groups were taken on an outing some distance from the camp. A truck was to go to town for food, but when everyone was hungry and ready to eat, it was found that the truck would not start, a situation that had been arranged by the researchers. The boys got a rope, and both groups pulled together to start the truck.

Yet the researchers found that joint efforts like these did not immediately dispel hostility:

> At first the groups returned to the old bickering and name calling as soon as the job at hand was finished. But gradually the series of cooperative acts reduced friction and conflict. The members of the two groups began to feel more friendly to each other. . . . The boys stopped shoving in the meal line. They no longer called each other names, and sat together at the table. New friendships developed between individuals in the two groups. In the end the groups were actively seeking opportunities to mingle, to entertain, and "treat each other."[29]

On the basis of such findings, Sherif concluded:

> What our limited experiments have shown is that the possibilities for achieving harmony are greatly enhanced when groups are brought together to work toward common ends. Then favorable information about a disliked group is seen in a new light, and leaders are in a position to take bolder steps toward cooperation. In short, hostility gives way when groups pull together to achieve overriding goals which are real and compelling to all concerned.[30]

Incentive Systems Wieland and Ullrich point out that "goal differentiation can also be reduced through the use of incentive systems designed to reward activities that benefit the larger system, as opposed to those that are primarily in the interest of subunits."[31] Many (perhaps most) organizational reward systems, by rewarding the performance of individuals (or individual departments), lead to a "win-lose" mentality in the organization. The quality control department, for example, may be rewarded for the number of defects it finds, but its rewards are obviously received at the expense of another department, usually production.

The Sears, Roebuck Company recently revised the method used in rewarding store managers, and the change is a good example of the use of reward systems to reduce intergroup conflict. For years, Sears store managers were rewarded for increasing the sales of their own stores. In recent years, however, it became apparent that this system was breeding conflictual behavior by store managers. For example, managers in the same geographical area were generally not inclined to advertise areawide sales, and they resisted transferring merchandise from one store to another. Under the new reward system, a store manager's reward is based not only on the sales of his own store but on the sales of all Sears stores in his area, and this has resulted in a marked increase in collaborative behavior by store managers.

• *Structural Approaches to Conflict Management*

You can also use various *structural* approaches to managing and resolving intergroup conflicts—for example, by having the groups appeal to a common superior.

Appeal to a Common Superior The most common way of resolving disagreements between departments is to refer the disagreements to a common superior. For example, if the vice-presidents for sales and production cannot reach agreement on some point, they would typically refer their disagreement to the president for a final, binding decision.

Stagner has made a study of how executives in major corporations typically resolve their conflicts.[32] The first thing he found was that conflicts are usually not resolved on the basis of logical arguments concerning profitability and so on, although the arguments are often couched in economic terms. Instead, most conflicts are resolved by resorting to power—power based on things like ability to provide rewards. Thus, the opponent who has the most "clout" is typically the one that prevails. Second, Stagner found that the chief executive is the most widely used arbiter of disagreements. In some cases, the chief executive simply resolves the conflict through decree; in other cases, he or she acts as a mediator or arbitrator. As an alternative, some corporations let the executive vice-president arbitrate the conflict; this leaves open the possibility of appealing the decision to the president if necessary. Although Stagner's study focused on the actions of executives, one would assume that the same general conclusions would apply for lower levels as well. For example, if the managers for quality control and production are in disagreement, referring the disagreement to the plant manager for a decision would probably be a logical step.

Reduce Interdependencies Conflicts rarely arise between groups not required to work interdependently, and so one way to reduce conflict is to reduce the required interunit interdependencies. James Thompson distinguished three types of interdependence—pooled, sequential, and reciprocal—and his proposal has recently received some empirical support.[33]

Pooled interdependence is exemplified by a fully divisionalized, decentralized organization in which the separate divisions are relatively self-contained and independent. On the other hand, as you can see in Figure 15-3, *sequential* interdependence results in a greater degree of interdependence between units, since the output of one unit now becomes the input to a second unit in the sequence, with the receiving unit quite dependent for its success on the sending unit. (An example here would be the dependence of a production department on a purchasing department.) Finally, Thompson suggests that units are most interdependent when that interdependence is *reciprocal*. In this situation, the output of various units become input for the others:

> This is illustrated by the airline which contains both operations and maintenance units. The production of the maintenance units is an input for operations, in the form of serviceable aircraft; and the product (or by-product) of operations is an input for maintenance, in the form of an aircraft needing maintenance. Under conditions of reciprocal interdependence, each unit involved is penetrated by the other. . . .[34]

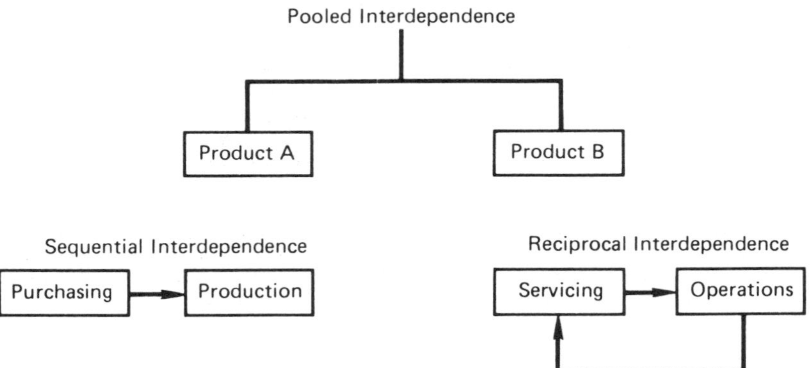

FIGURE 15-3 Types of Interdependence. *Source:* Based on James Thompson, *Organizations in Action* (New York: McGraw-Hill, 1967), Chap. 20.

Generally speaking, the potential for conflict should increase as the interdependencies between two groups increase. One alternative for preventing or managing conflicts is therefore to reduce interdependencies by moving from reciprocal to sequential and finally to pooled interdependence. At the extreme, this might involve what Galbraith calls the creation of "self-contained tasks," an arrangement that is thus useful for managing conflicts as well as for reducing the amount of information to be processed by the chief executive.

Rather than separating the units organizationally, a similar alternative involves separating them physically. Neilsen says that "physically separating the conflicting groups has the distinct advantage of preventing more damage from being done and of preventing the creation of further rationales for fighting." On the other hand, this tactic "may require continuous surveillance to keep the parties separate, especially if tempers are hot and energy levels high."[35] Also, physical separation does not encourage confronting basic problems or working through solutions; it is therefore more of a stopgap measure than a cure.

Reduce Shared Resources When two units are required to share scarce resources, the potential for intergroup conflict increases, and so another structural conflict-management approach involves reducing such sharing. March and Simon say that one technique for accomplishing this is increasing the available resources to the point where they are no longer considered "scarce."

Exchange of Personnel Conflict experts have long prescribed having conflicting groups trade personnel for a specified period as a way to reduce and manage conflicts. An exchange of people is very similar to a tactic psychologists call "role reversal," which is aimed at creating greater understanding between people by forcing each to present and defend the other's position.[36]

In one relevant study, 62 three-person groups composed of students each acted as either a "manufacturer" or a "wholesaler" of medical instruments; their goal was to get agreement on the selling price and quantity of these instruments. The researchers created a conflict situation in several ways. For example, they told the members of each group that their dollar earnings would depend on their group's performance relative to all other groups that had assumed corresponding positions in previous trials. To test the usefulness of role reversal, 30 minutes into the bargaining session, randomly selected groups were handed a memo that said the chief executive officers of each firm had decided to undertake a temporary exchange of personnel; to this end, the "manufacturer's salesman" and "wholesaler's purchasing agent" were to trade positions for 20 minutes. The subjects were physically exchanged, and when 20 minutes had elapsed, the "salesman" and the "purchasing agent" were returned to their "home" companies. The bargaining then continued until the trial ended.

The researchers concluded (from their analysis of various measures of intergroup conflict and collaboration) that the exchange-of-personnel program was effective at reducing conflict and speeding agreement. In fact, they point out, it was successful even though it was mandatory, involved the least influential members of the organizations, and was of relatively short duration.

Create Special "Integrators" In their study, Lawrence and Lorsch found that many companies reduce interdepartmental conflict by setting up special liaisons between the conflicting departments. In the high-technology plastics industry, for instance, successful companies set up special departments whose job it is to coordinate the work of the research, sales, and manufacturing departments, which in turn can each remain separate (more independent) organizationally. In the food industry (where technical changes are not as frequent), *individuals* are assigned the task of coordinating the work of the separate departments. In some industries, such as the container industry, in which technical changes are few, special liaisons are not necessary at all; here, instead, conflicts are ironed out by being referred to a common superior.

• *Interpersonal-Conflict Resolution Techniques*

There are many ways of settling an argument, and some are more effective than others. A list of the more popular conflict-resolution techniques would include these:

- *Competing:* "The other person took a stand and stuck to it."
- *Avoiding:* "The other person tried to avoid the task of negotiating."
- *Accommodating:* "The other person gave in to my position."
- *Compromising:* "The other person suggests a middle ground or compromise."
- *Collaborating:* "The other person communicated all of his/her information and encouraged me to do the same."

- *Confrontation:* "At first we did not have much agreement, but we kept confronting the issue until we agreed on the best solution."
- *Smoothing:* "The other person always tries to make a joke of the problem, in the hope that by sweeping it under the rug the problem will just go away."
- *Forcing:* "If the other managers are willing to go ahead my way, there is no problem, but if there is a conflict, then I take the decision to someone higher up."[37]

As you might expect, conflict resolution based on "confrontation" and "collaboration," in which both parties meet to confront the facts and hammer out a solution, is usually more effective than a technique like smoothing over the conflict, by "pushing the problems under a rug." Lawrence and Lorsch, for instance, in their study of differentiation and integration, found that managers in the highest-performing organizations usually rely on a confrontation approach, and only occasionally use a "backup" approach of forcing (appeal to a superior) when all else fails; managers in these companies rarely if ever use a "smoothing over" approach.[38]

The Renwick Study In another study, Patricia Renwick found that the topic and source of the disagreement influence the way the conflict is managed.[39] Subjects in her study were 72 employees from two large manufacturing firms in the San Francisco area. They were drawn from diverse departments, including sales, marketing, accounting, production, research and development, and computer operations, and occupied a variety of positions.

Employees were asked to indicate the extent to which they would use each of the conflict-management behaviors in Table 15-2 for conflicts involving each of three different topics: (1) salaries, promotions, and performance appraisals; (2) personal habits and mannerisms; and (3) physical working conditions and organiza-

TABLE 15-2 Modes of Conflict Resolution

Conflict-Management Behavior	*Questionnaire Items*
Withdrawal	Refrain from argument, try not to get involved. (very likely 1 2 3 4 5 very unlikely)
Smoothing	Play down the differences and emphasize common interests. (very unlikely 1 2 3 4 5 very unlikely)
Compromise	Search for an intermediate position, try to find a compromise. (very unlikely 1 2 3 4 5 very unlikely)
Forcing	Use the power of my position or knowledge to win acceptance of my point of view. (very likely 1 2 3 4 5 very unlikely)
Confrontation	Bring the problem clearly into the open and carry it out to resolution, even if feelings are likely to get hurt. (very unlikely 1 2 3 4 5 very unlikely)

tional policies and procedures. Then they were asked to indicate the extent to which they would use each of these behaviors if they thought the source of the conflict was (1) differences in knowledge of factual material, (2) personality differences, or (3) differences in attitudes or opinions.

Renwick found first that different *topics* are more likely to elicit different types of conflict-management behavior. For instance, employees "were inclined to *confront* topics involving salaries, promotions, or performance appraisals and were likely to rely on *compromise* to deal with conflicts concerning personal habits and mannerisms."[40] When the topic of the conflict concerned relatively unimportant matters such as physical working conditions and organizational procedures, however, no real preferences in conflict-management behaviors were observed.

The *source* of the conflict also affects the type of conflict-management behavior that is preferred. For example, disagreements originating from substantive factors (such as differences in knowledge or factual material) are more likely to elicit confrontation, and personality differences and differences in attitudes or opinions are more likely to elicit compromising or smoothing behavior.

Renwick, like Lawrence and Lorsch, also found a tendency for subjects to use "backup" behaviors should the primary conflict-management behavior fail. For example, she found that compromise and smoothing are likely to be used together, and that confrontation and compromise are often paired. Finally, her findings also suggest that people seem to have preferences for particular conflict-management behaviors, and that "they will be predisposed to adopt a specific method of conflict resolution to deal with a variety of topics and sources of disagreement."[41]

In summary, a confrontation approach usually has the best results, especially when the conflict involves major issues like salaries and promotions.[42] In other words, when it comes to important issues, the wisest strategy seems to be to confront the issues head-on and hammer out an agreement. On the other hand, smoothing over problems seems to work well enough for relatively minor issues, although for major ones it has insidious effects: Managers who are prone to smooth over problems by not taking definite stands and trying to "laugh off" disagreements eventually find that the cumulative effect of their mismanagement is an explosive situation, one they can no longer control.

Confrontation Meeting Some organizations have used a technique called *the confrontation meeting* to "clear the air" and resolve intergroup conflicts. The technique usually requires the use of a special consultant (sometimes called a "change agent") who is skilled in its use. Confrontation meetings seem to be especially useful when misperceptions are at the root of the intergroup conflict, such as when each group misperceives or misunderstands the opposing group's true position. The typical confrontation meeting lasts from four to eight hours and usually begins with the consultant discussing in general terms such topics as organizational communication, the need for mutual misunderstanding, and the need for members of the management team to share responsibility for accomplishing the organization's goals. The discussion might turn to an analysis of the organization's operating problems, including how advertising budgets are arrived at, how sales commissions are computed, and how financial controls are imposed. In any case, most confrontation meetings aim at reducing intergroup conflict, as between line and staff personnel.

Bennis describes a confrontation meeting that was aimed at dealing with this sort of intergroup conflict.[43] The meeting took place during a State Department conference held at the Massachusetts Institute of Technology and involved conflict between Foreign Service officers and the administrative staff of the State Department. The problem was that:

> . . . the stereotyping and mutual distrust, if not downright hostility, blocked communication and reduced effectiveness enormously, for each "side" perceived the other as more threatening than any realistic overseas enemy.[44]

The two groups of officers were assigned to separate rooms and were asked to discuss three questions:

1. What qualities best describe our group?
2. What qualities best describe the other group?
3. What qualities do we predict the other group would assign to us?

Each group was asked to develop a list of words or phrases that they felt best described their answers to each question. The results were as follows:

The Foreign Service officers saw themselves as being:

1. Reflective
2. Qualitative
3. Humanistic, subjective
4. Cultural, with broad interests
5. Generalizers
6. Interculturally sensitive
7. Detached from personal conflicts

The Foreign Service officers saw administrative officers as being (or having):

1. Doers and implementers
2. Quantitive
3. Decisive and forceful
4. Noncultural
5. Limited goals
6. Jealous of us
7. Interested in form more than substance
8. Wave of the future! [exclamation mark theirs]
9. Drones but necessary evils

The Foreign Service officers predicted that the administrative officers would see them as being:

1 Arrogant, snobbish
2 Intellectuals
3 Cliquish
4 Resistant to change
5 Inefficient, dysfunctional
6 Vacillating and compromising
7 Effete

The administrative officers saw themselves as being (or having):

1 Decisive, guts
2 Resourceful, adapative
3 Pragmatic
4 Service-oriented
5 Able to get along
6 Receptive to change
7 Dedicated to job
8 Misunderstood
9 Useful
10 Modest! [added by the person doing the presenting]

The administrative officers saw the Foreign Service officers as being:

1 Masked, isolated
2 Resourceful, serious
3 Respected
4 Inclined to stability
5 Dedicated to job
6 Necessary
7 Externally oriented
8 Cautious
9 Rational
10 Surrounded by mystique
11 Manipulative
11 Defensive

The administrative officers predicted that the Foreign Service officers would see them as being (or having):

1 Necessary evils
2 Defensive, inflexible

3 Preoccupied with minutiae
4 Negative and bureaucratic
5 Limited perspective
6 Less culture (educated clerks)
7 Misunderstood
8 Practical
9 Protected
10 Resourceful

The two groups of officers then assembled together and proceeded to discuss their own lists and those developed by the other group. They questioned each other about the lists, and after several hours, "it appeared as if each side moved to the position where they at least understood the other side's point of view."

• *Managing Intergroup Conflict: Summary*

Various techniques can be used to successfully head off or manage intergroup conflicts, so such conflict need not undermine the effectiveness of an organization or its structure. Common, "superordinate" goals can be established between the groups or departments—for example, through the use of incentive systems. Various structural approaches to conflict management can be used, including appealing to the superior, reducing interdependencies and shared resources, exchanging personnel, creating special integrators, and providing for frequent interaction. Finally, the evidence suggests that certain conflict-resolution behaviors, such as confrontation, are often more effective than are ones like the "smoothing over" of problems.

SUMMARY

Intergroup conflict has important implications for organization structure and theory. In this chapter, we discussed the sources, processes, and management of intergroup conflict. Sources include interdependencies and shared resources; differences in goals, values, and perceptions; authority imbalances; and ambiguities. The process, we said, can be viewed in terms of antecedents ⟶ moderators ⟶ and actual conflicts. Conflict-management strategies aimed at developing common goals, changing the organization structure, and choosing the best conflict-management behavior were shown to be effective.

How are organization structure and intergroup conflict related? In several ways. First, the effectiveness of a structure depends on the resulting departments' working together effectively. Intergroup conflict—between line and staff units, or production and sales units, for example—can be useful, but can also reduce communication and collaboration between departments so that the structure no longer functions effectively.

Second, there are several structural antecedents of conflict—for example, interdependencies, differences in goals and values (which may derive from the structural position of one department vis-à-vis another), authority imbalances, and ambiguity—that are based in the structure of the organization.

Finally, the structure of the organization provides a useful vehicle for reducing or managing conflict. This might involve, for example, referring conflicts to a common superior, reducing interdependencies, reducing shared resources, exchanging personnel, or creating special integrator departments or positions.

Discussion Questions

1 Compare and contrast the Pondy and Walton and Dutton models of intergroup conflict.
2 Does intergroup conflict always have to be dysfunctional? Explain the conditions under which it might and might not be dysfunctional.
3 Explain some of the techniques you could use to manage interdepartmental conflicts.
4 Explain the sources of intergroup conflict.
5 What is the relation between intergroup conflict and organization design?

APPENDIX TO CHAPTER 15
Reducing Organizational Conflict: An Incompatible-Response Approach

When it comes to confrontations at work, it is often not what you say but how you say it that determines whether you have a rational exchange of views or a gut-wrenching argument. Reporting the results of a recent study in this area, Baron concludes that you can disagree strongly with a person's views and still not cause anger, as long as you do it in a manner that elicits responses that are incompatible with anger and aggression.

His study was based on the idea that most people are incapable of simultaneous incompatible responses, like anger and sympathy. Applied to the control of anger and aggression, this principle suggests that if people who have been frustrated or annoyed are made to feel, say, sympathetic toward the person who has annoyed them, their anger and aggression should be markedly reduced.

In this study, male and female subjects played the role of executives in a large company and discussed important organizational issues with another person (issues like should their company manufacture a new product). Unbeknown to the subjects, the second person was actually the researcher's accomplice; his job was to disagree with the subject's views in all cases and to make it clear that he would reject any of the subject's efforts to get his or her views accepted. The *manner* in which he disagreed differed, though. First, he either simply disagreed with the subject ("Well, I can see how you feel that way, but I guess I disagree"), or was arrogant and condescending ("Hmph . . . that makes no sense to me at all"). Thus, the associate's manner during the discussion itself was one of either reasonable disagreement or condescension.

He also used different approaches with different subjects *after* the discussion took place. After the subject and the associate had discussed the problem, the researcher found an excuse to leave the two of them alone for several minutes. During this period, the associate either sat quietly and said nothing, or engaged in one of three distinct activities designed to induce positive feelings among the subjects. In the *gift* situation, the accomplice reached into his pocket, pulled out a package of Life Savers, and offered one to his subject. In the *sympathy* situation, he remarked that if he had seemed "uptight" during the first part of the study, it was because he had so many tests that week. Finally, in the *humor* condition, the accomplice took three cartons from an old book, explaining that he had to choose one for use in a communication course, and asked the subject to examine them and indicate which one he or she found most amusing. After a few minutes, the experimenter returned and had the subjects fill out a questionnaire in which they described their moods and how they thought they would deal with future conflicts with the accomplice.[45]

The findings of this study show that it wasn't so much what the accomplice said but how he said it that led to anger on the part of the subject. First, as one might expect, the subjects who were exposed to condescension rather than just rational disagreement reported themselves as being in a much more negative mood and as much less apt to engage in conciliatory, cooperative efforts in future conflicts with the associate than did those with whom the associate had simply disagreed. Specifically, those exposed to condescension were much less likely to engage in compromise or cooperation and more likely to engage in competition than those in a disagreement situation.

Furthermore, the study showed that inducing reactions that were incompatible with anger, such as sympathy or humor, could lead to less anger and a much more constructive approach to problem solving. Whether it was the small offer of a gift, or the humor, or the eliciting of sympathy, the three procedures significantly improved the subject's mood, enhanced the subject's readings of the accomplice, and increased the subject's reported preference for using constructive management of conflict when dealing with the accomplice in the future, while reducing the subject's preference for a less constructive tactic like competition.

There are at least two main implications. First, it seems apparent that even the small effort involved in inducing feelings incompatible with anger (actions like the gift, or sympathy, or humor) during and after a disagreement can make it easier to disagree strongly with someone but still maintain a good relationship.

The second implication concerns the powerful effect on the subject's behavior produced by the accomplice's personal style, and particularly whether he just reasonably disagreed or used a condescending style. Subjects exposed to the condescending style reported more negative moods, assigned lower ratings to the accomplice, and reacted to conflict in much less constructive ways than did subjects with whom he simply disagreed. In interpreting these findings, it is important to recall that in both cases, it wasn't what the person said but how he said it that made the major difference. In fact, whether he disagreed or was condescending, the accomplice *always* disagreed strongly with the subject's views and always based such disagreements on the identical arguments. The major difference in the accomplice's actions was the manner in which he disagreed, which made a world of difference in determining whether the disagreement was managed constructively or led to anger and destructive conflict.

Footnotes

[1]Steven Robbins, "Managing Organizational Conflict," in Jerome Schnee, E. Kirby Warren, and Harold Lazarus, *The Progress of Management* (Englewood Cliffs, N.J.: Prentice-Hall, 1977), pp. 163–76.

[2]I.L. Janis, *Victims of Group Think* (Boston: Houghton Mifflin, 1972); Robbins, "Managing Organizational Conflict."

[3]Robbins, "Managing Organizational Conflict."

[4]Kenneth Thomas and Warren Schmidt, "A Survey of Managerial Interests with Respect to Conflict," *Academy of Management Journal,* June 1976, pp. 315–18.

[5]Henry Landsberger, *Hawthorne Revisited* (Ithaca, N.Y.: Cornell University Press, 1968), p. 31.

[6]See, for example, John Rizzo, Robert J. House, and Sydney I. Lirtzman, "Role Conflict and Ambiguity in Complex Organizations," *Administrative Science Quarterly,* Vol. 15 (June 1970), 150–63.

[7]Harry Levinson, "The Abrasive Personality," *Harvard Business Review,* May–June 1978, pp. 86–94.

[8]M. Dalton, "Conflicts between Staff and Line Managerial Officers," *American Sociological Review,* Vol. 15, No. 3 (1950), 342–51. Also, "Changing Line–Staff Relations," *Personnel Administration,* March–April 1966), pp. 3–5.

[9]James A. Belasco and Joseph A. Allutto, "Line Staff Conflicts: Some Empirical Insights," *Academy of Management Journal,* Vol. 12, No. 4 (December 1969), 469–77.

[10]*Ibid.*

[11]Opinion Research Corporation, *The Conflict between the Scientific and the Management Mind* (Princeton, N.J.: ORC, 1959). See also Lyman Porter and Edward Lawler III, "Properties of Organizations in Relation to Job Attitudes," *Psychological Bulletin,* Vol. 64, No. 1 (1965), 23–51.

[12]Lyman W. Porter, "Job Attitudes in Management: III. Perceived Deficiencies in Need Fulfillment as a Function of Line versus Staff Type of Jobs," *Journal of Applied Psychology,* Vol. 47 (1963), 267–75.

[13]Dalton, "Conflicts."

[14]Richard Walton and John Dutton, "The Management of Interdepartmental Conflict: A Model and Review," *Administrative Science Quarterly,* Vol. 14, No. 1 (March 1969), 73–84.

[15]*Ibid.,* p. 82. For a good explanation of Ken Smith, "Studying Intergroup Relations in Better Organizations," *Administrative Science Quarterly,* Vol. 27, No. 1 (March 1982), 35–65.

[16]Walton and Dutton, "The Management of Interdepartmental Conflict."

[17]J.M. Dutton and R.E. Walton, "Interdepartmental Conflict and Cooperation: Two Contrasting Studies," *Human Organization,* Vol. 26 (1966), 207–20.

[18]M. Dalton, *Men Who Manage* (New York: John Wiley, 1959).

[19]H.A. Landsberger, "The Horizontal Dimension in a Bureaucracy," *Administrative Science Quarterly,* Vol. 6 (1961), 298–333.

[20]Paul Lawrence and Jay Lorsch, *Organization and Environment* (Boston Division of Research, Graduate School of Business Administration, Harvard University, 1967).

[21]John Seiler, "Diagnosing Interdepartmental Conflict," *Harvard Business Review,* (September–October 1963, pp. 121–132.

[22]Lewis Pondy, "Organizational Conflict: Concepts and Models," *Administrative Science Quarterly,* Vol. 12, No. 2 (1967), 296–320. For a description of other models of the conflict process, see, for example, Walton and Dutton, "The Management of Interdepartmental Conflict," pp. 73–84; Steward Schmidt and Thomas Kochan, "Conflict: Toward Conceptual Clarity," *Administrative Science Quarterly,* Vol. 17 (1972), 359–70; and Thomas Ruble and Kenneth Thomas, "Support for a Two-Dimensional Model of Conflict Behavior," *Organizational Behavior and Human Performance,* Vol. 16 (June 1976), 143–55.

[23]Dalton, "Conflicts"; and David Mechanic, "Sources of Power of Lower Participants in Complex Organizations," *Administrative Science Quarterly,* Vol. 2, No. 3 (December 1962), 349–64.

[24]Walton and Dutton, "The Management of Interdepartmental Conflict." Musser contends that the subordinate's desire to remain in the organization, his or her perceived congruence between the superiors and his or her own attitudes and beliefs, and the subordinates' perceived protection from arbitrary action all help to determine the conflict-reduction strategy that is chosen. See Steven Musser, "A Model for Predicting the Choice of Conflict Management Strategies by Subordinates in High-States Conflicts," *Organizational Behavior and Human Performance,* Vol. 29, No. 2 (April 1982), 257–69.

[25]See, for example, Schmidt and Kochan, "Conflict."

[26]Muzafer Sherif, "Experiments in Group Conflict," *Frontiers of Psychological Research,* ed. Stanley Coopersmith, *Scientific American,* November 1956, pp. 112–16; R.R. Blake and J.S. Mouton, "The Intergroup Dynamics of Win-Lose Conflict and Problem Solving Collaboration in Union Management Relations," in M. Sherif, ed., *Intergroup Relations and Leadership* (New York: John Wiley, 1962); D.W. Johnson and R.J. Lewicki, "The Initiation of Superordinate Goals," *Journal of Applied Behavioral Science,* Vol. 5 (1969), 9–24.

[27]Edgar Schein, *Organizational Psychology* (Englewood Cliffs, N.J.: Prentice-Hall, 1970).

[28]Sherif, "Experiments in Group Conflict."

[29]*Ibid.,* p. 116.

[30]*Ibid.,* p. 117. For an example of a study in which superordinate goals did *not* seem to reduce intergroup conflict, see Louis Stern, Brian Sternthal, and C. Samuel Craig, "Strategies for Managing Interorganizational Conflict: A Laboratory Paradigm," *Journal of Applied Psychology,* Vol. 60, No. 4 (August 1975), 472–82.

[31]George Wieland and Robert Ullrich, *Organizations: Behavior, Design, and Change* (Homewood, Ill.: Richard D. Irwin, 1976), p. 286.

[32]Ross Stagner, "Corporate Decision Making: An Empirical Study," *Journal of Applied Psychology,* Vol. 53 (1969), 1–13; George Wieland and Robert Ullrich, *Organizational Behavior, Design, and Change* (Homewood, Ill.: Richard D. Irwin, 1976), pp. 271–73.

[33]James Thompson, *Organizations in Action* (New York: McGraw-Hill, 1967); Thomas A. Mahoney and Peter Frost, "The Role of Technology in Models of Organizational Effectiveness," *Organizational Behavior and Human Performance,* Vol. 11 (1974), 122–38.

[34]Thompson, *Organizations in Action,* p. 55.

[35]Eric Neilsen, "Understanding and Managing Intergroup Conflict," in Paul Lawrence, Louis Barnes, and Jay Lorsch, *Organizational Behavior and Administration* (Homewood, Ill.: Richard D. Irwin, 1976), p. 297.

[36]J. Cohen, "The Technique of Role Reversal: A Preliminary Note," *Occupational Psychology,* Vol. 25 (1951), 64–66; M. Deutsch, "Psychological Alternatives to War," *Journal of Socia. .ssues,* Vol. 18 (1962), 97–119.

[37]Lawrence and Lorsch, *Organization and Environment,* pp. 74–75.

[38]*Ibid.,* p. 78.

[39]Patricia Renwick, "Impact of Topic and Source of Disagreement on Conflict Management," *Organizational Behavior and Human Performance,* Vol. 14 (December 1975), 416–25.

[40]*Ibid.*

[41]*Ibid.*, p. 424.

[42]*Ibid.*

[43]Warren Bennis, *Organization Development: Its Nature, Origins, and Prospects* (Reading, Mass.: Addison-Wesley, 1969).

[44]*Ibid.*, pp. 4–6.

[45]Robert Baron, "Reducing Organizational Conflict: An Incompatible Response Approach," *Journal of Applied Psychology*, Vol. 69, No. 2 (May 1984), 272–79.

16

Managing Change

OVERVIEW

The main purpose of this chapter is to explain how to manage organizational change.

Organizations and their contexts are dynamic and are constantly undergoing change. Competitors introduce new products, new production technologies are developed, employees retire or resign, intergroup conflicts arise, or productivity inexplicably drops. These changes and others are the kinds that managers face daily. And very often, an effective response involves the implementation of one or more of the organizational change and development techniques we discuss in this chapter. These include changing the structure of the organization (perhaps to make it more adaptable); changing the technology of the organization (to increase productivity); or changing the people (their attitudes and behavior, for example). Organizational change and development is thus important to a study of organization theory because it involves the modification of the structure, tasks, technology, and/or people in the organization for the purpose of increasing the organization's effectiveness.

The outline of this chapter is as follows:

A The organizational change process
- **1** A model of the organizational change process
- **2** Pressure for change
- **3** Recognize the need for change
- **4** Diagnose the problem
- **5** Plan the change

6 Implement the change
7 Follow up on the change
B Organizational change strategies
1 Changing organizations by changing structure
2 Changing organizations by redesigning tasks
3 Changing organizations by changing technology
4 Changing organizations by changing people: organizational development
5 Change as adapative behavior

THE ORGANIZATIONAL CHANGE PROCESS

• A Model of the Organizational Change Process

Effective organizational changes usually do not take place overnight, but instead proceed in stages. As illustrated in Figure 16-1, the six main stages in developing and implementing an organizational change are as follows:

- Stage 1: Pressure for change
- Stage 2: Recognize need for change
- Stage 3: Diagnose the problem
- Stage 4: Plan the change
- Stage 5: Implement the change
- Stage 6: Follow up on the change

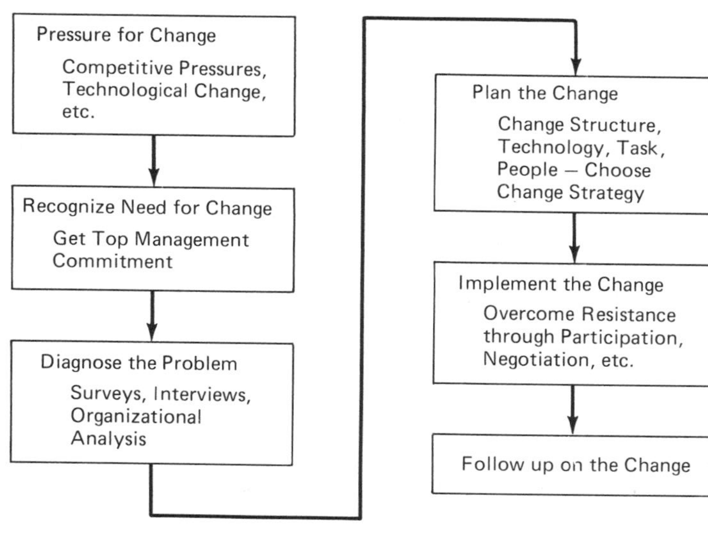

FIGURE 16-1 The Organizational Change Process

• *Pressure for Change*

Most organizational changes are carried out in reaction to or in anticipation of pressures from inside and outside the organization. Outside the organization, technological innovations like digital watches, microprocessors, personal computers, and cable television force managers to confront a changing competitive terrain. Within the organization, conflicts arise, employees retire or resign, and pressures mount as the organization outgrows its old way of doing things. In turn, pressures like these (or the anticipation of such pressures) demand changes in the structure, technology, tasks, and people in the organization.

• *Recognize the Need for Change*

The second stage of the change process involves the manager's recognizing and accepting the need for change. Lewin refers to this as the *unfreezing stage.* He says some provocative problem or event is usually necessary to get people to recognize the need for a change and to search for new solutions, and that without such "unfreezing," change will not occur.[1]

A Commitment Approach In this regard, House argues for a commitment approach to change and development.[2] His main point is that employees throughout the enterprise must be convinced that the top management is committed to the change before they themselves will accept it.

• *Diagnose the Problem*

The aim of the diagnosis stage is to identify the root cause of the problem so that an appropriate change can be planned and implemented.

Diagnostic Techniques The diagnostic techniques typically used at this stage include interviews, questionnaires, observations, and secondary data/unobtrusive measures.[3]

The major advantages and problems of these diagnostic techniques are shown in Table 16-1. Most organizational change and development programs involve preliminary interviews with (at least) a cross-section of employees, since interviews allow probing freely into a range of possible subjects, and help build rapport and support for the imminent change program. However, interviewing large numbers of employees can be expensive, and interviewers may advertently or inadvertently bias responses by reading more (or less) into an interviewee's response than is actually there.

Questionnaires are a second widely used technique. They are relatively easy to use with large numbers of employees, and the resulting information can be quantified and easily summarized. Survey data can also be a good starting point for gaining the commitment of the employees to the change, and for analyzing alternative solutions. On the other hand, the structured nature of most questionnaires means that the predetermined questions may miss important issues, and questionnaires themselves must be developed carefully so that questions are not ambiguous or incomprehensible.

A third technique is to simply *observe* the employees involved. This produces data regarding actual behavior (rather than reports of behavior), and it is real-time rather than retrospective (as are interviews and questionnaires). On the other hand, things are not always as they seem, so that observations are open to problems of misinterpretation and bias.

Finally, *secondary data* (for instance, regarding employee turnover or productivity) is easily quantified. However, accessing and retrieving this information from the employer's personnel files can be a problem, and the data must still be interpreted.

The breadth of the diagnosis will depend on how widespread the problem itself seems to be. In some cases, *organizational analysis*—in which the organization's goals, plans, environment, practices, and performance are investigated—is appropriate. At other times it may be fairly clear that the problem involves only one department, group, or individual and that the diagnosis can appropriately focus there.

TABLE 16-1 A Comparison of Different Methods of Diagnosis

Method	*Major Advantages*	*Major Potential Problems*
Interviews	1. Adaptive-allows data collection on a range of possible subjects 2. Source of "rich" data 3. Empathic 4. Process of interviewing can build rapport	1. Can be expensive 2. Interviewer can bias responses 3. Coding/interpretation problems 4. Self-report bias
Questionnaires	1. Responses can be quantified and easily summarized 2. Easy to use with large samples 3. Relatively inexpensive 4. Can obtain large volume of data	1. Nonempathic 2. Predetermined questions may miss issues 3. Data may be overinterpreted 4. Response bias
Observations	1. Collects data on behavior rather than reports of behavior 2. Real-time not retrospective 3. Adaptive	1. Interpretation and coding problems 2. Sampling is a problem 3. Observer bias/reliability 4. Costly
Secondary data/ unobtrusive measures	1. Nonreactive—no response bias 2. High face validity 3. Easily quantified	1. Access/retrieval possibility a problem 2. Potential validity problems 3. Coding/interpretation

Source: David Nadler, *Feedback and Organization Design: Using Data-Based Methods* (Reading, Mass.: Addison-Wesley, 1977), p. 119.

• *Plan the Change*

The fourth stage of the organizational change and development process is to plan the change. This involves answering the questions, *What* should we change? *When* should we change it? and, *How* should we change it?

Regarding *what* to change, Leavitt contends that all organizational changes can be classified as changes in structure, task, technology, or people.[4] Changing the *structure* might involve reorganizing departments, revising the span of control, or decentralizing. Changing the *task* might consist of enriching jobs or, at the other extreme, further specializing them. Changing the *technology* might include putting in a new production line, installing a new inventory control system, or instituting new selection procedures. Managers can also change the *people* in the organization—perhaps through training, confrontation meetings, or the sort of development activities explained in this chapter. Also at this stage, decisions are necessary regarding *how* the change will be made (specific development techniques to be used) and *when* to schedule each aspect of the change.

• *Implement the Change*

The next step is to actually change the structure, technology, task, or people in the organization—perhaps through a *reorganization,* or an on-the-job *training program,* for instance.

Why Do People Resist Change? Whether you are trying to implement small changes in work procedures or major changes like reorganizing the firm, overcoming or minimizing employees' resistance to the change will often be your major hurdle. Such resistance can quickly undermine and destroy your change efforts and can manifest itself in many ways, including decreased output, absenteeism, strikes, and hostility.

Lawrence says that resistance is not a necessary concomitant of change and that a change, if handled correctly, may evoke little or no resistance. He says this is because it is not the technical aspects of the change that employees resist, but rather its social consequences—"the change in their human relationships that generally accompany the technical change."[5] For example, they may see in the change diminished responsibilities for themselves and therefore lower status in the organization and less job security.

Three Approaches to Organizational Change There are two extreme approaches you can take to implementing an organizational change. On the one hand, you could *unilaterally decree* that the change will take place, and hope for the best. At the other extreme, you could *delegate the problem*—tell your employees what the problem is and let them come up with solutions and proposed changes.

Greiner says you needn't just deal in these two extremes; that a third, "middle ground" approach (which he calls "shared power") is possible. Here is how he categorizes his three approaches to making a change, with some examples:

A Unilateral Power

1 *The degree approach.* A "one-way" announcement originating with a person with high formal authority and passed on to those in lower positions.

2 *The replacement approach.* Individuals in one or more key organizational positions are replaced by other individuals. The basic assumption is that they will in turn change the organization's practices.

3 *The structural approach.* Instead of decreeing or injecting new blood into work relationships, management changes the required relationships of subordinates working in the situation. By changes in the structure of organizational relationships, organizational behavior is also presumably affected.

B Shared Power (participation)

4 *The group decision approach.* Here there is participation by group members in selecting from several alternative solutions specified in advance by superiors. This approach involves neither problem identification nor problem solving, but emphasizes the obtaining of group agreement to a particular course of action.

5 *The group problem-solving approach.* This takes "participation" one step further; it is problem identification and problem solving through group discussion. Here the group has wide latitude, not only over choosing the problems to be discussed, but in developing solutions to these problems.

C Delegated Power

6 *The data discussion approach.* Presentation and feedback of relevant data (for example, concerning decreasing product quality) to the "client," usually by a consultant. Organizational members are encouraged to develop their own analyses of the data, which are presented in the form of survey findings, data reports, etc.

7 *The sensitivity-training approach.* Here, managers are trained in small discussion groups to be more sensitive to the underlying processes of individual and group behavior. Changes in work patterns and relationships are assumed to follow from changes in interpersonal relationships. Sensitivity approaches focus on interpersonal relationships first, then hope for, or work toward, improvements in work performance. "Data discussion" and "sensitivity training" both give the employee much more latitude to analyze the data, identify problems, and develop solutions.[6]

Overcoming Resistance Through Participation Lawrence says that allowing affected employees to participate in developing and implementing the change can lower their resistance to it and thereby facilitate its implementation, and a study by Coch and French supports this contention.[7] As explained in Chapter 12, the researchers found that allowing employees to participate in planning and implementing the necessary procedural change made a significant difference in their acceptance of the change.

Other Methods for Overcoming Resistance Kotter and Schlesinger agree that employee participation can gain acceptance for a change, particularly where management does not have all the information it needs to design the change, and where the employees have considerable power to resist.[8] However, as summarized in Table 16-2, they say that in other situations, other actions are more effective in reducing resistance to change. For example, *education and communication* is appropriate where a lack of information or inaccurate information and analysis contributes to employees' resistance to the change. *Facilitation and support* (which might include

TABLE 16-2 Methods for Dealing with Resistance to Change

Approach	*Commonly Used in Situations*	*Advantages*	*Drawbacks*
Education + communication	Where there is a lack of information or inaccurate information and analysis	Once persuaded, people will often help with the implementation of the change.	Can be very time-consuming if lots of people are involved.
Participation + involvement	Where the initiators do not have all the information they need to design the change, and where others have considerable power to resist	People who participate will be committed to implementing change, and any relevant information they have will be integrated into the change plan.	Can be very time-consuming if participators design an inappropriate change.
Facilitation + support	Where people are resisting because of fear and anxiety	No other approach works as well with adjustment problems.	Can be time-consuming and expensive, and still fail.
Negotiation + agreement	Where someone or some group will clearly lose out in a change, and where that group has considerable power to resist	Sometimes it is a relatively easy way to avoid major resistance.	Can be too expensive in many cases if it alerts others to negotiate for compliance.
Manipulation + co-optation	Where other tactics will not work, or are too expensive	It can be relatively quick and inexpensive solution to resistance problems.	Can lead to future problems if people feel manipulated.
Coercion	Where speed is essential, and the change initiators possess considerable power	It is speedy, and can overcome any kind of resistance.	Can be risky if it leaves people mad at the initiators.

Source: John Kotter and Leonard Schlesinger, "Choosing Strategies for Change," *Harvard Business Review,* Vol. 57, No. 2 (March–April 1979), p. 111.

providing training in new skills, giving employees time off after a demanding period, or simply listening and providing emotional support) can reduce resistance where fear and anxiety lie at the heart of the resistance. On the other hand, where some group will clearly lose out in a change and where that group has power to resist, *negotiation and agreement* is in order. *Manipulation and co-optation* (for instance, by giving a main resister a key role in the change) works well where other tactics will not work or are too expensive. Finally, where speed is essential and the managers responsible for the change possess considerable power, they can deal with resistance by simply *coercing* others to go along with the change.

Given the variety of factors (the managers' power, the employees' ability to resist, and so on) that can influence the choice of approach, it is apparent that each approach can be appropriate under the right conditions. For example, in chaotic situations, a unilateral approach to change, in which the manager simply issues a decree and pushes through the change, may be appropriate. On the other hand, it is apparent that in many situations—such as where everything already seems to be going along fairly smoothly, but where some improvement is sought by management—a more shared approach can work well. Finally, as explained below, there are times when a more delegated, *developmental* approach is required. Here, the focus is on increasing the level of trust and open communication in the organization, on the assumption that this will make it easier for the organization to react to problems (such as the introduction of a new product by a competitor) and to change, by enabling the managers and groups to work more cooperatively.

• Follow Up on the Change

The next step is to evaluate the effects of the change. This means that objectives (in terms of improved performance or attitudes, for instance) must be set, so that the degree to which the change itself results in subsequent improvement can be assessed. An experimental design like one of those described in Chapter One can then be used to actually evaluate the effects of the change.

ORGANIZATIONAL CHANGE STRATEGIES

As mentioned above, Leavitt says that in solving an organizational problem, managers can pursue various *change strategies.* They can, in other words, change the *structure, tasks, technology,* or attitudes and skills of the *people* in the organization.

• Changing Organizations by Changing Structure

Reorganization involves a redesign of the organization structure—a change in the departmentalization, coordination, span of control, or centralization of decision making in the organization. Reorganization is a relatively direct and quick method for changing an organization, and the technique is widely used and often effective. In his studies, for instance, Chandler found that after World War II, the rapid rate of new-product development rendered ineffective the centralized organization structure at Westinghouse and General Electric.[9] In response, both firms decentralized their organizations. Recall that at Westinghouse, merchandise divisions were established for electrical appliances; these allowed a group of executives to make most of the sales, engineering, and manufacturing decisions for products in their own divisions. Similarly, General Electric established a decentralized, divisionalized organization with vice-presidents for such divisional groups as consumer products, aerospace, and construction of materials.

Another successful reorganization took place at General Motors. By the end of 1973, gas mileage had become an overriding concern for the automobile industry, and it was clear to GM that its entire product line would have to be redesigned and downsized. Normally, such product redesigning (which involved development of new soundproofing materials, shock absorbers, and so on) would have been done by each GM division, with some centralized policy making at headquarters. In this case, however, GM felt that its normal design organization was too ponderous, so in 1974, a project center was established to coordinate the efforts of the five automobile divisions. The project center is made up of engineers lent by the divisions, and it works on parts of engineering problems common to all divisions, such as frames, electrical systems, steering gear, and brakes.

According to *Fortune* magazine, the project center was probably GM's most important managerial tool in carrying out its downsize decision: "It has eliminated a great deal of redundant effort, and has speeded numerous new technologies into production."[10]

• *Changing Organizations by Redesigning Tasks*

Redesigning employees' tasks is another approach to organizational change. The classical examples of this are of the type proposed by Frederick Taylor and his disciples. They developed a new skill, industrial engineering, the purpose of which was to scientifically measure work methods and recommend improvements that usually meant creating highly specialized and routine jobs. Today, as explained earlier, the basic issue in job redesign is whether jobs should be highly specialized or enriched, with each approach having its own advocates and detractors.

• *Changing Organizations by Changing Technology*

Technological changes are changes in the work methods used by the organization to accomplish its tasks. These could be the introduction of new production technologies, industrial-engineering "time and motion" studies, introduction of new performance-appraisal procedures (including management by objectives), and so forth. Perhaps the most major and far-reaching technological change facing most organizations today is computerization—the use of computer systems on jobs formerly carried out by people—so we focus on the effect of computerization in this section.[11]

The Effect of Computers on Organization Structure Thomas Whisler studied the question of how computers affect organization structure. From his analysis of the research evidence, he concluded that the introduction of a computer system in an organization generally tends to cause the following changes in the structure of the organization:

1 Departments are consolidated.
2 The number of levels in the hierarchy is reduced.
3 The span of control is reduced.
4 Parallel departments are replaced by functional departments
5 Control becomes more centralized.
6 Control is shifted laterally between major executives and departments.
7 The technology becomes part of the control structure.[12]

Notice that most of the changes result in relatively more "mechanistic" organizations. For instance, spans of control are reduced (#3), divisionalized "profit-center" structures are replaced by the more traditional functional departmentation (#4), and control becomes more centralized. This is probably because such computer systems make their major contribution (according to Whisler) "by improving coordination and control." In other words, computer systems greatly increase management's capacity for monitoring and for processing information. Therefore, with the computer system, there is less need for organizational devices like profit centers and decentralization for reducing the information-processing load on top management.

Effect on Tasks and People Does modern technology such as computerization make man simply an appendage to a machine? That it does is a favorite argument of opponents of computerization, and some research lends support to their view.

In one study of computerization in an insurance company, it was found that more jobs were routinized than enlarged at the clerical level, whereas the reverse was true at the supervisory level. The enlargement in supervisory jobs appears to have been a consequence of having to understand computer systems and participate in their effective use. Even where supervisors have had their jobs enlarged, however, they still tend to have reduced control over the timing and patterning of their activities as a result of the deadline pressure imposed by computers. The results here seem to indicate that "where technology is important, complex, and directly involves others, the human being becomes an 'appendage' who must submit to the discipline of a routinized performance."[13]

Computerization also affects the communication patterns in the organization. It does this in two ways: First, in a "systems" sense, one person's actions directly affect more people more quickly than before. Ironically, though, computerization is also associated with reduced interpersonal communication, at least at the clerical level. In one study, it was found that computerization increased the percentage of time that clerks worked alone, so it also changed their pattern of communication; they spoke with other clerks less frequently, for example. On the other hand, interpersonal communication between managers increased.

Although computerization results in increased job routinization, the level of skills demanded of employees tends to increase. The explanation for this paradox is apparently that the demands on the employee increase: Each must perform precisely as the system demands, and greater *reliability* in performance is required. These new demands are translated into higher "skill" requirements.

Summary Technological changes like computerization often drastically change the organization and its people. Computerization, for example, is generally associated with increased centralization, a less "divisionalized" structure, and less discretion on the part of most employees.

• *Changing Organizations by Changing People: Organizational Development*

A variety of techniques can be used to change the people in the organization, but as House points out:

> If development is to be successful, it must be geared not only to the participants' needs and learning abilities, but also to the particular requirements and practices of the organization in which he manages.[14]

Similarly, Roger Harrison emphasizes that development methods require various degrees of emotional involvement, depending upon how private, individual, and hidden are the issues and processes concerned. He suggests that "surface" interventions, such as those stressing change in skills, are more appropriate where mechanistic conditions prevail. These surface development techniques include lectures, conferences, and reorganizations, for example.

On the other hand, says Harrison, "in-depth" interventions, such as *sensitivity training,* are more appropriate for developing organic organizations to meet rapidly changing conditions.[15] These organizations-development techniques are aimed at changing the attitudes, values, and behavior of participants with the specific objective of getting the people themselves to develop more open, supportive, organic types of organizations, in which innovation can then prevail.

Characteristics of Organizational Development (OD) Bennis lists seven distinguishing characteristics of organizational development.[16] First, OD is an *educational strategy* adopted to bring about some planned organizational change. Second, changes sought are usually directly related to the *exigency* or demand with which the organization is trying to cope. This demand, which typically arises in new and rapidly expanding organizations, frequently results in problems of communication, intergroup conflict, organizational identity and destination, and so forth, which are uniquely amenable to solution through organization development. Third, the OD effort almost always relies on a strategy that emphasizes *direct experience.* This may take the form of data feedback, sensitivity training, or confrontation meetings. Fourth, the OD effort utilizes a *change agent* who is almost always an external consultant. Fifth, the change agent enters into a *collaborative relationship* with organization members and works actively with them. Sixth, the change agent usually has a social philosophy or set of values concerning people and organizations that parallels those of *McGregor's "Theory Y"* (see Chapter 3). Seventh, the change agent often has a set of *normative* goals based on his social philosophy. Although the goals will differ from one agent to another, he most commonly seeks such goals as improvement in interpersonal competence, better methods of conflict resolution, more effective team management, increased understanding, and the establishment of a value system in which human feelings are considered legitimate. Furthermore, change agents usually aim at developing organic rather than mechanistic systems. These characteristics make OD a more appropriate strategy where organic systems are themselves appropriate.

Strategy in Organizational Development Organizational development's basic strategy consists of three steps:

1 Gathering of data about organizational operations, attitudes, and behavior
2 Feedback of data to the parties involved
3 Team planning of the solutions

Some OD practitioners refer to this three-step strategy as *action research,* implying, as Bennis puts it, that it is similar to all types of applied research except that "the relationship of researchers and subject may reverse—the subjects becoming the researchers."[17]

The data-gathering and feedback steps make up a diagnosis stage. Some applied-behavioral scientists also use the term *unfreezing* to denote this stage. The term implies that people in organizations have a tendency to become "frozen" into attitudes of conflict or competition, as well as into out-of-date operating policies and customs.

A preliminary step in the diagnosis is usually for the consultant and key client (the plant manager, company president, or division vice-president, for example) to meet and develop an initial assessment of the organization's strategic problems. Subordinates of the key client might also be interviewed at this point to obtain additional data. On the basis of this initial assessment, it may turn out that the problem is technological or that the key client is unwilling to delve more deeply into the organization's problems. But the diagnosis might also suggest a number of other alternatives, including postponing the development effort or hiring additional specialists (such as in finance or information systems), or it might lead to the second step of the process.

Assuming that the consultant and client agree that the development should continue, additional data are usually gathered. This is frequently done through interviews, at least in part, because this personal contact builds a cooperative relationship between the consultant and the client group. In addition, questionnaires in the context of what has been called *survey feedback* have also been used with success.

These data then form the basis for the feedback provided by the consultant to the client, often during two- or three-day off-site meetings. The consultant provides feedback in terms of some of the fundamental problems that have been identified during the data-gathering phase. The client group is then encouraged to set some priorities on the problems and to discuss them under the guidance of the consultant. Throughout these meetings, the consultant (who is also sometimes referred to as the change agent or the trainer) acts as an educator, training the participants in how to confront and analyze the problems under discussion.

Having eliminated some or all of the problems, the OD effort moves into its third, action-planning or refreezing stage. At this point, the client group sets about developing new ways of operating. The participants, having new attitudes and values, might at this point develop new job descriptions, policies and procedures, organization structures, and solutions to residual problems.

The specific OD method used will vary with the organization and the consultant. A great number are currently in use. In Chapter 15, we discussed confrontation meetings; in the following sections, we will discuss three other widely used, representative OD methods.

1 Survey feedback
2 Sensitivity training
3 The managerial grid

Some of the other methods are coaching and counseling activities, planning and goal-setting activities, third-party peacemaking activities, and technostructural activities.

Survey Feedback Many managers use attitude surveys, also though usually not as effectively as they might. In most cases, the forms are administered to employees by outside consultants, and the results are tallied and sent to top management. And as often as not, that is the last the employees hear about the attitude survey (at least, until next year's routine survey).

Attitude surveys can be quite useful as an organizational change technique. They can be used to dramatically underscore the existence of some problem (like low morale), thereby "unfreezing" the system. And they can be used as a basis for discussion among employees and for developing alternative solutions. Finally, they can also be used to follow up on the change to see if it has been successful ("refreezing"). Although it is an OD technique, survey feedback generally does not involve a high degree of emotional soul-searching on the part of participants.

Sensitivity Training *Sensitivity* or *T-group training* is a controversial development method that impinges upon the attitudes and personalities of the participants to a degree far exceeding that of other methods we discuss. The T-group, according to Argyris, is:

> . . . a group experience designed to provide maximum possible opportunity for the individuals to expose their behavior, give and receive feedback, experiment with new behavior, and develop . . . awareness and acceptance of self and others. . . .[18]

According to the National Training Laboratory (NTL), which specializes in conducting such training, the primary purposes of T-groups are:

1. To provide managers with the sensitivity for themselves and others and with skills necessary to more effectively guide and direct changes in social arrangements and relationships
2. To develop in managers the sensitivity, understanding, and skill to participate effectively both as group leaders and members
3. To discover and develop tested principles and improved methods of human-relations training

Although the T-group procedure varies from trainer to trainer, the usual framework has been described as follows: A group of 10 to 15 meets, usually away from the job, and no activities or discussion topics are planned. The focus is on the "here and now" (including the feelings and emotions of the group members), and the participants are encouraged to portray themselves *in the group* rather than in terms of past experiences or future problems. Breaks in the discussion are often filled by feelings of frustration, expressions of hostility, and eventual attempts by some to organize and impose a hierarchical structure on the rest. Such attempts are usually blocked spontaneously by the group or through the trainer's intervention. Since the group's behavior is the principal topic of conversation the success of the training group depends largely on the process of feedback. Specifically, participants must be able to inform each other of how their behavior is being seen, and be able to describe and interpret the kinds of feelings it produces. This feedback must be articulate and meaningful, since it is the primary channel through which the trainers learn. In turn, the success of the feedback process depends upon the member's being able to discover how deficient his or her earlier behavior was, and upon a climate of *psychological safety*. In other words, people should feel safe to reveal themselves in the group, to expose their feelings, drop their defenses, and try out new ways of interacting.[19]

T-group training is very personal in nature, so it is not surprising that it is an extremely controversial subject. Odiorne describes a training session in which, during one "horrible weekend," an inadequately trained trainer "broke down the barriers of formal courtesy that had substituted quite successfully for human relations in this successful lab for many years."[20] Everyone spoke frankly of his hostilities, and by the time the participants returned to their job, organized politicking and conflict reigned. Many senior scientists quit, and candid observations helped to sever ties between former colleagues. Odiorne points out several specific shortcomings of T-group training:

1 Not only are the participants unaware of what the outcome will be, but in many instances, since there are no controls, neither are the trainers.
2 Sensitivity training is based on creating stress situations for their own sake.
3 At present, anybody with a registration fee can attend.
4 Finally, the real flaw is that it isn't consistent with the business and economic world we live in.[21]

A number of writers have also attacked T-group training on the grounds that it may constitute an invasion of privacy. House points out that when participation in a T-group program is "suggested" by one's superior, attendance cannot be considered strictly voluntary.

The Managerial Grid The *managerial grid* is another technique sometimes used to bring about a change in employee attitudes or values. The grid itself, as summarized in Table 16-3, represents several possible leadership styles. The two basic orientations—concern for people and concern for production—are conceptually similar to the consideration and initiating-structure leader-behavior dimensions of the Ohio State LBDQ. The different leadership styles reflect different combinations of these two factors. For example, the 1-9 leader ranks high in concern for people but low in concern for production. At the opposite extreme, the 9-1 leader emphasizes production but deemphasizes the needs of people.

Blake and Mouton's managerial-grid program assumes that it is possible for managers to work toward and develop a 9-9 grid score.[22] It is a six-phase program that usually lasts three to five years:

- *Phase I* consists of laboratory-seminar training and is typically a one-week conference aimed at studying the theory of managerial effectiveness that underlies the grid program.
- In *phase II*, the superior and his group utilize the climate of openness—which phase I anticipates—to develop and analyze their managerial styles and group practices.
- In *phase III*, the experiences of phase II are extended to include the interrelationships of related organizational units. The objective here is joint problem solving.
- In *phase IV*, top management works with other groups to develop an ideal corporate model for the future management of the organization.

TABLE 16-3 Four Basic Leadership Styles Represented on the Managerial Grid

Type of Leader as Ranked on Grid	*Type of Concern for People*	*Type of Concern for Production*
(1-1)	Low	Low
(1-9)	High	Low
(9-1)	Low	High
(9-9)	High	High

Source: Based on material in Robert R. Blake and Jane S. Mouton, *The Managerial Grid* (Houston: Gulf Publishing, 1964).

- *Phase V* uses a number of the procedures of phase I to develop operational tactics for moving the company to the ideal organizational model developed in phase IV.
- Finally, in *phase VI*, the achievements of phases I through V are evaluated, with the objective of identifying weaknesses and taking corrective actions as necessary.[23]

• Change as Adaptive Behavior

Our discussion of organizational change strategies may imply that all or most organizational changes are planned and intentional, but this is not the case. Instead, most changes are informal and unplanned.

James March, for example, writes that "because of the magnitude of some changes in organizations, we are inclined to look for comparably dramatic explanations for change, but the search for drama may often be a mistake."[24] Most change in organizations, says March, results not from uncommon imagination, persistence, or skill, but from relatively stable, routine processes that relate organizations to their environment.

March's thesis is that most organizations are more adaptive than they appear to be, and that changes take place because most employees usually "do about what they are supposed to do; that is, they are intelligently attentive to their environments and their jobs." Neither success nor change requires dramatic action, says March; instead, the conventional, routine activities that produce most organizational changes require ordinary people to do ordinary things in a competent way.

It is thus appropriate that we conclude *Organization Theory: Integrating Structure and Behavior* with March's comments. As we explained in Chapter 4, organizational effectiveness adds up to organizational *survival*, and to survive, the organization must adapt to its environment. This may require a change technique like sensitivity training, but it is more often the routine efforts of employees that help ensure that adaptation takes place. In the final analysis, therefore, organizational change (and effectiveness) is accomplished not just through the use of change techniques, but by organizing and managing the enterprise in such a way that its members can and will be "intelligently attentive to their environments," as March says, and will willingly and enthusiastically make the extra effort required so that their firms can function effectively.

How can a manager do this? Organizing properly is the first step, since, as we saw in Chapters 4–10, organizational effectiveness begins with a structure that is appropriate for its task. Instituting the right degree of formalization is important as well, as is building in mechanisms (like those practiced by "excellent" firms) that encourage open, adequate communications.

Leadership processes and the culture you create are important, too. The most effective adaptors, we know, rely on a common culture—on a dependable system of shared beliefs about the common interests of the firm—rather than on just a formal structure and rules to motivate workers. And it is through leadership, myths, and reinforcement that one molds this culture. Encouraging the formation of positive, cohesive groups and managing intergroup conflict are also important.

In summary, the firm's ability to survive and effectively "bargain" with and adapt to crucial interest groups is the ultimate criterion of organizational effectiveness, and understanding how to cultivate such adaptability is one aim of *organization theory,* the subject concerned with understanding, explaining, and predicting how to best structure an organization to fulfill its goals.

SUMMARY

Maintaining organizational effectiveness inevitably requires *organizational change;* in other words, changing the structure, tasks, technology, and/or people in the organization for the purpose of increasing one or more criteria of organizational effectiveness like adaptability, innovativeness, or profitability. This chapter addressed the question of how to implement such changes successfully.

The organizational change process involves six steps—pressure for change, recognizing the need for change, diagnosis of the problem, planning the change, implementing the change, and following up on the change. Perhaps the most crucial part of the change process is overcoming employee resistance, and here we explained the advisibility of taking a "shared-power" or participative approach in order to overcome employees' resistance to the change. Organization change strategies include reorganization, redesigning tasks (for instance, via job enrichment), and changing technology, as occurs when all or part of the company's work system is automated.

Organizational development is a catchful phrase that includes various techniques whose overall objective is to change the values, attitudes, and behavior of employees in such a way as to get them to develop more open, supportive, organic types of organizations, in which innovation can prevail. Specific techniues here include survey feedback, confrontation meetings (as explained in Chapter 15), sensitivity training, and the managerial grid.

Discussion Questions

1 Why do people resist change?
2 Explain the techniques you would use to overcome resistance to change, and the conditions under which you would use them.
3 Explain why sensitivity training is a controversial development method and what you would do to minimize its adverse effects.
4 Explain how you would apply the six-stage change process to a reorganization; job-enrichment program; the installation of a new automated production line.
5 Explain why *managing change* is an important part of maintaining organizational effectiveness.

Footnotes

[1]K. Lewin, "Group Decision and Social Change," in T. Newcomb and E. Hartley, eds., *Readings in Social Psychology* (New York: Holt, Rinehart & Winston, 1947). In organizational change and development, attitudes, surveys, or interview results that show extremely low morale may suffice to galvanize a skeptical manager into action. Similarly, losing a big sale because of a communication breakdown or intergroup rivalry may convince top management that some changes are in order.

[2]See Robert J. House, *Management Development: Design, Evaluation, and Implementation* (Ann Harbor: Bureau of Industrial Relations, University of Michigan, 1967), p. 59.

[3]This is based on David Nadler, *Feedback and Organization Development: Using Data-Based Methods* (Reading, Mass.: Addison-Wesley, 1977), pp. 118–43. Depending on the apparent nature of the problem and the capabilities of the enterprise, these diagnostic techniques may be employed by the organization's managers or by a special consultant retained to diagnose the problem and implement the appropriate changes.

[4]Harold J. Leavitt, *New Perspectives in Organization Research* (New York: John Wiley, 1964).

[5]Paul Lawrence, "How to Deal with Resistance to Change," *Harvard Business Review,* (May–June 1954; For a fascinating description of the effects of resistance to change, see Nicole Woolsey Biggart, "The Creative-Destructive Process of Organizational Change: The Case of the Post Office," *Administrative Science Quarterly,* Vol. 22, No. 3 (September 1977), 410–26.

[6]Larry Greiner, "Patterns of Organization Change," *Harvard Business Review,* May–June 1967, pp. 623–24.

[7]Lester Coch and J.R. French, Jr., "Overcoming Resistance to Change," *Human Relations,* Vol. 1, No. 4 (1948); reprinted in Paul Lawrence, John Seiler, et al., *Organizational Behavior and Administration* (Homewood, Ill.: Irwin/Dorsey, 1965), pp. 931–32.

[8]John Keith Kotter and Leonard A. Schlesinger, "Choosing Strategies for Change," *Harvard Business Review,* Vol. 57, No. 2 (March–April 1979), 106–14.

[9]Alfred Chandler, *Strategy and Structure* (Cambridge, Mass.: M.I.T. Press, 1962).

[10]"How GM Turned Itself Around," *Fortune,* January 16, 1978.

[11]This section is based on Thomas Whisler, *Information Technology and Organizational Change* (Belmont, Calif.: Wadsworth, 1970).

[12]*Ibid.,* p. 68. See also Nancy Carter, "Computerization as a Predominant Technology: Its Influence on the Structure of Newspaper Organizations," *Academy of Management Journal,* Vol. 27, No. 2 (June 1984), 247–70.

[13]Whisler, *Information Technology,* p. 74. For a different point of view, see Herbert Simon, *The New Science of Management Decision* (Englewood Cliffs, N.J.: Prentice-Hall, 1977), Chap. 3.

[14]House, *Management Development,* p. 11.

[15]Roger Harrison, "Choosing the Depth of Organizational Intervention," *Journal of Applied Behavioral Science,* Vol. 2 (April/May/June 1970), 181–202.

[16]Warren Bennis, *Organization Development* (Reading, Mass.: Addison-Wesley, 1969), p. 10.

[17]Warren Bennis and H. Shepard, "A Theory of Group Development," *Human Relations,* Vol. 9, No. 4 (1965).

[18]Chris Argyris, "A Brief Description of Laboratory Education," *Training Director's Journal,* October 1963.

[19]Based on J.P. Campbell and M.D. Dunnette, "Effectiveness of T-Group Experiences in Managerial Training and Development," *Psychological Bulletin,* Vol. 70 (1968), 73–104. Reprinted in W.E. Scott and L.L. Cummings, *Readings in Organizational Behavior and Human Performance* (Homewood, Ill.: Richard D. Irwin, 1973), p. 571.

[20]George S. Odiorne, "The Trouble with Sensitivity Training," *Training Director's Journal,* October 1963.

[21]*Ibid.*

[22]Robert R. Blake and Jane S. Mouton, *The Managerial Grid* (Houston: Gulf Publishing, 1964).

[23]See R.R. Blake and J.S. Mouton, *Building a Dynamic Corporation through Grid Organizational Development* (Reading, Mass.: Addison-Wesley, 1969), p. 16.

[24]This section is based on James March, "Footnotes to Organizational Change," *Administrative Science Quarterly,* Vol. 26, No. 4 (December 1981), 563–77.

CASE FOR PART IV (Chapters 14–16) TEXANA PETROLEUM CORPORATION*

During the summer of 1966, George Prentice, the newly designated executive vice-president for domestic operations of the Texana Petroleum Corporation, was devoting much of his time to thinking about improving the combined performance of the five product divisions reporting to him (see Figure IV-1). His principal concern was that corporate profits were not reflecting the full potential contribution that could result from the close technological interdependence of the raw materials utilized and produced by these divisions. The principal difficulty, as Prentice saw it, was that the division general managers reporting to him were not working well together:

> As far as I see it, the issue is, where do we make the money for the corporation? Not how do we beat the other guy. Nobody is communicating with anybody else at the general manager level. In fact they are telling a bunch of secrets around here.

*This case was prepared by Jay W. Lorsch from data collected by Paul R. Lawrence, James A. Garrison, and himself. Case material of the Harvard Graduate School of Business Administration is intended as a basis for class discussion rather than to illustrate either effective or ineffective handling of an administrative situation. The case was reprinted in Robert Coffey, Anthony Athos, and Peter Reynolds, *Behavior in Organizations* (Englewood Cliffs, N.J.: Prentice-Hall, 1975), pp. 557–68.

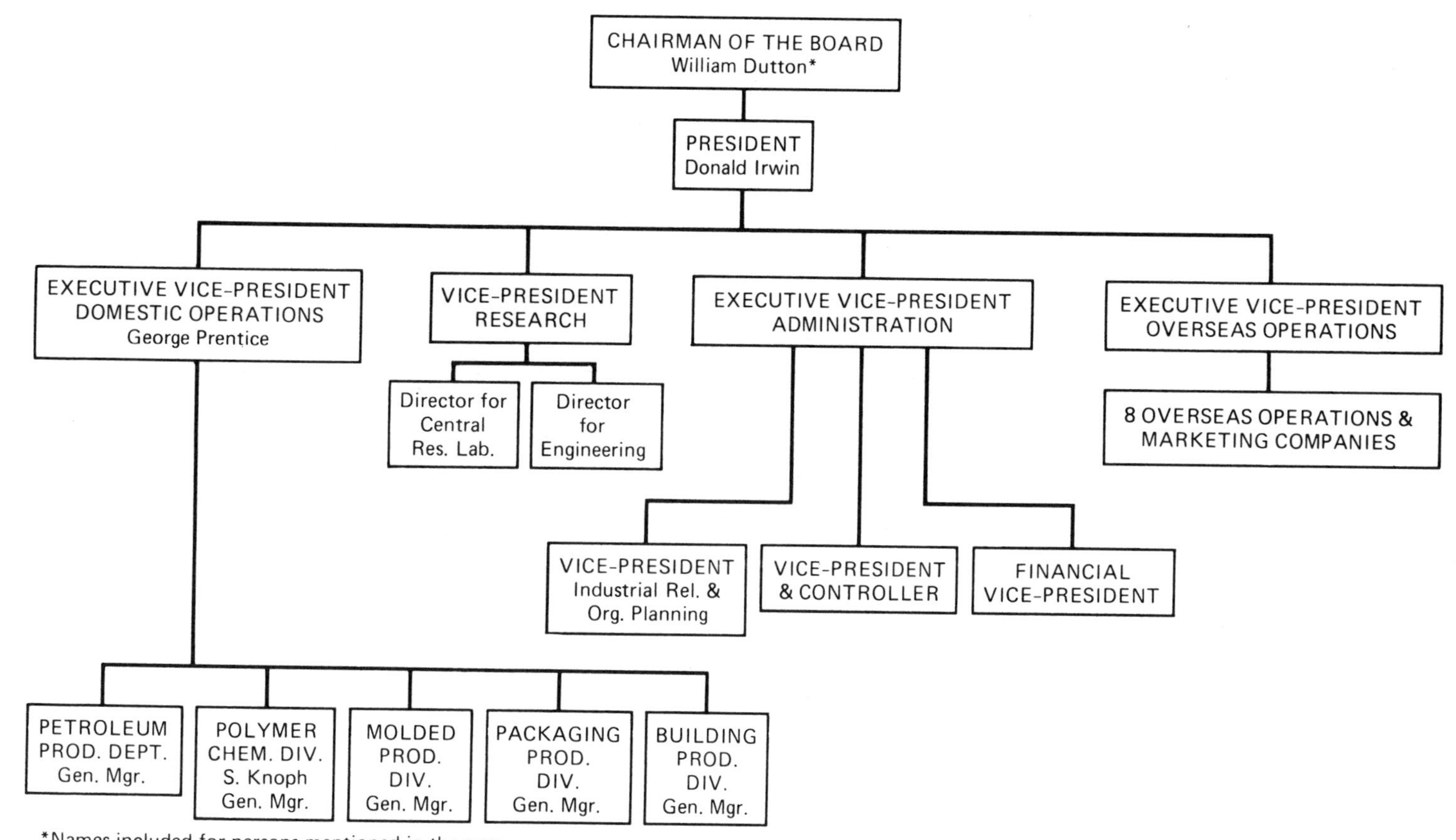

*Names included for persons mentioned in the case.

FIGURE IV-1 Texana Petroleum Company—Partial Organization Chart, 1966

• *Recent Corporate History*

The Texana Petroleum Corporation was one of the early major producers and marketers of petroleum products in the southwest United States. Up until the early 1950s, Texana had been almost exclusively in the business of processing and refining crude oil and in selling petroleum products through a chain of company-operated service stations in the southwestern United States and in Central and South America. By 1950, company sales had risen to approximately $500 million, with accompanying growth in profits. About 1950, however, Texana faced increasingly stiff competition at the retail service-station level from several larger national petroleum companies. As a result, sales volume declined sharply during the early 1950s, and by 1955, sales had fallen to only $300 million and the company was operating at just above the breakeven point.

At this time, because of his age, Roger Holmes, who had been a dominant force in the company since its founding, retired as president and chief executive officer. He was replaced by Donald Irwin, 49, who had been a senior executive with a major chemical company. William Dutton, 55, was appointed chairman of the board to replace the retiring chairman. Dutton had spent his entire career with Texana. Prior to his appointment as chairman, he had been senior vice-president for petroleum products, reporting to Holmes.

Irwin and Dutton, along with other senior executives, moved quickly to solve the problems facing Texana. They gradually divested the company's retail outlets and abandoned the domestic consumer petroleum markets. Through both internal development and acquisition, they expanded and rapidly increased the company's involvement in the business of processing petroleum for chemical and plastic products. In moving in this direction, they were rapidly expanding on initial moves made by Texana in 1949, when the company built its first chemical-processing plant and began marketing these products. To speed the company's growth in these areas, Irwin and Dutton selected aggressive general managers for each division and gave them a wide degree of freedom in decision making. Top management's major requirements was that each division general manager create a growing division with a satisfactory return on investment capital. By 1966, top management had reshaped the company so that in both the domestic and foreign market, it was an integrated product of chemicals and plastics materials. In foreign operations, the company continued to operate service stations in Latin America and in Europe. This change in direction was successful, and by 1966, company sales had risen to $750 million, with a healthy rise in profit.

In spite of this success, management believed that there was a need for an increase in return on invested capital. The financial and trade press, which had been generous in its praise of the company's recovery, was still critical of the present return on investment, and top management shared this concern. Dutton, Irwin, and Prentice were in agreement that one important method of increasing profits was to take further advantage of the potential cost savings that could come from increased coordination between the domestic operating divisions, as they developed new products, processes, and markets.

• *Domestic Organization 1966*

The product divisions reporting to Mr. Prentice represented a continuum of producing and marketing activities, from production and refining of crude oil to the marketing of several types of plastics products to industrial consumers. Each division was headed by a general manager. Although there was some variation in the internal organizational structure of the several divisions, they were generally set up along functional lines (manufacturing, sales, research and development). Each division also had its own controller and engineering activities, although these were supported and augmented by the corporate staff. Divisions had their own research effort, but there was also a central research laboratory at the corporate level, which carried on a longer-range research of a more fundamental nature, and outside the scope of the activities of any of the product divisions.

The *petroleum products division* was the remaining nucleus of the company's original producing and refining activities. It supplied raw materials to the polymer and chemicals division and also sold refining products under long-term contracts to other petroleum companies. In the early and mid-1950s, this division's management had generated much of the company's revenue and profits through its skill of negotiating these agreements. In 1966, top corporate management felt that this division's management had accepted its role as a supplier to the rest of the corporation, and that relations between it and its sister divisions were harmonious.

The *polymer* and *chemicals division* was developed internally during the late 1940s and early 1950s as management saw its share of the consumer petroleum market declining. Under the leadership of Seymour Knoph (who had been general manager for several years) and his predecessor (who was in 1966 executive vice-president of administration), the division had rapidly developed a line of chemical and polymer compounds derived from petroleum raw materials. Most of the products of this division were manufactured under licensing agreement or were materials whose formulation was well understood. Nevertheless, technical personnel in the division had developed an industrywide reputation for their ability to develop new and improved processes. Top management of the division took particular pride in this ability. From the beginning, the decision of what products to manufacture was based to a large extent upon the requirements of the molded and packaging products divisions. However, polymer and chemicals division executives had always attempted to market these same products to external customers, and had been highly successful. These external sales were extremely important to Texana, since they ensured a large enough volume of operation to process a broad product line of polymer chemicals profitably. As the other divisions had grown, they had required a larger proportion of the division's capacity, which meant that polymer and chemical division managers had to reduce their commitment to external customers.

The *molded products division* was also an internally developed division, formed in 1951. Its products were a variety of molded plastic items ranging from toys and household items to automotive and electronic parts. This division's major strengths were its knowledge of molding technology and particularly its marketing ability. Although it depended upon the polymer and chemicals division for its raw materials, its operations were largely independent of those of the packaging products and building products divisions.

The *packaging products division* was acquired in 1952. Its products were plastic packaging materials, including films, cartons, bottles, and so forth. All these products were marketed to industrial customers. Like the molded products division, the packaging division depended on the polymer and chemical division as a source of raw materials but was largely independent of other end-product divisions.

The *building products division* was acquired in 1963 to give Texana a position in the construction materials market. The division produced and marketed a variety of insulation roofing materials and similar products to the building trade. It was a particularly attractive acquisition for Texana, because prior to the acquisition, it had achieved some success with plastic products for insulation and roofing materials. Although the plastic products accounted for less than 20 percent of the total division sales in 1965, plans called for these products to account for over 50 percent of division sales in the next five years. Its affiliation with Texana gave this division a stronger position in plastic raw materials through the polymer and chemicals division.

• Selection and Recruitment of Management Personnel

The rapid expansion of the corporation into these new areas had created the need for much additional management talent, and top management had not hesitated to bring new men in from outside the corporation, as well as advancing promising younger men inside Texana. In both the internally developed and the acquired divisions, most managers had spent their careers inside the division, although some top division managers were moved between divisions or into corporate positions.

In speaking about the type of men he had sought for management positions, Donald Irwin described his criterion in a financial publication:

> We don't want people around who are afraid to move. The attraction of Texana is that it gives the individual responsibilities which aren't diluted. It attracts the fellow who wants a challenge.

Another corporate executive described Texana managers:

> It's a group of very tough-minded, but considerate gentlemen with an enormous drive to get things done.

Another manager, who had been with Texana for his entire career, and who considered himself to be different from most Texana managers, described the typical Texana manager as follows:

> Texana attracts a particular type of person. Most of these characteristics are personal characteristics rather than professional ones. I would use terms such as cold, unfeeling, aggressive, and extremely competitive, but not particularly loyal to the organization. He is loyal to dollars, his own personal dollars. I think this is part of the

> communication problem. I think this is done on purpose. The selection procedures lead in this direction. I think this is so because of contrast with the way the company operated ten years ago. Of course, I was at the plant level at that time. But today the attitude I have described is also in the plants. Ten years ago the organization was composed of people who worked together for the good of the organization, because they wanted to. I don't think this is so today.

• *Location of Division Facilities*

The petroleum products, chemical and polymer, and packaging products divisions had their executive offices on separate floors of the Texana headquarters building in the Chicago Loop. The plants and research and development facilities of these divisions were spread out across Oklahoma, Texas, and Louisiana. The molded products division had its headquarters, research and development facilities, and a major plant in an industrial suburb of Chicago. This division's other plants were at several locations in the Midwest and on the East Coast. The building products division's headquarters and major production and technical facilities were located in Fort Worth, Texas. All four divisions shared sales offices in major cities from coast to coast.

• *Evaluation and Control of Division Performance*

The principal method of controlling and evaluating the operation of these divisions was the semiannual review of division plans and the approval of major capital expenditures by the executive committee.[1] In reviewing performance against plans, members of the executive committee placed almost sole emphasis on the division's actual return on investment against budget. Corporate executives felt that this practice, together with the technological interdependence of the divisions, created many disputes about transfer pricing.

In addition to these regular reviews, corporate executives had frequent discussions with division executives about their strategies, plans, and operations. It had been difficult for corporate management to strike the proper balance in guiding the operations for the divisions. This problem was particularly acute with regard to the polymer and chemicals division, because of its central place in the corporation's product line. One corporate staff member explained his view of the problem:

> This whole matter of communications between the corporate staff and the polymer and chemical division has been a fairly difficult problem. Corporate management used to contribute immensely to this by trying to get into the nuts and bolts area within the chemical and polymer organization, and this created serious criticisms; however, I think they have backed off in this matter.

A second corporate executive, in discussing this matter for a trade-publication report, put the problem this way:

> We're trying to find the middle ground. We don't want to be a holding company, and with our diversity we can't be a highly centralized corporation.

• *Executive Vice-President, Domestic Operations*

In an effort to find this middle ground, the position of executive vice-president of domestic operations was created in early 1966, and George Prentice was its first occupant. Prior to this change, there had been two senior domestic vice-presidents—one in charge of the petroleum and polymer and chemicals divisions and the other in charge of the end-use divisions. Mr. Prentice had been senior vice-president in charge of the end-use divisions before the new position was created. He had held that position for only two years, having come to it from a highly successful marketing career with a competitor.

At the time of his appointment, one press account described Mr. Prentice as "hard-driving, aggressive, and ambitious—an archetype of the self-actuated dynamo Irwin has sought out."

Shortly after taking his new position, Prentice described the task before him:

> I think the corporation wants to integrate its parts better and I am here because I reflect this feeling. We can't be a bunch of entrepreneurs around here. We have got to balance discipline with entrepreneurial motivation. This is what we were in the past, just a bunch of entrepreneurs, and if they came in with ideas we would get the money, but now our dollars are limited, and especially the polymer and chemical boys haven't been able to discipline themselves to select from within ten good projects. They just don't seem to be able to do this, and so they come running in here with all ten good projects which they say we have to buy, and they get upset when we can't buy them all.
>
> This was the tone of my predecessors (senior vice-presidents). All of them were very strong on being entrepreneurs. I am going to run it differently. I am going to take a marketing and capital orientation. As far as I can see, there is a time to compete and a time to collaborate, and I think right now there has been a lack of recognition in the polymer and chemicals executive suite that this thing has changed.

• *Other Views of Domestic Interdivisional Relations*

Executives within the polymer and chemicals divisions, in the end-use divisions, and at the corporate level shared Prentice's view that the major breakdown in interdivisional relations was between the polymer and chemicals division and the end-use divisions. Executives in the end-use divisions made these typical comments about the problem:

> I think the thing we have got to realize is that we are wedded to the polymer and chemicals division whether we like it or not. We are really tied up with them. And just as we would with any outside supplier or with any of our customers, we will do things to maintain their business. But because they feel they have our business wrapped up, they do not reciprocate in turn. Now let me emphasize that they have not arbitrarily refused to do the things that we are requiring, but there is a pressure

on them for investment projects and we are low man on the pole. And I think this could heavily jeopardize our chances for growth.

. . . . .

I would say our relationships are sticky, and I think this is primarily because we think our reason for being is to make money, so we try to keep Polymer and Chemicals as an arm's-length supplier. For example, I cannot see, just because it is a polymer and chemicals product, accepting millions of pounds of very questionable material. It takes dollars out of our pocket, and we are very profit-centered.

. . . . .

The big frustration, I guess, and one of our major problems, is that you can't get help from them [Polymer and Chemicals]. You feel they are not interested in what you are doing, particularly if it doesn't have a large return for them. But as far as I am concerned, this has to become a joint venture relationship, and this is getting to be real sweat with us. We are the guys down below yelling for help. And they have got to give us some relief.

. . . . .

My experience with the polymer and chemicals division is that you cannot trust what they say at all, and even when they put it in writing, you can't be absolutely sure that they are going to live up to it.

Managers within the polymer and chemicals division expressed similar sentiments:

Personally, right now I have the feeling that the divisions' interests are growing further apart. It seems that the divisions are going their own way. For example, we are a polymer producer but the molding division wants to be in a special area, so that means they are going to be less of a customer to us, and there is a whole family of plastics being left out that nobody's touching, and this is bearing on our program. . . . We don't mess with the building products division at all, either. They deal in small volumes. Those that we are already making we sell to them, those that we don't make we can't justify making because of the kinds of things we are working with. What I am saying is that I don't think the corporation is integrating, but I think we ought to be, and this is one of the problems of delegated divisions. What happens is that an executive heads this up and goes for the place that makes the most money for the division, *but* this is not necessarily the best place from a corporate standpoint.

. . . . .

We don't have as much contact with sister divisions as I think we should. I have been trying to get a liaison with guys in my function but it has been a complete flop. One of the problems is that I don't know who to call on in these other divisions. There is no table of organization, nor is there any encouragement to try and get anything going. My experience has been that all of these operating divisions are very closed organizations. I know guys up the line will say that I am nuts about this. They say to just call over and I will get an answer. But this always has to be a big deal, and it doesn't happen automatically, and hurts us.

The comments of corporate staff members describe these relationships and the factors they saw contributing to the problem:

> Right now I would say there is an iron curtain between the polymer and chemicals division and the rest of the corporation. You know, we tell our divisions they are responsible, autonomous groups, and the polymer and chemicals division took it very seriously. However, when you are a three-quarter-billion-dollar company, you've got to be coordinated, or the whole thing is going to fall apart—it can be no other way. The domestic executive vice-president thing has been a big step forward to improve this, but I would say it hasn't worked out yet.
>
> . . . . .
>
> The big thing that is really bothering [the polymer and chemicals division] is that they think they have to go develop all new markets on their own. They are going to do it alone independently, and this is the problem they are faced with. They have got this big thing, that they want to prove that they are a company all by themselves and not rely upon packaging or anybody else.

Polymer and chemicals division executives talked about the effect of this drive for independence of the divisional operating heads on their planning efforts:

> The polymer and chemicals division doesn't like to communicate with the corporate staff. This seems hard for us, and I think the [a recent major proposal] was a classic example of this. That plan, as it was whipped up by the polymer and chemicals division, had massive implications for the corporation both in expertise and in capital. In fact, I think we did this to be a competitive one-up on the rest of our sister divisions. We wanted to be the best-looking division in the system, but we carried it to an extreme. In this effort, we wanted to show that we had developed this concept completely on our own. . . . Now I think a lot of our problems with it stemmed from this intense desire we have to be the best in this organization.
>
> . . . . .
>
> Boy, a big doldrum around here was shortly after Christmas (1965) when they dropped out a new plant, right out of our central plan, without any appreciation of the importance of this plant to the whole polymer and chemicals division's growth. . . . Now we have a windfall and we are back in business on this new plant. But for a while, things were very black and everything we had planned and everything we had built our patterns on were out. In fact, when we put this plan together, it never really occurred to us that we were going to get it turned down, and I'll bet we didn't even put the plans together in such a way as to really reflect the importance of this plan to the rest of the operation.

A number of executives in the end-use divisions attributed the interdivisional problems to different management practices and assumptions within the polymer and chemicals division. An executive in the packaging division made this point:

> We make decisions quickly and at the lowest possible level, and this is tremendously different from the rest of Texana. I don't know another division like this in the rest of the corporation.
>
> Look at what Sy Knoph has superfluous to his operation compared to ours. These are the reasons for our success. You've got to turn your guys loose and not breathe down their necks all the time. We don't slow our people down with staff. Sure, you may work with a staff, the wheels may grind, but they sure grind slow.
>
> Also, we don't work on detail like the other divisions do. Our management doesn't feel they need the detail stuff. Therefore, they're [Polymer and Chemical] always asking us for detail which we can't supply, our process doesn't generate it and their process requires it, and this always creates problems with the polymer and chemicals division. But I'll be damned if I am going to have a group of people running between me and the plant, and I'll be goddamned if I am going to clutter up my organization with all the people that Knoph has got working for him. I don't want this staff, but they are sure pushing it on me.

This comment from a molding division manager is typical of many about the technical concerns of the polymer and chemicals division management:

> Historically, even up to the not too distant past, the polymer and chemicals division was considered a snake pit as far as the corporate people were concerned. This was because the corporate people were market-oriented and polymer and chemicals division was technically run and very much a manufacturing effort. These two factors created a communication barrier and to really understand the polymer and chemicals division problems, they felt that you have to have a basic appreciation of the technology and all the interrelationships.
>
> Building on this strong belief, the polymer and chemicals divisions executives in the past have tried to communicate in technical terms, and this just further hurt the relationship, and it just did not work. Now they are coming up with a little more business or commercial orientation, and they are beginning to appreciate that they have got to justify the things they want to do in a business sense rather than just a technical sense. This also helps the problem of maintaining their relationships with the corporation, as most of the staff is nontechnical; however, this has changed a little bit in that more and more technical people have been coming on, and this has helped from the other side.
>
> They work on the assumption in the polymer and chemicals division that you have to know the territory before you can be an effective manager. You have got to be an operating guy to contribute meaningfully to their problems. However, their biggest problem is this concentration on technical solutions to their problems. This is a thing that has boxed them in the most trouble with corporation and the other sister divisions.

These and other executives also pointed to another source of conflict between the polymer and chemicals division and other divisions. This was the question of whether the polymer and chemicals division should develop into a more independent marketer, or whether it should rely more heavily on the end-use divisions to "push" its products to the market.

Typical views of this conflict are the following comments by end-use division executives:

> The big question I have about Polymer and Chemicals is, what is their strategy going to be? I can understand them completely from a technical standpoint, this is no problem. I wonder, what is the role of this company? How is it going to fit into what we and others are doing? Right now, judging from the behavior I've seen, Polymer and Chemicals could care less about what we are doing in terms of integration of our markets or a joint approach to them.
>
> . . . . .
>
> I think it is debatable whether the polymer and chemicals division should be a new product company or not. Right now we have an almost inexhaustible appetite for what they do and do well. As I see it, the present charter is fine. However, that group is very impatient, aggressive, and they want to grow, but you have got to grow within guidelines. Possibly the polymer and chemicals division is just going to have to learn to hang on the coattails of the other divisions, and do just what they are doing now, only better.
>
> . . . . .
>
> I think the future roles of the polymer and chemicals division is going to be, at any one point in time for the corporation, that if it looks like a product is needed, they will make it. . . . They are going to be suppliers, because I will guarantee you that if the moment comes and we can't buy it elsewhere, for example, then I darn well know they are going to make it for us regardless of what their other commitments are. They are just going to have to supply us. If you were to put the polymer and chemicals division off from the corporation, I don't think they would last a year. Without their huge captive requirements, they would not be able to compete economically in the commercial areas they are in.

A number of other executives indicated that the primary emphasis within the corporation on return on investment by divisions tended to induce, among other things, a narrow, competitive concern on the part of the various divisional managements. The comment of this division executive was typical:

> As far as I can see it, we [his division and Polymer and Chemicals] are 180 degrees off on our respective charters. Therefore, when Sy Knoph talks about this big project, we listen nicely and then we say, "God bless you, lots of luck," but I am sure we are not going to get involved in it. I don't see any money in it for us. It may be a gold mine for Sy but it is not for our company; and as long as we are held to the high profit standards we are, we just cannot afford to get involved. I can certainly see it might make good corporate sense for us to get it, but it doesn't make any sense in terms of our particular company. We have got to be able to show the returns in order to get continuing capital, and I just can't on that kind of project. I guess what I am saying is that under the right conditions we could certainly go in, but not under the present framework; we would just be dead in terms of dealing

with the corporate financial structure. We just cannot get the kinds of returns on our capital that the corporation has set to get new capital. In terms of the long run, I'd like very much to see what the corporation has envisioned in terms of a hook-up between us, but right now I don't see any sense in going on. You know, my career is at stake here too.

Another divisional executive made this point more succinctly:

Personally, I think that a lot more could be done from a corporate point of view, and this is frustrating. Right now all these various divisions seem to be viewed strictly as an investment by the corporate people. They only look at us as a banker might look at us. This hurts us in terms of evolving some of these programs because we have relationships which are beyond financial relationships.

The remarks of a corporate executive seemed to support this concern:

One of the things I worry about is where is the end of the rope on this interdivisional thing. I'm wondering if action really has to come from just the division. You know, in this organization when they decide to do something new, it always has been a divisional proposal—they were coming to us for review and approval. The executive committee ends up a review board; not us, working downward. With this kind of pattern, the talent of the corporate people is pretty well reduced into asking questions and determining whether a thing needs guidelines. But I think we ought to be the idea people as well, thinking about where we are going in the future, and if we think we ought to be getting into some new area, then we tell the divisions to do it. The stream has got to work both ways. Now it is not.

Discussion Questions

(Please answer the questions before proceeding to the conclusion below.)

1 What are the *antecedents* of conflict in this situation? The *moderating factors*? How is conflict *manifesting* itself?
2 How would you go about managing the conflict inherent in this situation? Texana has tried to handle it by appointing an executive vice-president for internal operations, but it is doubtful that this move by itself will be sufficient. Develop your own prescriptions for managing conflict at Texana. You might suggest, for example, such conflict-management techniques as developing superordinate goals, installing an improved incentive system, and structural approaches (special integrators, reduced interdependency, and the like); and conflict-resolution behaviors such as confrontation, smoothing, and forcing.
3 What organizational change and development techniques seem necessary here? Why?

4 Does there seem to be a high degree of "differentiation" between the end-use divisions and the polymer and chemical division? What implications does this have for how "integration" (coordination) should be achieved?
5 Is the organization structure adequate? How would you change it?
6 Is there a need to build more commitment on the part of employees? What do you base this on? How would you do so?

• *Conclusion*

This case helps illustrate, among other things, a number of the characteristics of intergroup relations and conflict we discussed in Chapter 15.

There are several sources or *antecedents* of conflict inherent in the way this company is now organized and managed. For one thing, the divisions are interdependent. The petroleum division is a supplier to other divisions, and the molded products, packaging products, and building products divisions are all dependent on the polymer and chemicals division for their raw materials. However, even though the divisions are highly interdependent, there are significant intergroup differences in terms of goals, values, and management styles. The performance of each division is measured by its own return on investment, a situation that seems to discourage interdivisional collaboration. And as an example of the differences in management styles between divisions, an employee says that in his division, they prefer making quick decisions at the lowest possible level, whereas in polymer and chemicals, employees always seem to want more "details," a process that slows down the decision process. By way of conflict antecedents, there is also some ambiguity. For example, there is no table of organization, so employees in each division don't know who their counterparts are in other divisions and can't communicate with them as they would like to.

Viewed in terms of the models of conflict we discussed, it is apparent why conflict has emerged at Texana. Not only are there numerous conflict antecedents, as we just discussed, but a number of moderating factors are acting to attenuate the effects of these antecedents. There is an absence of effective communication between divisions, and managers describe themselves as "180 degrees apart." Managers in the end-use divisions have come to assume that those in the polymer and chemicals division view them as "low man on the pole" and that "they have us wrapped up and do not reciprocate when we try to be helpful." There is no effective liaison between divisions. To make matters worse, the top executives in each division are assertive, aggressive, and competitive, a fact that probably increases further the likelihood that the conflict antecedents will lead to manifest conflict.

FOOTNOTES

[1]The executive committee consisted of Messrs. Dutton, Irwin, and Prentice, as well as the vice-president of research, executive vice-president of administration, and executive vice-president of foreign operations.

Index